Mapping
the Tibetan World

Kotan Publishing

Mapping the Tibetan World

Reprint Edition, September 2004
1st Edition, December 2000

Kotan Publishing, Inc.
1-3-441 Morino, Machida-shi, Tokyo 194-0022, Japan
E-mail: tibet-book@kotan.org   http://www.kotan.org

Distributed in North America, Latin America and Europe by
Tuttle Publishing
364 Innovation Drive, North Clarendon, VT 05759-9436
Tel: 800-526-2778   Fax: 800-329-8885   E-mail: orders@tuttlepublishing.com

Special Advisor .... Yukiyasu Osada

Editors .... Gavin Allwright, Atsushi Kanamaru

Translators .... Atsushi Kanamaru, Mari Sekizawa

Proofreaders .... Linda Armstrong, Scott Shibuya Brown, Sean Collins

Color Photographs ... Hiroyuki Nagaoka, Shintaro Matsui, Masashi Akiyama

Cover Photograph .... Hiroyuki Nagaoka

Cover Designer .... Jinichi Kuramae

Production .... Atsushi Kanamaru

Printer .... Sokosha Printing Ltd., Japan

Library of Congress Card Number: 00-191717

ISBN: 0-9701716-0-9

Text Copyright © Kotan Publishing 2000, 2004
Maps Copyright © Kotan Publishing & Ryokojin 2000
Photographs: Copyright is retained by each photographer.
Printed in Japan

The information contained in this book is accurate to the best of our knowledge at the time of editing. Things can and will change and we urge you to check any vital official information (visas, permits, etc.) before leaving on your trip. Kotan Publishing and the contributors accept no responsibility for any loss, damage or injury incurred through the use of the information included in this book.

Yukiyasu Osada

Born and raised in Aichi, central Japan, Yukiyasu first encountered the Tibetan world when he happened to visit a Tibetan refugee camp in Mussoorie in 1986. He made his first trip to Tibet in 1987 while a student at Waseda University, Tokyo. This was the start of a love affair that has lasted 17 years, during which he has returned 10 times and written 3 books in Japanese; 'My Own Lessons On Tibet' (1992), 'Guide To The Tibetan Area' (1998), and his latest book, 2 collections of travel essays (July, 2000). Yukiyasu gets back to the open skies, cool air and warm-hearted people of the region at every opportunity. He is a Tibet tour guide during the summer while during the rest of the year he works as a freelance writer. Visit his website 'I love Tibet!' at www.tibet.to/.

Gavin Allwright

Born in London and raised in Kent, south-east England, Gavin was bitten by the travel bug at an early age. He finally left England in 1993 and headed for Africa with a backpack. His fascination with the history, religion and culture of Asia meant that this year in Africa was quickly followed by 6 more years traveling and working throughout India, China, Japan and South-east Asia. After a spell of working as a teacher and then as a freelance photojournalist, he decided to go into publishing and was delighted to get the chance to work on the editing, research and writing of this exceptional project. He feels that this book will help to enrich travelers' experiences and help them to further understand the 'Tibetan World.' Gavin still travels the region whenever he can and currently lives and works in Tokyo, Japan.

Atsushi Kanamaru

Making the most of his school days at Japan's Waseda University, Atsushi visited over 20 countries including Tibet, China, Nepal, and India during that time. Despite his obsession with the 'Roof of the World' and its people, he decided to work at international airports in Tokyo and Amsterdam before moving on to a position in an airlines marketing department. After 6-1/2 years in the industry, he embarked for his 'New World,' publishing, where he has found his life's challenge and where he has finally come full circle back to Tibet. 'Mapping the Tibetan World' is one of the projects he is most proud of. Atsushi believes that the region introduced here will keep attracting travelers for a long time to come and may even change their lives, just as it changed his.

Key Contributors & Supporters

We would like to give our special thanks to Shozo Tominaga for contributing the complete set of maps. His dedication to his field has opened a great many doors for a great many people.

Thanks to
1) Yumi Twewan for her explanations and insights into the world of Mandala and Buddhist iconography. Her own work fuses Tibetan and Japanese styles and these have been exhibited both in Japan and the United States. Examples of her unique thangka can be found at http://members.xoom.com/thanka/

2) Tomoya Yuki for updating information on Western Tibet, Ladakh & Zanskar.

3) Kiyoaki Hirose & Ryosuke Tominaga for helping on the India & Nepal sections.

The Western Tibet section has been updated using 'West Tibet' by Shinya Takagi. (©Ryokojin 2000)

Thanks also go out to all of the staff at Ryokojin, Co., Ltd., who have all been very supportive and continued to give us great advice. Their unwavering enthusiasm for our project has helped to make the whole thing possible.

Ryokojin

Other Contributors

Chihiro Yatsu/Eiji Yamada/Hal Tanaka/Hiroshi Kitamura/Hiroyuki Ishii/Ike Kanata/Iwai Katuya/Karma Thupten/Keima Fukuda/Masaki Kobayashi/Masashi Akiyama/Mayumi Asai/Mito Masayoshi/Morimichi Tsuge/Naoko Morohashi/Naoko Sakuraba/Natsuko Miyake/Nobuhiko Miki/Satoshi & Riyomi Hirayama/ Takako Nakamura/Takashi Masubuchi/Takeshi Hara/Tamami Nishiyori/Yasuhiko Fujimura/Yoichi Yamakami/Yuriko Mizutani

Help Us Get It Right

We have made all efforts to make sure that this guidebook contains the most up-to-date and accurate information possible. The book has been translated and updated from the original 'Tibet' book published in Japan by Ryokojin, Co, Ltd. Things change with time and your help in informing us of any corrections or new information will be greatly appreciated and will help us to further improve this guide. We will endeavor to incorporate all these confirmed changes in subsequent editions of 'Mapping the Tibetan World.'

Message from the Publishers

As travelers and now as travel publishers, we have always felt that having the information and the means to truly appreciate the region that you are visiting is a vital asset. We hope that making this practical no-nonsense guide available to those interested in the Tibetan region will increase the understanding and appreciation of the people and culture in the area.

We have included all of the areas that can be classed as being within the 'Tibetan Cultural Region,' a classification that cuts across 'national' or 'geopolitical' boundaries and encompasses the areas where the people share a common ancestry, culture and religion.

To further the understanding of the region we are also the hosts of the 'Tibetan Cultural Region Web Directory,' which lists thousands of web sites, along with detailed descriptions of each one. If you want to find additional information, this is the place to go: http://www.kotan.org

Contents

TRAVEL IN TIBET **8**
Roads to Tibet 8
Borders 10
Visas 10
Visa Extensions 11
Permits to Enter Tibet 11
Alien Travel Permit 12
In Closed Areas 12
Making Arrangements in
Your Own Country 12
Making Arrangements with a
Travel Agency in Chengdu 13
Changing Money &
Exchange Rates 13
Budgets 13
Guesthouses 13
Transport 14
Hitchhiking in Tibet 14
What to Bring 14
Altitude Sickness 15
Dogs & Rabies 15
Vaccinations 15
Hospitals 20
Language 20
Other Guidebooks 20
Other Maps Available 20
Post & Telecommunications 22
Safety in Tibet 22
Illegal Matters 22
Customs & Taboos 23
Overview 23

MODEL TOURS **24**
Tibet in China 24
Ladakh (North-West India) 25
Encounter Tibet in Nepal 26
Darjeeling & Sikkim 27
Bhutan 27

COUNTRY INFORMATION
China 64
India 280
Nepal 320
Bhutan 376

NATURE IN TIBET **28**

HISTORY OF TIBET **30**

TIBETAN BUDDHISM **36**
The World of Tibetan
Buddhism 36
The Four Greatest Schools of
Tibetan Buddhism 38
Keywords for Prayer 40
The Prayer Scene 40

Entering the World of the Gompa 41
A Monk's Life 43
Buddhas, Deities, etc. in the
Mandala World **46**
Buddhas, Bodhisattvas &
Deities 47
Unraveling the Thangka Message 49
Buddhist Goods 49
Lucky Omen Symbols 50
Animals Found in Thangkas 51
Appreciating the Mandala 52
Fashions 54
Keywords for Tibetan Life **55**
Lives in Tibet 55
Things to Wear 55
Food 56
Customs 57
Tibetan Festivals **58**
Festival Dates 61

LHASA **63**
Access 65
Practical Information 67
Around the Barkhor **71**
Around the Potala Palace **78**
Around Lhasa **82**

AROUND LHASA **85**
Ganden Monastery **85**
Lhokha (Shannan) Prefecture ... **88**
Samye (Sangye) 88
Chimphu Hermitage 92
Dranang Valley (Zhanang) 92
Tsethang (Zedang) 92
South of Lhasa **95**
Nyetang Dolma Lhakhang &
Rock Image of Shakyamuni 95
Gongkar (Gongga) 95
Gongkar Choede
(Gongkar Dorjeden) 95
Mt. Chuwori 96
Shugseb Ani Gompa 96
Drakyul Caves &
Dorje Drak Gompa 97
Upper Reaches of the Kyi-chu
(NE from Lhasa) **98**
To the North of Lhasa **99**
Toelung (Duilongdeqingxian) .. **100**
Yamdrok Yumtso Lake to
Lhakhang **100**
Lhodrak (Luozha) 103
Lhakhang (Lakang) 103
To the East of Tsethang **103**
Chusum (Qusong) 103
Lhamo Latso Lake 104
Gyatsa (Jiacha) 104

Nang Dzong (Lang) 105
Tsari 105
Sangak Choeling 106
Lhuntse (Longzi) 106
Tsona (Cuona) 106
Namtso Lake and Nakchu **106**
Namtso Lake 106
Nakchu (Naqu) 108
Amdo (Anduo) 108

LHASA-KATHMANDU .. **109**
Tsang (Shigatse & Gyantse) **109**
Shigatse (Rikaze) 109
Gyantse (Jiangzi) 114
Around Shigatse **118**
Sakya (Sajia) 120
Lhatse to Dram **122**
Lhatse (Lazi) 122
Shelkar (New Tingri) 123
Jomolangma Trekking 123
Tingri (Dingri) 126
Lapchi 126
Nyalam (Nielamu) 126
Dram (Khasa) [Zhangmu] 127
To Nepal 128
Lhatse to Saga **129**
Kyirong Valley to Nepal **130**
Chumbi Valley to Sikkim &
Bhutan **131**

TO KAILASH **133**
Route to Mt. Kailash 137
Ali (Shiquanhe) 140
Mt.Kailash (Kang Rinpoche) 141
Mt.Kailash Khora
(Pilrimage Circuit) 143
Nangkhor
(Inner Pilgrimage Circuit) 145
Lake Manasarovar
(Mapham Yutso) 145
Langa Tso (Lake Rakshas Tal) ... 145
Memo Nani (Mt. Nemo Nanyi) ... 146
Sources of Asia's Great Rivers ... 146
Border Crossing
Purang-Simikot 147
The Guge Ruins 149
Tsamda (Zhada) 149
Tsaparang 152
Dungkar & Piyang 153
Tirthapuri 153
Rutok (Ritu) 156
Kashgar to Mt. Kailash
(Xinjiang-Tibet Highway) 156

KONGPO & CHAMDO
(Eastern Part of TAR) **159**

5

KONGPO [NYANGTRI
(LINZHI) PREFECTURE] 159
Lhasa to Bayi 162
Bayi 162
Basong Tso
(Lake Draksum Lhatso) 163
Nyangtri (Nyingtri)[Linzhi] 165
Mt. Bonri 165
Menling (Milin) 166
Mt. Namcha Barwa 167
Pemako (Metok) [Motuo] 167
Bayi to Pome 167
Lunang (Lulang) 167
Tang-me [Tongmai] 167
Pome (Powo) [Bomi] 168
CHAMDO (CHANGDU)
PREFECTURE 169
Rawok (Ranwu) 169
Dzayul (Chayu) 169
Pasho (Basu) 169
Pomda (Bangda) 169
Yunnan to Bayi 170
Yanjing 170
Markham (Mangkang) 170
Chamdo to Nakchu 171
Chamdo (Changdu) 171
Riwoche (Leiwuqi) 173
Tengchen (Dingqing) 173
Sok Dzong (Suoxian) 173
Lhorong (Luolong) 174
Pelbar (Bianba) 174
Lharigo (Jiali) 174
Dege in Sichuan to Chamdo 174
Chamdo to Pomda 174

AMDO
(Gansu, Qinghai & Sichuan) 175
GANSU PROVINCE 177
Lanzhou 177
Linxia 179
Gannan Tibetan Autonomous
Prefecture 181
Xiahe (Sang-chu) 182
Hezuo (Tsoe) 183
Luqu (Luchu) 184
Taktsang Lhamo (Langmusi) 185
Lintan 186
Zhuoni (Cho-ne) 186
Maqu (Machu) 187
Diebu (Thewo) 187
Zhouqu (Drukchu) 187
Boyu (Boeyul) 187
North-west of Gansu 187
Tianzhu (Pari) 187
Sunan Yugurzu Autonomous
County (Zhangye Diqu) 189
QINGHAI PROVINCE 190
Xining 190
Around Xining & Haidong
Diqu (District) 193
Huangzhong (Tsongkha) 193
Huzhu Tu Autonomous County
(Gonlung) 194
Ping'an (Tsongkha Khar) 194

Ledu (Drotsang) 195
Hualong Hui Autonomous
County (Bayan Khar) 195
Xunhua (Xunhua Salar
Autonomous County) [Dowi] 195
Xining-Golmud-Lhasa 195
Qinghai Hu (Lake Kokonor) 196
Golmud (Ge'ermu) 197
Huangnan Tibetan Autonomous
Prefecture 198
Tongren (Repkong) 198
Zeku (Tsekok) 200
Henan Mongol Autonomous
County (Sogwo) 201
Hainan Tibetan Autonomous
Prefecture 202
Gonghe (Chabcha) 202
Xinghai (Tsigorthang) 203
Guide (Trika) 204
Guinan (Mangra) 205
Tongde (Kawasumdo) 206
Guoluo (Golok) Tibetan
Autonomous Prefecture 207
Maduo (Mato) 207
Maqin (Dawu) 210
Gande (Gabde) 211
Dari (Jimai) [Darlag] 212
Banma (Padma) [Parma] 213
Jiuzhi (Jigdril) 214
Yushu Tibetan Autonomous
Prefecture (Jyekundo) 214
Yushu (Jyekundo) 214
Chengduo (Trindu) 218
Sumang (Zurmang) Region 218
To the Source of
the Mekong River 218
ABA (NGAWA) TIBETAN &
QIANG AUTONOMOUS
PREFECTURE (SICHUAN) ... 219
Wenchuan (Lungu) 220
Maoxian (Maowen Qiang
Autonomous County) 220
Heishui (Trochu) 221
Songpan (Zungchu) 221
Huanglong (Sertso) 222
Jiuzhaigou 223
Nanping (Namphel) 224
Lixian (Tashiling) 224
Ma'erkang (Barkam) 225
Jinchuan (Rabden) 226
Xiaojin (Tsenlha) 226
Rangtang (Zamthang) 227
Aba (Ngawa) 227
Hongyuan (Mewa) 228
Ruo'ergai (Dzoge) 229

EASTERN KHAM
(Ganzi Prefecture & Muli
County, Sichuan Province) 231
Chengdu 233
Ganzi (Kandze) Tibetan
Autonomous Prefecture 237
Kangding (Dartsedo) 237
Mugecuo Lake (Yeren Hai) 241

Around Kangding 242
Luding (Chakzamka) 242
Mt. Minya Konka
(Gongga Shan) 243
Hailuogou Glacier Park 243
Kangding to Ganzi, Dege, etc.
(Sichuan-Tibet Highway
North) 245
Danba (Rongtrak) 245
Jiulong (Gyezil) 246
Xinduqiao (Dzongzhab) 246
Tagong (Lhagang) [Hargong] 246
Bamei (Garthar) 247
Daofu (Tawu) 248
Luhuo (Drango) 249
Seda (Sertal) 250
Ganzi (Kandze) 250
Xinlong (Nyarong) 253
Baiyu (Pelyul) 253
Manigango 254
Xinluhai (Yilhun Lhatso) 254
Dege (Derge) 254
Monasteries around Dege 256
Shiqu (Sershul) [Serxu] 257
Kangding to Litang and Batang
(Sichuan-Tibet Highway
South) 258
Yajiang (Nyakchuka) 258
Litang (Lithang) 258
Batang (Bathang) 260
Yunnan to Litang (Lithang) 260
Xiangcheng (Chaktreng) 260
Daocheng (Dabpa) 260
Derong 260
Muli Tibetan Autonomous
County, Sichuan Province 260

DECHEN
(Diqing Tibetan Autonomous
Prefecture, Yunnan Province) .. 263
Yunnan to Tibet 263
Kunming 263
Dali (Dali Gucheng) 267
Lijiang (Jang Sadam) 268
Diqing Tibetan Autonomous
Prefecture 270
Zhongdian (Gyalthang) 270
Deqin (Dechen) [Jol] 274
Weixi (Balung) 275
Lugu Hu (Lake) 276
Ninglang 278
Yongning 278

LADAKH & ZANSKAR .. 279
Delhi 279
From Manali to Leh 283
Manali 283
From Srinagar to Leh 284
Srinagar 286
LADAKH 286
Leh 287
Leh to the South: Gompas in the
Indus Valley 291
Leh and the West: Gompas on the

Kargil Route 292
Trekking from Leh 293
Dha/Hanu Villages 294
Nubra Valley 295
East Ladakh 297
ZANSKAR 298
Padam (Padum) 298
Padam (Padum)-Phugtal-Darcha 299
Padam (Padum)-Zangla-
Lamayuru 299
Padam (Padum)-Sani-Kargil 302
LAHAUL 303
Keylong 303
SPITI 305
Kaza 305
KINNAUR 308
Shimla (Simla) 308
Sarahan 308
Rekong Peo 310
Kalpa 310
Sangla 310
Kanam 311
Puh 311
Nako 311
Chango 311
Shalkar 312
DHARAMSALA 312
OTHER AREAS SETTLED
BY TIBETAN REFUGEES
IN INDIA 315
Himachal Pradesh & Uttar Pradesh
[North-west India] 315
Karnataka State [Southern India] 317
Central India 317

NEPAL 319
Road to Nepal 323

Kathmandu 324
Trekking to the
Tibetan World 333
Route to Bigu Gompa &
Surrounding Area 336
Everest Trekking 336
Lukla to Hile 338
The Mt. Kangchenjunga Area 338
Langtang 338
Manaslu North 339
Pokhara 342
Annapurna Area Trekking 343
The Annapurna Sanctuary 343
Jomsom & Muktinath Area 346
Manang Area 349
Lo Manthang (Mustang) 351
Dolpo 354
Lumbini 355

SIKKIM 357
Kolkata (Calcutta) 357
West Bengal 360
Darjeeling 360
Kalimpong 364
Sikkim 365
Central & Eastern Sikkim 367
Gangtok 367
Northern Sikkim 370
Western Sikkim 371
Geyzing 371
Yoksum 372
Arunachal Pradesh 372

BHUTAN 375
Phuntsholing ('Free Zone') 383
Western Bhutan 384
Paro 384

Thimphu 386
Shopping in Thimphu 388
Punakha 390
Central Bhutan 391
Trongsa 391
The Bumthang Valleys 391
Eastern Bhutan 392
Mongar 392
Lhuntse 392
Tashigang 392
Samdrup Jongkhar 393
Tashi Yangtse 393

ARTICLES
Be Careful with
Mountain Sickness 21
The Dalai Lamas 35
Tibetan Buddhist Culture
Outside Tibet 54
Losar in Kathmandu 62
The 10th Panchen Lama 132
Hitchhiking in Tibet 189
Dolpo Flight Request 354

TIBET PHOTOS .. 262, 318, 394

APPENDIX 395
Survival Tibetan 395
Survival Chinese 398
Chinese Place Names 400
Embassies 404

INDEX
Tibet & China 406
India, Nepal & Bhutan 411
Map Index 414

Map Legend

⊕ Hotel	✉ Post Office	卍 Tibetan Buddhist Religious Site	×××× Disputed Area	
⊖ Restaurant	✚ Hospital	卐 Bon Religious Site	—··— State Border	
⊗ Shopping Center	🚌 Bus Terminal	▲ Chorten (Stupa)	--·-- District Boundary	
⊖ Bank	⚲ Bus Stop	∴ Ruins, etc.	★ Capital City	
❶ Tourist Information	🚢 Ferry	☾ Mosque	▣ City	
⑤ Money Changer	✈ Airport	Ⓧ Church	◎ Large Town	
⊕ Travel Agency	>< Pass (La)	⌒ Cave	○ Town	
☎ Telephone	♨ Hot Springs	+·H·+ National Border	● Village	

Useful Terms

CCP -- Chinese Communist Party
-chu -- River (Tibet/Bhutan)
CITS -- China International Travel Service
Daoban -- Road maintenance depot (China)
Dzong -- Monastery/Fortress (Bhutan/Tibet)
G.S. -- Gas station
He/Jiang -- River (China)

Khola -- River (Nepal)
La -- Mountain pass
Lhakhang -- Buddhist temple
PSB -- Public Security Bureau (China/Tibet)
Shan -- Mountain/Pass (China)
Tsangpo -- Large River (Tibet)
Tso/Cuo/Hu -- Lake

Travel in Tibet
Yukiyasu Osada

What is the Tibetan Cultural Area?

In general, these days the use of the term 'Tibet' refers to the Tibetan Autonomous Region (TAR) of the People's Republic of China (PRC). The sacred city of Lhasa and also Mt. Kailash (Kang Rinpoche) are to be found in this province. However, the 'Tibetan Cultural Area' covers not only the TAR and other Chinese territories annexed by the Chinese, but also areas outside of China (See the map below).

This chapter discusses the situation in the Tibetan areas within China. For information relating to other areas in India, Nepal and Bhutan, please refer to the relevant chapters.

ROADS TO TIBET

Travel information in Tibet is very fluid and the situation can change quickly, but if you are wondering if you can travel freely in this area, the answer would be that probably you can. It is true that besides a Chinese visa, a permit is also required for you to enter the TAR and there are also many places where lone foreign visitors are prohibited from entering.

Nonetheless, many individual travelers have found ways to travel relatively freely throughout Tibet and many of them have been enjoying this

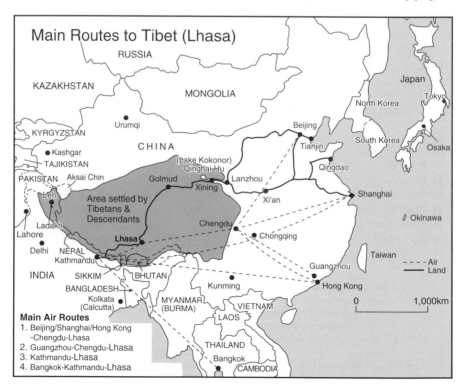

Main Routes to Tibet (Lhasa)

RUSSIA
KAZAKHSTAN
MONGOLIA
Japan
Tokyo
North Korea
KYRGYZSTAN
Urumqi
Beijing
South Korea
Kashgar
CHINA
Tianjin
Osaka
TAJIKISTAN
(Lake Kokonor)
Qinghai-Hu
Qingdao
PAKISTAN Aksai Chin
Golmud
Lanzhou
Leh
Xining
Shanghai
Area settled by
Tibetans &
Descendants
Xi'an
Ladakh
Chengdu
Okinawa
Lahore
Lhasa
Chongqing
Delhi NEPAL
Kathmandu
Taiwan
- - - - Air
INDIA SIKKIM BHUTAN
Guangzhou
——— Land
BANGLADESH
Kunming
Hong Kong
Kolkata
(Calcutta)
MYANMAR
(BURMA)
VIETNAM
0   1,000km
Main Air Routes
LAOS
1. Beijing/Shanghai/Hong Kong
   -Chengdu-Lhasa
2. Guangzhou-Chengdu-Lhasa
THAILAND
3. Kathmandu-Lhasa
Bangkok
4. Bangkok-Kathmandu-Lhasa
CAMBODIA

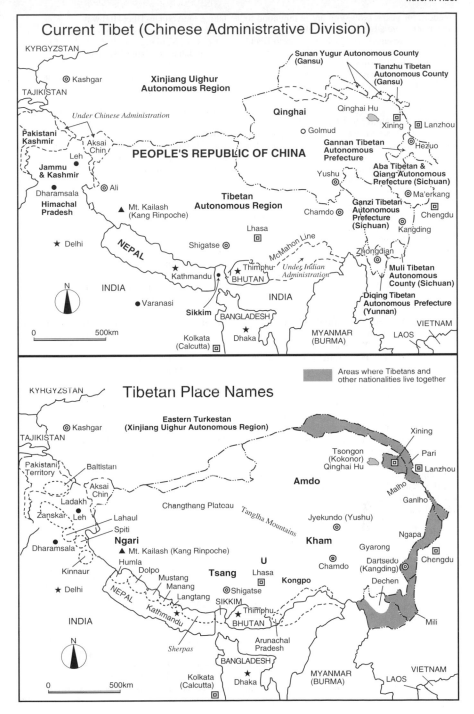

Current Tibet (Chinese Administrative Division)

KYRGYZSTAN

Sunan Yugur Autonomous County (Gansu)

Tianzhu Tibetan Autonomous County (Gansu)

◎ Kashgar

Xinjiang Uighur Autonomous Region

TAJIKISTAN

Qinghai

Qinghai Hu

Under Chinese Administration

Xining ⊡ ⊡ Lanzhou

○ Golmud

Pakistani Kashmir

Aksai Chin

PEOPLE'S REPUBLIC OF CHINA

Gannan Tibetan Autonomous Prefecture

Hezuo ◎

Leh

Jammu & Kashmir

Yushu ◎

Aba Tibetan & Qiang Autonomous Prefecture (Sichuan)

● Dharamsala

◎ Ali

● Ma'erkang ◎

Himachal Pradesh

▲ Mt. Kailash (Kang Rinpoche)

Tibetan Autonomous Region

Chamdo ◎

Ganzi Tibetan Autonomous Prefecture (Sichuan)

⊡ Chengdu

Lhasa ⊡

Kangding ◎

★ Delhi

NEPAL

Shigatse ◎

McMahon Line

Zhongdian ◎

Muli Tibetan Autonomous County (Sichuan)

★ Thimphu

Under Indian Administration

Kathmandu ●

BHUTAN

INDIA

INDIA

Diqing Tibetan Autonomous Prefecture (Yunnan)

● Varanasi

Sikkim

BANGLADESH

VIETNAM

N

0   500km

Kolkata (Calcutta) ⊡

★ Dhaka

MYANMAR (BURMA)

LAOS

Tibetan Place Names

Areas where Tibetans and other nationalities live together

KYRGYZSTAN

Eastern Turkestan (Xinjiang Uighur Autonomous Region)

Xining

◎ Kashgar

TAJIKISTAN

Pari

Pakistani Territory

Baltistan

Tsongon (Kokonor) Qinghai Hu

⊡ Lanzhou

Aksai Chin

Amdo

Malho

Ladakh

Changthang Plateau

Tanglha Mountains

Ganlho

Zanskar

Leh

Lahaul

Jyekundo (Yushu) ◎

Dharamsala

Spiti

Ngari

Ngapa

▲ Mt. Kailash (Kang Rinpoche)

Kham

Gyarong

Kinnaur

Humla

Dolpo

U

Chamdo ◎

Dartsedo (Kangding) ◎

Chengdu ⊡

★ Delhi

Mustang

Tsang

Lhasa ⊡

Dechen

NEPAL

Manang

Shigatse ◎

Kongpo

Langtang

SIKKIM

Kathmandu

★ Thimphu

Mili

INDIA

BHUTAN

N

Sherpas

Arunachal Pradesh

BANGLADESH

VIETNAM

0   500km

Kolkata (Calcutta) ⊡

★ Dhaka

MYANMAR (BURMA)

LAOS

freedom for years. Now, you are in the mood to embark on more adventurous travel than you have previously envisaged, let's look at 'Roads to Tibet.'

To get to the Tibetan capital, Lhasa, foreign travelers usually start from Chengdu in Sichuan, Xining in Qinghai or Kathmandu in Nepal:

[By Air]
1) Chengdu, Sichuan to Lhasa
Direct daily flights are available between Chengdu, Sichuan, and Lhasa. You can easily get a ticket through a travel agency in Chengdu. There is also a comfortable 2-hour flight twice weekly between Chongqing and Lhasa. (See page 234.)

2) Kathmandu to Lhasa
From April to November there are 2 flights a week available between the Nepalese capital and Lhasa. You can get to Lhasa whilst enjoying a spectacular flight over the Himalayas. However, individual travelers can get neither a visa nor an air ticket, which are only available to members of an organized group. (See page 325.)

[By Land]
1) Xining, Qinghai via Golmud to Lhasa
This bus trip is tough going and takes a minimum of 2 nights and 3 days along the Qinghai-Tibet Highway. Although uncomfortable this is still the most popular route for travelers sticking to land transportation. (See page 197.)

2) Kathmandu via Dram (Khasa) to Lhasa
As with the Qinghai-Tibet Highway, the China-Nepal Friendship Highway is a popular route for travelers. This route brings you close to a number of famous sights, such as Shigatse, Gyantse, and the Everest Base Camp. It takes 5-7 days of traveling over the Tibetan Highlands to get to Lhasa via this route. This overland trip also subjects individual travelers to the same restrictions as access by air from Nepal. (See page 325.)

Besides the legal routes listed above there are a number of others, where you'll need to rely on hitching a lift from a truck since commercial bus services are rarely available.

*Chengdu, Sichuan via Chamdo, Eastern Tibet to Lhasa taking the Sichuan-Tibet North Highway)
(For details, see page 236.)
*Chengdu, Sichuan via Bayi to Lhasa taking the Sichuan-Tibet South Highway)
(For details, see page 237.)
*Kunming, Yunnan via Bayi (Zhongdian and Dali -a popular travelers stop although the area north of it was damaged in an earthquake in 1995) to Lhasa taking the Yunnan-Tibet Highway
(For details, see page 265 & 267.)
* Kashgar, Xinjiang via Mt. Kailash to Lhasa
(For details see page 137 & 156.)

If you're interested in less travelled routes into Tibet, please refer to each chapter. For access to the areas outside of China, this book discusses these in the Indian, Bhutanese and Nepalese chapters.

Borders
India & Pakistan—The borders between the TAR and India/Pakistan have not been officially demarcated and the areas that are under actual control function as the defacto borderlines. These following areas have borders with Tibet that are disputed:

*The McMahon Line that separates north-east India and China.
*Sikkim, which in fact has been an Indian state since 1975, is disputed as China still regards Sikkim as an independent country.
*The area around the western Himalayas and K2.
*Aksai Chin is under the control of China.

Nepal—The Dram (Khasa)-Kodari crossing, on the China-Nepal border, is the only gateway that general travelers can pass through. Joining a package tour allows you to cross the border between Purang, south of Mt. Kailash (Kang Rinpoche), and western Nepal. All the borders between Tibet and India are closed to foreigners.

Bhutan—In principle the country only permits organized tours, however it has opened up the Phuntsholing area, making it into a 'Free Zone' on the border with India.

Visas
To go to Tibet you will require a Chinese visa. For Chinese Embassies & Consulates at home and abroad see Appendix.

In Hong Kong
The Visa Office at the Ministry of Foreign Affairs issues visas, but you can easily obtain a 3-month visa in Shenzhen and Macao. A 1-month visa costs HK$100 (US$12, single entry) and HK$150 (US$18, double entry). A 3-month visa costs HK$150 (US$18, single entry) and HK$180 (US$22, double entry).
As for a 6-month visa, the *Lucky Guesthouse* can arrange one for you. Hand in your passport and 1 passport photo to the guest house owner before 08:00. HK$750 (US$80) will secure you a visa in a couple of days, while an extra HK$100 (US$12) ensures same day delivery. If you apply

for the next day delivery on Friday, you'll get it on the next business day, usually a Monday, as the Consulate closes over the weekend.

The *Time Travel Service*, on the 16th floor of Chungking Mansions, also provides a similar service. If you produce a business card this reduces the cost from HK$850 (US$100) down to HK$600 (US$72) and it takes 4 working days. A 1-month visa costs HK$130 (US$15, single entry) and a 2-month visa costs HK$200 (US$24, single entry), both of which take 3-4 working days. For an extra HK$70-80 (US$8-10), the express service guarantees the visa will be delivered in the evening of the following day. Applications are accepted until 15:00 on weekdays and 11:00 on Saturdays.

In Nepal
Since May 1998, the Chinese embassy in Kathmandu has not accepted applications for individual tourist visas. Joining a tour organized by a travel agency gets you a group tour visa. The nature of these visas is not recorded in your passport and if you plan to leave the package tour in Lhasa or other cities in Tibet you need to make an arrangement with the travel agency to have the visa in your passport.

A major drawback to this is that the period of stay is extremely short. If you are lucky, you will get a maximum of 2 weeks. A few travel agencies have managed to arrange individual visas without package tours, but there is no guarantee this will be possible in the future.

A note of warning: a visa obtained in another country does not necessarily guarantee you entry to Tibet overland through Kodari. Some travelers have been known to get through while others have not. Check the present situation with the other travelers you meet in Kathmandu.

In Hanoi, Vietnam
Only 1-month visas, valid for 3 months, are available here. The Chinese Consulate visa section, next to the Chinese Embassy, 46 Hoang Dieu Street, is open from 08:30-11:00, Monday to Friday. It costs US$14 (payable in U.S. currency) if you don't mind waiting for about a week, or US$20 for next day delivery.

In Bangkok, New Delhi, and Islamabad
Only 1-month visas, valid for 3 months, are available in these cities.

Visa Extensions
You can extend your visa at the 'Foreign Affairs Section' of the local Public Security Bureau (PSB) in all of the major cities in the Peoples Republic of China (PRC). In Xining, Chengdu, Kunming, Lanzhou and other major centers outside the TAR,

the first extension generally gives you a 1-month extension and costs Y120 (US$15). The second extension usually allows you 2-4 weeks. You may or may not be able to get a third extension, as this seems to depend on the city and the official. The towns giving out the longer extensions vary, so keep your ears open.

In the TAR, you are unable to extend visas as much as you can in other areas. You should try to do it outside of Tibet, or obtain a longer visa in the first place. In Lhasa it is difficult to get even a 2-week extension on your first attempt.

You can also extend your visa in Shigatse, Tsethang, Bayi, Ali, etc, but the prices are not fixed. Some people have paid Y400 (US$50) for 3 days and others just Y120 (US$15) for 2 weeks. Both the length of stay and the price seem to be negotiable.

Permits to Enter Tibet
Of all the Tibetan areas in China, the TAR is a special case. Along with a visa, foreign visitors are officially required to have a permit issued by the PSB to enter the province. Without it, you'll be unable to buy air or bus tickets. However, you don't have to worry about where and how to get these permits. If you take common routes, such as Chengdu - Lhasa (Air), Golmud - Lhasa (Bus), etc., foreign travelers must buy both the permit and the ticket together through a travel agency.

You do not carry the permit, unless it is purchased outside the country, and inspections are rarely carried out to check if you have it with you. Instead, the 'Alien Travel Permit' mentioned next

---

Notes for Readers
Closed Areas (in China)
Those areas that are presently designated as 'Closed' have been indicated as such. These restrictions change over time and checking the most recent status of the 'Closed' area that you want to go to is a good idea. Most of these areas can still be reached by chartering a car or joining a package tour, except for some of the sensitive border regions.

Place Names
Under Chinese rule, there are many places in Tibet that have more than one name, either in Tibetan, Chinese, and/or the local dialect. This can be very confusing.
Instead of sticking to academic rules or conventions, we have adopted the most common and practical names in the area and introduce others when necessary. For example, we mainly use Tibetan first in the TAR.

is much more important. The areas of Tibet where travel has been liberalized are shown in the diagram below. As for Nepal, India, and Bhutan, please refer to the relevant chapter.

Alien Travel Permit

In China, there are open and closed areas for foreign visitors. Unfortunately, most areas in the TAR are closed. If you want to go to the closed areas, you need to have the local PSB near those areas issue an 'Alien Travel Permit' showing your destination. The availability of these very much depends on the situation at the time. To find out, either ask the PSB directly or gather some information from your fellow travelers.

In case you can't obtain a permit for yourself, the other option is to charter a car through a travel agent. Using this approach, you can get permits for many of the closed areas, except some of the more sensitive border areas. In Qinghai, Gansu, Yunnan and other areas outside of the TAR, many Tibetan places are open to foreigners.

In Closed Areas

In most cases, you can easily reach the closed areas when there are bus services running. In case you do turn up in a closed area without a permit by mistake you should be aware that you are breaking Chinese law and that you are all right as long as the PSB officers don't find you.

Staying at a plain guesthouse at the end of town is less conspicuous than staying at a hotel in the center. There are also many towns where a notification prohibiting foreigners to stay at a hotel will prevail. In this case, you have no choice but to stay at a designated hotel. Even so, some guesthouse owners will still allow you to stay at their place, even though they know the regulation is in force. Many of them are Hui or Tibetan. On the other hand, some of the owners will notify the PSB and there is also the real possibility of being found out in town.

If you are found in a town where there is no PSB foreign affairs section, your case might end simply by presenting your passport. In towns on a highway where foreigners often pass through, you are usually requested to move to a hotel designated by the PSB (even in closed areas, there are towns with designated hotels for foreigners on package tours). In most cases, the hotel that you are assigned will be the most expensive in that town. The PSB then puts a deposition on record and fines you.

If you stay just 1 night, the PSB might not be too strict; however, in the TAR the local PSB might fine you up to Y500 (US$60). Once again, this price is negotiable and the amount of the fine depends on the place and the official. Some PSB officials will just make foreigners buy a bus ticket for the following day to get them out of their hair as soon as possible. Strangers are a real nuisance for police officers!

In case you are caught on the way to, for example, Lhasa, some experienced travelers suggest that you tell the PSB that you actually came from Lhasa. Basically, the PSB then orders you to go back. Some foreigners have taken this a step further and prepared diaries to show local officials to prove this. In closed areas, you are frequently warned not to take photographs and the PSB have confiscated pictures from some tourists in the past. Even if you didn't intend to enter a restricted area, you should be careful. REMEMBER- You are still breaking the law!

Making Arrangements in Your Own Country.

If you have limited time for your trip, say a couple of weeks, pre-arranging things will save you time

---

TIBETAN-RELATED OPEN AREAS

TAR—Lhasa, Tsethang, Shigatse, Nakchu, Nyalam, Dram, Purang
*For Samye, Gyantse, Sakya, Lhatse, Tingri, etc., permits are issued to independent travelers. Although the town of Ali is closed, you can obtain one for Ali Prefecture there.
*For Dromo (Yadong), Lhodrak, Tso-me, Lhuntse, Tsona, Dzayul, ordinary individual travelers cannot obtain permits. But some reportedly got ones for Dzayul
Qinghai— Xining, Huangzhong, Ping'an, Ledu, Gangcha (Bird Island of Qinghai Hu), Wulan, Dulan, Golmud, Hualong, Xunhua, Jianzha, Tongren, Zeku, Henan, Guide, Tongde, Gonghe, Xinghai, Maqin (Dawu), Jiuzhi, Maduo, Yushu.
Gansu (Gannan Tibetan Autonomous Prefecture) — Xiahe (including Hezuo), Maqu, Diebu, Zhouqu. Outside of the prefecture, Lanzhou, Linxia, etc., are also open.
Sichuan (Aba Tibetan & Qiang Autonomous Prefecture) — Wenchuan, Maoxian (Maowen), Songpan, Nanping, Lixian, Ma'erkang, Xiaojin, Hongyuan, Ruo'ergai.
(Ganzi Tibetan Autonomous Prefecture)— All counties are now open. Outside of the prefecture, Muli has also recently become open.
Yunnan — All areas are open.

and trouble. You should confirm a return ticket and book any excursions through a travel agency in your home country, even though you will have to pay a commission.

You can easily fly to either Beijing or Shanghai and then take a connecting flight to Chengdu. The following day you can then get a flight to Lhasa.

Making Arrangements with a Travel Agency in Chengdu.

This has recently become available for the Chengdu-Lhasa leg of the journey. The arrangements can be made by fax and telephone. In this way, you can fly to Lhasa the morning after you arrive in Chengdu. A passport is not required to book a ticket, therefore a fax can be used. You then pay the fee after you arrive in Chengdu.

Changing Money & Exchange Rates

You can change the main currencies in Tibet, though, as in most parts of the world it is the mighty US dollar that is the most widely accepted. National currencies used in the region include Chinese Yuan (Y), Indian Rupees (Rs), Nepalese Rupees (NRs) and Bhutanese Ngultrums (Nu). (For exchange rates, see pages 64, 280, 320 & 376.)

Traveler's checks give you better rates in the banks, however, sometimes you need to pay for things in cash, and US dollars are the currency of choice in places such as travel agencies.

The usual place to change your foreign currency is at a branch of the Bank of China, however, these are usually closed on the weekend. At foreign tourist hotels, you can change money even on Sundays, but you'll get bad rates and have to pay a high commission. Many of these hotels only allow their guests to change money.

If you are traveling outside of the major centers and tourist areas, you will rarely find a Bank of China branch and you really must change more money than usual when planning to go to remote areas such as western Tibet. A good estimate is to budget for Y100 (US$12) a day + Y500-1,000 (US$60-120) on top.

Budgets

As long as you stay at guesthouses, move around by bus, and eat at local restaurants, you should be able to get by on less than US$10 a day.

Long-distance travel costs you the most. Tibet is a vast area, around the same size as Western Europe, and the main places to see are spread out over a wide area. Adding to this is the generally poor condition of the roads in the region.

To make the whole thing easier, you can pay a travel agency to arrange a 4-wheel drive car for you. In this case, the costs will be at least an additional Y1,000 (US$120) a day, as the agent also charges you for a driver and a guide. You will be able to share this amount with 3 or 4 other foreign passengers though.

See the Budget Price List for an estimate of the costs involved.

Guesthouses (Cheap Hotels)

For example, the well-known Yak Hotel in Lhasa is very popular among backpackers and starts at Y28 for a dormitory bed. In small towns, the price for dormitory beds ranges from Y10-20. Most

---

Budget Price List
$=US Dollar

Tibet (China)
G.H. dorm bed (Lhasa)
.... Y28+ ($3.40+)
Minibus (Lhasa-Shigatse) Y38 ($4.60)
Boiled dumplings (Large plate) ... Y3 ($0.36)
Chinese dish (3-4 people)
.... Y15 ($1.80)
Yoghurt Y2 ($0.24)
Beer Y5 ($0.60)
Color Print film
   (Chinese Kodak) Y25 ($3.00)
Cigarettes Y2 ($0.24)

India
G.H. dorm bed (Dharamsala)
.... 80Rs ($1.80)
Tibetan bread 3Rs ($0.07)
Vegetable fried rice 15Rs ($0.34)
Lemon curd cake 12Rs ($0.27)
Thali and tea 15Rs ($0.34)

Nepal
G.H. single room (Kathmandu)
.... 130NRs ($1.87)
Minibus (Kathmandu-Pokhara)
.... 200NRs ($2.88)
Dal baht 25NRs ($0.36)
Fried noodles 35NRs ($0.50)
Pizza 95NRs ($1.37)
Tea 8NRs ($0.12)
Beer 96NRs ($1.38)

Bhutan
Ema-datse 25Nu ($0.60)
Tukpa 20Nu ($0.48)
Chocolate cake 10Nu ($0.24)
Mineral water 15Nu ($0.36)
Beer (bottle) 30Nu ($0.72)
Camera film 100Nu ($2.40)

---

hotels outside major cities such as Lhasa have a common bathroom without a shower and boiling water in a teapot. You might also consider whether a hotel has a heater or an electric blanket on offer, as it gets very cold in some places, even during the summer months.

The number of hotels available to foreigners is limited and many foreign guests pay twice as much as the normal tariff. For that price though, you might get a better room in a closed town where foreigners rarely visit. Some large monasteries also have accommodation. It is the usual courtesy for guests to leave alms in return for their stay; around Y10-20 is an acceptable donation.

In India and Nepal, you shouldn't have much difficulty in finding a reasonable hotel. As for other Tibetan areas where you will mostly be trekking, carrying a tent can cut your costs substantially. For hotel details refer to each chapter. Bhutan has cheap accommodation but most caters to tour groups, as you are still required to spend a regulation amount per day (US$200-240).

Transport

Long-distance trips rely mostly on bus services. These days some long-distance routes have buses with sleeping berths and some mid-distance routes around the major cities operate good and reliable minibuses.

Rural area services are dominated by Chinese 5-seat-a-row cars, which are notoriously uncomfortable. Except for some highways connecting Lhasa with other major cities nearby, the roads are in very poor condition. Buses are unreliable and you may even be asked to help out if it breaks down.

Many of the interesting places to see on a trip to Tibet are the monasteries and temples that are designed for ascetic practices in remote areas. Access to these is naturally quite difficult. Like local people, you'll have to walk from the highway or hitch a lift on infrequent tractors and the like.

If you're not into such hardships, you should charter a 4-wheel drive car such as a Toyota Land Cruiser or a Beijing Jeep. Of course, this arrangement costs and may simply be unavailable in some of the more remote areas. Another option is to hire a horse from the local people. This is not out of the ordinary as this means of travel is nothing special in the Tibetan countryside.

In Ladakh, Zanskar, Nepal, etc., most visitors rely on walking to get around since the primary reason for coming to these regions was to trek in the mountains. You can get around in Bhutan by bus, but most people still enter the country on package tours with a driver and an English-speaking guide.

Hitchhiking in Tibet

The bottom line is that it is illegal for foreigners to hitchhike in Tibet. Foreign travelers may feel that it is only an inconvenience to be caught, but for drivers the offense is much more serious. A hefty fine is bad enough but you should bear in mind that the driver's license may also get suspended, depriving him of the means of making a living. Many drivers still risk it and they may charge foreigners more than local people.

There are many truck stops along the major routes and you'll find many drivers staying at the hotels in these places to negotiate with. On the streets, ask the local people where to find hitchhiking points as they usually vary, according to the destination.

A truck cabin accommodates 3 people and it's not necessarily any more comfortable than the loading platform behind. The back often affords you a lot of space and the best views, although it is dangerous in winter as temperatures go well below freezing. As with a bus, the front of the loading platform shakes less than the back. You must prepare for cold weather because you often have to stay out overnight and it gets especially cold when it rains.

A final tip is that mail trucks seem to have less chance of getting inspected at checkpoints and may take you farther than ordinary trucks.

What to Bring

*Clothing—You probably think of Tibet as always being extremely cold, but it is often warm enough for just a T-shirt in Lhasa. Temperatures do vary substantially during the day, though, and it gets chilly at night. You will encounter the more extreme cold when you cross the high mountain passes. You should take clothes to match these variable conditions and wet weather gear is an important consideration.

*Sun protection—The intense ultra-violet light makes it vital for you to have sunglasses and a brimmed hat. To prevent sunburn, you should also have a liberal amount of sunblock. This is not widely available in Tibet, so you'll have to bring it with you.

*Trekking equipment—Even if you're not planning to go trekking, a water bottle and a sleeping bag are really important considerations when packing. You should also choose trekking boots that fit well and have been thoroughly broken in, since you will often find yourself walking long distances.

You can get both brand new and second-hand trekking gear, such as sleeping bags and down jackets in Kathmandu. In Ladakh and Zanskar, however, it is difficult to get these things. You may also find some stuff for sale on guesthouse notice boards in Lhasa and Chengdu.

Altitude Sickness

Possibly the greatest concern for travelers to mountainous regions is altitude sickness. The deadly headache, loss of appetite, lethargy and sleeplessness are the less-severe symptoms of the condition. These warning signs can also be accompanied by swelling, nausea, nightmares, diarrhea and fever. This debilitating condition varies from person to person and is caused by the body's inability to adjust to lower atmospheric pressure and decreased oxygen. Age, gender and physical strength are not seemingly important factors in determining who will suffer from it. The people who you think are most likely to be seriously affected are often the people that remain relatively untouched by it. Furthermore, people who have been unaffected before are in no way immune to altitude sickness the next time around.

Serious or 'acute' altitude sickness is a very dangerous condition and can ultimately lead to death. The symptoms include hallucinations, 'cyanosis' (a lack of oxygen in the blood, characterized by the face and limbs turning blue), severe breathlessness, a great difficulty in walking properly, disorientation, and the inability to concentrate on anything. Although there is no established means to prevent this condition, the most important thing to do when you first arrive in a high altitude region is to take it extremely easy for the first couple of days. Many cases of altitude sickness follow a first day of vigorous activity after which the person suddenly collapses.

A common suggestion is to drink a lot of water and avoid alcohol. This is because the dry air prompts your body to lose a lot of water and this dehydration puts a burden on your heart, which in turn affects the rest of the body. Drinking will also get you drunk very quickly at this altitude and this reduces your body temperature dramatically, too.

Smoking can also reduce your ability to deal with the rarefied mountain air. Cutting down on cigarettes, or cutting them out completely, can really ease the discomfort in breathing that you'll feel.

If you're planning on trekking in these regions, you should try to gradually build up to tackling the longer distances and higher altitudes. Among Western tourists and trekkers, in particular, it is also well-known that taking a medicine called Diamox (acetazolamide) is very effective. You need to be very careful with how and when you take this drug. Consult a doctor!

Once you realize you or a companion is suffering from any of the symptoms mentioned, you should try to stay calm or try to calm your companion. A mistake is deciding to just lie down as this actually disrupts your metabolism, thus worsening the condition. You should try to adjust your body to the environment through light and moderate exercise and it is not unusual that just getting up and walking around can get rid of the pounding headache and nausea one had while lying down. The most effective measure to deal with altitude sickness is to breathe oxygen. Hotels catering to foreign tourists usually keep an oxygen refill and of course, hospitals definitely have them available.

If you are up a mountain and start to suffer from these same symptoms it is absolutely vital that you drop to a lower altitude as quickly as possible. If your condition continues or worsens, all that is left for you to do is to leave the region and return to a low-lying area immediately.

Dogs & Rabies

Wherever you are in Tibet, you can't miss the dogs and getting bitten happens more often than you might expect. These dogs are fearless and throwing stones or brandishing a stick won't deter them.

One thing you can do is to check with someone at the monastery or house you are going to visit to see if they keep one of these savage beasts. The dogs are trained to attack dubious strangers making foreigners prime targets.

In rural areas a typical encounter starts more than 200m from a nomads tent, with a huge Tibetan Mastiff guard dog barking and coming hurtling towards you at high speed. Be sure to call a resident to hold it off before you approach their tent.

Should you get bitten, you must get the vaccine immediately. If rabies sets in, it has a 100% death rate. The vaccine is available in Lhasa and must be taken 5 times a month. A preventive injection is also available in your home country, which covers you for about 3 years.

If you are unfortunate and get bitten in a rural area, you have a serious problem, as the vaccine is rarely available there. You should return to Lhasa as soon as you possibly can, even if you've had the preventative vaccination. There is nothing better than avoiding being bitten in the first place.

Vaccinations

You should consult your doctor at best a couple of months before your planned departure to allow ample time to have all the required vaccinations. Although doctors are aware of the basic requirements concerning travel to Tibetan areas, it is wise to consult specialists in the tropical medicine field.

*Recommended vaccinations include: Rabies, Meningitis, Typhoid, Hepatitis A, Hepatitis B, Tetanus, Yellow Fever, Japanese Encephilitis,

Bus Service Routes
in Tibetan Cultural Region

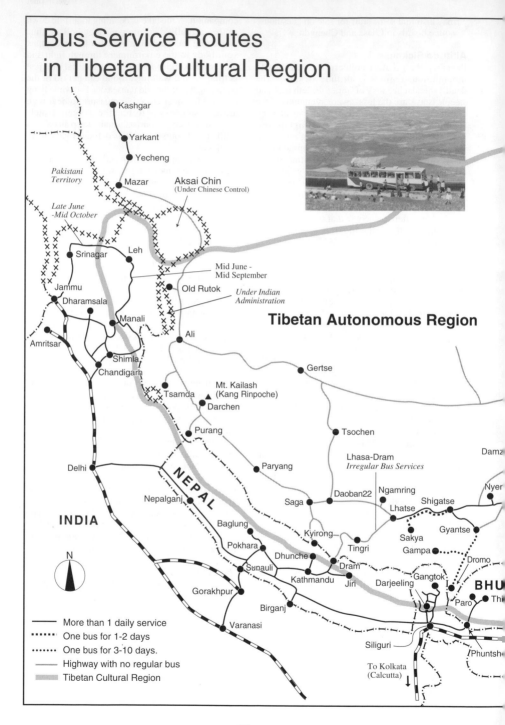

Kashgar

Yarkant

Yecheng

Pakistani Territory

Mazar

Aksai Chin
(Under Chinese Control)

Late June -Mid October

Leh

Srinagar

Mid June - Mid September

Jammu

Old Rutok

Under Indian Administration

Dharamsala

Manali

Tibetan Autonomous Region

Amritsar

Ali

Shimla

Chandigarh

Gertse

Tsamda

Mt. Kailash (Kang Rinpoche)

Darchen

Tsochen

Purang

Damz

Lhasa-Dram
Irregular Bus Services

Paryang

Delhi

Ngamring

Nyer

Nepalganj

Daoban22

Shigatse

Saga

Lhatse

INDIA

Baglung

Gyantse

Kyirong

Sakya

Pokhara

Tingri

Gampa

Dhunche

Dromo

Sunauli

Dram

Kathmandu

Jiri

Darjeeling

Gangtok

BHU

Gorakhpur

Paro

Thi

Birganj

Varanasi

Siliguri

Phuntsh

To Kolkata
(Calcutta)

N

——— More than 1 daily service

••••••• One bus for 1-2 days

••••••• One bus for 3-10 days.

——— Highway with no regular bus

▓▓▓ Tibetan Cultural Region

16

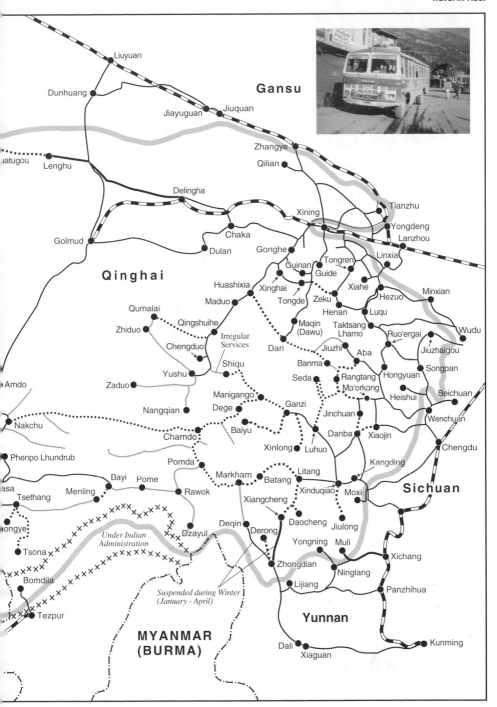

Gansu

Qinghai

Sichuan

Yunnan

MYANMAR
(BURMA)

*Under Indian
Administration*

*Suspended during Winter
(January - April)*

*Irregular
Services*

Liuyuan

Dunhuang

Jiayuguan Jiuquan

uatugou

Lenghu

Zhangye

Qilian

Tianzhu

Yongdeng

Delingha

Xining

Lanzhou

Golmud

Chaka

Dulan

Gonghe

Tongren

Linxia

Guinan

Guide

Xiahe

Huashixia

Xinghai

Zeku

Hezuo

Minxian

Maduo

Tongde

Henan

Luqu

Qumalai

Qingshuihe

Maqin
(Dawu)

Taktsang
Lhamo

Ruo'ergai

Wudu

Zhiduo

Jiuzhi

Aba

Jiuzhaigou

Chengduo

Dari

Banma

Hongyuan

Songpan

Yushu

Shiqu

Seda

Rangtang

Ma'orkang

Heishui

Beichuan

Amdo

Zaduo

Manigango

Ganzi

Jinchuan

Wenchuan

Nangqian

Dege

Danba

Xiaojin

Chengdu

Nakchu

Baiyu

Phenpo Lhundrub

Chamdo

Xinlong

Luhuo

Pomda

Kangding

Bayi

Pome

Markham

Litang

asa

Menling

Batang

Xinduqiao

Tsethang

Rawok

Xiangcheng

Moxi

ongye

Deqin

Daocheng

Jiulong

Tsona

Dzayul

Derong

Yongning

Muli

Xichang

Bomdila

Zhongdian

Ninglang

Panzhihua

Tezpur

Lijiang

Kunming

Dali

Xiaguan

17

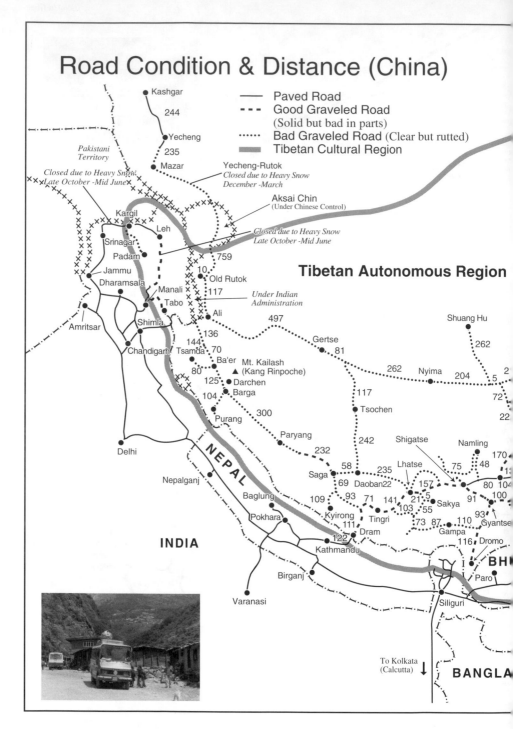

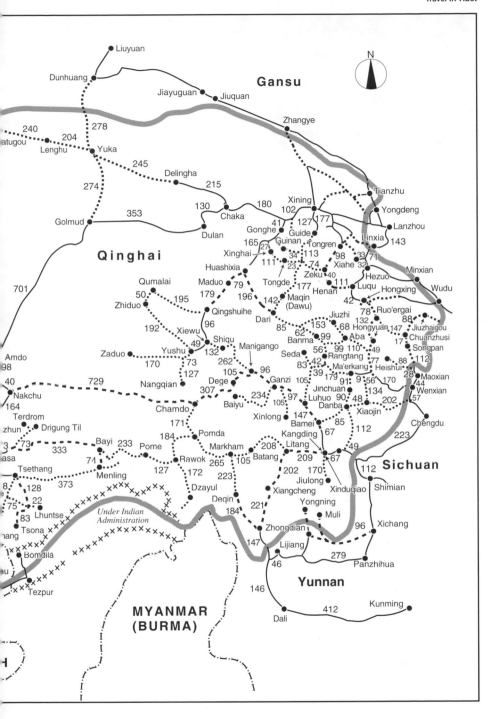

N

Liuyuan

Dunhuang

Jiayuguan   Jiuquan

Gansu

240   278
atugou 204
Lenghu   Yuka

Zhangye

245

Delingha

274   215

130   180   Xining
Chaka   102   Tianzhu
Golmud   353   41   127   177   Yongdeng
Dulan   Gonghe   Guide   Lanzhou
Qinghai   165   Guinan   Tongren   Linxia   143
Xinghai   27   34   113   98   33   71
Huashixia   111   23   74   Xiahe   32
701   Zeku   40   111   Minxian
Qumalai   Maduo   79   Tongde   177   Hezuo   Wudu
50   195   179   196   142   Henan   Luqu   Hongxing
Zhiduo   192   Qingshuihe   Maqin   42   Ruo'ergai
Xiewu   96   Dari   (Dawu)   Jiuzhi   78   132   88
Zaduo   49   Shiqu   85   62   153   68   Hongyuan   147   Jiuzhaigou
Yushu   132   Manigango   Banma   99   Aba   99   110   49   17   Chuanzhusi
170   73   262   Seda   56   Rangtang   77   88   Songpan
Nangqian   127   105   96   83   42   Ma'erkang   Heishui   112
729   Dege   Ganzi   39   179   91   9   56   170   28   Maoxian
Nakchu   307   234   105   Luhuo   90   48   134   44   Wenxian
164   Chamdo   Baiyu   97   Danba   202   57
Terdrom   171   Xinlong   147   Xiaojin   Chengdu
zhun   Drigung Til   184   Pomda   Bamei   85   Chengdu
73   Bayi   233   Pome   Kangding   67   112   223
333   74   Markham   208   Litang   209   49
Tsethang   127   Rawok   265   105   Batang   202   170   67
Menling   172   223   Jiulong   Xinduqiao   112   **Sichuan**
128   373   Dzayul   Xiangcheng   Shimian
75   22   Deqin   221   Yongning
Lhuntse   83   184   Muli   96   Xichang
Tsona   Zhongdian   Xichang
hang   *Under Indian*   147   Lijiang   279
Bomdila   *Administration*   46   Panzhihua
Tezpur   **Yunnan**

MYANMAR   146   Kunming
(BURMA)   412
Dali

Elementary School

Polio, Tuberculosis, Cholera.
*Other health concerns include: Malaria (especially for Nepal and India), Dysentery (Bacilliary & Amoebic), Giardia.

You should always be careful with drinking water. Make sure it is either boiled or treated with iodine to avoid waterborne disease (Dysentery and Giardia). In malaria areas, you should cover up, use liberal amounts of repellent and seriously consider taking prophylactics. These danger areas change and the emergence of drug resistant strains means you should check with a vaccination or tropical medicine center before you travel.

Hospitals
In Tibet, the standard of the hospitals is not very high and some of them, even in Lhasa, are without sufficient electricity or heating systems. Foreign patients face exorbitant prices for treatment. In one instance, a traveler was charged Y6,000 (US$720) for a single day's hospitalization and this figure was only after serious negotiation. This makes travel insurance seem rather appealing.

If you have mild altitude sickness or need a rabies vaccine, a small clinic in the city might be more practical. These days, every clinic uses disposable syringes, but you should check beforehand just in case and have a supply of sterile ones yourself. You should leave Tibet immediately if you come down with anything more serious and seek medical attention in a more developed area.

Language
English is spoken at foreigner's hotels in the cities, restaurants popular with tourists, the Foreign Affairs Section of the PSB, travel agencies, etc. Many signs, buses, ticket offices, menus, etc., show only Chinese characters.

Ordinarily, the Tibetans speak Tibetan, and the Chinese, Chinese. The Tibetans can also speak Chinese pretty well, as they must learn it at school. Still, many Tibetan people who did not study Chinese at school, such as monks, understand only their own language. On the other hand, very few Chinese people understand Tibetan. Basically, most Tibetans don't like hearing Chinese and some of them will ignore you or get angry with you if you speak to them in Chinese. (See Appendix.)

For travelers who have come from China, the Chinese that you've learnt is easier and can help you get most things done, however you should bear in mind the feelings of Tibetans.

With the exiled Tibetan government in India, you sometimes meet Tibetans in remote areas who speak English, having learned it in India.

Other Guidebooks
To supplement this book there are numerous other titles on the market.

*Footprint Tibet Handbook with Bhutan (Footprint)
This is a detailed guidebook to all of Tibet, including Kham, Amdo and Bhutan. The writer gives a detailed explanation about monasteries and sacred grounds.

*Tibet-A Travel Survival Kit (Lonely Planet)
It only covers the Tibetan Autonomous Region but contains detailed information for the areas around Lhasa.

*The Tibet Guide: Central & Western Tibet (Wisdom Publications)
This book also only covers the Tibetan Autonomous Region, however the writer is a scholar of Buddhism and the descriptions and explanations of the monasteries and sacred grounds are detailed and reliable.

*Tibet Handbook (Moon Publications)
This is a detailed book that contains over 1,000 pages and covers most of the places and routes for pilgrimages in the Tibetan Autonomous Region. It's good for reference but not good to carry.

*The Power-Places of Central Tibet (RKP)
This is a detailed guidebook covering only Central Tibet. Its maps are pretty good for this area.

*Trekking in Tibet (The Mountaineers)
Covering the destinations in Kham and Amdo as well, this is a detailed trekking and pilgrimage guidebook.

Other Maps Available

*China Tibet Tour Map-Chinese & English (Mapping Bureau of the TAR)
You can pick this map up at the Jokhang, Norbulingka, foreigner's hotels, etc. It is easy to read but has some inaccuracies.

Be Careful with Mountain Sickness

Chihiro Yatsu

Tourists in Tibet are always fretting about altitude sickness. It's a mysterious condition! The symptoms vary, with some people bed-bound for most of their stay in Lhasa while others really active on the day they arrive.

Our first experience with mountain sickness was in July, twelve years ago. We traveled from Golmud to Lhasa by bus and although the temperature down on the Silk Road was a blistering 40°C, we were soon cloaked in falling snow as we climbed into the Tibetan highlands. Some hours after we left Golmud, I realized that I was becoming ill. As the bus climbed, a terrible headache, endless nausea, and cold chills swept over me, all aggravated by the fact that the bus had no heater.

I wondered whether this was mountain sickness but as I slipped in and out of consciousness, all I could think about was reaching Lhasa as soon as possible. As we neared a pass, the bus gasped hard and with a laboring sigh it dropped speed. I glanced through the window at a sign reading 5,231m above sea level, and at that point I really started to regret ever getting on-board.

That night we stayed in Amdo and I just flaked out on the bed in the pitch-black guesthouse. My condition wasn't improving and I couldn't sleep for the hammers in my head, and vague fears for my future. All the while I listened to another backpacker beside me who was asleep but having trouble breathing. It was a comfort to know that I wasn't the only one suffering. Calmed a little by this, I was asleep before I knew it. Next morning, with the bus descending gradually throughout the day I realized that I was starting to feel better and when we finally arrived in Lhasa my spirits were high and my condition was almost back to normal.

Some years later, we decided to skip the bus and instead we flew into Lhasa. Nothing happened to me on our first day and I was very relieved, thinking, "I am all right this time!" Two days later, it caught up with my partner and I with headaches, nausea, and high fevers. Although I was experienced in this area, I still had difficulty overcoming my anxiety, worrying about what on earth I would do if my condition got worse. My fever remained high, so we decided that it was better to be safe than sorry and off to the People's Hospital we went. The hospital was a real disappointment; first we were directed to different departments and finally the staff told us there was no medicine in stock. All this effort just seemed to make my condition worse.

When I explained our situation to the receptionist at our hotel, they introduced us to a clinic nearby. It was tiny and not very hygienic, but the doctor examined me and using a disposable syringe gave me the required injection. Moreover, this angel of mercy visited our hotel room and made sure there was an intravenous drip set-up, though the instructions to pull out the needle when it was finished was a bit surprising.

The following year we decided on another route and entered Tibet from Nepal overland. By this time we knew a lot about the hardships caused by altitude sickness, so we finally decided to execute a 'Diamox' tactic. It's a famous medicine among trekkers in the Himalayas, so we bought a substantial amount of it in Kathmandu, smiled, and said "With this, no pain!" Before we got in the chartered Land Cruiser in Dram (Khasa), we took a bit more of the medicine than instructed just to make sure. Within half-an-hour we had to stop the car for a call of nature. After that brief stop, the car pulled away again but within minutes I was bursting to go again. Yes, the medicine also has a diuretic effect.

We had to stop the car numerous times which annoyed the driver but gave the poor local women who was carsick the whole journey some relief. Finally after crossing another 5,000m pass, we safely reached Lhasa. After the ill effects subsided we were once again able to enjoy the Tibet of our dreams.

*Map Book of the 'Tibetan Autonomous Region' (Chinese)
This is a detailed map book and is colored by region.

*Traffic Map of the 'Tibetan Autonomous Region'
This map is as big as a broad-sheet newspaper and shows distances well.

*Himalayas (Melles Maps)
Geographical features on this map are easy to understand. Unfortunately, it has some mistakes concerning roads and the borders. It's available at bookstores in Kathmandu, Pokhara, Bangkok's Khaosan Rd, etc. US$3-9.

Post and Telecommunications
In the TAR international calls are available in Lhasa and Shigatse. You can make phone calls without going through an operator in Lhasa. You can also send faxes at hotels and telephone exchanges in the city. Outside the TAR there are many places where you can make international calls, such as Chengdu in Sichuan, Xining in Qinghai, Lanzhou in Gansu, and other regional centers.

As for postal service, it takes the mail about 7 days from Lhasa to reach the outside world. You can receive mail at the post restante counter at the post office, but it is easier to use the mailbox at your guesthouse. For anyone in a rush there is EMS (Express Mail Service) available.

Considering the current political situation in Tibet, you should bear in mind that letters, telephone calls and faxes may be censored, and likewise the new Lhasa phenomenon, the Internet café. There have been situations where foreign visitors have been ordered to leave the country due to the content of their fax messages.

Safety in Tibet
There is little danger in Tibet unless you do things that you wouldn't normally do in other places, such as walking alone at night, though reports of people being robbed are extremely rare.

Tibet is a politically unstable place with ethnic conflicts and an active independence movement. There is no denying the possibility that you may face a serious situation if, for example, a sudden demonstration occurs at the Barkhor in Lhasa. As a foreigner, you shouldn't even think of getting involved. In case you come across a demonstration, refrain from taking pictures or video. Something that has happened recently is that the PSB will not order you to stop immediately but instead will allow you to take as many photographs as you like and then confiscate the film, using it to arrest Tibetan participants in the demonstration.

Illegal Matters
As already mentioned, Tibet has an active independence and anti-government movement and the Chinese authority's suppression of these movements has intensified. It has mainly focused on things that have to do with the exiled Tibetan leader, the 14th Dalai Lama.

Materials that will be confiscated include Tibetan National Flags, Dalai Lama pictures, Free Tibet T-shirts, and other such items that are all easily available in Nepal and India. There have been reports that even a guidebook page with the Dalai Lama's picture was destroyed during a baggage inspection and that a traveler wearing a Free Tibet T-shirt was ordered out of the country.

Up to 1995, Dalai Lama pictures were still being sold in public at the Barkhor in Lhasa, but this was banned in the fall of that year. In 1996, the pictures hanging in major monasteries and temples, such as the Jokhang, Sera, Drepung, Ganden, and Ramoche also were removed. His pictures also supposedly disappeared from all public places, such as restaurants. With the exception of government staff and Chinese Communist Party members, Tibetan people are not prohibited to privately own Dalai Lama pictures; however, it is illegal for foreigners to bring them in and distribute them among local people.

Naturally, banning them increases Tibetans' desire to have one and some of them will ask you for one by simply saying 'Dalai Lama photo.' If you do pass them out nothing will happen immediately, but you'll never know what became of the recipient after you left. You should also be careful because there are spies, even among the Tibetans, who will approach foreigners in a sting operation.

Just carrying the Tibetan flag can make for an extremely serious crime, labeled as an 'Offense Against State Security,' a crime that prior to 1997 had been labeled as a 'Counter-revolutionary Act.'

If you are arrested, the worst that will happen to you is that you will be ordered to leave the country. The penalties for Tibetan people, if he or she is branded as a 'separatist' with 'Dalai Lama clique sympathies,' can be very harsh indeed, including severe physical maltreatment and sentencing without a proper trial. Tibet ranks high among nations in its numbers of political prisoners.

Customs & Taboos

*Unlike India or Islamic areas, Tibet has few religious restrictions on daily life. Both the consumption of meat and alcohol are permitted and even monks eat meat. What most concerns Tibetan people about foreigners is whether these strangers respect Buddhism or not.

*Asian travelers may have a hard time because many Tibetans will initially take you to be Chinese. A way to diffuse this concern is to show your respect for the Buddhist images by offering a prayer and remembering to move clockwise around the monasteries and sacred grounds, just as the Tibetans themselves do.

*Following Tibetan customs such as wearing a rosary, even if you don't meditate, can ease people's concerns. You never know but repeatedly visiting monasteries in this manner 'may' eventually shape you into a Buddhist and make you a part of the Tibetan landscape.

*Monasteries are mainly supported by alms given by believers. Such alms may be money, yak butter for the offering lamps, tea, or *tsampa*, the staple food. Helping with the building of a monastery is also an acceptable gift. It is simply good manners to leave some alms for the maintenance of these places of worship in return for your visit. But this is up to you.

*Some Tibetans still practice a polygamous marriage system, where a wife can have more than 1 husband and husbands numerous wives. The Tibetans are surprisingly free in this respect and this may have developed due to men being away selling goods for half of the year, making it difficult to keep a close relationship going. Getting involved in this tradition is a personal judgement call.

*Another well-known Tibetan custom is the solemn practice of sky burial, where the body of the deceased is dismembered and left for wild birds to pick the bones clean. Since Tibet was opened to foreigners, observation of these rites has become a morbid fixture on tourist's sightseeing schedules.

Relatives undoubtedly will not appreciate strangers coming to see their loved one's funeral. It is officially forbidden for foreigners to observe the ceremony and the fine is in the region of Y1,000 (US$120).

Overview

In many ways Tibet at first glance reminds you of a remote and unexplored region, but in recent years the transport system has greatly improved, making the movement of people and materials much easier. This has also resulted in many changes, a visible one being the large number of empty noodle cups scattered about, even in rural areas without electricity.

Access has improved, but there seems to be no sign that the number of areas in the TAR open to foreigners will increase in the near future; indeed, government controls have intensified. Under these circumstances, it will take a substantial amount of time for all the towns introduced in this book to be opened up to foreigners. Watch out for any change in status in these closed areas, although if nothing changes you can still reach many of them by chartering a car through a travel agency.

Please write to us with your impressions and information about Tibet to help make the next edition of this guide as up-to-date and relevant as possible. Hopefully this book can help put you in touch with the fascination of Tibet, guide you, and assist you in communicating with the Tibetan people and their culture. Have a wonderful trip!

Tibet is certainly huge but as mentioned before there is a limit on the number of places that foreign visitors can go. Here are some routes that are easier for independent travelers to take and some alternative routes where a chartered car is necessary. One unavoidable aspect is that it takes time to get around in these areas, so here are some ideas to help you plan your own itineraries — an exciting chore made much easier with the detailed maps included in this book.

TIBET IN CHINA

A: Lhasa by Air (6 Days)

This course focuses solely on Lhasa. You should take it easy for the first and second days so you can adjust to the high altitude. Return plane tickets to depart from Lhasa must be bought on arrival. The starting point for this one is Chengdu.

Day 1: Chengdu (By Air) - Lhasa (PM: Barkhor)
Day 2: Lhasa (Jokhang Temple, Norbulingka, etc.)
Day 3: Lhasa (Potala Palace)
Day 4: Lhasa (Drepung & Sera Monasteries)
Day 5: Lhasa (Day Trip to Ganden Monastery)
Day 6: Lhasa (By Air) - Chengdu (or Kathmandu, Nepal)

B: Tibetan Areas in Qinghai and Gansu +Tibet Overland (12 Days)

By traveling to Lhasa overland one can visit the Tibetan cultural areas in Qinghai and Gansu. The Labrang and Rongbo monasteries are large. The starting point is Lanzhou.

Day 1: Lanzhou, Gansu (By Bus) - Xiahe
Day 2: Xiahe (Labrang Monastery)
Day 3: Xiahe (By Bus) - Tongren, Qinghai (Rongbo Monastery)
Day 4: Tongren (By Bus) - Xining
Day 5: Xining - Ta'er Monastery (Day Trip)
Days 6-8: Trip to Qinghai Hu
Day 9: Xining City Trip
Day 10: Xining (By Night Bus or Train) - Golmud
Day 11: Arrival at and departure from Golmud (By Night Bus for 30-40hrs)
Day 12: Arrival at Lhasa

C: Excursions around Lhasa (7 Days)

Visiting Shigatse, Gyantse, and Sakya is one of the most common routes around central Tibet.

Day 1: Lhasa (By Bus) - Shigatse
Day 2: Shigatse (Tashilhunpo Monastery, etc.)
Day 3: Shigatse - Sakya (Sakya North Monastery, etc.)
Day 4: Sakya (AM: Sakya South Monastery)- (PM: By Bus) - Shigatse
Day 5: Shigatse (By Bus) - Gyantse
Day 6: Gyantse (Pelkhor Choede)
Day 7: Gyantse (By Bus) - Shigatse (By Bus) - Lhasa
*It is possible to get from Sakya to Gyantse in a single day.

D: Excursions around Lhasa (9 Days)

Another common tour is visiting the Tsethang area, where the Tibetan royal family was born.

Day 1: Lhasa (By Bus) - Entrance (2hr Walk) - Mindroling Monastery (Stay)
Day 2: Mindroling Monastery (Walk, Hitch, Boat, and Truck) - Samye (Stay)
Day 3: Samye
Day 4: Samye - Chimphu Hermitage (Day Trip)
Day 5: Samye (By Boat, Bus, etc.) - Tsethang
Day 6: Tsethang - Kings' Tombs at Chongye (Stay)
Day 7: Chongye - Tsethang (Yumbu Lagang, Tradruk Temple)
Day 8: Tsethang (By Bus) - Lhasa

E: From Lhasa to Tsethang Area (By Land Cruiser) (3 Days)

To see the Tsethang area quickly, arranging a Land Cruiser makes it much easier. The price of a 3-day tour ranges from Y2,500-3,000 (US$300-360).

Day 1: Lhasa - Mindroling Monastery - Tsethang
Day 2: Tsethang Area (Kings' Tombs, Yumbu Lagang, Tradruk Temple)
Day 3: Tsethang (Both Ways by Boat) - Samye - Lhasa

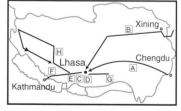

F: From Lhasa to Kathmandu (By Land Cruiser) (9 Days)

To make efficient use of your time, your only option is to arrange for a Land Cruiser. This is because it is difficult to get buses between Shigatse and Dram.

Day 1: Lhasa - Yamdrok Yumtso Lake - Nangartse - Gyantse
Day 2: Gyantse (Pelkhor Choede, etc.)
Day 3: Gyantse - Zhalu Monastery - Shigatse
Day 4: Shigatse (Tashilhunpo Monastery) - Sakya
Day 5: Sakya (Sakya South Monastery) - Shelkar
Day 6: Shelkar- Everest [Jomolangma] Base Camp
Day 7: Everest [Jomolangma] Base Camp
Day 8: Everest [Jomolangma] Base Camp - Tingri - Milarepa Monastery - Dram (Border. Land Cruiser terminates here.)
Day 9: Dram - Kodari (Nepalese Border) - Kathmandu

G: From Lhasa to Kongpo (By Land Cruiser) (9 Days)

If it is beautiful scenery that you are after, Kongpo to the east of Tsethang is a must. Without chartering a Land Cruiser, though, it is difficult to get a permit.

Day 1: Lhasa - Kongpo Gyamda
Day 2: Kongpo Gyamda - Basong Tso Lake
Day 3: Basong Tso Lake
Day 4: Basong Tso Lake - Bayi
Day 5: Bayi - Nyangtri - Serkhyim La (View of Mt. Namcha Barwa) - Menling
Day 6: Menling - Lhopa village - Nang Dzong
Day 7: Nang Dzong - Tsethang
Day 8: Tsethang Area (Kings' Tombs, Yumbu Lagang, Tradruk Temple)
Day 9: Tsethang - Mindroling Monastery - Lhasa

H: To Mt. Kailash (Kang Rinpoche) and Guge Ruins (By Land Cruiser) (3 Weeks)

A Land Cruiser is a real must for this one!

Days 1-6: Lhasa (North Route) - Ali
Day 7: Ali - Toling
Day 8: Toling - Guge Ruins (R/T)
Day 9: Toling - Montser
Day 10: Montser - Tirthapuri - Darchen (Mt. Kailash)
Days 11-15: Pilgrimage to Mt. Kailash
Day 16: Darchen - Lake Manasarovar
Days 17-22: Lake Manasarovar (South Route) - Lhasa

I: From Yunnan to Lhasa (2-3 Weeks)

The following courses are not acknowledged by the government and as a traveler, you must rely on buses and hitching lifts from trucks. The itinerary really depends on how lucky you are.

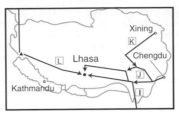

(1) Dali, Yunnan - Zhongdian - Markham - Pomda - Pome - Bayi - Lhasa
*The best season to visit is from April to May and again from October to November.

(2) Dali, Yunnan - Zhongdian - Markham - Pomda - Chamdo - Nakchu - Lhasa
*There is no real problem on this route during the rainy season, however it gets bitterly cold in winter. A trip along this route can be arranged through travel agents in Kunming, etc.

J: From Chengdu to Lhasa (2-3 Weeks)

(1) Sichuan-Tibet Highway North: Chengdu - Kangding - Ganzi - Dege - Chamdo - Nakchu -Lhasa
*A bus runs to Dege.
(2) Sichuan-Tibet Highway South: Chengdu - Kangding - Litang - Batang - Markham - Pomda - Pome - Lhasa
*A bus runs to Markham.

K: Via Yushu from Xining (2-3 Weeks)

Xining, Qinghai - Yushu - Manigango, Sichuan - Dege - Chamdo - Nakchu - Lhasa
*Though frequent, the only bus service is between Xining and Yushu.

L: From Kashgar to Lhasa, via Mt. Kailash (Kang Rinpoche) (35-50 Days)

Bus services terminate at Yecheng. This becomes a legal trip on the way, as it is possible to get a permit at Ali (at the time of going to print).
Kashgar - Yecheng - Ali - Guge Ruins - Mt. Kailash - Lhasa

LADAKH (NORTH-WEST INDIA)

Ladakh is often referred to as 'Little Tibet' and the best time to see it is from June to September. Those who plan to fly in at this time should make early reservations as flights fill up rapidly. The main draw is the big festival at Hemis Gompa.

Land transport is also available between late-June and mid-September with a bus service that runs from Manali to Leh and takes 2-3 days. The bus service from New Delhi to Manali takes 15-16 hours. The territorial dispute in the region between India and Pakistan has made the popular Srinagar route bus hazardous. This bus operates from June to October.

The Ladakh area has little snowfall, even in winter, and you can get more of a feel for ordinary Ladakhi life from fall to spring when there are fewer tourists around. There are also many festivals from December to February.

Monastery Tour in Ladakh (11 Days)

Day 1: Delhi (Early morning flight) - Leh (PM: Leh Town, Sankar Gompa)
Day 2: Leh Town (Leh Palace, Bazaar, etc.)
Day 3: Leh - Lamayuru Gompa - Alchi Gompa
Day 4: Alchi Gompa - Likir Gompa
Day 5: Likir Gompa - Serzang [Basgo] Gompa - Leh
Days 6-8: Leh - Hemis Gompa - Taktok Gompa - Tikse Gompa - Shey Gompa - Stok Gompa - Matho Gompa - Stakna Gompa - Leh
Day 9: Leh - Phyang Gompa - Spituk Gompa
Day 10: Leh Town - Choglamsar (Tibetan Refugee Settlement)
Day 11: Leh (By Air) - Delhi

*The above tour is for those who charter a car. If you use local bus services, it will take longer. Many backpackers spend 20-30 days completing this same route.

ENCOUNTER TIBET IN NEPAL

The regions that are populated by many Tibetan people and their descendents can be reached by trekking. They include the Sherpas in the Solu Khumbu Region, the Tamangs to the north of Mt. Annapurna, the Gurungs in Manang, etc.

There are many Tibetan monasteries and temples around Swayambhunath and Bodhnath in Kathmandu. The dry season from October to April is the best time to visit this area. This is also a good opportunity to visit many Nepalese sights, such as temples and the Royal Palace. You will need at least 4-5 days to see the Kathmandu area thoroughly.

Visit Tibet in Kathmandu (3 Days)

Day 1: Swayambhunath and around
Day 2: Bodhnath - Kopan Gompa - Phulvari Gompa
Day 3: Carpet factories (Tibetan Refugee Settlements at Pharping and Patan), etc.

Visit Tibet in Kathmandu, Pokhara, and Lumbini (9 Days)

Days 1-3: (Same as above, 'Visit Tibet in Kathmandu')
Day 4: Kathmandu - Pokhara
Day 5: Pokhara Town (Tibetan Temples, Tibetan Refugee Settlements, etc.)
Day 6: Pokhara - Bhairawa - Lumbini

Day 7: Lumbini (Birthplace of Buddha Shakyamuni)
Day 8: Lumbini - Bhairawa
Day 9: Kathmandu

Everest Trekking

While you are trekking, you can visit Sherpa villages around Mt. Everest (*Sagarmatha* in Nepal, *Jomolangma* in Tibet). Flying from Kathmandu to Lukla is common, but the 10-day walk is also a good option and you can visit the Tibetan temples in the Solo Khumbu Region on the way.

Round Trip by Air (12 Days)

Flying from Kathmandu to Lukla, you head for Kala Pattar, known as the observatory of Mt. Everest. On the return you get to see Gokyo Peak and enjoy some great Himalayan panoramas. If you try to visit both of these peaks, it will take at least 12 days to return to Namche Bazaar (the large bazaar is held every Saturday morning here). You should make a reservation early for the return flight.

Day 1: Kathmandu (Preparation, etc.)
Day 2: Kathmandu (By Air) - Lukla - Chumoa
Day 3: Chumoa - Namche Bazaar
Day 4: Namche Bazaar
Day 5 to Day 11: Namche Bazaar (Round Trip) - Kala Pattar (c.7 days)
Day 12: Namche Bazaar (Break)
Day 13: Namche Bazaar - Chablung
Day 14: Chablung - Lukla
Day 15: Lukla (By Air) - Kathmandu

OTHERS

* Namche Bazaar - Gokyo Peak
  (Round Trip for c.7 days)
* Namche Bazaar - Kala Pattar - Gokyo Peak - Namche Bazaar (12-14 days)
*It takes around 8 days to travel from Namche Bazaar to Jiri but you may need at least 10 days if you want to stop at Thubten Choeling Gompa on the way. A bus runs from Jiri to Kathmandu and takes more than 10 hours.

Dhaulagiri

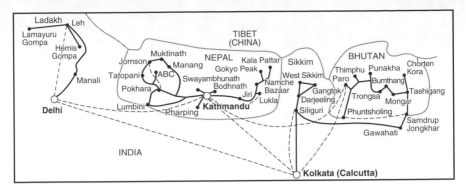

Annapurna Trekking

Day 1: Kathmandu - Pokhara
Day 2: Pokhara (Preparation)
*You may also do it in the capital.
Days 3-11: Pokhara - Annapurna Base Camp
(Round Trip for 9 days)
Days 3-9: Pokhara - Ghandrung - Tatopani -
Pokhara (7 days)
Days 3-16: Pokhara (By Air) - Jomsom (R/T) -
Muktinath - Baglung - Pokhara (14 days)
Days 3-22: Pokhara - Besisahar - Manang - Thorung
La - Muktinath - Ghorepani - Pokhara (20 days)
*It takes 1 day from Pokhara to Kathmandu.

DARJEELING AND SIKKIM

The tourist season is from October to May, which
is the dry season. But it might be better to avoid
April and May to visit Darjeeling and Gangtok, as
the resorts are packed with Indian tourists. For a
trip to Sikkim, you need a travel permit, which can
be obtained at Darjeeling, etc.

The starting point is Kolkata (Calcutta).
Day 1: Leave Kolkata (Calcutta) [At Night]
Day 2: Arrive at Darjeeling
Day 3: Darjeeling Town
Day 4: Darjeeling (Early Morning) - Tiger Hill -
Ghoom Gompa - Thupten Sang-Ngag Choeling
Gompa
Day 5: Darjeeling - Kalimpong
Day 6: Kalimpong (Town, Gompas, etc.)
Day 7: Kalimpong - Gangtok (Town)
Day 8: Gangtok (R/T) - Rumtek Gompa
Day 9: Gangtok - Phodang Gompa - Phensang
Gompa - Gangtok
Day 10: Gangtok - Geyzing - Pemayangtse Gompa
Day 11: Pemayangtse
Day 12: Pemayangtse (Walk) - Tashiding Gompa
Day 13: Tashiding Gompa (Walk) - Legship -

Siliguri (Night Departure)
Day 14: Kolkata (Calcutta)

BHUTAN

Bhutan's best season is the dry season that stretches
from October to May, even if it is freezing in the
morning. It rarely snows at places below 2,000m.
At many lhakhangs and gompas, you will get to
see only their exteriors, as they do not allow tourists
inside. Even if you travel alone, you will be
accompanied by a guide. The starting point is either
Kolkata (Calcutta) or Kathmandu.

Paro, Thimphu, and Punakha (9 days)

Day 1: Kolkata (Calcutta) or Kathmandu (By Air)
- Paro
Day 2: Paro Town (Paro Dzong, Ta Dzong, Dungtse
Lhakhang)
Day 3: Paro Town (Taktsang Monastery, Drukgyel
Dzong, Kyerchu Lhakhang)
Day 4: Paro - Thimphu
Days 5-6: Paro Town (Tashi Chodzong, etc.)
Day 7: Thimphu - Punakha
Day 8: Punakha - Paro
Day 9: Paro - Kolkata (Calcutta) or Kathmandu

All Bhutan (14 days)

Days 1-7: (See above)
Day 8: Punakha - Trongsa
Day 9: Trongsa
Day 10: Trongsa - Bumthang
Day 11: Bumthang - Mongar
Day 12: Mongar - Tashigang (R/T for Chorten
Kora)
Day 13: Tashigang - Samdrup Jongkhar
Day 14: Samdrup Jongkhar - (India) - Gawahati
(By Air) - Kolkata (Calcutta)
*Phuntsholing can also be a gateway in or out of
Bhutan.

THE SOURCE OF ASIAN CIVILIZATION?

The Tibetan Plateau is north of the Himalayas. To the north it meets the Kunlun Range, to the east China, and in the west the Pamir. Tibet is called the 'Roof of the World,' and so it should come as no surprise that most of the area is over 4,500m above sea level and has the thin air that goes with such a high altitude.

The Tibetan cultural area is roughly the size of Western Europe and the TAR makes up a little less than half of that. This vast area has only a population of around 6 million thanks mainly to the region's harsh climate.

Tibet is the highest place in the world now; however 100 million years ago it was at the bottom of the sea. Continental plate movements raised the sea bottom and 3 million years ago, the pressure created by the Indian continent colliding with the Eurasian land mass thrust the land up to form the Tibetan Plateau. This collision folded and creased the land to produce the Himalayan Range. Throughout the Tibetan areas you can still find much fossilized sea life, even on the highest peaks.

That the Tibetan Plateau was brought into being by the movement of the Indian landmass is an apt story of genesis, as the Buddhism that defines much of Tibetan culture also came from the Indian subcontinent.

Some Tibetans boast that all the great rivers that gave birth to the great civilizations of the east have their sources on the Tibetan Plateau. These include the Yellow River (Ma-chu or Huang He), the Yangtse River (Dri-chu or Jinsha Jiang), the Ganges (Karnali River), the Mekong (Dza-chu or Lancang Jiang), the Brahmaputra (Yarlung Tsangpo) and the Indus (Senge Tsangpo or Shiquanhe), etc. This is a natural occurrence due to the altitude of Tibet, but for Tibetans it is meaningful to be able to trace all these cultures back to their homeland.

FROM WOODLAND TO DESERT

The Tibetan Plateau is traditionally divided into three parts, U and Tsang (Central Tibet), Kham (North-Eastern Tibet) and Amdo (Far Eastern Tibet). Out of these areas, the most severe environment is on the Changthang Plateau, in the north of Central Tibet, a vast lake studded wilderness where nomads seek out pastureland and live out traditional lives.

Amdo is also a nomadic area, but lies in a vast plain with rich grazing land that stretches to Mongolia. These grasslands rely on the blessing bestowed by the Yellow River (Ma-chu or Huang He) that winds through the area.

Kham has a mild climate affected by the monsoon weather system and is partly covered in thick forest. The region's water is primarily supplied by the upper reaches of the Mekong (Dza-chu or Lancang Jiang).

The Kongpo Region, in the south-east of Tibet is also at a low altitude and it is heavily forested. The Yarlung Tsangpo, running from the west to the east of Tibet, changes its name to the Brahmaputra River after it turns south in this region. The river's source is at the foot of Mt. Kailash (Kang Rinpoche) in Western Tibet and forms rich farmland in its basin. Most of the population of Central Tibet has settled along its banks and it is considered the cradle of Tibetan civilization.

IS TIBET COLD?

The climate of Tibet is characterized by little rainfall and dry weather in general. The Himalayas rising in the south of Tibet intercept the monsoon from the

Indian Ocean. Lhasa has over 300 days of fine weather a year and richly deserves its title of 'City of the Sun.'

This is great for visitors but the fundamental problem is that when there is no rain there are also no crops. Generally, the rainy season falls between June and September and during this period most of the annual rainfall is recorded. The yearly precipitation in the TAR is about 360mm, which is equal to a single rainy spring month in New England or the same as in the Kalahari Desert. This rainfall comes in short bursts with blue skies and sunshine returning swiftly afterwards.

Tibetans have nicknamed their land, calling it *Kangjong* and *Kawachen* meaning 'Land of Snows.' Snow does fall in Tibet, but it rarely settles for long unless it is at high altitude, as the weather is too dry. Although it is warm enough to walk around in a T-shirt in Lhasa in summer, it is often said that there are 4 seasons in a day. Thanks to little dust and moisture in the atmosphere and extremely strong UV rays, you will feel warm out in the sun but cold in the shade. The difference between daytime and nighttime temperatures can be more than 25°C.

THE CHANGING TIBETAN PLATEAU

Driving through Tibet, you will come across many small creatures skipping around. These are marmots that rush into their burrows when startled by the sound of an approaching car. These inquisitive but easily scared animals are common here and the Tibetan Plateau is a paradise for a wide variety of other flora and fauna. The region was a virgin area

that had been hardly touched by human hands until quite recently.

There are many rare animals in these areas including, *Kyang* (Wild Asses), the Tibetan Antelope (Tsod), Tibetan Gazelle, and the snow leopards among others. One should not forget the Giant Panda (Thomtra), which lives at the eastern end of the Tibetan Plateau and is under the protection of the Chinese government.

Qinghai Hu (Lake Kokonor) and Yamdrok Yumtso Lake are famous as breeding areas for flocks of migratory birds. Tibet's high altitude also makes it a treasure trove of alpine plants. In the hills surrounding Ganden Monastery in Lhasa, you can admire the Himalayan Blue Poppy during the short mountain summer.

As in many other places in the world these precious animals and plants are under threat of extinction. Animals in particular can be sold to merchants for their furs and for use in Chinese medicine. These fetch very high prices, an especially attractive incentive in this desperately poor region. Poaching is very common, though more depressing is the hunting tour for foreign tourists, an undesirable link in the chain of the tourist industry.

The rich woodlands of eastern Tibet have been devastated by ill-conceived logging practices and this is continuing to cause huge problems with the silting-up of riverbeds and the subsequent flooding of immense areas of low-lying land in India, Bangladesh and China. The effects of nuclear testing and uranium ore mining are also long term environmental and health concerns. At first glance, the nature of the Tibet Plateau may seem untouched and untamed, however the future holds no guarantees.

Tibet's close proximity to China has meant that much of Tibetan history has been written down and recorded by the Chinese. The Chinese have a much longer history of written language and it wasn't until the 7th century that the Tibetans adopted a writing system of their own. This script seems to have been created for the sole purpose of translating the Buddhist Canons brought from India. The recording of Tibetan history was definitely not a high priority, mirroring the example of India, which also has scarce historical records from the time.

Bearing in mind the upheavals that China has endured with invasions, revolutions and civil wars, there is no way of telling how and to what degree the history of centuries has been adapted, corrupted or simply rewritten. This situation has been compounded by a lack of archeological evidence and the cultural destruction inflicted on Tibet during the Cultural Revolution.

In fact, there is a hopeless gap between the history of Tibet as accepted by the Tibetans themselves and the one put forward by the Chinese and taught to Tibetan children using Chinese texts.

A very rough summary of these divergent views goes something like this:

China: "Tibet has always been a part of China."
Tibet: "Gee, we never thought of it that way."

The Tibetan side of the story doesn't often get a chance to be aired, though. So here is an attempt, possibly a reckless one for a guidebook, to discuss both the Tibetan and Chinese versions of the history of the area. Each is the 'truth' seen from their respective points of view.

TIBETAN HISTORY FROM THE CHINESE POINT OF VIEW

Tibet as we call....

Tibet is the south-western border region of China. The people inhabiting Tibet have a long history dating back to the Neolithic Age and from early times already had connections with the Han Chinese living in Zhongyuan to the east.

During the Tang period (618-907), there were intermarriages between the royal families of the 2 peoples and treaties were signed bringing close political, economic, and cultural ties. This strong connection, over time, built a solid base for the establishment of a unified nation.

Even now, at the Potala Palace in Lhasa, there stands a statue of Princess Wengcheng, who came from the Tang royal family and in 641, married King Songtsen Gampo (c.618-649), ruler of T'u-Fan (Tibet). The square in front of the Jokhang Temple in the city, is also home to a stone obelisk erected in 823 to commemorate the Sino-Tibetan peace treaty signed the year before.

The inscription reads:

"The conference on the uniting of the country of the father-in-law and the country of the nephew, and the conclusion of the peace treaty, eternally never changing, has been witnessed and recognized by both the gods and the people, and shall be praised for ages and generations to come."

TIBETAN HISTORY FROM THE TIBETAN POINT OF VIEW

Legend has it that the first Tibetans were born from the union of a monkey and an ogress. The first king of Tibet appeared 2,000 years ago, 418 years after the death of the Buddha Shakyamuni, (Prince Gautama Siddharta) and the king's arrival is marked as the beginning of the Tibetan calendar. It is either said that the king descended from heaven or that he came from India. Since then, different tribal groups have joined together and gradually formed the country of Tibet.

The 32nd king, Namri Songsten, expanded the influence of Tibet, making expeditions as far afield as Persia, but it was his successor, Songsten Gampo (c.618-649), who actively spread the teachings of Buddhism throughout the areas under his control. The king had 3 Tibetan empresses, but as Tibet grew in power and influence the adjacent countries of Nepal and China sought out alliances and wished to remain on friendly terms with their neighbor. As a sign of friendship, royal princesses were sent to marry Songsten Gampo and these 2 women played very important roles in the development of Buddhism in the Tibetan lands. During this time the famous Jokhang Temple was constructed.

In the 8th century, during the reign of King Trisong Detsen, Tibet finally occupied Xi'an, the imperial capital of the Tang Dynasty. During this

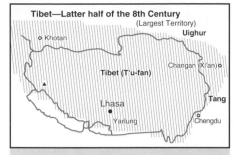

Tibet—Latter half of the 8th Century
(Largest Territory)

period, Guru Rinpoche (Padmasambhava) was invited from India to help with the spread of Buddhism in Tibet and Indian-style Buddhism was adopted as the official national religion.

During the reign of King Tri Relpachen in the 9th century there was again war between Tibet and China, in which Tibet emerged victorious. The countries signed a peace treaty which defined the borders between the 2 countries and stone pillars were erected in 823 to mark this agreement, one in Lhasa, one in Xi'an, and one at Mt. Gungu Meru on the border. These stone pillars carry the following inscriptions in both Tibetan and Chinese:

"Tibet and Tang shall respect the current borders. Hereafter, neither country shall invade the adjacent land with armed force."

The Revival of Buddhism

In the early 13th century, the Mongolian leader Genghis Khan established the kingdom of Mongol Khan in northern China. Tibet, led by the Tibetan religious leader Sakya Pandita (head of the Sakyapa order), decided to submit to the powerful Mongols.

In 1279, the Mongol Khan administration unified all of China, establishing the Yuan Dynasty. They established a central government following the example of the Han and the Tang before them, which allowed them to rule over every area and people of China. Tibet was one of those areas that officially became an administrative region ruled by this central government. Despite the repeated rise and fall of the many dynasties that ruled over China, Tibet has always been under the control of the central government.

The 14th century saw the rise of the Ming Dynasty and the third emperor Chengzu, who ruled from 1403 to 1424, and who granted Tibetan local religious leaders titles such as 'Religious King' and 'King.'

Tibet continued to increase the lands under its control until 841 when the Bonpo king Langdarma was assassinated due to his harsh oppression of Buddhism. This action plunged Tibet into 3 centuries of political upheaval and warlord rivalry.

Buddhism was gradually revived starting in the Guge Kingdom in Western Tibet. High priests from India were invited to Tibet to help spread the teachings across the country.

In the 13th century, Tibet came under threat from the advancing Mongols who had already subjugated China and had even reached as far as Eastern Europe. The Mongol Army attacked Tibet and in the face of this aggression the country was forced to accept them as their rulers. The Mongol emperors were impressed by the teachings of Tibetan Buddhism and the religion spread to Mongolia. The Mongols became zealous advocates and during the Yuan Dynasty, established by Kublai Khan in 1260, the head lama of the powerful Sakyapa order in Tibet was appointed as the head religious figure in the empire, enabling the Sakyapa to take control of Tibet.

The Dalai Lama Administration

The Qing Emperor Shizu, who ruled from 1645 to 1661, established the political and religious positions of 'Dalai Lama' and 'Panchen Lama' and appointed an ambassador to Tibet to supervise the Tibetan regional administration, which was also extensively reformed. He also determined the exact borders between Tibet and Sichuan, Yunnan, and Qinghai.

The Gelukpa order, founded by Tsongkhapa (1357-1419), became the dominant school of Tibetan Buddhism in the 16th century. The Gelukpa leader Sonam Gyatso (1543-88) received the title of 'Dalai Lama' from the Mongolian leader Altan Khan. Since then, the Dalai Lamas, who are revered as the incarnation of Avalokiteshvara, have weilded both political and religious power over the country.

After the Manchu Qing Dynasty came to power in China, ambassadors were placed in Lhasa. The Qing emporers had been followers of Tibetan Buddhism for generations and the relationship

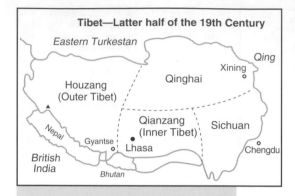

Tibet—Latter half of the 19th Century

Eastern Turkestan

Qing

Xining

Qinghai

Houzang
(Outer Tibet)

Nepal

Gyantse

Qianzang
(Inner Tibet)

Sichuan

Lhasa

Chengdu

British
India

Bhutan

between Tibet and China was one of 'temple and patron.' Even so, contacts with the Qing Dynasty gradually declined and by the 19th century Tibet had entered into a state of self-imposed isolation with its doors tightly closed to foreigners. Meanwhile the situation in the Asian areas surrounding Tibet changed dramatically, especially during the administration of the 13th Dalai Lama (1876-1933).

The British Invasion

Since the Opium War in 1840, the imperial powers have continuously attacked China, leading the country down the road towards semi-colonization. Britain invaded Tibet on a number of occasions and during one of these incursions in 1903 they actually overran Lhasa and proceeded to expel the 13th Dalai Lama.

Even though the British acknowledged Chinese sovereignty over Tibet in the Sino-British negotiations held between 1904 and 1906, they still conspired to win control over the Tibetan Plateau.

Around the end of the 19th century, the British colonial government in India began looking to open trade links with Tibet and to assert its control over the country to stop Russian designs on the region. To further these aims, the British invaded in 1903-4 led by Colonel Francis Younghusband. A treaty was signed with the independent, sovereign Tibetan administration but this was contested by the Chinese. The Qing emperor insisted that the British go through them when dealing with Tibet. The British agreed and signed a separate treaty in 1907 that recognized Chinese sovereignty over Tibet.

The Administration by the People's Republic of China

In the fall of 1911, the Nationalist Xinhai Revolution overthrew the Qing Dynasty and established the Republic of China. Immediately after its establishment, the Republican government proclaimed China was a united country consisting of the Han, the Man (Manchus), the Hui, and the Tibetans. Taking advantage of the confusion generated by this declaration, Britain expelled the Chinese ambassador from Tibet, and pushed the Tibetan regional government into a declaration of independence.

However, both the Dalai and Panchen Lamas repeatedly proclaimed their wish to protect the unity of the Motherland and their support for the central government.

In 1930, the 13th Dalai Lama stated:

"What I wish from the bottom of my heart is the true peaceful unity of China."

The confusion created by invasions and provocation by imperialists gradually subsided and the bonding between Tibet and the Motherland was allowed to strengthen.

In 1910, the Qing Army attacked Lhasa and the 13th Dalai Lama fled into exile in India. The following year a revolt broke out in China and the Qing Dynasty was deposed and the Nationalists came to power and proclaimed a republic. The Qing soldiers that had been stationed in Lhasa in an attempt to control Tibet were driven out and the 13th Dalai Lama returned to the country victorious and declared Tibet independent.

These years of freedom unfortunately lasted only until 1950 when 35,000 Chinese Communist troops, fresh from the victory against the Nationalists, invaded Tibet and seized Chamdo, the capital of eastern Tibet in a matter of days. Tibet, under the leadership of the newly enthroned 15-year old, 14th Dalai Lama, had virtually no armed forces and it was powerless to resist the onslaught.

The Tibetan government delegation that was summoned to Beijing the following year was forced to sign the 17-point agreement for the 'Peaceful Liberation of Tibet' under threat of war if they didn't sign. At the signing of the treaty a fake official seal was used to legitimize the document. Neither India, Britain nor the United Nations would come to the assistance of Tibet and the promises

Barley Harvest

In 1949, the Chinese people won a glorious victory in the People's War of Liberation, establishing the People's Republic of China. Although American and British imperialists continued to scheme for an independent Tibet, the People's Liberation Army (PLA), on its way to accomplishing the complete liberation of all of China, reached Chamdo in 1950. The following year the 17-point, 'Agreement Between the People's Central Government and Tibetan Regional Government Regarding the Method for Peaceful Liberation of Tibet,' was signed by the 2 governments.

Anti-Chinese forces abroad and many of the nobility within Tibet could not tolerate the peaceful integration of Tibet into the Motherland. These anti-revolutionaries often engaged in antagonistic and destructive activities, and finally raised arms against the People's government in 1959.

The 14th Dalai Lama had decided, of his own free will, to attend a theatrical performance at the Tibetan Military Area Auditorium. The rebels used this as an excuse to begin spreading rumors that the Hans were attempting to kidnap the Dalai Lama or that they were going to poison him. They attempted to stir up the people of Lhasa and coerced about 2,000 citizens into surrounding the Norbulingka, his residence. They threatened the Dalai Lama and then took him from Lhasa to Lhokha, in southern Tibet, where the rebellious forces were based.

Once the Dalai Lama had been removed from Lhasa, these counter-revolutionaries then gathered a mob of some 7,000 people to attack the political organizations, government offices, and the People's Liberation Army (PLA). The actions of loyal patriotic Tibetans and the PLA thwarted this attempt and the revolt was completely suppressed in the city of Lhasa in just 2 days. The defeated rebels, who had been fleeing to Lhokha, then made their escape to India.

Thanks to the 'Democratic Revolution,'

of regional autonomy, freedom of religion and the guarantee of the Dalai Lama's position were all reneged on quickly by the Chinese.

The Tibetan people put up a fierce resistance in which hundreds of thousands of people were murdered. Even more people died of starvation as farmers were forced to turn their agricultural land over to wheat production instead of the far better suited traditional crop of barley. This disastrous policy, combined with a dramatic increase in the urban population due to Chinese immigration, caused chronic food shortages across the country.

In 1959, the Chinese commander in Lhasa ordered the 14th Dalai Lama to attend a theater performance at a Chinese military compound. Fearing for his holiness's safety, Tibetan people surrounded his summer palace, the Norbulingka, to protect him. The Chinese Army tried to intervene and the clash resulted in thousands of Tibetan deaths. To avoid an even worse tragedy, the Dalai Lama slipped out of the palace and fled to India where he established his government-in-exile in the Indian town of Dharamsala.

Later, the Communist government divided Tibet into an autonomous region, provinces, prefectures and counties, and it has continued to assert its control over the 6 million Tibetan people, labeling them as 'minority peoples.' Since the occupation, over 100,000 Tibetan people have fled to India, Nepal, Bhutan and elsewhere in the world.

The Cultural Revolution arrived in Tibet in 1966. Many monasteries and temples had already been severely damaged during the invasion and occupation of the country; these and many others were now razed to the ground. Along with the destruction of the buildings, much of the artwork and many religious objects were also destroyed or stolen. Anything that was seen to be traditional was seen as a threat to the revolution and all things Tibetan were banned. During this period, thousands lost their lives and more were imprisoned in forced labor camps.

White Palace, Potala Palace

the Tibetan people have managed to cast off the cruel yoke of feudal serfdom and for the first time in their history, they have achieved their freedom. Democracy was in place, farmers and herdsmen were highly motivated in their production to benefit the masses and modern industrialization began. All these glorious achievements have improved the Tibetan people's standard of living immensely.

Throughout the Cultural Revolution, Tibet, just as other regions in China, had the freedom of religion curtailed and many religious complexes were destroyed. After that period, though, freedom of religion in Tibet was totally restored. Religious activities were revived and shattered temples are undergoing vigorous, government-assisted reconstruction. In 1995, the Potala Palace's restoration was completed in time for the Tibetan Autonomous Region's 30th anniversary celebrations.

At the present time, we still see the Dalai Lama group and other 'Splitist' forces abroad at work, scheming to undermine the stability of the People's Republic of China and separate Tibet from the Motherland through the spreading of false rumors, counter-revolutionary propaganda and the inciting of riots.

Although some limited freedoms were restored immediately after the end of the Cultural Revolution, there was a great repulsion felt by the Tibetan people as they were obliged to act as Han Chinese. This antipathy has been further fueled by the continued influx of Chinese migrants, which has actually turned Tibetans into a minority in Lhasa.

Since the fall of 1987 there have been a scattering of demonstrations and each time the Chinese authorities have brutally suppressed them, with loss of life or liberty for many of the participants. In Lhasa, martial law was imposed in 1989 and this lasted for a year and 7 months. Over time, the Dalai Lama has actually conceded the demand for full independence and he has called on the Chinese to hold peace talks, but China has chosen to ignore this. The Dalai Lama was awarded the Nobel Peace Prize in 1989 for his efforts to reach a solution without resorting to violence, however the Chinese have only responded by stiffening their attitude towards his Holiness and his government-in-exile. Estimates put the number of political prisoners jailed in Tibet today at more than 400.

The Dalai Lamas

Yukiyasu Osada

The Dalai Lama is regarded as the embodiment of Avalokiteshvara (Bodhisattva of Compassion). As Religious King, the highest authority of Tibetan Buddhism, and also the Tibetan political leader, the Dalai Lamas have reigned over both Tibetan religious and secular life.

1st	Gendun Drupa (1391-1474)
2nd	Gendun Gyatso (1475-1542)
3rd	Sonam Gyatso (1543-1588)

The head of Drepung and Sera Monastery, Sonam Gyatso was invited by Altan Khan of Mongolia to Chabcha, Amdo (Gonghe, Qinghai Province) in 1578 and received the title of *Dalai Lama* (Ocean of Wisdom). The title of Dalai Lama started with the third incarnation, and the 2 predecessors were named Dalai Lama only later.

4th	Yonten Gyatso (1589-1616)
5th	Lobzang Gyatso (1617-1682)

The 5th Dalai Lama is commonly known as *Gyalwa Ngapa* (5th, the Great). Supported by Gushi Khan of Mongolia, Lobzang Gyatso became the head of all Tibet in 1642 and established the Dalai Lama's government. In the reign of the 5th Dalai Lama, Tibetan culture flourished, and this led to the construction of the Potala Palace.

When the 5th Dalai Lama passed away, the great regent, Desi Sangye Gyatso, who held absolute power in the country, suppressed the news of the death for 14 years while he was grooming the sixth incarnation and completing the Potala Palace.

6th	Tsangyang Gyatso (1683-?)

Tsangyang Gyatso was born to a Nyingmapa family in Monyul (Tawang, Arunachal Pradesh in India). Maybe because he was offended by the dogged struggle for power, Tsangyang Gyatso grew to become a lover of the fast life and fell well short of the regent's expectations. He often escaped from the Potala Palace to play around and eventually decided to return to secular life. Nonetheless, his personality and down-to-earth nature continues to appeal to Tibetans, and his love songs still delight the people.

It is said that Tsangyang Gyatso was relieved of the title of Dalai Lama by Lhazang Khan, who occupied Lhasa, due to his bad behavior, and he later died in Amdo, as he was being sent under escort to Beijing. His body was not preserved.

7th	Kelzang Gyatso (1708-1757)
8th	Jampal Gyatso (1758-1804)
9th	Lungtok Gyatso (1805-1815)
10th	Tsultrim Gyatso (1816-1837)
11th	Khedrub Gyatso (1838-1855)
12th	Trinle Gyatso (1856-1875)

After the 7th Dalai Lama passed away, there was a deadly struggle amongst the country's nobles for the seat of regent, who ruled for the Dalai Lamas until they came of age. All of the Dalai Lamas from the 9th to the 12th died unnaturally in their teens and early twenties.

13th	Tubten Gyatso (1876-1933)

A pawn in the struggle between the Qing (Manchu) Dynasty and Britain, which eventually invaded Tibet, Tubten Gyatso was the first Dalai Lama to really be dragged onto the world stage.

14th	Tenzin Gyatso (1935-)

Born in Taktser, Amdo, Tenzin Gyatso ascended to the throne in Lhasa at the age of 4. In 1950 the Chinese Communists invaded Tibet, and the Dalai Lama assumed his majority in the face of the aggression. After failed attempts to work with the Chinese, the Dalai Lama finally secretly fled to India in 1959. Since then, Tibet has lost its independence, and the Dalai Lama heads the government-in-exile in Dharamsala, India.

Appreciated for his adherence to non-violent struggle against the Chinese occupation, he won the Nobel Peace Prize in 1989. Although he lives in exile, the 14th Dalai Lama is still seen as the highest leader of Tibet and has continued with his pleas to the Chinese government for negotiations, while appealing to the international community for support.

THE WORLD OF TIBETAN BUDDHISM

Possibly because of the impressive, intimidating, and at times, erotic murals decorating Tibetan monasteries, Tibetan Buddhism was often misunderstood and classed by many outsiders as an eccentric cult until quite recently. In reality, it is basically the same as the Buddhism practiced elsewhere. The fundamentals of Tibetan Buddhism are:

1. Refuge in 'The Three Precious Jewels' (Kunchok Sum): Buddha (Shakyamuni), Dharma (his teachings), and Sangha (the monastic community).
2. 'Bodhicitta' (Jangchup Sempa), or the fervent wish for the salvation of all living things and the desire to free them from their worldly suffering.
3. 'Altruism,' a dedication to bring happiness to others.

This is *'Tekpa Chenpo'* (Mahayana) or the 'Greater Vehicle' style of Buddhism that is practiced throughout East Asia, including China, Korea and Japan. These teachings focus on the securing of enlightenment for all, unlike the *'Tekmen'* (Hinayana) or 'Lesser Vehicle' style of Buddhism practiced in South Asia, which emphasizes the individual path to enlightenment.

So why does Tibetan Buddhism look so different if it is basically so similar in its teachings to the Buddhism found in other East Asian countries?

Shakyamuni

What Makes Tibetan Buddhism Different

The style of Buddhism that spread along the Silk Road through China, then into the Korean Peninsula, and which finally reached Japan in the 6th century was one that originated in India around the 1st century.

Tibet, on the other hand, remained untouched by this early spread of Buddhism, even though India was an immediate neighbor and there were many contacts between the countries. Buddhism was finally introduced into Tibet in the 7th century and the religion took root in the country over the following century.

Thus, the Buddhism found across East Asia and Tibetan Buddhism were brought from India along different routes. With its highly developed civilization, China seems to have added its own interpretation to the Buddhist texts it received. As for Korea and Japan further to the east, not only did China act as a cultural filter of Buddhism, but the practice of religion in these countries also was influenced by their own strong indigenous cultures.

Tibet however received a more 'pure' form of Buddhism as the religion came straight from the country where it originated. The translation of the Indian texts became a national undertaking and it was to make this endeavor possible that the Tibetan written script was created. The Tibetan scholars concentrated on as faithful a translation as possible and it was for that reason that the texts closest to the original material were preserved in Tibet after the dramatic decline of Buddhism in India. This fact led a couple of monks from

Guru Rinpoche who introduced Tantric Buddhism to Tibet

Japan, the most famous being Ekai Kawaguchi (author of *Three Years in Tibet*), to risk their lives to reach Tibet to study these texts around the turn of the century despite the country being tightly closed to foreigners.

Another important factor that helps explain the differences in Buddhism has to do with when Buddhism was introduced into Tibet. This occurred 10 centuries after Buddhism was born and when the religion in India had entered an age of a highly animistic and shamanist-like 'Late Tantric Buddhism.' Because Tibet faithfully inherited this late Tantric Buddhism, strange images of wrathful deities and father-mother Buddhas appear on the Buddhist murals produced in the country, giving it the air of a cultish religion.

Tantric Ascetic

Exoteric Buddhism and Tantric (Esoteric) Buddhism
Those who have followed the order and its teachings of open, general 'Exoteric' Buddhism are entitled to be given the teachings of 'Tantric' Buddhism. These teachings are at an even higher level of secrecy and they are not restrained by ethical codes. Tantric Buddhism is made up of many kinds of meditation and symbolic rituals, and this is thought to be the main characteristic of Tibetan Buddhism. However, all the esoteric Buddhist practices are based on exoteric Buddhist texts known as *Do* or *Sutras*. The esoteric texts are called *Gyu* or *Tantras*.

Reincarnation and Incarnated Lamas
All living things eternally repeat the cycle of life and death in the 'Six Realms' (Hell, Hungry Ghost, Animal, Human Being, Asura, and Deva Realms) according to their deeds in their previous life. As long as one is born as a living thing, all kinds of agony ensue. Escaping this circle of reincarnation is what is called 'emancipation from worldly attachments' or 'enlightenment.' In the 'Six Realms,' only human beings are allowed to train for enlightenment, so it is considered a precious opportunity to be born as a human.

Thangka of the Wheel of Existence

In the incarnated lama system, which is unique to Tibet, when a high-ranking monk or nun dies, he or she is born again and the child is sought out and educated as a successor. Sometimes the high-ranking lamas leave a prophecy that they will be reborn in a certain place or an oracle is relied on in cases where there are no clues. Such lamas could have actually reached enlightenment and chosen not to be born again into this world but they have decided to return to the world to help the people still suffering and confused. The idea is based on the altruism of the 'Greater Vehicle' of Buddhism. The most famous one is the Dalai Lama, revered as the living embodiment of Avalokiteshvara, the Bodhisattva of Compassion.

Bon
One can't understand either Tibetan Buddhism or Tibetan culture without also looking at the Bon religion. Bon is a collection of folk religions that existed in Tibet and flourished for thousands of years prior to Buddhism's arrival. Although Tibetan life has become intertwined with Buddhism, it is Bon that is the religion unique to the Tibetan people.

A Hanging Goat in a temple, a vestige of Bon

Legend has it that the founder of Bon, Shenrab Miwoche, descended from heaven and chose to land on Mt. Kailash in Western Tibet. He introduced this combination of animist and shamanist traditions that involve the use of magic rituals and prayers.

After Buddhism was introduced into Tibet, Bon lost most of its power and gradually Tibet became a Buddhist country. Yet Bon's influence has remained strong among the people. Bon elements can be found in some festivals and rituals and Bon still retains considerable influence in certain regions of Tibet.

The Bon that survives today is quite different from its original form. The teachings were reorganized in order to withstand the challenge from Buddhism and these days there is not much distinction separating them.

Visible differences between Buddhism and Bon are:

- The *Yungdrung* or 'Swastika' symbol: Buddhism 卐, Bon 卍
- The pilgrimage route taken around a temple or other sacred place: Clockwise for Buddhism, counter-clockwise for Bon.
- Common chanted prayer phrases: *Om Mani Padme Hum* for Buddhism, *Om Matri Muye Saledu* for Bon.
- The principle temples of traditional Bon are Tashi Menri Monastery and Yungdrungling Monastery (both to the east of Shigatse). However, as most of the leaders have gone into exile in India, the newer Tashi Menri Monastery in Dolanji, northern India, now functions as the head monastery of the religion.

THE FOUR GREATEST SCHOOLS OF TIBETAN BUDDHISM

At present there are 4 major schools: Nyingmapa, Kagyupa, Sakyapa, and Gelukpa.

Nyingmapa (Red Hat Sect)
Founder: Guru Rinpoche (Padmasambhava)
Head Monastery: Mindroling Monastery (Southern Treasures), Dorje Drak Monastery (Northern Treasures)

Guru Rinpoche

Nyingma means 'Old' and as the name suggests, Nyingmapa is the oldest school of Tibetan Buddhism. The Indian master Guru Rinpoche, who laid the foundations of Tibetan Tantric Buddhism in the 8th century, founded the school. With a strong influence from Bon, the Nyingmapa are still very active in eastern Tibet, Nepal, Bhutan, and other smaller areas.

The Nyingmapa order has been persistent in keeping the tradition of taking religious training without renouncing the world. It also has a system of discovering *Terma* (Concealed Teachings), the whereabouts of which are revealed by revelations or visions. This adds a mystical flavor to the order.

Prominent Figure 1: Guru Rinpoche (Padmasambhava)
The Indian founder of Tibetan Buddhism used his strong Tantric Buddhist power to subdue the local deities who interfered with the construction of Samye Monastery, which was being built by Shantaraksita, a venerable exoteric Buddhist philosopher also from India. He is also famed for rushing from place to place in Tibet and systematically transforming the local Bon deities into Buddhist protectors, thus making Tibet into a Buddhist country. Although many of the accounts of his life and exploits have passed into myth and legend, Guru Rinpoche remains overwhelmingly popular among the Tibetan people regardless of which schools' teachings they adhere to.

Milarepa, Wandering Minstrel

Prominent Figure 2: Longchen Ranbjampa (1308-63)
In the 14th century Longchen Ranbjampa reorganized the teachings of the order to defend against the criticisms made by the other increasingly influential Buddhist schools. He introduced the teachings of the *Dzogchen* which are still regarded as the principal teachings of the present-day Nyingmapa.

Kagyupa
Founder: Marpa (1012-96)
Head Monasteries: Tsurphu Monastery (Karma Kagyupa Black Hat Sect), Yangpachen Monastery (Karma Kagyupa Red Hat Sect), Drigung Til Monastery (Drigung Kagyupa), Sangak Choeling (Drukpa Kagyupa), Taklung Monastery (Taklung Kagyupa), Jomonang Monastery (Jonang Kagyupa).

The 14th Dalai Lama, now in exile in India

Maybe because the founder himself was a Buddhist lay practitioner, the Kagyupa has not developed as well-coordinated within the school. It is roughly divided into 6 major subdivisions from which a number of smaller groups have been derived. The largest of these, the Karma Kagyupa, is known to have introduced the 'Incarnated Lama System' into Tibet. Another major one, the Drukpa Kagyupa, is the national religion of Bhutan. The Kagyupa has a strong Tantric Buddhist flavor.

Prominent Figure: Milarepa (1052-1135)
Regretful over killing a large number of people with black magic, Milarepa decided to become master Marpa's pupil. Only after long, relentless and extremely arduous training did he receive the teachings. Later, he became a Buddhist ascetic and wandering minstrel. Milarepa is one of the historical figures who is also beloved among Tibetans.

The late 10th Panchen Lama

Sakyapa
Founder: Konchok Gyalpo (1034-1102)
Head Monasteries: Sakya Monastery, Ngor Monastery, and Gongkar Choede.

In the 11th century the Khon family of Sakya established Sakyapa with the construction of Sakya Monastery. Later in the 13th century, the leader of the order became the mentor to the Mongolian Emperor and seized enormous power across Tibet. While many of the other Buddhist schools practice the 'Incarnated Lama System,' the head of the Sakyapa is a hereditary position. The present Sakyapa though is not directly descended from the Khon family.

Prominent Figure 1: Sapan (Sakya Pandita) (1182-1251)
The greatest monk and scholar in the history of the Tibetan Tantric Buddhism. Sapan is also credited with spreading Tibetan Buddhism to Mongolia.

Prominent Figure 2: Phakpa (1235-80)
A nephew of Sapan, Phakpa became the Emperor's mentor and created the Mongolian script of *Phakpa*.

Gelukpa (Yellow Hat Sect)
Founder: Je Rinpoche (Tsongkhapa) (1357-1419)
Head Monastery: Ganden Monastery
The Six Greatest Monasteries: Ganden, Drepung, Sera, Tashilhunpo, Labrang, Ta'er (Kumbum)

Tsongkhapa, Founder of Gelukpa

Gelukpa is the newest and the largest school. Although the Dalai Lama belongs to this school, the actual patriarch of Gelukpa is Ganden Tripa, the elected head of the Ganden Monastery.

The founder of Gelukpa, Tsongkhapa, opened the doors and allowed a fresh breeze to blow into a Tibetan Buddhism world that had been corrupted by some sexually oriented Tantric practices. In the early 15th century, Tsongkhapa, who considered the ethical codes to be all-important, established the system that dictated that only those who had mastered exoteric Buddhism were allowed to proceed onto the esoteric Tantric Buddhist practices. With this religious reform and the introduction of the incarnated lama system that produced the Dalai Lama, Gelukpa developed dramatically. Among the major Buddhist schools, Gelukpa does not allow its monks to marry.

Prominent Figure 1: The Dalai Lama
Revered as the embodiment of Avalokiteshvara, the Bodhisattva of Compassion, the Dalai Lama is the leader of both politics and religion in Tibet. The most recent 14th incarnation is Tendzin Gyatso who assumed power in 1950. For details see page 35.

Prominent Figure 2: The Panchen Lama
Revered as the embodiment of the Buddha Amitabha, the Panchen Lamas's base is the Tashilhunpo Monastery in Shigatse. A dispute over acknowledgment of the present incarnation, the 11th Panchen Lama, has led to a serious confrontation between the Dalai Lama and the Chinese Government.

KEYWORDS FOR PRAYER

Most of the places you visit in Tibet will be monasteries, temples or other sacred places. You will also meet pilgrims everywhere you go. Whether it is a day-long picnic in the city, or a month-long walking tour in a remote mountainous region, the Tibetan world of prayer is one that is filled with delight that has touched many foreign visitors.

THE PRAYER SCENE
Tar-choks
Five-colored prayer flags that flutter in the breeze on the roofs of Tibetan houses, in gardens, from atop nomads' tents, in mountain passes, on sacred peaks and holy lakes, in monasteries and other revered places. These flags are printed with Buddhist scriptures and they spread the Buddhists' word to the outside with every gust of wind.

Lungta (Wind Horse)
A common image found printed on *tar-choks* -- the horse is pictured galloping across the sky spreading the teachings of Buddhism whenever the flags are blown by the wind. You can also buy sheaves of thin square paper with the image of the 'Wind Horse' printed on them and these are also called *Lungta*. Shouting *Lha Gyal Lo!* (Victory

Tar-choks in a mountain pass

over God!), Tibetans scatter these *Lungta* as they go through mountain passes.

Lungta

Dar-shing
The white banners such as *Dar-shing* are also prayer flags that are found in sacred places. These are particularly common in Kham, Sikkim and Bhutan.

Chorten (Stupa)
Originally, these were built as reliquaries for the cremated remains of high-ranking lamas. These structures are now built when a memorial service is held for them, too. *Chorten* are also constructed as offerings to local mountain or river deities. *Tsatsa* statuettes and other offerings are found inside the structures.

Tsatsa
Small statues made from sun-baked mud or pottery. These are made in the image of Buddha or other religious symbols. At pilgrimage sites you can usually buy the ones made from mud from stalls set-up to cater to pilgrims.

Khora

Khora (Clockwise Pilgrimage Circuit)
Making a clockwise pilgrimage circuit around a holy site, such as a temple, monastery, chorten, sacred mountain or lake. The followers of the Bon religion make a circuit in the opposite direction.

Mani-stones (Prayer Stones)
Tibetans make piles of stones whenever the opportunity presents itself. This custom is said to have originated prior to the arrival of Buddhism and it spread across the Tibetan world. *Mani*-stones are those stones and rocks that have been painted or engraved with Buddhist images. They come in a variety of sizes and shapes, ranging from small stones on which only a single character has been engraved to massive rocks decorated with Buddhist images. The most common one of these carries the 6 characters that spell out *Om Mani Padme Hum*.

Om Mani Padme Hum
This *mantra* connected to Chenrezik (Avalokiteshvara), the Bodhisattva of Compassion, means 'Oh Jewel of Lotus in Me.' All Tibetans are familiar with this prayer phrase. Every Buddha, bodhisattva and deity has their own *mantra*. (See page 47 & 48).

Mani-stone of 'Om Mani Padme Hum'

Sang (Fragrant Grass)
Burnt in an incense burner during Buddhist memorial services and other special occasions. When you see the clouds of smoke and there is a heavy smell of *Sang* in the town, it must be a festival day.

Rangjung
Meaning 'Self-Arising,' they can be found at most sacred places. This group of objects includes rocks on which a letter 'A' has appeared miraculously and images of Buddha that have been engraved in a similar mysterious way.

ENTERING THE WORLD OF THE GOMPA
Gompa (Monastery)
Gompas are where monks live together and receive the Buddhist teachings. There used to be over 6,000 monasteries in Tibet, but the vast majority of these were first dissolved during the early years of

Sang Burner

Lhakhang

Mani prayer-wheels

Prostration

the Chinese occupation. They were not seen by the Communists solely as centers of religion but also as a centers for the ruling theocratic class that owned the means of production and exploited the masses. These institutions were further decimated during the Cultural Revolution (1966-76), which was an attempt by Chairman Mao Zedong to reinvigorate the Chinese revolution.

Since the early 1980's, there has been considerable reconstruction of these buildings, though many of the artifacts that were destroyed or stolen are irreplaceable. This resurgence has been made possible by the Chinese government's policy of 'Open-and-Reform.'

Large-scale complexes consist of the *Tsokchen* (Great Assembly Hall), the *Dukhang* (Assembly Hall), *Tratsang* (Colleges), *Lhakhangs* (Temples/Shrine), and clusters of monks' lodgings. The larger monasteries function like a small town.

Lhakhang (Temple or Shrine)
These temples or shrines are dedicated to various Buddhas, bodhisattvas, and deities. They can be found both as a part of a gompa or by themselves.

Gonkhang (Protector Chapel)
A special type of lhakhang that is dedicated to *Choekyong* (Dharma Protector Deities)

Manikhor (Mani Prayer-wheel)
Turning a *Manikhor* means that you have then read all the Buddhist scriptures that are inside the wheel. This convenient religious tool ranges in size from hand-held ones to huge ones that can only be turned with the help of someone else.

Surrounding lhakhangs, there are usually *Manikhor* corridors or groups of prayer wheels strung out in lines. As you make your *Khora* you turn each wheel. Be careful, as doing this to excess can really hurt your hands after a while.

Kyangcha (Prostration)
By prostrating oneself, you demonstrate your devotion with all your body and soul. *Kyangcha* is the conventional way of praying in Tibet and you will meet pilgrims wearing padding on their chest and cloth padding on their hands to protect them when repeatedly performing this ritual. Tibetans prostrate themselves when entering a lhakhang or in the presence of a revered image of Buddha or a high-ranking lama.

The *Kyangcha* follows these steps:

1. Begin with joining your hands in prayer in front of your chest. The formal way is to arrange both of your hands so they are not completely together.
2. Move your joined-together hands above the head. (Prayer by body)
3. Put your joined-together hands down to your mouth. (Prayer by words)
4. Keep your hands joined together and move them further down to your chest. (Prayer by the heart)
5. Unclasp your hands and then put both your hands and knees to the ground.
6. Lay prone on the ground and stretch out your body.
7. Join your hands in prayer again with your arms fully stretched out.
8. Get up and repeat it from Step 1.

Choeme (Butter Lamp)

If you decide to bring something on a pilgrimage to a gompa, you should consider bringing *Mar* (Butter). Tibetan lamps use it as fuel and they are kept burning thanks to the offerings of butter that pilgrims pour into them one after another.

Choepa (Offerings)

Besides butter, Tibetans present various other offerings to the images of Buddha. Common *Choepas* are *Poe* (Incense sticks), fruits, flowers, bread, rice and money.

Offerings

Torma

Made from butter, tsampa, and sugar, a *Torma* is a vividly colored offering sculpted into different forms. A common shape is that of a chorten and the forms reflect the skills and artistic sensibility of each monastery. After the ritual, the cake is eaten.

Katak

A thin silk scarf that is used at festivities or when biding farewell to someone. You place a piece of *Katak* around the neck of the other party while saying *Tashi Delek* (Congratulations). The offer of the scarf is also accompanied by a wish for the recipient's happiness. To be given a blessing by a high-ranking lama, you bring the cloth for him to put around your neck. When you worship an image of Buddha, you do it all yourself.

Gau

A *Gau* is carried in either the front or back pocket of your *chuba* (Jacket). Inside it contains either an image of Buddha or an amulet.

Torma

Kyilkhor (Mandala)

Various styles of paintings and structures are used to visualize the world of Buddhas and deities: 2-dimensional paintings and murals, sand *mandalas* formed with only colored sand, 3-dimensional *mandalas* copying the palaces of deities, and even buildings themselves arranged to form a *mandala*. The type of *Kyilkhor* also varies from ones depicting concrete images of Buddhas and deities to abstract ones formed using only their symbols. (For more, see page 52 & 53.)

Thangka (Buddhist Painting)

Framed by a silk brocade, *Thangka* are Buddhist paintings that were originally designed for use as religious items, but they have also become popular among the people as they portray the very essence of Tibetan art. (For more, see pages 49-51.)

Gau

A MONK'S LIFE

Lama (Guru or Master)

Originally meaning 'Guru,' but in many cases to the general public it simply means 'Monk.' However, the term *My Lama* means the 'Master' or 'Guru' from whom the person receives his teachings. Tibetan Buddhism used to be called *Lamaism* because the religion considers the relationship between master and pupil as very important. As the first stage of learning, a devout belief in the *Lama* is strongly emphasized.

Trapa (Monk)

In the monasteries *Trapa* is the lowest-ranking monk. Monks may

Debating at Sera Monastery

get promoted through exams and debates, however most of them end their lives without rising above the rank of *Trapa*. However, there are still various areas in which they can demonstrate their skills: drawing *thangka*, managing the kitchen, or succeeding in business, among others.

Tulku (Emanation, Incarnated Lama)
Originally the meaning was 'Reincarnation' and these highly revered lamas are born again and again so that they can continue to help people.

Rinpoche (High-Ranking Lama)
Generally a title conferred on a high-ranking and revered lama -- it means 'Jewel.' A *Rinpoche* does not have to be a *Tulku* and, as a matter of fact, some highly learned monks are also called *Rinpoche*.

Geshe (Philosophical Degree)
While the *Trapa* is the entry level, the *Geshe* is the highest title that can be attained by a scholar-monk. Only after a monk passes a number of exams and debates can he attain this title and the preparation normally takes 30 years. Finding a *Geshe* in the Chinese-occupied areas of the Tibetan world is not easy, as most high-ranking lamas have sought refuge abroad to further their training and take their examinations.

Khenpo (Abbot)
Roughly, the *Khenpo* occupies the highest position at a monastery. When the *Khenpo* from a leading monastery leaves to give teachings, a number of Land Cruisers will be arranged and the highly revered lama is placed under the escort of public security officers.

Ani (Nun)
At an *Ani Gompa* (Nunnery), an *Ani* receives her training and performs rites similar to the ways that monks do.

Umdze (Chanting Master)
When a *sutra* is recited the *Umdze* is the one that takes the lead. They are chosen for their strong and clear voices.

Young monks practicing Tibetan Horns

Ngakpa (Ascetic)
Ngakpas do not stay at one particular monastery and instead practice their asceticism in caves far from human habitation. The Nyingmapa and Kagyupa have many *Ngakpas* who look similar to Indian *Saddhus* as they have long hair and grow beards.

Pecha (Buddhist Scriptures)
Buddhist scriptures are printed using wood blocks. The general collection of Buddhist scriptures is the 'Tibetan Buddhist Canon' consisting of the *Kangyur*, the scriptures themselves, and the *Tengyur*, a set of commentaries. These texts are sacred writings and should be given the same respect as the actual spoken word of Buddha.

Terma (Concealed Teachings)
The *Terma* are said to be the Buddhist scriptures that Guru Rinpoche (Padmasambhava), the founder of Tibetan Tantric Buddhism, buried in various places in expectation that they would be recovered when the time was right. As Guru Rinpoche foretold in the 8th century, these will be found by a *Terton* (Treasure Finder) inspired by a spiritual

Nuns printing Buddhist scriptures

revelation concerning the whereabouts of the hidden text.

This tradition is unique to the Nyingmapa and some viewing this objectively have argued that these are wrong teachings. The *Tibetan Book of the Dead* that helped to bring Tibetan Buddhism world recognition is one of these *Terma*.

Bardo Thoedrol (Tibetan Book of the Dead)

The original title is 'A Profound Teaching: Self-liberation Through the Meditation of Peaceful and Wrathful Deities.' *Bardo Thoedrol* was one of the *Terma* teachings concealed by Guru Rinpoche.

A lama reads the book beside a dying person so that it can help him or her to attain a better reincarnation. *Bardo* means the 'intermediate stage between death and reincarnation,' while *Thoedrol* means 'liberation through listening.' The best result is if one breaks out from the cycle of reincarnation and is not reborn, but there are very few who can do this. Thus, the *Tibetan Book of the Dead* appears to be more realistic as it promises even a slightly better reincarnation.

Bardo Thoedrol discusses in detail how the body changes while dying and where the consciousness goes. Furthermore, the book teaches how a dead person copes with visions and how to be reborn better.

Originally, one had to receive solid Buddhist training while he or she was alive to obtain a better life after death. However, the *Bardo Thoedrol* is based on a positive interpretation that you can be reborn better if you do your best in the last moments before death.

Pecha

Lamp and mani prayer-wheel that is turned by air currents from the lamp

Shelves full of Buddhist scriptures

Shakyamuni

Thousand-armed Avalokiteshvara

Rigsum Gonpo: Vajrapani (Chakna
Dorje), Manjughosa (Jampeyang),
Avalokiteshvara [Left to right]

BUDDHAS, DEITIES, ETC., IN THE MANDALA WORLD

When you visit Tibetan temples, you will encounter a great number of images of Buddhas and deities. According to one accepted convention, there are 5,000 different images. All these Buddhas and deities have their roles and they appear in the secular world in response to a person's invitation or request. This book discusses some of the important figures but categorization of the images can't always be definite. As a matter of fact, a bodhisattva can be a guardian deity, a dharma protector (protector deity), or assume some other role. In Tibetan Buddhism, pious people look at the nature of the whole rather than the style of the individual figure.

Buddhas (Tathagata)

The word *Buddha* reminds many people of the historical figure Shakyamuni (Prince Gautama Siddhartha) but there are many others who have attained spiritual enlightenment. All of them are referred to as *Buddha* or 'Awakened One.'

Besides Shakyamuni (Shakya Thubpa or the founder of Buddhism), Vairocana, Aksobhya, Ratnasambhava, Amitabha, and Amoghasiddhi are representative Buddhas; collectively, they are known as the 'Buddhas of the Five Families.' Other well-known important Buddhas are Bhaisajyaguru (Sangye Menla), who is common throughout East Asia, Vajrasattva (Dorje Sempa) and Varadhara (Dorje Chang) who are both regarded as highly positioned Tantric Buddhas.

Even though the images of the Buddhas are not as lavishly decorated as the various other deities, they are without doubt at the center of the 'Mandala World.'

Lamas (Guru or Spiritual Teacher)

Lamas come in different forms; they are the founders of each Buddhist order, famous figures who achieved spiritual awakening, teachers, and so on. They may also be regarded with higher appreciation than the Buddhas and deities themselves, as without them it would be impossible to receive the Buddhist teachings.

Bodhisattvas (Jangchub Sempa)

Buddhas who have already freed themselves from worldly attachments never return to the secular world where human beings suffer from the cycle of reincarnation. However, *Bodhisattvas* are beings who have attained this enlightenment but have decided to stay in the world to help liberate others from all their worldly desires and worries. Bodhisattvas embody true altruism, which is at the core of the *Mahayana* (Greater Vehicle of Buddhism), the heart of Tibetan Buddhism .

The number of bodhisattvas is countless but the most famous and popular in Tibet are Avalokiteshvara (Chenrezik), an embodiment of compassion, Manjughosa (Jampeyang), an embodiment of wisdom, Goddess Tara (Dolma), wrathful Vajrapani (Chakna Dorje), etc. Although

Maitreya (Jampa) is a bodhisattva, this is the 'Future Buddha' who is supposed to appear in 5,670,000,000 years time.

Choekyong (Dharma Protector or Protector Deity)

Choekyong are deities that protect Buddhism and many of these used to be Hindu or Bonpo deities. For example, Nechung who protects the Dalai Lamas, used to be a local Bonpo deity.

Mahakala (Gonpo) is a famous choekyong and is the embodiment of Shiva. Although Hayagriva (Tamdrin) is a bodhisattva, it can also be considered a dharma protector or protector deity. The 'Four Guardian Kings,' including Vaishravana and the lute-playing Sarasvati (Yangchenma), are also popular choekyong.

Yidam (Guardian Deity)

Buddhist followers, monks, temples, etc., have their own *Yidam* to protect them. The lama introduces you to your deity when you start receiving his teachings.

Many *yidams* are depicted as images of *Yabyum* (Father and Mother Buddha), in which they have a number of arms and legs, striking wrathful red or blue faces, tiger skins wrapped around their waists, and are holding onto a goddess. Despite his fearful, brutal-looking bull's face, the Yidam Vajrabhairava (Dorje Jigje) is actually the embodiment of the calm Manjughosa (Jampeyang), one of the most important bodhisattvas.

Yidam's wife is called *Kandroma* (Dakini) and is herself a religious figure revered by the people. The goddess Palden Lhamo is the yidam that protects the whole of Tibet.

Choekyong (Dharma Protector)

Goddess Palden Lhamo

BUDDHAS, BODHISATTVAS & DEITIES

The followings are extracts from the more than 5,000 Buddhas, Bodhisattvas, and Deities to be found in the 'Mandala World.' These are the popular and most common images that you will find depicted on *thangkas*.
*The names are first given in Tibetan and then in Sanskrit. Following each name is the *mantra* for each one.

སྤྱན་རས་གཟིགས།

Chenrezik/Avalokiteshvara
(Om Mani Padme Hum)
White bodhisattva of compassion and mercy with a white lotus in the left hand, a Buddhist rosary in the right, and the *Cintamani* or 'Jewel of the Heart' in the center. The white lotus symbolizes the purity of wisdom and the rosary the power of *mantra*. The most popular form of the bodhisattva has 4 hands. The Thousand-Armed Mahakarunika and Eleven-Faced Avalokiteshvara are also well known.

སངས་རྒྱས་སྨན་བླ།

Sangye Menla/
Bhaisajyaguru (Bhaisajya Guru Vaidurya Prabharajah Tayatha Om Beekhenze Beekhenze Maha Beekhenze Radza Samunggate So Ha)
Sangye Menla takes care of worldly interests. His blue-bodied image pictures him with *Myrobalan* (Medicinal herbs that cure all illness) and other implements in his hands. His hand gesture is the same as that of Shakyamuni. Sangye Menla is popular among the people and you cannot miss his image if you visit a Tibetan hospital.

Jamyang/Manjushri
(Om Arapatsana Dhi)
The red bodhisattva of wisdom is most commonly pictured in the sitting position with a burning sword held in the right hand to renounce worldly desires, and the 'Perfection of Wisdom' scripture to symbolize wisdom and lotus flowers in the left. Some images of Jamyang have him astride a *Senge* (Lion).

འཇམ་དབྱངས།

Dolma/White Tara
(Om Tare Tutare Ture So Ha)
Painted in white, red, green, among other colors, Dolma (Tara) helps people cross the 'Sea of the Cycle of Reincarnation' and she is a popular goddess in Tibet. The white Tara has a white shiny face and body and she keeps watch over the people with her 7 eyes and helps them when they are in need.

སྒྲོལ་དཀར།

Kandroma/Dakini (Om A Bum Guru Harinisa Sidhi Hum)
Kandroma, the 'Space Voyager,' is a female spirit who lives in either the 'Pure Realm' or in the people's world with its cycle of reincarnation. She can fly freely through the emptiness and she brings protection to Buddhist practitioners. This *Machik Labdron* or *Dakini* acts like a shaman. She is pictured with a white body and she carries a *Damaru* (Hand-drum) in her right hand and a *Drilbu* (Bell) in her left. Her figure is shown dancing wearing a white bone necklace.

མཁའ་འགྲོ་མ།

Jampa/Maitreya
(Om Budha Metri Mem So Ha)
The time of Jampa, the 'Future Buddha,' is said to come after that of Shakyamuni. He is usually pictured seated so that he is ready to come to the world soon. With a teaching gesture, both of his hands hold lotuses, each of which has either the 'Wheel of Dharma' or a vase. The body of Jampa is either gold or red.

བྱམས་པ།

Dolma Marpo/Red Tara
(Om Tare Tutare Ture So Ha)
Dolma is said to have been born from the tears that were shed by Chenrezik (Avalokiteshvara) when he observed the people's sufferings. Dolma depicted in colors other than white have a *Udumbara* (Blue Lotus Flower) in the left hand and the bottle of *Amrita* (Nectar of Immortality) in the right hand. The bodhisattva's right foot rests on a lotus.

སྒྲོལ་མ་མར་པོ།

Sangye/Shakyamuni Buddha
(Tayatha Om Muni Muni Mahamuni Shakyamuni Ye So Ha)
The founder of Buddhism, Sangye is the 'Historical Buddha' who was known as 'Prince Gautama Siddharta' before attaining enlightenment. To show his renouncing of the world and his asceticism, Sangye is depicted in a simpler way compared to that of the bodhisattvas. The 'Past Buddha' (Sangye Marmedze/ Kashyapa) and the 'Future Buddha' (Jampa/Maitreya) and the 'Historical Buddha' (Sangye/Shakyamuni) are often portrayed as the 'Buddhas of Three Times.' Nampar Nangze (Vairocana), Mikyopa Dorje Sempa (Aksobhya), Rinchen Jungne (Ratnasambhava), Opame (Amitabha) and Donyo Drupa (Amoghasiddhi) are called the 'Buddhas of the Five Families' and their images are painted in white, blue, yellow, red, and green, respectively.

སངས་རྒྱས།

UNRAVELING THE THANGKA MESSAGE

The *Thangka* is a hanging scroll-like painting depicting Buddhist themes and scenes from legend. The word was derived from *Pata*, the Indian paintings made on cloth. The artist makes a preliminary sketch with a pencil on the cotton cloth, trying to duplicate the original picture. Paint or decorations of mineral pigments, smashed precious stones (turquoises, corals, etc.) and shells are then added. The 4 edges are decorated with red, yellow, and blue cloth. In addition to the ones that are painted, there are those that are embroidered or woven, as well as prints and appliqués. *Thangkas* are used for meditation, visualization and other religious rites.

Common Thangka Imagery

Sky/Namkha ནམ་མཁའ།
Clear blue symbolizes 'Emptiness.'

Nimbus/Woekor འོད་ཀོར་
The cloud is a 'Halo.'

Back Curtains/Gyabyol རྒྱབ་ཡོལ།
Golden ones are behind 'Buddha.'

Hand Seal/Chokgya ཕྱག་རྒྱ།
'Mudra,' the patterns created by the way hands and fingers are folded, have various meanings. The putting of the hand on the ground symbolizes 'Having reached Enlightenment.'

Robe/Nasa ན་བཟའ།
Shakyamuni's robe is yellow, the color of the monkhood.

Rhinoceros Horns/Seru'ira བསེ་རུའི་རྭ།
A precious treasure.

Gold Rings/Khorlo Nacha འཁོར་ལོ་སྣ་ཆ།
Given as an offering.

Jewels/Norbu ནོར་བུ།
When accompanied by fire, they have a 'Supernatural' but 'Essential' brilliance.

Gold Offerings/Tsunmo Nacha བཙུན་མོ་སྣ་ཆ།
With the gold rings these make a set.

Rainbow/Ja འཇའ།
Symbolizes 'Spiritually Awakened.'

Clouds/Trinpa སྤྲིན་པ།
White symbolizes 'Purity.'

Leaves/Loma ལོ་མ།
Green symbolizes 'Life Force.'

Mountains/Pang སྤང་ས།
Depict the lush, green 'Pure Realm.'

Lotus Flower/Pema པད་མ།
Blossom in the mud. Symbolizing 'Innocence' and 'Mercy,' they experience life on earth and then blossom in heaven.

Lakes/Tso མཚོ།
Also depict the 'Pure Realm,' blessed with bountiful water.

Lotus Seal/Pema'i den པད་མའི་གདན།
Symbolizes reaching 'Enlightenment' and the attainment of 'Buddhahood.'

Coral/Churu
Especially precious in landlocked Tibet.

Elephant Tusks/Langpoche'l Chewa གླང་པོ་ཆེའི་མཆེ་བ།
A precious treasure.

BUDDHIST GOODS

Vajra or Dorje རྡོ་རྗེ།
Meaning 'Thunder' and 'Diamond,' a *Dorje* hand-held scepter indicates the power of emptiness to harmonize all confrontations.

པི་ཝང་།

Instruments/Dramnyen
One of the common offerings, the Tibetan guitar represents the sense of hearing. These offerings represent the 5 senses of hearing, taste, smell, sight, and touch, which arouse the desire for worldly things.

འཁོར་ལོ།

Wheel of Dharma/Khorlo
Represents the teachings, especially those concerning Karma.

དྲིལ་བུ།

Bell/Drilbu
Many bells have *Dorje* for their grips. The *Drilbu* also represent the elementary sound, the teachings beyond ordinary hearing, and the emptiness itself.

Hand-drum/Damaru
Represents the bonding of the dualism of secular and heavenly truth.

Hooked Knife/Driguk
The S-shaped edge and hilt of the *Dorje* symbolizes the cutting off of ego and attachment to worldly things.

Skull Cup/Kapala
Possessing magical properties, the 'Skull Cup' is often filled with blood as a symbol of the life force.

Conch Shell/Dung
This stands for the elementary sound that leads all living things to the truth.

Mirror/Melong
Another offering, the *Melong* stands for the sense of sight. It is used for magic rituals and fortune-telling.

Short Dagger/Phurbu
Triangle-shaped short sword with a hilt of *Dorje* that controls spiritual power. Used for magical rituals.

Buddhist Rosary/Trengwa
This indicates that the chanting of *mantra* brings power. The 108 balls forming the rosary are equal to the number of people's desires for worldly things. Chenrezik (Avalokiteshvara) and other bodhisattvas and deities carry one of these.

Butter Offering/Torma
Representing the sense of taste, the *Torma* is an offering made from butter and tsampa. The form that this offering takes varies according to whether it is being offered to Buddhas or deities.

- -

LUCKY OMEN SYMBOLS

The *Tashi Tagye* or 'Eight Auspicious Symbols' are seen everywhere in Tibet and the Tibetan Cultural Region. When a high-ranking monk is invited to a monastery, *Tashi Tagye* are drawn on the street. Others are used as decorations during the *Losar* (Tibetan New Year) celebrations.

Precious Parasol/Duk
This carries the power to save the bearer from any harm and bring peace to their life.

Banner of Victory/Gyaltsen
Standing for the power and determination to eradicate all desires for worldly things.

Conch Shell with Clockwise Twist/Dung
This produces the elementary sound that leads all living things to the truth.

Knot of Eternity/Pelbeu
The endless thread that symbolizes total harmony and the boundless scope of Buddhist mercy.

Golden Dharma Wheel/Khorlo
By rotating the wheel, the teachings of Buddha are spread, especially those concerning Karma.

Vase/Bumpa
Containing *Amrita*, the 'Nectar of Immortality' that you can get by following the true teachings.

Two Golden Fishes/Sernya
These stand for riches, wealth, or freedom. The laying-out of treasures to heaven.

Lotus Flower/Pema
Transcendence over ordinary things and pure mercy.

Many animals are included alongside the Buddhas, bodhisattvas and deities in *thangkas*. In addition to those you can actually see, there are also imaginary beasts or 'Protector Animals' and each of these has a Buddhist meaning.

Makala/Chusin
Living in the water, the *Makala* has an elephant-like head and a crocodile-like body. It appears behind Buddhas or in water.

Garuda/Khyung
The *Garuda* is a mythical bird that serves as a protector for Buddhas. Depicted above the head of the Buddha, it has a *Cintamani* or 'Jewel of the Heart' in its mouth and a snake in its hand.

Lion/Senge
Commonly seen as part of the seat of Buddha, the *Senge* is a dog and lion-like animal that looks friendly. It also appears on the Tibetan flag.

Naga/Lu
The 'Water-Dragon' or 'Water Deity' takes care of people's health. The upper half of many *Naga* is a woman but there are some whose whole body is a snake. This mythical creature is a very popular figure in folklore and it is evoked to help in the recovery from sickness.

Dragon/Druk
The most popular among these beasts is the *Druk*, which stands for power. With a *Cintamani* or 'Jewel of the Heart' in its hand, the dragon has free run of the sky.

Cock/Cha, Pig/ Phak & Snake/Drul
These 3 animals are commonly seen in the center of the 'Thangka of the Wheel of Existence.' The cock stands for appetite, the pig for ignorance, and the snake for anger.

APPRECIATING THE MANDALA

Mandala means the 'Indication of the Essence' or the 'Circle' in Sanskrit and it depicts the Buddhist vision of the universe. The *Mandala* represents the unification between directly opposing ideas, such as the 'part' and the 'whole,' the 'individual' and the 'universe,' and the 'sacred' and the 'secular.' It allows the people to see the perspectives of those who have been spiritually awakened. It is called *Kyilkhor*, which is derived from *Kyil* meaning 'Center' and *Khor* meaning 'To make a circle.'

Mandala of Dorje Phagmo (Diamond Sow)

Symbolizing the birth of the world, *Dorje Phagmo* or 'Diamond Sow' is in the center of the inverted triangle surrounded by 8 lotus petals. *Vajra* and 5-color frames surround the innermost circle. *Dorje Phagmo* with her red face wears bones, and has a hooked knife in her right hand and a *Kapala* in her left. She has the power to transform ignorance and desire into enlightenment.

Monks are supposed to draw mandalas as part of their religious training and they follow the Buddhist scriptures to produce all the fine details. Characteristically made with vibrant colors and strict symmetry, they are used for special Buddhist rituals or as the principal image for a religious service, etc. Typical examples have a Yidam (Guardian Deity) in the figure symbolizing the universe. The outside is surrounded by earth, water, fire, and wind (yellow, white, red, and blue respectively). Mandalas are created in the form of thangkas and wall paintings, as well as made from colored sand.

There are countless ones for each Buddha, bodhisattva, and deity. Most of those found in the Tibetan cultural region are from the 'Late Tantric' period of Buddhism and the oldest example in the area is at Alchi Gompa in the north Indian area of Ladakh. (See page 292.)

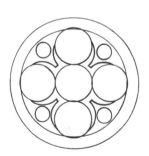

Mandala of Buddhas of the Five Families

Common in Nepal, the 'Buddhas of the Five Families' appear in the form of Jampel (Manjushri) carrying swords, bells, etc. Mikyopa Dorje Sempa (Aksobhya) is in the center, Nampar Nangze (Vairocana) to the east, Rinchen Jungne (Ratnasambhava) to the south, Opame (Amitabha) to the west, and Donyo Drupa (Amoghasiddhi) to the north.

Sand Mandala

These are recognized as the most formal way of producing a mandala. They are formed by intricate combinations of colored sand and when the ritual is finished, it is destroyed and then dispersed in water. This total eradication of the mandala is also meant to sever the desires for worldly things.

Mandala of Samvara Tantra

This has Demchok (Chakrasamvara) as the principle image. Four different colors are used with the east in white, the south in yellow, the west in red, and the north in green. The 4 gates are decorated with Dharma wheels, a pair of deer, bottles, and the 'Seven Treasures.' Lotus flower circles, *Dorje*, frames, and the 'Eight Graves' surround the outer edge.

Kalachakra Mandala

This is one of the most typical mandalas in Tibet. Based on the teachings of the *Kalachakra Tantra*, which is regarded as the ultimate teaching of Tantric Buddhism, it is drawn for the rituals when high-ranking monks offer their teachings to their disciples. The 4-layer structure stands for the relationship between the universe and the micro-cosmos, and between the Buddha and oneself. During the *Dukhor Wangchen*, a ceremony that can only be performed by Dalai Lama, a grand sand *Kalachakra* mandala is created.

Three-Dimensional Mandala

This is a common sight in Tibet and a famous example of this is the 3-dimensional Kalachakra mandala in the Potala Palace. The photograph is of a mandala depicting the 'Protector Deities of the Four Directions' (North, South, East and West), which is used for rituals.

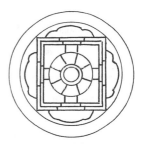

Mandala of Purification

The typical pattern's principle image is Nampar Nangze (Vairocana) whose brilliance, like the sun, illuminates the entire world. The mandala saves the souls of the dead from descending into hell and so it is often used in funerals.

The Five Buddhas in Mandalas and Thangkas

Direction	Buddha / Body Color / Hand Gesture / Vehicle / Symbol
Center	Vairocana / White / Turning the Dharma Wheel / Senge / Wheel of Dharma
East	Aksobhya / Blue/ Touching the earth/ Elephant / Dorje
South	Ratnasambhava / Yellow/ Fulfilling wishes / Horse / Cintamani
West	Amitabha / Red / Meditation / Peacock / Lotus Flower
North	Amoghasiddhi / Green / Calming fear / Garuda / Double Dorje

[Thangka Photographs]

Karma Thupten/ Born in Kham, eastern Tibet. Karma Thupten escaped from Tibet at the age of 5. After over 20 years of religious training, he became a thangka artist in the most traditional style of *Karma Kawdi*. He gives thangka classes in Kathmandu.

Yumi Twewan/ Since 1994, Yumi Twewan has been receiving Karma Thupten's instruction in the making of thangka.

Tibetan images are clothed in unique garments and ornaments. The ascetic Buddhas are dressed simply whilst the bodhisattvas wear sumptuous clothing. It is said that people's yearning to reach the Buddhist paradise has shaped the style of these bodhisattvas.

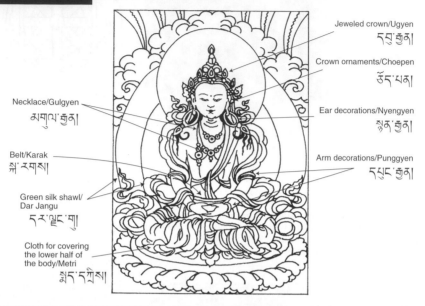

Jeweled crown/Ugyen
དབུ་རྒྱན།

Crown ornaments/Choepen
ཅོད་པན།

Necklace/Gulgyen
མགུལ་རྒྱན།

Ear decorations/Nyengyen
སྙན་རྒྱན།

Belt/Karak
སྐེ་རགས།

Arm decorations/Punggyen
དཔུང་རྒྱན།

Green silk shawl/Dar Jangu
དར་ལྗང་གུ

Cloth for covering the lower half of the body/Metri
སྨད་དཀྲིས།

TIBETAN BUDDHIST CULTURE OUTSIDE TIBET

Yukiyasu Osada

Tibetan Buddhism has also extended beyond the areas inhabited by Tibetans. The spread of its teachings was mainly due to the Mongols who became enthusiastic followers of the religion. The Mongolian Empire that sprawled across Eurasia also spread Tibetan Buddhism in its wake. Most of the areas that were converted during this time fell under the control of the now-defunct Soviet Union and were subjected to bans on religious activities and at times, the severe persecution of religious followers. Since the collapse of the USSR, Buddhism has seen a rapid revival.

Tibetan Buddhism is once again thriving in Buryat and Tuva to the north of Mongolia. In Ulan-Ude, the capital of Buryat, you will find Ivolginsk Tratsang, the largest monastery in the former Soviet Union. Further to the west, on the northern side of the Caspian Sea, Kalmyk has a president who is enthusiastic enough to say that he will try to set-up a Vatican-like country by inviting the Dalai Lama to relocate to the region. Since 1991, the Dalai Lama has visited these countries and has been enthusiastically welcomed by the people.

Mongolia brought all of Tibet under its control during the 13th century and introduced the Sakyapa School of Tibetan Buddhism to all parts of its empire. Successive Mongolian emperors had Tibetan monks as their teachers and it was the support of later Mongolian emperors that helped the Dalai Lama's government to unify Tibet.

At the time of the establishment of a socialist republic in Mongolia in 1924, there were over 700 monasteries in the country. These were all devastated and 17,000 monks were reportedly murdered by the regime, an experience similar to what Tibet has experienced under Chinese control. Since 1989, the democratization of Mongolia has led to a revival of Buddhism and the Dalai Lama has been invited to the country several times. The head religious center is Gandan Monastery in the capital Ulaan Baatar. There are also several Tibetan temples in the Inner Mongolian Autonomous Region of China.

KEYWORDS FOR TIBETAN LIFE

Lives in Tibet
Yak and Dri
The *Yak* and *Dri* are longhaired cow-like animals found on the Tibetan Plateau. Not only are they used as beasts of burden but they also produce milk for butter, cheese, and yoghurt. Their meat, internal organs, and blood are all turned into food and their fur is used for clothing and their hair for weaving clothes and tents. Even their dung is a vital resource since it is used as fuel in Tibet, which is blessed with few trees. These animals richly deserve the appreciation of the Tibetan people, as they are the source of so much that is necessary for life in the region.

Yak and Nomad

The name *Yak* is for the male and *Dri* is for the female. Aside from them, there are also the *Dzomo* (female) or *Dzo* (male), which are crosses between a bull and a dri. The huge wild yak is known as a *Drong*.

Drokpa (Tibetan Nomads or Stock Farmers)
Living in a *Gur* (Tent), the Drokpas raise and tend their livestock on the plateau grasslands. In Tibet, pure nomadic life is not a very common practice and instead most of the nomadic groups move between designated areas with the changing of the season.

The traditional *Gur* is made from thickly woven yak hair that is ink black, which is possibly made from this material to absorb as much heat from the sun as possible. Inside, the tents are spacious and warm and usually they contain a Buddhist altar, a set of solid furniture and other family items. There are often bicycles parked outside the tents, too. Even if there is a water supply nearby, the nomads seldom take a bath.

Zhingpa (Farmers)
The most common lifestyle in Tibet is a combination of farming and stock-raising. The farms produce barley for tsampa and also potatoes. The farmers' diet is supplemented by the milk that they get from their herd of dri, etc. The most common style of house in farming villages in Tibetan areas has 2 or 3 storys and many Tibetan families use the 1st floor as a barn.

Kham Guys

Tsongpa (Merchants or Traders)
Tsongpas roam all over Tibet and even appear as far as Beijing, Shanghai, Hong Kong, India, and Nepal. Thanks to the improvements in the transport system and the Chinese Open-and-Reform policy, they have been increasingly active in trading their wares. In Lhasa there are also many Tsongpas from eastern Tibet and other outlying areas, and they often rent rooms in the city with others from the same home districts.

Things to Wear
Chuba (Sheep Skin Coat)
The *Chuba* is a gown-like Tibetan dress made of wool or furs. Tibetans in the cities wear it only at the New Year but it is still common everyday dress in rural areas. The chuba's long sleeves keep you very warm.

Nomadic Family, Kham

Kneading Tsampa

Butter Tea Preparation

Momos

Tukpa

Panden
Woven of *Nambu* (Wool), the *Panden* is a striped patterned apron that used to be worn only by married women. This tradition seems to not hold true these days as some unmarried girls also choose to wear it.

Dashe
The *Dashe* is the turban-like hair ornament worn by the men of Kham. You are most likely to see these in either red or black.

Lhamko
The name for Tibetan boots is *Lhamko* and these are made from woolen cloth, felt, and leather. Although the boots are water-resistant they are also rather heavy to wear.

Food
Tsampa
Tibet's staple food is *Tsampa*, which is powdered roasted barley. Tibetans eat tsampa in the form of a ball formed by kneading the powder along with butter tea.

Ja (Tea)
One experience to be had in Tibetan areas is the drinking of *Ja* or so-called 'butter tea.' In fact it tastes more like soup than tea. The common recipe is one combining churned tea leaves from Yunnan Province in China, butter, and salt. It is a woman's job and the preparation is heavy physical work. Traditionally, they use a tool called a *Trongmo* (Churn) but in larger cities an electric blender is often used to mix a small amount.

Ja Ngarmo (Milk Tea)
Common in Central Tibet, *Ja Ngarmo* is a sweet Indian-style tea that has fewer spices than the Indian version called *Chai*. In Tibet, tea leaves from India and Nepal are also available for preparing this.

Ja Thang (Black Tea)
Salted black tea or *Ja Thang* is a drink from eastern Tibet.

Wanzi (Muslim Tea)
In Amdo you will find *Wanzi*, a sweet tea that people make by pouring hot water into a lidded cup containing tea leaves, rock sugar, and loganberries. They then sip the drink with the cover slightly shifted to the side.

Momo
Tibetan-style steamed dumplings are called *Momos*. You can also get these boiled, too. In Central Tibet yak meat is the most common filling but other meats such as mutton, pork, beef, etc., are also used. Tibetans eat momos with *Sepen* (Chili sauce).

Tukpa
Tukpa is Tibetan-style noodles in soup and different types of noodles are found in different varieties of tukpa, such as Chinese-style *Gyathuk* and *Tenthuk*, which has flour dumplings boiled in soup.

Chang
Made from barley, *Chang* is unrefined Tibetan beer. It tastes a bit sour but is pleasant enough. It is available from *Changkhang* (Chang

Bars) and also is sold at liquor stores. You will notice the difference in quality if you can find a place that sells higher quality stuff.

Customs
Chadur (Sky Burial)
The tradition of sky burial is to leave the mortal remains of the deceased for vultures to consume. Some say that the birds take the spirit from the bodies to heaven. However, this is a complete misunderstanding of the process as the souls of the dead have already left the bodies by the time of the sky burial. The correct interpretation is that as the souls are already on their way to their life after death, or reincarnation, the bodies are now unnecessary. Based on altruism, the sky burial allows these unnecessary human remains to be used by other living things. Probably another major reason that this custom persists is that cremation is impractical and costly as fuel is very scarce in many areas of Tibet. Indeed, cremation is a common practice in the Tibetan areas that are covered in woodland.

Lingka (Picnic)

After the appropriate ceremony, the sky burial is held at the site, which is usually on the hill at the back of a monastery or on other religious grounds. Attendants use hatchets to cut up the body into small pieces to make it easier for the vultures to feed.

This ritual is a solemn family affair and visits by inquisitive foreigners are extremely offensive. You can also expect to pick up a hefty fine of US$120 when you are reported to the authorities.

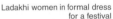
Lingka and Gambling

Lingka (Picnic)
On holidays a picnic to the park, the riverside, or to the grasslands is one of the major Tibetan pastimes. Besides food, tea, and liquor, Tibetans bring tables, mah-jongg sets, radio-cassette players, and so on. They give themselves up to singing, dancing, or gambling the day away.

Tsezang Duezang (Festivals)
Most Tibetan festivals are related to Buddhism and the dates of these are dictated by the Tibetan calendar, which is different from both the Chinese and Western ones. The Tibetan New Year's Day falls between February and March.

No matter what the point of the particular festival is, the people end up drinking and feasting after paying their visit to the temple.

Ladakhi women in formal dress
for a festival

There are countless festivals held all over Tibet and this section highlights only the major ones in and around Lhasa. Horse racing festivals in the summer and harvest festivals during the fall are held throughout the region. The dates of even the same festival may vary from region to region. For example, the New Year's Day in Shigatse is celebrated at the beginning of December on the Tibetan calendar.

Gutor = Day before New Year's Eve (29th day of the 12th lunar month)

Usually, explanations of festivals start by looking at the New Year's Day celebrations. However, the year's end is also of special importance and Tibetans observe *Gutor* while they are busy preparing for the New Year's Day.

Preparations for New Year start about 2 weeks before the day and people arrange their religious offerings, buy new dress clothes and food and drink for the feasts. The feasts include a substantial amount of *Dresi*, a sweet buttered rice with raisins; *Droma*, which is rice boiled with small potatoes, various meats, fruits, breads, chang, butter tea, among other ingredients; and *Kapse*, a fried sweet that comes in different shapes and forms. Tibetans are supposed to see in the New Year with these sweets piled high on their tray.

On *Gutor*, Tibetan families eat *Guthuk*, a soup with dumplings, in the evening. The dumplings contain beans, broken pieces of wood, chilies, wool, charcoal, or pieces of paper on which various words are written. People eat them in turn and they tell their New Year's fortune by checking the ingredients of the bowl that they are served. There is also a game played at this time where some of the family members decide on an unlucky mark in advance and the one who picks it has to do a forfeit.

Following this, everyone participates in the original purpose of *Gutor*, which is to exorcise the evil spirits from the previous year by running around with a doll representing a fierce god, and setting-off fireworks and hand-held firecrackers. On the 30th, New Year's Eve, Tibetans clean their houses and then wait in anticipation for the following day's festivities.

Losar (1st-3rd day of the 1st lunar month)

The Tibetan New Year is known as *Losar*, and it is the most popular of all the festivals of the year, when even young Tibetans wear chuba and pay their first visit of the year to a temple with their family early in the morning. On New Year's Day, Tibetans are supposed to offer chang beer and ornaments called *Chemar* to their household's deity and to the water dragon that takes care of their water supply. Be careful, as the chang gruel that is served is strong enough to get you drunk.

After saying *Tashi Delek* and exchanging greetings with neighbors, Tibetans do nothing but feast on the food and drink that they have painstakingly prepared. They visit each other's feasts and have parties full of drinking and singing. The men don't miss an opportunity to enjoy gambling, with games of *Sho* (Dice), *Pakchen* (Mah-jongg), etc.

On New Year's Day, everyone spends time with family or the neighbors. They then visit their relatives on the second day. Children

The Build-Up to the Tibetan New Year

On the day before New Year's Eve, Tibetans come together to enjoy themselves; New Year's Eve itself is for cleaning houses and quiet relaxation.

Monks start performing *Cham* dances in the morning. From 09:00 until dusk, the dance of the *Mahakala*, a great picture roll based on the Buddhist scriptures, is performed. It is believed that watching these dances will leave you untouched by sickness for the coming year. The dance reaches its climax when the image of Mahakala is engulfed in flames.

Filled with the atmosphere of the year's end, Tibetans eat *Guthuk*, a gruel made with dumplings, at home. They say that this is the only day when all Tibetans, including the Dalai Lama, eat the same food. On opening the dumpling, you will find an 'oracle': a white thread is for longevity, a white stone indicates a pure heart, charcoal means a black or foul mouth, a black stone symbolizes a black heart, a chili is for the talkative, etc.

Mine? It was a white stone and not a chili as everyone had expected. Everyone then delights in showing-off their 'oracle' to one another and the year's end is ushered in with hearty laughter.

Yumi Twewan

also have a good time on New Year's with gifts of candies, etc.

On the third day, Tibetans replace the year-old *Tar-choks* and *Dar-shings* on the roof of their houses with new ones and burn thick bunches of *Sang* . After so much feasting it is no wonder that Tibetans take days off after the celebrations. Other nationalities such as the Han and Hui have their own New Year celebrations according to different calendars but the shopkeepers among them are said to be too scared to even open their shops during Tibetan *Losar*, due to the mobs of drunk Tibetans.

Jokhang Temple whilst burning 'Sang'

Monlam = Prayer Festival
(4th-11th day of the 1st lunar month)

Monlam means 'Prayer' and at monasteries a great Buddhist service is held and *Cham* (Buddhist dances) are performed. From New Year's Day until the end of *Monlam*, people continue to eat, drink and make merry.

In Lhasa, an offering carefully crafted from butter and standing over 10m-high was put in the Jokhang Temple, where most of the monks from the monasteries around Lhasa would gather and hold the *Monlam Chenmo* or 'Great Prayer Festival.' This festival was banned during the Cultural Revolution and although it was revived once in 1985, it was once again prohibited in 1990, perhaps because the festival too strongly encourages Tibetan identity.

Putting tsampa on one other in celebration

Chunga Choepa = Memorial Service on the 15th
(15th day of the 1st lunar month)

Also called the 'Butter Lamp Festival.' On the day of *Chunga Choepa* the Barkhor Square in Lhasa turns into a grand exhibition site for huge *Tormas* sculpted from butter in the form of various auspicious symbols and lamps. It is a fantastic night.

Chunga Choepa used to be the highlight of *Monlam* in Lhasa and in the past the Dalai Lamas would come to the Jokhang Temple and perform the great Buddhist service. The debating examination for the highest-ranking monk or *Lharampa Geshe* was also held before the Dalai Lama during this festival. These events are now carried out in Dharamsala where the Dalai Lama's government is in exile.

Tibetan Uprising Day (Mar 10, Western calendar)

To commemorate the people's uprising in Lhasa on March 10, 1959, demonstrations and Buddhist memorial services are held in the countries where Tibetans have sought refuge (other than China). The Dalai Lama makes a statement at this time every year.

Saka Dawa Festival (15th day of the 4th lunar month)

The most important festival for Tibetan Buddhism, the *Saka Dawa Festival* commemorates Shakyamuni's Buddhahood and the death of his mortal body. At every monastery sutras are recited and *Cham* dances are performed. It is said that good deeds in the month of this festival deserve 300-fold in return and this leads many people to donate large sums to the religious orders, monasteries and to the beggars that gather at this time of year.

Saka Dawa Festival at Mt. Kailash

Horse Racing Festival in Gyantse
(18th day of the 4th lunar month)

The Unveiling of the Great Thangka at Tashilhunpo Monastery (15th day of the 5th lunar month)

Celebration of the Dalai Lama's Birthday (Nepal)

The unveiling of the Grand Thangkas at the Potala Palace

Tsechu (Hemis, Ladakh)

Birthday of the 14th Dalai Lama (July 6, Western calendar)

Of course, this is not a recognized, official event in main Tibetan areas under Chinese control, however Tibetans everywhere continue to celebrate it unashamedly. Conversely, Tibetans do not possess the custom of celebrating the birthday of ordinary people, and although people remember their own birth sign and the day of the year, few Tibetans actually know the date on which they were born.

Zamling Chisang = Universal Prayer Day (15th day of the 5th lunar month)

Zamling Chisang was originally meant to commemorate Guru Rinpoche's subjugation of the local deities and the founding of Samye Monastery. In Lhasa, there is the spectacle of large amounts of *Sang* being burned up on the hills of Chakpori, Bumpari (on the southern side of the Kyi-chu) and Gephelri (behind Drepung Monastery), etc.

Choekhor Duechen (4th day of the 6th lunar month)

Also called *Drukpa Tsezhi* or 'June 4,' *Choekhor Duechen* is a commemoration of Shakyamuni's first teachings at Buddha Gaya, which he gave at the age of 35. After paying a visit to the temple, Tibetans then proceed to enjoy a picnic.

Guru Tsechu (10th day of the 6th lunar month)

This festival is to celebrate the birthday of Guru Rinpoche. This festival is held in higher regard in the outlying Tibetan areas of Bhutan and Ladakh.

Zhoton (30th day of the 6th lunar month)

When the summer retreat for their intensive training is over, monks are served with yoghurt. That is said to be the origin of *Zhoton*, which is also called the 'Yoghurt Festival.' At Drepung Monastery there are *Cham* dances and the grand thangka is unveiled early in the morning. After devoutly viewing the thangka, the people go onto the Norbulingka and other popular spots for a picnic. *Zhoton* is also known as the 'Tibetan Opera Festival' due to the competitive performances of *Ache Lhamo* (Tibetan Opera) that are held at the Norbulingka.

Bathing Festival (27th day of the 7th lunar month)

On this starlit night Tibetan people take a ceremonial wash in the waters of their local rivers or natural springs. This is a seductive and tranquil festival.

Changthang Horse Racing Festival at Nakchu (Aug 10, Western calendar)

Harvest Festival (Early in the 8th lunar month)

These festivities are not related to Buddhism and the date of them is dictated by the ripening of the crops. The liveliest places to catch this festival are in farming villages.

Lhabab Duechen (22nd day of the 9th lunar month)

Celebrating Shakyamuni's descent from the god realm to the human realm. On the day of the festival the number of pilgrims to the sacred places increases substantially as this also corresponds with the agricultural off-season.

Palden Lhamo Festival (15th day of the 10th lunar month)
Tibet's protector deity Palden Lhamo's festival.

Ngachu Chenmo=Tsongkapa Butter Lamp Festival (25th day of the 10th lunar month)
The anniversary of the death of Tsongkhapa, the founder of the Gelukpa order. Houses, streets, and temples are lit by numerous lamps, and it is also known as the 'Tsongkhapa Butter Lamp Festival.'

	Year 2131 Wood-Monkey (2004-2005)	Year 2132 Wood-Cock (2005-2006)	Year 2133 Fire-Dog (2006-2007)
Gutor	Feb 7	Feb 27	Feb 16
Losar (Tibetan New Year)	Feb 21	Feb 9	Feb 28
Monlam (Great Prayer Festival)	Feb 28-Mar 7	Feb 16-25	Mar 7-15
Chunga Choepa (Butter Lamp Festival)	Mar 6	Feb 23	Mar 14
Tibetan Uprising Day	Mar 10	Mar10	Mar 10
Saka Dawa	Jun 3	May 23	Jun 11
Zamling Chisang (Universal Prayer Day)	Jul 2	Jun 22	Jul 11
Birthday of H.H. the 14th Dalai Lama	Jul 6	Jul 6	Jul 6
Choekhor Duechen (Six-Four Festival)	Jul 21	Jul 10	Jul 29
Guru Tsechu (Birthday of Guru Rinpoche)	Jul 27	Jul 16	Aug 4
Changthang Horse Racing	Aug 10-16	Aug 10-16	Aug 10-16
Zhoton (Yoghurt Festival)	Aug 15-22	Sep 3-10	Aug 23-31
Bathing Week	Aug-Sep	Aug-Sep	Aug-Sep
Lhabab Duechen	Nov 4	Nov 23	Nov 12
Ngachu Chenmo (or Tsongkhapa Festival Butter Lamp Festival)	Dec 7	Dec 26	Dec 15

Lingka (Picnic) during Zhoton

Cham Dance

LOSAR IN KATHMANDU

Yumi Twewan

Losar Decorations

"Tashi Delek, Losar." Tibetan voices echo in the chilly morning air. This is the land where the Tibetan culture called *'Swayambhunath'* originates, on the outskirts of Kathmandu. My Buddhist painting master Karma Thupten invited me to the *Losar*, the biggest and most eagerly anticipated event in the Tibetan year.

Momo, Karma's mother who also plays the role of my grandmother, braided my hair, weaving in embroidery threads called *Dashe*. Tibetans wear all kinds of jewels at Losar and people watching at this time of year is a lot of fun. My excitement really started to rise as I put on turquoise earrings, *DZi* stone (An antique precious stone), Buddhist rosaries, and *Gau* (A case for a good luck charm). Dressing up in a lavender *Unjuk* (Blouse), burgundy *Chuba* (Long dress), and a vivid *Panden* (An apron traditionally worn only by married women) transformed me into a Tibetan girl.

Master Karma's 6 children were all extremely excited as though Christmas, New Year's Day and their birthdays had all come at once.

The first morning of Losar starts when tsampa is tossed into the air. After that, a special annual feast is served. It begins with *Kapse* (Tibetan cookies) and butter tea. This is followed by *Chang* (Sweet liquor), *Dresi* (Buttered rice with raisins and root vegetables), and *Sho* (Yoghurt). Each dish has a special meaning, *Dresi* is for long life, *Sho* is for the purity of the heart, and so on. I was surprised at the buffalo meat being sliced in front of us. Your chuba gets very tight with all the food you eat at this time of year as there are many invitations from Tibetans in the area and we visited house after house to join other New Year's feasts.

Adults party through the night, dancing, gambling, and feasting, and people are said to spend their entire year's income during these 3 days.

The main event during the celebration is the great Bodhnath prayer on the third morning. A monk holding up a portrait of the Dalai Lama reads a prayer and hundreds of Tibetans from various regions throw tsampa into the air to mark the start of the year in Tibet.

It is quite a scene to see Tibetans dressed-up for Losar in all kinds of jewels, furs and lavish hats, making their khora around the chorten and showing off their respective regional styles from as far afield as Kham and Amdo. Children dressed in their miniature chuba are very cute. "Wow, those Kham people are really something." "It's no wonder Amdo people like tigers." I, just in Tibet overnight, could do nothing but marvel at their original fashion sense and sigh as the night of Losar quickly passed.

Monks reciting prayers and holding up portraits of the Dalai Lama

LHASA

གནས་མཆོག་ལྷ་ས།

Lhasa, the capital of Tibet, means 'God's Land' or the 'Place of the Deity' in Tibetan. With words used to describe it such as 'mysterious,' 'unexplored region,' and 'sacred place,' the city has continued to attract and enchant foreigners. For Tibetans, it is one of the sacred places they wish to visit at least once in their lifetime. The Potala Palace, where the Dalai Lamas, the embodiment of Avalokiteshvara, had lived for centuries, and the Jokhang Temple, with its endless procession of prostrating pilgrims, make for an awe-inspiring atmosphere, which certainly earns the city its heavenly title.

From prostrating pilgrims to the Tibetan Mafia and prostitution, Lhasa is the greatest city in Tibet for both religious and secular life. Bazaars and department stores have a wide range of goods to offer, not only from China but also from India and other Asian countries. At the restaurants, pizzas are on the menus alongside more traditional fare, and high-class boutiques have clothes imported straight from Hong Kong. Tourists arriving on non-stop international flights can slip into city life without any dramatic culture shock. For travelers arriving here after the hardships of hitchhiking across the Tibetan Plateau, Lhasa is an oasis.

The city, as the center of the region, is also politically very sensitive. The cause of a one-and-

a half year long martial law proclaimed across all of Tibet in March 1989 were demonstrations calling for independence in Lhasa. Occasional demonstrations and bomb attacks still occur in the city.

Going by another title, the 'City of the Sun' combines strong sunlight all day and very limited rainfall to create a really comfortable climate for tourists. Even when it does rain, it doesn't last long, and blue skies quickly return. After one of these infrequent cloud bursts you may catch sight of a rainbow framing the immense Potala Palace, and at that point the city will have cast its spell and captured your heart forever.

According to Chinese statistics, the area of Lhasa Chengguanqu (Metropolitan area) is 523 sq km, and its population is around 130,000. Lhasa City, including the 7 counties surrounding it, covers 30,000 sq km, and there is a total of 400,000 people living in the area.

The town is roughly divided into 2 parts. The first part is the old town found around the Barkhor and the Ramoche Temple, where Tibetans are still in a majority. The other part is the Chinese town stretching from the Potala Palace to the west. The feel of these 2 quarters is very different, but with urban development projects encroaching into the

CHINA

Formal Name of the Country
People's Republic of China (PRC)
Time Difference
8 hrs ahead of GMT (Beijing Time)
International Dialing Code
86
Currency
Yuan(Y)=10 Jiao, 1 Jiao=10 Fen
Exchange Rates

Australian Dollar	Y4.80
Bhutan Ngultrum (100)	Y18.60
British Pound	Y12.40
Canadian Dollar	Y5.60
Dutch Guilder	Y3.50
French Franc	Y1.20
German Mark	Y4.00
Hong Kong Dollar	Y1.05
Indian Rupee (100)	Y18.60
Japanese Yen (100)	Y7.60
Nepalese Rupee (100)	Y11.70
New Zealand Dollar	Y3.80
Pakistan Rupee (100)	Y15.70
Singapore Dollar	Y4.70
Swedish Krona	Y0.95
Swiss Franc	Y5.00
US Dollar	Y8.30

Language
Mandarin Chinese (Putonghua), the dialect in Beijing, is widely spoken. English is also understood at travel agencies, hotels, etc., in major tourist areas.
Inhabitants
Han Chinese 91.9%; Tibetan, Hui, Qiang, Uighur, and other nationalities make-up the remainder of the population.
*According to Chinese statistics, more than 94% of inhabitants in the Tibetan Autonomous Region are Tibetan.
*According to Tibetan sources, Tibetans are now a minority in their own country, and with the continuing immigration of Chinese, the percentage of ethnic Tibetans is dropping.
Capital
Beijing (Population of 12,000,000)
Regional Capitals
Lhasa (Tibetan Autonomous Region), Xining (Qinghai Province), Lanzhou (Gansu Province), Chengdu (Sichuan Province), Kunming (Yunnan Province).

Population
Over 1.2 billion people.
The population growth has slowed to around 1% per year.
Land Area
Approximately 9,595,000 sq km.
Climate
The air up on the Tibetan Plateau is extremely dry and temperatures vary dramatically between day and night. The south-east area of the Tibetan Plateau is affected by the monsoon weather patterns and the rainy season lasts from June to September.
Electricity
AC220V, 50Hz
Office Hours
Monday-Friday 09:00-13:00 & 15:00-18:00. The opening and closing hours vary. Saturday 09:00-12:00. Some offices, stores, etc. are open on Sunday even though it is officially a day off.
National Holidays
New Year's Day (January 1st)
Chinese Lunar New Year's Day (January-February)
Losar, Tibetan New Year (February-March)
International Women's Day (Mar 8th)
International Labor Day (May 1st)
International Children's Day (June 1st)
Chinese Communist Party's Foundation Day (July 1st)
People's Liberation Army's Foundation Day (August 1st)
National Day (October 1st)
Religion
Officially atheist

old town, this is changing.

Many of the Tibetans previously living in the old town have been pushed out into the suburbs of the city. This resettlement of people has extended the city towards the north and the west. Although Lhasa is the Tibetan capital, the accepted opinion is that Tibetans are now a minority due mainly to the influx of great numbers of Chinese immigrants.

Lhasa has also gained a degree of international infamy for the unusually high number of political prisoners. Although a relatively small city, it has quite a number of prisons, detention centers, and labor camps.

There is also a huge People's Liberation Army (PLA) base that crouches over the city, placing it under a watchful eye.

History
In the 7th century, the Tibetan king, Songtsen Gampo, transferred the capital from the Yarlung Valley to Lhasa, which was called *Ra-sa* or 'Place of the Goat' in those days. This name was quickly supplanted by the present name, *Lha-sa*, meaning 'Place of the Deity,' as Buddhism took hold throughout the Tibetan lands.

Later in the 17th century, the Dalai Lama's government completed the unification of Tibet and constructed the huge Potala Palace here to symbolize their authority in both the religious and secular life of the country. This time was the golden period for all aspects of Tibetan culture, and the city further flourished, as it was a vital focal point for trade between China and India.

Tibet lost its independence following the invasion by Chinese Communist forces in 1950, and since the 14th Dalai Lama fled to India in 1959, Lhasa has been losing its identity. The ruling Communist Party has been proceeding with a model of development aimed at turning the city into just another typical Chinese-style regional center.

ACCESS
To Lhasa
By Air
Flying into Lhasa allows passengers to get an excellent view of the Himalayas below. No question about it — Get a window seat!

Whether you are coming in from Chinese cities or from Kathmandu, air tickets to Lhasa are supposed to be sold through travel agencies.

*Chengdu—2-3 flights a day (2 in winter). All of these flights leave in the morning, usually between 06:30 and 07:00, and there's another at 11:20. (2 hrs). Costs: Y1,580. You have to buy a ticket through a travel agency in Chengdu, as the offices of China Southwest Airlines (SZ) in

Barkhor, Lhasa

the city do not sell tickets to foreigners. (For details, see Chengdu section.)

*Chongqing—2 flights a week on Monday and Sunday. (2 hrs 20 min). Costs: Y1,900.

*Xi'an—One flight a week on Thursday. Costs: Y1,670.

*Kathmandu—Tuesday and Saturday, April to November (Check a recent schedule.), China Southwest Airlines (SZ). Costs: US$190. Airport tax at Nepal is 700NRs. Chinese visas are not issued in Kathmandu to individual travelers. Moreover, even if you have one issued in a different country, you cannot obtain a ticket as long as you are an individual tourist.

Gongkar Airport to Lhasa
There are buses from the airport to the town office of CAAC, and the 100km trip costs Y25. Within an hour and a half heading towards Lhasa, some passengers will start to have symptoms of mountain sickness, as the airport is at an altitude of 3,600 m.

Over Land
There are only 2 routes that individual travelers are permitted to take:

*Xining in Qinghai Province-Golmud-Lhasa
        (Qinghai-Tibet Highway)
*Kathmandu-Kodari-Dram (Zhangmu)-Lhasa
        (China-Nepal Highway)

From Golmud
There are both trains and buses between Xining and Golmud, and to continue on to Lhasa, there are buses. (For details, see Golmud section.)

From Kathmandu
You cross the border at Kodari on the Nepalese side and then head for Dram (Zhangmu) on the Tibetan side, and from there you continue on to Lhasa. However, this border is more than likely closed to individual travelers with or without a Chinese visa. Traveling in the opposite direction poses none of these problems.
(For details, see Dram [Zhangmu] section.)

Other Routes

*Chengdu to Lhasa (Sichuan-Tibet Highway)
*Dali, Yunnan Province to Lhasa via Bayi
  (Yunnan-Tibet Highway)
*Xining, Qinghai Province, to Lhasa via Yushu
  (Jyekundo), Derge, and Chamdo
*Kashgar to Lhasa via Yecheng, Ali, and Mt.
  Kailash
*Simikot, western Nepal, to Lhasa via Purang
(For details on each of these routes, refer to the
relevant sections.)

From Lhasa
By Air

Tickets for Chinese cities are available at the CAAC
office to the east of Potala Palace, though ones for
Kathmandu can be bought at the ticket office in
the Tibet Hotel. This is not a permanent
arrangement, and the situation may change in the
future.

*Chengdu—2-3 flights a day (summer), 2 flights
  (winter). Departures: 09:25, 10:30, 14:10.
  Costs: Y1,580 or Y1,200 in winter. (1 hr 45 min).
*Chongqing—2 flights a week. Tuesday and
  Sunday. Costs: Y1,900. (2 hrs).
*Beijing—One flight a week. Thursday.
  Costs: Y2,910. (3 hrs).
*Xining—2 flights a week. Monday and Friday.
  Costs: Y1,980 (2 hrs).
*Xi'an—2 flights a week. Wednesday and Sunday.
  Costs: Y1,980 (2 hrs).
*Kathmandu—3 flights a week. Tuesday, Thursday
  and Saturday, (April to November).
  Costs: US$190+Y90 (Airport tax).

Between the city and the airport, there is a bus that
leaves the CAAC office at 06:00 and costs Y25.
There are also a number of shared-taxis waiting
for passengers at the airline office. The fare is Y50
per person, and the trip takes a couple of hours.

Buses
Mid & Long-distance Buses

On the street to the east of the Yak Hotel (See the
map on pages 72-73.), buses wait for passengers
from 07:00-09:00. For the following destinations,
you do not have to go all the way out to the long-
distance bus station. Another advantage of catching
the bus from here is that there is no additional
charge for foreigners.

*Shigatse—There are numerous buses operating
  on this route, and they cost Y38.
*Tsethang—A number of buses leave from here,
  and the fare is Y30.
*Samye—A single bus leaves each day for Y23.
*Nakchu (Naqu)—Also only one bus is available

Jokhang, Lhasa

each day, and the fare is Y40.
*Damzhung (Dangxiong)—One bus runs each day,
  costing Y30.

Buses at the Long-distance Bus Station

At the long-distance bus station, ticket prices for
foreigners are 3 times as much as for locals, but
having a Chinese student card can get you a
moderate discount. Generally, tickets are available
3 days before departure, but foreigners are not
permitted to buy ones for Chamdo and Bayi.

*Golmud—There is a daily bus that covers the trip
  in 26-30 hours. Buses run overnight, and even
  in summer it gets cold. The foreigners' fare for
  an ordinary bus is Y270, and one for a bus with
  sleeping berths is Y470. (1,165km)
*Chengdu (via Xining, Lanzhou)—There is a daily
  sleeping berth bus that takes 4 nights, and the
  tickets cost Y514. Foreigners are allowed to use
  this service. (3,280km)
*Nakchu (Naqu)—There is a bus each day that
  takes 8 hours. (326km)
*Chamdo (Changdu)—It is advisable to check the
  departure board for the dates of the 3-5 buses a
  month. The journey takes 3 nights. (1,121km)
*Bayi—This is an overnight trip with a daily
  service. There are also sleeping buses and
  minibuses operating on this route. (406km)
*Tsethang—This 5-hour trip is serviced by daily
  buses. (191km)
*Shigatse—This trip takes 6 hours, and there is at
  least 1 bus a day. (280km)
*Dram (Zhangmu)—There are 3 buses a month,
  and the trip takes 2 nights. Check the bus station
  for the most recent schedule. (755km)

To Nepalese Border by Land Cruiser

For Dram (Zhangmu), on the Tibetan side of the
border, it is quite easy to find travel companions
with which to share a car. Staying overnight at
Shelkar (Xindingri), a Land Cruiser for 4 passengers
or so costs Y3,000-4,000. Many tours add a number
of additional stops along the way, such as Yamdrok

Yutso Lake, Gyantse, Tashilhunpo Monastery, Sakya, and Everest B.C., among others. A trip including a selection of these sights will take 5-6 days and costs Y6,000-7,000.

You can book a seat at a travel agency or check message boards at guesthouses that are popular among backpackers.

Tourist Buses to the Nepalese Border
Tourist buses from Lhasa to Dram (Zhangmu) stay overnight at Shigatse and arrive at the Nepalese side the following day. There is 1 bus or so a week, and the fare is Y350. This service is usually suspended during the winter. You reserve a seat at the Banok Zhol Hotel, Snowlands Hotel, Kyire Hotel, etc.

Buses to the Outskirts of Lhasa
(Lhasa City Long-distance Buses)
Between 06:30 and 09:00 there are buses to Tsurphu Gompa, Ganden Gompa, Nyemo (Nimu), Phenpo Lhundrub (Linzhou), Meldro Gungkar (Mozhugongka), Chushul (Qushui), Taktse (Dazi), Gongkar (Gongga), and other nearby areas. (See the route map on page 86.) You can catch one either in the front of the Jokhang Temple in the early morning or at the car park near Jokhang Temple later on. (See the map on pages 72-73.) Tickets are available at the ticket office in the car park or when you board the bus.

Local Transportation
Minibuses are reasonable and convenient for getting around to areas such as the Norbulingka, Sera Monastery, Drepung Monastery, and other nearby sights. The fare charged on these is Y2, and there are frequent ones from 07:00-22:00. Before and after that there are some minibuses, but these are few and far between. (For minibus routes, see the map on page 68.) There are also a number of taxis, and the basic fare is Y10 for the first ride. For a longer trip, you will have to use your negotiation skills, but most places in town can be reached for the basic fare.

PRACTICAL INFORMATION
Visa Extensions and Travel Permits
Visa Extension (Lhasa City PSB)
(See the map on pages 68-69.)
You can get your visa extended at the Foreign Affairs Office of the Lhasa City PSB, Linkuo Beilu. Business hours: Monday to Friday 09:00-13:00 & 15:30-18:30. However, the office in Lhasa is very strict, and you are lucky if you can get even a 10-day extension. Securing an extension in Shigatse may be a better option.

Travel Permit (Public Security Office)

- (See the map on pages 68-69.)
A travel permit (See page 12.) is required to visit closed areas. Although the document is actually issued at the Foreign Affairs section of the Public Security Office, Beijing Donglu, individual travelers are not entitled to this. To get around this, there should be no problem arranging one through a travel agency.

Nepalese Visa
Royal Nepalese Consulate General
Norbulingka Rd. 13, Lhasa.
Tel: 0891-36890/ 22881 Fax: 0891-633 6890
Business hours: Monday to Saturday 09:30-12:30.
You can get a 1- or 2-month visa, valid for 6 months at the Nepalese consulate. One photograph is required, and the visa is issued after payment in Yuan.

Also, 15-day visas for US$15 and 30-day visas for US$25 are available at the border and at Kathmandu Airport. These also require 1 photograph.

Changing Money
The best place to change foreign currency is at the *Bank of China*, Lhasa head office, to the west of the Potala Palace. Business hours: Monday to Friday 09:30-12:30 & 14:00-17:30. Saturday 09:30-12:30. You can also change your money at the *Beijing Donglu Branch* between the Kyire and Banok Zhol Hotels. Business hours: Monday to Friday 10:00-13:00 & 15:00-17:00.

Post & Telecommunications
There is a post office at the *Post & Tele-communications Building*, to the east of Potala Palace. The international mail counter is at the left end of the building, and the postal workers speak English and are very efficient. Boxes and packing materials are also on sale here.
They also have a Poste Restante service.
Business hours: Winter 09:30-18:30, Summer & Fall 09:00-20:00, and 10:00-18:00 on Sunday.

There is also a telephone exchange in the same building, and direct international calls are available from telephone booths 24 hours a day here. You can also make international calls from the business center on the 2nd floor of the Pentoc Guesthouse, and they charge a Y10 commission for these. Faxes can also be sent and received from here. When a fax message arrives, one of the business center clerks calls you at your hotel.
*Fax Submission: Y12.7 per minute + Y10 commission. Fax Receipt: Y5.

Local calls can be made at most hotels in town free of charge. You can make long-distance domestic calls from telephone service offices that display a *Quanguozhibo* sign.

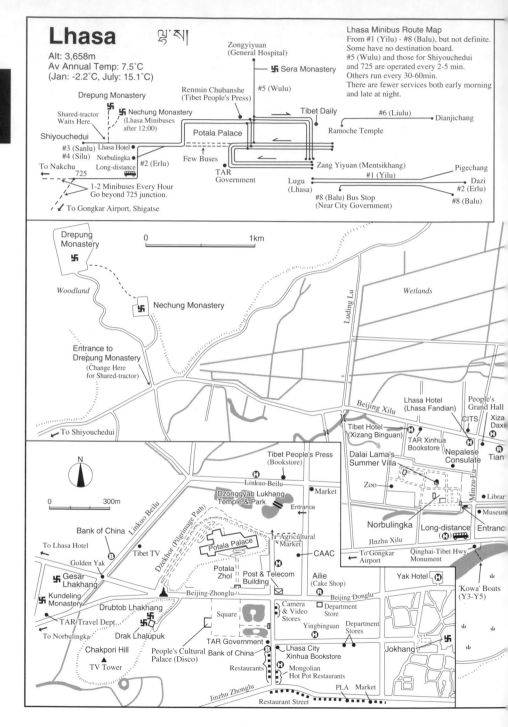

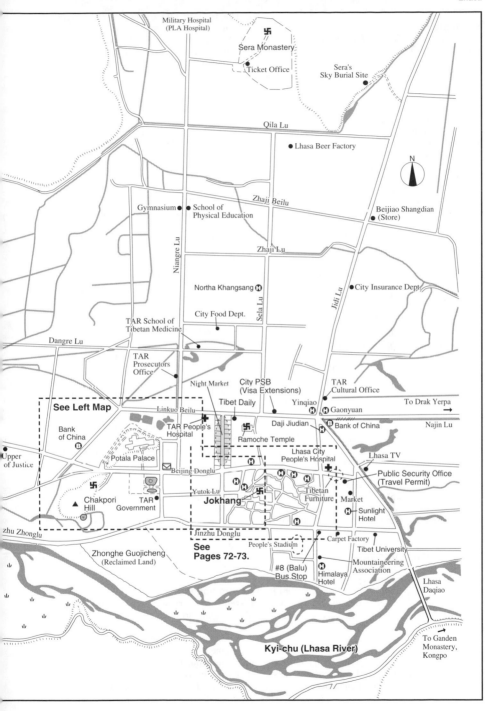

Military Hospital
(PLA Hospital)

Sera Monastery

Ticket Office

Sera's
Sky Burial Site

Qila Lu

● Lhasa Beer Factory

N

Zhaji Beilu

Gymnasium ● ● School of
Physical Education

Beijiao Shangdian
● (Store)

Niangre Lu

Zhaji Lu

Northa Khangsang ⊕

City Insurance Dept.

Sela Lu

Jidi Lu

City Food Dept.

TAR School of
Tibetan Medicine

Dangre Lu

TAR
Prosecutors
Office

Night Market

City PSB
(Visa Extensions)

TAR
Cultural Office

To Drak Yerpa →

See Left Map

Linkuo Beilu

Tibet Daily

Yinqiao

Gaonyuan

Bank
of China
Ⓑ

TAR People's
Hospital

Daji Jiudian

Ⓑ Bank of China

Najin Lu

Upper
of Justice

Potala Palace

Ramoche Temple

Lhasa City
People's Hospital

Lhasa TV

Public Security Office
(Travel Permit)

Beijing Donglu

Chakpori
Hill

TAR ●
Government

Yutok Lu

Jokhang

Tibetan
Furniture

Market

Sunlight
Hotel

zhu Zhonglu

Jinzhu Donglu

See
Pages 72-73.

People's Stadium

Carpet Factory

Tibet University

Zhonghe Guojicheng
(Reclaimed Land)

#8 (Balu)
Bus Stop

Himalaya
Hotel

Mountaineering
Association

Lhasa
Daqiao

To Ganden
Monastery,
Kongpo

Kyi-chu (Lhasa River)

Hospitals

TAR People's Hospital (Zizhiqu Renmin Yiyuan)— The TAR People's Hospital is a huge hospital on the Linkuo Beilu. For emergency treatment for ailments such as mountain sickness, go to the *Jijiu Zhongxin* (Emergency Treatment Center) in the building right next door. There are doctors who speak English here, and if you can't find them, ask at reception for them to be called on their pagers. If necessary, you can be admitted to the hospital here.

Chuanwang Zhensuo (Clinic)—The clinic is approximately 5 minutes from the Yak Hotel to the east on Beijing Donglu. A doctor will come to your hotel to see you, and this would be very helpful even if you only need to have an intravenous drip. Ask the hotel receptionist to arrange the doctor's visit.

Tibetan Medical and Astrological Institute (Mentsikhang)—Opposite the Barkhor Square, the Mentsikhang is a Tibetan medicine hospital. The staff here is very kind, the prices are reasonable, and there are doctors who understand English. Opening hours: Monday to Saturday 10:00-13:00. Closed on Sunday and national holidays.

Lhasa City People's Hospital (Lhasa Renmin Yiyuan)—This hospital sits on the eastern side of the junction where the Beijing Donglu meets the Linlang Donglu.

Major Travel Agencies

Tibet International Sports Travel (TIST)—At the Himalaya Hotel, they have good experience in mountaineering and trekking.

CITS—At 208, Beijing Xilu.

CITS Shigatse Branch—At the Tibet Hotel.

Tibet Linzhi Travel—With good experiences in the Linzhi area, it is on the other side of the road from the Snowlands Hotel.

CYTS—At the entrance of the People's Stadium. At all of these agencies there are staff that speak English. Besides the ones listed above, there is also a number of other travel companies at the Lhasa Hotel and the Tibet Hotel.

Tips for Arranging Trips in Lhasa

Many travelers will have to arrange a trip in Lhasa, as there are a number of places that are inaccessible using public transportation. There are a number of problems and pitfalls that people experience time and again when dealing with travel agencies in the city.

Problems:

1) Although the travel agent promised to arrange a Land Cruiser, it turned out to be a less comfortable and reliable 'Beijing Jeep.'

2) The driver and the guide continually ignored requests for photo stops.

3) The trip was extended due to poor road conditions, and the extra charges for this were extremely high.

4) Other problems include: additional minor charges, last minute changes to the itinerary, and general deviations from the original proposal.

Solutions:

1) Prepare a written contract (in English) laying out in black and white the conditions, such as itinerary, type of car, and payment. Then, at the very least, get the agent to sign it. There is no other way to legally protect yourself in this situation.

2) Don't pay all the money in advance. Split it with half paid before the trip and the rest on completion.

3) Remember to get receipts for everything, and keep them.

4) Most importantly, you have to find a reliable travel agency. Rumors spread quickly among travelers, so try to get the most up-to-date information you can before you decide on a particular company.

Bookstores (Tibetan Resources)

TAR Xinhua Bookstore—Next to the Tibet Hotel.

Lhasa City Xinhua Bookstore—Opposite the TAR Government buildings.

Xinhua Bookstore (Tibetan)— Behind the Jokhang Temple, it has a good selection of books in Tibetan.

Tibet People's Press (Renmin Chubanshe)—There are a lot of titles that you may be unable to find at the Xinhua Bookstore.

*The store at the Lhasa Hotel or the one at the Norbulingka, which has a good collection of photographs.

Study in Lhasa

Foreigners are only allowed to study at the *College of Tibetan Language, Tibet University* (Xizang Daxue). Tuition is US$1,000 per year, and the accommodation is expensive at Y40 a day for a room without a heater and unreliable warm showers.

Accommodation

Listed below are some of the more popular places to stay in Lhasa.

The *Pentoc Guesthouse* (Tel: 63-30700) has dormitory beds from Y35, which is reduced to Y25 during the fall and winter. There are also separate rooms for women. Double rooms cost from Y60. Heaters are provided, and warm showers are available 24 hours a day. The Pentoc is new and clean and has good facilities. There is a gift store on the 1st floor that has a good selection of souvenirs. At the business center on the 2nd floor you can make international calls, send and receive faxes, and use the color photocopier and a host of other services. Western videos are played every night.

The *Banok Zhol Hotel* (Tel: 63-23829) charges Y25-30 for a dormitory bed, Y35 for a single room, and Y62 for a double. A suite of rooms here will cost you from Y140. There is a free laundry service available. If you submit your clothes for laundering by 09:00, you can get them back by the evening. Bags are stored for free too. You can take in the view from the roof of the building, and there is a small kiosk and the Kailash Restaurant in the hotel.

The *Yak Hotel* (Tel: 63-23496) is popular among Japanese travelers. It has dormitory beds for Y25-36 (starting at Y20 in the fall and winter). Single rooms go for Y30-70, and doubles cost upwards of Y60. There is a warm shared shower, and you can wash your clothes in the courtyard. Bags can be stored here for free. There is a new 4-story building that has double rooms with a bathroom, television, heater, and writing desk. Prices start at Y200.

The *Kyire Hotel* (Tel: 63-23462) charges Y33 for a dormitory bed and Y66 for a double room. There is a free laundry service available.

The *Snowlands Hotel* (Tel: 63-23687) is the hotel closest to the Jokhang Temple. Dormitory beds cost Y24-Y35, and double rooms are Y60-80. You can wash your clothes in the courtyard. There is a high-class restaurant on the 1st floor.

The *Bus Station Guesthouse* is at the long-distance bus station, which is convenient for those early morning departures.

Mid and Top Range Hotels

The *Lhasa Hotel* (Lhasa Fandian) (Tel: 68-32221) is a popular choice for group tours, and the hotel enjoys the reputation as the best quality accommodation in Lhasa. It used to be run by the Holiday Inn Group, but the contract was not renewed in 1997. However, the level of services has not diminished, and for around Y600, you can get a nice double room here. There are a number of travel agencies in the hotel, and there is even a resident doctor.

The *Tibet Hotel* (Xizang Binguan) (Tel: 68-34966) has double rooms for Y460 and up. There are a number of travel agencies in the building.

The *Himalaya Hotel* (Tel: 63-34082) charges from Y250 for its double rooms. *Sports Travel Agency* is in this hotel.

The *Sunlight Hotel* (Riguang Binguan) (Tel: 63-22227) has doubles for Y200. There is a restaurant and also a travel agency here.

Restaurants

There is a wide selection of food available in the city though the quality is extremely variable. You can sample Tibetan food, Sichuanese *huoguo* (Mongolian hotpot), Shandong *jiaozi* (boiled dumplings), Western food, Nepalese *dal bhat* (lentil curry), and Uighur *shish kebab* to name a few.

Popular Restaurants for Foreigners:

Tashi Restaurant 1 and *Tashi Restaurant 2* are both foreigners' hangouts that have travel information notebooks. Tashi 1 is near the Yak Hotel, and Tashi 2 is at the Kyire Hotel. These restaurants serve Western and Tibetan food. The chocolate cake and cheesecakes are worth a try.

The *Kailash Restaurant* is on the 1st floor of the Banok Zhol Hotel and serves Western, Nepalese-style Tibetan, and Japanese food.

The *Snowland Restaurant* is on the 1st floor of the Snowlands Hotel. It is a neat and clean restaurant serving Western and Tibetan meals. There are good but expensive cakes available here too.

The *Barkhor Café* is run by the Lhasa Hotel (Lhasa Fandian), and it is a relatively high-class restaurant on the 2nd floor of the building on the southern side of the Barkhor Square. There is Chinese, Western, Nepalese, and Japanese food on the menu.

The *Hard Yak Café* is actually at the Lhasa Hotel, and it serves pizza, Great Yak Burgers, etc. The coffee and cakes here are also good.

If you want to try plain Tibetan food, such as *momos* and *tukpa*, check out the restaurants around the Barkhor or Ramoche Temple.

AROUND THE BARKHOR

Jokhang Temple (Tsuglagkhang)

For Tibetan pilgrims heading for Lhasa from all over Tibet this holiest of temples is their ultimate destination.

In front of Jokhang Temple, pilgrims repeatedly prostrate themselves. The common image of Tibetan religion and its practitioners is that of a severe form of asceticism. However, if your first encounter of this is at this temple, you will go away with a feeling that the pilgrims actually enjoy it.

When approaching the Jokhang, your nose is assaulted by the rich blended aroma of butter lamps and burning incense. On Buddhist holidays the incense is at its strongest with clouds of smoke shrouding the temple in a swirling mist.

The real date when the Jokhang Temple was founded is still unknown. One accepted version of events is that in the 7th century the late King Songtsen Gampo's Nepalese Queen, while grieving for her dead husband, was inspired to build the

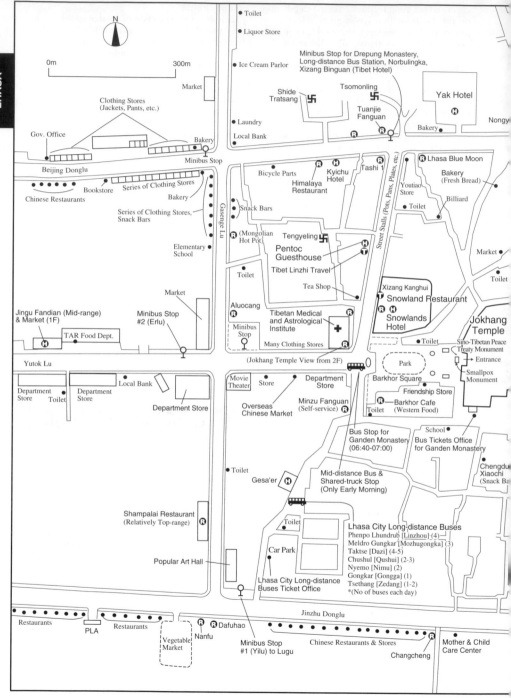

N

0m 300m

Toilet
Liquor Store
Ice Cream Parlor

Minibus Stop for Drepung Monastery,
Long-distance Bus Station, Norbulingka,
Xizang Binguan (Tibet Hotel)

Shide Tratsang
Tsomonling
Yak Hotel

Tuanjie Fanguan

Laundry
Local Bank

Bakery

Nongy

Market

Clothing Stores
(Jackets, Pants, etc.)

Gov. Office

Bakery

Minibus Stop

Beijing Donglu

Bookstore Series of Clothing Stores

Chinese Restaurants

Series of Clothing Stores,
Snack Bars

Bakery

Elementary School

Market

Jingu Fandian (Mid-range)
& Market (1F)

TAR Food Dept.

Minibus Stop
#2 (Erlu)

Gasenge Lu

(Mongolian Hot Pot)

Snack Bars

Toilet

Aluocang

Minibus Stop

Tengyeling

Pentoc Guesthouse

Tibet Linzhi Travel

Tea Shop

Tibetan Medical
and Astrological Institute

Many Clothing Stores

Bicycle Parts

Kyichu Hotel

Himalaya Restaurant

Tashi 1

Street Stalls (Pots, Pans, Plates, etc.)

Lhasa Blue Moon

Bakery
(Fresh Bread)

Youtiao Store

Billiard

Toilet

Market

Toilet

Xizang Kanghui

Snowland Restaurant

Snowlands Hotel

Jokhang Temple

Sino-Tibetan Peace
Treaty Monument

Toilet

Park

Entrance

Smallpox Monument

Barkhor Square

(Jokhang Temple View from 2F)

Yutok Lu

Department Store

Toilet

Local Bank

Department Store

Department Store

Department Store

Movie Theater

Store

Overseas Chinese Market

Department Store

Minzu Fanguan
(Self-service)

Friendship Store

Barkhor Cafe
(Western Food)

Toilet

School

Bus Stop for
Ganden Monastery
(06:40-07:00)

Bus Tickets Office
for Ganden Monastery

Chengdu
Xiaochi
(Snack Ba

Toilet

Gesa'er

Mid-distance Bus &
Shared-truck Stop
(Only Early Morning)

Shampalai Restaurant
(Relatively Top-range)

Toilet

Car Park

Lhasa City Long-distance Buses

Phenpo Lhundrub [Linzhou] (4)
Meldro Gungkar [Mozhugongka] (3)
Taktse [Dazi] (4-5)
Chushul [Qushui] (2-3)
Nyemo [Nimu] (2)
Gongkar [Gongga] (1)
Tsethang [Zedang] (1-2)
*(No of buses each day)

Popular Art Hall

Lhasa City Long-distance
Buses Ticket Office

Restaurants

PLA

Restaurants

Vegetable Market

Nanfu

Dafuhao

Minibus Stop
#1 (Yilu) to Lugu

Jinzhu Donglu

Chinese Restaurants & Stores

Changcheng

Mother & Child
Care Center

Around Jokhang Temple

གཙུག་ཆེ་ར་ལྷ་ས།

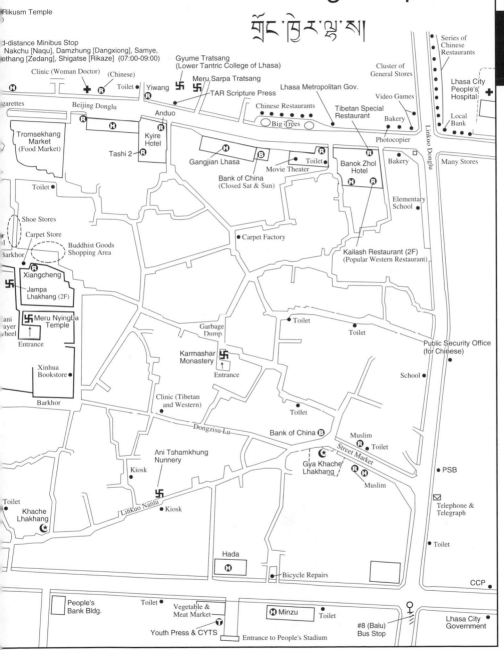

Rikusm Temple

d-distance Minibus Stop
Nakchu [Naqu], Damzhung [Dangxiong], Samye,
ethang [Zedang], Shigatse [Rikaze] (07:00-09:00)

Clinic (Woman Doctor)   (Chinese)

garettes

Beijing Donglu

Tromsekhang
Market
(Food Market)

Tashi 2

Toilet

Shoe Stores

Carpet Store

Barkhor

Buddhist Goods
Shopping Area

Xiangcheng

Jampa
Lhakhang (2F)

ani
ayer
heel

Meru Nyingba
Temple

Entrance

Xinhua
Bookstore

Barkhor

Toilet

Khache
Lhakhang

Series of
Chinese
Restaurants

Cluster of
General Stores

Lhasa City
People's
Hospital

Gyume Tratsang
(Lower Tantric College of Lhasa)

Meru Sarpa Tratsang

Yiwang

TAR Scripture Press

Lhasa Metropolitan Gov.

Anduo

Chinese Restaurants

Tibetan Special
Restaurant

Video Games

Bakery

Photocopier

Linkuo Donglu

Local
Bank

Kyire
Hotel

Big Trees

Gangjian Lhasa

Movie Theater

Toilet

Bank of China
(Closed Sat & Sun)

Banok Zhol
Hotel

Bakery

Many Stores

Elementary
School

Carpet Factory

Kailash Restaurant (2F)
(Popular Western Restaurant)

Garbage
Dump

Toilet

Toilet

Karmashar
Monastery

Entrance

Public Security Office
(for Chinese)

School

Clinic (Tibetan
and Western)

Toilet

Dongzisu-Lu

Bank of China

Muslim

Toilet

PSB

Ani Tshamkhung
Nunnery

Kiosk

Street Market

Gya Khache
Lhakhang

Muslim

Toilet

Linkuo Nanlu

Kiosk

Telephone &
Telegraph

Toilet

Hada

Bicycle Repairs

CCP

People's
Bank Bldg.

Toilet

Vegetable &
Meat Market

Youth Press & CYTS

Entrance to People's Stadium

Minzu

Toilet

#8 (Balu)
Bus Stop

Lhasa City
Government

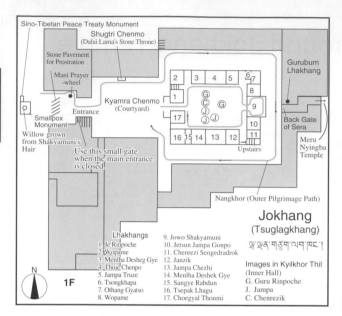

Sino-Tibetan Peace Treaty Monument
Shugtri Chenmo
(Dalai Lama's Stone Throne)
Stone Pavement for Prostration
Mani Prayer -wheel
Kyamra Chenmo (Courtyard)
Entrance
Smallpox Monument
Willow grown from Shakyamuni's Hair
Use this small gate when the main entrance is closed!
Gurubum Lhakhang
Back Gate of Sera
Meru Nyingba Temple
Upstairs
Nangkhor (Outer Pilgrimage Path)

Jokhang
(Tsuglagkhang)

ཇོ་ཁང་གཙུག་ལག་ཁང་།

Lhakhangs

1. Je Rinpoche
2. Wopame
3. Menlha Desheg Gye
4. Thuje Chenpo
5. Jampa Truze
6. Tsongkhapa
7. Othang Gyatso
8. Wopame

9. Jowo Shakyamuni
10. Jetsun Jampa Gonpo
11. Chenrezi Sengedradrok
12. Janzik
13. Jampa Chezhi
14. Menlha Deshek Gye
15. Sangye Rabdun
16. Tsepak Lhagu
17. Choegyal Thonmi

Images in Kyilkhor Thil (Inner Hall)
G. Guru Rinpoche
J. Jampa
C. Chenrezik

N
1F

distinguished services by the goats, Jampa Chezhi Lhakhang (13), on the 1st floor of the Jokhang, holds a small image of a goat.

Visit to the Jokhang Temple

The entrance to the Jokhang is usually open after 08:30. Once it is open, the impatient pilgrims from the countryside crowd into the structure. There is a lot of noise and commotion that is quite irreverent, and the visitors from Lhasa, on the other hand, remain cool and look on in an aloof manner.

Jostled by the crowd, you turn the huge *mani*-prayer wheel on the left and then enter the building. Soon after you pass under the watchful eyes of the Four Guardian Kings, you reach the spacious courtyard, Kyamra Chenmo.

Although the whole site is commonly referred to as the Jokhang Temple, in reality it is not just a single building. Jokhang Temple is the main structure, and another building, the Trulnang Temple, surrounds it. The generic name for the site though is Jokhang Temple.

After the courtyard you come to a number of Buddhist statues standing together in the main temple. These are impressive, but the pilgrims simply pass by and go straight into the chapel on the left without paying much attention to them.

Now, let's start making a pilgrimage circuit, clockwise as tradition stipulates.

Straight to the left side is Je Rinpoche Lhakhang (1). This chapel accommodates images of Tsongkhapa, the founder of Gelukpa, and his 8 disciples.

At the first corner is Wopame Lhakhang (Infinite Light Chapel) (2), dedicated to Amitabha. The popular Eight Medicine Buddhas are at Menlha Deseg Gye Lhakhang (3). The next important chapel is Thuje Chenpo Lhakhang (4), housing the Eleven-faced Avalokiteshvara, one of the most sacred Buddhist images in Tibet. It is said that part of the statue was secretly taken out to Dharamsala, India, where the 14th Dalai Lama now lives in exile.

Next is Jampa Truze Lhakhang with an image of Jampa (Maitreya). At the second corner are both the Tsongkhapa Lhakhang (6) and Othang Gyatso

temple with its statue of Buddha, the eleven-faced Avalokiteshvara. Therefore, the main temple faces the west toward her home, Nepal. The Jokhang is dedicated to the image of Jowo Rinpoche (Shakyamuni) that Princess Wengcheng, the Chinese Queen of King Songtsen Gampo, brought as an offering for the marriage. This image of Jowo Rinpoche (Shakyamuni) is an auspicious statue that was originally a gift from India.

Another legend has it that it was Princess Wengcheng who decided where to construct the Jokhang Temple. By consulting astrological charts, she was told to build the temple on this site by reclaiming the land from the Othang Lake. Goats were used to carry the earth used to fill in the lake, and this is why the area came to be called *Ra* (Goat)-*Sa* (Place). This may sound strange, but it is a widely held belief. To show appreciation for the

Image of Jowo Rinpoche (Shakyamuni)

Jokhang Temple

of the chapels have their own rich history, and there is lots of interest. At the 3rd corner, you can go upstairs to the 3rd floor. On the landing between the 2nd and 3rd floors is the image of Palden Lhamo, guardian goddess of Tibet, which is the Jokhang Temple's second highlight. From the temple roof you can see the imposing spectacle of the Potala Palace.

On leaving the main shrine there is a *Nangkhor* (Pilgrimage Path). Again, there are a number of chapels in the corridor along with a lot of *mani* prayer wheels strung out in long lines. Gurubum Lhakhang (Hundred thousand images of Guru Rinpoche), behind the image of Jowo Rinpoche, is also well worth seeing.

Lhakhang (7), dedicated to the filled-in lake upon which the Jokhang is built. Wopame Lhakhang (8) is right next to these. During the pilgrimage season this section turns into a bottleneck, and it is the scene of some frustrated jostling. Though the highlight of the Jokhang is in the next chapel, the crowds tend to move slowly, and as you wait, you are engulfed by thick wafts of incense and butter lamp smoke intermingled with pilgrims' chants.

On the other side of the entrance, Jowo Shakyamuni Lhakhang (9) houses the image of Jowo Rinpoche (Shakyamuni), the most revered image in Tibet. At the back of the chapel is the gold image representing Buddha around the age of 12. You are finally there, and you just have to try to forget the mirror ball above your head.

At the front, pilgrims offer a *katak* (white prayer scarf) and vigorously rub their foreheads against the image of Jowo Rinpoche (Shakyamuni). Then, they repeat the same thing on the left-hand side. At this point they are making a wish, and this slows the flow of people through the chapel. Although there are temple monks to hurry them along, the crowds keep to their own pace and do it again, moving to the right-hand side around the back of the image. On leaving the temple you relax, but some of the pilgrims again prostrate themselves here too.

The trip hasn't finished yet — though most of the pilgrims seem to have done their piece, and there is a more relaxed atmosphere. Of course, the rest

Admission in the Afternoon

Jokhang Temple is open during the morning. In the afternoon, the temple is for tourists paying admission of Y25, but you can only see the Buddhist images at a distance, as the chapels are locked. Enter the small gate on the right (the main entrance is closed), and then go upstairs.

The gate was used by the *Substitute*, a person chosen soon after *Monlam Chenmo* (New Year's Great Prayer Festival) and then expelled to a remote area of the country, taking with him all of the year's bad luck.

A Buddhist service is held after 19:00, and it might be fun to join the event. The basic rule is that photographs are not allowed inside the buildings and chapels.

Barkhor Square

The square in front of the Jokhang functions as an important meeting place. In the evening, a number of Tibetans gather here after school or work, making the place very lively. Local women come to enjoy the cool breeze, and young men check out prospective girlfriends. It is understandable that this is a time that people can enjoy suspicious chats, as in the evening the surveillance cameras can't catch the activities on film so well, and public security officers have gone off duty. The square was built approximately 15 years ago by destroying old nobles' houses, similar to the ones that surround the Barkhor.

The Yutok Lu, which used to be a river, heads straight to the west from the square and leads to the seat of the TAR Government.

Barkhor (Eight Corners Street)

The Barkhor is the circular bazaar around the

Prostration, Jokhang Temple

Barkhor, Lhasa

Jokhang Temple. People usually move clockwise around it, keeping the temple to their right, but you may also see a few walking in the opposite direction. These may be either Chinese or residents taking a shortcut, as even the followers of the Bon religion are said to move around this sacred site clockwise.

You will also encounter groups of monks or nuns sitting and chanting *sutras* in the midst of the throng of people. They are probably collecting donations for the reconstruction of their monasteries or nunneries.

No matter how pious they are, many Tibetans make it a daily rule to make circuits around the Barkhor, and the number of times depends on the person. Although you see some prostrating themselves earnestly, most pilgrims have a look at or drop in to the street stalls while at the same time undertaking their religious duty.

These stores and stall keepers deal in striped wool for women's aprons, yak furs, jewels, accessories, popular music tapes, and all manner of other household and daily goods. There is also a good selection of Buddhist images, Buddhist altar fittings, *sutras*, *thangkas*, and other religious items available, and even the monks have to get tough to get discounts on these goods for their temples.

Everything that Tibetans need is available at the Barkhor. There used to be a number of photographs

Ramoche Temple

of the Dalai Lama in exile on street stalls, which attracted pilgrims, but after the fall of 1995, these disappeared from Lhasa due to stricter government controls.

Of course, the square is also a great shopping center for foreign visitors. You can enjoy haggling with the vendors, but you have to be careful, as overcharging tourists is common practice. All in all, the bargaining experience is a lot less hassle than similar negotiations in India.

The quality of the goods on sale at the Barkhor varies from top rate to third rate. You have to watch out in particular for fake jewelry, such as turquoise. Many of the Buddhist goods on sale are imports from India, but the number of those made locally in Lhasa and Shigatse has been increasing recently. Also, many of the sweaters and bags are from Nepal, so if you are continuing on to Kathmandu, it would be cheaper to buy one there. There are some sweaters made in Lhasa also available these days.

While walking around the Barkhor, you may hear a secretive whisper 'Master, Master' from behind you. In most cases the guy approaching you is an underling of Khampa merchants from the east of Tibet trying to sell dubious antiques. If he suddenly draws a short sword from inside his jacket, don't worry, as he just wants to sell it to you. If you are interested in buying something, you will be taken to a lodging house nearby, where they will show you a lot of *thangkas* and antiques. These may be of dubious origin, and the prices are probably higher than you expected. But these merchants are not too persistent, and after a cup of tea, you are free to leave again.

In the evening, a number of Han and Hui stall keepers join the crowds and start up bargain sales for all manner of everyday items by trumpeting '*Jianjia! Jianjia!*' The mix of pilgrims, monks chanting *sutras*, and the shouts of '*Jianjia! Jianjia!*' form a fairly harmonious backing soundtrack for an evening in the Barkhor.

One further possible problem is for travelers of Asian descent being mistaken for Chinese, as there are regularly a number of drunken Tibetans hanging around the square in the evenings.

All the buildings around the Barkhor have a history of their own. One used to be a noble's house, and another was a labrang, or house for an incarnate lama, and so on. Most of these have now been converted into apartments since all the major nobles and high-ranking lamas sought refuge abroad.

Ramoche Temple

Like the Jokhang, Ramoche Temple is an old and revered temple. It is said to have been built in dedication of the image of Jowo Rinpoche

(Shakyamuni) that Princess Wengcheng, King Songtsen Gampo's Chinese Queen, brought with her. The image was removed and taken to the Jokhang Temple sometime later without any record of the undertaking surviving. Admission to the site is Y20.

At Ramoche Temple is the Gyuto Tratsang (Upper Tantric College of Lhasa), one of the 2 great tantric colleges in Lhasa — though the actual college seat has been relocated to India.

Meru Nyingba Temple

Right behind the Jokhang, Meru Nyingba Temple looks like a part of Jokhang Temple, but it is a separate Nyingmapa temple. Like the Jokhang, it has a history stretching back to the 7th century, and the founder was Tonmi Sambhota, who also created the Tibetan alphabet during the reign of King Songtsen Gampo. Later, the site was destroyed by King Langdarma, who oppressed Buddhism throughout Tibet. In the 16th century, Atisha, the high-ranking Indian lama who laid the foundations of the Gelukpa order, reconstructed it.

The oldest part of the temple is the Jampa Lhakhang, on the 1st floor, and a branch of Sakyapa's Gongkar Choede near the Gongkar Airport is on the 2nd floor.

Jampa Lhakhang

Also called Jamkhang for short, it is at the entrance to the Meru Nyingba Temple when coming from the north of the Barkhor. With a large image of the Sitting Jampa (Maitreya), the structure is said to have been built by one of Tsongkhapa's disciples in the 15th century.

The highlight to a visit here is a ceremony to exorcise evil spirits, held in the mornings on the 2nd floor. With a bell, a lama chanting *sutras* burns incense and puts holy water on your head while you kneel in the usually crowded room.

Ani Tshamkhung Nunnery

Ranked alongside the Drubtob Lhakhang and Chubzang Gompa, Ani Tshamkhung Nunnery is

Ani Tshamkhung Nunnery

one of the 3 great nunneries in Lhasa. Although small, the site houses over 100 calm but friendly, young nuns. The nunnery was established in the 7th century, and the main temple is dedicated to Chenrezik (Thousand-armed Avalokiteshvara). For entry into King Songtsen Gampo's meditation place (Tshamkhung), take the path to the right of the building. The nun's lodgings have recently undergone renovation. For some reason the nuns here seem to like learning English. Admission is Y6.

Gyume Tratsang
(Lower Tantric College of Lhasa)

Along with the Gyuto Tratsang at the Ramoche Temple, this is one of the 2 great tantric colleges in Lhasa. The site is opposite the Kyire Hotel. The college has also been reconstructed in southern India by Tibetans living in exile there.

Meru Sarpa Tratsang

Next to the Gyume Tratsang, this college was once occupied by a theater troupe for a while, but now it functions as a monastery where religious services and catechism, a form of oral instruction, are practiced.

Karmashar Monastery

Along with the State Oracle of Tibet, whose seat is at Nechung Monastery at the foot of Drepung Monastery, the Oracle at Karmashar Monastery used to divine the destiny of Tibet. The site is to the east of the Barkhor.
(See the map on pages 72-73.)

Shide Tratsang

Approximately 200m to the west of the Yak Hotel on Beijing Donglu, take a path to the north, and you will soon reach the courtyard of the temple. Shide Tratsang is said to have been constructed by King Relpachen in the 9th century. At the site is Reting Labrang, the residence for the incarnate Reting Rinpoches. The Chinese government recognized a 2-year-old as the most recent incarnation in 2000 to replace the previous Rinpoche, who passed away in Lhasa in 1997. The 14th Dalai Lama has refused to recognize the Chinese choice. (See page 99.)

Ling Shi (Four Regency Temples)

Ling Shi is the generic name for the 4 temples that acted as the Dalai Lama's regency and seized enormous power during the 19th century. This period saw a lot of political scheming and upheaval among the nobility of the country. During this time all the Dalai Lamas from the 9th, Lungtok Gyatso, through to the 12th, Trinle Gyatso, met with untimely deaths.

Kundeling Gompa

Kundeling Gompa is at the foot of Parmari, to the west of the golden statue of a yak. Although its scale has been diminished, the site is being gradually revived. (See page 81.)

Tengyeling

This one can still be found behind the Mentsikhang (Institute of Tibetan Medicine and Astrology).

Tsomonling

To get to the temple, take the path beside the Tuanjie Fanguan (Restaurant) on the same side of the street as the Yak Hotel. Although a section of it still works as a temple, the rest has been converted into apartments.

Drib Tsechokling

Drib Tsechokling used to be in Drib Village, south of the Kyi-chu. A good copy of this temple has also been constructed in Dharamsala, and the incarnate lama also lives in India.

The Mentsikhang (Institute of Tibetan Medicine and Astrology)

The hospital's doctors practice Tibetan medicine, and there is a tour available during which you can observe them at work. The hospital has English-speaking doctors. You can buy a copy of the *Gyuzhi* (The Four Secret Oral Tantras of the Eight Branches of the Medical Tradition), the complete works of beautiful medical *thangka*, which can be regarded as the bible of Tibetan medicine.

If you have a minor ailment, such as a cold, it might be good to see a doctor here. A medical examination is based on taking your pulse, and the treatment provided will be a mild and safe mixture of crude drugs made from plant extracts. Admission for the tour is Y15, and the hospital is open 10:00-13:00.

Along with medicine, the Mentsikhang also prepares the Tibetan calendar on which all Buddhist events across Tibet are based. There is also a Mentsikhang that has been built in Dharamsala, India. Like its counterpart in Lhasa, the institute takes care of medicine and calendars too.

Carpet Factory

Tibetan carpets and handwoven small articles are available here, and you will find the factory near the Sunlight Hotel (Riguang Binguan). Admission is free, and it is open 08:00-12:30 and 15:30-18:30. Closed on Sunday.

Kyi-chu River

The river flows through the southern part of Lhasa. Traditional *Kowa* boats, made of yak skin, still play an active role on the river, and foreigners are charged Y3-5. Recent development has destroyed the popular picnic and dating spot on Jamalingka Island, in the middle of the Kyi-chu, and land along the river has been prepared for new commercial buildings.

Gya Khache Lhakhang

The street on the southern side of the Jokhang Temple leads straight to Muslim Town with a number of Muslim restaurants and this green-roofed mosque. You are permitted to enter and look around except during praying time.

Khache Lhakhang

In the south of the Barkhor, this is a small mosque for the Khache people, who are Muslims from Kashmir. Unlike the Huis, who are more recent migrants from China, the Khache have lived in Tibet, traded, and worked as merchants for hundreds of years. They speak using extremely polite Tibetan honorific words — much better than the Tibetans use themselves.

AROUND THE POTALA PALACE

Potala Palace (Podrang Potala)

Rather than the whole of Lhasa, it is the Potala Palace that really symbolizes Tibet. Built in the 17th century on Mt. Marpori (Red Hill), at the western end of Lhasa, the palace, according to one version of events, replaced a fortress that had been on this spot since the reign of King Songtsen Gampo in the 7th century.

Potala means 'The Place where Avalokiteshvara Lives,' of whom the Dalai Lama is the embodiment. In 1645 the 5th Dalai Lama started construction on the White Palace on the right, as you look from the front, and 3 years later the structure was completed. Since the Dalai Lama moved his residence from Ganden Podrang at Drepung Monastery to the Potala Palace later, it has been the political and religious center of Tibet. After the 5th Dalai Lama passed away, his powerful regent, Desi Sangye Gyatso, built the Red Palace (Podrang

Potala Palace from Chakpori Hill

78

White Palace

Marpo). Until the Red Palace was completed 14 years later, the death of the revered leader wasn't revealed.

During the Chinese invasion and the Cultural Revolution, it is consoling to think that the palace survived with only minor damage, as the site was under control of the Beijing government and protected as a national asset. Regarded as a piece of history, however, the site has taken on the look of a museum. In 1994 after the completion of extensive repairs, 2 huge *thangkas* were draped on its walls for the first time since the 14th Dalai Lama fled into exile in India.

It is said that there are 999 rooms, but most of them are not open to public, and you are not allowed to walk around the buildings freely. Camera fees are high, and there are surveillance cameras installed along the tourist routes. It takes a couple of hours for a full visit.

Admission is Y45 for a foreigner, Y20 for a student with an ID (Chinese, domestic, or

international), and the same for a Chinese national. In addition, there is an insurance charge of Y2. One thing to be very careful about here is the variable charges for taking photos, as they are extremely high — as much as hundreds of yuan. The palace grounds are open between 09:00 and 12:00.

Zhol Village

Following the solid-looking gate on the Beijing Donglu, there are a number of buildings that do not look special. The village of Potala Zhol, at the foot of the Potala Palace, used to be home to a wide range of facilities, from the Tibetan government, to houses for government officials, a settlement for craftsmen, and schools. Recent rezoning has transferred most of these functions out to the north of Lhasa.

White Palace (Podrang Karpo)

Through the entrance pathway with its gift stores, you make your way up the stairs on the left. These are long and not too easygoing. If you keep heading straight ahead, it brings you to the Red Palace, but tourists must take the other way to reach the entrance.

Soon after you go into the first building, you reach the spacious courtyard called Deyang Shar. The structure in front of you is the White Palace. The structure housed the political activities of the palace and private quarters for the Dalai Lama.

Nyiwo Shar Ganden Nangsel

This was the Dalai Lama's living quarters, and the 14th Dalai Lama actually spent much of his time here. Along with an audience chamber and a gonkhang, there are also more private rooms, such as a living room, etc.

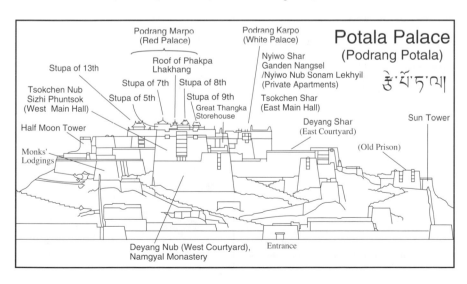

Potala Palace
(Podrang Potala)

ཀྲེ་པོ་ད་ལ།

Podrang Marpo (Red Palace)
Podrang Karpo (White Palace)
Nyiwo Shar Ganden Nangsel /Nyiwo Nub Sonam Lekhyil (Private Apartments)
Stupa of 13th
Roof of Phakpa Lhakhang
Stupa of 7th | Stupa of 8th
Tsokchen Nub Sizhi Phuntsok (West Main Hall)
Stupa of 5th
Stupa of 9th
Great Thangka Storehouse
Tsokchen Shar (East Main Hall)
Half Moon Tower
Deyang Shar (East Courtyard)
Sun Tower
Monks' Lodgings
(Old Prison)
Deyang Nub (West Courtyard), Namgyal Monastery
Entrance

Tsokchen Shar (East Main Hall)

The East Main Hall is an assembly hall built in a bell shape going up to the 3rd floor. This is the place where each successive Dalai Lama was enthroned and other important ceremonies were held.

Red Palace (Podrang Marpo)

Among the structures at the Potala, the Red Palace is the most striking building with its dark-red painted facade. This is the center of religious activities, and besides the huge mausoleum for successive Dalai Lama's mummies, there are many richly decorated chapels.

Some have it that the building has 13 floors including the roof. This book regards the floor on which the reliquary stupa of the 5th Dalai Lama stands as the 1st floor.

The size of the stupas here vary from the small ones on the 4th floor to the huge ones on the 1st floor, the tops of which reach the 4th floor. Entry from the roof of the White Palace leads you to the 4th floor of the Red Palace. In the center you will see the roof of the Tsokchen Nub Sizhi Phuntsok (West Main Hall). A tour of the White Palace starts from here and then takes you down to the 1st floor.

Fourth Floor

*Phakpa Lhakhang

This is the most sacred chapel at the Potala Palace, and it is said to be part of the original 7th century structure. The sandalwood image of Avalokiteshvara here is *Rangjung* (Self-arising). Also, the structure houses the stone footprints of Guru Rinpoche that he left at Gungtang La pass when he entered Tibet for the first time.

*Great Reliquary Stupa of the 13th Dalai Lama

The path on the western side leads to the mausoleum of the 13th Dalai Lama with his stupa standing at 13m. There is a *mandala* here that is said to be made up of 200,000 pearls as well as precious stones, etc.

*On the roof, you can get a good view of the *Sertoks* (Golden Roofs) laid out side by side.

Third Floor

*Dukhor Lhakhang

There is a 3-dimensional *mandala* depicting the teachings of *Kalachakra*.

*Chogyel Drupuk

It is said to be the oldest chapel for King Songtsen Gampo's meditation at the Potala Palace.

Second Floor

There are no chapels currently open to visitors on this level, but the walls are spectacularly painted with stories concerning the foundation of the Red Palace and the monasteries of Lhasa. There are also panels that detail old Tibetan customs. To appreciate the flow of the stories, you must go in a clockwise direction. Near the end of the wall paintings, you can get a view overlooking the 5th Dalai Lama's stupa.

First Floor

*Tsokchen Nub Sizhi Phuntsok (West Main Hall)

The largest room in the Potala Palace, it is a great assembly hall designed in a bell shape with a roof that rises up to the 3rd floor.

*Lamrim Lhakhang

The chapel is dedicated to the ancient founders of the Gelukpa order. The teachings of *Lamrim* are currently the main stream of Gelukpa practices.

*Rigdzin Lhakhang

This chapel is dedicated to the ancient founders of Nyingmapa.

*Serdung Dzamling Gyenchik

Named 'Unique Ornament in the World,' this chapel

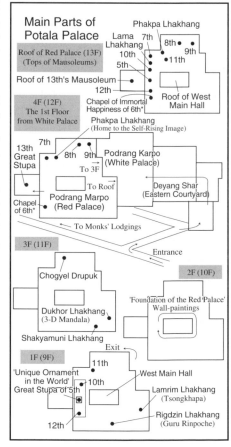

Main Parts of Potala Palace

Roof of Red Palace (13F) (Tops of Mausoleums)

Roof of 13th's Mausoleum

4F (12F) The 1st Floor from White Palace

13th Great Stupa

Chapel of 6th*

Podrang Marpo (Red Palace)

To Monks' Lodgings

3F (11F)

Chogyel Drupuk

Dukhor Lhakhang (3-D Mandala)

Shakyamuni Lhakhang

1F (9F)

'Unique Ornament in the World' Great Stupa of 5th

12th

Phakpa Lhakhang

Lama Lhakhang 7th
10th
5th
8th
9th
11th

12th

Chapel of Immortal Happiness of 6th*

Roof of West Main Hall

Phakpa Lhakhang (Home to the Self-Rising Image)

7th
8th 9th Podrang Karpo (White Palace)

To 3F

To Roof

Deyang Shar (Eastern Courtyard)

Entrance

2F (10F)

'Foundation of the Red Palace' Wall-paintings

Exit

11th

10th

West Main Hall

Lamrim Lhakhang (Tsongkhapa)

Rigdzin Lhakhang (Guru Rinpoche)

Annual unveiling of the thangka at Drepung Monastery, one of the largest monasteries in Tibet. (HN)

Potala Palace. (HN)

The colorful Zhoton (Yoghurt) Festival
held annually in Lhasa. (HN)

Taking a break at the sacred Lake
Yamdrok Yumtso, near Lhasa. (MA)

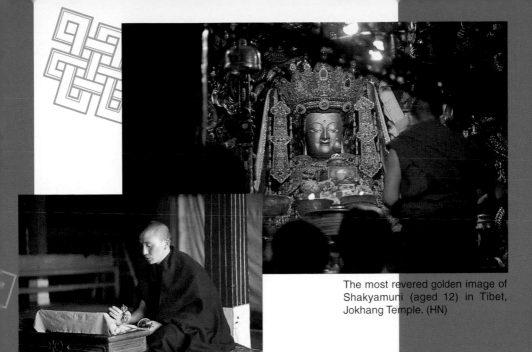

The most revered golden image of Shakyamuni (aged 12) in Tibet, Jokhang Temple. (HN)

Sera Monastery. (MA)

Outside the Jokhang
Endless procession of pilgrims visit the Jokhang Temple, Lhasa. (HN)

(SM)

(HN)

(SM)

(MA)

(MA)

could be regarded as the highlight of a trip to the Red Palace. Among 3 reliquary stupas, the one dedicated to the 5th Dalai Lama at 14m is overwhelming. This monument to the great leader is decorated with 3,700kgs of gold and a large quantity of precious stones and jewels. The other 2 next to it are for the 10th and 12th Dalai Lamas.

Dago Kani
At the western end of Mt. Marpori and to the side of Beijing Donglu, this chorten used to be the West Gate of the capital and was rebuilt in 1995.

Dzonggyab Lukhang Temple
Dedicated to *Naga* (Water-dragons), the temple was constructed right behind the Potala in the 17th century. Also called the Water-dragon Chapel, the sight is a popular picnic spot, although the Norbulingka attracts more people. Construction of the Potala Palace required massive amounts of earth, and much of this was taken from this site. The holes left after the building work filled with water, creating the ponds here. This temple used to have elephants too.

Chakpori Hill
With a radio mast atop it, the hill commands a good view of the Potala. Although nothing now remains, this was once the site of the Tibetan College of Medicine. Built by the 5th Dalai Lama, the structure was here from 1413 until 1959.

On the hillside, you can see a number of rock paintings, and on the hillside facing the south-east, you will find Drak Lhalupuk.

Drak Lhalupuk & Neten Lhakhang

Drak Lhalupuk
Clinging to the south-eastern side of Chakpori Hill, this cave-temple is a pilgrimage place, which many Tibetans visit along with the Potala. Drak Lhalupuk is regarded as the place where the water-dragon that resided in Othang Lake was imprisoned while the lake was drained and filled in during the construction of the Jokhang Temple.

The highlight to a visit here is the 2nd floor cave at the back on the right. Filled with a mystical atmosphere, the narrow cave holds 71 stone images of Buddha carved into rocks. The oldest one dates from the 7th century, and later ones were created between the 12th and 15th centuries.

Neten Lhakhang
Adjacent to Drak Lhalupuk, Neten Lhakhang is a new, yellow, 3-story temple with a terrace on the top floor that commands a great view of the Potala Palace.

Drubtob Lhakhang
Higher up on the hillside, Drubtob Lhakhang is on the right-hand side of Drak Lhalupuk. As a branch of Shugseb Ani Gompa, the small Nyingmapa nunnery was built at the cave where Thangtong Gyalpo, nicknamed Drubtob, meditated. Thangtong Gyalpo (1385-1464) was the founder of traditional Tibetan opera, *Ache Lhamo*, and the expert bridge builder who constructed 108 bridges throughout the Tibetan world.

Kundeling Monastery
To the west of the Potala, on Beijing Donglu, and after the golden yak junction, you come to Parmari (Bonpori) on the left. At the foot of Parmari you will find Kundeling Gompa, which used to wield enormous political power. The structure in front of it is the Dolma Lhakhang, dedicated to Dolma (Tara).

Gesar Lhakhang
Gesar Lhakhang is nestled peacefully on the top of Parmari. The chapels here were built in the early 1790s and are dedicated to King Ling Gesar, the Tibetan legendary hero who helped defeat the invading Gorkhas from Nepal. Although there are monks here, the site is maintained by an ordinary Tibetan family.

Norbulingka
In the reign of the 7th Dalai Lama, the Norbulingka was built as the Summer Palace in the woods outside of the capital in 1755. The name is created by the words *Norbu* meaning 'Treasure' and *Lingka* meaning 'Park.' Take a minibus to Shuinichang (Cement Factory) and get off at the Lhasa Hotel, or you can catch a #725 local bus (Erlu bus) and

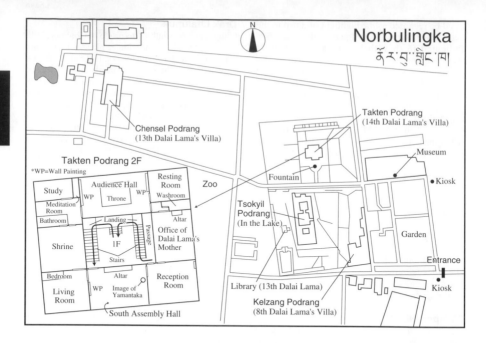

Norbulingka
ནོར་བུ་གླིང་ཁ

Chensel Podrang
(13th Dalai Lama's Villa)

Takten Podrang
(14th Dalai Lama's Villa)

Museum

Takten Podrang 2F

*WP=Wall Painting

Study	Audience Hall	Resting Room	Zoo
	WP Throne WP	Washroom	
Meditation Room			
Bathroom	Landing	Altar	
Shrine	1F Passage	Office of Dalai Lama's Mother	
	Stairs		
Bedroom	Altar	Reception Room	
Living Room	WP Image of Yamantaka		
South Assembly Hall			

Fountain

Kiosk

Tsokyil Podrang
(In the Lake)

Garden

Entrance

Library (13th Dalai Lama)

Kelzang Podrang
(8th Dalai Lama's Villa)

Kiosk

get off at the Norbulingka.

The highlight here is the Takten Podrang Palace where the 14th Dalai Lama actually lived. Maybe because the Dalai Lama is very fond of novelties, this relatively new structure, built in 1954, was furnished with a number of European items. It was from here that, only 5 years after its completion, the Dalai Lama fled into exile in India.

The Norbulingka is the place for picnics and going on dates in Lhasa. On Sundays and national holidays, the grounds are crowded with families bringing huge tents, karaoke machines, mah-jong sets, pieces of furniture, etc. They come early in the morning to secure a good spot. Under the trees, where the crowds are lighter, couples whisper sweet nothings to one another. In summer, during the

Zhoton (Yoghurt) festival, an *Ache Lhamo* (Tibetan opera) contest is held here. Admission is Y15 for foreigners.

AROUND LHASA

Drepung Monastery
Founded in 1416 by Jamyang Choeje, one of Tsongkhapa's disciples, this was once a huge monastery city, where over 10,000 monks studied. Although the monastery now houses only about 500, it is still one of the largest monasteries in Tibet. This vast site with its many slopes is 12km to the north-west of Lhasa, and an extensive tour with Tibetan pilgrims takes 3-5 hours. Admission is Y15, but the photo fees vary according to the room. Be careful of the dogs, as there are many roaming around.

After the Dalai Lama fled to India, Drepung Monastery was rebuilt in Mundgod, Karnataka, in southern India, and this new one houses 3,500 monks.

Ganden Podrang (Ganden Palace)
Ganden Podrang was given to the 2nd Dalai Lama in 1518. The palace housed the Dalai Lamas until

Norbulingka

Drepung Monastery
འབྲས་སྤུངས་དགོན་པ།
Jamyang Lhakhang
Jamyang Drubpuk
Tashi Gomang Tratsang
Ngakpa Tratsang
Tsokchen
Loseling Tratsang
Deyang Tratsang
To Nechung Monastery
Thangka Wall
Ganden Podrang (Dalai Lama's Palace)
Ticket Office
To Lhasa City
N

Nechung Monastery

the Potala Palace was completed.

Tsokchen (Great Assembly Hall)

Tsokchen is the largest building at Drepung. On the 1st floor are the reliquary stupas of the 3rd and 4th Dalai Lamas, which are open to the public during the *Zhoton* (Yoghurt) festival. On the 2nd floor is Jampa Thongdrol Lhakhang, the most sacred chapel of Drepung, which is dedicated to 15-meter-high Jampa (Maitreya). The section above the breast can be seen from the 3rd floor. The 3 images of Dolma (Tara) at Dolma Lhakhang on the 3rd floor are self-arising and speaking.

Ngakpa Tratsang

This is a tantric college for monks who have mastered esoteric studies.

Jamyang Lhakhang (Manjushri Temple)

Behind the Great Assembly Hall, this shrine houses an image of Manjushri.

Jamyang Drubpuk (Manjushri Meditation Cave)

This is the cave where Jamyang Choeje, the founder of Drepung Monastery, meditated.

Loseling Tratsang

For dialectics, this is the largest college at Drepung Monastery.

Tashi Gomang Tratsang

This is the second largest college, with many monks traditionally from Amdo and Mongolia.

Deyang Tratsang

Dedicated to Menla Sangye (Medicine Buddhas),

this is the smallest college.

Access

Take one of the frequent minibuses to Shiyouchedui operating along the Beijing Donglu, which stops off at the foot of Drepung Monastery. From the stop a tractor takes you up to the entrance.

Minibuses with a destination board showing Zhebangsi or ones with guys shouting *'Drepung Topche'* go directly to the entrance of the monastery.

Nechung Monastery

Before Drepung, the Nechung Monastery is the old seat of the State Oracle, who decided the destiny of Tibet during the reigns of the Dalai Lamas. After Drepung Monastery, follow the pilgrims, and you will reach Nechung Monastery in about 15 minutes. In the afternoon, minibuses heading for Lhasa wait for passengers at the exit of the monastery.

The Oracle sought refuge along with the Dalai Lama, and there is a new Nechung Monastery that has been built in Dharamsala.

Sera Monastery

In the north of Lhasa, Sera Monastery is a great Gelukpa monastery. It was constructed in 1419 by Jamchen Choeje Sakya Yeshe, one of Tsongkhapa's disciples. Even before this time, Sera Utse on the hill was a place where Tsongkhapa's disciples practiced asceticism.

During the period when Tibet closed its doors to foreigners, 2 Japanese monks, Ekai Kawaguchi and Tokan Tada, were able to get into the country and stayed here to study Tibetan Buddhism.

Like Drepung Monastery, Sera is very large, and an intensive tour takes 3-5 hours to get around the 3 colleges that are here now. Admission is Y15, and the photo fee is not fixed. It opens between 09:30 and 16:30, but there is a lunch break.

Again, like Drepung, Sera Monastery has been rebuilt in Mundgod, Karnataka in southern India. This new monastery accommodates approximately 3,000 monks.

Sera Me Tratsang

This is a college for learning the foundation of

Drepung Monastery

esoteric studies. The Chanting Hall is dedicated to the image of Sakya Yeshe.

Ngakpa Tratsang
This is the smallest college for monks to master tantric studies after esoteric studies.

Sera Je Tratsang
This is the largest college in Sera Monastery for esoteric teachings. Traditionally, it accommodates many monks from eastern Tibet and Mongolia.

At Sera Je Tratsang, Tamdrin Lhakhang (Horse-necked Avalokiteshvara Chapel) is home to the most sacred image at the monastery, Hayagriva, sculpted by Lodro Rinchen, another of Tsongkhapa's disciples. Female pilgrims put their foreheads onto the foot of the image, as it is believed to bring them a child.

Next to the chapel is a pleasant *Chora* (Courtyard), where monks have a catechism session, usually on weekday afternoons.

Hamdong Khangtsang
This is the accommodation for monks studying at Sera Je College.

Tsokchen (Great Assembly Hall)
A 4-story building that is the largest structure at the monastery, the hall houses an image of Sakya Yeshe, the founder of Sera, and a 6m-tall image of Jampa (Maitreya).

Choeding Khang
Walking up the hillside from the Tsokchen, you

Sera Monastery

get to the Choeding Khang. Tsongkhapa meditated here.

Sera Utse
Walk uphill for an hour and a half, and you will reach the hermitage where Sera Monastery started. There is a chapel, and you get good views from here.

Access
There are a number of minibuses to Selasi (Sera Monastery) from town, and it costs Y3. Some of them go right up to the front of the monastery, but the rest make a turn before it. Around the junction of Beijing Donglu and Niangre Lu, there are also shared-jeeps going out to the site.

Pawangka Gompa
North-west of Sera Monastery, take a left at the point where the minibuses from Lhasa to Sera Monastery make their turn before reaching the Military Regional Hospital. You will see Pawangka Gompa up on the left-hand side and Chubzang Nunnery on the right.

Some people believe that Pawangka Gompa is older than both the Jokhang and Ramoche Temples. The site is home to a cave where Songtsen Gampo meditated. The main temple lies on the huge rock, and a pilgrimage to this site is believed to be as blessed as a visit to Kusinagara in India, where the Buddha died.

Ngakpa Tratsang
Sera Je Tratsang *Mt. Purbuchok*
(Home to Hayagriva)
To Sera Utse
(Uphill for 1.5 hr)
Debating
Courtyard
Hamdong
Sera Me   Tsokchen   Khangtsang
Tratsang
Choeding Khang
Scripture
Press
N
To Lhasa
Town   **Sera Monastery**
Ticket Office   སེ་ར་ཐེག་ཆེན་གླིང་།
Minibus Stop

AROUND LHASA

དབུས་དང་ལྷོ་ཁ

GANDEN MONASTERY

On the southern side of the Kyi-chu (River), 45km to the east of Lhasa, Ganden Monastery is the head monastery of the Gelukpa order of Tibetan Buddhism. Its large temples and other buildings are spread out over slopes near the peaks of 2 mountains. From the pilgrimage path at over 4,200m, you can enjoy a great view of the site.

Ganden Monastery was built in 1409 by Tsongkhapa, the founder of Gelukpa, and it is said that the construction was foretold by Shakyamuni.

After the Chinese Army completed their takeover of Tibet in 1959, the site was utterly destroyed. In the 1980s some of the monks who had fled from the monastery returned, and there has been a level of reconstruction, especially over the last few years. Nonetheless, many parts still remain in ruins, and the monastery, which used to house 7,500 monks (another historical account puts the figure at only 3,500), now accommodates a mere 400 of them.

Rarely seen in Tibet, the Ganden Tripa, head of Ganden Monastery, is chosen from among monks in Lhasa. He is neither an incarnate lama

nor the son of a particular family. Along with the 14th Dalai Lama, the Ganden Tripa went into exile, and Ganden Monastery was reestablished in Mundgod, Karnataka State in southern India.

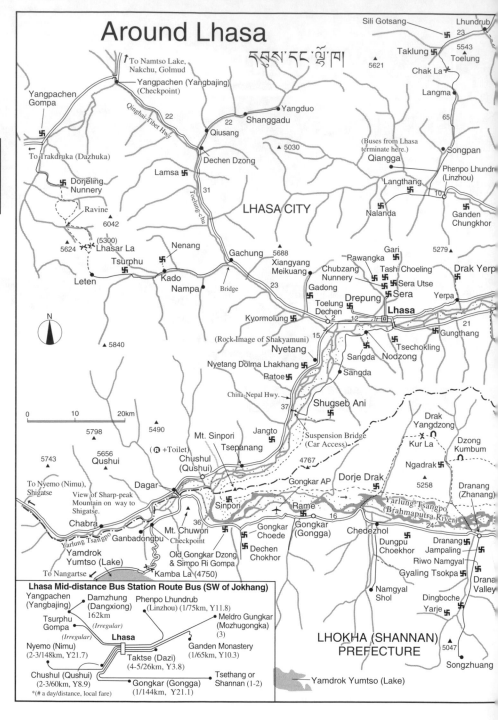

Around Lhasa

དབུས་དང་ལྷ་ས།

Sili Gotsang — Lhundrub
Taklung ‖ 23
▲ 5621 5543
Toelung
Chak La ‖

To Namtso Lake,
Nakchu, Golmud
Yangpachen (Yangbajing)
(Checkpoint)
Langma

Yangpachen
Gompa
Yangduo
65

Qinghai-Tibet Hwy 22
22 Shanggadu
Qiusang
(Buses from Lhasa
terminate here.)
Songpan

To Trakdruka (Dazhuka)
▲ 5030
Qiangga
Phenpo Lhundru
(Linzhou)

Dechen Dzong
Lamsa ‖
Langthang
10

Dorjeling
Nunnery
Nalanda
Ganden
Chungkhor

Ravine
LHASA CITY
▲ 6042

(5300)
5624 ⚔ Lhasar La
Nenang
Gachung 5688
Gari 5279 ▲

Tsurphu ‖
Xiangyang
Meikuang
Rawangka ‖
Tashi Choeling ‖
Drak Yerp ‖

Leten
Kado
Nampa
Bridge 23
Chubzang
Nunnery
Sera Utse ‖

Gadong
Toelung
Dechen
Drepung
Sera ‖
Yerpa

Kyormolung ‖
2 12
Lhasa
Gungthang
21

N
(Rock-Image of Shakyamuni) 15
Nyetang
Sangda
Tsechokling ‖
Nodzong

▲ 5840
Nyetang Dolma Lhakhang ‖
Ratoe ‖
Sangda

China-Nepal Hwy.
37
Shugseb Ani ‖
Drak
Yangdzong

0   10   20km
▲ 5490
Jangto
Tsepanang
Suspension Bridge
(Car Access)
Kur La
Dzong
Kumbum

5798
Mt. Sinpori
(ℝ +Toilet)
4767
Ngadrak ‖

5743
▲
5656
Qushui
Chushul
(Qushui)
Gongkar AP
Dorje Drak
5258
Dranang
(Zhanang)

To Nyemo (Nimu),
Shigatse
Dagar
Sinpori ‖
Rame ‖
Gongkar
(Gongga)
Chedezhol
Dungpu
Choekhor
Dranang ‖
Jampaling

View of Sharp-peak
Mountain on way to
Shigatse.
Gongkar
Choede
Yarlung Tsangpo
(Brahmaputra River) 24

Chabra
Mt. Chuwori ‖ 36
Dechen
Chokhor
16
Riwo Namgyal
Gyaling Tsokpa ‖

Yarlung Tsangpo Ganbadongbu
Checkpoint
Drana
Valley

Yamdrok
Yumtso (Lake)
Old Gongkar Dzong
& Simpo Ri Gompa
Namgyal
Shol
Dingboche
Yarje ‖

To Nangartse
Kamba La (4750)
LHOKHA (SHANNAN)
PREFECTURE
▲ 5047

Lhasa Mid-distance Bus Station Route Bus (SW of Jokhang)

Yangpachen
(Yangbajing)
Damzhung
(Dangxiong)
162km
(Irregular)
Phenpo Lhundrub
(Linzhou) (1/75km, Y11.8)

Tsurphu
Gompa
(Irregular)
Meldro Gungkar
(Mozhugongka)
(3)

Lhasa

Nyemo (Nimu)
(2-3/148km, Y21.7)
Taktse (Dazi)
(4-5/26km, Y3.8)
Ganden Monastery
(1/65km, Y10.3)

Chushul (Qushui)
(2-3/60km, Y8.9)
Gongkar (Gongga)
(1/144km, Y21.1)
Tsethang or
Shannan (1-2)

*(# a day/distance, local fare)

Songzhuang

Yamdrok Yumtso (Lake)

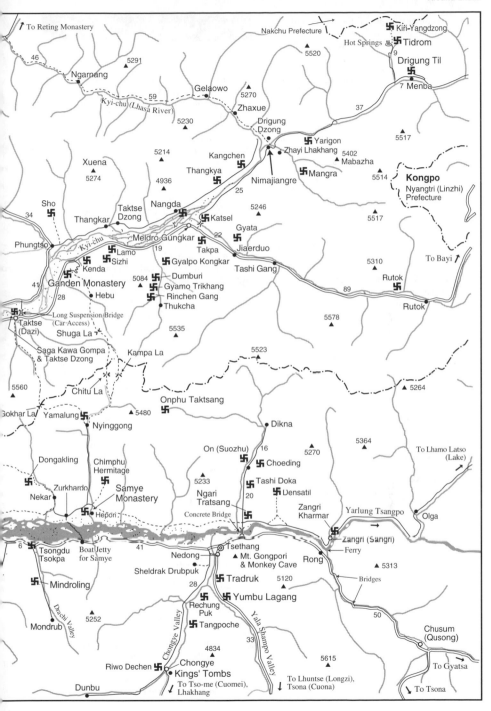

To Reting Monastery
Nakchu Prefecture
Kiñ-Yangdzong
Hot Springs
Tidrom
Drigung Til
5520
46
9
7 Menba
5291
Ngarnang
Gelaowo
5270
37
59
Kyi-chu (Lhasa River)
Zhaxue
5517
5230
Drigung
Dzong
Yarigon
Zhayi Lhakhang
5402
Mabazha
Xuena
5214
Kangchen
Mangra
5514
Kongpo
Thangkya
Nimajiangre
Nyangtri (Linzhi)
5274
4936
25
Prefecture
Sho
Nangda
5246
5517
Taktse
Dzong
Katsel
Thangkar
Gyata
34
Phungtso
Meldro Gungkar
Takpa
Jiaerduo
To Bayi
Lamo
19
22
5310
Sizhi
Gyalpo Kongkar
Tashi Gang
Rutok
Kenda
5084
Dumburi
89
41
Ganden Monastery
Gyamo Trikhang
Rutok
28
Hebu
Rinchen Gang
5578
Thukcha
Long Suspension Bridge
(Car Access)
5535
Taktse
(Dazi)
Shuga La
Saga Kawa Gompa
& Taktse Dzong
Kampa La
5523
5560
5264
Chitu La
Gokhar La
Yamalung
5480
Onphu Taktsang
Nyinggong
Dikna
5364
To Lhamo Latso
Dongakling
(Lake)
Chimphu
Hermitage
On (Suozhu)
16
5270
Zurkhardo
Choeding
5233
Nekar
Samye
Monastery
Ngari
Tratsang
Tashi Doka
20
Densatil
Hepori
Concrete Bridge
Zangri
Kharmar
Yarlung Tsangpo
Olga
6
Tsongdu
Tsokpa
Boat Jetty
for Samye
41
Nedong
Tsethang
Zangri (Sangri)
Ferry
Mindroling
Sheldrak Drubpuk
Mt. Gongpori
& Monkey Cave
Rong
5313
Bridges
Tradruk
5120
Yumbu Lagang
5252
Rechung
Puk
50
Mondrub
Tangpoche
33
Chusum
(Qusong)
4834
Riwo Dechen
Chongye
5615
To Gyatsa
Kings' Tombs
Dunbu
To Tso-me (Cuomei),
Lhakhang
To Lhuntse (Longzi),
Tsona (Cuona)
To Tsona

Admission is Y15-30 for foreigners with the price varying from person to person. You can make a pilgrimage circuit in around 50 minutes. There are many shrines here that women are not allowed to enter. On June 15 and November 25 in the Tibetan lunar calendar, huge *thangkas* are unveiled here.

Access

At the fountain in front of the Jokhang Temple in Lhasa there is a bus that leaves between 06:40 and 07:00. The trip takes about an hour and 40 minutes. Tickets go on sale at a small office on the southern side of the Jokhang (See the map on pages 72-73.) after 16:00 on the day before departure. You can also pick one up on the same day you're leaving. The fare is Y8 one-way and Y16 for a return ticket.

For the return leg, a bus leaves Ganden Monastery for Lhasa at 14:00. It stops over at Saga Kawa Gompa, Taktse (Dechen/Dazi) on the way for about 15 minutes.

Accommodation & Restaurants

At Ganden you may be able to stay on the 2nd floor of the kiosk building at the entrance of the monastery. The cost of a night's stay is Y6.

For food they will serve you typical Tibetan fare, such as *tukpa*.

Ganden — Samye Trekking

This is a very popular trekking course that starts at Ganden Monastery, then turns south, and heads for Samye Monastery on the banks of the Yarlung Tsangpo (Brahmaputra River). In summer you will meet other trekkers almost every day. Normally the trek takes 4-5 days, though fast walkers can complete it in only 3 days. There shouldn't be a problem tackling this route without a guide, but it is still advisable to check the topography before you leave and ask nomads along the way, as at some points the place where the track changes course is not easy to find. You can easily get up-to-date information before you set off and en route during the summer. Officially, a trekking permit is required.

The season is from June, when snow starts melting, to late September. Even in summer it snows sometimes but melts during the daytime. It is advisable to carry a tent, as you will have to sleep in the open. There are no villages between Hebu Village and Nyinggong Village, but you will probably see nomads in the area during the summer, and you may be able to stay with them. In one of the villages you may also be able to stay at a local's house for around Y5, but you will need to put your negotiation skills to the test, as overcharging is quite common. For this trip it would be best to bring enough food to last 5-7 days.

LHOKHA (SHANNAN) PREFECTURE

The area between the Yarlung Tsangpo (Brahmaputra River), to the south of Lhasa, and the border with Bhutan, is the Lhokha Prefecture. Covering the Yarlung Valley, which can be regarded as the birthplace of Tibetan civilization, Lhokha Prefecture is one of the most fertile areas in Tibet.

In Chinese, it is called *Shannan*, and its administrative center is Tsethang, in the heart of Yarlung Valley. The road between Lhasa and Tsethang has now been completely paved, allowing for easier access.

SAMYE (SANGYE) (CLOSED)

Samye Monastery was the first monastery to be built in Tibet, and it lies on rich and fertile land on the northern side of the Yarlung Tsangpo. The entire site of the monastery is in the village of Samye. From the top of Hepori, a hill to the east of the monastery, you can see that this village-monastery, surrounded by oval walls, forms a *mandala* demonstrating the Buddhist vision of the universe, with the main temple in the center.

Samye is where the important 792 debate was held to decide whether Indian-style Buddhism or its Chinese counterpart would become the national religion of Tibet. At the conclusion of the debate, the Indian form was adopted.

A travel permit is required to visit Samye, and independent travelers used to be able to get one in Lhasa for Y300. Recently these have been unavailable, and although some travelers have managed to get there without one, others have been turned back.

Access

Near the Yak Hotel in Lhasa, there is a minibus that will take you out to the boat jetty on the opposite bank of the river from Samye. This sets off when it is full of passengers, which is usually around 08:00-09:00. The trip takes around 4 hours and costs Y23-25.

The bus crosses the Yarlung Tsangpo to the southern side after Chushul (Qushui). You then pass through Gongkar and finally reach the jetty to cross the river to Samye. Travel permits are sometimes checked here. At the jetty there are boats that can carry about 50 passengers each, and these take around an hour to get over to Samye and about 40 minutes for the return journey. The boat fare is Y3-10 for a foreign passenger. During the fall and winter the quantity of water is decreased, and the windy and cold boat trip takes twice as long.

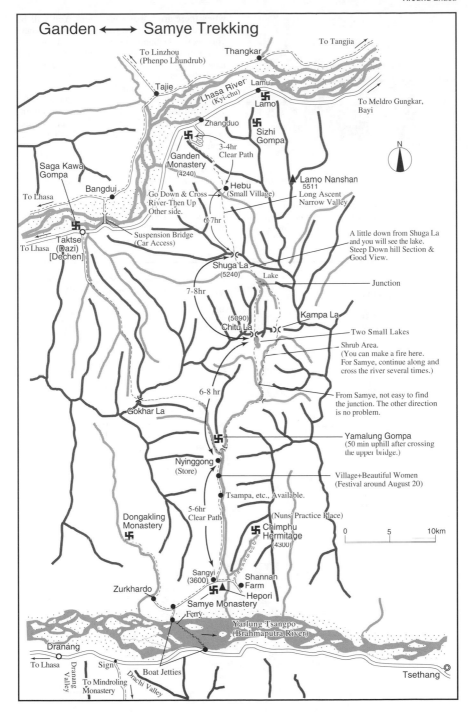

Ganden ⟷ Samye Trekking

AROUND LHASA

- To Linzhou (Phenpo Lhundrub)
- Thangkar
- To Tangjia
- Tajie
- Lhasa River (Kyi-chu)
- Lamu
- Lamo
- To Meldro Gungkar, Bayi
- Zhangduo
- Sizhi Gompa
- 3-4hr Clear Path
- Saga Kawa Gompa
- Ganden Monastery (4240)
- To Lhasa
- Bangdui
- Go Down & Cross River-Then Up Other side.
- Hebu (Small Village)
- Lamo Nanshan 5511
- Long Ascent Narrow Valley
- 6-7hr
- Suspension Bridge (Car Access)
- Taktse (Dazi) [Dechen]
- To Lhasa
- A little down from Shuga La and you will see the lake. Steep Down hill Section & Good View.
- Shuga La (5240)
- Lake
- Junction
- 7-8hr
- (5090) Chitu La
- Kampa La
- Two Small Lakes
- Shrub Area. (You can make a fire here. For Samye, continue along and cross the river several times.)
- 6-8 hr
- From Samye, not easy to find the junction. The other direction is no problem.
- Gokhar La
- Yamalung Gompa (50 min uphill after crossing the upper bridge.)
- Nyinggong (Store)
- Village+Beautiful Women (Festival around August 20)
- Tsampa, etc., Available.
- 5-6hr Clear Path
- (Nuns Practice Place)
- Dongakling Monastery
- Chimphu Hermitage (4300)
- 0   5   10km
- Sangyi (3600)
- Shannan Farm
- Hepori
- Zurkhardo
- Samye Monastery
- Ferry
- Yarlung Tsangpo (Brahmaputra River)
- Dranang
- To Lhasa
- Dranang Valley
- Sign
- Boat Jetties
- Drachi Valley
- To Mindroling Monastery
- Tsethang

Samye Monastery

when there are fewer passengers. You will be dropped off in front of the great main temple, where you can see the Samye Guesthouse on the left.

For the return journey, a shared-truck leaves from the same spot around 08:00, and when you reach the other side of the river by boat, there is a minibus to Lhasa waiting for you.

For Tsethang, you will have to catch a bus for Tsethang (destination board shows Shannan) coming from Lhasa. There are also shared trucks operating on the route, and the trip to Tsethang takes around 30-40 minutes.

Accommodation

The *Samye Guesthouse* is at the monastery itself and has dormitory beds for Y15. If you have a good grasp of the Chinese language, this would not be a place to practice it, as those using it are ignored. You can arrange a lift on a tractor to take you to the

On the monastery side of the river there is a large-size truck or a tractor waiting for boat passengers. The truck charges Y3 for the half-hour ride, while the tractors charge Y3-6 and take about 50 minutes. The fare for both of these increases

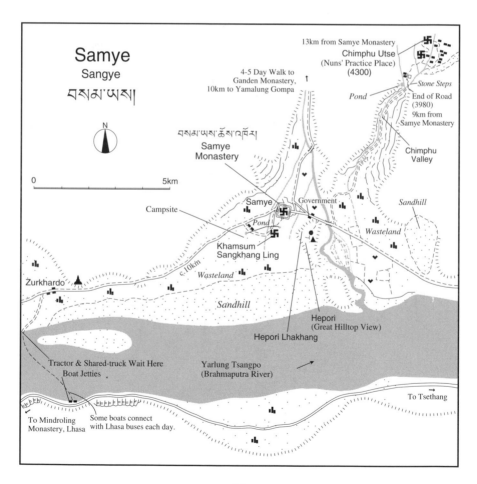

Samye
Sangye
བསམ་ཡས།

བསམ་ཡས་ཆོས་འཁོར།
Samye
Monastery

13km from Samye Monastery
Chimphu Utse
(Nuns' Practice Place)
(4300)

4-5 Day Walk to
Ganden Monastery,
10km to Yamalung Gompa

Pond

Stone Steps

End of Road
(3980)
9km from
Samye Monastery

Chimphu
Valley

N

0   5km

Campsite

Samye

Pond

Government

Sandhill

Khamsum
Sangkhang Ling

Wasteland

Zurkhardo

Wasteland

c. 10km

Sandhill

Hepori
(Great Hilltop View)

Hepori Lhakhang

Tractor & Shared-truck Wait Here
Boat Jetties

Yarlung Tsangpo
(Brahmaputra River)

To Tsethang

To Mindroling
Monastery, Lhasa

Some boats connect
with Lhasa buses each day.

Chimphu Hermitage entrance at the guesthouse. Another possibility is arranging to stay at one of the private houses here.

Restaurants

There are a handful of restaurants, and at one on the northern side of the main temple, Chinese meals and rice are available. Near the east gate is *Gompo's Snowland Restaurant*, where the staff understands English. There are also 7-8 kiosks here.

Samye Monastery (Sangyesi)

Founded by King Trisong Detsen, who adopted Buddhism as the national religion, Samye Monastery was the first Tibetan monastery. True, the Jokhang and Ramoche Temples in Lhasa and the Tradruk Temple in Tsethang are older, but these are temples and not monasteries, where monks live together and undertake their religious duties.

When the great Main Temple was completed in 779, Shantaraksita, a venerable philosopher invited from Nalanda Buddhist University in India, ordained 7 Tibetans, who became the first ever Tibetan monks.

Guru Rinpoche (Padmasambhava), the founder of the Nyingmapa order later, had been also invited from India. It is said that he subdued local demons that were disturbing the construction of the monastery and made them followers of Buddhism as he completed the work.

King Trisong Detsen is said to have encouraged the Buddhist masters from China and India to debate at Samye Monastery, and on the decision to follow the Indian version, the Chinese proponent was expelled from the country.

Called the 'Solid Mandala,' Samye Monastery has its buildings arranged in the shape of a *mandala* to represent Buddhist cosmology. The main temple of Utse represents Mt. Sumeru, the center of the universe. To the north is Dawa Lhakhang (Moon Temple) and to the south Nyima Lhakhang (Sun Temple). The other 4 temples represent the 4 continents, and there are 4, different colored chortens that surround the main temple. This monastery was completely razed by the Chinese, but the site underwent rapid rebuilding just before the last Panchen Lama passed away.

At the Utse Temple there are Tibetan, Chinese, and Indian artwork, and visitors must go up to the 3rd floor. Although repainted in the 18th century, these wall paintings depict various legends and actual events concerning Tibet, Samye Monastery itself, and elsewhere. The paintings are well worth seeing. Admission is Y30 for a foreign visitor, and you will have to ask one of the monks to unlock the door.

Hepori

To the east of Samye, Hepori was originally a sacred mountain for the followers of Bon until Buddhism started to prosper. It is said that King Trisong Detsen and Guru Rinpoche climbed the hill to decide where to construct Samye Monastery. On the summit is a temple called Hepori Lhakhang, and there is also a cave where Guru Rinpoche meditated.

*Along with Samye Monastery, there is Khamsum Sangkhang Ling a little to the south. A chorten and

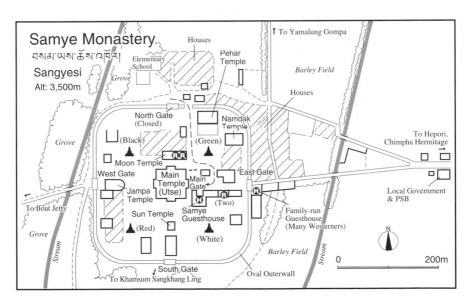

Dongakling Monastery are also nearby at the village of Zurkhardo, about 10km to the west of Samye.

Yamalung Gompa

On a hill around 15km to the north of Samye, this monastery can be used as a stopover halfway along the Ganden-Samye trekking course. The cave here is another sacred place that is famous for its connection with Guru Rinpoche, and it is said that this is the place where Guru Rinpoche concealed a *Terma* text.

CHIMPHU HERMITAGE (CLOSED)

Around 13km to the north north-east from Samye are a group of caves in the Chimphu Valley, which is one of the most active hermitages for the practice of Nyingmapa *tantras*. Ascetics from eastern Tibet and other regions where the Nyingmapa are active shut themselves away in the caves here. There are also young monks and nuns at the hermitage.

Near a ridge is one cave where Guru Rinpoche and his partner, Yeshe Tsogyal, worked hard on their religious practices. Moreover, Nyingmapa's great master, Longchen Ranbjampa, is said to have died in the woods of Chimphu. During the Cultural Revolution, the site was ravaged completely.

From Samye to the site it is a 4-5 hour walk, with the return trip taking around 3 hours. A tractor carrying 7-8 people can be arranged for about Y50. If necessary, ask for one at the Samye Guesthouse the day before you want to go.

DRANANG VALLEY (ZHANANG)
(CLOSED)

On the way from Lhasa to Samye and Tsethang, you go through a town called Dranang (Zhanang), the center of Dranang County that covers the Samye and Mindroling areas. To the south of the town spreads the Dranang Valley that produced prominent Nyingmapa figures, such as Longchen Ranbjampa, Orgyen Lingpa, and Minling Trichen, among others. Along the valley there are a number of monasteries related to these ascetics scattered about. Its eastern neighbor is Drachi Valley, where Mindroling Monastery is located.

Mindroling Monastery

Around 10km before you reach the boat jetty for Samye, the road from Lhasa to Tsethang branches off to the south and the Drachi Valley, where the head monastery of the Nyingmapa Southern

Treasures is located.

It is said that the original structure dates from the 10th century, but Mindroling Monastery itself wasn't opened until 1676, when Terdak Lingpa from the neighboring Dranang Valley expanded the site. Called 'Minling Trichen' (Great Treasure Finder Terton of Mindroling), Terdak Lingpa served as the 5th Dalai Lama's teacher.

From the 1950s to the 1960s, most of buildings here were destroyed to the point where even explosives were used. The main temple was used as a storage place, but now the structure has been rebuilt. Luckily, the wall paintings on the 3rd floor of the main temple have survived intact. The beautiful low rock walls around the monastery have also survived. Admission is Y15 for a foreign visitor, and there is no accommodation nearby.

Mindroling Monastery was rebuilt in Clement Town, Dehra Dun in northern India. Minling Trichen Rinpoche, the head of the monastery, also lives in exile there.

Access

On the bus route from Lhasa, you will see a sign in English that announces the Mindroling entrance. This is 5km after Dranang (Zhanang) or 10 before the boat jetty for Samye. It takes around an hour and a half after passing Gongkar Airport. At the sign, take a right off the main road, and take the graveled road for about 8km. This is a half-hour ride or a 2-hour walk. For the return journey there is a shared-truck that sometimes leaves from a spot near the monastery around 08:30.

TSETHANG (ZEDANG)

To the south-east of Lhasa, it is a 200km journey from the TAR capital to Tsethang, the capital of Lhokha (Shannan) Prefecture. The town lies in the Yarlung Valley called, among other things, the 'Birthplace of Tibetan Civilization' and 'Valley of Kings.' Legend has it that the first Tibetans were born here after the mating of a male monkey and a rock ogress. The graves of a succession of Tibetan kings are found in the valley.

Tsethang itself has little of special interest for visitors. If you need to get around this large new Chinese-style town, there are 3 minibus routes, and the fare is Y1. The town's old Tibetan quarter is at the foot of Mt. Gongpori, a sacred mountain to the east of the town.

To the south from the Tsethang Hotel (Zedang Fandian) is Nedong in Naidong County, which is a rather nondescript town even though it was the Tibetan capital during the 15th century.

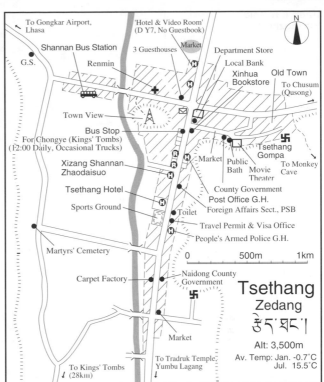

Pearl Thangka, Tradruk Temple

Map labels:
To Gongkar Airport, Lhasa
'Hotel & Video Room' (D Y7, No Guestbook)
Shannan Bus Station
3 Guesthouses
Market
Department Store
G.S.
Renmin
Local Bank
Xinhua Bookstore
Old Town
To Chusum (Qusong)
Town View
Bus Stop
For Chongye (Kings' Tombs) (12:00 Daily, Occasional Trucks)
Tsethang Gompa
Xizang Shannan Zhaodaisuo
Market
Public Bath
Movie Theater
To Monkey Cave
Tsethang Hotel
County Government
Post Office G.H.
Sports Ground
Toilet
Foreign Affairs Sect., PSB
Travel Permit & Visa Office
People's Armed Police G.H.
Martyrs' Cemetery
0   500m   1km
Carpet Factory
Naidong County Government
Tsethang
Zedang
ཙེ་ཐང་།
Alt: 3,500m
Av. Temp: Jan. -0.7°C
Jul. 15.5°C
Market
To Tradruk Temple, Yumbu Lagang
To Kings' Tombs (28km)

AROUND LHASA

Access
From Lhasa
There are 3 ways to get to Tsethang by bus. Many people use minibuses, and a Land Cruiser would get you there in 4 hours.

*Minibus—Leaving the bus stop, 100m to the east from Yak Hotel, between 08:00 and 09:00. The trip costs Y30 and takes around 5 hours.

*Bus—Leaving the long-distance bus station at 09:00. The fare is Y70-90 for foreign passengers.

*Bus—Leaving from the mid-distance bus station, 200m south-west of the Jokhang Temple at 08:30. The fare is Y30.

From Tsethang
Buses to Lhasa leave Shannan Bus Station at 08:00, 10:00, and 12:00. There are also minibuses leaving from the center of town.

For Tsona (Cuona), near the Indian border, there is a bus leaving at 07:00 every Thursday. However, this service is not available to foreigners.

Accommodation
The *Tsethang Hotel* (Zedang Fandian) is where foreigners are advised to stay. It is a well-equipped top range hotel. Rooms cost Y240-420 for foreigners.

The *Friendship Hotel* (Youyi Binguan) and *Tsethang Guesthouse* (Zedang Zhaodaisuo) are also available to foreigners.

The *Post Office Guesthouse* (Youdian Gongwan) is a relatively new hotel with dormitory beds for Y80.

Changing Money
It is advisable to change enough money in Lhasa, as there are no Bank of China branches in Tsethang.

Visa Extensions
These are unavailable.

Places to See
Mt. Gongpori and the Monkey Cave
The sacred mountain to the east of Tsethang is Mt. Gongpori at about 4,130m high. It is believed that there is a door to a secret paradise hidden somewhere on the mountain. The birthplace of the Tibetan people, Monkey Cave (4,060m) is 70m down from the summit. The mountain is surrounded by pilgrimage paths, and along these you will find Tsethang Gompa and Sangak Samteling Nunnery, among others.

Tsethang Gompa (Ganden Choekhorling)
Tsethang Gompa is in a Tibetan village at the foot of Mt. Gongpori. It was constructed as a Kagyupa monastery in 1351 but later came to belong to the Gelukpa. Destroyed in the 1960s, the site has been undergoing reconstruction.

Tradruk Temple (Changzhusi)

Five kilometers to the south of Tsethang, Tradruk Temple is said to be the oldest temple in Tibet, with a legend that King Songtsen Gampo exterminated 5 dragons in a lake here and then constructed the temple on the site of his victory. It was first built like a miniature of the Jokhang Temple in Lhasa in the 7th century and later expanded in the 14th and 17th centuries. On the top floor of the temple is a famous *thangka* made of pearls. Admission is Y3 for a foreign visitor, and the temple remains open during holidays.

Yumbu Lagang

On a hill 7km to the south-east of Tradruk Temple stands Yumbu Lagang. It is a reconstruction of the structure that was said to have been the oldest in Tibet.

According to legend, the first king of Tibet, Nyatri Tsenpo landed here when he descended from the heavens and built the original Yumbu Lagang in 127 BC (The Tibetan calendar started from this year.) Destroyed in the 1960s, the site was rebuilt after 1982.

Further up the valley, the road leads to Podrang, one of the oldest Tibetan villages, Yarto, and Tsari, which is one of the 3 most sacred places in Tibet. The entire area is rich in historical remains.

To get to Tradruk Temple and Yumbu Lagang, ask for a lift from a tractor driver near the Xinhua Bookstore in Tsethang. If you can find some other passengers with which to share the tractor, it will cost you around Y2 for Yumbu Lagang. Chartering a car costs Y30-40 for a round trip. One car carries 7-8 passengers. If you decide to walk to the site, it will take 2.5 hours. Admission to Yumbu Lagang is Y10 for foreigners, and it remains open on holidays.

Sheldrak Drubpuk

On the other side of Mt. Gongpori is Sheldrak Drubpuk, the first cave in Tibet where Guru Rinpoche meditated. Ranked alongside Chimphu and Yerpa, it is one of the greatest caves for religious practices and is an important pilgrimage place.

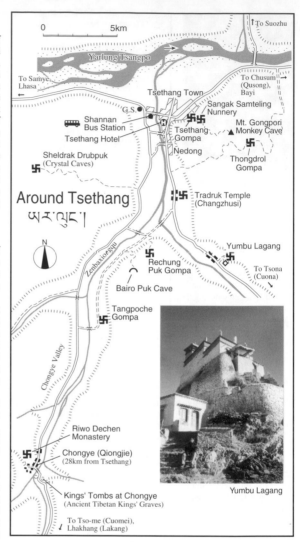

Map: Around Tsethang ཡར་ལུང་།

0   5km

To Suozhu

Yarlung Tsangpo

To Samye, Lhasa

To Chusum (Qusong), Bayi

Tsethang Town

Sangak Samteling Nunnery

G.S.

Shannan Bus Station

Tsethang Hotel

Tsethang Gompa

Mt. Gongpori Monkey Cave

Nedong

Thongdrol Gompa

Sheldrak Drubpuk (Crystal Caves)

Tradruk Temple (Changzhusi)

Yumbu Lagang

N

Rechung Puk Gompa

To Tsona (Cuona)

Bairo Puk Cave

Tangpoche Gompa

Zenbaxioxigu

Chongye Valley

Riwo Dechen Monastery

Chongye (Qiongjie) (28km from Tsethang)

Kings' Tombs at Chongye (Ancient Tibetan Kings' Graves)

To Tso-me (Cuomei), Lhakhang (Lakang)

Yumbu Lagang

Rechung Puk Gompa

This is the cave temple where Rechungpa, Milarepa's most illustrious disciple, practiced asceticism. *Puk* means a 'Meditation Cave.' The present site doesn't at all reflect the place's history. It used to flourish as a great Kagyupa monastery with 1,000 monks.

Tangpoche Gompa

Further to the south from Rechung Puk is Tangpoche Gompa. Although it is not so striking, the gompa is said to have had less damage than other monasteries during the Cultural Revolution. Wall paintings and other decorations have been relatively well preserved.

Kings' Tombs at Chongye (Closed)
Twenty-eight kilometers to the south of Tsethang is Chongye, the ancient capital of Tibet until King Songtsen Gampo transferred it to Lhasa. Chongye is well known as the 5th Dalai Lama's birthplace. On a rocky mountain behind the village is an old fortress called Chingwa Taktse Dzong. The Riwo Dechen Monastery, which is still under construction, is also on a hillside here. On the other side of the village across the river, there are groups of ancient tombs that are regarded as the graves of successive Tibetan kings, including Songtsen Gampo himself.

From Tsethang, you can get to the site by bus or shared-truck. There is a bus leaving around 12:00 every day from near the Xinhua Bookstore. The trip takes an hour and 20 minutes and costs Y3. At Chongye, the bus leaves for Tsethang at 07:30.

There are 2 guesthouses at Chongye, and you'll need to ask a local where they are as there are no signs. A bed costs Y5-6. Some travelers have been reported to the PSB, but they were only requested to give their names to the officials. There are a number of restaurants and kiosks in the village.

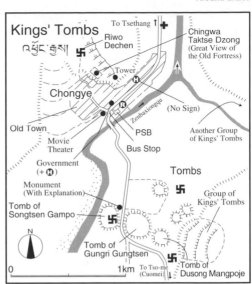

SOUTH OF LHASA

NYETANG DOLMA LHAKHANG & ROCK IMAGE OF SHAKYAMUNI

When you go south on the highway from Lhasa to Tsethang along the Kyi-chu, you will see a large colorful painted image of Shakyamuni on the rock to the right-hand side. Another 5km to the south from here is Nyetang Dolma Lhakhang.

Nyetang Dolma Lhakhang is famous for its connection with the high-ranking Indian monk Atisha. Invited by the Guge king, Atisha traveled all over Tibet during the 11th century and laid the foundation of Kadampa, the origin of the Gelukpa order.

Born in Bengal, Atisha is a historical figure who has been adopted as a national symbol by Bangladesh. The government of Bangladesh requested Zhou Enlai, the Chinese premier, to protect the temple, and he ordered the Red Guards (Hongweibing) to refrain from damaging the lhakhang. It is one of the few temples that survived the Cultural Revolution intact.

GONGKAR (GONGGA)

Although famous for the airport now, Gongkar was home to a fortress called Gongkar Dzong approximately 10km from the airport to Lhasa. To get there, take a bus to Tsethang or Gongkar. On the way from Lhasa to Gongkar there are some small temples and monasteries other than the ones mentioned below.

GONGKAR CHOEDE (GONGKAR DORJEDEN)

Around 7-8km before the airport from Lhasa, take the branch off the highway heading south, and you will find Gongkar Choede monastery. Be careful, as the junction doesn't have a sign. Although not very popular among travelers, Gongkar Choede is the head monastery of the Sakyapa's Gongkar school. Constructed in the 15th century, the site was destroyed during the Cultural Revolution but has been fully restored now.

Dechen Chokhor
Approximately 4km to the south of Gongkar Choede, this Drukpa Kagyupa monastery used to be much larger than it is now.

AROUND LHASA

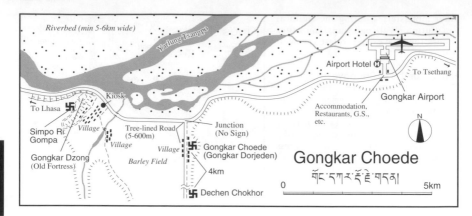

Gongkar Choede

གོང་དཀར་རྩེ་རྫེ་གདན།

Simpo Ri Gompa

On the mountain next to the old Gongkar Dzong, to the west of Gongkar Choede, is the small Simpo Ri Gompa. There is a great view from here. When approaching the gompa, signal one of the monks so that he can control the huge guard dog. There is a possibility of staying here. It is advisable to bring food with you.

MT. CHUWORI (CLOSED)

On the southern side of the point where the Kyi-chu meets the Yarlung Tsangpo (Brahmaputra River), there is the sacred Mt. Chuwori. It is said that there used to be 108 sacred springs and 108 hermitages here. On the summit there is a cave where Guru Rinpoche once meditated.

The Qushui Bridge at the foot of Mt. Chuwori may not now catch your attention, but before this modern structure was put up, there was an iron-made suspension bridge constructed by the talented Thangtong Gyalpo (1385-1464). Using iron chains, he bridged 108 rivers in Tibet and also worked in Bhutan. In *thangkas* he is easy to recognize as he carries chains in his hand. Not only famous for building bridges, he also founded the traditional Tibetan opera, *Ache Lhamo*.

SHUGSEB ANI GOMPA (CLOSED)

This Nyingmapa nunnery has the sacred Mt. Gangri Toekar at its back. On the mountain there are caves used for ascetic practices.

Machik Labdron, a female ascetic, founded the site, and Shugseb Jetsun Rinpoche, regarded as her incarnation, has taken the head seat of the nunnery from generation to generation. Historically, Shugseb Ani Gompa belongs to the Nyingmapa, but the last Jetsunma Rinpoche (Ani Longchen) opened it to other schools.

The style of ascetic practice that Machik Labdron developed, *Chod* (Object of Cutting), is still practiced actively in Tibetan *tantra*. By separating the spirit from the body, the physical part is left to the demons. The rite is especially necessary for the sky burial ceremony.

The great Nyingmapa master, Longchen Ranbjampa, was also led to Shugseb later. While practicing asceticism on Mt. Gangri Toekar, he was inspired to unearth the *Nyingthig of Dzogchen* that Guru Rinpoche had buried here. These became the foundation of the present Nyingmapa teachings.

The site is said to have held 700 nuns in 1959, but the nunnery was devastated in the Cultural Revolution. In the 1980s, reconstruction started with about 30 nuns, and the nunnery now houses about 250. At the actual practice site you will see a number of nuns practicing *Chod* with mallets and drums in their hands. Many of them are very kind and friendly, and they're around 20 years old.

Gongkar Choede

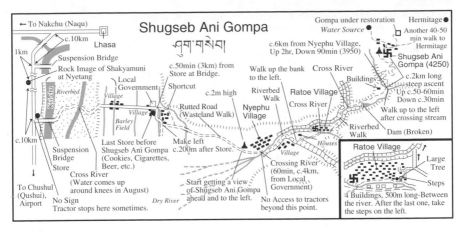

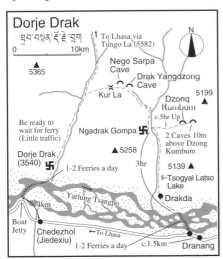

Access

From Lhasa

At the mid-distance bus station south-west of the Jokhang Temple, you can take a bus to Qushui twice a day or to Nyemo (Nimu) 2-3 times a day. Get off just before the suspension bridge on the left approximately 10km after the image of Shakyamuni at Nyetang. (See the map above.) Tell the bus conductor the place you want to get off at in advance. The fare is Y5.

After getting off the bus, it is a 6-7 hour walk up hill to Shugseb Ani Gompa. The return trip is roughly 15km and takes about 4 hours. To get back to Lhasa, catch a truck or bus on the highway. The fare is Y4-5.

Accommodation

By making a donation of Y10 or Y15 to the nunnery, you may be able to arrange accommodation here. You will be offered hot water and something to eat, but it is better to bring some food with you.

DRAKYUL CAVES & DORJE DRAK GOMPA (CLOSED)

On the northern side of the Yarlung Tsangpo, the Drakyul Caves and Dorje Drak Gompa are pilgrimage places famous for their connection with Guru Rinpoche. As usual, there is a concentration of caves where Guru Rinpoche meditated. The pilgrimage course is as follows:

Dorje Drak Gompa-Drak Yangdzong-Dzong Kumbum- Tsogyal Latso

It takes about 4 days, and during the trip you can stay at gompas along the way.

Dorje Drak Gompa

The Nyingmapa order is divided into the Southern Treasures and the Northern Treasures. While Mindroling Monastery is home to the former, Dorje Drak Gompa is the head monastery of the latter.

Four kilometers before Chedezhol on the highway connecting Lhasa with Tsethang, take a ferry to the northern side of the river. Then, you will see Dorje Drak Gompa on the hill. Regarded as the incarnation of Guru Rinpoche, Godemchen founded the monastery. In 1959 the site housed 400 monks, but it too was destroyed in the 1960s. Restoration of the gompa started in 1985.

The ridge where the gompa is situated is said to look like a *Dorje* (Scepter) if viewed from the opposite side of the river.

Drak Yangdzong

To the north of Dorje Drak Gompa and after the

Kur La pass are the Drak Yangdzong groups of caves. These are roughly divided into 3 groups.

Dzong Kumbum

To the south of Drak Yangdzong is Ngadrak Village, with its Karma Kagyupa Ngadrak Gompa. Walk up to the east from here, and you will reach a ridge at approximately 4,800m. The Dzong Kumbum group of caves, where Guru Rinpoche once meditated, is found here. The caretaker of the caves lives in Ngadrak Village, and it might be better to ask him to guide you to the site. You'll need a flashlight to see the splendid wall paintings in the caves.

Tsogyal Latso

Further to the south from Ngadrak Village is Drakda, the village with the small lake, Tsogyal Latso. This lake is said to be the resting place of the spirit of Yeshe Tsogyal, Guru Rinpoche's wife.

UPPER REACHES OF THE KYI-CHU (NE FROM LHASA) (CLOSED)

Approximately 100km up the Kyi-chu from Lhasa are Drigung Til Gompa, the head monastery of Drigung Kagyupa, and Tidrom Gompa (Terdrom Nunnery), where you can also enjoy hot springs.

Access
From Lhasa

Chartering a car such as a Land Cruiser is easy, and the trip takes 4-5 hours. These 4-wheel drive cars can carry 6 passengers and cost Y1,500-2,000 for the 2-night trip. A Beijing Jeep costs Y1,000-1,500 for the same trip.

If you want to get there by yourself, catch a bus from Lhasa to Meldro Gungkar (Mozhugongka). There are 3 buses operating on this route, leaving at 10:00, 14:00, and 18:00. The trip takes 2 hours. At Meldro Gungkar, charter or hitch a tractor to the site. It is 16km from Drigung Til to the Tidrom (Terdrom) Hot Springs.

Drigung Til Gompa

Drigung Til acts as the head monastery of the Drigung Kagyupa order. This school of Buddhism was founded in the 12th century. It continued to expand its sphere of influence until the 13th century, when it made an enemy of Kublai Khan, who was trying to bring all of Tibet under his control. The Mongol emperor was a great Sakyapa supporter and set about the devastation of all of the Drigung Kagyupa monasteries. Unsurprisingly, Drigung Til Gompa was again destroyed after the Chinese invasion, but the site has been well restored.

Structurally, the buildings of the Drigung Kagyupa are like those in India or Western Tibet (around Tsaparang, etc.), dating from the 10th to 11th centuries.

Sharing many similarities with the Nyingmapa, Drigung Kagyupa are also known for their ascetic practice in caves. It is said that there are *tantric* ascetics called the 80 Hermits living at Drigung.

Drigung Kyabgon Rinpoche, the head of the Drigung Kagyupa order, was arrested by the Chinese and held in detention for 16 years. In 1975, he managed to escape to India, and his current base is in Dehra Dun in northern India. At Drigung Til Gompa a dormitory bed costs Y5-7. The monks here are kind, and hot water is provided.

Tidrom (Terdrom) Hot Springs

Surrounded by rocks, the hot springs at Tidrom (Terdrom) used to be reserved only for the head of Drigung Til Gompa. The pools are fed by gushes of crystal clear water. Admission is free, and there is a separate room for female bathers.

The *Hot Spring of Tidromm Digong Guest House* has dormitory beds for Y13, or you could stay at the nunnery, which charges foreigners Y15 and Chinese Y5. Hot water is served here.

Terdrom Gompa

Legend has it that in 772 King Trisong Detsen offered Yeshe Tsogyal, one of his queens, to Guru

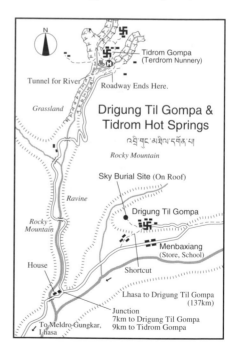

Drigung Til Gompa & Tidrom Hot Springs

འབྲི་གུང་མཐིལ་དགོན་པ།

Rocky Mountain

Sky Burial Site (On Roof)

Drigung Til Gompa

Menbaxiang (Store, School)

Shortcut

Lhasa to Drigung Til Gompa (137km)

Junction
7km to Drigung Til Gompa
9km to Tidrom Gompa

To Meldro Gungkar, Lhasa

Tidrom Gompa (Terdrom Nunnery)

Tunnel for River

Roadway Ends Here.

Grassland

Ravine

Rocky Mountain

House

Rinpoche, whom he had invited from India. That action alienated the Bonpo aristocrats, who were still very influential, and thus Guru Rinpoche and Yeshe Tsogyal had to flee into hiding, seeking refuge in these caves at Tidrom (Terdrom). It is also said that some *termas* were discovered here, and the name *Tidrom* or *Terdrom* means a 'Concealed Treasure Box.'

Further up from the gompa, there are caves where Guru Rinpoche meditated, and the site is an important pilgrimage destination.

TO THE NORTH OF LHASA (CLOSED)

Drak Yerpa

Approximately 30km to the east of Lhasa is Drak Yerpa, with caves where both Guru Rinpoche and Atisha meditated. Earlier in the 7th century King Songtsen Gampo also meditated here. Each cave has a detailed history of who did what in which one. One of these caves is where Lhalung Peldor meditated for 22 years. He is famous for having assassinated King Langdarma, the 9th century suppressor of Buddhism, and he came to the site after the deed was done.

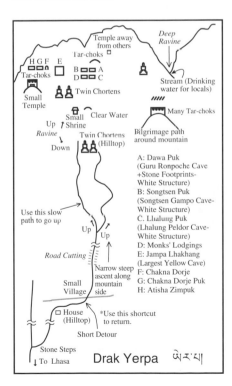

Yerpa Gompa, at the foot of the ridge, used to house 300 monks, and the monastery acted as a summer resort for the Gyuto Tratsang (Upper Tantric College) in Lhasa.

From Lhasa, take the road on the northern side of Kyi-chu, and then make a left to the north along another river at Yerpa. Even on foot from Lhasa, you can get here within a day. A good option is to visit Drak Yerpa, Taklung, and Reting in one trip by chartering a car.

Taklung Gompa

Founded in 1180 by Taklung Tangpa Tashipel, the site is where the Potowa of Kadampa lived. It is 140km to the north of Lhasa, and Taklung is the head monastery of the Taklung Kagyupa.

Around the 13th century Taklung Kagyupa dominated the Tibetan world with 7,000 monks. However, the Gelukpa introduced the incarnated lama system in the 17th century and began to prosper. This seriously affected the Taklung Kagyupa and made them relocate their base to Riwoche, to the west of Chamdo in Kham. During the Cultural Revolution, the monastery was dynamited.

From Lhasa there are 4 buses to Phenpo Lhundrub (Linzhou) daily. After Phenpo Lhundrub the road goes through Chak La pass (5,300m) before reaching the monastery.

Nalanda Gompa

Approximately 20km to the west of Phenpo Lhundrub (Linzhou) is Nalanda Gompa. The Sakyapas' Rongton Sheja Kunrig and Kunkhyen Tashi Namgyal founded the monastery in 1425. At its peak the monastery boasted a population of 2,000 monks, but the number later declined. The monastery was destroyed during the Chinese invasion, and restoration work began in 1980. Nalanda Gompa is now home to 50 monks.

Reting Gompa

Further to the north of Taklung, you will come to the Gelukpa monastery of Reting. Dromtonpa, the founder of Kadampa (the root of Gelukpa), established Reting Gompa in 1056. In 1397 Tsongkhapa, the founder of Gelukpa, visited Reting and had a vision of Atisha, the great Indian scholar and Dromtonpa's teacher. He was inspired to write the *Lamrim Chenmo*, which laid down the tenets of *Lamrim*, the Gelukpas' most important teachings. Since that time, Reting Gompa has been an important center for the Gelukpa. Some abbots of the monastery were appointed as regents for the Dalai Lama until he would reach his majority, and during those periods, it wielded absolute power.

The residence of the incarnate Reting Rinpoche is the Reting Labrang, and the Chinese government recognized a 2-year-old as the most recent incarnation in 2000 to replace the previous Rinpoche, who passed away in Lhasa in 1997. The 14th Dalai Lama has refused to recognize the Chinese choice.

TOELUNG (DUILONGDEQINGXIAN)
(CLOSED)

Near Toelung (Duilongdeqingxian), to the west of Lhasa, is a concentration of major monasteries, such as Tsurphu Gompa, belonging to the Karma Kagyupa.

Tsurphu Gompa

Founded by the 1st Karmapa in 1189, Tsurphu Gompa is the head monastery of the Karma Kagyupa order. Among the incarnate lamas of the Karma Kagyupa, the Karmapa holds the highest ranking.

After fleeing into exile in India, the late 16th Karmapa made Rumtek Gompa in Sikkim into his base and enthusiastically set about spreading the order's teachings in the West. He died in 1981, but his transmigration was not found until 1992 in the Kham region of Tibet. Recognized by both China and the Dalai Lama, the present 17th Karmapa assumed his position at Tsurphu Gompa. Despite his young age, he was treated as a VIP in China, meeting with the Chinese president Jiang Zemin.

In 2000, however, he escaped from China to Dharamsala, the Dalai Lama's home in exile, sought asylum in the country, and stated that he is against the Communist government in Tibet.

The Karma Kagyupa has many high-ranking lamas in exile who have been very active and gained many Western followers. Perhaps due to the good financial situation of the order, Tsurphu Gompa was impressively restored after the 17th Karmapa had taken his seat here. The majority of Karma Kagyupa followers are from eastern Tibet, and there is no end of pilgrims from there to the gompa.

Admission is Y10, and the general rule is that neither cameras nor bags are allowed in the monastery.

Access

A minibus leaves at 07:00 from in front of the Jokhang Temple in Lhasa. The trip takes 2 hours and 30 minutes, and the fare both ways is Y30. It would also be good to arrange a car with some other travelers.

Yangpachen Gompa & Hot Springs

Roughly 90km from Lhasa along the Qinghai-Tibet Highway are the Yangpachen Hot Springs. To bathe

Tsurphu Gompa

in them, you will need a swimsuit. Many travelers join a tour to visit the site along with Namtso Lake. Yangpachen Gompa is the head monastery of the Karma Kagyu Zhamarpa.

Historically, the Zhamarpa has tended to be anti-Gelukpa. When Nepali Gorkhas invaded Tibet in the 18th century, the Zhamarpa formed an alliance with them. That aroused the wrath of the Dalai Lama's government, and the Zhamarpa were prohibited from confirming incarnate lamas by the Tibetan government. Lately, the Zhamarpa did not recognize the 17th Karmapa confirmed by both the 14th Dalai Lama and the Chinese government but instead chose a different 17th Karmapa in India. Zhamar Rinpoche (Shamar Rinpoche), the head of Zhamarpa, uses the *Karmapa International Buddhism Centre* in Delhi as his base.

Tsurphu - Yangpachen Trekking

This is a popular trekking route from Tsurphu Gompa to Yangpachen, and if you give it 4 days, that should be enough.

Day 1—Tsurphu - Leten
Day 2—Leten - Lhasar La pass (5,300m) - Ravine
Day 3—Ravine - Dorjeling Nunnery
Day 4—Dorjeling Nunnery - Yangpachen

YAMDROK YUMTSO LAKE TO LHAKHANG (CLOSED)

Until some years ago the buses from Lhasa to Gyantse ran alongside the 'Lake of Turquoise,' or Yamdrok Yumtso Lake, via Nangartse. Since a new road was completed to the north, the only way to get out to the lake is by either hitchhiking or chartering a car.

The area between the southern side of Yamdrok Yumtso Lake and Bhutan, behind Mt. Kulha Kangri, is called the Lhodrak Region. Marpa, the founder of Kagyupa, and his disciple and poet, Milarepa, one of the most popular saints in Tibet, were both born in Lhodrak. Scattered around this area are a number of sacred places and monasteries that are famous for their connection with Marpa and Milarepa. The Lhodrak region could easily be ranked as the 4th greatest sacred place in Tibet.

If you charter a Land Cruiser in Lhasa or elsewhere, you can easily get a permit allowing you to travel up to around Monda La, to the south of Phuma Yumtso Lake. To get to Lhakhang (Lakang), check with the PSB as to whether a permit can be issued. Without permission, the local PSB officials will expel you from the area around Lhodrak (Luozha).

The original pilgrimage route in the area starts at the Yarlung Valley (Tsethang) and goes south down to Lhakhang via Tso-me (Cuomei). It then continues north up to Phuma Yumtso Lake, in a clockwise direction. It is an extremely long way to go but good for a pilgrimage.

Yamdrok Yumtso Lake

Meaning the 'Lake of Turquoise,' Yamdrok Yumtso Lake is one of the 4 greatest sacred lakes in Tibet, and the soul of Tibet is believed to reside here. As its name suggests, this 638 sq km lake is a beautiful turquoise color. You can get to see the lake by chartering a car, or you can enjoy trekking through the area around the vast lake. The Chinese have been constructing a massive hydroelectric power station at the lake.

Access

Chartering a Land Cruiser in Lhasa or another large town is an easy option. Alternatively, you can also get here by joining a tour to the Nepalese border via Yamdrok Yumtso Lake.

If you are making your way there by yourself, take a bus to Nyemo (Nimu) or Gongkar (Gongga) and stop over at the Yarlung Tsangpo (Brahmaputra River) Bridge just beyond Chushul (Qushui). After crossing the bridge, hitch a lift on the road to Nangartse though there is little traffic and the paved

road lasts for only another 10km. From Kamba La pass (4,750m) on the way, you get a view of the strikingly blue Yamdrok Yumtso Lake below.

On the way to Nangartse is Pelde, a lakeside village, which is a good place to take a rest.

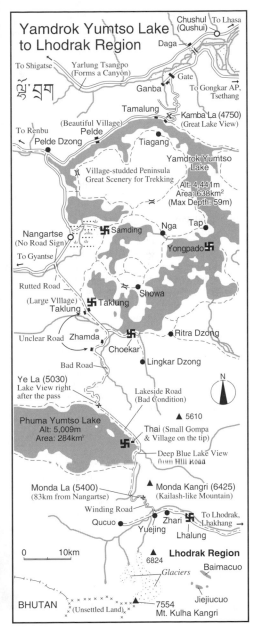

Yamdrok Yumtso Lake

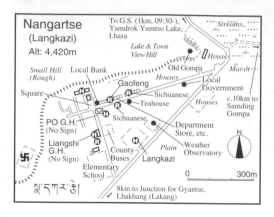

Nangartse
(Langkazi)
Alt: 4,420m

To G.S. (1km, 09:30-),
Yamdrok Yumtso Lake,
Lhasa

Streams

Lake & Town
View Hill

Houses

Small Hill
(Rough)

Local Bank

Old Gompa

Marsh

Gaofeng

Houses

Local
Government

Square

Sichuanese

Teahouse

Houses

c.10km to
Samding
Gompa

PO G.H.
(No Sign)

Sichuanese

Department
Store, etc.

Liangshi
G.H.
(No Sign)

County
Buses

Plain

Langkazi

Weather
Observatory

N

Elementary
School

0   300m

8km to Junction for Gyantse,
Lhakhang (Lakang)

Nangartse (Closed)

With only a few people on the streets, this is a rather deserted and uninviting town. The small hill to the north commands a lovely view.

Accommodation

The *Post Office Guesthouse* doesn't have a sign outside it. A dormitory bed here costs Y12.
The *Liangshi Zhaodaisuo* (Guesthouse) is also without a sign. A bed without a shower costs Y10 for a foreign guest. These rooms are really just for an overnight stay, and the toilet is in a different building.

Restaurants

You cannot expect too much from the food here. The restaurant next to Liangshi Zhaodaisuo charges Y5 for *tukpa* and Y8 for egg *tukpa*. Some Chinese meals are also on the menu here. Although the restaurant opens at 08:00, it is better to tell them the day before if you want to come to the restaurant in the morning so they have time to prepare something for you.

Samding Gompa

Home to a female incarnate lama, Samding Gompa is on the rocky hill beside Yamdrok Yumtso Lake. The nunnery is 10km to the east of Nangartse, roughly a half-hour ride.

According to legend, Samding Gompa was built here to save all of the Tibetan lands from a flood caused by the Yamdrok Yumtso Lake. It is believed that if this gompa were ever destroyed, there would be a disaster.

Another well-known legend concerns the Dzungar armies from Mongolia that attacked Samding Gompa in 1716. When the soldiers broke into the nunnery, the courtyard was full of pigs. They were so shocked that they broke ranks and

fled without looting anything. The female incarnate lama had transformed her nuns into sows and changed herself into the largest of the bunch to protect them and the nunnery. Since then, the female incarnation was granted great privileges by the Tibetan government. Called *Dorje Phagmo*, meaning 'Diamond Sow,' the post has been popular for generations, but the present Samding Dorje Phagmo returned to secular life after the Cultural Revolution, and she is now an executive in the government.

Karo La Pass (5,045m)

From Khari La you can get a close look at the glaciers of Mt. Nojin Gangzang (7,191m) rising to the north of here.

Yongpado Gompa

On an island in Yamdrok Yumtso Lake is Yongpado Gompa. This small monastery is a branch of Lhalung Gompa to the east and is famous for its connection with Guru Rinpoche.

Phuma Yumtso Lake

Starting from the western side of Yamdrok Yumtso Lake, you make your way to Taklung Gompa and Zhamda Village. You will see Phuma Yumtso Lake after you go through Ye La pass (5,030m). The lake is at an altitude of 5,009m, and it covers an area of 284 sq km.

Meaning the 'Lake of Flying Turquoise,' Phuma Yumtso Lake, according to legend, flew here from the sea at the end of the universe. Guru Rinpoche designated the salt lake as an important pilgrimage place. On the eastern side of the lake there is a village that is home to Thai Gompa and should probably be recognized as the highest village in the world at 5,050m.

Monda La Pass (5,400m)

Monda La pass commands a great view of Mt. Kulha Kangri (7,554m) on the border with Bhutan.

Lakeside Village, Phuma Yumtso

Lhalung Gompa

After Monda La pass, Lhalung Gompa is on the way to Lhodrak (Luozha). Lhalung Peldor, renowned for having assassinated King Langdarma (the 9th century oppressor of Buddhism), built the monastery. The 108 chortens at the gompa used to form a *mandala* by surrounding the monastery, but these were destroyed and are yet to be reconstructed. However, the holy footprints of Marpa and Milarepa survived the Cultural Revolution intact, as they were hidden from the Red Guards.

LHODRAK (LUOZHA) (CLOSED)

Lhodrak is on the road from Lhalung Gompa to Lhakhang. With a strong Chinese flavor, it is the administrative center of Lhodrak County. Even by arranging a Land Cruiser at a travel agency, it is far from guaranteed that an ordinary foreign visitor will be issued a permit for this area.

Although there is a road connecting Lhakhang with Lhalung, the real pilgrimage path to Lhalung Gompa heads a little to the east of Lhalung via Sekhar Gutok and the sacred Pemaling Tso, and not through the town of Lhodrak itself.

Pemaling Tso

East of Lhalung, take a branch off the main road and then head south. After going through Drum La pass, you will see this small sacred lake on the eastern side of Mt. Kulha Kangri (7,554m). The pilgrimage path circles the lake, and there are a number of important points along it, such as caves where Guru Rinpoche once meditated. Some rank Pemaling Tso as one of the 4 greatest sacred lakes of Tibet.

Sekhar Gutok Gompa

The site is home to the 9-story tower that is said to have been built independently by Milarepa and then dedicated to the son of his master, Marpa.

Regretting a killing he performed using black magic, Milarepa visited and begged Marpa to give him Buddhist instruction. Marpa, however, refused to take Milarepa as his disciple and instead ordered him to undergo a series of ordeals as penance.

Marpa then ordered Milarepa to construct a tower using only his own labor. The master continually criticized his efforts and forced Milarepa to repeatedly start again from scratch. After Milarepa had been plunged into the depths of despair 9 times, Marpa recognized that Milarepa's heart had finally been freed from the obstacles to the pursuit of enlightenment and accepted him as his leading disciple.

LHAKHANG (LAKANG) (CLOSED)

Only 15km from the Bhutanese border, Lhakhang is located at the confluence of the Kuru-chu and the Tamzhol Rivers, 364km to the south of Lhasa. The town used to be an important center for the trade with Bhutan. There are several hotels and restaurants in the town. There is no public transportation serving Lhakhang, and even arranging a Land Cruiser at a travel agency does not guarantee you a travel permit for the area.

Khothing Lhakhang

In Lhakhang Village, you will find Khothing Lhakhang, a temple constructed by King Songtsen Gampo in the 7th century. This is one of the 108 geomantic lhakhang that radiate out from Lhasa in Tibet, which form 3 distinct groups, the *Runon* (Inner- sanctuary Temples), the *Tandul* (Border-taming Temples), and the *Yangdul* (Further-taming Temples). These temples were intended to subdue the great ogress that straddled the Tibetan lands.

This ogress symbolizes the anti-Buddhist forces in the country at the time, and this lhakhang is meant to pin down the left elbow of the evil monster and so help to maintain the peace and harmony in the land and allow Buddhism to prosper.

Kharchu Gompa

This used to be a prosperous monastery, and although it belongs to the Nyingmapa, Kharchu Gompa also has a strong connection with the Drukpa Kagyupa order. The monastery has recently been under reconstruction.

TO THE EAST OF TSETHANG

CHUSUM (QUSONG) (CLOSED)

Chusum means 'Three Rivers,' and in the north of the town there is the Si-chu. Between Tsethang and Gyatsa, Chusum is a 100m to the north of the highway. From Tsethang, the 50-km trip takes approximately 2 hours by Land Cruiser, and bus services are irregular.

Chusum used to go by the old name, *Lhagyari*, meaning 'Royal Family of God.' The Buddhist Tibetan Royal family was forced to flee to Western Tibet to escape from King Langdarma's oppression of Buddhism during the 9th century. After King Langdarma was assassinated, Tibet split into a confusion of small kingdoms and fiefdoms.

Descendants of the royal family who had taken shelter in the west then moved to Lhagyari near

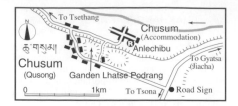

the Yarlung Valley, the original birthplace of the family. They then constructed Ganden Lhatse Podrang. It is said that Songtsen Gampo's direct descendants still live in the village.

At the *Anlechibu Restaurant* there are *momos*, *tukpa*, and alike available, but foreign visitors can expect to be overcharged.

LHAMO LATSO LAKE (CLOSED)

Said to be the place where the spirit of the Dalai Lama resides, Lhamo Latso Lake is one of the most holy lakes of Tibet. The lake is also revered, as mystical messages appear on its surface. Successive Dalai Lamas have come here to foretell their own

futures and that of the country.

When the 13th Dalai Lama passed away in 1933, Regent Reting Rinpoche visited Lhamo Latso Lake and saw a vision of the birthplace of the future Dalai Lama on the surface of the lake. That sign led the searchers to discover the present Dalai Lama quickly. When the search was on for the 11th Panchen Lama, acknowledged in 1995, high-ranking lamas from the Tashilhunpo Monastery visited the lake to help find the location of the new incarnation on behalf of the 14th Dalai Lama in exile.

To get to the lake by yourself, there are 2 ways — starting at Sangri, on the northern side of the Yarlung Tsangpo (Brahmaputra River), or going through Tsethang and Gyatsa. For accommodation, you can stay at Chokhorgyal Gompa, south of the lake.

GYATSA (JIACHA) (CLOSED)

Approximately 90km to the east of Chusum, along the Yarlung Tsangpo, Gyatsa on the southern side of the river is the center of Gyatsa County. There is an irregular bus service out here from Tsethang.

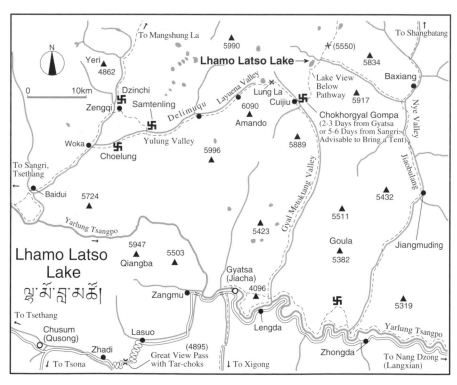

Accommodation & Restaurants

There are 2 guesthouses in the town. *The County Guesthouse* (Xian Zhaodaisuo) has rooms for Y7-20. The Y20 rooms are clean and equipped with television sets. Unfortunately, there are no showers in the guesthouse.

There are several restaurants on the main street with both Tibetan and Chinese food available. These restaurants open after 09:00.

NANG DZONG (LANG) [LANGXIAN] (CLOSED)

Another 70km further down the Yarlung Tsangpo from Gyatsa is Nang Dzong (Lang). This town is a starting point for pilgrimages to Tsari. There are 2 buses from Bayi each week on Wednesday and Saturday.

Accommodation & Restaurants

The *County Government Guesthouse* (Xianzhengfu Zhaodaisuo) has dormitory beds for Y10-15.
The *Post Office Guesthouse* (Youdian Zhaodaisuo) has rooms for Y26, though this is negotiable. Both of the guesthouses provide clean bed sheets but have no showers.

There are 3-4 restaurants here, and the one near the bridge has Chinese food on the menu. Prices vary from Y10 to Y15 for a dish.

TSARI (CLOSED)

In the north of the Indian state of Assam is the sacred mountain Dakpa Shelri (5,735m). With this peak at its center, Tsari is one of the most important pilgrimage destinations in Tibet, ranked alongside Mt. Kailash, Lapchi Gang, Mt. Amnye Machen of Amdo, and so on. For ascetic practices and pilgrimages, the holy site of Cakrasamvara is very important. Originally founded by Phakmodrupa Dorje Gyalpo of the Phakmodrupa Kagyupa, Tsari is especially revered by the Drukpa Kagyupa and Drigung Kagyupa, as both are descendants of Phakmodrupa Kagyupa.

The main pilgrimage route is called the *Kyilkhor* (Inner Pilgrimage Circuit), which circles around Mt. Dakpa Shelri and takes about a week to complete. Starting at Nang Dzong and heading

south, cross the Sur La pass (4,850m), and you will reach Choezam in the Tsari Valley. Further to the east along the valley is Chikchar, the starting point of the *Kyilkhor*. Then, go to the south and walk around Mt. Dakpa Shelri to reach Choezam in the west, and you will have completed the pilgrimage circuit. Although there are 7 passes along the route, you will not go above 5,000m. The trekking season

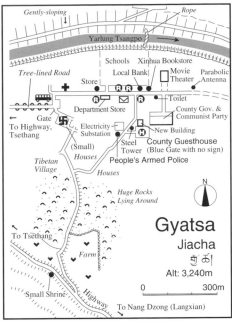

is only between July and September, as the weather is strongly influenced by the monsoons, and snowfalls shut the passes during the rest of the year.

There are other pilgrimage places to the east, such as Tsokar Lake and Tsari Sarma, that were established by Nyingmapa master Longchen Ranbjampa's teacher.

SANGAK CHOELING (CLOSED)

Head south from Nang Dzong (Langxian) and continue on after Choezam. You will reach the site at the western end of the Tsari Valley. Founded in 1512 by the religious King Jamyang Choekyi Dragpa III, Sangak Choeling is the head monastery of the Drukpa Kagyupa order. Before the Chinese came, the site housed 400 monks. Later the monastery was rebuilt in Darjeeling, India, and the 12th Drukchen Rinpoche, head of the Drukpa Kagyupa, now lives in exile there. Drukpa Kagyu is Bhutan's state religion.

LHUNTSE (LONGZI) (CLOSED)

The county is roughly 120km to the south of Tsethang. The administrative center of Lhuntse County is actually Xinbazhen, which is larger than Lhuntse Dzong, a little to the west. However, the latter is the original center and is where the buildings housing the Tibetan government before the Revolution are to be found. In 1959, the 14th Dalai Lama established his temporary government at Lhuntse Dzong on his way to India. In his first autobiography, *My Land and My People*, he said that the fortress at Lhuntse Dzong was like a miniature of the Potala Palace.

TSONA (CUONA) (CLOSED)

Although he established his temporary government at Lhuntse, the 14th Dalai Lama still decided to flee into exile and passed through Tsona on his way to India. The town is around 210km to the south of Tsethang and is near the Bhutanese and Indian borders. The administrative center of Tsona County, Cuonazhen is located 2km to the north from the old town, Tsona Dzong.

NAMTSO LAKE AND NAKCHU

NAMTSO LAKE (CLOSED)

At the eastern end of the Changthang Plateau, 190km to the north of Lhasa, lies the sacred Namtso Lake. It is the second largest salt lake in Tibet and China after Lake Kokonor (Qinghai Hu) in Amdo. The area is 70km by 30km at an altitude of over 4,700m. Yaks, sheep, goats, and horses roam the vast grassland surrounding the lake. Beyond the blue lake and across the grasslands, the snow-covered Nyenchen Tanglha (7,162m) can be seen. On the southern side of the lake there is a peninsula with a rocky end, which is home to a cave hermitage, Tashidor Gompa.

It is advisable to get acclimatized before you get here because of the altitude. Although a travel permit is said to be required, there are almost no PSB officers in the area.

Access
Independent Trip from Lhasa
At the long-distance bus station in Lhasa, take a bus to Nakchu (Naqu) and stop off at Damzhung (Dangxiong) 3-4 hours later. You can also take a minibus, which leaves from near the Yak Hotel, Jokhang Temple, and other points in the city every day.

For the section beyond Damzhung, catch a truck to Namtso Village, to the east of the lake. It is easy to find and negotiate with drivers at Damzhung, as there are a number of roadside restaurants for them. The 40-km trip to Namtso Village takes about 2 hours, and the climbs are not easy even for 4-wheel-drive cars. When crossing the Lhachen La pass (5,132m), you will get a view of the deep blue Namtso Lake spreading out below you.

From the village to the rocky mountain by the lakeside, you can share the Y200 cost of a tractor if you are in a group. You can also hire a horse for

Namtso

Y100 after some negotiating. It is a 40-km plain road out to the peninsula, and at the entrance to the peninsula, there are endless wire fences. You must pay Y10 as an admission fee at the gate.

Trekking from Damzhung to Namtso Lake is popular, but this route is dangerous without knowledge of mountaineering.

*Taking the Namtso Village Shortcut:
Damzhung - Military Airport - Kong La Pass (5,200m) - Namtso Lake.
This 2-3-day trek requires a tent, as there is no accommodation along the way.

Group Tour from Lhasa
In the summer Namtso Lake is such an easy-to-reach and popular spot that you can easily find other travelers at a guesthouse with which to share a Land Cruiser. A common 2-night tour goes to Yangpachen Monastery and the hot springs beyond Namtso Lake. A Land Cruiser with 5-6 seats costs Y2,500-3,000, not including food and accommodation. When the summer is over, the price for hiring the cars is reduced.

Accommodation
There is a small hut in front of Tashidor Gompa with only 2 rooms, and a bed here costs Y30. Needless to say, there is neither electricity nor a

Around Tashidor Gompa

toilet, but there is beer, precooked Chinese noodles, and some other food. You will appreciate the heater provided, as it snows here even in summer. Hot water is served to guests, but campers outside have to pay for this service. The friendly guesthouse guy used to be a nomad.

The guesthouse at Namtso Village has dormitory beds for Y10.

Rocky Hill Caves & Tashidor Gompa
On the peninsula jutting into the lake there is a rocky hill pockmarked by limestone caves and reminiscent of an ant nest. You can do a bit of exploring in them, but be careful. As you move from one to another in the strong wind, you can loose

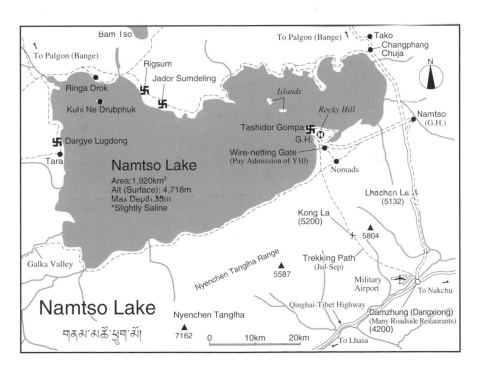

your footing. The caves are still used by occasional Nyingmapa and Kagyupa hermits.

The rocky mountain itself is a holy place. Although there is nothing special inside, Tibetans look into each cave and put their hair and pieces of their clothing into the caves. On the pilgrimage path along the lake you will see no end to *mani*-stone piles.

In the caves at the foot of the rocky mountain is the small Tashidor Gompa. New *thangkas* and Buddhist altar fittings here have been bought recently in Lhasa and donated to the monastery by nomads in the area. Some monks and nuns reside here.

NAKCHU (NAQU)

Important for traffic on the Qinghai-Tibet Highway, Nakchu is a large town that also acts as a good hitchhiking point. It has a road leading to Mt. Kailash, through the Changthang Plateau in the west and another going to Chamdo and Sichuan Province in the east along the Sichuan-Tibet Highway.

In town there are markets, a department store, hotels, and restaurants. You can usually find everything you need for traveling around. Although Nakchu is a large Chinese-looking town, there are still a lot of Tibetans around. In August there is a

big festival during which nomads demonstrate their horse-riding skills, etc.

Access
From Lhasa there are minibuses leaving around 07:00 daily from in front of the Jokhang Temple or near the Yak Hotel. There is also a bus that leaves daily from the long-distance bus station, which takes approximately 6 hours.

From Nakchu you can find the places from which to catch a lift on the map below.

Accommodation & Restaurants
The Naqu Fandian (Hotel) is the one that most foreigners are ordered to stay at. A dormitory bed here costs Y20.

The Zhaodaisuo (Guesthouse) is another one at which some foreign visitors have reportedly been allowed to stay.

There are a number of Chinese and Muslim restaurants in the town.

Zhabten Gompa
In the western end of town is Zhabten Gompa. This small Nyingmapa monastery is still home to many young monks.

Samtenling Gompa
On the western hill is a nunnery, Samtenling Gompa, with approximately 20 young nuns. It is not a good idea to try to enter without notifying one of the nuns, as there is a vicious guard dog. The hill is a good place to lay back and relax in the sun.

AMDO (ANDUO) (CLOSED)

Constructed on the southern side of the Dangla Mountains, Amdo is a Chinese-style town on the Qinghai-Tibet Highway. The road here leads off to the west, heading towards the Mt. Kailash area via the Changthang Plateau. Many of the buses from Golmud to Lhasa used to stay overnight here.

Checkpoint ● ↑ To Amdo (121km), Golmud (838km)
Hill
Samtenling Gompa (On the Hill)
Qinghai-Tibet Highway
Minibuses for Lhasa & Golmud (from Lhasa)
Naqu Fandian
Stores, Restaurants
Shopping Street
Bus Stop for Lhasa
Renmin
Xinhua Bookstore
Renmin Lu
To Chamdo (729km)
Zhabten Gompa
Market
Elementary School
Hitchhiking Point
Buses from Golmud ● PSB
To Lhasa (327km)
Av. Temp: Jan -13.9°C
Jul 8.9°C
Nakchu
Naqu
Alt: 4,507m

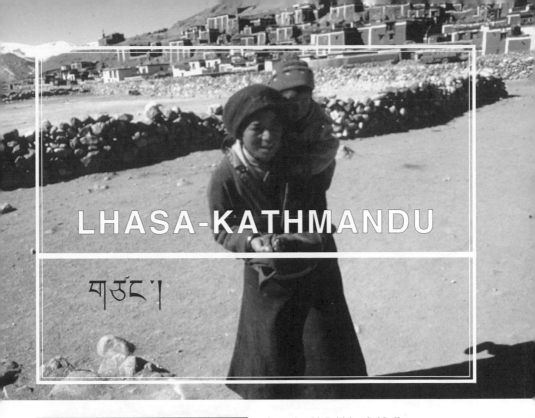

LHASA-KATHMANDU

གཙང་།

TSANG (SHIGATSE & GYANTSE)

Lhasa is the center of Central Tibet, an area called *U* in Tibetan. In the west of the traditional province lies the Tsang region, including Tibet's second largest city, Shigatse, as its center. These 2 adjacent Tibetan provinces of U & Tsang struggled against each other for supremacy for centuries. Since the 9th century, the power has alternated between the two.

Especially during the 17th century, when the Gelukpa Dalai Lama's government was established, the Tsang region, with the Panchen Lama as its head, confronted the government in Lhasa in one way or another for years. The friction between the provinces was really taken advantage of by 2 of the regional powers that had interests in Tibet, Britain and China. After the Dalai Lama fled to India in 1959, the Panchen Lama became an executive in the Chinese government in Beijing, highlighting their contrasting approaches.

Go south-east along the Nyang-chu that meets the Yarlung Tsangpo (Brahmaputra River) at Shigatse, and you will reach Gyantse. This other important town in Tsang used to prosper as a center for trade with British-ruled India.

The Friendship Highway (China-Nepal Highway) connecting Lhasa with Kathmandu is one of the highlights of a trip to Tibet. You will have a chance to trek to Mt. Jomolangma (Everest) Base Camp along the way.

SHIGATSE (RIKAZE)

With a population of around 45,000, Shigatse is the center of the Tsang region and the second largest city in Tibet. The city is about 280km to the south-west of Lhasa. It is home to the splendid and massive Tashilhunpo Monastery.

Access
From Lhasa
In front of Nongye Bank, 100m to the east of the Yak Hotel, the minibuses to Shigatse wait for passengers between 07:00 and 09:00. The 280km trip costs Y38 and takes roughly 6 hours along the well-paved highway. The minibuses arrive in front of the Renmin Bank at the entrance to the old town. There are also larger buses leaving from the long-distance bus station at 07:30.

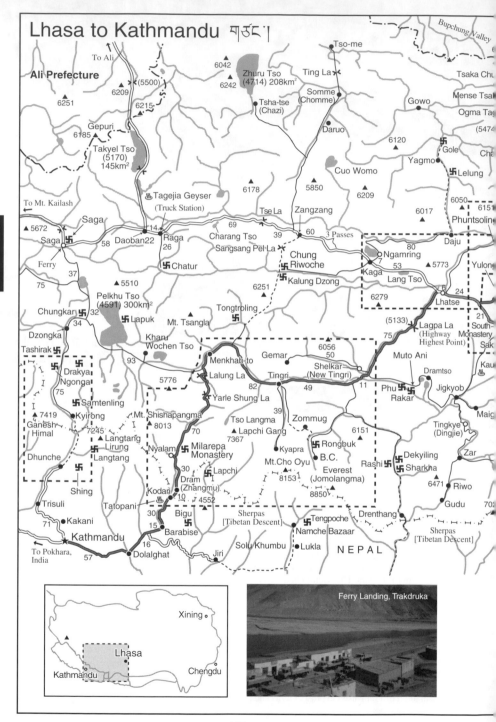

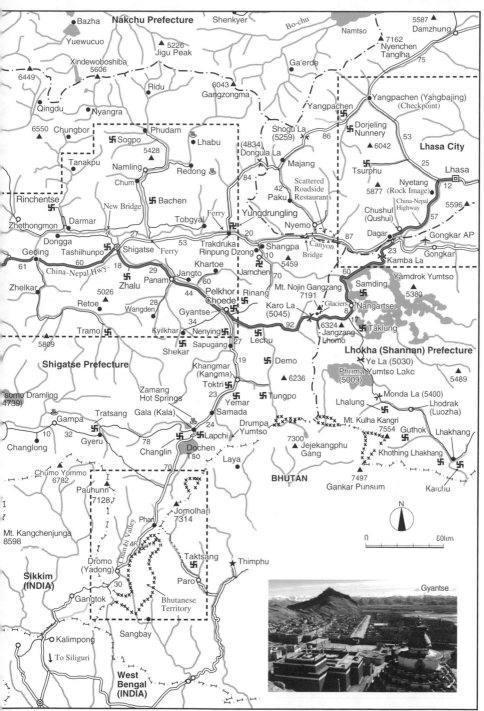

Gyantse

From Shigatse

*Lhasa—Minibuses to Lhasa leave many places in town between 07:00 and 11:00. Major stops are in front of Tashilhunpo Monastery, Tenjin Hotel, Renmin Bank, and the bus station. The fare to Lhasa is Y38. There is also a larger bus that leaves from the bus station every morning.

*Gyantse—See Gyantse section.

*Lhatse—There are 2 minibuses everyday.

*Sakya—See Sakya section.

*Dram (Zhangmu)—(Suspended late 1997.)

*Dromo (Yadong)—Two departures each week on Tuesday and again on Saturday. There is a checkpoint on the way.

*Khangmar (Kangma)—Twice a week on Wednesday and Sunday.

*Gampa (Gangba)—Once a week on Tuesday.

Public Security Bureau (PSB)

Compared to other places in the TAR, Shigatse is a relatively easy place to have your visa extended. There are reports of 20-day extensions costing Y120 being given and that third time extensions have been allowed. It is also relatively easy for independent

travelers to get a travel permit for Gyantse, Sakya, etc., for Y50.

Office hours: Monday-Friday 09:30-13:00 & 15:00-18:00, Saturday 09:30-12:00. Closed on Sunday and national holidays.

Changing Money

Travelers' checks are accepted at the *Bank of China* in the city.

Office hours: Monday-Friday 09:30-12:30 & 15:30-18:30, Saturday 09:30-12:00. Closed Sunday and national holidays.

Post & Telecommunications

There is a Post & Telecommunications office about 300m north-west of the bus station.

Office hours: Monday-Friday 09:30-12:30 & 15:30-18:30, Saturday 09:30-12:00. Closed Sunday and national holidays.

(International calls are still available.)

Hospitals

The *People's Hospital* (Renmin Yiyuan) is 500m north of the bus station on the right-hand side of

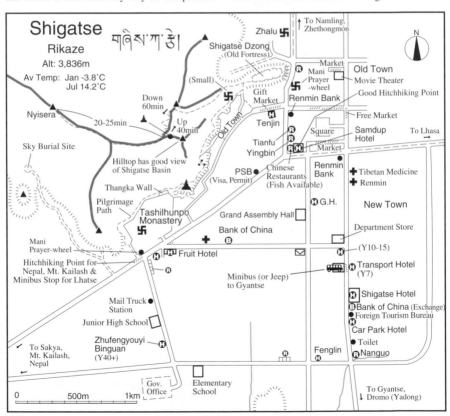

112

Tashilhunpo Monastery

the road. It is open every day 09:00-12:00 & 16:00-18.50. English is spoken here.

Next door to this one is a Tibetan medicine hospital.

Accommodation
For Backpackers
The *Tenjin Hotel* in front of the gift market is popular with backpackers. They have dormitory beds for Y20 and single rooms for Y50. There is also a CITS office in the hotel.
The *Fruit Hotel* is opposite the entrance to the Tashilhunpo monastery. The hotel charges Y15 for a dormitory bed.
The *Samdup Hotel* (Sangzhuzi Fandian) doesn't have any dormitories but has double rooms for Y80. The courtyard here is a good place to find and

negotiate for lifts.
Top-range Hotels
The *Shigatse Hotel* (Rikaze Fandian) has double rooms that start at Y300. All the rooms are equipped with hot showers and toilets, and they even have satellite television.

There are also a number of other choices, and group tours typically stay at the *Youdian Binguan* and the *Zhufengyouyi Binguan*, among others.

Restaurants
There are some restaurants with English signs on the right side of the street as you make your way from the Samdup Hotel to the Tenjin Hotel. There are Chinese and basic Western meals available at these places. There are also some Tibetan restaurants serving the usual Tibetan fare.

Places to See
Tashilhunpo Monastery
The massive Tashilhunpo Monastery is one of the 6 greatest monasteries of the Gelukpa. Founded by the 1st Dalai Lama in the 15th century, the site has flourished since the Panchen Lama, the head of the monastery, was recognized as the embodiment of Buddha Amitabha in the reign of the 5th Dalai Lama. During that period the Panchen Lama served as the Dalai Lama's tutor.

The monastery opens around 08:00 and closes near noon for cleaning. It is better to visit here early in the morning to get a good look around.

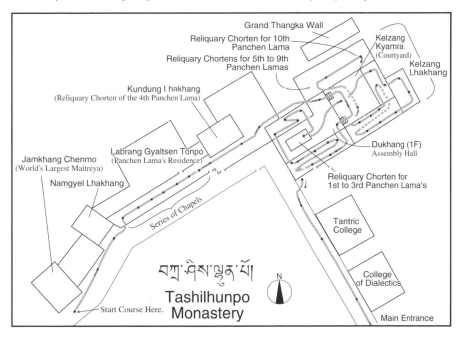

Admission is Y40 for a foreign visitor, and the photo fees vary.

For a tour around the monastery, you start at the western end of the complex and move gradually toward the eastern end. It is unlikely that you will have time to even quickly look into every structure, as the monastery is massive and houses many chapels and temples, etc. The highlights, including the Jamkhang Chenmo, Labrang Gyaltsen Tonpo, Kundung Lhakhang, and Kelzang Lhakhang, are at the beginning and end of the tour.

Jamkhang Chenmo
At the western end of the monastery is the Jamkhang Chenmo. This relatively new building was constructed in 1914. The tall structure is home to the world's largest statue of Maitreya, which is 26m high and fashioned from 300kg of gold and 150 tons of copper and brass.

Labrang Gyaltsen Tonpo
This acted as the residence of successive Panchen Lamas. Opposite the structure, there are 7 small chapels.

Kundung Lhakhang
With a gold roof, the Kundung Lhakhang accommodates the 11m-tall reliquary chorten of the 4th Panchen Lama, who was the first to be recognized as the incarnation of Buddha Amitabha. As this was the burial place of the first acknowledged Panchen Lama, the structure was not destroyed even during the Cultural Revolution.

Kelzang Lhakhang
First go into the courtyard, where the monastery's monks perform *Cham* dances during festival times. On the 1st floor of the western building is the Dukhang (Assembly Hall). This is the oldest part of Tashilhunpo, and it is said to have been originally built on the rock for sky burial.

Around the Dukhang there are a number of chapels, and after you've looked around the southern and northern wings, you finally go into the Tongwa Donden Lhakhang, just above the Dukhang. The structure contains the reliquary chortens of the 1st and 3rd Panchen Lamas. There are still a number of chapels left at the eastern and southern ends of the courtyard, but many visitors save their remaining energy for the last building on the northern side of the courtyard.

To the left is a row of mausoleums of the 5th to 9th Panchen Lamas, and although they were destroyed during the Cultural Revolution, the bodies were hidden from the Red Guards. In 1989 the 10th Panchen Lama completed the restoration of the monastery. The Panchen Lama who was living in Beijing returned to Shigatse to celebrate

Tashilhunpo Monastery

the completion of the reliquary chortens. Six days after the ceremony, he died. On the right-hand side is the chorten for him, which was completed in 1994. The propaganda value alone may justify the US$10 million spent on the lavish decoration by the Chinese government.

Shigatse Dzong (Old Fortress)
At the site where the old residence of the kings of Tsang was located, there used to be a fortress that could be compared to the Potala Palace in Lhasa. This dzong was destroyed in 1959.

GYANTSE (JIANGZI) (CLOSED)

By the Nyang-chu, Gyantse is regarded as the third largest city in Tibet. It once flourished as a trading center with India, and in 1904 the city became a battlefield when the British Army that had invaded Tibet under Colonel Francis Younghusband attacked the city.

The temple town stretches southwards from Pelkhor Choede, and Gyantse Dzong (Fortress) is where the road makes a great curve towards the east.

Travel Permit
A permit is required to visit Gyantse, and these can be easily obtained at the PSB office in Shigatse for Y50.

Access
From Shigatse
*There are 5-6 minibuses that depart from in front of the bus station from 08:00-17:00. The trip

takes over 2 hours and costs Y25. On occasion, some drivers will not let foreign passengers board the bus. A larger bus from Shigatse is operated every other day. Minibuses arrive near the roundabout in the center of the town.

*Buses to Dromo (Yadong) and Khangmar (Kangma) also stop at Gyantse.

From Gyantse

*Shigatse—There are some minibuses or jeeps that leave the southern side of the roundabout between 08:00 and 17:00. If you leave Gyantse early in the morning, you may be able to get to Lhasa via Shigatse in a day, and the fare to Shigatse is Y25.

*Although not daily, there are buses heading for Dromo (Yadong) and Khangmar (Kangma) that come and go after noon.

Hitchhike at Gyantse

*For Yamdrok Yutso Lake you may have a hard time, as there are few trucks. See the map to the right for the hitching point.

*For Khangmar (Kangma), there are shared-trucks.

Accommodation

The *Fuzhuang Guesthouse* (Fuzhuang Zhaodaisuo) is popular among backpackers. Dormitory beds cost Y20, but there are no showers.

The *County Government Hotel* (Xianzhengfu Binguan) has dormitory beds and clean rooms for Y25.

The *Gyantse Hotel* (Jiangzi Fandian) is a top-range establishment. Group tours stay here, and a double room costs Y287. You can stay in Tibetan-style rooms, and if you want to eat here, you will need to make a reservation.

Restaurants

Opposite the County Government Hotel and the Gyantse Hotel there are some relatively clean restaurants. They have a wide variety of dishes but are a little expensive. Try to order from the menus in Chinese if possible, as the ones in English show higher prices for the same dishes. There are also many Tibetan restaurants.

Places to See
Pelkhor Choede

Regarded as the center of Gyantse, Pelkhor Choede was established by the King of Gyantse from eastern Tibet in the 15th century. The monastery doesn't belong to any particular Buddhist order.

The site is home to only about 30 monks now, but it is said that it used to contain 17 colleges covering all manner of different religious activities. All the structures were destroyed, but now the Tsuklakhang in front of the entrance, Rinding Temple (Zhalupa Tradition), and a number of other structures have been restored. The monastery opens at 09:00, and admission is Y30.

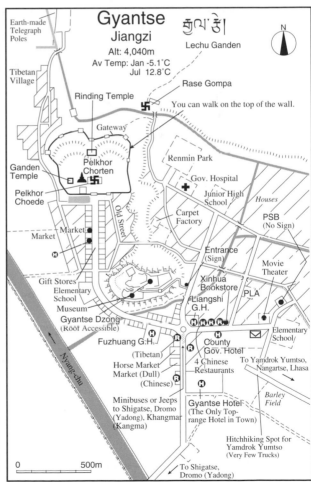

Gyantse ཀ྄ུལ་རྩེ
Jiangzi
Lechu Ganden
Alt: 4,040m
Av Temp: Jan -5.1°C
Jul 12.8°C
Rase Gompa
You can walk on the top of the wall.
Earth-made Telegraph Poles
Tibetan Village
Rinding Temple
Gateway
Renmin Park
Ganden Temple
Pelkhor Chorten
Gov. Hospital
Pelkhor Choede
Junior High School
Houses
Carpet Factory
PSB (No Sign)
Market
Market
Entrance (Sign)
Movie Theater
Gift Stores
Old Street
Xinhua Bookstore
PLA
Elementary School
Museum
Liangshi G.H.
Gyantse Dzong (Roof Accessible)
Elementary School
Fuzhuang G.H. (Tibetan)
County Gov. Hotel
Horse Market (Dull) (Chinese)
4 Chinese Restaurants
To Yamdrok Yumtso, Nangartse, Lhasa
Minibuses or Jeeps to Shigatse, Dromo (Yadong), Khangmar (Kangma)
Gyantse Hotel (The Only Top-range Hotel in Town)
Barley Field
Nyang-chu
Hitchhiking Spot for Yamdrok Yumtso (Very Few Trucks)
0   500m
To Shigatse, Dromo (Yadong)

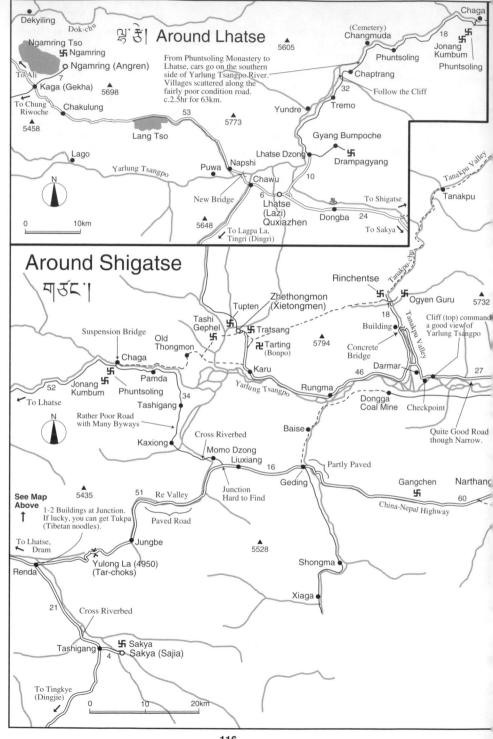

Around Lhatse

ཞ་རྩེ།

Dekyiling
Dok-chu
Ngamring Tso
卐 Ngamring
○ Ngamring (Angren)
To Ali
Kaga (Gekha)   7
5698
To Chung
Riwoche   Chakulung
5458
Lang Tso   53
5773
5605
(Cemetery)
Changmuda
Phuntsoling   18
卐
Jonang
Kumbum
Phuntsoling
Chaptrang
32   Follow the Cliff
Yundre   Tremo
Gyang Bumpoche
卐
Drampagyang

From Phuntsoling Monastery to
Lhatse, cars go on the southern
side of Yarlung Tsangpo River.
Villages scattered along the
fairly poor condition road.
c.2.5hr for 63km.

Lago
Yarlung Tsangpo   Puwa
Napshi   Lhatse Dzong
New Bridge   Chawu
N
0   10km   5648   Lhatse
(Lazi)
Quxiazhen   6
10   ♨
Dongba   24   To Shigatse
Tanakpu Valley
Tanakpu
To Sakya
To Lagpa La,
Tingri (Dingri)

Around Shigatse

གཙང་།

Rinchentse
卐   Ogyen Guru   5732
Zhethongmon
(Xietongmen)   18   Cliff (top) command
a good view of
Yarlung Tsangpo
Tupten
Tashi
Gephel   卐   Tratsang
Old
Thongmon   卍 Tarting
(Bonpo)   5794
Building   Concrete
Bridge
Darmar   46   27
Suspension Bridge
Chaga   卐   Karu
Jonang
Kumbum   52   Pamda
卐   Phuntsoling   Rungma
Dongga
Coal Mine   Checkpoint
To Lhatse   Tashigang   34
Yarlung Tsangpo
Rather Poor Road
with Many Byways   Quite Good Road
though Narrow.
N
Kaxiong   Cross Riverbed
Momo Dzong
Liuxiang
Baise
16   Partly Paved
Geding
Gangchen
卐   Narthang
60
China-Nepal Highway
See Map
Above   5435
↑   1-2 Buildings at Junction.
If lucky, you can get Tukpa
(Tibetan noodles).
51   Re Valley
Junction
Hard to Find
Paved Road
5528
To Lhatse,
Dram   Jungbe
Renda   Yulong La (4950)
(Tar-choks)
Shongma
Xiaga
21   Cross Riverbed
卐 Sakya
Tashigang   4   ○ Sakya (Sajia)
To Tingkye
(Dingjie)
0   10   20km

116

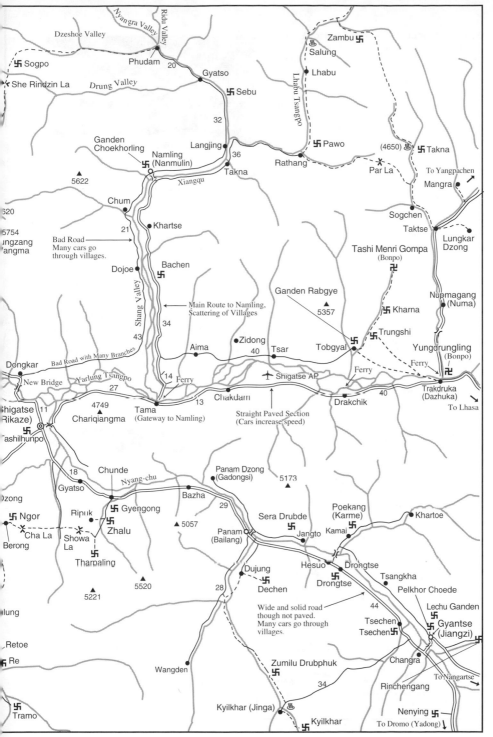

Dzeshoe Valley

Nyangra Valley

Ridu Valley

卐 Sogpo

✕ She Rindzin La

Phudam 20

Drung Valley

Gyatso

卐 Sebu

Zambu 卐
♨ Salung

Lhabu

Lhabu Tsangpo

32

Ganden
Choekhorling

Langjing

卐 Pawo

(4650) ♨ 卐 Takna

Namling
(Nanmulin) 卐

36

Rathang

✕ Par La

To Yangpachen

▲
5622

Takna

Xiangqu

Mangra

Chum

620

Khartse

21

5754
ungzang
angma

Bad Road
Many cars go
through villages.

Bachen

Dojoe

Shang Valley

34

43

Main Route to Namling,
Scattering of Villages

Sogchen

Taktse

Lungkar
Dzong

Tashi Menri Gompa
(Bonpo)
卐

Ganden Rabgye

▲
5357

卐 Kharna

Nupmagang
(Numa)

卐 Trungshi

Aima

Zidong
40

Tsar

Tobgyal 卐

卐

Yungdrungling
(Bonpo)

Dongkar

Bad Road with Many Branches

Yarlung Tsangpo

14

Ferry

Ferry

卍

New Bridge

27

13

Chakdam

Shigatse AP

Drakchik

Ferry

40

Trakdruka
(Dazhuka)

higatse
Rikaze) 11

▲ 4749

Chariqiangma

Tama
(Gateway to Namling)

Straight Paved Section
(Cars increase speed)

To Lhasa

卐
ashilhunpo

Chunde

Nyang-chu

Panam Dzong
(Gadongsi)

▲ 5173

18

Gyatso

Bazha

29

Sera Drubde

Poekang
(Karme)

Khartoe

Dzong

卐 Ngor

Ripuk

卐 Gyengong

▲ 5057

Panam
(Bailang)

Jangto

Kamai

Zhalu

✕ Cha La

Showa
La

卐

Dujung

Hesuo

Drongtse

Tsangkha

Berong

卐

Tharpaling

5520

▲
5221

28

Dechen

Drongtse

Pelkhor Choede

Lechu Ganden

44

卐 Gyantse
(Jiangzi)

lung

Wide and solid road
though not paved.
Many cars go through
villages.

Tsechen
Tsechen 卐

Retoe

卐 Re

Wangden

Zumilu Drubphuk
卐

Changra

To Nangartse

34

Rinchengang

卐
Tramo

Kyilkhar (Jinga)

♨

卐 Kyilkhar

Nenying 卐

To Dromo (Yadong)

Gyantse Kumbum (Pelkhor Chorten)

At Pelkhor Choede, the Gyantse Kumbum is the largest chorten in Tibet at over 37m. *Kumbum* means 'A Hundred Thousand Buddha Images,' and the 8-story structure is said to have 100,000 Buddhist images drawn on the walls.

There are 75 chapels in total, and as you ascend in a clockwise direction viewing the Buddhist images on the walls of each room, you may feel that you too are being brought toward spiritual enlightenment just as the wall paintings show. The whole atmosphere inside the chorten has a mysterious, mystical feel.

On the 1st floor are painted images familiar to exoteric Buddhism, such as Shakyamuni. As you go upstairs, you will get more of a tantric Buddhism feel with images and *mandalas*, which themselves depict the historical process of how the *Tantric* scriptures (Tantras) were formed. On the 6th and 7th floors of Unsurpassed Yogatantras are a number of Yabyum (father and mother Buddhas), where a male deity holding his queen is depicted. On the top floor is the Dorje Chang, the main image of

Gyantse Kumbum

Gyantse Kumbum.

Many of the wall paintings are badly damaged or poorly repaired. Some of them have been well preserved, and you can really appreciate the quality of the artwork influenced by the Nepalese Newar-style of the 15th century. All the surviving works at Gyantse Kumbum are valuable enough to have produced many collections of photographs.

It is advisable to bring a flashlight with you, as it is dark inside. Admission is Y30 for foreign visitors.

Gyantse Dzong (Gyantse Fortress)

Gyantse Dzong is the solid old fortress that accommodated the kings of Gyantse from the 14th century onwards. Even the British Army, which invaded Tibet in 1903, had a hard time taking the fortress. The entrance is on the eastern side, and admission to the museum is Y20 for foreign visitors.

AROUND SHIGATSE (CLOSED)

All the area around Shigatse is closed, and you need to apply for a permit at the PSB in the city.

Zhalu Monastery

This small monastery dates back to the 11th century, and Buton, the great scholar and translator, stayed here in the 14th century. To get to Zhalu you have to travel about 20km to the south-east of Shigatse, towards Gyantse on the highway, and then an additional 4km to the south off the main road. Admission is Y15 for a foreign visitor.

Ngor Monastery

The head monastery of Ngor Sakyapa is approximately 30km to the south-west of Shigatse. The monastery was built in the 15th century and is ranked second in the Sakyapa order after Sakya Gompa. The site used to have 18 colleges and housed 400 monks, but there

Gyantse Kumbum
(Pelkhor Chorten)

- 8F — Dorje Chang (Principal Image)
- 7F — Mother Class of Unsurpassed Yogatantras
- 6F — Father Class of Unsurpassed Yogatantras
- 5F — Yogatantras
- 4F — Chapels of Various Schools
- 3F — Yogatantras
- 2F — Caryatantras
- 1F — Kriya-tantras

South Gate

- 8F (1R)
- 7F (1R)
- 6F (1R)
- 5F (4R)
- 4F (12R)
- 3F (20R)
- 2F (16R)
- 1F (20R)

Route

0 10m 20m South Gate Outer Wall R=Rooms

are now less than 30 monks here. The 4 highest-ranking monks all went into exile abroad, and Ngor Monastery was rebuilt in Dehra Dun, northern India. From Zhalu Monastery, there is a roughly 20km trekking route to the monastery via Showa La pass.

Narthang Monastery
Narthang was founded as a Kadampa (Old Gelukpa) monastery in the 12th century, and it is famous for the Tibetan Buddhist Canon of Narthang. Between 1730 and 1742, the woodblock for the canon was prepared at the monastery. Reconstruction was started here in 1987. The monastery is approximately 20km to the south-west of Shigatse.

Yungdrungling Monastery
Yungdrungling Monastery is at Trakdruka (Dazhuka), approximately 80km to the east of Shigatse. Take a ferry to the northern side of the Yarlung Tsangpo (Brahmaputra River) and then walk for an hour to reach the site. From Shigatse to Trakdruka (Dazhuka), it takes about an hour and a half by minibus.

Constructed in the 19th century, Yungdrungling Monastery is a Bonpo monastery. Before the Chinese invasion, there were 700 Bonpo monks from all over Tibet. Now it is home to only about 30 monks.

Yungdrungling was destroyed twice — once during the Chinese invasion and again in the Cultural Revolution. The present buildings are of recent construction. The monastery is regarded as the center of Bonpo in Central Tibet, but it is said that there are very few Bonpos now living in the area.

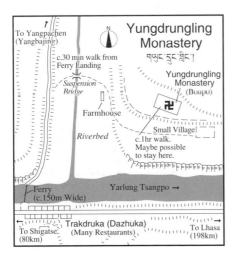

To Yangpachen (Yangbajing)

Yungdrungling Monastery

ग্অুংদুং গ্নীং।

c.30 min walk from Ferry Landing

Yungdrungling Monastery (Bonpo)

Suspension Bridge

Farmhouse

Small Village c.1hr walk. Maybe possible to stay here.

Riverbed

Ferry (c.150m Wide)

Yarlung Tsangpo →

Trakdruka (Dazhuka) (Many Restaurants)

To Shigatse (80km)

To Lhasa (198km)

Tashi Menri Gompa
Around 30km to the north, north-west of the ferry stop at Trakdruka (Dazhuka), Tashi Menri Gompa is further up Zhung-chu from Tobgyal. Constructed by Nyame Sherab Gyaltsen in the early 15th century, Tashi Menri is another important Bonpo monastery. According to one theory, Tonpa Shenrab, the founder of Bon, gave teachings as early as 3,000 B.C. When he visited here, he decided to establish a monastery on the site in the future and left his footprints on the rock to mark the spot.

After the Chinese invasion, the monastery was rebuilt in Dolanji, northern India. Under the 33rd Menri Trizin, the head of the Tashi Menri Monastery who is now living in exile, this new monastery now functions as the center of Bon.

Menri means 'Mountain of Medicine,' and the mountains in the area are said to be rich in medicinal herbs and hot springs.

Rong Jamchen Gompa
From Trakdruka (Dazhuka) with the ferry jetty, go down 20km along the Yarlung Tsangpo (Brahmaputra River), and make a right at the truck station after crossing the river. Then, go for another 5km or so south-east, and you will reach the Tibetan town of Rinpung Dzong. Five kilometers further on is the Chinese-style town of Renbu in Rinpung County.

Constructed by King Rinpung, who seized power in the Tsang region during the 14th century, Rong Jamchen Gompa in Rinpung is a Gelukpa monastery that used to house 1,500 monks.

Namling
You will have to hitch a lift on a truck or charter a Land Cruiser to get to Namling from Shigatse, as there are no buses operating on this section. There are 2 routes, but travelers usually use the one via the ferry, roughly 27km to the east of Shigatse. The combination of Land Cruiser and ferry gets you to Namling in just over 2 hours. The other land-only route via the Dongkar Bridge takes over 2 hours, as the road is in a bad condition. Both routes are 75km.

Go up the Shang Valley, following the Shang-chu to the north, and the Gelukpa's Ganden Choekhorling will come into view, spreading over the slope on the approach to Namling. Although small, the town of Namling has a market and is a lively place.

There is a guesthouse without a sign here, and a bed costs from Y15 to Y25. Opposite the entrance to the guesthouse is the only Chinese restaurant in Namling. But Chinese food is only served in the evenings, and noodles are all that is available in the afternoon.

Namling
Nanmulin
ཉམ་གྲོང་།

- Pilgrimage Path
- Ruined Fortress (Can climb up here from the rear)
- Pilgrimage Path
- Main Temple
- Ganden Choekhorling
- Obo
- Slope
- Local Gov.
- **Old Town**
- Deji (Tibetan Teahouse)
- Market
- Entrance
- Local Bank
- People's Armed.Police
- Gov. G.H. (No Sign)
- Chinese Food (Nights only)
- County Gov.
- Tar-choks
- After Bridge 75km to Shigatse
- Bad Road
- Shang-chu
- Suspension Bridge
- Local Banks
- Junior High School
- 700-800m
- 75km to Shigatse via Ferry (This main route takes less time.)
- Alt: 4015m
- 0 — 300m

46km from Darmar. With stores, guesthouses, a PSB office, and other amenities, this is the largest town in the region. There are a number of monasteries around here, such as Tashi Menri Gompa, Gelukpa Tratsang Gompa, and Tarting Gompa, the third most influential monastery of the Bonpo after Yungdrungling Monastery.

Further to the north from Zhethongmon is Ngangtse Tso Lake, and then the road continues on to the Changthang Plateau.

Phuntsoling and Jonang Kumbum

Heading south-west from Zhethongmon you will pass Old Thongmon and then reach a suspension bridge spanning the Yarlung Tsangpo (Brahmaputra River). On the other side of the river is Phuntsoling Monastery (Jomonang Gompa). From Shigatse, the monastery is 111km to the west, and the trip takes just over 3 hours by Land Cruiser.

Phuntsoling is the head monastery of the Jonang Kagyupa order. During the reign of the 5th Dalai Lama, the Gelukpa government oppressed this small school of Tibetan Buddhism. During that period the order had to shut down all of its monasteries and was prohibited from spreading its teachings.

Within a 2-hour walk from Phuntsoling you will catch sight of Jonang Kumbum. With exquisite Tibetan art, influenced by the 15th century Nepalese Newar-style, the 20m-high chorten is important enough to be compared to Gyantse Kumbum (Pelkhor Chorten), and fortunately, the structure has been recently restored. Jonangpa now has many temples, especially in the Amdo region of Sichuan Province.

Rinchentse Gompa

From Shigatse, go north and cross the bridge to Dongkar, on the northern side of the Yarlung Tsangpo, and then go west in the opposite direction to Namling. About 27km after the bridge is Darmar, and from here you start going north up the Tanakpu Valley along the Tanakpu-chu. After around 18km, you will find Rinchentse Gompa, a Nyingmapa monastery built in the 15th century. There are also a number of Buddhist and Bon temples in the Tanakpu Valley. Further to the north in the valley is the Kyaring Tso (Lake). The road then finally leads up to the Changthang Plateau, where you will experience the harshest climate and one of the strongest Tibetan atmospheres in the country.

Zhethongmon (Xietongmen)

The western neighbor of the Tanakpu Valley is the Yeshung Valley, whose center is Zhethongmon,

Sakya is the birthplace of the Sakyapa, one of the 4 greatest schools of Tibetan Buddhism. What sets Sakya apart from other towns is the colors of its walls. The white and dark-red stripes on a dark-blue background are peculiar to this area.

Huge temples used to be clustered together on both sides of Trum-chu in the past, but now only the South Monastery functions fully. The North Monastery, where Sakyapa was founded, was destroyed and is yet to be rebuilt. Sakya lies in the valley of the Trum-chu, about 152km to the south-west of Shigatse via Tso La pass (4,500m).

Phuntsoling Monastery

Sakya

Access
To Sakya
At the bus station in Shigatse there is a daily bus during the summer. Tickets are available the day before departure, and foreigners are charged Y54, while locals are charged Y27.

The bus leaves Shigatse at 08:00 and arrives at the County Guesthouse in Sakya around 13:00, with an hour long break along the way. It is advisable to bring some food with you, as only tea and other beverages are available during stops.

From Sakya
*Shigatse—When a bus from Shigatse arrives at

the guesthouse in Sakya, tickets go on sale at the guesthouse reception for the return journey leaving at 11:00 the next day.

*Lhatse—Take a bus heading for Shigatse and get off at the junction with the China-Nepal (Friendship) Highway. From here you can hitch a lift on a truck to Lhatse, and this takes an hour to cover the 24km. There is accommodation at the junction.

Accommodation & Restaurants
The *Sakya County Guesthouse* has dormitory beds for Y8-Y10.
The *Sakya Tibetan Hotel* also has dormitory beds that start from Y15.

There are several Chinese restaurants with rice, noodles, beer, etc., on the menu. Prices are relatively expensive.

Places to See
Sakya Gompa
In 1073 Konchok Gyalpo of the Khon family founded Sakya Gompa, the headquarters of Sakyapa, on the northern side of Trum-chu. His son, Sachen Kunga Nyingpo, further developed the site and established the name of the monastery.

Later, Sakyapa was given absolute power to rule

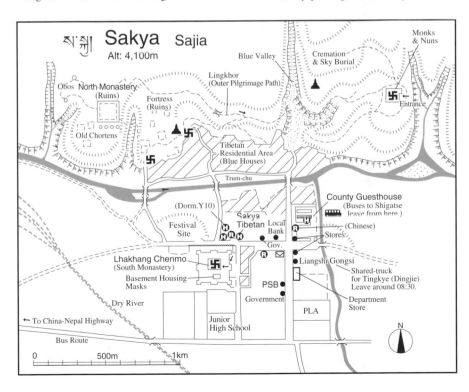

ས་སྐྱ Sakya Sajia
Alt: 4,100m

Monks & Nuns

Blue Valley

Cremation & Sky Burial

Lingkhor
(Outer Pilgrimage Path)

Obos North Monastery
(Ruins)

Entrance

Fortress
(Ruins)

Old Chortens

Tibetan
Residential Area
(Blue Houses)

Trum-chu

County Guesthouse
(Buses to Shigatse
leave from here.)

(Dorm. Y10)

Festival
Site

Sakya
Tibetan

Local
Bank

(Chinese)

Stores

Gov.

Lhakhang Chenmo
(South Monastery)

Liangshi Gongsi

Basement Housing
Masks

PSB

Shared-truck
for Tingkye (Dingjie)
Leave around 08:30.

Department
Store

Dry River

Government

PLA

← To China-Nepal Highway

Junior
High School

Bus Route

0   500m   1km

N

Sakya South Monastery
Walking on Outer Wall is Allowed.

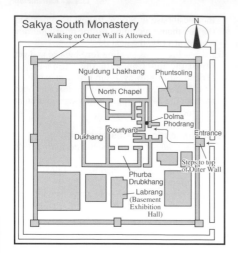

Nguldung Lhakhang
Phuntsoling
North Chapel
Dolma
Phodrang
Courtyard
Dukhang
Entrance
Steps to top
of Outer Wall
Phurba
Drubkhang
Labrang
(Basement
Exhibition
Hall)

Sakya South Monastery

LHATSE TO DRAM

LHATSE (LAZI) (CLOSED)

over Tibet by the Mongols in the 13th century. The order prospered during this period, and in 1268 Phakpa constructed the South Monastery on the southern bank of the Trum-chu.

After the Chinese invasion, the North Monastery, said to have housed 3,000 monks in its 108 buildings, was completely destroyed. Sakya Trizin Rinpoche, the head of Sakyapa, fled to India, and a new Sakya Monastery was built in Rajpur, northern India.

**South Monastery
(Lhakhang Chenmo)**
Surrounded by solid walls, the South Monastery is a fortress-like structure. After you pass through the entrance, you come to the Dukhang (Main Assembly Hall) straight in front of you. Nguldung Lhakhang, to the right, is home to 11 reliquary chortens dedicated to successive Sakya Rinpoches.

The main temple opens at 09:00 though the other buildings open earlier. You can also make a circuit by walking on top of the outer wall. Admission for foreign visitors is Y20, and a morning visit is recommended.

Old North Monastery
Go up the hill through the Tibetan houses with the Sakyapa coloring and you will reach the site of the old North Monastery. The majority of the monastery is still to be rebuilt. There are only a couple of chapels and the white chorten dedicated to Sachen Kunga Nyingpo here now.

Lhatse is a town on the China-Nepal (Friendship) Highway, 155km to the west of Shigatse. The junction, 4.5km to the west of town, is well known as a point to catch a lift on a truck for Mt. Kailash (Kang Rinpoche), and there is no checkpoint here. In town there are a number of restaurants and rooms to stay in. Travel permits for Lhatse can be obtained in Shigatse.

Eleven kilometers to the north of the center is the old town, Lhatse Dzong. On the peak of the rocky hill here is the old dzong (fortress) itself.

By walking 12km towards Shigatse, which takes about 3 hours, and then going 300m off the highway to the north, you will get to some hot springs. In the large building at the springs there are 4 rooms with baths. If you are planning to stay overnight here, you should bring some food with you.

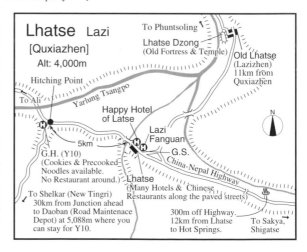

Lhatse Lazi
[Quxiazhen]
Alt: 4,000m

To Phuntsoling
Lhatse Dzong
(Old Fortress & Temple)
Old Lhatse
(Lazizhen)
11km from
Quxiazhen

Hitching Point
To Ali
Yarlung Tsangpo

Happy Hotel
of Latse
Lazi
Fanguan
5km
G.H. (Y10)
(Cookies & Precooked
Noodles available.
No Restaurant around.)
G.S.
China-Nepal Highway
Lhatse
(Many Hotels & Chinese
Restaurants along the paved streets)

To Shelkar (New Tingri)
30km from Junction ahead
to Daoban (Road Maintenace
Depot) at 5,088m where you
can stay for Y10.

300m off Highway.
12km from Lhatse
to Hot Springs.
To Sakya,
Shigatse

From Lhatse

*Dram—You can arrange a lift on a truck in the courtyard of the *Lazi Fanguan*, which has dormitory beds for Y15, and the fare is Y100-150.

*Shigatse—A minibus leaves Lhatse around 10:00 everyday, and the trip takes 4 hours. It takes closer to 3 hours by Land Cruiser.

SHELKAR (NEW TINGRI) [XINDINGRI] (CLOSED)

Meaning 'Crystal,' Shelkar is a starting point for trekking up to Jomolangma (Everest) Base Camp. About 30km to the south of Lhatse on the China-Nepal (Friendship) Highway is Lagpa La pass (5,250m), the highest pass on the road. From the pass with its stone monument and fluttering *tarchoks*, you can get a good view of the Himalayan Range.

At the distance marker sign (5,133km), about 50km after the Lagpa La pass, you leave the highway and head for the *Jomolangma Guesthouse* (Zhufeng Binguan) just after a bridge. There are also 2 guesthouses at the junction before the bridge. You will also find another one at the distance marker (5,134km), 400m further on, though this guesthouse has no sign outside.

Most travelers joining a Land Cruiser tour are booked into the *Jomolangma Guesthouse*, where a dormitory bed costs Y40. Double rooms go for Y260, but you may be able to get a discount if you negotiate a little. The more expensive rooms are equipped with showers, but for the price, the facilities are poor and the restaurant's meals are expensive.

A further 7km to the west is the town of Shelkar, which is the center of Dingri County. This Chinese-style town has nothing outstanding to see, but you may be interested in the old Shelkar Dzong in the center of the old town and Shelkar Gompa (Shelkar Choede Monastery).

Checkpoint

There is a gate at the 5,139km distance marker on the China-Nepal (Friendship) Highway that is a checkpoint for foreigners. You are requested to present your passport here. There is a guesthouse with dormitory beds for Y15 that also serves meals.

JOMOLANGMA TREKKING (CLOSED)

Needless to say, Mt. Jomolangma (Everest) is the world's highest mountain at 8,850m. You can trek up to the Base Camp (Camp 1, A.B.C.), but the site is also accessible by Land Cruiser, which can be arranged in either Lhasa or Shigatse. The best season is from May to October, but the peak is often covered in clouds from July to August. There are 2 trekking routes. (See the map on pages 124-125.)

Peruche Route

Shelkar - Checkpoint - 200m after 5,145m Marker - Chay Village (Checkpoint)- Pang La pass - Peruche Village - Paksum Village - Choesang Village - Rongbuk Monastery - Base Camp.

Following this route you can clearly see the path to take, as there is also a roadway. If you rent a donkey or a horse in a village along the way, your guide will take you on a different path for more than half the way.

*Donkey—Carries 2 large backpacks & 1 daypack. Costs Y40-50 per day.

*Horse—Carries 4 large bags. Costs Y70-100 per day.

*Normally, there is no fee for a guide, but some may ask for one.

Tingri Route

Tingri - Lungjang Village - Lamma La Pass - Zommug Village - Rongbuk Monastery - Base Camp

It is better to have a guide for this route, as the path is hard to follow. If you don't have a tent, you will have to stay at Zommug Village for the night. Snow begins to settle in the area around October.

Accommodation & Restaurants

Staying at private houses is the most common practice. You can get relatively good meals at the lodge in Paksum Village, and at *Ganden's House* in Lungjang Village you may even be served rice dishes. At other villages, however, *tukpa* and the like are the best available. At Rongbuk there is neither food nor hot water available. On this route, the accommodation costs Y4-5 at a private house or Y10-15 at a lodge. The price of a bowl of *tukpa* varies from Y2-5.

Rongbuk Monastery

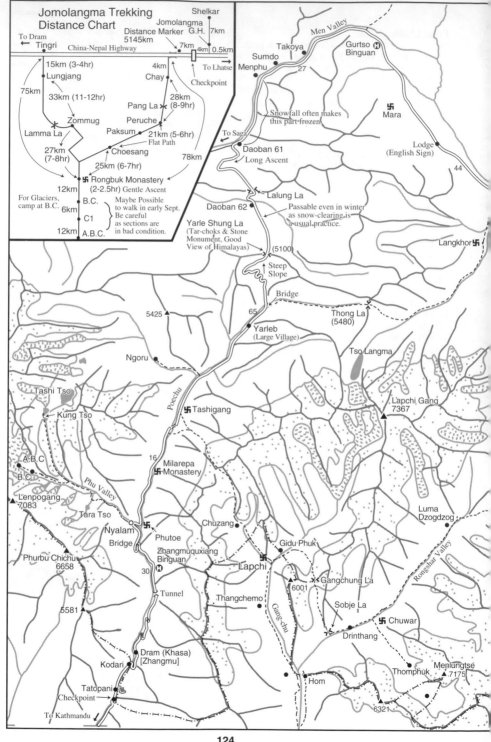

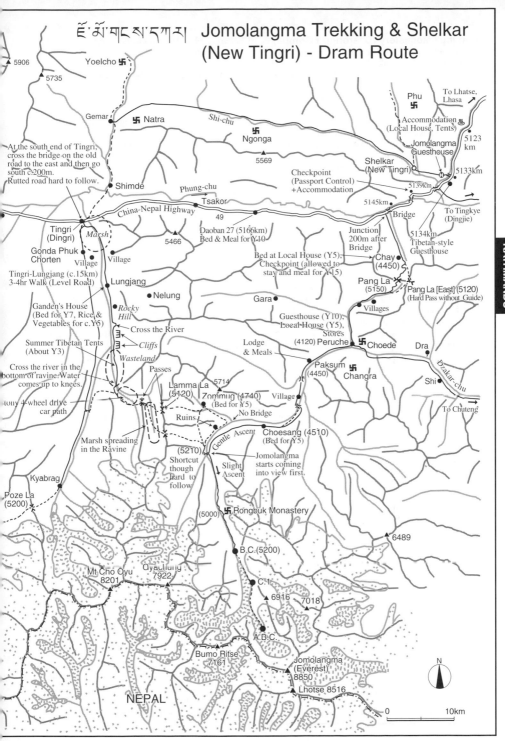

ཇོ་མོ་གངས་དཀར། Jomolangma Trekking & Shelkar (New Tingri) - Dram Route

▲5906
5735

Yoelcho 卍

Gemar 卍 Natra   Shi-chu

卍 Ngonga

▲5569

At the south end of Tingri, cross the bridge on the old road to the east and then go south c.200m. Rutted road hard to follow.

Shimde   Phung-chu   Tsakor

China-Nepal Highway   49

Tingri (Dingri)   Marsh   Daoban 27 (5166km)
Bed & Meal for Y10
Gonda Phuk Chorten   ▲5466
Village   Village   Bed at Local House (Y5);
Checkpoint (allowed to stay and meal for Y15)
Tingri-Lungjang (c.15km)   Lungjang   Gara
3-4hr Walk (Level Road)

Ganden's House   Nelung   Guesthouse (Y10);
(Bed for Y7, Rice & Vegetables for c.Y5)   Rocky Hill   Local House (Y5), Stores
Cross the River   Lodge   (4120) Peruche
Summer Tibetan Tents   & Meals
(About Y3)   Cliffs   Paksum
Wasteland   (4450)
Cross the river in the   Passes   Changra
bottom of ravine.Water   Lamma La   ▲5714
comes up to knees.   (5120)   Zommug (4740)   Village
Stony 4-wheel drive   (Bed for Y5)
car path   Ruins   No Bridge   Choesang (4510)
Marsh spreading   (5210)   Gentle Ascent   (Bed for Y5)
in the Ravine   Shortcut   Jomolangma
though   Slight   starts coming
Kyabrag   hard to   Ascent   into view first.
follow
Poze La   (5000) 卍 Rongbuk Monastery
(5200)

Phu
Accommodation
(Local House, Tents)
Jomolangma   5123
Guesthouse   km
Shelkar
(New Tingri)   5133km
5139km
Checkpoint   5145km   5134km
(Passport Control)   Tibetan-style
+Accommodation   Bridge   Guesthouse
Junction   To Tingkye
200m after   (Dingjie)
Bridge   Chay
(4450)
Pang La   Pang La [East] (5120)
(5150)   (Hard Pass without Guide)
Villages
Choede   Dra

Shi
To Chuteng

To Lhatse,
Lhasa

B.C.(5200)   ▲6489

Mt Cho Oyu   Gyachung
8201   7922   C.1
▲6916   ▲7018
A.B.C.
Bumo Ritse   Jomolangma
7161   (Everest)
8850
NEPAL   Lhotse 8516

N

0   10km

LHASA-
KATHMANDU

Rongbuk Monastery (Dzarongpu Gompa)

At the foot of the glaciers on the north face of Mt. Jomolangma is Rongbuk Monastery. Built in 1902, it is said to be the highest monastery (5,000m) in the world, and the site used to be home to 500 monks and nuns. It is said that the site also functioned as a hermitage for nuns from Mindroling Monastery for centuries before the Nyingmapa monastery was constructed. Trulzhik Rinpoche, the incarnate lama of the monastery, now resides in Nepal. From the junction of the China-Nepal (Friendship) Highway, it takes about 2 hours by Land Cruiser.

TINGRI (DINGRI) (CLOSED)

On the way from Kathmandu to Lhasa, most travelers stay at Tingri on the second night of the journey, and many get their first taste of altitude sickness. For those heading for Kathmandu from Lhasa, most spend their last night in Tibet here. Besides, Tingri is another one of the starting points for trekking up to the Jomolangma Base Camp.

There is nothing special to see in town, but the spectacular views of Mt. Jomolangma and Mt. Cho Oyu that you can get from the old Tingri Dzong's hilltop will more than make up for it.

Access

From Lhasa and Shigatse

Take one of the irregular buses to Dram that stop over at Tingri.

From Tingri

At Tingri you may have to hitchhike, as catching a bus at this intermediate stop is usually difficult.

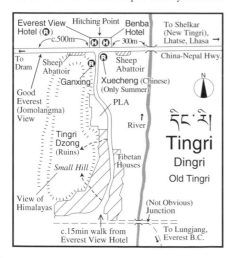

Chartering a Land Cruiser is the surest way to leave when you want to.

Accommodation & Restaurants

Most travelers who arrive by Land Cruiser stay at the *Everest View Hotel*. A dormitory bed here costs Y20 for foreign guests.

There are 2 lodges with English signs along the road toward Dram from Tingri. The first can be found around 10km from Tingri, and the second one is the same distance further on. At Gurtso, 39km from Tingri, there is the *Gurtso Binguan* (Hotel) and also some army facilities. These seem to be closed to foreign tourists, so you will have to wait until the *Daoban* (Road Maintenance Depot) to find available accommodation.

LAPCHI (CLOSED)

The sacred mountain of Lapchi Gang (7,367m) is approximately 40km to the south-west of Tingri, to the north-east of Nyalam. *Lapchi* means 'Noble Mountain,' and the Nyalam Valley area is regarded as one of the 3 holiest places in Tibet, as the great Milarepa lived in the area. To make a pilgrimage to the area, you will start at Tingri and then go south, finishing at Milarepa Monastery (Pelgyeling) and its caves. This route always keeps the sacred mountain to your right-hand side.

On the China-Nepal (Friendship) Highway, both the points for starting and finishing the pilgrimage are in Chinese territory. You must cross the Nepalese border during the trip though, as Lapchi was actually ceded to Nepal by China in 1962. There is a checkpoint before you reach Lapchi Gompa.

NYALAM (NIELAMU)

After Tingri, the China-Nepal (Friendship) Highway heading for Kathmandu goes through the Lalung La and Yarle Shung La passes and then on to Nyalam. Decorated with many *tar-choks*, Yarle Shung La commands a great view of Mt. Lapchi Gang to the south-east and Mt. Shishapangma (8,013m) to the west. At Nyalam you will find Milarepa Monastery, which, as its name suggests, is famous for its connection with Milarepa.

Access

From Lhasa or Shigatse, take one of the irregular buses to Dram and get off at Nyalam (Nielamu). Between Nyalam and Dram there is also an irregular schedule, and most travelers arrange a lift

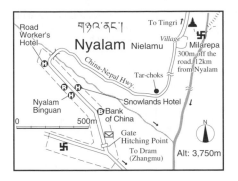

Nyalam Nielamu

གཉའ་ནང་། To Tingri ↑
Village
Milarepa
300m off the road, 12km from Nyalam
Tar-choks
Road Worker's Hotel
Nyalam Binguan
Snowlands Hotel
Bank of China
Gate Hitching Point
To Dram (Zhangmu)
0   500m
China-Nepal Hwy.
Alt: 3,750m
N

on a truck or a Land Cruiser from here. For Tingri, it is the same situation. The point for catching a lift is at the gate at the southern end of town.

Accommodation
The *Nyalam Binguan* (Hotel) has rooms for foreign guests from Y50.
The *Snowlands Hotel* (Xueyu Luguan) charges Y20 for a single room.
The *Road Worker's Hotel* is another option down near the bridge.

Milarepa Monastery (Nyalam Pelgyeling)
Halfway up the hill overlooking the Nyalam Valley stands Milarepa Monastery. It is around 12km to the north of Nyalam town, and the walk should take 3-4 hours. Set back 300m from the road, the monastery is said to have been built on the spot where Milarepa and his disciple, Rechungpa, meditated. Besides the caves here, there are a number of other spots associated with Milarepa, such as a rock that the great master lifted with his supernatural powers, a place where he laid his *tsampa* bowl, etc.

The present structures were rebuilt starting in 1983 in cooperation with Nepalese craftsmen. The original buildings had been destroyed during the Cultural Revolution. Although it used to belong to the Kagyupa, Milarepa Monastery is now under the wing of the Gelukpa. The site is home to approximately 15 monks, and one speaks English.

DRAM (KHASA) [ZHANGMU]

It is only 30km between Nyalam at 3,750m and Dram at 2,350m. After a trip featuring the endless stark vistas of the Tibetan Plateau, Dram, with its rich greenery, brings it home to you that you are finally leaving Tibet. The town compounds this feeling, as the people are mostly Nepalese, and it also has the Nepalese name of Khasa. On the other hand, travelers from Kathmandu to Lhasa may feel that this town is the very gateway into China, not Tibet, as you can see a dramatic increase in the number of Chinese signs and people.

Spreading over a steep hill, Dram has a number of 4- and 5-story buildings. It is a bustling and prosperous border town full of goods from both China and Nepal. Prices here are the highest in Tibet — 2-3 times as expensive as Lhasa.

Immigration and customs are to be found at the gate at the end of the town. From here, you go 10km down a mountain trail, and you'll reach the Friendship Bridge over the river that marks the border. The Nepalese immigration and customs offices are at Kodari on the other side of the bridge.

The section between Nyalam and Dram is the hardest part of the China-Nepal (Friendship) Highway. During the rainy season, landslides often make this section impassable.

Access
To Dram
*Lhasa and Shigatse—There is a long-distance bus service along these routes, though these departures are infrequent and irregular. The service is suspended during the winter, and at other times of the year it is dependent on the snowfall. The trip from Lhasa takes 2 nights, and the one from Shigatse is an overnight trip.

From Dram
*Lhasa and Shigatse—See details above.
*Nyalam—Check locally for the most recent information on buses operating on this section.
*At Dram there is a CITS office, where you can arrange a Land Cruiser to Lhasa. Without additional stops, a trip from Dram to Lhasa takes 1 night and costs around US$80 per person. The cost includes the fee for travel permits required for the trip. (No permit is required for the return journey from Lhasa to Dram.)
*For a lift on a Land Cruiser or truck, you can find

Dram

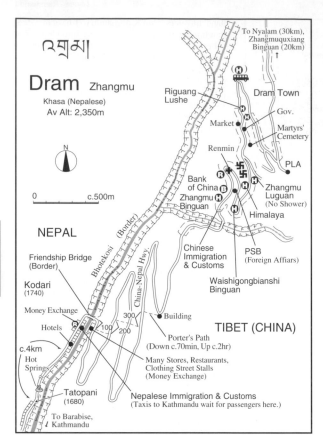

Dram Zhangmu
Khasa (Nepalese)
Av Alt: 2,350m

NEPAL

Friendship Bridge
(Border)

Kodari
(1740)

Money Exchange

Hotels

c.4km

Hot
Springs

Tatopani
(1680)

To Barabise,
Kathmandu

To Nyalam (30km),
Zhangmuquxiang
Binguan (20km)

Riguang
Lushe

Dram Town

Gov.

Market

Martyrs'
Cemetery

Renmin

PLA

Bank
of China

Zhangmu
Binguan

Zhangmu
Luguan
(No Shower)

Himalaya

Chinese
Immigration
& Customs

PSB
(Foreign Affiars)

Waishigongbianshi
Binguan

Building

TIBET (CHINA)

Porter's Path
(Down c.70min, Up c.2hr)

Many Stores, Restaurants,
Clothing Street Stalls
(Money Exchange)

Nepalese Immigration & Customs
(Taxis to Kathmandu wait for passengers here.)

0   c.500m

The *Zhangmu Luguan* and the *Himalaya Hotel* both have dormitory beds for Y10. The *Waishigongbianshi Binguan* charges Y18-20 for dormitory beds.

The *Zhangmuquxiang Binguan* is 20km from Dram, at 3,350m. This is a hotel for group tours, and although a little difficult to get to and from, the hotel is well equipped.

Changing Money

The *Bank of China* office does not change Nepalese Rupees for Chinese Yuan.

Business hours: Monday to Saturday 09:00-12:00 & 15:00-18:00.

To change from Yuan into Nepalese Rupees, you may get a better rate in Dram on the Chinese side. Stores, restaurants, etc., at Dram, Kodari, and Tatopani accept or change both Chinese and Nepalese currencies.

TO NEPAL

The Nepalese immigration is near the Friendship Bridge, and you can obtain a Nepalese visa at the border. Customs checks are not a usual occurrence. From the border there are 2 major ways of getting to Kathmandu — a taxi or the bus.

Taxis

Taxis to Kathmandu wait for passengers in front of the immigration building. You will need to employ your negotiation skills with the driver, but the trip usually costs from US$30-32 (equivalent to 2,050-2,200NRs). The trip takes 4 hours and is the easiest way to go.

Bus (via Barabise)

At the Kodari border crossing, there is usually only a single direct bus for Kathmandu a day. Most travelers take the bus to Barabise, where they change onto one that proceeds to the capital.

From Kodari to Barabise, there are a number of mid-sized buses each day. The police check foreigners on the way. The 30km trip costs around 30NRs and takes 3 hours.

a driver in front of the Zhangmu Binguan (Hotel) or the Waishigongbianshi Binguan (Guesthouse), and they are open to negotiating. For Shigatse, a Land Cruiser costs around Y200 and a truck from Y100 to Y150.

Between Dram and Kodari

You have 2 options, one is to walk, and the other is to hitchhike, though you may be overcharged. If you want to go directly to Kathmandu by taxi, you can find one before you get to the immigration office. There are also baggage porters costing 30NRs to 40NRs per porter. If you take the road, it is approximately 10km. If you walk, the shortcut is approximately 3km.

Accommodation & Restaurants

The *Zhangmu Binguan* is close to the immigration office, and a bed in a 4-person room costs Y30. Double rooms cost Y160. There are a lot of Chinese restaurants around the hotel.

At Barabise, there are buses to Kathmandu every 30 minutes that depart from an area just after the bridge. The 88km trip costs 50NRs and takes 5-6 hours, as the buses stop at many places along the way.

Tatopani

Four kilometers to the south of Kodari is Tatopani, with its hot springs. In Nepalese *Tatopani* means 'Hot Water.' Bathing in the open air will definitely refresh you after a long trip through the dry and dusty highlands. There are nearly a dozen guesthouses, and the costs of beds range from 25NRs to 50NRs. There are also a lot of restaurants and kiosks.

LHATSE TO SAGA (CLOSED)

The road to the west from Lhatse, on the China-Nepal (Friendship) Highway, leads to Mt. Kailash. The area around here is closed, but if you arrange a Land Cruiser at a travel agency, you can get a travel permit.

This section discusses the route: Lhatse - Ngamring - Zangzang - Raga - Daoban 22 (Junction) - Saga

Ngamring (Angren)

To the west of Lhatse, cross the Yarlung Tsangpo (Brahmaputra River) to the north side of the river and then continue on to the Lang Tso (Lake) to get to Kaga (Gekha), 53km from Lhatse.

Seven kilometers to the north-east from the main road at Kaga (Gekha) is the town of Ngamring. The lake here is called Ngamring Tso, and there is a monastery from the 13th century, Ngamring Gompa.

Zangzang (Sangsang)

There is nothing special to see in this town, 60km to the west of Kaga (Gekha). Go to the south, and cross the Sangsang Pel La pass to reach the Yarlung Tsangpo. In this area is the massive chorten of Chung Riwoche. (See the map on page 110.) At the *Sangsang Binguan* there are dormitory beds costing Y25.

Raga

Going to the west of Zangzang for 120km, you come to the truck stop of Raga. There are 2 guesthouses here with dormitory beds for Y10, and meals are also available.

Daoban 22

Daoban 22 at 4,725m is 235km west of Lhatse. This is where the northern road to Ali (Shiquanhe), going through the Changthang Plateau, and the southern road, up along the Yarlung Tsangpo (Brahmaputra River) to Mt. Kailash, meet.

Saga

There are 3-5 shared-trucks a day between either Lhasa or Shigatse and Saga, but many of the drivers won't take foreign passengers. You can stay at the *County Government Guesthouse* for Y50, and this is popular with truck drivers. There are 4 restaurants and a lot of stores in town. There are no checkpoints in Saga, and the PSB officers here generally leave travelers alone.

Chung Riwoche

Chung Riwoche was constructed by the great bridge builder, Thangtong Gyalpo (1385-1464), in the middle of the 15th century. Although a little smaller than Gyantse Kumbum (Pelkhor Chorten), this massive chorten miraculously survived the Mongolian invasion during the 18th century, and due to its remote location, was not very damaged even during the Cultural Revolution. The structure is a well-preserved example of the Tibetan arts that flourished from the 14th to the 15th century.

From Lhatse by car, leave the main route at Kaga (Gekha) to cross to the northern side of the Yarlung Tsangpo. Continue to the west following the course of the river, and you will finally get to Chung Riwoche. The best seasons to try it are in either the spring or fall. During the rest of the year the level of the river makes it impassable to vehicles.

As mentioned before, there is also a route that starts at Zangzang and crosses the pass to reach the site on foot. From Tingri, you may also walk there from the south.

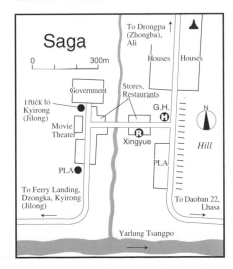

KYIRONG VALLEY TO NEPAL
(CLOSED)

In general, travelers are not allowed to enter Nepal via this route:

[Saga - Kyirong (Jilong) - Kathmandu]
The Kyirong Valley is to the west of the Nyalam Valley over Mt. Shishapangma. This valley is the area of Milarepa's birthplace, and along with Lapchi and Lhodrak, Kyirong is made famous by the connection to him. Near the Nepalese border, the town of Kyirong (Jilong) is below 3,000m, and the climate is mild with temperatures that don't go below 10°C even in winter.

Saga - Dzongka
At the south end of Saga, take a ferry for Y0.2 to cross the Yarlung Tsangpo. For Dzongka, catch a China Post truck, which will take you the 103km, crossing several passes along the way.

Dzongka
Dzongka is where the kings who ruled over the Kyirong Valley once lived. Like a fortress, massive 8m-high and 2m-thick walls surrounded the old town. In this instance it was not the Chinese but the Gorkha armies from Nepal that destroyed most of the town in the 19th century, but some parts are still left to see. Dzongka is presently the administrative center of Jilong County. Dzongka is known as the birthplace of Rechungpa, Milarepa's greatest disciple.

At the *Post Office Guesthouse* a bed costs Y7. Dzongka is a good place for food, and there are 5-6 kiosks here.

Dzongka - Gun - Kyirong (Jilong) (73km)
Around 20km to the south of Dzongka is the village of Gun. Another 10km to the east of Gun is Tsalung, the birthplace of Milarepa. At Kyirong (Jilong) Town (2,774m) is a Nepalese-style temple called Phakpa Wati Lhakhang.

To Nepal
From Kyirong (Jilong) it is 20km to the Nepalese border. At the border there is a bridge but no immigration or customs offices. Tibetan villages are on both sides of the bridge, and you can change money with villagers near the border.

It is 30km from the border to Dhunche via Syabunbesi. At Dhunche there is a bus departing at 07:00 and arriving in Kathmandu at 16:00.

With a pre-arranged Nepalese visa, a traveler will be able to cross the border, but soon after they

will be found and taken to Kathmandu by the police. In one case, a fine of 1,000NRs (US$140) was negotiated with the immigration officials, and an entry stamp was made in his passport, though he was still without his Chinese exit stamp.

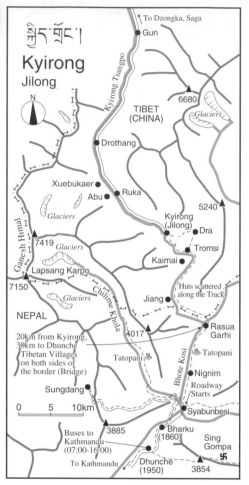

Lhatse -Daoban 22

Pelkhu Tso

To the east of Dzongka is Pelkhu Tso, which is mentioned in Milarepa's literary work. The road going along the southern lakeshore leads to the China-Nepal (Friendship) Highway.

CHUMBI VALLEY TO SIKKIM & BHUTAN
(CLOSED)

*Ordinary travelers are not permitted to take this route.

[Gyantse - Dromo (Yadong) - Bhutan]

Between Bhutan and Sikkim, the Chumbi Valley is a historically important point for traffic connecting Tibet with Darjeeling in India. The British Army invaded Tibet through the Chumbi Valley, to the south of Gyantse. This scenic area covered in lush vegetation is all closed, and it is hard to even obtain a permit through a travel agency.

The center of the Chumbi Valley is Dromo (Yadong). Although 2 buses connect Shigatse with Dromo (Yadong) each week on Tuesday and Saturday, foreign passengers are routinely ordered to turn back at the checkpoint on the way. Between Gyantse and Dromo (Yadong) there are 4 of these checkpoints even though it is only 200km or so, highlighting the sensitivity of this border area with India.

Gyantse - Khangmar (Kangma)

On the Gyantse side of Khangmar (Kangma) is where you will run into the first checkpoint, and most travelers are sent back from here. Good luck!

Gala (Kala)

With a checkpoint, Gala (Kala) is where the road branches off to the west until it reaches Gampa (Gangba) and Tingkye (Dingjie). In the south of Gala (Kala) there is a lake called Dochen Tso (Bam Tso).

Phari

Phari means 'Pig Mountain,' and it is said that a mountain nearby looks like a pig. It is only 7km from Phari to the Bhutanese border after you cross the Tremo La pass.

Drotoe (Shangyadong)

The area around Phari and Shangyadong is a place where Bon still flourishes, and there are 4 temples scattered around here.

Sharsingma (Xiasima)

The town commonly referred to as *Dromo (Yadong)* is Sharsingma, which is around 15km from the Sikkim border and less than 20km from the Bhutanese one. There is a PSB office here, and although this is a sensitive border area, merchants are still able to move freely between the 3 countries.

Dromo (Yadong) - Sikkim

There are 2 paths that take you from Dromo (Yadong) to the border of Sikkim and onto Gangtok. These go through either the Natu La pass or the Dzaleb La pass, though the route over the Dzaleb La pass is the more common of the two. At present the border is still closed.

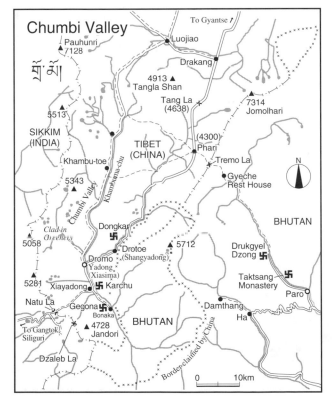

Chumbi Valley

131

The 10th Panchen Lama

Yukiyasu Osada

Since photographs of the Dalai Lama have disappeared from monasteries across Tibet, the most common images that you will encounter inside these religious centers are pictures of the late 10th Panchen Lama. Because the late 10th Panchen Lama received the title of Vice Chairman of the National People's Congress from the Chinese government, there are no problems displaying his picture, unlike that of the Dalai Lama's.

The title of 'Panchen Lama' or 'Panchen Rinpoche,' meaning 'Great Scholarly Lama,' has been given to successive abbots of the Tashilhunpo Monastery in Shigatse. Regarded as the embodiment of the Buddha Amitabha (Opame), he is ranked second in the order of Tibetan religious leaders, after the Dalai Lama. Although he is a high-ranking religious leader, the Panchen Lama originally carried no political authority; however, successive Panchen Lamas were used by both Britain and China in their efforts to subjugate the Dalai Lama's government in Lhasa.

Even after the 14th Dalai Lama fled to India during the 1959 upheaval in Tibet, the 10th

Panchen Lama, then 21-years-old, decided to stay in Tibet. Some say that he collaborated with the Chinese government. However, by the early 1960s, he observed that the Chinese policies at work in Tibet were resulting in hunger, death and suffering for the Tibetan people. He decided to use his position to deliver a report critical of the Chinese methods and the report became known as the '70,000 Character Petition.' The Chinese government replied by imprisoning him in Beijing for 9 years and 8 months. He was then placed under house arrest in the capital for another 14 years. He was finally allowed to return to his homeland in 1982.

In 1983 the 10th Panchen Lama married a Chinese woman and a girl was born to them. Though this was a violation of the ethical codes governing the life of a monk, this has never affected Tibetans' belief in him. It is probably the case that most Tibetans feel that he was in Beijing to support the Tibetan cause.

On his return, the 10th Panchen Lama devoted all of his energies to the revival of Tibetan religion and culture, which had almost been totally annihilated during the Cultural Revolution. Unfortunately, these efforts were short-lived. In January 1989, he returned to Shigatse after his long absence and was welcomed home by 30,000 Tibetans jubilant at his return. He made a statement to this crowd that could be interpreted as a criticism of the Chinese government, saying: 'Tibet has paid a price that could never be met by the development achieved over the last 30 years.' Five days later he suffered a massive heart attack and died. He was only 50 years old.

TO KAILASH
(Western Tibet = Ngari)

སྟོད་མངའ་རིས།

The western part of the Tibetan Plateau is called *Ngari* in Tibetan. Mt. Kailash (Kang Rinpoche), the most sacred place in Tibet, is a destination that many backpackers want to visit, and it is easily the most famous sight in the area. Although group tours are presently available, anyone who has managed to visit Mt. Kailash has accomplished something special.

Besides Mt. Kailash and Lake Manasarovar, there are a number of other highlights in the area, such as the Guge ruins, Tirthapuri Gompa, Purang (near the Nepalese border), and Panggong Tso (Bangong He).

Ngari & Past Glory

Ngari is now classed simply as a remote region in the far west of China. However, it was for a long time the center of Tibet.

Usually, most Tibetan history discussions start with the kings of the Yarlung Valley. This does not take into account that there was a country called *Zhangzhung* near Mt. Kailash long before that, where the Bon religion flourished. The people of this area moved to the east along the Yarlung Tsangpo (Brahmaputra River) and reached the Yarlung Valley and the further easterly area of Kham. This migration shaped the origin of the

Boepa (Tibetan people). In fact, various regions in Tibet have continued oral traditions that trace their origin to Western Tibet. For example, the eastern end of the Tibetan Plateau around Aba Prefecture, in present day Sichuan Province, is called *Ngawa* in Tibetan, and according to many, this means 'People of Ngari.'

Ngari was again thrust under the spotlight during the 9th century with the ascendancy of King Langdarma, whose belief in Bon led him to suppress Buddhism in central Tibet. After his assassination by the devout Buddhist Lhalung

Pilgrims, Darchen

133

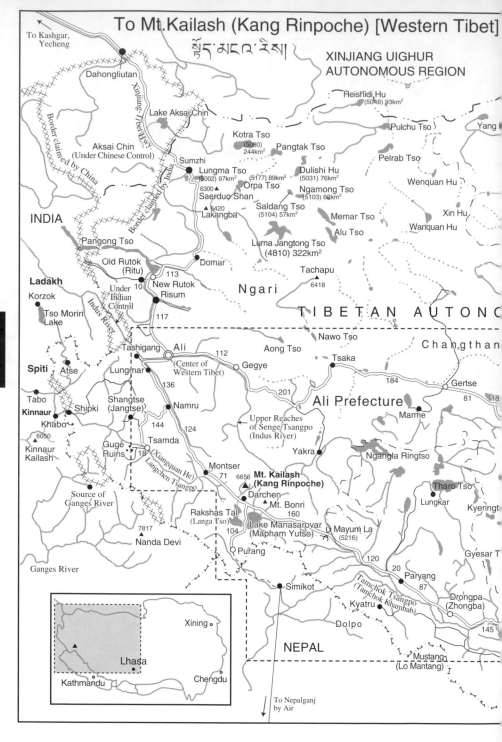

To Mt.Kailash (Kang Rinpoche) [Western Tibet]

གྲོང་མངའ་རིས།

XINJIANG UIGHUR
AUTONOMOUS REGION

To Kashgar,
Yecheng

Dahongliutan

Lake Aksai Chin

Heishidi Hu
(5048) 93km²

Pulchu Tso

Yang

Kotra Tso
(5080)
244km²

Pangtak Tso

Pelrab Tso

Aksai Chin
(Under Chinese Control)

Sumzhi

Lungma Tso
(5002) 97km²

6300 ▲
Saerduo Shan

Orpa Tso

(5177) 89km²

Dulishi Hu
(5031) 76km²

Wenquan Hu

Ngamong Tso
(5103) 62km²

Xin Hu

Border claimed by China

Border claimed by India

▲ 6420
Lakangba

Saldang Tso
(5104) 57km²

Memar Tso

Wanquan Hu

INDIA

Alu Tso

Pangong Tso

Luma Jangtong Tso
(4810) 322km²

Old Rutok
(Ritu)

Domar

Tachapu
▲
6418

Ladakh

113

Korzok

10

Under
Indian
Control

New Rutok
Risum

N g a r i

Tso Moriri
Lake

117

TIBETAN AUTONO

Nawo Tso

Changthan

Tashigang

Ali

112

Aong Tso

Spiti

Atse

Lungmar

(Center of
Western Tibet)

Gegye

Tsaka

184

Gertse

Tabo

136

201

81

18

Kinnaur

Shipki

Shangtse
(Jangtse)

Namru

Ali Prefecture

Marme

Khabo

144

124

Upper Reaches
of Senge Tsangpo
(Indus River)

Ngangla Ringtso

6050

Kinnaur
Kailash

Tsamda

Guge
Ruins

18

(Xiangquan He)
Langchen Tsangpo

Yakra

Montser

Tharo Tso

71

6656

Mt. Kailash
(Kang Rinpoche)

Lungkar

Kyeringt

Source of
Ganges River

▲ Mt. Bonri
160

Darchen

Rakshas Tal
(Langa Tso)

104

Lake Manasarovar
(Mapham Yutso)
(5216)

Mayum La

7817

Nanda Devi

Purang

120

Gyesar T

Ganges River

20

Paryang

87

Simikot

Tamchok Tsangpo
(Tamchok Khambab)

Drongpa
(Zhongba)

Kyatru

145

Dolpo

Xining

NEPAL

Mustang
(Lo Mantang)

Lhasa

Chengdu

Kathmandu

To Nepalganj
by Air

TO
KAILASH

Source of
Ganges River

Indus River

Xinjiang-Tibet Hwy.

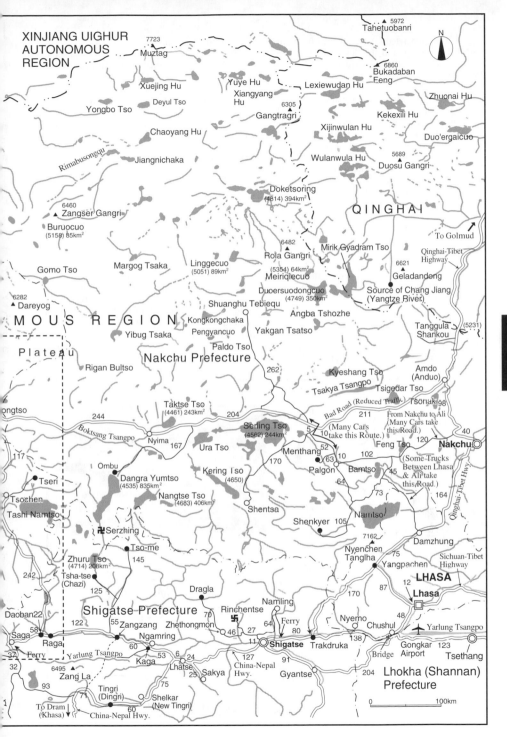

XINJIANG UIGHUR
AUTONOMOUS
REGION

N

▲ 5972
Tahetuobanri

7723
Muztag

▲ 6860
Bukadaban
Feng

Xuejing Hu

Yuye Hu

Lexiewudan Hu

Zhuonai Hu

Yongbo Tso

Deyul Tso

Xiangyang
Hu

Kekexili Hu

Chaoyang Hu

6305
Gangtragri

Xijinwulan Hu

Duo'ergaicuo

Rimabusongqu

Jiangnichaka

Wulanwula Hu

5689
Duosu Gangri

QINGHAI

Doketsoring
(4814) 394km²

6460
▲ Zangser Gangri

Buruocuo
(5158) 85km²

Margog Tsaka

Linggecuo
(5051) 89km²

6482
▲
Rola Gangri
(5354) 64km²
Meiriqiecuo

Mirik Gyadram Tso

To Golmud

Qinghai-Tibet
Highway

6621
Geladandong

Gomo Tso

Duoersuodongcuo
(4749) 350km²

Source of Chang Jiang
(Yangtze River)

6282
▲ Dareyog

Shuanghu Tebiequ

Angba Tshozhe

Tanggula
Shankou

(5231)

M O U S   R E G I O N

Kongkongchaka
Pengyancuo

Yakgan Tsatso

Yibug Tsaka

Paldo Tso

Plateau

Rigan Bultso

Nakchu Prefecture

262

Kyeshang Tso

Amdo
(Anduo)

Tsakya Tsangpo

Tsigedar Tso

Tsonak 98

ongtso

244

Taktse Tso
(4461) 243km²

204

Bad Road (Reduced Traffic)

211
From Nakchu to Ali
(Many Cars take
this Road.)

40

Boktsang Tsangpo

Serling Tso
(4562) 244km²

5
10

(Many Cars
take this Route.)

Feng Tso

120

Nakchu

Nyima

167

Ura Tso

52

63

10

102

(Some Trucks
Between Lhasa
& Ali take
this Road.)

117

Ombu

Menthang

170

Palgon

Bamtso

45

164

Tseri

Dangra Yumtso
(4535) 835km²

Kering Tso
(4650)

64

73

Namtso

Tsochen

Nangtse Tso
(4683) 406km²

Shentsa

Shenkyer 105

7162

Tashi Namtso

Serzhing

Tso-me

Nyenchen
Tanglha

75

Damzhung

Zhuru Tso
(4714) 208km²

145

Yangpachen

Sichuan-Tibet
Highway

242

Tsha-tse
(Chazi)

125

Dragla

170

87

12

LHASA

Lhasa

Daoban22

Shigatse Prefecture

122

55

Zangzang

Namling

Rinchentse

70

Nyemo

48

Chushul

Yarlung Tsangpo

58

Raga

Ngamring

60

Zhethongmon

46

27

64

Ferry

80

138

Gongkar
Airport

123

37 Ferry

Yarlung Tsangpo

Kaga

53

6

24

11

Shigatse

Trakdruka

Bridge

Tsethang

32

6495 ▲

Zang La

75

Lhatse

25

Sakya

127
China-Nepal
Hwy.

91

Gyantse

204

Lhokha (Shannan)
Prefecture

93

Tingri
(Dingri)

71

Shelkar
(New Tingri)

60

China-Nepal Hwy.

To Dram
(Khasa)

0

100km

TO
KAILASH

Peldor, Tibet separated into small rival fiefdoms, and during this period the descendants of the Yarlung royal family escaped from Lhasa to Western Tibet and Ladakh. Once there they tried to revive Buddhism, and one of their bases was the kingdom of Guge with Tsaparang at its center.

The Ngari area is now known as the Ali Prefecture of the TAR. Commonly called Ali, the Chinese-built town of Shiquanhe is the administrative center of the area.

Taking China as your center, you may feel that Ngari is an extremely remote area, as even the shortest journey from Lhasa to Mt. Kailash is around 1,200km. On the other hand, if you trace the old trading routes from India (Ladakh and Zanskar) and Nepal, you won't get the same feeling. Even now, merchants still use these routes to transport their wares.

Although the area of Ali Prefecture is around the same size as Italy or the state of Arizona (300,000 sq km), it is dominated by the barren Changthang Plateau and is sparsely populated with only approximately 70,000 people.

Travel Permits
The whole of Western Tibet is closed, but still a number of foreigners actually visit the area, and most of them end up paying fines to the PSB at either Ali or Darchen.

Strangely, you can get a permit once you get to Ali or Darchen, and normally, a 15-day permit costs Y10. You may also be able to obtain one for 21 days if your negotiation skills are good enough or you are simply lucky. Permits are available for 9 places, including Rutok (Ritu), Tsamda (Guge Ruins), Mt. Kailash & Lake Manasarovar, Purang, Montser, Gertse (Gaize), and Tsochen (Cuoqin).

Trip to Western Tibet
*With fine weather during the summer, May through October is the best time to visit the area, although the peak of Mt. Kailash is frequently covered with clouds between mid-June and mid-September.

*For hitchhiking, wrap up warm, as the nights are freezing even in summer.

*Carry enough food and water for the journey, as these are in limited supply.

*You should change enough money into local currency in either Lhasa or Shigatse, as there are very few places to change in Western Tibet.

*Minimum costs will be at least Y3,000 for a 4-6 week stay. This includes PSB fines and admission to the Guge ruins, which are fairly expensive.

*You may be able to change US dollars in either Ali or Purang.

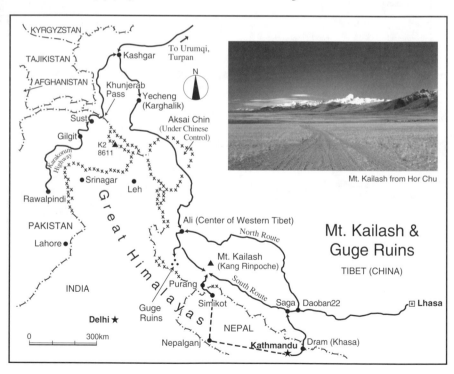

Mt. Kailash from Hor Chu

Mt. Kailash & Guge Ruins
TIBET (CHINA)

ROUTE TO MT. KAILASH

Mt. Kailash is the most likely destination for travelers heading to Western Tibet. There are 4 routes to Darchen, the village at the foot of Mt. Kailash. (For details, see the map to the left.)

To the west beyond Lhatse there are no buses operating, and you will have to charter a Land Cruiser or hitch a lift on a truck. The cost for hitching is about Y1 per 5-8 km.

Northern Route from Lhasa
Lhasa - Shigatse - Lhatse - Daoban 22 (Road Maintenance Depot) - Tsochen - Gertse (Gaize) - Ali - Darchen (1,945km, 7-9 days)

This is the most common route on which ordinary trucks run. The journey is a rather monotonous drive across the vast Changthang Plateau. (See page 129 and pages 138-139.) From Lhasa to Ali, the 1,625km trip costs around Y200. Some drivers charge foreigners more- Y300-500. The trip takes 5-7 days by truck or 4-5 days by Land Cruiser.

Southern Route from Lhasa
Lhasa - Shigatse - Lhatse - Daoban 22 (Road Maintenance Depot) - Saga - Paryang - Darchen (1,280km, 5-7 days)

This route is via the Lhasa-Purang Highway following along the Yarlung Tsangpo. During the rainy season ordinary trucks avoid this route, as the level of the river rises. Army trucks overcharge you. (See page 129 and pages 138-139.)

Xinjiang-Tibet Highway Route from Kashgar
Kashgar - Yecheng - Ali - Darchen
(1,670km, 7-8 days)
(See pages 154-155 and page 156.)

From Kathmandu, Nepal
Kathmandu - Simikot - Purang - Darchen
(See page 147.)

Paryang

Group Tours
A number of travelers visit Mt. Kailash by organizing groups and then hiring a Land Cruiser through a travel agency in Lhasa. You will often read about these on message boards in Lhasa guesthouses, such as the Yak Hotel, Snowlands Hotel, etc. In this case, you can easily get a travel permit issued in a couple of days. A popular course that takes 22-25 days is as follows:

*Days 1-8: Lhasa - Lhatse - Tsochen (Northbound) - Ali
*Days 8-13: Ali - Tsamda (Toling Gompa) - Guge - Tirthapuri - Mt. Kailash
*Days 13-18: Mt. Kailash (4 days) - Lake Manasarovar (1 day)
*Days 18-23: Lake Manasarovar - Lhasa (Southbound)
*Add a couple of days for poor road conditions, even if you go by Land Cruiser.

Chartering a car following this itinerary costs Y25,000-30,000 (US$3,100-3,600) during the summer. You may be able to negotiate a 10% discount during the spring or fall, but this varies depending on the travel agency.

The 4-wheel-drive cars can accommodate 4-5 passengers, but 3 is the best number, for with any more than 3, someone will have to sit in the cargo space. Japanese-made Land Cruisers are the most comfortable.

The price includes the car, fuel, permit fees, accommodation, and meal expenses for the driver and the guide (not including those for the passengers). If you include accommodation and want meals, a cook will accompany you and the cost will go up sharply. It is also possible to rent a tent through a travel agency.

To get there cheaply, you may have the option of chartering a large-size truck costing Y15,000-20,000 (US$1,800-2,400). These can take approximately 15 passengers, but they are extremely uncomfortable and more prone to breakdowns and accidents. The availability of these trucks on this route is not guaranteed, and you should check locally for the most recent information.

Make sure that you prepare a written contract when you make your arrangements with a travel agency. Pay half on departure and the rest on your return. It is also advisable to view the car in advance. Otherwise, you might wind up with a less reliable Chinese-made jeep rather than the Land Cruiser you expected.

The journey out to Mt. Kailash is a long and arduous month, and this will be made all the harder if you get off on the wrong foot with your driver and guide, let alone your other traveling

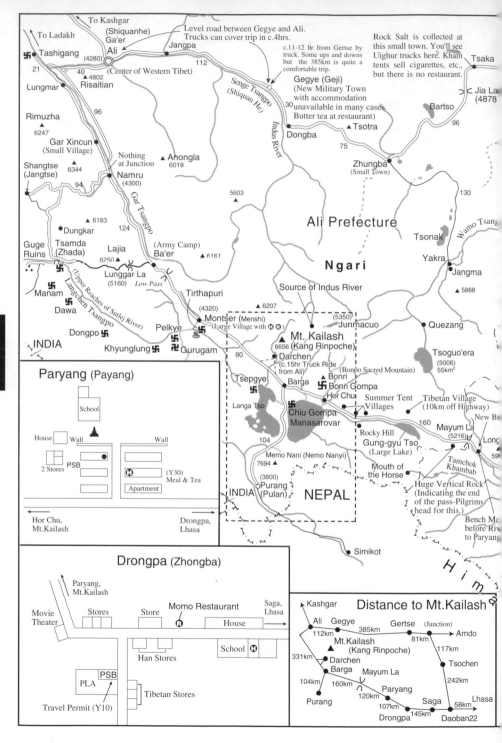

To Ladakh

To Kashgar
(Shiquanhe)
Ga'er
Ali
(4280)
(Center of Western Tibet)

Jangpa

112

Tashigang
21
40 ▲ 4802
Risaitian

Lungmar

96

Rimuzha
▲
6247

Gar Xincun
(Small Village)

Shangtse
(Jangtse)
94

▲ 6344

Nothing
at Junction

Namru
(4300)

Dungkar

Guge
Ruins

Tsamda
(Zhada)

Lajia

Ba'er
(Army Camp)

6250 ▲

Lunggar La
(5160) Low Pass

Manam

Dawa

Dongpo

Pelkye

Khyunglung

Gurugam

INDIA

▲ 6183

124

Gar Tsangpo

▲ 6161

(Upper Reaches of Sutlej River)
Langchen Tsangpo

Level road between Gegye and Ali.
Trucks can cover trip in c.4hrs.

c.11-12 hr from Gertse by
truck. Some ups and downs
but the 385km is quite a
comfortable trip.

Gegye (Geji)
(New Military Town
with accommodation
unavailable in many cases.
Butter tea at restaurant)

Senge Tsangpo
(Shiquan He)

Indus River

30

Dongba

75

Zhungba
(Small Town)

▲ 5603

Ali Prefecture

Ngari

▲ 6207

Source of Indus River

Tirthapuri

(4320)

Montser (Menshi)
(Large Village with 🏨 ®)

80

Tsepgye

Langa Tso

Rock Salt is collected at
this small town. You'll see
Uighur trucks here. Kham
tents sell cigarettes, etc.,
but there is no restaurant.

Tsaka

Jia La
(4878

Bartso

Tsotra

96

Tsonak

Yakra

Jangma

▲ 5888

130

Wamo Tsang

(5350)
Junmacuo

Mt. Kailash
6656 (Kang Rinpoche)

Darchen
(c.15hr Truck Ride
from Ali)

Barga

Bonri
Bonri Gompa

Hor Chu

Chiu Gompa
Manasarovar

104

Memo Nani (Nemo Nanyi)
7694 ▲

(3800)
Purang
(Pulan)

INDIA

NEPAL

(Bonpo Sacred Mountain)

Summer Tent
Villages

Rocky Hill

Gung-gyu Tso
(Large Lake)

Mouth of
the Horse

Quezang

Tsoguo'era
(5006)
55km²

Tibetan Village
(10km off Highway)

160

Mayum La
(5216)

New B

Long

59

Tamchok
Khambab

Huge Vertical Rock
(Indicating the end
of the pass-Pilgrims
head for this.)

Bench Ma
before Riv
to Paryang

Simikot

Him

TO
KAILASH

Paryang (Payang)

School

House

Wall

Wall

2 Stores

PSB

🏨

(Y30)
Meal & Tea

Apartment

Hor Chu,
Mt.Kailash

Drongpa,
Lhasa

Drongpa (Zhongba)

Paryang,
Mt. Kailash

Movie
Theater

Stores

Store

Momo Restaurant
®

House

Saga,
Lhasa

School 🏨

Han Stores

PLA

PSB

Tibetan Stores

Travel Permit (Y10)

Distance to Mt.Kailash

Kashgar

Ali
112km

Gegye
385km

Gertse
81km

(Junction)

Amdo

117km

Mt.Kailash
(Kang Rinpoche)
▲

331km

Darchen

Barga

Mayum La

Tsochen

242km

104km

160km

Paryang
120km

Saga
58km

Lhasa

Purang

Drongpa
145km

107km

Daoban22

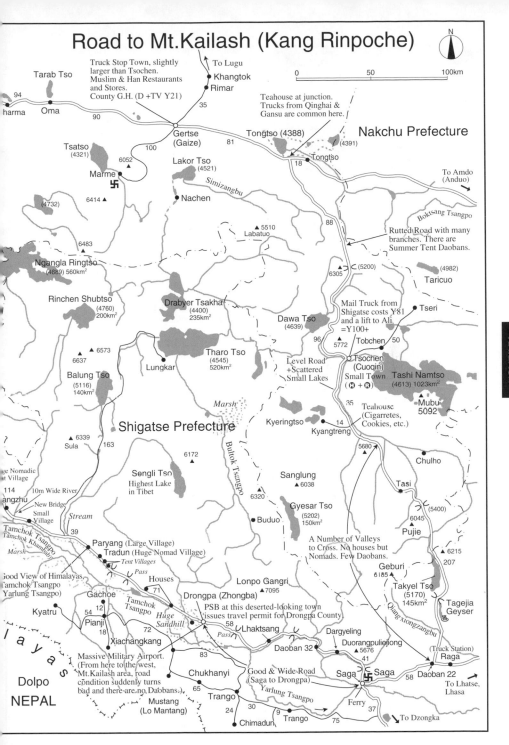

Road to Mt.Kailash (Kang Rinpoche)

N

Tarab Tso

Truck Stop Town, slightly larger than Tsochen. Muslim & Han Restaurants and Stores. County G.H. (D +TV Y21)

To Lugu

Khangtok
Rimar

94
harma   Oma
90

35

0   50   100km

Teahouse at junction. Trucks from Qinghai & Gansu are common here.

Gertse
(Gaize)   81   Tongtso (4388)   (4391)

Nakchu Prefecture

Tsatso
(4321)   100   18   Tongtso

6052
Marme   Lakor Tso
(4521)
Simizangbu

6414 ▲   Nachen

To Amdo
(Anduo)

(4732)

88

Boktsang Tsangpo

6483
▲ 5510
Labatuo

Rutted Road with many branches. There are Summer Tent Daobans.

Ngangla Ringtso
(4689) 560km²   ▲ (5200)   (4982)
6305   Taricuo

Rinchen Shubtso
(4760)
200km²   Drabyer Tsakha
(4400)
235km²   Dawa Tso
(4639)   Mail Truck from Shigatse costs Y81 and a lift to Ali =Y100+   Tseri

6573   96   5772   Tobchen   50
6637   Tharo Tso
(4545)
520km²   Level Road +Scattered Small Lakes   Tsochen
(Cuoqin)
Small Town
(🏥+🏤)   Tashi Namtso
(4613) 1023km²

Lungkar

Balung Tso
(5116)
140km²

Marsh   Mubu
5092

▲ 6339   Kyeringtso   14   Teahouse
(Cigarretes, Cookies, etc.)
Sula   163   Kyangtreng

Shigatse Prefecture

6172
▲   5680   Chulho

Sengli Tso
Highest Lake in Tibet   6320   Sanglung
▲ 6038   Tasi

Bulok Tsangpo

Gyesar Tso
(5202)
150km²   6045
▲   (5400)
Buduo   Pujie

ge Nomadic
t Village

114
angzhu   10m Wide River
New Bridge
Small
Village   *Stream*   A Number of Valleys to Cross. No houses but Nomads. Few Daobans.   ▲ 6215
207

Tamchok Tsangpo
Tamchok Khambab   39   Paryang (Large Village)
Tradun (Huge Nomad Village)   Geburi
6185
Marsh   *Tent Villages*   Takyel Tso
(5170)
145km²   Tagejia
Geyser

Pass
Good View of Himalayas
Tamchok Tsangpo
Yarlung Tsangpo)   Houses   Lonpo Gangri
▲ 7095   Takyel Tso
Gachoe   71   Drongpa (Zhongba)   *Qiang xiongzangbu*
Kyatru   54   12   Tamchok
Tsangpo   PSB at this deserted-looking town issues travel permit for Drongpa County   (Truck Station)
Pianji   *Huge
Sandhill*   58   Raga
18   72   Lhaktsang   Dargyeling
Xiachangkang   *Pass*   Duorangpuliejiong
83   Daoban 32   ▲ 5676   To Lhatse,
Massive Military Airport. (From here to the west, Mt.Kailash area, road condition suddenly turns bad and there are no Daobans.)   Saga   41   Saga   Lhasa
Chukhanyi   Good & Wide Road
(Saga to Drongpa)   58   Daoban 22

Dolpo
NEPAL

Mustang
(Lo Mantang)   65   Trango   *Yarlung Tsangpo*   Ferry   37   To Dzongka
24   30   9
Chimadun   Trango   75

l a y a s

To Mt. Kailash

Tibetans who speak good English. They are experienced and used to negotiating with travelers. In most cases, they start with Y500 and agree on around Y400 for the fine.

Ali Prefecture Travel Permit
You can obtain these at the PSB office, and the fee doesn't depend on the number of towns you apply for. A single payment of Y50 will allow you to go to Mt. Kailash, Lake Manasarovar, Purang, Guge, etc. Even if your itinerary is not fixed, it is better to apply for as many towns as possible. When you try to find a room or organize transportation, you are often asked whether you are carrying a permit.

Visa Extensions
At the PSB, you can get your visa extended for a maximum of an additional 30 days. And this costs Y120. This town is probably where you can get the longest extensions in the TAR. Extensions are not available in either Darchen or Purang.

Accommodation & Restaurants
The *Ali Fandian* charges Y40 for a bed in a 4-person room. There are no showers, and the toilets are outside. Hot water is available here. Perhaps the only good thing about this place is that it gets a lot of sunshine. Without a permit, you will be reported to the PSB immediately.

The *Ali Dajiudian* is a relatively new hotel, which has become popular lately. A 3-person room costs Y25 per person.

There are a number of Chinese restaurants in

companions. Another thing to bear in mind is that if one of the participants gets sick, your whole itinerary may change on short notice. This is even more reason to make sure everyone is fully acclimatized before setting off and to keep an eye on your condition as you go.

ALI (SHIQUANHE) (CLOSED)

Built by the Chinese, Ali (Shiquanhe) is the administrative center of Western Tibet (Ali Prefecture). In town you will often see Uighurs too. Ali is the destination for most trucks heading for Western Tibet. This is the town to get caught in, as it is a closed area. Without a permit, you will definitely be reported to the PSB by the guesthouse you stay in, and it is difficult to avoid this.

If you are heading for Guge or Mt. Kailash from Ali, it seems better to get caught here than later on. You will get a travel permit for the Ali Prefecture issued to you right after being fined Y400-500. This may sound illogical, but this is the way it goes. Once you have the permit, you don't have to worry about checkpoints, and you can move around or book a room with confidence.

Foreign Affairs Branch, Public Security Bureau (PSB)
The office used to be at the Ali Fandian, but it is presently at the PSB office. Most of the offices here are staffed by

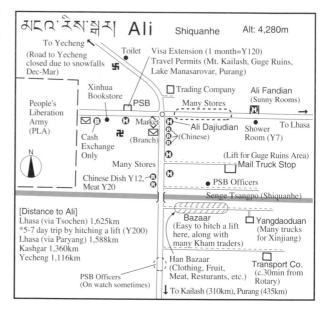

᠌᠊ Ali Shiquanhe Alt: 4,280m

To Yecheng
(Road to Yecheng closed due to snowfalls Dec-Mar)

Toilet

Visa Extension (1 month=Y120)
Travel Permits (Mt. Kailash, Guge Ruins, Lake Manasarovar, Purang)

Xinhua Bookstore
People's Liberation Army (PLA)
PSB
Trading Company
Many Stores
Ali Fandian (Sunny Rooms)

Market
Cash Exchange Only
(Branch)
Ali Dajiudian (Chinese)
Shower Room (Y7)
To Lhasa

Many Stores
(Lift for Guge Ruins Area)
Mail Truck Stop

Chinese Dish Y12,
Meat Y20
PSB Officers

Senge Tsangpo (Shiquanhe)

[Distance to Ali]
Lhasa (via Tsochen) 1,625km
*5-7 day trip by hitching a lift (Y200)
Lhasa (via Paryang) 1,588km
Kashgar 1,360km
Yecheng 1,116km

PSB Officers
(On watch sometimes)

Bazaar
(Easy to hitch a lift here, along with many Kham traders)

Han Bazaar
(Clothing, Fruit, Meat, Resturants, etc.)

Yangdaoduan
(Many trucks for Xinjiang)

Transport Co.
(c.30min from Rotary)

↓ To Kailash (310km), Purang (435km)

town, and on the southern side of the bridge, there are many Tibetan restaurants.

MT. KAILASH (KANG RINPOCHE)
(CLOSED)

Commonly known as Mt. Kailash, Kang Rinpoche is the holiest place in the world for Hindus, Jains, Bonpos, and Buddhists.

Hindus—Regarding the peak as Shiva's symbolic *Lingam* or Phallus, Hindus, especially devotees of the Shiva sect, worship Mt. Kailash (Sanskrit name).

Bonpos—Bonpos believe the sacred mountain is the place where Shenrab Miwoche, the founder of Bon, landed when he descended from the sky.

Tibetan Buddhists—Kang Rinpoche meaning 'Precious Snow Mountain' is a natural *mandala* representing the Buddhist cosmology on the earth. The mountain itself is Shakyamuni, and the surrounding peaks are Bodhisattvas or deities.

Jains—Established around the time of Buddhism, they believe this holy site to be the place where their founder was spiritually awakened.

No matter what has actually transformed Mt. Kailash into such a holy place, you will be convinced of its status when you first catch sight of this awe-inspiring mountain. The old Tibetan policy of isolation, Chinese border disputes with India, the Chinese communists' ban on religion, and other factors have conspired to separate Mt. Kailash from the outside world. This has further intensified the mystique of the mountain, and only since the mid-1980s were pilgrimages again permitted and foreigners allowed to visit the site.

The white stripes on the side of the mountain's north face are believed to be imprints left by ropes with which a demon tried to carry the mountain to Sri Lanka. Shakyamuni came and persuaded him to stop, and Shakyamuni's footprints can be seen in the stone along the pilgrimage path. To date, no one has ever reached the summit of Mt. Kailash.

Mt. Kailash (Kang Rinpoche)

Darchen
Right in front of Mt. Kailash, Darchen is the starting point for pilgrimages in the area, and it is here that many pilgrims pitch their tents. They prepare butter tea with water drawn from the Darchen-chu nearby and eat *tsampa*. Traditionally, it is said that Tibetans don't kill anything during their pilgrimage to Mt. Kailash, thus refraining from eating meat.

The PSB & Permits.
*PSB officers are stationed at a guesthouse next to the Ganges Guesthouse from spring until October each year. They are strict about checking permits, and if you don't have one (e.g. you came from Lhasa on the southern route along the Yarlung Tsangpo), you should report to them as soon as possible and pay the Y50 fine. Otherwise, you may be fined a non-negotiable Y500.

*Ali Prefecture Permits cost Y50, and it will cost Y10 for a 10-day permit extension.

*The PSB officers are good-natured, except for their Han Chinese leader who has been known to get violent with travelers.

Accommodation & Restaurants
The *Ganges Guesthouse* has double rooms for Y50, but overcharging is a common problem here. If you ask the staff before they have their meal breaks, you can usually arrange something to eat.

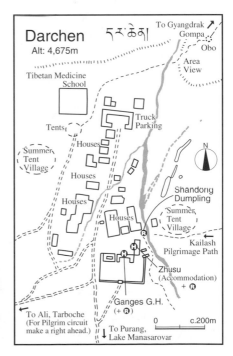

Darchen ད་ར་ཆེན།
Alt: 4,675m

Tibetan Medicine School
Tents
Houses
Summer Tent Village
Houses
Houses
Houses
Houses
Truck Parking
To Gyangdrak / Gompa
Obo
Area View
N
Shandong Dumpling
Summer Tent Village
Kailash Pilgrimage Path
Zhusu (Accommodation)
Ganges G.H.
To Ali, Tarboche (For Pilgrim circuit make a right ahead.)
To Purang, Lake Manasarovar
0   c.200m

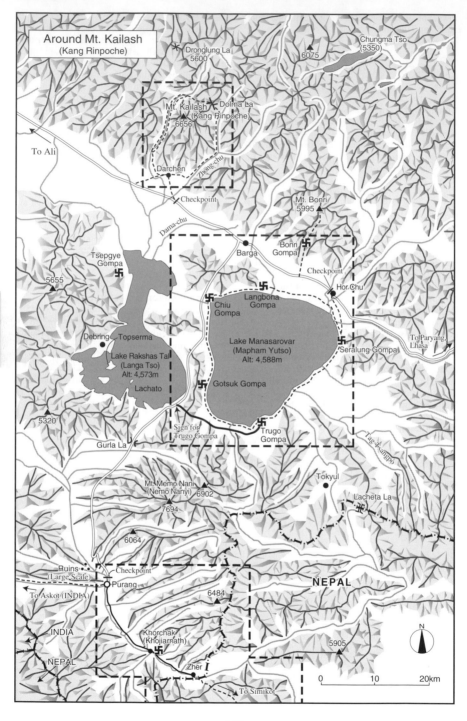

Around Mt. Kailash
(Kang Rinpoche)

Dronglung La
5600

6075

Chungma Tso
(5350)

Mt. Kailash
(Kang Rinpoche)
6656

Dolma La

To Ali

Zhong-chu

Darchen

Checkpoint

Mt. Bonri
5995

Dama-chu

Tsepgye
Gompa

Barga

Bonri
Gompa

Checkpoint

5655

Chiu
Gompa

Langbona
Gompa

Hor Chu

To Paryang,
Lhasa

Debring
Topserma

Lake Manasarovar
(Mapham Yutso)
Alt: 4,588m

Seralung Gompa

Lake Rakshas Tal
(Langa Tso)
Alt: 4,573m

Lachato

Gotsuk Gompa

5320

Tag-tsangpo

Sign for
Trugo Gompa

Trugo
Gompa

Gurla La

Mt. Memo Nani
(Nemo Nanyi) 6902

Tokyul

Lacheta La

7694

6064

Ruins
(Large Scale)

Checkpoint

Purang

To Askot (INDIA)

6484

NEPAL

INDIA

Khorchak
(Khojiarnath)

5905

NEPAL

Zher

N

0   10   20km

To Simikot

TO
KAILASH

The *Zhusu* is next door, and dormitory beds cost Y50. If you are lucky, you may be able to get a discount rate of Y30. The toilet is outside, and there is a restaurant.

The *Shandong Dumpling* is a popular restaurant with an English-speaking owner who is the brother of one of the PSB officers. There are some other restaurants, and the availability of food in the town has been improving. A number of stores and kiosks, including Khampa tent stores, have a good variety of goods on sale.

MT. KAILASH KHORA (PILGRIMAGE CIRCUIT)

A pilgrimage to Mt. Kailash involves nothing more or less than making circuits around the sacred mountain. One circuit is about 52km, and Tibetans can complete a circuit in a day. The number of times varies from person to person and can also depend on their physical condition, but the majority seem to go for 13 circuits if they can. Many of those attempting a large number of circuits will make at least one of them while performing *Kyangcha* (Prostration). While a circuit takes roughly 14 hours to complete, it takes a couple of weeks when prostrating oneself. Some pilgrims try for the ultimate act of devotion and make 108 circuits, thus securing their path to enlightenment.

Those moving in a clockwise direction, keeping Mt. Kailash to their right, are usually Buddhists and Hindus, while Bonpos go counter-clockwise. Hindus call this circuit *Parikrama*.

Many travelers may feel hard-pressed to complete a circuit in just a day, and of course, not all Tibetans are able to either. There are 3 places to stay along the way, and you can camp at these points, though carrying a tent will slow you down even more.

On the eastern side of the course there is a small tent kiosk where you can buy precooked noodles. This is the only place to get food on the pilgrimage path

Many travelers take 3 days to complete their circuit. The second day is the hardest as you have to cross the Dolma La pass. For the route, refer to the map.

Day 1: Darchen - Drirapuk Gompa
Day 2: Drirapuk Gompa - Zutrulpuk Gompa
Day 3: Zutrulpuk Gompa - Darchen

Darpoche

An hour from Darchen, Darpoche is famous for the *Saka Dawa Festival*, celebrating the birth, Buddhahood, and death of Shakyamuni. This is held on the full moon day of April 15 in the Tibetan calendar. *Darpoche* originally meant '13m Pole with *Tar-choks*,' and each year on this day the pole is knocked down and then erected again with new *tar-choks* fluttering from it. This is, of course, all done manually.

Tibetans tell their fortunes from how the new pole stands: standing straight means good luck, leaning towards Mt. Kailash signifies bad luck, and leaning away from the mountain infers that caution should be taken. During the Cultural Revolution, the festival was banned, and the way to raise the pole properly was forgotten, resulting in failures or broken poles in attempts since then.

Chogu (Chuku) Gompa

Built in the 13th century, Chogu (Chuku) Gompa is a Drukpa Kagyupa monastery. The site was rebuilt during the late 1980s. A limestone image called Chuku Rinpoche at the main temple is regarded as the most important image at Mt. Kailash. You can stay at the lodge here that has dormitory beds for Y30 and hot water.

Tamdrin Dronkhang

Tamdrin Dronkhang is dedicated to Tamdrin (Hayagriva), a deity with the head of a horse. There is also a set of Milarepa's footprints nearby.

Drirapuk Gompa

Founded in the 13th century, Drirapuk Gompa is also a Drukpa Kagyupa monastery, and it was restored in 1986. *Drirapuk* means 'Cave of the Female Yak Horn,' and the shape of this is said to have come to the surface of the cave's roof. At the lodge here a bed in a 6-person room costs Y35. There is an additional Y3 charge for hot water.

Dolma La Pass

At 5,630m, Dolma La is the hardest point along the Mt. Kailash circuit.

Kandro Sanglam Pass

This is a secret pilgrimage path on which you can get to the eastern side of the mountain without crossing the Dolma La. Only pilgrims who have finished 12 circuits can take this short cut, and the Goddess Dakini keeps a watchful eye on this section of the route.

Zutrulpuk Gompa

Zutrulpuk Gompa is famous as the site of the fight between the Buddhist Milarepa and the Bonpo Naro Bonchung as they struggled for supremacy over the sacred mountain. During the 1st round, they decided to build a cave to find out who had stronger powers. Milarepa prepared the roof by chopping up a huge rock with his hands and then making it float in midair. Although Naro Bonchung was supposed to construct the walls, he was so overwhelmed by Milarepa's display that Milarepa had to complete the cave by himself, thus winning the contest. This is the cave of Zutrulpuk, and an image of Milarepa in the cave is believed to have been made by him before he died.

For the 2nd round, the challenge was to see who could fly to the peak of Mt. Kailash first. Riding on a drum, Naro Bonchung started out before dawn and reached the foot of the mountain before daybreak. However as the sun rose, Milarepa was transported by the sunlight and reached the summit in an instant.

Since then, the humiliated Bonpos have basically given up Mt. Kailash, and in its place they were offered Mt. Bonri, a smaller mountain to the east, north of Lake Manasarovar.

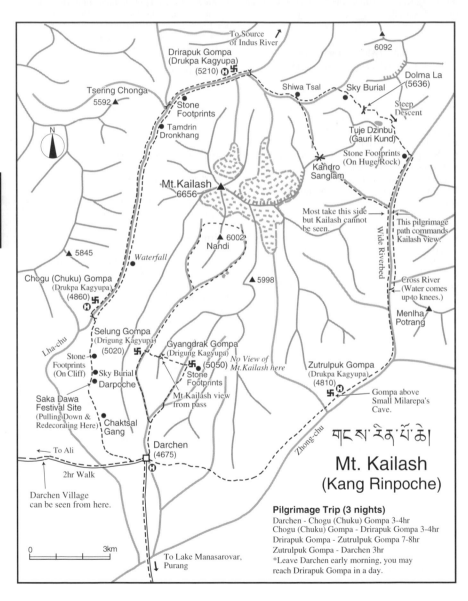

To Source of Indus River

6092

Drirapuk Gompa (Drukpa Kagyupa) (5210)

Dolma La (5636)

Shiwa Tsal   Sky Burial

Tsering Chonga 5592

Stone Footprints

Steep Descent

N

Tamdrin Dronkhang

Tuje Dzinbu (Gauri Kund)

Stone Footprints (On Huge Rock)

Kandro Sanglam

Mt.Kailash 6656

Most take this side but Kailash cannot be seen.

This pilgrimage path commands Kailash view.

5845

Waterfall

6002 Nandi

5998

Cross River (Water comes up to knees.)

Menlha Potrang

Chogu (Chuku) Gompa (Drukpa Kagyupa) (4860)

Selung Gompa (Driugung Kagyupa) (5020)

Gyangdrak Gompa (Drigung Kagyupa) (5050)

No View of Mt.Kailash here

Zutrulpuk Gompa (Drukpa Kagyupa) (4810)

Lha-chu

Stone Footprints (On Cliff)

Sky Burial

Darpoche

Stone Footprints

Mt.Kailash view from pass

Gompa above Small Milarepa's Cave.

Saka Dawa Festival Site (Pulling Down & Redecorating Here)

Chaktsal Gang

To Ali

Darchen (4675)

2hr Walk

Zhong-chu

གངས་རིན་པོ་ཆེ།

Darchen Village can be seen from here.

Mt. Kailash (Kang Rinpoche)

0   3km

To Lake Manasarovar, Purang

Pilgrimage Trip (3 nights)
Darchen - Chogu (Chuku) Gompa 3-4hr
Chogu (Chuku) Gompa - Drirapuk Gompa 3-4hr
Drirapuk Gompa - Zutrulpuk Gompa 7-8hr
Zutrulpuk Gompa - Darchen 3hr
*Leave Darchen early morning, you may reach Drirapuk Gompa in a day.

There is a guesthouse here, and a bed costs Y35. There is an additional charge of Y5 for hot water.

NANGKHOR (INNER PILGRIMAGE CIRCUIT)

Pilgrims who have made 12 (though the number can vary) circuits on the *Chikhor* (Outer Pilgrimage Circuit) are only then allowed to enter the *Nangkhor* (Inner Pilgrimage Circuit). You can try this route too, and there are 2 rebuilt monasteries belonging to the Drigung Kagyupa along the way.

Gyangdrak Gompa
Rebuilt in the 1980s, Gyangdrak Gompa is the largest monastery in the area. It is a branch of the Drigung Til Gompa to the north of Lhasa. Gyangdrak Gompa is said to have been constructed on the very site where Shenrab Miwoche first offered teachings of Bon, a couple of thousand years ago.

Selung Gompa
Selung Gompa is another recently rebuilt branch of Drigung Til Gompa. From the monastery, you can get a good view of the impressive southern face of the sacred mountain.

LAKE MANASAROVAR (MAPHAM YUTSO) (CLOSED)

Together with Mt. Kailash, the sacred lake is a pilgrimage site. *Mapham* means 'Unconquered' in Tibetan. Mahatma Gandhi's ashes were scattered in this lake. The freshwater lake is 30km to the south of Mt. Kailash.

There is a pilgrimage path around the lake, and a circuit is a little over 100km, taking 4-5 days to complete. Along the route there are 5 gompas where you can stay, though it is still advisable to bring a tent with you. You have to cross a number of rivers while making a circuit of the lake.

Lake Manasarovar Khora (Pilgrimage Circuit)
Chiu Gompa, 30km to the south of Darchen, is a good starting point for your circuit around the lake. Here is a sample schedule for a 4-day circuit.

Day 1: Chiu Gompa - Langbona Gompa
Day 2: Langbona Gompa - Seralung Gompa

Prostration, Mt. Kailash

Day 3: Seralung Gompa - Trugo Gompa
Day 4: Trugo Gompa - Chiu Gompa

*Traditional pilgrims start their trip from Hor (Hor Chu), at the north-east end of the lake, on the highway. To the north of Hor is the sacred mountain of Bon, Mt. Bonri, and Bonri Gompa.

Chiu Gompa
Chiu Gompa is a branch of Drirapuk Gompa at Mt. Kailash. Although located very far away, it belongs to the Drukpa Kagyupa Dingpoche Gompa in Dranang Valley near Tsethang. The name *Chiu* means 'Bird' in Tibetan.

Under the main temple there is a cave in which Guru Rinpoche is said to have lived for the 7 years before his death. To the south of the Ganga-chu (Channel) there are some hot springs.

Trugo Gompa
Rebuilt in 1984, Trugo Gompa is a Gelukpa monastery that is the most important and active among the 5 functioning monasteries at Lake Manasarovar. The monastery is also home to a young incarnate lama.

Hindus ritually bathe themselves at this point, and although Tibetans do this too, it is not to the same degree. There is a guesthouse that charges Y25 for a dormitory bed.

LANGA TSO (LAKE RAKSHAS TAL) (CLOSED)

Lake Manasarovar's western neighbor is the slightly smaller lake, Langa Tso (Rakshas Tal). Connected with Lake Manasarovar via a water channel, the Ganga-chu, Langa Tso is called the 'Lake of the Demon' or 'Lake of Poisoned Water,' although it has a beautiful surface. This provides a balance to Lake Manasarovar, but there is only a single gompa at Langa Tso, while there are 8 sites (5 have been rebuilt to date) at Lake Manasarovar. The reason for this imbalance is a mystery.

It is believed that when the level of the water flowing from Lake Manasarovar into Langa Tso through the Ganga-chu is high, this is a good omen. Although this channel has been dry for many years, water has been flowing again recently.

MEMO NANI (MT. NEMO NANYI)
(CLOSED)

Between Lake Manasarovar and Purang, Memo Nani (7,694m) is another sacred mountain known as *Gurla Mandhata* to Hindus.

SOURCES OF ASIA'S GREAT RIVERS
(CLOSED)

From ancient times, Tibetans and Indians alike have regarded Lake Manasarovar as the source of 4 mighty rivers. Tibetans give the names of animals to these sources to illustrate where each river flows from.

Mouth of the Horse .... Tamchok Khambab
    (Yarlung Tsangpo-Brahmaputra River)
Mouth of the Peacock .... Mapcha Khambab
    (Mapcha Tsangpo-Karnali/Ganges River)
Mouth of the Elephant ..... Langchen Khambab
    (Langchen Tsangpo-Sutlej River)
Mouth of the Lion .... Senge Khambab
    (Senge Tsangpo-Indus River)

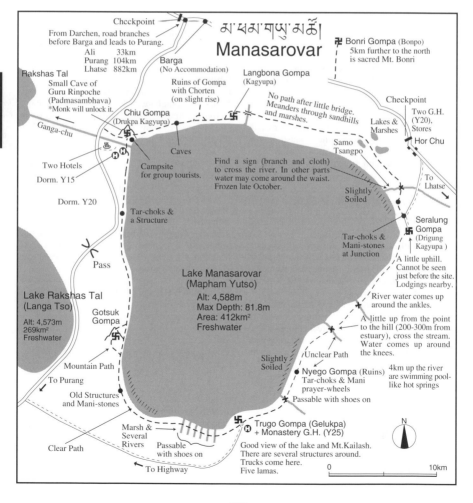

TO KAILASH

Checkpoint
From Darchen, road branches before Barga and leads to Purang.
Ali 33km
Purang 104km
Lhatse 882km

ম'ধম'মৃত্যু'মর্ক্ট
Manasarovar

Bonri Gompa (Bonpo)
5km further to the north is sacred Mt. Bonri

Barga (No Accommodation)
Langbona Gompa (Kagyupa)

Rakshas Tal
Small Cave of Guru Rinpoche (Padmasambhava) *Monk will unlock it.

Ruins of Gompa with Chorten (on slight rise)

No path after little bridge. Meanders through sandhills and marshes.

Checkpoint
Two G.H. (Y20), Stores

Chiu Gompa (Drukpa Kagyupa)

Ganga-chu

Caves

Lakes & Marshes

Samo Tsangpo

Hor Chu

Two Hotels
Dorm. Y15

Campsite for group tourists.

Find a sign (branch and cloth) to cross the river. In other parts water may come around the waist. Frozen late October.

To Lhatse

Slightly Soiled

Dorm. Y20

Tar-choks & a Structure

Seralung Gompa (Drigung Kagyupa)

Tar-choks & Mani-stones at Junction

A little uphill. Cannot be seen just before the site. Lodgings nearby.

Pass

Lake Manasarovar (Mapham Yutso)
Alt: 4,588m
Max Depth: 81.8m
Area: 412km²
Freshwater

River water comes up around the ankles.

Lake Rakshas Tal (Langa Tso)
Alt: 4,573m
269km²
Freshwater

Gotsuk Gompa

A little up from the point to the hill (200-300m from estuary), cross the stream. Water comes up around the knees.

Mountain Path
To Purang

Old Structures and Mani-stones

Slightly Soiled

Unclear Path

Nyego Gompa (Ruins)
Tar-choks & Mani prayer-wheels

Passable with shoes on

4km up the river are swimming pool-like hot springs

N

Marsh & Several Rivers

Clear Path

Passable with shoes on

Trugo Gompa (Gelukpa) + Monastery G.H. (Y25)

Good view of the lake and Mt.Kailash. There are several structures around. Trucks come here. Five lamas.

0   10km

To Highway

146

In fact, only the water of the Langchen Khambab can actually be traced back to the Lake Manasarovar, and the other rivers flow from different sources in the area.

Yarlung Tsangpo (Brahmaputra River)
Called 'Mouth of the Horse,' the source of the Yarlung Tsangpo (Brahmaputra River) is not found at Lake Manasarovar but to the east of the lake.

Langchen Tsangpo (Sutlej River)
Called 'Mouth of the Elephant,' the source of the Sutlej River is Langa Tso. This means that Lake Manasarovar could be regarded as the source, as the western lake is connected to Lake Manasarovar via the Ganga-chu.

Mapcha Tsangpo (Karnali/Ganges River)
Called 'Mouth of the Peacock,' the Karnali River, which later becomes the Ganges River, starts to the south of Lake Manasarovar.

Senge Tsangpo (Indus River)
The source of the river is to the north of Mt. Kailash. From Drirapuk Gompa, the journey takes about 3 days. Start from the gompa heading along the Tseti Valley to the north, and you will reach Tseti Lachen La pass (5,466m). After crossing it, head for Senge Phuk along the Indus River, and then go upstream until you reach the source.

BORDER CROSSING
PURANG - SIMIKOT (CLOSED)

Mt. Kailash is really close to western Nepal along an old trade route. The border between Simikot, Nepal and Purang (Taklakot), Tibet is open to pilgrims and group tourists. The situation for independent travelers is continually changing, and you should try to get the most recent information you can locally.

Purang to Simikot
Group tour members usually have no problem crossing the border. However, if you are an independent traveler, you are not allowed to obtain a Chinese exit stamp in your passport at the immigration office in Purang, although there have been reports to the contrary. If you are planning to enter Nepal without a Chinese exit stamp, here is one traveler's experience:

"On the Nepal side of the border there is a checkpoint at Yari. When I reported to the office and told the officer that I came from China, I was advised to go on to Muchu to get a trekking permit. The condition was that I had to be accompanied by a police officer from Muchu to Simikot and that I must pay 500NRs (US$8 or Y60) per day for the 4-day trip. (A 2,000NRs charge is levied even if you arrive in Simikot earlier.) At Muchu I then had to pay US$90 for the trekking permit and then continue under escort to Simikot. Along the way the policeman paid for the accommodation. You'll need to have a Nepalese visa, which can be issued in Lhasa, and these 30-day visas are valid for 6 months."

Day 1: Purang (3,800m) - Zher (Zhera) (3,720m)
  Flat.
Day 2: Zher - Yari (3,670m)
  Climbs 800m before crossing a pass.
Day 3: Yari - Muchu (2,920m)
  Gradually descends and then crosses the river.
Day 4: Muchu - Yalbang (2,890m)
  Cross the river once again.
Day 5: Yalbang - Tuling (2,270m)
  Descends slightly, though there's a lot of ups and downs.
Day 6: Tuling - Simikot (2,910m)
  Difficult to cross the pass on this section.

Simikot to Kathmandu
At Simikot there are hotels (lodges), restaurants, and stores. Prices here are 35NRs for *dal bhat* (lentil curry), 20NRs for fried noodles, 10NRs for *momo*, and 5NRs for tea.

For Nepalganj, it costs US$88 on a Royal Nepal Airline flight (5 flights a week). There is a student discount for those under 25 years old.

From Nepalganj to Kathmandu or Pokhara
*Kathmandu—There is a bus at 05:30 (177NRs). Also, 3 night buses leave between 15:00 and 18:00 (225NRs), and the trip takes 16 hours. There is also a daily flight to Kathmandu (US$99).
*Pokhara—There is a night bus, and the 16-hour trip costs 225NRs.

Simikot to Purang
At Kathmandu, get a trekking permit to the Humla Region (Simikot - Yari). A 7-day permit costs US$90. If you need more than a week, you have to pay US$15 per extra day. There is no guarantee that these will be issued to independent travelers. Another serious problem is that you may not be able to get a Chinese entry stamp at the Purang immigration office. Check the latest information on this situation before setting off. There are no problems for group tourists.

Day 1: Simikot (2,910m) - Tuling (2,270m)
  After going through a pass (3,200m), you descend about 900m down to Tuling.

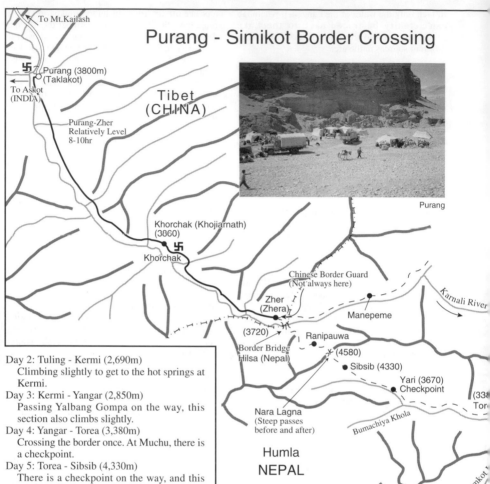

Purang - Simikot Border Crossing

To Mt.Kailash

卐 Purang (3800m)
(Taklakot)
To Askot
(INDIA)

**Tibet
(CHINA)**

Purang-Zher
Relatively Level
8-10hr

Purang

Khorchak (Khojiarnath)
(3060)
卐
Khorchak

Chinese Border Guard
(Not always here)

Zher
(Zhera)

Manepeme

Karnali River

(3720)

Ranipauwa

Border Bridge
Hilsa (Nepal)

(4580)

Sibsib (4330)

Yari (3670)
Checkpoint

(33
Tor

Nara Lagna
(Steep passes
before and after)

Bumachiya Khola

**Humla
NEPAL**

Tumkot

Day 2: Tuling - Kermi (2,690m)
Climbing slightly to get to the hot springs at
Kermi.

Day 3: Kermi - Yangar (2,850m)
Passing Yalbang Gompa on the way, this
section also climbs slightly.

Day 4: Yangar - Torea (3,380m)
Crossing the border once. At Muchu, there is
a checkpoint.

Day 5: Torea - Sibsib (4,330m)
There is a checkpoint on the way, and this
section climbs around 1,000m from Torea
(3,380m) to Sibsib.

Day 6: Sibsib - Purang (3,800m)
This section drops 800m after crossing a high
pass (4,580m) down to a flat road.

Purang (Pulan)

Called *Taklakot* in Nepalese, Purang, to the south
of Gurla Mandhata, is a center for trade between
Tibet and Nepal, and the Mapcha Tsangpo (Karnali
River) flows through the town. For the Nepalese
and Indians, Purang is a gateway for pilgrimages
to Mt. Kailash. On the hill, west of the town center,
are Simbiling Gompa and the old Purang Palace.
(See page 150.)

From Darchen, hitch a lift on a pilgrimage truck
or other vehicle to get to Purang. There is a
checkpoint where the road from Darchen meets the

one to Barga. Further on from Barga there is another
checkpoint just before you reach Hor Chu and
another at the tent market, north of Purang. With a
travel permit, you'll have no problem. For Lake
Manasarovar, Darchen, and surrounding areas, this
is the hitching point.

Accommodation & Restaurants

The *Pulan Binguan* has rooms for Y175, though
for an independent traveler you may get a bed for
as little as Y40.

The *Government Guesthouse* charges Y10 for
dormitory beds, and the *People's Armed Police
Guesthouse* charges Y15.

There are a number of Chinese, Tibetan, and
Nepalese restaurants in the town. You can buy

mineral water at the stores here.

Changing Money
You can change only cash at the bank in Purang. You may also be able to change cash with traders here, but their rates will be a little lower.

THE GUGE RUINS (CLOSED)

When King Langdarma, the 9th century oppressor of Buddhism in central Tibet, was assassinated, Tibet broke up into small rival fiefdoms, and Namde Osung, one of his sons, established the kingdom of Guge in Western Tibet.

Yeshe-o, Guge King during the 10th century, was an enthusiastic advocate of reviving Buddhism. He sent Rinchen Zangpo, a translator and monk, to India and invited a number of Indian scholars to Tibet. Yeshe-o is also well known for a story about his kidnapping by a Turkish army. He made his people use his ransom to pay to bring the Indian scholar, Atisha, to the country, thus sacrificing himself for his beliefs.

Entering Tibet in 1042, Atisha stayed at Toling, the capital of Guge in those days, and then spread Buddhism across Tibet. Rinchen Zangpo is believed to have built 108 temples in Western Tibet, Ladakh, Lahaul, and Spiti, after

coming back from India. Toling Gompa is one of his works.

The kingdom of Guge had 2 centers, Toling and Tsaparang. Both capitals prospered for 5 centuries or so. However, Tsaparang was suddenly abandoned in 1650, perhaps due to changes in the underground water supply. Toling functioned as the religious center until 1960. During the Cultural Revolution, Red Guards (Hongweibing) even bothered to come to this remote region just to destroy the temples at Toling.

In the realm of Buddhist art history, both old capitals are important places, as there are many relatively well-preserved examples of wall paintings in the Guge-style, influenced by Nepalese and Kashmiri arts. The landscape here is overwhelming, and some describe the Guge area as a 'Hundred times as splendid as the Grand Canyon.'

TSAMDA (ZHADA) (CLOSED)

This Chinese-built town is in the place originally called Toling. The north-south main street has government buildings along the southern half and stores, restaurants, Khampa tent stores, Toling Gompa, and some chortens along the northern half. With a permit obtained in Ali, you should have no problems hitching a lift, etc.

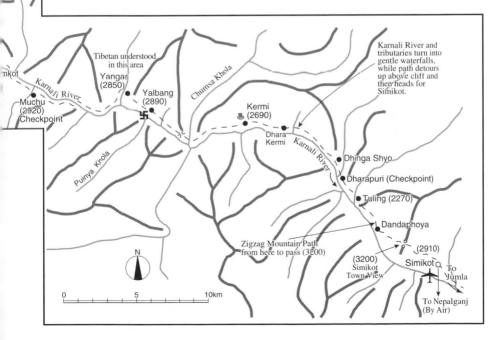

Access

From Ali to Tsamda, a good option is to try to catch a lift on a China Post truck. There is an Ali to Tsamda truck every Saturday, and it returns from Tsamda the day after. The 15-hour trip costs Y100. You can also charter a Land Cruiser.

Accommodation

The *People's Armed Police Guesthouse* charges Y50 for a bed in a 4-person room. There are no showers, but hot water is available.

The *Tuolin Binguan* is busy with tour groups and members of excavation teams. All the rooms here cost more than Y80.

Toling Gompa

Rinchen Zangpo founded Toling Gompa in the early 11th century. The most popular monk and translator in Western Tibet, Rinchen Zangpo studied Buddhism in India for 17 years and upon his return made efforts to translate all the Sanskrit script *sutras* into Tibetan.

At Toling, there used to be 6 temples, but now there are only Lhakhang Marpo (Red Temple), Lhakhang Karpo (White Temple), and the Mandala Chapel of Yeshe-o. You are only allowed into Lhakhang Marpo and Lhakhang Karpo, and admission is Y105. You may be able to negotiate the camera fee down to Y300. There has been an excellent photographic collection of this area's artwork already published. A flashlight is an absolute must.

Lhakhang Marpo (Red Temple)

This was the largest temple of the 6 at Toling, and the number and quality of the wall paintings here are overwhelming. Some say that they are Guge-style dating from the 13th and 14th centuries while another theory says that they date from the 15th and 16th centuries. The temple now houses 4 monks.

Lhakhang Karpo (White Temple)

Restoration work on the temple is quite recent. Wall paintings here depict images from the Gelukpa, Drigung Kagyupa, and other schools. These relatively new pieces are said to date from the 16th century.

Mandala Chapel of Yeshe-o

The chapel occupies the western half of the gompa. The central hall is surrounded by corridors, and outside of these are chapels and shrines. This layout forms a 3-dimensional *mandala*. The site is not open to the public at present, as it is being excavated.

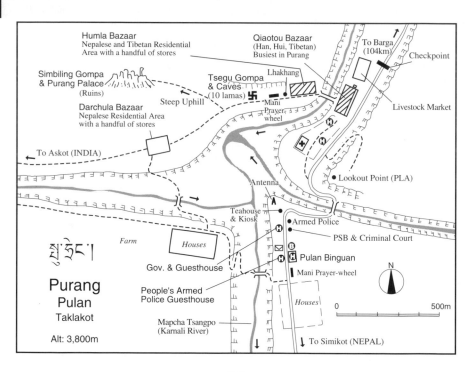

Chortens

Along the edge of the site, to the north of Toling Gompa, there are numerous chortens arranged in rows. Originally these stupas were collected together in groups of 108.

Southern Ruins

On the southern hillside along the road to Tsaparang, there are a number of caves and the remains of buildings. The site is believed to have been the summer residence for the monks at Toling.

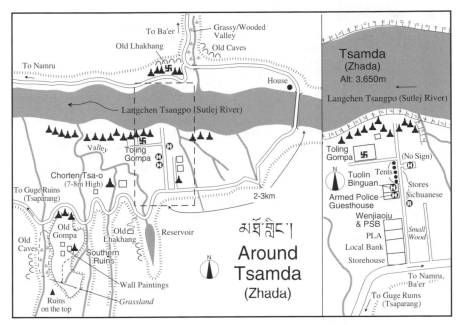

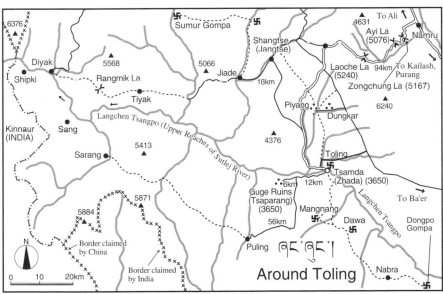

Chorten Tsa-o

Also called the Chorten of Yeshe-o, this huge stupa is 7-8m tall and is famous enough to be the most photographed structure at Toling.

TSAPARANG (CLOSED)

The remains at Tsaparang are also important to the history of Buddhist art. The different styles of the wall paintings here were influenced by the changes in the political situation at the time. They are divided roughly as follows:

11th Century—The oldest are in the Kashmiri-style that was popular in Western Tibet and Ladakh during this period. These are similar to those of Alchi Gompa in Ladakh and Tabo Gompa in Spiti.

14th & 15th Century—Similar to the Sakyapa-style that was heavily influenced by the Newar-style from Nepal, these are reminiscent of the wall paintings at Gyantse Kumbum (Pelkhor Chorten).

17th Century—With the ascendancy of the Gelukpa in central Tibet, the Guge Kingdom started to decline. The art became more Tibetan in style while keeping Indian and Nepalese influences. Finally, it disappeared.

Archeologists are now excavating the Tsaparang ruins. Six temples and a citadel are the only ones open to visitors. There are also a number of ruins around the main site.

Visit Arrangements (At Tsamda)

Go to the PSB office and have an officer write a pass approval document. These cost Y10, and a travel permit is required.

After receiving the approval, take it to the *Culture and Education Bureau* (Wenjiaoju) on the 2nd floor of the northern building. The pass costs Y360 if you want one that covers entering the buildings or Y120 for one that just allows you access to the site. Without a pass, you will not be able to enter the buildings, as the chapels are kept locked. You should also make sure that your pass is valid for enough days, as transport from Toling to Tsaparang can be difficult to arrange.

Tsamda to Tsaparang

The easiest way to complete this trip is by

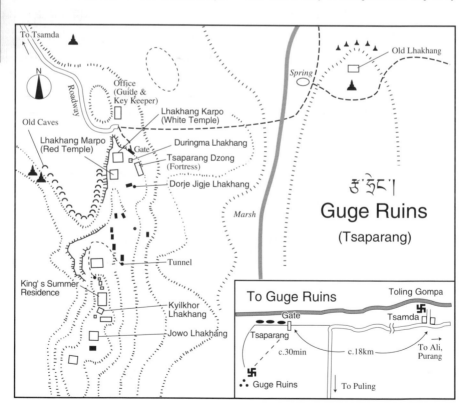

ཙ་རྩིང་།

Guge Ruins

(Tsaparang)

Labels on map: To Tsamda · Old Lhakhang · Spring · N · Roadway · Office (Guide & Key Keeper) · Old Caves · Lhakhang Karpo (White Temple) · Lhakhang Marpo (Red Temple) · Gate · Duringma Lhakhang · Tsaparang Dzong (Fortress) · Dorje Jigje Lhakhang · Marsh · Tunnel · King's Summer Residence · Kyilkhor Lhakhang · Jowo Lhakhang

Inset map: To Guge Ruins · Toling Gompa · Gate · Tsamda · Tsaparang · c.30min · c.18km · To Ali, Purang · Guge Ruins · To Puling chartering a Land Cruiser at the Tuolin Binguan (Hotel). You could also rent a horse. It is hard to hitch lifts on this route, as there is little traffic.

Walking the 20km to the site takes nearly 8 hours. Bringing your own food and water is a must. With little shade, it is hot during the summer, and it is freezing cold during the rest of year.

Accommodation & Restaurants
At Tsaparang there is no accommodation, and many visitors turn this into a day trip. There is a place where you can camp, and the excavation staff and workers live at the site. There is a village, but this has neither a restaurant nor a store.

Visit to the Ruins
*You can get to the entrance of the ruins by car. Traveling on foot from Tsaparang Village takes about half an hour. Go up the hill on the right, to the south, just after the gate at the eastern end of the village.
*Before you reach the gate to the ruins, there is an office on the left where you will find a guide and the gate keeper. On presenting your pass, the guide must escort you around the site. You should bring a flashlight with you.

Starting on the northern side, there are 4 lhakhangs. Then, you are taken up through a tunnel, and you can see the fortress and palace on the southern side.

Lhakhang Karpo (White Temple)
This is the white building on the right-hand side after the gate. This is the highlight of your visit with wall paintings that are considered the oldest at Tsaparang. On either side of the entrance tower stand 5m-high, wrathful, guardian deities. The red one on the left is Tamdrin (Hayagriva), the horse-headed deity, and the blue one on the right is Chakna Dorje (Vajrapani).

Duringma Lhakhang
This is a small temple just after the gate. The Buddhist paintings here date from around the 16th century.

Lhakhang Marpo (Red Temple)
The wall paintings in this lhakhang are believed to date from around 1630, just before the Guge Kingdom began to decline. Only the pedestal that used to support the large central statue of Buddha remains.

Dorje Jigje Lhakhang (Vajrabhairava Temple)
The structure must have been dedicated to Dorje Jigje (Vajrabhairava), but the image has not survived. There are wall paintings depicting Tsongkhapa, the founder of Gelukpa, and other

Tsaparang

religious figures. After passing through some other groups of ruins, go up the steep tunnel stairs to reach the top of the hill.

King's Summer Residence
This white building on the hill has nothing special to see, but you can admire the view.

Kyilkhor Lhakhang (Demchok Mandala Shrine)
The lhakhang is home to a 3-dimensional *mandala* depicting the meditational deity, Demchok (Cakrasamvara).

DUNGKAR & PIYANG (CLOSED)

Heading north on the way from Toling to Namru, you will reach Piyang and then a fork in the trail with a branch going of to the east. This leads to Dungkar Village.

The area was thrust into the limelight in 1992 when a large number of old cave temples were discovered near the villages of Dungkar and Piyang, 2km to the west. There are over 2,000 caves and a total of 4,000 to 5,000 people are believed to have lived here. Some of the Buddhist wall paintings at Dungkar are reminiscent of the caves at Dunhuang on the ancient Silk Road.

Both ruins are presently under excavation, and the surrounding area promises to yield more cave temple discoveries. This major find has highlighted the early importance of this upper part of the Sutlej River basin.

TIRTHAPURI (CLOSED)

Tirthapuri is another important sacred place, 10km to the south-west of Montser. It is said that neither Hindus nor Buddhists feel that a pilgrimage to Mt. Kailash and Lake Manasarovar is complete without visiting Tirthapuri. It is also famous for the Peldung

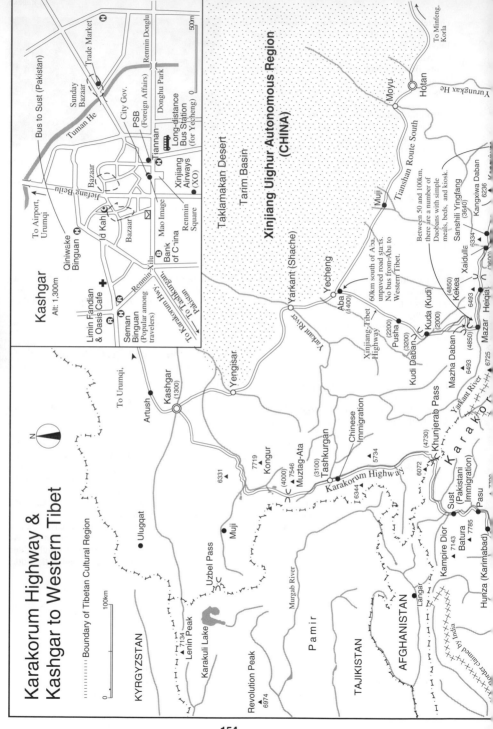

Karakorum Highway &
Kashgar to Western Tibet

N

KYRGYZSTAN

0   100km

.... Boundary of Tibetan Cultural Region

To Urumqi

Artush

Kashgar
(1300)

Uluqqat

Lenin Peak
▲7134

Karakuli Lake

Uzbel Pass

Revolution Peak
▲6974

6331 ▲

7719
Kongur ▲

Muji ●

7546 ▲
Muztag-Ata
(4000)

Murgab River

P a m i r

TAJIKISTAN

AFGHANISTAN

Langar

Yengisar

Tashkurgan
(3100)

Chinese
Immigration

Karakorum Highway

6344 ▲

5734

Khunjerab Pass
(4730)

6072 ▲

Sust
(Pakistani)
Immigration

Kampire Dior
7143 ▲
Batura
▲ 7785

Hunza (Karimabad)

Pasu

K a r a k o r u m

Yarkant River

border claimed by India

Kashgar
Alt: 1,300m

To Airport,
Urumqi

Qiniwake
Binguan

Id Kah

Bazaar

Seman
Binguan
(Popular among
travelers)

Liman Fandian
& Oasis Cafe

Bus to Sust (Pakistan)

Sunday
Bazaar

Tuman He

Trade Market

Bazaar

Jiefang Beilu

City Gov.

PSB
(Foreign Affairs)

Tiannan

Long-distance
Bus Station
(for Yecheng)

Renmin Donglu

Donghu Park

Xinjiang
Airways
(XO)

Mao Image
Renmin
Square

Bank
of China

Bank of China

To Karakorum Hwy.

Renmin Xilu.

To Tashkurgan.

500m

Xinjiang Uighur Autonomous Region
(CHINA)

Taklamakan Desert

Tarim Basin

To Minfeng,
Korla

Moyu

Hotan

Yurungkax He

Muji ●

Tianshan Route South

Sanshili Yingfang
(3640)

Kangxiwa Daban
6236 ▲

Xaidulla
6334 ▲
3600

Kekea
(4850)

6493 ▲

Mazar
(4850)

Heiqia

6493 ▲

6725 ▲

Yarkant River

Between 50 and 100km,
there are a number of
Daofbans with simple
meals, beds, and kiosk.

Yecheng

Aba
(1400)

60km south of Aba,
unpaved road starts.
No bus from Aba to
Western Tibet.

Xinjiang-Tibet
Highway
(2200)

Pusha
(3200)

Kuda (Kudi)
(2000)

Kudi Daban

Mazha Daban

Yarkant (Shache)

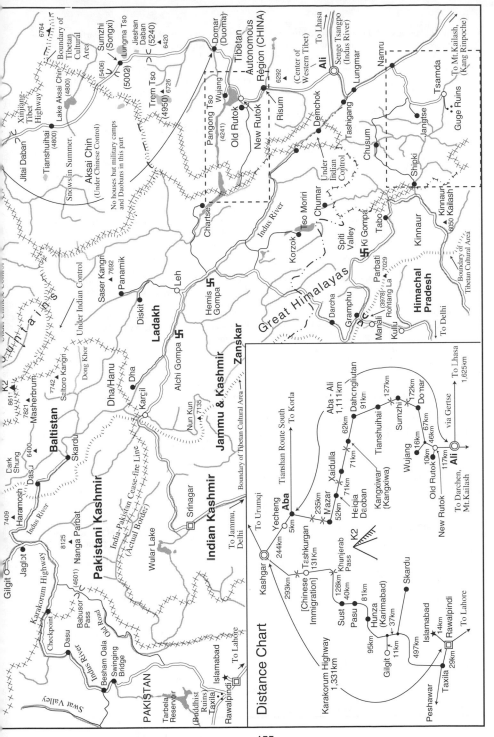

6764

Boundary of
Tibetan
Cultural
Area

Sumzhi
(Songxi)

Lungma Tso

Jieshan
Daban (5240)

6420

Domar
(Duoma)

Tibetan
Autonomous
Region (CHINA)

To Lhasa

Senge Tsangpo
(Indus River)

To Mt.Kailash,
(Kang Rinpoche)

Xinjiang-
Tibet
Highway

Lake Aksai Chin
(4800)

(5406)

(5002)

Trem Tso
(4950)

6726

Pangong Tso
(4241)

Wujang

Old Rutok

New Rutok

Risum

6292

(Center of
Western Tibet)

Ali

Lungmar

Namru

Tsamda

Guge
Ruins

Tianshuihai
(4800)

Aksai Chin
(Under Chinese Control)

Snows in Summer.

No houses but military camps
and Daobans in this part

Demchok

Tashigang

Jangtse

Jitai Daban

Chartse

Tso Moriri

Chumar

Chusum

Shipki

Kinnaur
Kailash

6050

Boundary of
Tibetan Cultural Area

Indus River

Korzok

Spiti
Valley

Ki Gompa

Tabo

Kinnaur

Under
Indian
Control

Under Indian Control

Saser Kangri
7692

Panamik

Leh

Hemis
Gompa

Great Himalayas

Parbati
7029

Himachal
Pradesh

Darcha

Gramphu

Manali
(3978)

Rohtang La

To Delhi

Kullu

To Lhasa

Dong Khor

Diskit

Ladakh

Alchi Gompa

Zanskar

K2
861

7821

7742

Seltoro Kangri

Dha

Karçil

Nun Kun
7135

Masherbrum

Dha/Hanu

Jammu & Kashmir

Boundary of Tibetan Cultural Area

Baltistan

Dark
Shung

Das

6400

Skardu

India-Pakistan Cease-fire Line

Indian Kashmir

To Jammu,
Delhi

7409

Haramosh

Indus River

Pakistani Kashmir

India-Pakistan Cease-fire Line
(Actual Border)

Srinagar

Wular Lake

Nanga Parbat
8125

(4601)

Gilgit

Karakorum Highway

Checkpoint

Babusor
Pass

Old Road

Dasu

Besham Oala

Swinging
Bridge

Indus River

Swat Valley

PAKISTAN

Tarbela
Reservoir

Buddhist
Ruins

Taxila

Islamabad

Rawalpindi

To Lahore

Distance Chart

To Urumqi

To Korla

Tianshan Route South

To Kashgar

Yecheng

5km

244km

Aba

235km

Mazar

Xaidulla

62km

Heiqia
Deoban

52km

71km

71km

71km

Kangxiwar
(Kangxiwa)

Tianshuihai

Aba - Ali
1,111km

Dahcngliutan

91km

127km

Sumzhi

72km

Do nar

16km

67km

46km

Wujang

10km

Old Rutok

46km

117km

Ali

To Darchen,
Mt.Kailash

via Gertse

To Lhasa
1,625km

New Rutok

Kashgar

293km

[Chinese
Immigration]

Tashkurgan

131km

Khunjerab
Pass

128km

Sust

40km

Pasu

81km

Hunza
(Karimabad)

37km

K2

Skardu

95km

Gilgit

11km

497km

Islamabad

14km

Rawalpindi

To Lahore

Karakorum Highway
1,331km

Peshawar

Taxila

29km

155

Chutsen, hot springs, which are believed to have healing power, and there are hot water geysers in the area. With the blue sky framing them, the innumerable *tar-choks* that decorate the valley are a sight to see.

Pilgrims to Tirthapuri Gompa come to the hot springs and surrounding area in search of a powdered residue called *Ringsel*. Authentic *Ringsel* is believed to be an incredibly effective medicine that lays dormant in the body until sickness or injury befalls the person. Once the *Ringsel* has cured everything, it then dissipates. If you believe in these mystical healing powers, the best time to try it is on a full moon day. You may come across hawkers selling the powder here.

Until 1941, when the Kazakhs invaded the area, Tirthapuri Gompa belonged to Hemis Gompa in Ladakh. There are footprints here made by Guru Rinpoche and his partner, Yeshe Tsogyal.

At Montser there are guesthouses and restaurants. Between Montser and Tirthapuri it takes about 3 hours on foot, including a short rest, and the path is easy to follow.

Khyunglung

At the fork in the road about 8km west of Montser, take the left-hand road, to the south, and you will reach Tirthapuri. The other road leads you the 15km to Gurugam Gompa, the only Bon monastery in Western Tibet.

A further 10km down the Senge Tsangpo is Khyunglung (Garuda Valley) on its northern side.

The site is said to be the ruins of the earliest city in Tibet, and Khyunglung is regarded as the ancient capital of Zhangzhung, the oldest known Tibetan kingdom, dating from as early as 2000 B.C. The city was home to thousands of people, and there is still a small village here now.

Namde Osung, the son of the 9th century anti-Buddhist King Langdarma, was himself a Buddhist, and when he fled to Ngari, he divided the region into 3 kingdoms: Guge, Rutok, and Purang. Then he let his 3 sons each govern one of the regions. Rutok became the capital of Northern Ngari, and later, Rutok strengthened its ties with Ladakh.

The small town is 127km to the north of Ali and about 10km to the west off the Xinjiang-Tibet Highway. There is nothing special in the town, but compared to other stops on the Xinjiang-Tibet Highway, New Rutok is relatively well stocked with restaurants and stores.

In 1985 a large number of sculptures were discovered in the area. These were found in roughly 3 groups:

*Rimotang—Located 1.5km to the south-east of Risum, on the Xinjiang-Tibet Highway. Risum is 40km to the south of New Rutok.
*Luri Langkar—12km to the west of Old Rutok.
    *Karke Sang—25km to the south of Domar (Duoma).

All the statues have been dated from before the 7th century, and thus prior to the diffusion of Buddhism. There are many images of yak, sheep, the sun and moon, and the *swastika*.

KASHGAR TO MT. KAILASH (XINJIANG-TIBET HIGHWAY)
(CLOSED)

Among the routes to Mt. Kailash, this is the most difficult, as it grazes the Taklamakan Desert and crosses the Kunlun mountain range.

At Kashgar, take a bus to the open town of Yecheng (*Karghalik* in Uighur). Hitching a lift from Aba, to the south of Yecheng, gets you started on your journey to the sacred mountain.

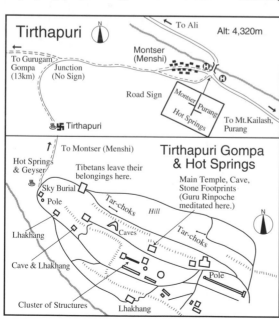

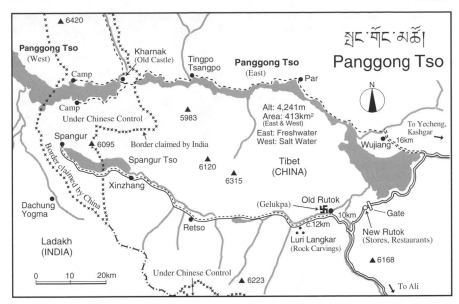

ཤྱང་གོང་མཚོ།

Panggong Tso

Kashgar
This Uighur town is a real oasis on the Tianshan Route South section of the Silk Road.

Access
At the bus station in Urumqi there are more than 10 buses to Kashgar each day. Many of the sleeping berth buses leave at 18:00, and the trip takes 35 hours. These sleeping berth buses cost Y440, or you can pay Y230 for an ordinary bus. There is also a daily flight departing in the evening for Y1,220.

Accommodation & Restaurants
A popular choice among backpackers, the *Seman Binguan* is a half-hour walk to the north-west of the long distance bus station. Dormitory beds cost Y15, and doubles go for Y140-280. If you prefer a suite of rooms, these cost Y500 or Y800. Hot showers are available. At the No.3 building across the street, there are double rooms for Y60 and triples for Y90.

The *Qiniwake Binguan* has beds in triples for Y30, and for Y25 you get a bed in a 4-person room. Single rooms cost Y120, and doubles are Y180 and Y220. This hotel is popular for Pakistani merchants and traders traveling through the area.

The *Tiannan Fandian* is conveniently located opposite the long-distance bus station, and you can buy bus tickets to Yecheng here. There are dormitory beds for Y16 and double rooms for Y30, Y60, and Y90.

The *Oasis Cafe* (Limin Fandian) is opposite Seman Binguan and serves Western and Chinese meals. You can get up-to-date travel information here.

Sust (Pakistan) to Kashgar
The Karakorum Highway is also an attractive route. It starts at Gilgit in the northern mountains of Pakistan and finishes at Kashgar going via Hunza and the Khunjerab Pass.

There are daily buses, except during the winter, that make an overnight stay at Tashkurgan (Chinese Immigration), and the bus trip arrives the following day. Officially, the service is available between May 1 and October 31, but the period is sometimes stretched from mid-April to late December. You can obtain a Chinese visa in Islamabad or New Delhi, but most of the visas issued in these cities are only valid for a month.

From Kashgar to Pakistan, you may be able to obtain a 7-day transit visa in Sust. This service is changeable, and you should check recent information before you decide upon this option.

Kashgar to Ali
Kashgar to Yecheng (Karghalik) - There are several buses leaving the long distance bus station in Kashgar each day, and the 6-hour trip costs Y37.5 for foreign passengers.

Yecheng to Aba (3-4km) - There are a number of minibuses from Yecheng for Aba, a hitchhiking point for Ali. These leave from an area next to the bus station, and the 15-minute trip costs Y2.5. If locals don't understand your pronunciation of Aba, try *Linggongli*.

Aba Town - The Aba PSB officers are said to regularly check the accommodation and garage at the truck stop at the end of town. Some foreigners have reportedly been caught here. There are a lot of trucks during the daytime, but drivers don't seem to stay here. A double room at the *88 Hotel* costs Y25. There are no showers, and the toilet is outside. There are a lot of restaurants in town.

Hitchhiking from Aba - Most trucks to Ali leave at 07:00-09:00. There are also a few that depart around noon or in the evening. Approximately 10 trucks leave in this direction each day, but many drivers refuse to give foreigners a lift. They are worried about possible security checks even though there are no permanent checkpoints along the way. It is also possible to hitch lifts from army trucks along this section of the route.

For a lift straight through to Ali from Aba, drivers ask for Y500-600, and it is difficult to negotiate a better deal. The trip to Ali usually takes 3 nights, but make sure that you are in the cab as it gets bitterly cold.

Aba to Mazar [237km] - This section takes up to 11 hours from Aba (1,400m) by truck. You cross 2 high passes, Kudi Daban (3,200m) and Mazha Daban (4,850m) on the way. At Kuda (Kudi, 2,000m) there are only a couple of restaurants to choose from, and the ones in Mazar are expensive.

Xinjiang-Tibet Highway

Mazar to Dahongliutan [256km] - From Mazar (3,790m) it takes around 9 hours by truck. At Xaidulla there is only a *Daoban* (Road Maintenance Depot). On the northern side of the river, the old-looking fortress is actually a relatively new structure built during the Kuomintang (Nationalists) Government period. Another 20 minutes further on is Sanshili Yingfang (3,640m), where there is a People's Liberation Army (PLA) base. There are also a number of small restaurants here. Kangxiwa Daban (4,240m) is the next pass, and this is just a gentle climb. At Kangxiwar (Kangxiwa) there are only some ruins. Dahongliutan (4,200m) functions basically as a truck station with an army facility and some restaurants.

Dahongliutan to New Rutok [503km]— The trip takes 16-18 hours by truck. About an hour and a half from Dahongliutan, you will cross the Jitai Daban pass and then reach the ruins at Quanshuigou. Here the road branches off to the interior of Aksai Chin. At Sumzhi (Songxi, 5,000m) there are a handful of small restaurants. You then cross the highest pass on the Xinjiang-Tibet Highway, Jieshan Daban (5,240m), with its fluttering *tar-choks* letting you know that you have finally arrived in Tibet. At Domar (Duoma, 4,450m) there are a number of restaurants. You will also start seeing chortens and *mani* temples here. Roughly 2.5 hours later, Panggong Tso comes into view to the west. There is a gate before you reach New Rutok (4,250m), and it is about 5 minutes beyond this to the town. New Rutok has a number of restaurants and numerous government and military facilities.

New Rutok to Ali (Shiquanhe) [117km]—This section takes over 3 hours by truck. You pass through Risum (Risong) on the way, but there are only a few buildings and little else.

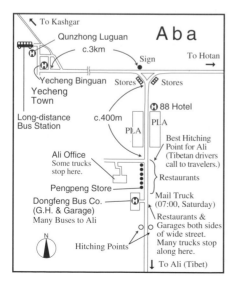

158

KONGPO & CHAMDO

ཀོང་པོ་དང་ཆབ་མདོ།

Eastern Part of TAR

The Kongpo region covers an area along the Sichuan-Tibet Highway South connecting Lhasa and Sichuan. The districts of Kongpo Gyamda, Nyangtri (Nyingtri or Linzhi), and the area surrounding Mt. Namcha Barwa all lie within this region. The Nyangtri (Linzhi) Prefecture, (Chinese Administrative Division), contains nearly the entire Kongpo region. The Yarlung Tsangpo flows from west to east until it reaches *Kongpo Chulak*, which means 'Where the Water Disappears.' Here it makes a sharp 180 degree turn and then winds its way southward, becoming the Brahmaputra River.

Unlike most parts of Tibet, the altitude in this area gets down as low as 3,000m, and due to the many passes through the Himalayan range, the weather system here is influenced by the monsoon. There is a lot of rainfall here, which waters the lush forests that blanket the region and keep the Kongpo climate mild. The people here wear poncho-like outer clothes that are totally different from the *Chubas* worn throughout Central Tibet, making them conspicuous even in Lhasa.

Highlights in the Kongpo region include the Bonpo's sacred peak, Mt. Bonri, the forests around Nyangtri, the sacred lake of Basong Tso (where the spirit of a Tibetan hero lives), Mt. Namcha Barwa, and visits to the Monpa, Lhopa, and Tengpa villages.

Unfortunately the area is closed, but it is possible to visit a number of places if you arrange a car through a travel agency in Lhasa, etc. Kongpo is a scenic area with a comfortable atmosphere, but the area was once used as a penal colony by the Lhasa government. Although this green land is the kind of place that most Tibetans would usually love, Kongpo carries an image of an undeveloped, ominous, and terrifying place for those living in central Tibet. Many Tibetans still say: "Are you going to Kongpo? You should be careful with the food. Don't let them poison you!" One Kongpo tradition that is said to have survived is the sacrificing of a stranger to drive out an evil spirit, and an unwitting traveler could be the perfect candidate. An invitation to share a meal could be dangerous, as the poison supposedly has no visible

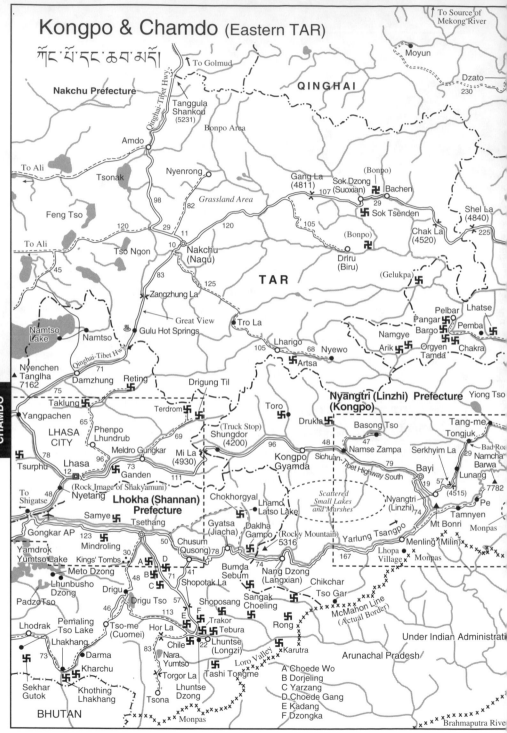

Kongpo & Chamdo (Eastern TAR)

ཀོང་པོ་དང་ཆབ་མདོ།

To Source of
Mekong River

To Golmud

Nakchu Prefecture

QINGHAI

Moyun

Dzato
230

Tanggula
Shankou
(5231)

Amdo

Bonpo Area

Tsonak

Nyenrong

(Bonpo)

Gang La
(4811)   Sok Dzong   Bachen
107   (Suoxian)
29

Shel La
(4840)

To Ali

Feng Tso

98   Grassland Area   Sok Tsenden

82

120   29   11   120   105   Chak La
10   (Bonpo)   (4520)   225

To Ali   Tso Ngon   Nakchu
45   (Naqu)   Driru
(Biru)

T A R

(Gelukpa)

83   125

Zangzhung La   Pelbar   Lhatse

Great View   Pangar   Bargo   Pemba
Gulu Hot Springs   Tro La   Namgye   Orgyen
Namtso   Lharigo 68 Nyewo   Arik   Tamda   Chakra
Lake   Namtso   105   Artsa

Nyenchen   Reting   Drigung Til
Tanglha   Toro   **Nyangtri (Linzhi) Prefecture**   Yiong Tso
7162   Damzhung   **(Kongpo)**
75   Drukla   Basong Tso   Tang-me
Taklung   Terdrom   Tongjuk
Yangpachen   (Truck Stop)   Namse Zampa   Serkhyim La   Bad Roa
65   Phenpo   Shungdor   96   48   47   29 Namcha
LHASA   Lhundrub   69   (4200)   Sichuan   79   Bayi   Barwa
CITY   Kongpo   Tibet Highway South   57   Lunang
78   Meldro Gungkar   Mi La   Gyamda   19   7782
Tsurphu Lhasa   96   73 (4930)   (4515)
12   Ganden 111   Nyangtri
(Rock Image of Shakyamuni)   Chokhorgyal   (Linzhi)   Pe
To   Nyetang   **Lhokha (Shannan)**   Lhamo   Scattered   74   Tamnyen
Shigatse 48   **Prefecture**   Latso Lake Small Lakes   Mt Bonri
Samye   Tsethang   Gyatsa   Daklha   and Marshes   Monpas
Gongkar AP 123   (Jiacha) Gampo (Rocky Mountain) Yarlung Tsangpo   Menling (Milin)
Yamdrok   Mindroling   50 Chusum   5316   167   Lhopa   Monpas
Yumtso Lake Kings' Tombs   30   (Qusong) 78   Village
Meto Dzong   A D 41   Bumda   Nang Dzong
Lhunbusho   48 B 71   Sebum   (Langxian) Chikchar
Dzong   Drigu   C   Shopotak La   Sangak   Tso Gar
Padzo Tso   Drigu Tso 57   Shoposang   Choeling
46   113 F   Rong   McMahon Line
Lhodrak   Pemaling   Trakor   (Actual Border)
Tso Lake Tso-me   Hor La   Tebura   Arunachal Pradesh
Lhakhang   (Cuomei)   Lhuntse   Karutra
Darma   83   Chile 22   (Longzi)   **Under Indian Administratic**
73   Nara   Loro Valley
Kharchu   Yumtso Tashi Tongme
Sekhar   Torgor La Lhuntse
Gutok   Khothing   Dzong   Monpas
Lhakhang
BHUTAN   Tsona   Monpas   Brahmaputra Rive

A Choede Wo
B Dorjeling
C Yarzang
D Choede Gang
E Kadang
F Dzongka

120

Phenpo
Lhundrub

Qinghai-Tibet Hwy

Qinghai-Tibet Hwy

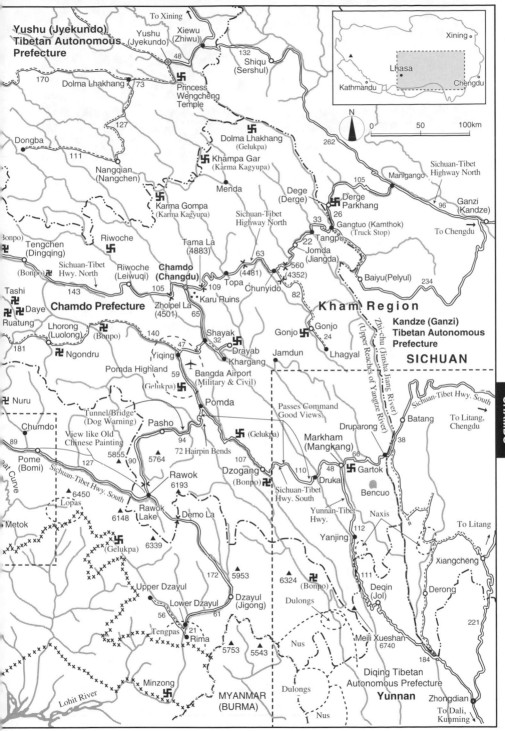

To Xining

Yushu (Jyekundo)
Tibetan Autonomous
Prefecture

Yushu (Jyekundo)　Xiewu (Zhiwu)

48　　132　Shiqu (Sershul)

170　Dolma Lhakhang　73

Princess Wengcheng Temple

127

Dongba

111　Nangqian (Nangchen)

Dolma Lhakhang (Gelukpa)

Khampa Gar (Karma Kagyupa)

Menda

262

Sichuan-Tibet Highway North

Manigango

105

Dege (Derge)　Derge Parkhang

33　26　Gangtuo (Kamthok) (Truck Stop)

Ganzi (Kandze)

96

To Chengdu

(Bonpo)
Tengchen (Dingqing)

Riwoche

Karma Gompa (Karma Kagyupa)

Sichuan-Tibet Highway North

Tama La (4883)

63

22　Tangpu

Jomda (Jiangda)

560　(4352)

Baiyu (Pelyul)

234

(Bonpo)
Sichuan-Tibet Hwy. North

Riwoche (Leiwuqi)

Chamdo (Changdu)

105　2　109　Topa

(4481)

Chunyido

82

Kham Region

Tashi

Daye

Ruatung

143

Zholpel La (4501)

Karu Ruins

65

Kandze (Ganzi) Tibetan Autonomous Prefecture

SICHUAN

Lhorong (Luolong)　(Bonpo)

140

Shayak

32

Gonjo　Gonjo

24

181　Ngondru

Yiqing

47　Drayab Khargang

Jamdun

Lhagyal

Pomda Highland

59

Bangda Airport (Military & Civil)

(Gelukpa)

Passes Command Good Views

Nuru

Tunnel/Bridge (Dog Warning)

Pasho

Pomda

(Gelukpa)

Druparong

Batang

Sichuan-Tibet Hwy. South

To Litang, Chengdu

Chumdo

View like Old Chinese Painting

94

Markham (Mangkang)

38

89

Pome (Bomi)

127

5855　90

5764

72 Hairpin Bends

107

Dzogang (Bonpo)

110

48　Gartok

66

Druka

Bencuo

6450
Lopas

Rawok

6193

Sichuan-Tibet Hwy. South

Yunnan-Tibet Hwy.

Naxis

To Litang

Metok

6148

Rawok Lake

Demo La

Yanjing

112

6339

Xiangcheng

(Gelukpa)

172　5953

6324

(Bonpo)

111

Deqin (Jol)

Derong

Upper Dzayul

Dzayul (Jigong)

Dulongs

221

56　Lower Dzayul

61

Tengpas　21　Rima

5753　5543

Nus

Meili Xueshan 6740

184

Minzong

Nus

Diqing Tibetan Autonomous Prefecture

MYANMAR (BURMA)

Dulongs

Yunnan

Zhongdian

To Dali, Kunming

Lohit River

N

0　50　100km

Xining

Lhasa

Kathmandu

Chengdu

161

effect until it is already too late.

In Kongpo, the calendar is also different from that of other Tibetan areas, and the New Year is celebrated in October on the mainstream Tibetan lunar calendar.

LHASA TO BAYI

If you do decide to go to Kongpo by yourself, you will need to head for Bayi from Lhasa by either truck or bus. One problem is that bus tickets for Bayi are not available to foreigners at the long-distance bus station in Lhasa. The buses often stay overnight at Kongpo Gyamda, 270km to the east of Lhasa, and unfortunately the *Bus Stop Guesthouse* here overcharges foreigners with beds costing Y120. To head for Basong Tso, you need to get off at a junction 50km after Kongpo Gyamda the following day and then take the route to the north.

Sample of Arranged Tours from Lhasa (Major Sites)
Ten Nights
Lhasa - Basong Tso (Lake Draksum Lhatso) - Bayi & Mt. Bonri - Serkhyim La (Seqila) (View of Mt. Namcha Barwa) - Menling (Milin) - Gyatsa (Jiacha) - Tsethang - Lhasa

The total trip costs Y8,500, which includes the fees for the Land Cruiser, guide, driver, fuel, and permits needed for the area. Meals and accommodation are not included.

Be careful if you are on a tight schedule, as these tours often have to be extended due to bad road conditions.

BAYI (CLOSED)

The name *Bayi* means the 'August 1st,' which is the foundation day of the People's Liberation Army. As this name suggests, it is a Chinese town built by the army on a piece of wasteland along the banks of the

Bayi - Lunang

Nyang-chu. Bayi, the capital of Nyangtri Prefecture, is home to around 20,000 and is at about 3,000m surrounded by mountains covered in thick vegetation.

Besides the large-scale wool mills and the *Tibetan College of Agriculture and Animal Husbandry*, there are a lot of military facilities due to its proximity to the sensitive Indian border. For tourists, Bayi is the starting point for trips out to Mt. Namcha Barwa (7,782m) or Menling (Milin). You will have no problem with accommodation in the town if you arrange a car through a travel agency. However, many foreigners traveling in this

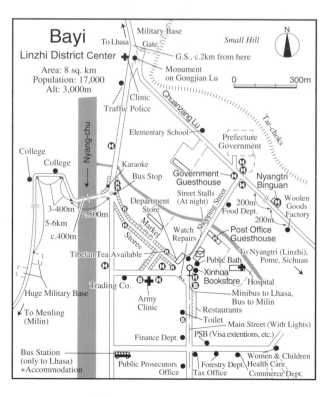

162

area without a permit are often caught by the PSB personnel here. A visa extension can be obtained at the PSB office and costs Y25 for 15 days.

Access

At Lhasa, there is a daily bus that departs for Bayi from the Tibet Long-Distance Bus Station at 07:30. However, the office at the bus station will not sell tickets to foreigners. There is also a minibus that also covers the 406km trip. Both of these take roughly a day and a half, but if you hire a Land Cruiser, the journey takes around half a day.

Bus from Bayi

*Foreign passengers have to pay twice as much as the locals.

*Lhasa—There is a bus leaving the bus station at 06:00 every day. The trip takes 15 hours, and foreigners pay Y122. There is also a minibus leaving from outside the Xinhua Bookstore at 06:00 every day. By taking the minibus you actually have a fighting chance of avoiding the foreigner's price.

*Menling (Milin)—There is a daily bus leaving at 11:00.

*Nang Dzong (Langxian)—Two buses a week operate on this route — one on Wednesday and the other on Saturday.

*Nyangtri (Linzhi)—Numerous shared-jeeps are available.

Accommodation & Restaurants

The *Nyangtri Hotel* and *Post Office Guesthouse* are the hotels supposedly designated by the PSB for foreigners.

The *Nyangtri Hotel* is relatively new (1996). It has double rooms for Y190.

The *Post Office Guesthouse* has dormitory beds for Y15 and singles that start at Y80.

The *Government Guesthouse* has beds in 3-person rooms for Y30. You need to get permission from the PSB to stay here.

The *Bus Stop Guesthouse* is handy if you want to take the 05:30 bus for Lhasa. Once again you will

Kongpo Gyamda རྒྱ་མདའ།

Alt: 3,400m ⊢——— c.1km ———⊣

N

need PSB permission to stay here.

Bayi is a fairly large town with a lot of restaurants to choose from.

Mt. Bayi Pelri

To the east of Bayi town, this sacred mountain is a place of pilgrimage. Guru Rinpoche (Padmasambhava) fought and defeated a local monster here, when the area was at the bottom of a lake. The pilgrimage route takes about 3 hours to complete.

BASONG TSO
(LAKE DRAKSUM LHATSO) (CLOSED)

In the grand heroic epic 'Gesar,' King Ling Gesar was an energetic player in the extermination of the pagans. His spirit now resides in this sacred lake, which is known as Draksum Tso in standard Tibetan, or Basong Tso in the Kongpo dialect.

Guru Rinpoche (Padmasambhava), the Nyingmapa founder, visited the lake in the 8th century, and Sangye Lingpa, a high-ranking Nyingmapa lama, built a monastery here in the 14th century, making the lake an important sacred site. Local people regard the shape of the lake as that of a dragon.

Basong Tso nestles among mountains covered in greenery. A common pilgrimage course is a 2-day circuit around the lake, stopping at Tsosum Gompa along the way. For most foreign tourists, there will be little to worry about, as the trip will have been arranged in advance by a travel agent in Lhasa. If you try it by yourself, you will need to get off the bus or truck at the Bahel Bridge (Namse Zampa), 48km to the east of Kongpo Gyamda. Then you have to take the road that branches off to the north of the Sichuan-Tibet Highway. After the village of Shoga, you will finally reach the lake. There are both restaurants and places to stay at Namse Zampa.

The pilgrimage course starts with a visit to Tsosum Gompa on its island. If the boat service is suspended, you may have to cross by the rope-

Serkhyim La (Seqila)

163

pulled raft ferry. The gompa was rebuilt by Dudjom Rinpoche, the high-ranking Nyingmapa lama from Kongpo, who now lives in exile. On the route, there are many interesting religious points. These include the hoof prints of King Gesar's horse and the footprints of Sangye Lingpa's female tiger that carried a chorten made by Guru Rinpoche here, among others.

Accommodation

A little further to the left from the entrance to Basong Tso is a guesthouse with a campsite. A dormitory bed here costs Y30.

There is also a high-class resort hotel halfway around the lake, 9km from the junction. It has a set of parasols standing in a row in front of it. On the island close to this site stands Tsosum Gompa.

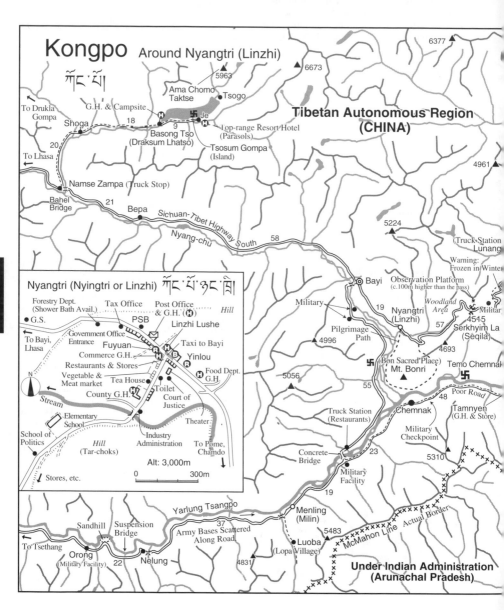

NYANGTRI (NYINGTRI) [LINZHI] (CLOSED)

Located 20km to the south-east of Bayi, this small town is on the Sichuan-Tibet Highway. There are a number of places to stay, including the *County Guesthouse*, *Nyangtri Guesthouse* (with foreigner's

tariff), and the *Post Office Guesthouse*. The woodland around here is famous for a huge juniper tree, which is around 2,500 years old.

MT. BONRI (CLOSED)

This mountain is about 10km to the south of

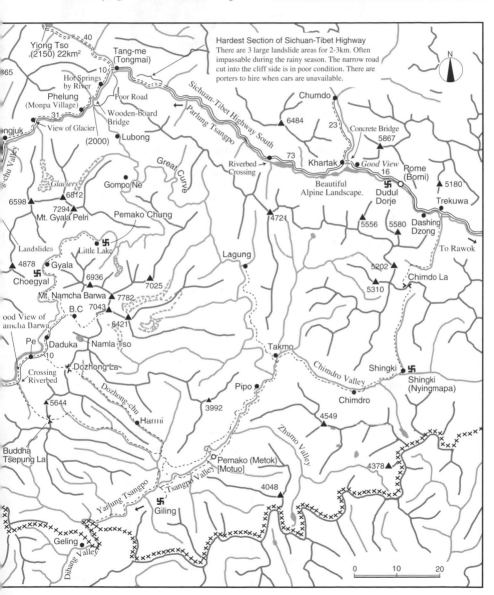

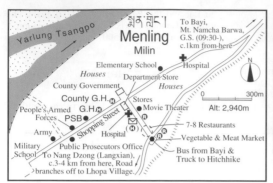

Menling / Milin map labels:
ཞུན་གླིང་ / Menling / Milin
To Bayi, Mt. Namcha Barwa, G.S. (09:30-), c.1km from here
Yarlung Tsangpo
Elementary School
Hospital
Houses
Department Store
County Government
Houses
Stores
County G.H.
G.H.
Movie Theater
People's Armed Forces
PSB
Shopping Street
Hospital
Army
7-8 Restaurants
Military School
Public Prosecutors Office
Vegetable & Meat Market
To Nang Dzong (Langxian), c.3-4 km from here, Road branches off to Lhopa Village.
Bus from Bayi & Truck to Hitchhike
Alt: 2,940m
0 — 300m

Lhopas

Nyangtri and is ranked along with Mt. Kailash (Kang Rinpoche) as the most important sacred pilgrimage destination for Bonpos. The name itself means 'Bon Mountain.'

Buddhist pilgrims follow the Bon order's practice of circumambulating the mountain in a counter-clockwise direction. On the pilgrimage route, there are many places that are related to the great activities of Shenrab Mibo, the founder of Bon, who is said to have fought local demons with magic here.

For a typical Mt. Bonri pilgrimage route taking 2 nights, it is a good idea to take food, a tent, sleeping bag, etc., as there is no accommodation in the area.

Day 1:
Departing around noon, travel along a level road with the river to the right and the huge, gently-sloping Mt. Bonri on the left. There are 1 or 2 stores where you can buy precooked noodles, etc. Sleep under canvas.

Day 2:
Start early in the morning. This stage is really hard going, and you will reach a pass decorated with tar-choks by about 15:00-16:00. You really don't have time to stop, as the descent is very dangerous if you attempt it in the dark. Pitch your tent halfway down the hill.

Day 3:
Soon after resuming your walk, you will reach the town of Nyangtri. It may be possible to complete this section in a night.

Mt. Bonri is surrounded with ancient stories, legends, and myths. It is believed to be the place where Nyatri Tsenpo, said to be the first king of Tibet, landed when he descended from heaven. This is not unique to Mt. Bonri, as there are a number of places throughout Tibet that claim the same honor.

Another story tells of a royal gravesite that is even older than the ones found in the Yarlung Valley. There is also a legend that says that Trena Village, on the pilgrimage route, is where Avalokiteshvara, disguised as a monkey, and the offspring of Tara, disguised as a rock ogress, mated and gave birth to the Tibetan people.

The agricultural off-season sees an increase in pilgrims, especially from the eastern areas of Tibet, such as Chamdo, Kyungpo, etc. In the villages along the pilgrimage route, it is either the Bon or Nyingmapa order that is most prevalent.

MENLING (MILIN) (CLOSED)

From Bayi, there is a bus every 1-2 days, and there are a number of military bases on the way. At the County Guesthouse, the cost of a bed for foreign guests is Y18 though there are no showers. About 10km to the south of Menling (Dungdor) is a Lhopa village. Around 300,000 Lhopa, meaning 'Southern People' in Tibetan, live in this disputed border area in the southern end of Kongpo. There is no exact number, as there is a lot of cross border movement.

Although the Lhopa speak their own languages, they also use Tibetan and Tibetan script when they

Map labels:
Yarlung Tsangpo
To Nang Dzong (Nangxian)
3-4km
Menling (Milin)
Gate
Kiosk c.1.5km
Visit Lhopas
Government
Army
Bad Road
6-7km
Lhopa Village
No Entry Beyond Village.
No Accommodation

Map labels:
ཀུ་ནང་ / Lunang (Lulang)
Tang-me, Pome
Restaurants
G.H.
Lumbermill
Nyangtri, Bayi
Alt: 3,370m
Tar-choks

166

write. They also eat *tsampa* and drink butter tea, while they farm and hunt for a living. Unlike Tibetans though, they follow their own animist faith rather than either Buddhism or Bon.

MT. NAMCHA BARWA (CLOSED)

Just before the great curve of the Yarlung Tsangpo are 2 high mountains, Mt. Namcha Barwa (7,782m) and Mt. Gyala Pelri (7,294m). There is only 21km between them, and the river valley is as deep as 5,000m in parts. To reach Mt. Namcha Barwa, take the road opposite Mt. Bonri on the southern side of the Yarlung Tsangpo and follow this route: Demo Chemnak- Luzhar - Tamnyen- Pe - Daduka -Base Camp.

En route you will pass through the Chinese village of Luzhar and then on to the village of Tamnyen, where you will find accommodation, stores, and the ferry that will take you across the river. Further down the road is the Chinese village of Pe (also called Dozhong), which has an excellent view of Mt. Namcha Barwa. There are 2 stores and a guesthouse in the village, but foreigners may be charged excessively to stay there. As you continue towards the Base Camp, the imposing figure of Mt. Namcha Barwa comes fully into view.

Although there is a truck between Pe and Menling (Milin), you may have to wait 1-2 days between each one, and the road is in extremely poor condition.

PEMAKO (METOK) [MOTUO] (CLOSED)

This natural paradise spreads out over the area between the southern foot of Mt. Namcha Barwa and the McMahon Line, which functions as the defacto border with India. Due to the influence of the monsoon, the climate in this area is both mild and wet. The best seasons to visit Pemako are between April and May, before the rainy season sets in, and again from October to November. The winters here see the mountain passes clogged with snow and generally impassable.

Pemako is called a *Beyul*, or 'A Hidden Heaven on Earth,' and it is said there are 16 *Beyuls* in existence. These mystical places are where all wishes are said to come true. When the Chinese Army invaded eastern Tibet, many Tibetans tried to escape to this mysterious place in search of salvation, but sadly to no avail. The area is also famous for sightings and stories of the Yeti.

The area is also known as *Metok* meaning 'Flower,' and it has around 500 mainly Monpa

residents, who were still practicing slash-and-burn agriculture until quite recently. Pemako is the only one of roughly 3,000 Chinese counties with no road leading to another county. It is surrounded by high mountains with a lot of rainfall — thus, road construction is particularly hazardous, and numerous attempts have all met with failure. Though there are no roads, this is still an area of strategic importance due to its proximity to the border, and thus, it is connected with Nyangtri by helicopter.

To get to this dreamland of Pemako, travel to the south-east from Pe (Dozhong) and then cross the Dozhong La (5,287m). Along the way you may be accompanied by local Monpas, as they also use this route to and from Kongpo. The trip will take you 4 days without stopping at monasteries, etc. There is also another route from around Pome to the east.

BAYI TO POME

After Kongpo, this route leading to Chamdo goes through the canyon to the north of the great curve of the Yarlung Tsangpo. With numerous passes to cross, the trip is hard-going, though the scenery definitely makes it worthwhile. After Nyangtri and its vast woodland areas and huge trees, you will see Mt. Namcha Barwa on the eastern side of Serkhyim La (Seqila) pass (4,515m). The road branches off here, and there is a roadway that goes up for about 100m. From there you'll get a great view of Mt. Gyala Pelri and the surrounding area.

LUNANG (LULANG) (CLOSED)

About an hour down from the Serkhyim La (Seqila) pass is Lunang Village (3,370m). The village has about 10 restaurants on both sides of the road, and there are also some places to stay. The scenery is like a true Shangri La around Lunang.

TANG-ME [TONGMAI] (CLOSED)

Another 3-hour ride further on is Tang-me. Up to here the road is extremely poor, with only a rough, stone surface. This section dips below 2,000m at times, and you will pass through the Monpa village of Phelung along the way.

With only a few restaurants and a guesthouse, Tang-me is a rather lonesome village nestling in woodland. The restaurants charge from Y12 per

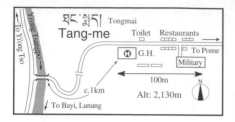

བང་ཐེད། Tongmai
Tang-me
Toilet Restaurants →
☉ G.H. ▭▭ To Pome
▭▭ ▭ Military
← 100m →
c.1km
Alt: 2,130m N
To Yiong Tso
To Bayi, Lunang

Pome

dish, and you should be careful as they may overcharge you.

Several kilometers towards Pome from here, there is an area that is prone to landslides, and it is often closed during the rainy season. The rest of the road is in relatively good condition. It is possible to hire a baggage porter for the trek.

POME (POWO) [BOMI] (CLOSED)

Sometimes referred to as the 'Switzerland of Tibet,' Pome is an area of scenic beauty with views of stunning snow-covered mountains. It is a relatively big town surrounded by some of the most fertile

land in Tibet. It has a fairly good selection of produce on sale, from camera film to mineral water.

The transportation system leaves a lot to be desired, and the bus service here is almost non-existent. There are checkpoints on the way to Tang-me that are very thorough, and even non-local Tibetans have to be careful. The PSB officials in the towns in the area are the same.

The town was once the capital of the Pome Kingdom that lasted from the 16th century up until the Chinese occupation. Pome is no longer what it used to be and now acts more like a truck stop. The

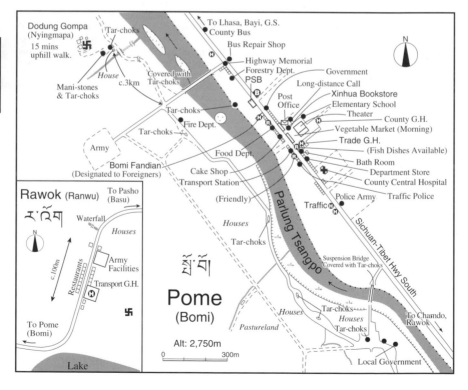

Dodung Gompa (Nyingmapa) Tar-choks
15 mins uphill walk.
House Covered with Tar-choks c.3km
Mani-stones & Tar-choks
Tar-choks
Tar-choks Fire Dept.
Army
Bomi Fandian
(Designated to Foreigners)
Food Dept.
Cake Shop
Transport Station

To Lhasa, Bayi, G.S.
County Bus
Bus Repair Shop
Highway Memorial
Forestry Dept. Government
PSB
Long-distance Call
Post Office Xinhua Bookstore
Elementary School
Theater
County G.H.
Vegetable Market (Morning)
Trade G.H.
(Fish Dishes Available)
Bath Room
Department Store
County Central Hospital
Police Army Traffic Police
Traffic
Parlung Tsangpo
Sichuan-Tibet Hwy South
N

Rawok (Ranwu)
ར་འོག
To Pasho (Basu)
Waterfall
Houses
Army Facilities
Transport G.H.
To Pome (Bomi)
Lake
N
c.100m
Restaurants

(Friendly)
Houses
Tar-choks
མེ་གི

Pome
(Bomi)
Alt: 2,750m
0   300m

Houses
Suspension Bridge
Covered with Tar-choks
Tar-choks
Pastureland
Houses
Tar-choks
Tar-choks
To Chamdo, Rawok
Local Government

town is well known as the breeding center for the famous Pome hunting dog and for Jomolangma tea that is sold in Lhasa and other major centers in Tibet. This is grown along the Yi'ong Tsangpo, to the west of the town.

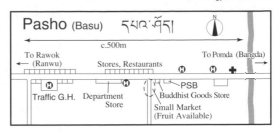

Pasho (Basu) དཔའ་ཤོད།

c.500m

To Rawok ← (Ranwu)

Stores, Restaurants

To Pomda (Bangda) →

PSB

Traffic G.H. Department Store

Buddhist Goods Store

Small Market (Fruit Available)

Accommodation & Restaurants

The *Pome Hotel* has dormitory beds for Y10, including electric blankets and televisions.

The *Trade Guesthouse* charges Y13 for dormitory beds and Y25 per person in a double room. There are a lot of restaurants in town that stay open until 22:00.

CHAMDO

CHAMDO (CHANGDU) PREFECTURE, TIBETAN AUTONOMOUS REGION

On the Sichuan-Tibet Highway South, Chamdo (Changdu) Prefecture starts at Rawok (Ranwu) to the east. The district covers an area of 109,000 sq km, a little larger than Hungary or the state of Kentucky, and has a population of around 510,000. Although the Chinese administrative division of Chamdo (Changdu) Prefecture is very large, the area normally referred to as *Chamdo* by Tibetans is only in and around Chamdo County itself.

RAWOK (RANWU) (CLOSED)

Surrounded by mountains, Rawok (3,850m) is a small town beside a lake. It is about 4 hours from Pome by Land Cruiser and around 3 hours from Pasho. The eateries in the town serve good food, but the prices are relatively high, starting from Y15. You can stay at the *Transport Guesthouse* with dormitory beds for Y12.

To the south, there is Rawok Lake, which is 1-2km wide and 26km long. The lake is surrounded by beautiful woods, glaciers, hot springs, etc. On the route of the Sichuan-Tibet Highway, Chamdo Prefecture is to the east.

DZAYUL (CHAYU) (CLOSED)

Heading south from Rawok towards the Myanmar (Burma) border, you reach this low-lying area (2,300m), which is inhabited by the Tengpa people. You can get here by chartering a Land Cruiser from Rawok, and these take 6 hours or so. One problem with visiting the area though is that permits are not always issued to foreigners.

Dzayul is famous as a treasure trove of rare butterflies and attracts the attention of serious enthusiasts and scholars from around the world. Around the Nu Jiang River, in the eastern part of the county near the border with Yunnan, there are Dulong and Nu villages scattered. Administratively, Dzayul belongs to Nyangtri (Linzhi) Prefecture.

PASHO (BASU) (CLOSED)

After passing through a lot of towns on the Yunnan route heading for Lhasa, Pasho is the first town you come to with electricity. There are no problems staying at the *Traffic Guesthouse* in town. This is also home to the 500-year-old Pasho Gompa, which has approximately 350 monks now.

POMDA (BANGDA) (CLOSED)

If you take either the southern route, via Nyangtri, or the northern route, via Chamdo, to get to Lhasa from Yunnan, you will inevitably pass through Pomda. Though there is little of interest at this transportation hub, it is not too difficult to catch a truck heading for Pasho (Basu) or Chamdo. The trip to Chamdo by Land Cruiser takes about 6 hours. There are beds available at the *Transport Guesthouse*, among others. Most of the restaurants in Pomda charge from Y10 per dish.

Between Pomda and Pasho (Basu) there is an expanse of beautiful grassland called the Pomda Highlands. The trip out here takes around 5 hours by Land Cruiser. This section of the journey is definitely the hardest part of the route and features the infamous '72 Hairpin Bends' that take you down into the Ngul-chu (Nu Jiang) Valley.

Pomda was once the site of a military airport, but this was converted to civilian use and reopened

KONGPO & CHAMDO

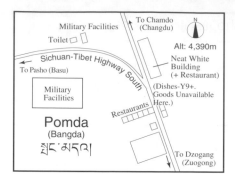

as Chamdo Airport (Bangda Airport, 4,334m) in 1995. China Southwest Airlines (SZ) has flights between Chengdu and Pomda. For foreigners, tickets are only available to members of group tours.

YUNNAN TO BAYI

There is a minibus from the open town of Dechen (Deqin), in Yunnan, to Yanjing, in the Tibetan Autonomous Region. Beyond Yanjing, hitchhiking is the only way to go.

The major points on the route are as follows: Dechen (Deqin), Yunnan - Yanjing (Checkpoint)- Mangkang (Checkpoint)- Zuogong - Pomda - Pasho - Rawok - Pome - Bayi. (You're most likely to be fined here.)

As there is little transportation on this route, many truck and jeep drivers overcharge foreigners. It is also possible to hitch lifts from army cars too. The trip from Dechen (Deqin) to Lhasa takes 10-14 days.

YANJING (CLOSED)

Yanjing is the first town in the TAR that you will reach on your way from Yunnan. The town is a little set back from the main road. There is a daily

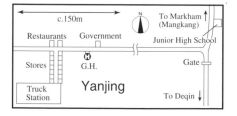

minibus from Dechen (Deqin) to Yanjing, and the trip takes 6-7 hours. There should be no problem with staying at the guesthouse in town. To catch a lift with a truck, simply go down to the truck station, though there are usually only a few trucks there at any one time.

In the past there have been PSB checks looking for foreigners traveling along this route at the entrance to the town.

MARKHAM (MANGKANG) (CLOSED)

Markham is where the Yunnan-Tibet Highway meets the Sichuan-Tibet Highway. This town, along with Yanjing, is where a traveler who is chancing this route should be cautious, as the PSB are especially enthusiastic here. Many travelers have been fined and ordered back to where they came from. The trip from Yanjing by Land Cruiser takes over 4 hours.

Trucks from Markham
If you are able to continue your journey from Markham, head for Dzogang to the west. The number of trucks from Markham (Mangkang) to Dzogang (Zuogong) seems to be less frequent than on any other section of the Yunnan route. The hitching point is at the T-junction in town, and catching a lift with a truck heading to Druka (Zhuka) may be the only way to leave town quickly.

You have the option of taking one of the infrequent minibuses for Dechen (Deqin) and Bathang, which both depart from the truck depot next to the post office once every 4 -5 days. There are also jeeps available here.

Trucks and jeeps also start from the Government Guesthouse, etc. These are usually destined for Dzogang, Bathang, and Dechen (Deqin). A final possibility is taking the bus that makes the trip between Markham and Chamdo once every 5 days.

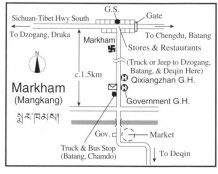

Nomads, Paho-Rawok

Sichuan to Markham

There is a bus from Bathang in Sichuan to Markham, which takes around 3 hours. At a bridge over the Dri-chu (Jinsha Jiang River) there is a checkpoint, though they are not primarily concerned with foreigners.

Druka (Zhuka)

Druka (Zhuka) is a small town around 40km to the south-west of Markham. The river flowing through the town is the Dza-chu, which finally matures into the mighty Mekong River. You can stay at the *Zhuka Restaurant & Guesthouse*.

Unfortunately, the number of civilian trucks that travel on to Dzogang are very few. There is apparently a bus from Markham to Dzogang once every 5 days. It is 126km to Dzogang, and the scenery between the Joba La pass (Jiaobashan, 3,908m) and Rongshoe (4,100m) is stunning.

Dzogang (Zuogong)

The trip from Druka (Zhuka) by Land Cruiser takes about 5 hours and from Pomda around 4 hours, and the road is relatively level. The *Wuzhuanbu Guesthouse* here is not supposed to accept foreign guests but you may be able to arrange this with the help of a fellow passenger. No registration is required, and a dormitory bed costs from Y8. You can also get dormitory beds at the *Shilang Guesthouse* for Y12. The restaurants here may overcharge you.

CHAMDO TO NAKCHU

The trip by truck from Chamdo to Nakchu usually takes 2 nights and costs Y70-100. Many trucks stay overnight at Tengchen and Bachen. On this route there are refreshing open grassland vistas and towns that are at once forgettable. However, there are a number of noted monasteries along the way, although these are not well known among travelers.

CHAMDO (CHANGDU) (CLOSED)

Chamdo (3,240m) is the largest town in the eastern Tibetan province of Kham. Administratively, it is Chamdo Town, Chamdo (Changdu) County, and it has a population of around 25,000. This center of the Chamdo (Changdu) Prefecture is where the Dza-chu intersects with the Ngom-chu. Roughly speaking, the Ngom-chu divides the town into 2 parts, with a Chinese and a Tibetan section.

The center of the Tibetan area is the huge Jampaling Monastery on the hill, and there are plenty of Tibetan goods on sale in the market here. There are also the Chamdo (Changdu) County Government offices in this section. The Chinese part has a number of buildings, including the Changdu Prefectural Government offices and a fine-looking department store.

In 1950, Chamdo was surrendered to the advancing Chinese army without permission from the central command in Lhasa. This single action really clinched the swift PLA victory over the small ill-equipped Tibetan forces.

Access by Bus
To Chamdo

Although there are buses from Chengdu and Lhasa, these are not supposed to take foreign passengers, and hitchhiking is really the only alternative. The ones from Chengdu leave from the *Chamdo Transport Co.*, 5-6 km to the south-west of Wuhou Temple. There are buses leaving at 06:00 on

Tuesdays and Fridays, and the trip (via Dege) takes 4 nights.

From Chamdo
*Lhasa—There is a single bus on Monday that goes via Nakachu.
*Chengdu—The buses on Wednesday and Saturday leave at 06:00.
*Tengchen (Dingqing)—One bus every 5 days.

All these buses leave from the Chamdo Transport Co. Tickets are available on the 2nd floor of the guesthouse at the bus station.

Hitchhiking
See the map to the right for the hitchhiking points. Truck information can be obtained at the Chamdo Transport Co., Changdu Lushe (Hotel), etc. It is possible to catch a truck going to Lhasa, via Nakchu, once a day. The trip costs locals between Y100 and Y150. The morning trucks often

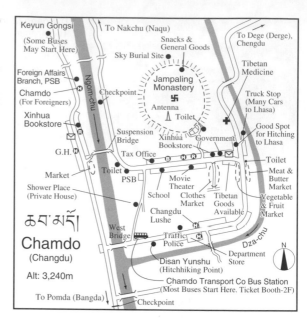

stop overnight at Tengchen (Dingqing), and the ones starting around noon spend the night at Riwoche.

Accommodation & Restaurants
The *Chamdo Hotel* is the one where foreigners are supposed to stay, and although it is a large hotel, the services are nothing special. Double rooms start at Y40. It is next door to the Public Security Bureau. The *Changdu Lushe* (Hotel) has dormitory beds for Y9.
The *Chamdo County Trade Co. Guesthouse* is at the foot of the Jampaling Monastery, opposite the movie theater. A bed in a double room with a television costs Y12. Although the rooms are clean, the toilets are shared and there are no showers.
Next to the department store is a place with beds in 3-person rooms that cost Y10.

There is a Tibetan-run private shower house halfway between the monastery and the bus station, and this costs Y2. The place looks like a normal private house, and you should be careful of the dog. Many of the restaurants in Chamdo are either Chinese or Muslim.

Foreign Affairs Branch, Public Security Bureau (PSB)
The office is next door to Chamdo Hotel. If you are caught in Chamdo, you will be taken to the Chamdo Hotel and fined Y100. You will then be

ordered to buy a ticket for the direct bus to Chengdu. After they have punished a traveler in this fashion, they do not seem to mind you going to see the monastery or whatever.

Jampaling Monastery
On the hill looking down on Chamdo is the great Gelukpa monastery of Jampaling, which seems to house about 1,000 monks now. Armed with a proposal from Tsongkhapa, the founder of the Gelukpa order who visited here in the 14th century, Jangsem Sherab Zangpo, Tsongkhapa's pupil, established the site in the 15th century. Although the Chinese destroyed the monastery twice in this century, the large 3-story assembly hall and other buildings have been restored.

Houses, Chamdo

Mt. Namcha Barwa

The attractive 4-story building on the northern side is the former palace, which is now the labrang for the incarnate 11th Phakpalha Gelek Namgyel. He is the vice-chairman of the National People's Congress, and this VIP now lives in Lhasa.

Karma Gompa

At the foot of Baixishan, 130km to the north of Chamdo, Karma Gompa is a Karma Kagyupa monastery. It was constructed by the 1st Karmapa in the 12th century, and the great assembly hall here was once the largest in Tibet.

RIWOCHE (LEIWUQI) (CLOSED)

The relatively large town of Riwoche is 105km from Chamdo, and there is nothing especially noteworthy along the main road. However, the Riwoche Tsuklakhang, the center of Taklung Kagyupa, is about 30km towards Qinghai from here. The site was established in the 13th century.

There are a number of places to stay in the town including the *Post Office Guesthouse* and the *Meteorological Agency Guesthouse*. The *County Government Guesthouse* has dormitory beds for Y10. Whether you are allowed to stay at these guesthouses or not seems to be a matter of luck.

TENGCHEN (DINGQING) (CLOSED)

At first glance this town seems to be nothing more than a large truck stop. However, Tengchen is a great Bon religious center. The town is often called Khyungpo Tengchen, as the area surrounding the town is the Khyungpo District.

The *Dingqing Liangyou Guesthouse* has dormitory beds for Y8 and ones with a television for Y12, though it is right next door to the PSB office. Buses and trucks often use this guesthouse as their overnight stop.

Before the Chinese built the Sichuan-Tibet Highway to help with the subjugation of the Tibetan Plateau, the main trade route connecting Chamdo with Lhasa went from Chamdo down to the south through Tengchen and headed for Shopado, Pelbar, and Lharigo after the Salween River. The route then crossed the Yi'ong Tsangpo to reach Gyamda, on the present Sichuan-Tibet Highway South, and finally completed its way to Lhasa. There are a number of old Bon and Buddhist monasteries along this old main road.

SOK DZONG (SUOXIAN) (CLOSED)

This is a small town, 240km to the east of Nakchu, though it has a central government office, a post office, and even a hospital, unlike most other places in this area. A lift in a truck from Nakchu will cost you Y20.

The stores, hotels, restaurants, etc. are concentrated around the only junction in town where the 3 roads meet. There is a nameless guesthouse with a couple of 5-person rooms, and a bed in one of these costs Y8, though there is no toilet. This guesthouse is run by Hui brothers from Qinghai, and it has a restaurant and general store. Other options are the *Post Office Guesthouse* and the *Wuzhuanbu Guesthouse*.

Sok Tsanden Gompa

Standing on a hill, Sok Tsanden Gompa is an imposing fortress-like monastery. The Mongolian Gushi Khan Tenzin Choegyal founded this Gelukpa

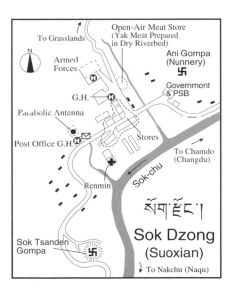

Sok Tsanden Gompa

monastery in the 17th century, and the word *Sok* means 'Mongolian' in Tibetan.

The monastery reputedly housed around 650 monks until Chinese forces from Yushu (Jyekundo) destroyed it in 1959. Nonetheless, a substantial number of the monks, in typical Khampa fashion, refused to leave, and the gompa is still being rebuilt with about 250 friendly monks engaged in the work. This is also home to the incarnated lama, Ganden Ngawang Ziktrul Rinpoche.

LHORONG (LUOLONG) (CLOSED)

On the old main road (discussed in the Tengchen section) you will find Shopado, which is home to Shopado Gompa. This monastery belongs to the very small Martsang Kagyupa order and used to be home to 300 monks. Also, at Dzitho, the center of Lhorong County, you will find both Dzitho Gompa and Nyiseb Gompa.

PELBAR (BIANBA) (CLOSED)

Pelbar is also on the old main road and is home to the Pelbar Gompa, a great Nyingmapa monastery, which used to house about 200 monks.

LHARIGO (JIALI) (CLOSED)

Although it is also on the old main road, Lharigo used to be an important trading post, connected with Pome to the east and Nakchu to the west by the road along the Yi'ong Tsangpo. It now belongs to the Nakchu Prefecture. The 11th Panchen Lama, selected by the Dalai Lama in 1995, and the opposing candidate, appointed by China, are both from Lharigo.

DEGE IN SICHUAN TO CHAMDO

From Dege to Chamdo, hitchhiking is your only option, and the trip usually takes 2 days. (For hitchhiking from Dege, see the Dege section on page 254.) After the bridge over the Dri-chu (Jinsha Jiang River), the Tibetan Autonomous Region (TAR) begins, and there seems to be no problem with the checkpoint here. Several kilometers past the border is the truck stop of Kamthok (Gangtuo). The first place after crossing into the TAR that really looks like a town is Jomda (Jiangda). Trucks from Dege are fairly likely to stay overnight here, and there is accommodation at the truck stop, though a report is often forwarded to the local PSB. As you continue on to Chamdo from here, there are numerous mountain passes to go through.

CHAMDO TO POMDA

To the south of Chamdo is Drayab (Chaya), and the area to the south is called *Tsawarong* or 'Warm Valley.' This was one of the most fertile and wealthy regions in Tibet, at least before the Chinese took over. The area is also home for the Jorkhe Ritro, which is said to be the largest nunnery in Tibet, and Jamdun Bugon.

AMDO
Tibetan Areas in Gansu, Qinghai, and Sichuan

ཨ་མདོ།

If your image of Tibet includes vast steppes and nomads, then the Amdo region could be the area that you are thinking of.

The Yellow River (Huang He), recognized as the birthplace of Chinese civilization, is itself born in Amdo and meanders its way down off the Tibetan Plateau from here. The nomads of Amdo live out their pastoral existences on the vast plain of fertile grassland created by the great river and its tributaries. Since early times various peoples, the Tibetans, Mongolians, and Turkish-related ethnic groups, have intermingled, and each of their distinctive cultures has been assimilated into that of the area, shaping the present *Amdo-wa*, as the Tibetan people of Amdo are known.

Tibetan nomads are big-hearted and freely welcome strangers, but those in this region are also shrewd in their dealings with others. It may be due to their history of trying to peacefully co-exist, with such ethnically diverse groups in such close proximity to one another, which has taught the people of the Amdo region how to play their cards so well. This panned out during the Communist Revolution, the subsequent takeover of Tibet, and during the Cultural Revolution that followed, as they were able to save quite a few monasteries in the area from total destruction. The religious life

of Amdo is dominated by the Gelukpa order, and a very serious interpretation with strict precepts has prevailed here. The founder of the Gelukpa order, Tsongkhapa, was from Amdo, and the present 14th Dalai Lama, who was also born in the region, has strengthened this connection.

Gannan Prefecture (Gansu Province)
At the eastern end of the Tibetan Plateau, the main highway connecting Lanzhou with Chengdu makes for easy access to the prefecture. Gannan is famous for the Labrang Monastery, one of the 6 leading Gelukpa monasteries, and also the area, like

Labrang Monastery, Xiahe

175

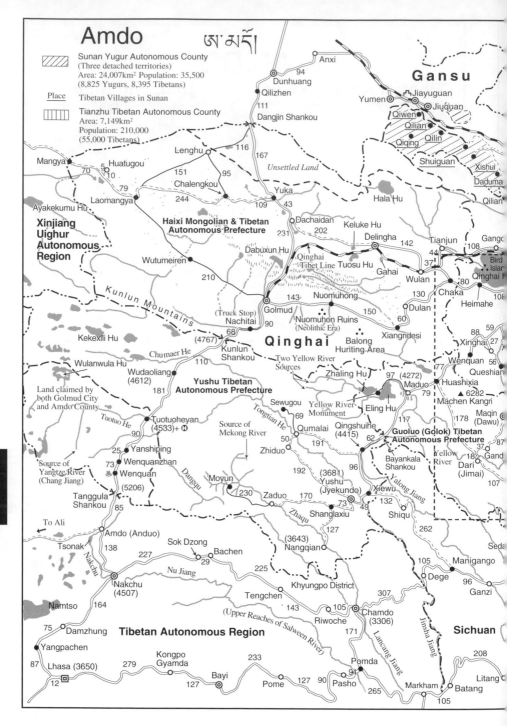

Amdo অ་མདོ

Sunan Yugur Autonomous County
(Three detached territories)
Area: 24,007km² Population: 35,500
(8,825 Yugurs, 8,395 Tibetans)

Place   Tibetan Villages in Sunan

Tianzhu Tibetan Autonomous County
Area: 7,149km²
Population: 210,000
(55,000 Tibetans)

Gansu

Anxi
94
Dunhuang
Qilizhen
111
Dangjin Shankou
116   167
Lenghu
151   95
Chalengkou
244
Laomangya
79
Huatugou
70 5
10
Mangya
Ayakekumu Hu
Yuka
109   43
Hala Hu
Qilian
Xishui
Daduma
Shuiguan
Qiqing Qilin
Qiwen
Qilian
Jiuquan
Yumen Jiayuguan

Unsettled Land

**Xinjiang
Uighur
Autonomous
Region**

**Haixi Mongolian & Tibetan
Autonomous Prefecture**
231
Dachaidan
202
Keluke Hu
Delingha 142
Tianjun Gango
44   108
37   Bird
Islan
Qinghai H
Wulan
80
Chaka
108
Heimahe
Dulan
130
60
Xiangridesi

Dabuxun Hu
Qinghai-
Tibet Line Tuosu Hu
Gahai
210

Kunlun Mountains
Wutumeiren

(Truck Stop)
Nachitai
Golmud
143
Nuomuhong
150
Nuomuhon Ruins
(Neolithic Era)
90

Kekexili Hu
68
(4767)
Kunlun
Shankou
Qinghai
Balong
Hunting Area
88   59
Xinghai 27
Wenquan 56
Queshian
Huashixia
79 ▲ 6282
Machen Kangri
Maqin
(Dawu)
87
37

Wulanwula Hu
Chumaer He
110
Wudaoliang
(4612)
181
**Yushu Tibetan
Autonomous Prefecture**
Two Yellow River
Sources
Zhaling Hu
97 (4272)
Maduo
177
178

Land claimed by
both Golmud City
and Amdo County
Tuotuo He
90
Tuotuoheyan
(4533)+ ☉
Source of
Mekong River
Sewugou
69
Yellow River
Monument
Eling Hu
Qingshuihe
(4415)
62
117
**Guoluo (Golok) Tibetan
Autonomous Prefecture**
Yellow
River
18
Dari
(Jimai)
Gand
107

Source of
Yangtze River
(Chang Jiang)
25 Yanshiping
73 Wenquanzhan
Wenquan
(5206)
Tanggula
Shankou 85
To Ali
Tsonak
Amdo (Anduo)
138
227
Sok Dzong
29 Bachen
Nu Jiang
225
Nakchu
(4507)
Namtso
164
Moyun
230
Zaduo
170
Zhaqu
(3681)
Yushu
(Jyekundo)
Xiewu
132
Shiqu
262
Seda

Qumalai
191
50
Zhiduo
192
96
Bayankala
Shankou
Yalong Jiang
49 73
Shanglaxiu
127
(3643)
Nangqian
105
Manigango
Dege 96
Ganzi

Tengchen
143
(Upper Reaches of Salween River)
Khyungpo District
105   307
Riwoche
171
Chamdo
(3306)
Sichuan

75 Damzhung
Yangpachen
87 Lhasa (3650)
12
Tibetan Autonomous Region
279
Kongpo
Gyamda
Bayi
127
233
Pome
127
90 Pasho
Pomda
94
265
Markham Batang
105
208
Litang

Lancang Jiang
Jinsha Jiang

176

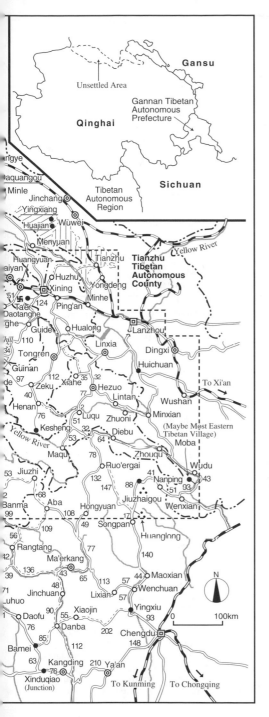

Qinghai, is home to many nomadic people. Gansu Province still has many Tibetan inhabitants, who are concentrated in areas such as the Tianzhu Tibetan Autonomous County, among others. Wudu and Wenxian, in the east of Gannan Prefecture also have Tibetan villages, while Moba in Wudu County marks the eastern boundary of the Tibetan region.

Aba (Ngawa) Prefecture (Sichuan Province)
Going south down the main road from Gannan Prefecture into the north of Sichuan Province, you will reach the Aba (Ngawa) Tibetan & Qiang Autonomous Prefecture. Like Qinghai, its northern half, is made up of grassland steppe, through which the upper reaches of the Yellow River (Huang He) flow. As the prefecture spreads south, getting closer to the Sichuan Basin, the altitude gets lower, and the grasslands give way to woodland watered by the Min Jiang and Dajinchuan tributaries of the mighty Yangtze River (Chang Jiang). In this vicinity there is a very famous area of natural beauty called Jiuzhaigou.

Qinghai Province
The province is famous for Qinghai Hu (Lake Kokonor) and the Ta'er Monastery (Kumbum). Many simply regard this as their starting point for the route from Xining via Golmud to Lhasa. In reality, there are numerous interesting things to see, and many of the villages scattered throughout the countryside are open to foreigners, making it far more accessible than other areas to the south. Yushu (Jyekundo), to the south-west, is actually in the Kham region, but will be discussed in this chapter, as Xining is a gateway for a visit to this prefecture.

GANSU PROVINCE

LANZHOU

Having once been an important trading post on the Silk Road, Lanzhou has maintained its influence as the provincial capital of Gansu. The city itself does not have much to do with Tibet and its culture, but it is a staging point for trips out to the Tibetan areas, such as Gannan Prefecture, Tianzhu, etc. At 1,520m, the area has a moderate average temperature of 22.6°C in July, which drops to a chilly -6.8°C in January. Although the average temperature in July is quite pleasant, it can get

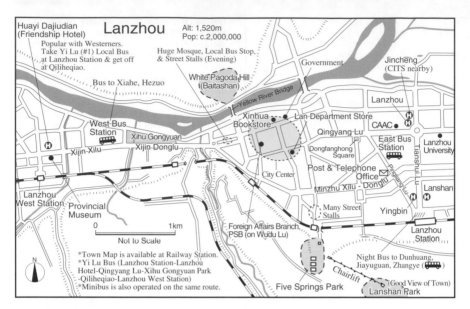

Huayi Dajiudian
(Friendship Hotel)
Popular with Westerners.
Take Yi Lu (#1) Local Bus
at Lanzhou Station & get off
at Qiliheqiao.

Lanzhou

Alt: 1,520m
Pop: c.2,000,000

Bus to Xiahe, Hezuo

Huge Mosque, Local Bus Stop,
& Street Stalls (Evening)

White Pagoda Hill
(Baitashan)

Government

Jincheng
(CITS nearby)

Yellow River Bridge

Lanzhou

Xinhua
Bookstore

Lan-Department Store

West Bus
Station

CAAC

Qingyang-Lu

Xihu Gongyuan

Xijin-Xilu

Xijin-Donglu

Dongfanghong
Square

East Bus
Station

Lanzhou
University

Post & Telephone
Office

City Center

Minzhu Xilu - Donglu

Lanzhou
West Station

Provincial
Museum

Many Street
Stalls

Yingbin

Lanshan

0   1km

Not to Scale

Foreign Affairs Branch,
PSB (on Wudu Lu)

Lanzhou
Station

*Town Map is available at Railway Station.
*Yi Lu Bus (Lanzhou Station-Lanzhou
Hotel-Qingyang Lu-Xihu Gongyuan Park
-Qiliheqiao-Lanzhou West Station)
*Minibus is also operated on the same route.

N

Night Bus to Dunhuang,
Jiayuguan, Zhangye

Chairlift

Five Springs Park

(Good View of Town)
Lanshan Park

uncomfortably hot here during the day in the summer.

To Lanzhou
Access by Rail
*No. 43 Special Express
  Beijing 11:01-Lanzhou 16:57 (1 night)
*No. 75 Special Express
  Beijing West 08:50-Lanzhou 13:11 (1 night)
*No. 172 & 173 Special Express
  Qingdao 18:49-Lanzhou 06:03 (2 nights)
*No. 376 & 377 Express
  Shanghai 22:01-Lanzhou 12:13 (2 nights)

There are daily trains from Guangzhou, Chengdu, Xi'an, Xining, Urumqi, and other major centers in the region.

Access by Air
*Beijing—Two flights daily. Costs: Y1,280 (2 hrs).

Grassland, Gannan Prefecture

*Shanghai—Monday, Wednesday, Thursday, Friday, & Sunday.
  Costs: Y1,690 (2 hrs 10 mins).
*Guangzhou—One daily flight. Costs: Y1,830
  (2 hrs 45 mins).
There are flights from Xi'an, Chengdu, Urumqi, etc., almost daily.

The airport is 70km to the north of the town, and the trip takes 2 hours by CITS bus.

From Lanzhou
Access by Rail
*No. 44 Special Express
  Lanzhou 13:05-Beijing 19:47 (1 night)
*No. 76 Special Express
  Lanzhou 12:37-Beijing West 16:53 (1 night)
*No. 171 & 174 Special Express
  Lanzhou 17:44-Qingdao 06:52 (2 nights)
*No. 375 & 378 Express
  Lanzhou 19:55-Shanghai 07:44 (2 nights)

Access by Air
There are regular flights to Beijing, Shanghai, Guangzhou, Xi'an, Chengdu, Urumqi, and other regional centers almost every day.

Bus Trip Insurance & Foreign Tourist Fares
In Gansu, foreign tourists are supposed to get insurance for bus trips and are charged bus fares that are as much as twice the fare paid by locals. This is not the whole story though, as you may be able to get reasonably priced tickets without

AMDO

insurance in non-tourist areas outside of Lanzhou, Xiahe, Dunhuang, etc.

You can buy the insurance at travel agencies in Lanzhou, such as *Gansu Silk Road Travel*, 361 Tianshui-lu, Lanzhou, Tel. 27931-597 or at the *Lanzhou Hotel*. The policy is valid for 1-2 weeks. *CITS* also issues a 2-week insurance policy for Y5, and the *People's Insurance Company of China* (PICC) charges Y20 for one too.

Buses from Lanzhou

Lanzhou has 2 bus stations, one at the eastern end of town and the other to the west. For Gannan, you will need to go to the western station, and you'll find connections for Dunhuang at the eastern one. The following schedule is for buses going out to the Tibetan areas.

From the Western Bus Station

To get out to the station, take a local bus #1 (Yilu).
*Linxia—There are frequent services every day, and the156km trip takes 4-5 hours.
*Xiahe—There is a daily departure at 07:30.
*Hezuo (via Linxia)—There are a number of buses going via Linxia, and the earliest one leaves at 07:30.
*Minxian (via Lintao, Huichuan)—Departs at 06:30, or you can catch the one going to Zhouqu (Drukchu) that also stops off here.
*Zhouqu (via Minxian, Dangchang)—There is a daily service leaving at 07.30.

From the Eastern Bus Station

Tickets are available between 06:00 and 19:00, and the window where you can purchase night bus and sleeping berth tickets for Xiahe, Jiayuguan, Yumen, Dunhuang, etc. is reached by going through the waiting room to the bus departure area and then taking a left. In the daytime, the buses with sleeping berths also stop in front of the railway station in Lanzhou.

*Other destinations serviced from the station are Xining, Wudu, Jiuquan, etc.

Local Transportation

The #1 (Yilu) bus is really useful for getting around the town, and there is also an extensive network of minibuses that will take you to where you want to go.

Accommodation

The *Lanzhou Fandian* (Hotel) is located on a roundabout directly north from the railway station. Its clean rooms are reasonably well equipped, and a 3-person room with a shower costs Y50 per person.
The *Jincheng Binguan* (Hotel) is next to the

Lanzhou Fandian, and this relatively new hotel has a CITS office.
The *Huayi Dajiudian* (Hotel) has a dormitory in a building at the back. A bed costs Y33, and there are usually many western tourists staying here. Take the local #1 (Yilu) bus and get off at Qiliheqiao.

Places to See

White Pagoda Hill (Baitashan), the Five Springs Park (Wuquanshan Gongyuan), and the Yellow River Bridge (Zhongshan Qiao), also known as Huang He Tieqiao (Iron Bridge), are some of the highlights in the city. Taking the lift at the Lanshan Park will also give you a thrill.

LINXIA

This city of around 170,000 is about a 4-hour bus ride from Lanzhou and the capital of the Linxia Hui Autonomous Prefecture. There are numerous mosques here catering to the Muslim Hui population. You can change foreign currency at the *Bank of China* in the city.

Access by Bus

There are many buses from the Western Bus Station in Lanzhou, and there are also buses coming from Xining, Xiahe, Hezuo, etc. At Linxia there are also

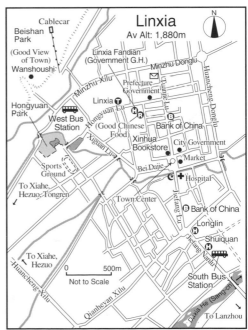

179

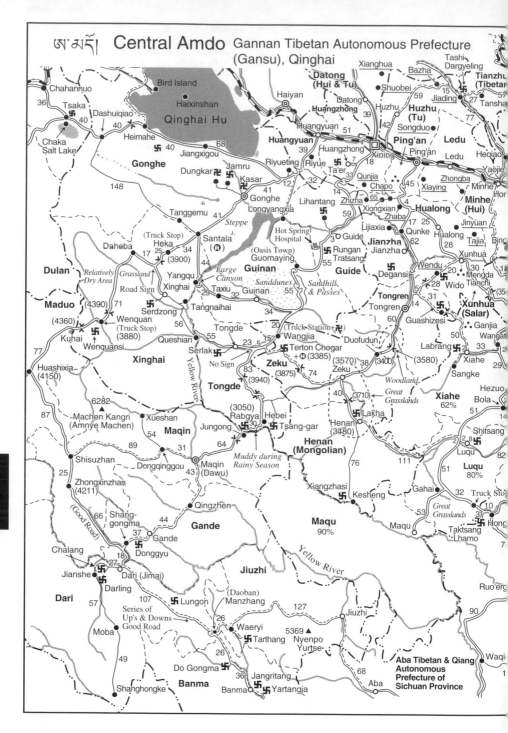

Central Amdo

ཨ་མདོ

Gannan Tibetan Autonomous Prefecture (Gansu), Qinghai

Chahannuo
Tsaka
36
Dashuiqiao
40
40
Heimahe
40
Bird Island
Haixinshan
Qinghai Hu
Jiangxigou
68
Haiyan
Xianghua
Bazha
Tashi Dargyeling
Tianzhu (Tibetan)
Datong (Hui & Tu)
Shuobei
Huzhu
15
59
Jiading
27
Tansha
Datong
Huzhu (Tu)
77
Chaka Salt Lake
Gonghe
148
Dungkar
Tanggemu
41
Jamru
Kasar
Gonghe
41
Longyangxia
12
Riyueting
Riyue
Ta'er
33
Huangyuan
51
Huangzhong
39
Huangzhong
39
Xining
Ping'an
7
18
142
Songduo
Ping'an
Ledu
Ledu
Heqiao
Yaojie
Zhongba
Qunjia
Chapo
45
Xiaying
Minhe
14
Lihantang
Zhizha
65
Xiongxian
Zhaba
4
Minhe (Hui)
Hor
Steppe
Dulan
Relatively Dry Area
Grassland
Road Sign
Daheba
Heka
34
25
17
(3900)
Santala
(Oasis Town)
Guomaying
Hot Spring Hospital
Rungan Tratsang
3
Guide
Jianzha
Jianzha
62
Hualong
Hualong
28
Zhaba
Lijiaxia
Qunke
Jinyuan
Tajia
Xunhua
17
25
59
Xiongxian
(Truck Stop)
(3900)
44
55
Guide
Degansi
Wendu
20
Mengda Tianchi
30
Yangqu
Xinghai
Taxiu
Guinan
Guinan
Sanddunes
Sandhill & Passes
55
Tongren
Tongren
14
Xunhua (Salar)
Wangat
5
28
Wido
31
(35
Maduo
(4390)
71
Serdzong
Wenquan (Truck Stop)
(3880)
Tangnaihai
34
Guashizesi
60
Ganjia
50
Labrang
33
2
(4360)
56
Tongde
20
(Truck Station+ 卍)
Duofudun
Kuhai
Wenquansi
Queshian
55
Wangjia
Terton Chogar
+ (3385)
(3570)
38
(3400)
(3580)
Xiahe
29
Sangke
77
Huashixia (4150)
Xinghai
Serlak
No Sign
23
15
83
(3940)
Zeku
(3875)
Zeku
74
Woodland
Hezuo
Bola
Tongde
40
(3710)
Great Grasslands
Xiahe
62%
51
Shitsang
6282
Machen Kangri (Amnye Machen)
Xueshan
(3050)
Rabgya
Jungong
30
Hebei
Tsang-gar
Henan (3480)
Lakha
Henan (Mongolian)
Luqu
82
Maqin
54
89
31
64
Luqu
80%
87
Shisuzhan
Dongqinggou
Maqin (Dawu)
43
Muddy during Rainy Season
76
111
Gahai
32
Truck Stop
10
25
Zhongxinzhan (4211)
Xiangzhasi
Kesheng
Great Grasslands
3
Hong
(Good Road)
66
Shanggongma
44
Qingzhen
Maqu
90%
Maqu
Taktsang Lhamo
53
7
37
Gande
Gande
Chalang
Donggyu
18
27
Dari (Jimai)
Jiuzhi
Yellow River
Jianshe
Darling
Dari
57
107
Lungon
(Daoban) Manzhang
127
Jiuzhi
90
Moba
Series of Up's & Downs Good Road
26
Waeryi
Tarthang
5369
Nyenpo Yurtse
68
Ruo'erg
49
26
Do Gongma
Jangritang
36
Aba
Waqi
1
Shanghongke
Banma
Banma
Yartangja
Aba Tibetan & Qiang Autonomous Prefecture of Sichuan Province

AMDO

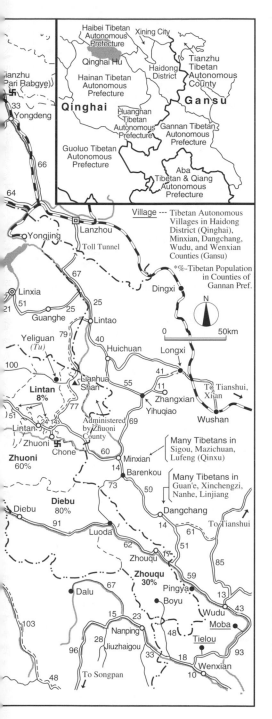

Village --- Tibetan Autonomous
Villages in Haidong
District (Qinghai),
Minxian, Dangchang,
Wudu, and Wenxian
Counties (Gansu)

*%-Tibetan Population
in Counties of
Gannan Pref.

2 bus stations, a southern and a western one, with
many of the buses heading towards Lanzhou
leaving from the southern one. Many of those for
Xiahe, Hezuo, and Tongren depart from the west.
Depending on the destination, there are also a
number of buses heading in the same direction that
leave from both of the stations.

Accommodation

There is a wide range to choose from in the town,
from small guesthouses to a massive hotel. Many
of these are located around the Southern Bus
Station.

The *Government Guesthouse* (Linxia Fandian) has
dormitory beds for Y20, but only the more
expensive rooms are equipped with hot water
showers. The guesthouse also has a restaurant.

The *Huaqiao Fandian* (Hotel) is one of those near
the Southern Bus Station, and a double room with
a television and an electric blanket costs Y60.

The majority of restaurants in Linxia serve
Islamic food.

GANNAN TIBETAN AUTONOMOUS PREFECTURE

Follow the well-paved highway along the Daxia
He River (Sang-chu) from Lanzhou, and you will
reach the Hui town of Linxia. After passing the
town, you will start seeing Tibetan signposts along
the road indicating that you have entered the
predominantly Tibetan-populated Gannan
Prefecture.

Facing Qinghai and Aba (Ngawa) Tibetan &
Qiang Autonomous Prefecture in Sichuan, Gannan
is in the southern part of Gansu Province and
spreads out over an area dominated by the
tributaries of the Yellow River (Huang He). In an
area roughly the same size as the Netherlands, there
are only around 600,000 people, consisting mainly
of Tibetans, Hui, Han Chinese, and some other
minority groups and immigrants. Visiting the great

Mandala, Labrang Monastery

AMDO

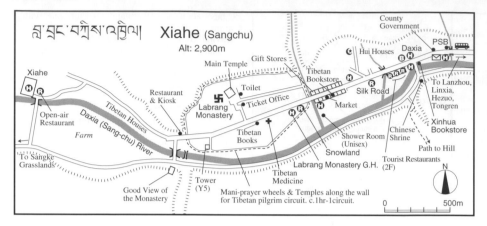

ह्र'ह्रूद'वग्रूब'वहिया। Xiahe (Sangchu)
Alt: 2,900m

Labrang Monastery in Xiahe and taking in the vast panoramic views of the grasslands here are the highlights in this region.

XIAHE (SANG-CHU)

Located on the banks of the Daxia He (Sang-chu), this village at 2,900m was built around the Labrang Monastery. The average temperature in August is 15°C, and it falls to -12°C during January, with the first snowfalls starting in October. On the main street of this important monastery town there are not only new buildings and public offices but also many stores stocking Tibetan goods. You will see a lot of young monks from the gompa wandering around the town, and the pilgrims riding into town on horseback will remind you that you are in an authentic Tibetan town.

Access

There are direct buses to Xiahe from both of the bus stations in Lanzhou. The trip requires a travel insurance policy and takes about 7 hours. From Hezuo there are a lot of minibuses that service the route, and there are also a few buses each day that come in from Linxia, which takes just over 2 hours.

Buses from Xiahe (Bus Station)

*Tongren (via Ganjia)—Departing daily at 07:30, the trip costs Y11 and takes 4 hours.
*Lanzhou—This trip takes 7 hours, and the bus leaves at 07:20 each day.
*Hezuo—There are a lot of minibuses everyday, and the 2-hour trip costs Y7.

At the station ticket booth, foreigners are requested to show their travel insurance, but this may not be a problem if you get on the bus out in the street.

Accommodation & Restaurants

The town welcomes not only tourists but also pilgrims, and thus there are over 30 guesthouses and hotels of various standards.

The *Daxia Binguan* (Hotel) has dormitory beds for Y15 and double rooms for Y80. The hot water showers are only available for an hour at night.

The *Labrang Monastery Zhaodaisuo* (Guesthouse) is popular among backpackers, and it charges Y10 for a bed in its dormitory. There are only cold water showers available.

The *Xiahe Binguan* (Labrang Hotel) is a Tibetan-style establishment that has dormitory beds for Y20 and double rooms for Y150. There are hot showers and heaters available. You might get somewhat hassled by the dogs at night on the route home from the town center, as it is around 30 minutes on foot. The *Minzu Fandian* (Hotel) is another cheap option for staying near the bus station. Here a dormitory bed will cost you Y12, and there is a hot water shower in the courtyard.

An alternative to staying in a recognized hotel or guesthouse is to stay with a Tibetan family, as some are willing to take in foreign visitors.

With many foreign tourists visiting the town, many of the restaurants here have English menus. In addition to Chinese and Islamic places, there are Tibetan restaurants serving *momos* and *tukpa*.

Places to See
Labrang Monastery

Labrang is among the 6 leading Gelukpa monasteries in the Tibetan world, and it is has been constructed on an enormous scale. Along with Kumbum (Ta'er Monastery), it wields a great deal of influence and attracts a large number of pilgrims from throughout the Amdo region. If you're enticed to enter the monastery by the sight of the Maitreya Hall's (Main Assembly Hall) glittering golden roof, you will be asked to buy a *Foreign Tourist* ticket

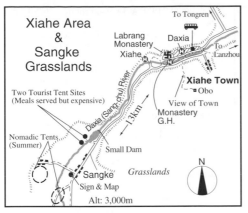

Xiahe Area & Sangke Grasslands

To Tongren
Labrang Monastery
Daxia
Xiahe
To Lanzhou

Xiahe Town
Obo

Two Tourist Tent Sites
(Meals served but expensive)

Daxia (Sang-chu) River

13km

View of Town
Monastery
G.H.

Nomadic Tents
(Summer)

Small Dam

Sangke
Sign & Map

Grasslands

Alt: 3,000m

N

costing Y22.5. Single visitors are not supposed to enter the monastery, so if you are traveling alone or in a non-organized group, it would be better to try after 09:00, when the large tourist groups crowd into the monastery.

If you take the pilgrim's circuit around the monastery, rotating *mani* prayer-wheels as you go, you can get a good view of the back of the monastery. In front of the main gate there is a cluster of buildings that act as lodgings for the monks, giving the area the feel of a maze. You may be befriended by a monk in town, who will invite you to his place to watch him or his colleague making statues of the Buddha, while you enjoy a cup of butter tea.

Labrang originally meant 'Dormitory for Incarnate Lamas.' With 6 colleges for the study of astronomy, Tibetan medicine, and other religious and cultural pursuits, this huge monastery covers all the aspects of Tibetan Buddhism. The monastery was founded in the 18th century by the 1st Jamyang Zhepa. In 1957 the monastery housed 4,000 monks, and at its peak, there were approximately 500 incarnate lamas from all over the country in residence. This made the monastery function as an elite religious training school up until the Chinese occupation of the region.

It was shut down by the Chinese, and although there have been substantial restoration efforts, there are still only as few as 1,000 monks in residence now. The great incarnated lama, the 6th Jamyang Zhepa, now lives in Lanzhou.

In accordance with its size and importance, this monastery hosts many festivals corresponding to the dates of the Tibetan Buddhist calendar, especially during *Monlam* (Great Prayer Festival), held during the 1st lunar month (February-March).

Sangke Grasslands
Traveling about 13km south-west of Xiahe, you

will reach the area known as the Sangke Grasslands. There are tents laid out for tourists, and there is also food available, although it is relatively expensive. In summer, you can probably stay in local nomad's tents, but it is advisable to bring your own food.

There is an intermittent bus service, which is scheduled to leave Xiahe at 13:30, but this is unreliable, and at times simply doesn't happen at all. The best way to get to this area is to rent a bicycle at your guesthouse or hotel in Xiahe. The Y10 a day ride takes between an hour and 90 minutes.

Ganjia
This is a grassland area that you will pass through on the way to Tongren in Qinghai Province after leaving Xiahe. The incarnate lamas of the Ganja Drakar Gompa, to the north-east of Ganjia, have been women for generations, and the present incarnation holds an executive position in the government.

HEZUO (TSOE)

When you approach Hezuo from Lanzhou by bus, you will first see gompas that look like modern buildings that appear wider than they are long. With a population of 35,000, this town is the capital of Gannan Prefecture, and it commands an important position on the highway connecting Lanzhou with Chengdu. There are many Hui and Han people in the town, and at the northern end is Tsoe Gompa (Hezuo Monastery).

Access
There are many buses from Xiahe and Linxia, and trips from both of these towns take 2 hours. There are also direct buses leaving from both the eastern and western stations in Lanzhou, and the trip to Hezuo takes 7 hours.

From Hezuo there are a few buses each day for Lanzhou, Xining, Linxia, and Xiahe. There are also bus services from Hezuo to other towns in Gannan Prefecture, such as Lintan, Zhuoni (Chone), Minxian, Dingxi, Luqu, Maqu, Diebu (Thewo), and Zhouqu. The towns of Henan in Qinghai and both Aba (Ngawa) and Ruo'ergai in Sichuan are also connected by bus with Hezou.

Accommodation
There are some places to stay in the bus station. The *Gannan Binguan* (Hotel) is opposite the station, and it has clean rooms. A double with a private bath and a television is Y25 per person, and hot water is available for about an hour each night

AMDO

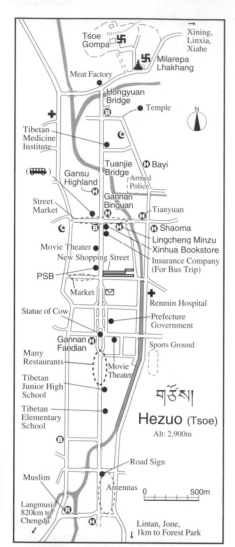

Tsoe Gompa

Xining, Linxia, Xiahe

Milarepa Lhakhang

Meat Factory

Hongyuan Bridge

Temple

N

Tibetan Medicine Institute

Tuanjie Bridge — Bayi

Gansu Highland — Armed Police

Street Market

Gannan Binguan — Tianyuan

Shaoma

Lingcheng Minzu

Movie Theater — Xinhua Bookstore

New Shopping Street — Insurance Company (For Bus Trip)

PSB

Market

Statue of Cow

Renmin Hospital

Prefecture Government

Gannan Fandian

Sports Ground

Many Restaurants

Movie Theater

Tibetan Junior High School

Tibetan Elementary School

मर्ठेंबा

Hezuo (Tsoe)
Alt: 2,900m

Road Sign

Muslim

Antennas

0   500m

Langmusi 820km to Chengdu

Lintan, Jone,
↓ 1km to Forest Park

AMDO

Milarepa Lhakhang

starting at 21:00. A 3-person room costs Y15 per person.

The *Gansu Highland Travel* is a guesthouse to the north of the bus station, and a bed in the dormitory costs Y15.

The *Lingcheng Minzu Lushe* (Hotel) is another cheap alternative, which has 3-person rooms costing Y8 per person.

Places to See
Tsoe Gompa (Hezuo Monastery) & Milarepa Lhakhang

Built on a hillside, Tsoe Gompa was constructed in the 17th century and used to house 500 monks, but now as few as 80 live here. The most striking building here is a 13-story Milarepa Lhakhang, which stands at the foot of the hill. The dark-red colored, 9-story part is said to symbolize the tower, with 9 levels that Milarepa spent all his energy on and built by himself to honor the son of his revered master, Marpa. The present building was reconstructed some years ago, and the design has remained faithful to the original that was destroyed by the Chinese Communist forces.

LUQU (LUCHU) (CLOSED)

To the north of the Luqu River, which is a tributary of the Yellow River (Huang He), is the small town of Luqu. Although it is 2-3km to the east off the main road connecting Hezuo with Ruo'ergai (Dzoge), most long-distance buses are stationed at Luqu. The name *Luchu* means 'The River of the Dragon God.' About 8km to the east of the town is Shitsang Monastery, and to the south is the scenic Haihu Lake that you can see from the bus.

Access

There are 4-5 buses each day from Hezuo to Luqu, and the 2-hour trip costs around Y7. Most of the buses that are continuing on to points beyond Luqu still stop at the town. At Luqu, the buses leave from the Luqu Bus Station. A bus departs from Luqu for Hezuo at 06:30, and between 09:00 and 11:00 there are at least 5-6 buses that stop at Luqu before continuing on to their destinations. There are a number of other buses leaving the town right up into the evening.

If you are heading south, there is a bus for Maqu that leaves around 09:00 and another at 13:00. There is also one that heads for Langmusi (Taktsang Lhamo) around 09:00, and though locals are charged Y7 for the trip, many foreigners are overcharged to the tune of Y30 or more. Buses for Diebu and Zhouqu stop at the town between 08:00 and 11:00.

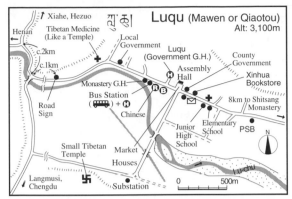

```
Xiahe, Hezuo      ग'क्षु|   Luqu (Mawen or Qiaotou)
                                        Alt: 3,100m
Henan    Tibetan Medicine
         (Like a Temple)    Local
c.2km                       Government   Luqu
                                        (Government G.H.)    County
   c.1km                                                     Government
                            Assembly                Xinhua
         Monastery G.H.     Hall                     Bookstore
           Bus Station                              8km to Shitsang
Road      (🚌) + 🏥                                   Monastery
Sign           Chinese
                         Junior  Elementary  PSB    N
                         High    School
         Small Tibetan   School
         Temple    Market
                   Houses
    Langmusi,                      0        500m
    Chengdu    Substation
```

that Guru Rinpoche, who brought esoteric Buddhism to Tibet, destroyed a demon in this valley.

*Note: This section also includes a description of Kirti Gompa even though it is on the Sichuan side of the border.

Access

From Hezuo and surrounding areas, catch a bus destined for towns in the south of Gannan Prefecture or Sichuan, such as Ruo'ergai, Songpan, Zhouqu, Diebu, etc. Get off at Langmusi-chakou, but you must be careful, as there are no signs for the stop. There is sometimes a tractor waiting at the entrance to ferry passengers from there, and you can share this for Y1. If there is no tractor, it is either a 3km walk up the mountain path, or you may be able to hitch a lift.

Coming from the Ruo'ergai area, you will need to take a bus heading for Hezuo, Lanzhou, etc.

Accommodation

You can stay at the bus station, and a dormitory bed costs Y8. There are showers, and the staff is kind.

The *Luqu Binguan* (Hotel) is a new establishment, and the rates start at Y20.

Places to See
Shitsang Monastery (Xicangsi)

Eight kilometers to the east of Luqu is the monastery of Shitsang, a branch of the Labrang Monastery in Xiahe. The monastery, next door to a mosque, used to house as many as 500 monks but now has only about 150 in residence. While it is about a 2-hour walk from the town, you should be able to get a lift on a shared farm tractor heading out that way.

Transportation from Langmusi

Whether you are going to either Hezuo or Ruo'ergai, it is easiest to hitch a lift in a car or truck leaving the village. If you can't find a lift, walk down to the entrance, Langmusi-chakou, to catch a bus. Some buses heading in the Ruo'ergai direction should arrive at 11:00-12:00, and the trip costs Y13. For Hezuo, 4-5 buses should arrive at 08:00-09:00, and the fare is also Y13. It is advisable to check the most recent bus schedules with local people or other travelers, since these times are subject to change. Some buses on these routes require that you show a valid travel permit.

If you have trouble getting on the buses or there are simply none around, you can try to hitch a lift on a truck with other locals, many of whom are monks from Langmusi. Trucks heading for the Ruo'ergai area may actually be faster and more comfortable than the bus, since the trucks can really get up some speed on this flat stretch. There is a checkpoint on the way.

TAKTSANG LHAMO (LANGMUSI)

On the 2 tree-covered hills that face each other across the valley, there are 2 large monasteries, one on either hill. The Sertri Gompa is on the northern hill, and Kirti Gompa is on the southern one. There is a water mill along the stream that flows through the valley separating them, which has a *mani* prayer-wheel that is turned by the water in the stream. The village has a very peaceful and calm atmosphere.

It is said that the boundary separating the provinces of Gansu and Sichuan cuts through the center of the village, and this places Sertri Gompa in Gansu and Kirti Gompa in Sichuan.

This village is called Taktsang Lhamo in Tibetan, with the *Taktsang* meaning 'Tiger's Cave.' The story goes that the woodlands in the valley are home to a cave where a tiger has its lair. *Lhamo* means 'Goddess,' and it is believed that a goddess also lives in these same woods. Another legend tells

Accommodation
& Restaurants

The *Langmusi Binguan* (Guesthouse) is facing the high street, but set back in a courtyard. Beds with a common shower cost Y15, and the rate for a dormitory bed is Y10. Coal heaters provided.

The *Taktsang Lhamo Sertri Monastery Hostel* has dormitory beds at Y11 for foreigners. There are no showers, and the toilet is not in the same building as the rooms. There is a water pump that allows you to wash your clothes.

AMDO

The village has a couple of restaurants with English menus where you'll be served rather simple Western or Chinese food.

Places to See
Sertri Gompa
(Dacanglangmu Saichisi)

This large Gelukpa monastery is on the hill to the north of the village, and you may hear the locals refer to it as Sechi Gompa. The head priest of Ganden Gompa, the head monastery of the Gelukpa order, is called Ganden Tripa, and the 53rd Ganden Tripa was the one that founded the gompa in 1748. *Sertri* means 'Seat of Gold' and is the other name given to Ganden Tripa.

During the Cultural Revolution, the monastery was totally devastated, but reconstruction started in 1981, and a monk at the site said that the monastery is now home to approximately 400 monks.

Kirti Gompa
(Dacangnama Ge'erdisi)

This other great Gelukpa monastery stretches over the southern hill from north to south, and its large chorten is a beautiful sight.

Like Sertri Gompa, the monastery was in ruins after the Cultural Revolution, and it is said that there are now about 700 monks in residence. The great incarnated lama, Kirti Tulku, fled to India and founded a monastery in Dharamsala where he has also held office in the Tibetan government-in-exile.

Both Kirti and Sertri Gompas have engaged in an age-old power struggle for control of the surrounding nomadic areas. This competitive relationship may still be continuing, therefore setting the provincial boundary straight through the middle of the village.

Chorten, Sertri Gompa

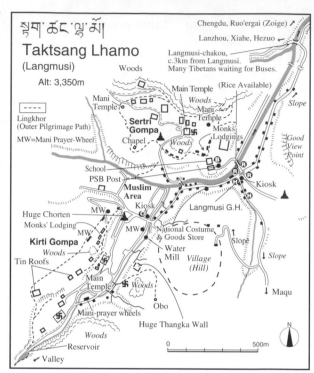

 སྟག་ཚང་ལྷ་མོ།

Taktsang Lhamo
(Langmusi)
Alt: 3,350m

Chengdu, Ruo'ergai (Zoige)
Lanzhou, Xiahe, Hezuo
Langmusi-chakou, c.3km from Langmusi.
Many Tibetans waiting for Buses.

Woods

Main Temple (Rice Available)

```
----
```
Lingkhor
(Outer Pilgrimage Path)
MW=Mani Prayer-Wheel

Mani Temple
Woods
Mani Temple
Slope

Sertri Gompa
Chapel
Woods
Monks Lodgings
Good View Point

School
PSB Post
Muslim Area
Kiosk

Langmusi G.H.

Huge Chorten
Monks' Lodging
MW
Kirti Gompa
Woods
Tin Roofs
MW
Kiosk
MW
National Costume & Goods Store
Water Mill
Village (Hill)
Slope
↓ Slope

Main Temple
Mani-prayer wheels
Woods
Obo
↓ Maqu

Huge Thangka Wall

Woods
Reservoir
↙ Valley

0   500m

N

LINTAN (CLOSED)

More than 70% of those living in Lintan County are Han Chinese, and the Tibetan people here only make up about 6% of the population. This county was probably formed by putting Han-dominated areas together within the Tibetan Autonomous Prefecture, as the county boundaries are complicated. There is also a detached territory that is incorporated into this administrative unit. In Mandarin the county is called *Lintan*, but the local pronunciation is *Lintai*.

You can get to Lintan by taking a bus from Hezuo, and at the northern end of the county there is a scenic area called Lianhuashan.

ZHUONI (CHO-NE) (CLOSED)

Cho-ne Gompa
(Gonchen Shedrubling)

In 1295, Phakpa, who was trusted with governing Tibet by Kublai Khan (the emperor of the Yuan

Dynasty), visited Cho-ne Gompa (Gonchen Shedrubling). Until that time Bon had prospered in these parts, but Buddhism was soon to take over that position, and the predominant school of Buddhism at that time was Sakyapa. Later the Cho-ne version of the Tibetan Buddhist canon, the *Kangyur* and *Tangyur* that are housed here, made the monastery famous. The gompa now belongs to the Gelukpa order.

Hezuo is also the gateway for Zhuoni, with regular buses going to and from the town.

MAQU (MACHU)

Maqu is on the Yellow River (Huang He), which flows from the west up to here, and then the river makes a huge curve at this point and proceeds to flow back in the opposite direction. Maqu County is between the provinces of Sichuan and Qinghai, and most of the inhabitants here are Tibetan. The county is accessible by bus from Hezuo, Xiahe, etc.

DIEBU (THEWO)

There are many Tibetans in this county, and as 60 % of Diebu County is covered with woodland, forestry is unsurprisingly an important activity. The southern part of the county faces Aba (Ngawa) County in Sichuan Province, and it is said that there is ongoing nuclear research in the area using uranium mined here since the 1960s. Diebu can be reached by bus from Hezuo.

ZHOUQU (DRUKCHU)

This county is along the Bailong Jiang (Druk-chu or Dragon River), and like Diebu, the area is heavily wooded, and the endangered Panda is reported to still inhabit this region. There are buses taking you out to Zhouqu from Hezuo.

BOYU (BOEYUL)

In the south of Zhouqu County, across a mountain from Jiuzhaigou in Sichuan, is Boyu. It is said that the ancestors of those living here came from Chamdo in the Tibetan Autonomous Region to the west. The name *Boeyul* means 'Tibetan Village.'

The story goes that this name was adopted so as to remind the inhabitants that their real roots were in Tibet, even though they had moved to the very edge of Chinese territory.

At the flower festival held here, *Metho Dusang*, the girls wear really unique colorful costumes and ornaments on their heads.

NORTH-WEST OF GANSU

TIANZHU (PARI)
(Tianzhu Tibetan Autonomous County) (Closed)

The Tianzhu Tibetan Autonomous County, facing Qinghai, is about a 3-hour ride by bus from Lanzhou to the north-west. Around one-third of the population are Tibetans, but it looks very much like a Han Chinese town. If you take a closer look at the people here, you will see that some of the women, said to be the Tibetan womenfolk, knot their hair back with towel-like cloths. You will also see Tibetan characters on the signboards at government offices and on storefronts.

Access by Bus
There are many buses from both of the bus stations in Lanzhou, and you will need to take a bus going to Wuwei, Jinchang, etc. and then get off along the way. The 3-hour journey costs Y10.8.

At Xining, you have to catch the bus heading for Jinchang, which leaves at 07:45 each day, and get off on the way. It arrives around 15:00, and the fare is Y20.3.

Access by Rail
There are only 3 local trains that stop at the station of Huacangsi, and these arrive around midnight, which makes them rather inconvenient.

Buses from Tianzhu (Tianzhu Bus Station)
*Lanzhou, Wuwei—There are many buses
   that leave from the road in front of the station.
*Tiantangsi Temple—There is a bus leaving at
   09:00, and the 92-km trip costs Y7.5.
*Huzhu in Qinghai (via Jiading)
   There is a daily departure at 07:40.
*Ta'er Monastery (Kumbum) in Qinghai
   This route is serviced by a bus leaving at 08:00.

There are a lot of buses for other destinations, and there are also minibuses for Yongdeng.

Accommodation & Restaurants
The *Tianzhu Binguan* (County Government Guesthouse) is a 7- to 8-minute walk from the bus station. A 2-person room here costs Y12-15 per

AMDO

person, and a 4-person room is Y7 per bed. Rates for beds in double rooms are Y20-50, and although none of the rooms have a shower, there is a pool for bathing in front. The guesthouse also has a restaurant.

There are a number of hotels and guesthouses in and around the bus station, and the rates are Y5-10.

For eating out, there are restaurants serving mainly Sichuanese food around the station and near the market.

Places to See
Pari Rabgye Gompa (Huacangsi)
This is a small Gelukpa monastery, and there are numerous minibuses from town to the gompa.

Tashi Dargyeling (Tiantangsi)
This is the largest monastery in this region, though it is not on as massive a scale as other regional religious centers. Legend has it that the monastery was based on a Bon temple that had been here since the 9th century, and it eventually came to belong to the Gelukpa order after having been in the hands of the Sakyapa and Karma Kagyupa orders. In this area are many indigenous people called *Hor* (*Tu* in Chinese), who are also followers of Tibetan Buddhism.

Admission charges at the Tiantangsi Temple are Y1 for the Shakyamuni Lhakhang and Y2 for the Dukhor Lhakhang (Kalachakra Temple).

Access by Bus
For Tashi Dargyeling (Tiantangsi), there is a single daily bus leaving Tianzhu at 09:30. The bus journey takes you through a 3,560m high pass and then the Zhuchaxiang area, with its large population of indigenous people. It arrives sometime after 14:00, and Tashi Dargyeling is about 300m from the bus stop.

Buses from Tianzhu to Huzhu do not make a stop at Tiantangsi, but go on to Jiading (Beishan) on the other side of the river. It is approximately 4km between Tiantangsi and Jiading, and it takes about an hour. A bus leaves for Tianzhu at 08:30, and there is a bus from Jiading to Huzhu (Weiyuan), which sets off at 09:00 every day. The bus from Huzhu to Tianzhu also stops at Jiading (Beishan) around 10:30, and the one from Minhe to Menyuan and another from Menyuan to Minhe both arrive here around 11:00. In addition, there is a bus from Tianzhu to Huzhu that stops at Jiading (Beishan) between 12:00 and 13:00 every day.

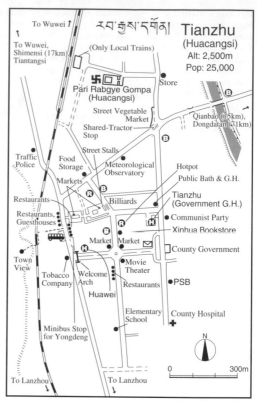

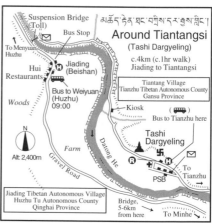

Accommodation
The *Bus Station Guesthouse* is in front of the bus station at Tiantangsi and has beds for Y5. There is also a guesthouse in Jiading.

There are a couple of restaurants at Tiantangsi and a handful of Islamic restaurants in Jiading. There seem to be no Chinese restaurants in the area.

SUNAN YUGURZU AUTONOMOUS COUNTY (ZHANGYE DIQU) (CLOSED)

On the northern side of the Qilian Mountains, separating the provinces of Gansu and Qinghai, is an area that was once part of the Silk Road. This area is home to Tibetan people who live by rearing livestock on the grasslands that cover this highland region.

This area used to be called *Yugur* in Tibetan, which originally meant *Uighur*, but the transliteration of the word into Chinese characters led to the adoption of the name *Yugur*. The Yugur people living in the area are also engaged in rearing livestock, and they also follow the teachings of the Gelukpa order, just as the Tibetans do here.

Taje Gompa (Matisi Monastery)
Sixty kilometers to the south of the Silk Road oasis of Zhangye you will find the monastery of Taje Gompa (Matisi), which is famous for its stone cave. The monastery is said to have once housed approximately 1,000 monks, but there are only a few left here now.

Hitchhiking in Tibet

Yasuhiko Fujimura

Many trips around the vast expanses of Western Tibet will take at least 2 days and during these journeys you will probably have to sleep out in the open, as few truck drivers stay in hotels. It is definitely advisable to take warm clothing with you as the nights get bitterly cold. I myself nearly died from the cold twice while traveling in the area.

The most serious problem on these truck journeys, though, is probably the unrelenting shaking and vibration of the trucks and the stomachaches you can get from it. After a pilgrimage to Mt. Kailash I had to take a place at the very back of a truck (a position best avoided), as the vehicle was already full of passengers. With the truck running on unpaved wasteland, there was endless shaking and bumps to contend with for the entire 6 hours. After finally being released from this hell, I thought my brains had turned to liquid and I had a terrible ache in my stomach. It was easily the worst drive of my life.

These appalling road conditions cause the Chinese-made trucks to deteriorate rapidly. A brand-new one becomes unreliable and prone to breakdowns within a couple of years. Although the Tibetan drivers are hardened by their grueling experiences and toughened by

having to make frequent repairs, they are still kind to their passengers. Those I met spared me some of their tsampa and butter tea on a number of occasions and these truck journeys turned out to be a good exercise in getting used to the unique foods of Tibet.

One final cautionary note is to avoid throwing cigarettes from a moving truck. In Tibet the strong winds and the dry air combine to make it easy for cargo to catch on fire. Trucks also carry gasoline as gas stations are very few and far between in this remote region. In my case, I was fortunate that my cigarette only set fire to my backpack and some other stuff near it, otherwise I might not have survived.

AMDO

QINGHAI PROVINCE

XINING

The large city of Xining (2,250m) is the capital of Qinghai Province and acts as one of the major gateways to the Tibetan Plateau. This is a popular starting point for those heading for the Amdo region or for Lhasa via Golmud. Though the city itself has a strong Islamic flavor, as it is home to many Hui people, you will start getting a more Tibetan feel as you move away from the city. There are many Tibetan sites in the area, such as Qinghai Hu (Lake Kokonor), Ta'er Monastery (Kumbum), etc. The city is known in Tibetan as *Sulang*.

Access by Rail
To Xining
*No. 75 Special Express
Beijing West 08:50-Xining 17:26 (1 night)
(Lanzhou-Xining, every other day)
*No. 376 & 377 Express
Shanghai 22:01-Xining 16:52 (2 nights)
*No. 172 & 173 Special Express
Qingdao 18:49-Xining 10:14 (2 nights)
(Lanzhou-Xining, every other day)
*No. 575 Express
Xi'an 15:15-Xining 11:17 (1 night)
*Lanzhou-Xining
There are a number of trains every day. (For trains from Golmud, see the Golmud section.)

From Xining
*No. 76 Special Express
Xining 08:49-Beijing West 16:53 (1 night)
(Lanzhou-Xining, every other day)
*No. 375 & 378 Express
Xining 15:45-Shanghai 07:44 (2 nights)
*No. 171 & 174 Special Express
Xining 13:26-Qingdao 06:52 (2 nights)
(Lanzhou-Xining, every other day)
*No. 576 Express
Xining 14:08-Xi'an 08:58 (1 night)

From Xining to Golmud
*No. 759
Xining 12:23-Golmud 09:52 (1 night)
*No. 603 Rapid
Xining 18:30-Golmud 12:00 (1 night)
These trains are in service on alternate days, and you can normally purchase a ticket for the following day's train at Xining.

Access by Air
To Xining
The city is connected to most of the major national and regional centers by air. Flights are on various different airlines including: China Northwest Airlines (WH), China Southwest Airlines (SZ), Air China (CA), Xinjiang Airways (XO), Sichuan Airlines (3U), Zhongyuan Airlines (Z2), Changan Airlines (2Z), and Shanghai Airlines (FM).

*Beijing
Mon (WH), Tue (SZ), Wed (CA), Thu (SZ), Fri (SZ), Sat (WH), Sun (AC & CSW).
Costs: Y1,530. (2 hrs)
*Shanghai
Tue (FM), Sat (FM). Costs: Y1,720. (3 hrs 35 mins)
*Guangzhou
Tue (XO), Sat (XO). Costs: Y1,790. (3 hrs)
*Chengdu
Tue (SZ), Wed (3U), Fri (SZ), Sun (SZ & 3U).
Costs: Y1,050. (1 hr)
*Urumqi
Mon (XO), Tue (WH & XO), Wed (XO), Sat (XO). Costs: Y1,340. (2-3 hrs)
*Xi'an
Mon (SZ), Tue (FM & 2Z), Thu (FM), Fri (SZ), Sat (FM & 2Z). Costs: Y730. (1 hr)
*Lhasa
There are 4 flights per week, and the day of departure varies seasonally. (2 hrs)

There are also a few flights from Chongqing, Kunming, Shenyang, Dunhuan, and Golmud (Geermu). The airport is 15km south, south-east of the city, and from the CAAC office you can take a limousine bus for Y10.

Bus from Xining to Golmud and Lhasa
For Golmud - There are a lot of buses leaving from the bus station and from the main railway station in Xining.

From Xining Station
Night Bus (seat) - The bus leaves Xining at 13:00-14:00 and arrives in Golmud around 09:00 the next morning.
Night Bus (sleeping berth) - The bus leaves Xining at 16:00 and arrives in Golmud at 10:00 the next morning.

There is also a direct bus to Lhasa, and if you are lucky, you may be able to obtain a through ticket. Although this is possible, many foreigners have reportedly been forced to get off the bus at Golmud and then buy a ticket at the foreigner's price. If you can buy a through ticket to Lhasa, this should cost you about Y500.

AMDO

Buses at the Long-Distance Terminal

The bus routes from Xining out to various points within the province are in relatively good condition for a Tibetan area. Tickets are available a day in advance, and a nice surprise is that these buses don't charge special rates for foreign passengers.

Major Services:
To the West:
*Chaka (via Heimahe)—There is a daily bus leaving at 08:00. (298km)

*Dulan (via Chaka)— Two departures daily at 08:30 and 09:00. (428km)

*Golmud—There are a lot of buses servicing this route. (781km)

*Wulan (via Chaka)—The bus leaves at 08:00 every day and arrives in the evening. (374km)

*Lenghu (via Delingha)—This is a 3-day trip with a bus leaving every other day at 07:30. (975km)

*Delingha - Departing every day at 07:30, these buses have sleeping berths available. (511km)

*Huatugou (via Lenghu)—Leaves at 07:30 every other day.

*Haiyan (via Huangyuan)—Three departures a day at 14:00, 15:00, and 17:00. (90km)

*Gangcha (via Haiyan)—08:30 departure every day. (196km)

*Tianjun (via Gangcha)—There is a bus every other day at 08:00. (310km)

To the North:
*Menyuan—There are 5 buses a day. (155km)

*Qilian—Two departures a day at 08:30 and 09:30. (288km)

*Zhangye—Daily bus leaving at 07:30. (347km)

*Jinchang (via Tianzhu)—Daily bus leaving at 07:45.

To Huangnan & Surrounding Area:
*Tongren—There are a lot of minibuses on this route. (191km)

*Jianzha—One departure a day between 08:00 and 13:30. (131 km).

*Hualong—There are a lot of minibuses on this route. (114km)

*Henan (via Tongren and Zeku) - There is a daily service on this route. (325km)

*Xunhua—There are a lot of minibuses on this route. (159km)

To Gannan (Gansu Province):
*Linxia—There are a lot of buses each day. (266km)

*Hezuo (via Hualong and Xunhua)—There is a bus leaving a 07:45 every day. (331km)

To the South-west:
*Gonghe (via Daotanghe)—There are a lot of minibuses on this route. (144km)

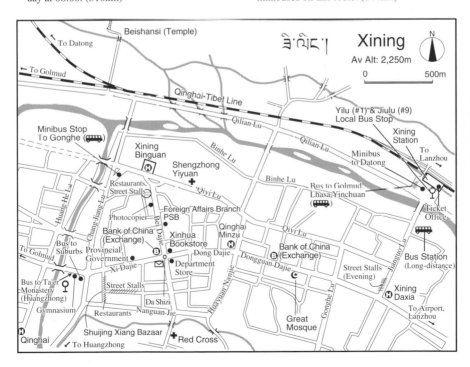

AMDO

*Xinghai (via Gonghe and Heka)—Three departures a day. (267km)
*Guide—There are a lot of minibuses on this route. (116km)
*Guinan (via Gonghe)—Daily departure at 09:30. (299km)
*Guinan (via Guide)—Also departs at 09:30. (255km)
*Tongde (via Gonghe and Guinan)—There is a bus every other day leaving at 08:30.
*Tongde (via Guide)—Daily departure also leaving at 08:30.
*Maqin (Dawu)—There is a daily bus with sleeping berths.
*Dari (Jimai)—It leaves at 09:45 on days with dates including either 2, 5, or 8 (e.g. 2, 15, 28, etc.), and the trip takes 2 days. (607km)
*Banma—Also leaves at 09:45 on days with dates including 4 or 0 (e.g. 4, 14, 24, 30, etc.), and this trip takes 3 days. (776km)
*Qumalai—Has buses on days with dates including 1 or 5 (e.g. 1, 5, 15,31, etc.), and the trip takes 3 days. (807km)
*Yushu (Jyekundo)—A daily bus with sleeping berths leaves at 13:00. There is also an ordinary bus that leaves at 10:00 every day, and the trip takes about 25 hours without an overnight stop. (819km)

Accommodation
The *Xining Hotel* has a dormitory that is popular with backpackers.
The *Xining Binguan* (Hotel) is a short bus ride from the main railway station in Xining. Take a # 9 (Jiulu) route bus and get off at the Binguan stop, and you will find this massive hotel on the Qiyi Lu. It looks like a historical landmark, and its rooms are well equipped. The front desk is in building No. 2 (the 2nd building after the gate), and the receptionists here speak English. The 3-person dormitories are in building No. 4 (the building at the far end of the complex), and a bed in one of these with a hot shower costs Y48. If you'd prefer a double room with satellite television, these are available in building No. 2 and cost Y216 a night. There is a *CITS* office on the 1st floor of building No. 1 (the building just after the gate), and *Qinghai Minzu Travel* is also in the same building.
The *Xining Dasha* (Mansion) is on the left corner of the T-junction about 20 minutes on foot along the Jianguo Lu from the railway station. You can also get there by taking a # 1 (Yilu) bus. A bed in a double room here costs Y23.
The *Qinghai Minzu Binguan* (Hotel) is on the Dong Dajie and you can get there by taking either the #1 (Yilu) or the # 32 (Sanshi'er Lu) bus and getting off at Huangguang. A dormitory bed costs from Y25, and the double rooms here have private

bathrooms, though the availability of hot water is very limited. Rooms for 2 people start at Y38. There is also an office of *Qinghai Minzu Travel* at the hotel.

Restaurants
There are many Islamic restaurants in the town, reflecting the number of Hui people living here. However, there are still a lot of other options available with food ranging from Guangdong and Sichuanese cuisine to Uighur *shish kebabs*.
There is a restaurant area right next to the Shuijing Xiang Bazaar, in the center of the city, and throughout the evening and into the night there are many street stalls serving good food around Ximen and on the western side of Jianguo Lu (Xining Mansions street). If you want to eat at these food stalls, dishes cost Y5-10.

Foreign Affairs Branch, Public Security Bureau (PSB)
The office on the eastern side of Bei Dajie is open 09:30-12:30 and again at 15:30-17:30. A 30-day visa extension costs Y125.
You may be told to go to the CITS office if you apply for a travel permit, and they are notorious for overcharging applicants.

Changing Money
If you are heading out into the rural provinces from here, it would probably be better for you to change more money than you think you will need before you go. In Qinghai Province, Xining and Golmud are the only cities where you are guaranteed to get your foreign currency changed.
The *Bank of China* branch on Da Shizi is open for foreign currency transactions at 10:00-15:00, and travelers' checks are accepted. The bank is closed on the weekends.
The *Bank of China* branch on Dongguan Dajie is open for foreign currency transactions at 10:00-12:00 and 15:00-17:00. Travelers' checks are accepted here, and this branch is also closed on the weekends.

Post & Telecommunications
There is a post office on Da Shizi, which is open 08:30-17:30 daily. You can send parcels from here, and on the 2nd floor of the building there is a telephone service. International calls are also available at night.

Bookstores
The *Xinhua Bookstore* is opposite the post office, and it has a good selection of Tibetan-related books.
Another place to look for books on Tibet is on the 2nd floor of the long-distance bus station, where there are also Tibetan clothes on sale.

Hospital

The best hospital in the city is the Shengzhong Yiyuan on Qiyi Lu. There are English-speaking staff here, but there is an additional tariff on the treatment of foreign patients.

Places to See
Beishansi (Temple)

In the north of the town is a stone-cave temple called Beishansi, and from here you can get a good view of the town.

Dongguan Qingzhen Dasi (Great Mosque)

This is the largest mosque in Xining, and you are permitted to visit at 10:00-12:00 and 15:00-18:00, except on Fridays. These are the times when prayers are not being held at the mosque.

AROUND XINING AND HAIDONG DIQU (DISTRICT)

HUANGZHONG (TSONGKHA) [LUSHAER]

Huangzhong is about 28 km to the south-west of Xining, and although it is only a small town, it is an extremely important place for Tibetans. This is the birthplace of Tsongkhapa (Je Rinpoche), the founder of the Dalai Lama's Gelukpa order, and it is the site of Ta'er Monastery (Kumbum), one of the 6 greatest Gelukpa monasteries. There are many Han and Hui in the town itself, but the area around the monastery is full of tourists mingling among the throngs of Tibetan pilgrims who flock to the site from across the Amdo region.

Access

A normal-size bus leaves from Xining Tiyuguan (Gymnasium) every half hour between 07:30 and 18:00, and there are also minibuses. Some buses have their destinations indicated as *Lushaer*, but they still go to Huangzhong. After about an hour, the buses arrive at Ta'er Monastery (Kumbum). The bus station is about 2km down the road towards Xining from Ta'er Monastery (Kumbum), and the walk takes just 30 minutes. There are also direct buses to Gonghe, Huangyuan, Datong, Menyuan, and Ping'an.

Accommodation

Most visitors just come to the town on a day trip, but staying here for the night and visiting the monastery in the morning and evening when there are fewer tourists is definitely worthwhile.

Ta'er Monastery

The *Ta'ersi Binguan* (Hotel) is where many foreign tourist groups stop to have lunch, and there is a souvenir store that caters to them. A bed in a 3-person room with a hot shower costs Y55, a double room charges Y180, and a suite is Y280.

The *Kumbum Motel* is located in the monastery itself, and this Tibetan-style guesthouse is popular among pilgrims. The cost of a bed in a dormitory is Y20, and there is also a restaurant here.

Places to See
Ta'er Monastery (Kumbum)

Kumbum means 'A Hundred Thousand Buddha Images' in Tibetan, and it is one of the 6 great Gelukpa monasteries boasting enormous influence in both the religious and secular life of the Amdo region. The monastery is said to have originated with a chorten that Tsongkhapa's mother constructed in the 14th century. Later, the Manchu emperor gave a large sum of money to further expand the site, allowing the temples and accommodation for the monks to sprawl over the hills, across the valley, and into the surrounding areas.

The present 14th Dalai Lama, the late 10th Panchen Lama, and many other great incarnate lamas studied at this spiritual site. The monastery is said to have once housed more than 4,000 monks, but there are only 500 at most here at present.

The monastery has now been transformed into a major tourist site, and visitors are supposed to buy an entry ticket at the booth provided. You can purchase tickets at 08:30-17:30 for Y22.5, and the monastery is actually open 09:30-18:00. Once inside the monastery you can visit the 6 designated temples, which all have information boards, etc., and you will be requested to show your ticket at each one so that it can be punched. This routine gives you the impression of visiting a museum rather than a thriving religious site.

Butter engraving, in which images of Buddha, other religious figures, and sacred symbols are fashioned, is a popular draw for visitors here. There are also 3-dimensional scroll-like sculptures telling

AMDO

famous stories, such as the one detailing when Princess Wengcheng, the daughter of the Tang Emperor, marries into Tibet. To view the butter engravings you need to go through the Tsokchen Dukhang (Great Assembly Hall) and cross the bridge in front of the Dukhor Dratsang (Kalachakra Temple), and you will reach Jetsunpei Gyencho Zhengsa where they are on display.

These artworks were originally meant as religious offerings, but there was another piece entitled 'Tiananmen Square' on show alongside the more traditional artworks.

If you walk along the *Lingkhor* (Pilgrimage Path) surrounding the monastery and up the hill at the back, you will get a view of the fields of barley stretching out towards the snow-covered mountains in the distance.

There are many Tibetan souvenir stores on the road leading up to the monastery, and this is something of a honey trap for the unwary visitor. High prices and menacing peddlers are there to greet the unprepared shopper, so be careful.

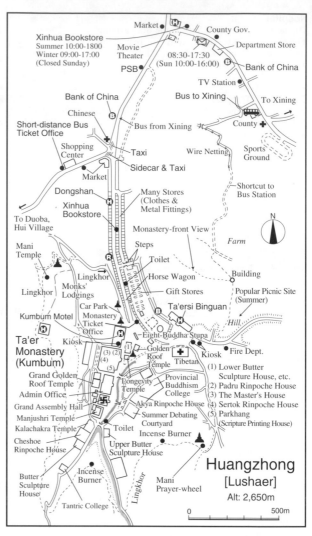

HUZHU TU AUTONOMOUS COUNTY (GONLUNG) (CLOSED)

Gonlung Jampaling (Youningsi)

Gonlung Jampaling is to the north-east of Xining, and this was formerly a great monastery that was founded in the 17th century. Incarnate lamas here were taken into the confidence of the Qing (Manchu) Dynasty rulers, and the monastery boasted 7,000 monks at the peak of its influence. Yong He Gong in Beijing was opened by the great incarnated Changkya Lama from this monastery.

Gonlung Jampaling is located in the village of Wushixiang, to the south-east of Huzhu, and there are over 20 buses a day from Xining to Huzhu, but the town is currently within a closed area.

PING'AN (TSONGKHA KHAR)

Home of the 14th Dalai Lama (Taktser)

Qijiachuan, in present-day Ping'an County (Tsongkha Taktser), is the place where the exiled Dalai Lama was born in 1935. A place with such strong political symbolism inevitably requires you to apply for a permit to visit the actual village of Taktser, unlike the other places in Ping'an County, which are open. Some people have reportedly been able to visit the site by arranging a car through a

Home of the 14th Dalai Lama

by Lama Dondrub Rinchen, the teacher of Tsongkhapa, the founder of the Gelukpa order. It was to this monastery that Tsongkhapa came and renounced the world, and thus it could be regarded as the birthplace of the Gelukpa. The gompa is still home to about 500 monks.

Take a bus from either Xining or Ping'an heading for Hualong, and get off at the village of Zhaba. There are jeeps or tractors that will take you the rest of the way to Chapo, where the monastery is located.

travel agency in Xining.

The house in which the Dalai Lama was born was rebuilt in 1986, and his relatives now live there. There is also an elementary school on the site.

If you try to get there by yourself, you will need to take a bus to Ping'an from Xining. For this 34km section of the journey there are a lot of buses to choose from. Then continuing on from Ping'an, you can either hitchhike or walk.

LEDU (DROTSANG)

Drotsang Gompa (Qutansi)

Constructed in the 15th century, this old monastery is to the south of Ledu and used to be home to 2,300 monks. During the Cultural Revolution it was used as a storehouse and now houses 10 monks at most. *Qutan* is an honorific title bestowed upon the Buddha, and this monastery is famous for a wall painting depicting his life. There is a chorten in the courtyard, and admission to the grounds is Y5.

To reach the monastery you will first need to leave Xining for Ledu, and there are a lot of minibuses that cover this 65km trip. An alternative is to take a car to Minhe, which costs Y5.8. From Ledu, there are a number of minibuses each day covering the 20km to Qutan, and the fare is Y3. A day trip from Xining would leave you little time to look around unless you leave at the crack of dawn. There is a guesthouse near the monastery with dormitory beds costing Y7.

HUALONG HUI AUTONOMOUS COUNTY (BAYAN KHAR)

Jakhyung Gompa (Xiaqiongsi)

This monastery was founded in the 14th century

XUNHUA (XUNHUA SALAR AUTONOMOUS COUNTY) [DOWI]

There are a large number of Salar people living in this area. These people are Muslim, but speak their own language, *Salar*, which is related to Turkish, unlike the Hui who also follow Islam. They are said to have migrated here after Genghis Khan had surrounded Samarkand. They now play an active role in peddling wares all over Tibet.

Wendo Gompa (Wendusi) and the Late Panchen Lama's Home (Birthplace)

Seventeen kilometers south-west of Xunhua, this monastery houses about 200 monks. Wendu is the village where the late 10th Panchen Lama was born. He later went on to study at Wendo Gompa in his early days. The village is on the way from Xunhua to Tongren, and there are a few buses per day along the route between the 2 towns that passes near to the village.

Mengda Tianchi Lake

About 40km south of Jishizhen, this scenic spot is sometimes compared to the beautiful area of Xishuangbanna in Yunnan. This lovely lake is surrounded by mountains, and the area is covered in virgin forest.

XINING-GOLMUD-LHASA

The Qinghai-Tibet Highway, which stretches for around 1,940km in total, connects Xining with Lhasa. On leaving Xining, the road between Riyueting and Golmud climbs to 3,000-3,700m above sea level, and after crossing the Kunlun Shankou at 4,767m, 150km south of Golmud, the bus continues through this highland region at altitudes of around 4,500m. The highest point along the way is Tanggu La Shankou (on the border between Qinghai and Tibet), which stands at 5,206m.

AMDO

195

QINGHAI HU (LAKE KOKONOR) [TSO NGONBO]

Traveling 200km west of Xining, you will come to the Qinghai Hu (Lake Kokonor), which is the largest salt lake in China. The Qinghai Hu is *Kokonor* in Mongolian, which means 'Blue Lake,' and the Tibetan name, *Tso Ngonbo*, means the same. In the center of the lake there is an island called Haixinshan (Tso Nying) on which there is a temple.

You can either take a bus from Xining to Heimahe on the southern side of the lake, or to Gangcha, on the northern side. If you want to visit the tourist sights though, it would be better to join a group tour from the *Xining Binguan* (Hotel), etc. or simply charter yourself a car.

There is accommodation available at Hudong Muchang (Pasture) and Heimahe, and you can get some tasty fish in the restaurants around the lake.

Riyueting

If you are going to Qinghai Hu (Lake Kokonor) from Xining, you will cross the pass called Riyueshan (3,520m) along the way. There are 2 shrines here, called Riting (Sun Shrine) and Yueting (Moon Shrine), and this is the place where Princess Wengcheng, daughter of the Tang Emperor, said goodbye to her homeland while still worrying about

Riyueting

her fate with her marriage into the Tibetan royal family in the 7th century. After the pass, the landscape totally changes and is transformed into a Tibetan world, with wild yaks wandering among its peaks and grazing in the highland passes. Get off the bus in the vicinity of the pass, and it is about a kilometer on foot to the site.

Bird Island (Niaodao)

This island is a breeding ground for migratory birds on the western side of Qinghai Hu (Lake Kokonor), and as the name infers, the island is completely covered with birds, especially during the peak season from May to June. Admission is Y50.

There are only 1-2 buses a day from Heimahe, and you will have to walk more than 2 hours after

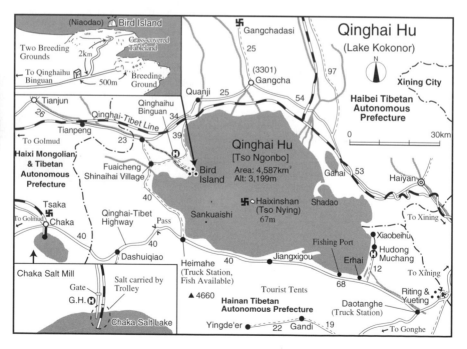

196

the Qinghaihu Binguan (Hotel) stop to reach the site. Most people wanting to visit Niaodao join a group tour at Xining.

Shaobei Hu (Lake)

To the north-east of Qinghai Hu (Lake Kokonor) is Shaobei Hu, a much smaller but possibly even more beautiful lake than Kokonor. There are tents available for visitors, and these are pitched on the lake shore.

Chaka (Tsaka) Salt Lake

This salt lake lies at 3,104m and 80km from Heimahe, to the west of Qinghai Hu (Lake Kokonor). There are buses from Xining to the town of Chaka, which is around 6km from the salt-producing lake. There is a guesthouse here, and you can visit Tsaka Gompa in the town.

GOLMUD (GE'ERMU)

This is an important transportation hub on the Qinghai-Tibet Highway, connecting Xining with Lhasa. Golmud seems to be an artificially constructed town used simply to connect Qinghai Province with the TAR. There is also another highway leading to Dunhuang. Whether you arrive here by bus or rail, you will need to take either a hotel bus, the #1 (Yilu) local bus, which comes around every 30 minutes, or a taxi to get to a place to stay for the night. On foot, it will take you more than 30 minutes to get to any of the guesthouses.

Accommodation & Restaurants

The *Golmud Binguan* (Hotel) is expensive, and there is a CITS office in the hotel.

The *Golmud Zhaodaisuo* (City Government Guesthouse) has dormitory beds starting at Y17, and a double room here will cost you Y60 per person. During the winter months there are heaters supplied.

Public Security Bureau (PSB)

You can get visa extensions here, and a 1-month one will cost you Y120.

Access

Bus to Lhasa

The only reason that most travelers visit this town is as a stopover before continuing on to Lhasa. The biggest issue here is how cheap the journey is going to be. Chinese people can get a ticket costing as little as Y300, while foreigners have to pay more than Y1,000 for the same trip. With this kind of discrepancy, it is little wonder that many backpackers try to find unofficial and secretive methods of reaching Lhasa for a reasonable price. The cost of a sleeping berth on a bus is almost as expensive as the airfare from Chengdu to Lhasa.

Another drawback in trying to enter the TAR from Golmud is that the route is sometimes closed and the ticket situation changes quite frequently.

Make sure that you take cold weather gear, as it is cold here even in summer. It is also important to be careful about acclimatizing yourself while in the town, as the altitude climbs dramatically after you start the trip.

CITS

Buying a ticket at the CITS office, in the Golmud Binguan (Hotel), is the official way to go about things. An ordinary bus ticket costs Y1,180, and a bus with sleeping berths costs Y1,600, which both include the fee for the required permit. Passengers are sometimes requested to put together a group of 4 people or more in order to get their tickets. The bus leaves Golmud in the afternoon and arrives in Lhasa 2 days and 2 nights later.

Unofficial Taxis & Bus

You may be offered a lift around the bus station or alternatively find one there if you want. The fare is negotiable but generally is

Qinghai-Tibet Highway (1 hour after Golmud)

gauged by the number of passengers and the type of car. The standard price per person is said to range from Y300-500, and these cars will usually get through checkpoints quite easily.

Checkpoints
On the 1,160km trip between Golmud and Lhasa there is most likely to be an inspection, with officials specifically looking for foreigners and checking their documents. These checks take place around 30km after leaving Golmud and again at Yangbajing just before you reach Lhasa.

From Lhasa to Golmud, Xining
When you arrive at the bus station in Golmud on the way from Lhasa, many Tibetans on board change to a bus with sleeping berths to complete their journey onto Xining. If you follow their example and everything goes smoothly, you can save a fair amount of time.

From Golmud to Xining by Rail
*No. 604 Rapid
    Golmud (14:30)-Xining (07:46) (1 night)
*No. 760
    Golmud (20:45)-Xining (17:58) (1 night)

On the 2nd floor of the station, you can purchase a ticket for the No. 604 a day before your planned departure. Tickets for the No. 760 are available on the same day as departure. These 2 trains are operated on an alternate basis (i.e. Sunday-No. 604, Monday-No. 760, Tuesday-No. 604, Wednesday-No. 760, etc.).
(For trains from Xining to Golmud, see the Xining section.)

Bus from Dunhuang to Golmud
A bus from Dunhuang to Golmud leaves the bus station in Dunhuang at 07:30 every morning, and you can get a ticket through the CITS office. The fare for local people is set at Y44, while foreigners have to pay Y400. If you don't have a travel insurance certificate, you will have to pay another

Y20. There are unconfirmed rumors that it is possible to get tickets at local prices in Qilizhen.

Bus from Golmud to Dunhuang
A bus from Golmud to Dunhuang leaves the bus stop opposite the station at 07:30 every morning. The trip takes around 12 hours, and you can get a ticket at the CITS office at the Golmud Binguan. A travel permit is also required.

HUANGNAN TIBETAN AUTONOMOUS PREFECTURE

TONGREN (REPKONG)

Tongren (Repkong) is a town formed around Rongbo Gompa (Longwusi), along the Longwu He River (Rongbo Guchu), a tributary of the mighty Yellow River (Huang He).

The Repkong region is endowed with more monasteries than any other area within Huangnan Prefecture, and around Rongbo, the villages of Sengeshong (Wutunsi), Gashari (Kasar), Nyentok, and Gomar are all famous for their *Repkong Art*, with the 4 of them being regarded as a great center for Tibetan Buddhist arts.

Access
From the bus station at Xining, there are many buses and minibuses to the area, and the trip takes 5-6 hours. At Tongren, you may be requested to get off a bus at a roundabout in the town before you reach the bus station. There is a guesthouse at the junction, though foreigners are not supposed to stay there. You can also get to Tongren by bus from Xiahe in Gansu Province and other surrounding centers.

Buses from Tongren:
These depart from the bus station in Huangnan, near the roundabout.
*Xining—There are a large number of buses and minibuses taking this route, and the 5-6 hour trip costs Y16.2.

Tongren

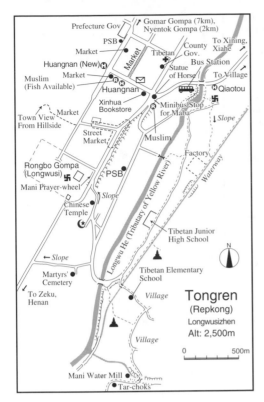

Map labels:
Prefecture Gov / Gomar Gompa (7km), Nyentok Gompa (2km)
PSB
Market
Huangnan (New)
Muslim (Fish Available)
Market
Huangnan
Town View From Hillside
Market
Xinhua Bookstore
Street Market
Rongbo Gompa (Longwusi)
Mani Prayer-wheel
Chinese Temple
Slope
Martyrs' Cemetery
To Zeku, Henan
Mani Water Mill
Tar-choks
Village
Village
Tibetan Elementary School
Tibetan Junior High School
Muslim
Factory
Slope
PSB
Minibus Stop for Maba
Slope
County Gov.
Tibetan
Statue of Horse
To Xining, Xiahe
Bus Station
To Village
Qiaotou
Longwu He (Tributary of Yellow River)
Waterway
Market

Tongren
(Repkong)
Longwusizhen
Alt: 2,500m
0   500m

*Xunhua (via Wendu)—There are 4 departures a day at 07:00, 09:30, 11:00, and 12:00. (76km)
*Linxia—The bus departs at 07:00 daily, and the trip takes 7-8 hours. (183km)
*Henan (via Zeku)—Daily bus leaves at 07:30 every day, and the trip takes 5 hours. (137km)
*Zeku—There is usually a bus leaving at 07:00 every day, but sometimes it runs every other day.
*Xiahe (via Guashizesi)—Leaving at 08:00 every day, this trip takes 4 hours. (104km)
*Lijiaxia—There is a minibus leaving around noon. (104km)

Accommodation & Restaurants

The *Huangnan Binguan* (Hotel) is the place where foreigners are supposed to stay when in town, and the hotel has a special tariff for them. A bed in a 2-person room costs Y38-68, and one in a 3-bed room goes for Y20-24. For Y60 you can get a room equipped with a bathroom and a hot shower that is available for an hour in the evening, after 20:30. There is a restaurant in the hotel.
The *Qiaotou Lushe* is a small hotel near the river that has dormitory beds for Y5.

Places to See
Rongbo Gompa (Longwusi)

Originally founded as a Sakyapa monastery in the 12th century, the great Rongbo Gompa housed well over 2,000 monks at the peak of its power. Now, it belongs to the Gelukpa order and has only about 400 monks. But the gompa has maintained considerable influence in the region with 4 incarnate lamas, such as the young but revered 8th Rongbo Kyabgon, calling this monastery home. There are also a number of other high-ranking lamas holding the title of *Geshe*, which corresponds to a doctorate in Buddhist theory.

Sengeshong (Wutun Shangzhuang/Wutun Xiazhuang)

The village is 6km north of Tongren and consists of Wutun Shangzhuang (Senge Yagotsang) and Wutun Xiazhuang (Senge Magotsang). Both parts have gompas that are famous for their *Repkong* Buddhist artwork. In the villages around the monasteries there are the houses of the *thangka* painters and their workshops. You can find out where these are by asking one of the monks from the monastery. You can also pick up some of the paintings that are on sale, though the quality of these varies considerably.

To get to Sengeshong, take a minibus to Maba from the roundabout in Tongren and get off on the way. It is also possible to hitch a lift with a truck or tractor. Wutun Shangzhuangsi is a bit far off the main road, and on arrival you will have to go around to the far side to find the entrance.

Gomar Gompa (Guomarisi)

From Sengeshong, you will catch sight of a large chorten on the other side of the river. This is the great chorten of Gomar, and you can actually climb to the top floor via a staircase decorated with images of Buddha and other Buddhist paintings. The ascent

AMDO

Gomar Gompa

can be rather unnerving, as there is neither a handrail nor anything to break a fall. The key to the chorten is kept by one of the monks.

The monastery is right across the river from Sengeshong, but you have to walk (or possibly hitchhike) 2.5km down the river to cross it, as there aren't any bridges nearby. It might be possible to cross the river in the shallows, but you should be very careful, as the water level can be quite deceptive. If you are visiting the gompa from Tongren, you don't have to worry about crossing the river.

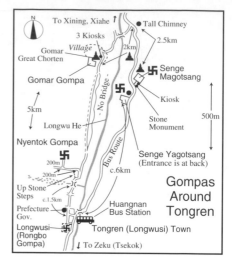

Gompas Around Tongren

ZEKU (TSEKOK)

This small town is set in vast tracts of grassland roamed by Tibetan nomads, and the streets are filled with a nomadic atmosphere. The town itself is simply a relay point on the bus route connecting Xining with Henan. In the west of the town there is a small hill, where you can get a good view out across the steppe.

Access
To Zeku
The town is 285km from Xining, and to get there you will need to catch a bus destined for Henan and then get off along the way. The trip takes 9-10 hours.

From Zeku
There is no bus station at Zeku, and all the buses arrive at and leave from the area in front of the Nongye Yinhang (Bank).

*Xining—There is a bus that passes through the town around 07:20 each day.
*Henan—A bus passes through town twice a day. The first one is around 13:00 and the second one

at 17:00. The earlier service is sometimes cancelled.
*Tongde—A bus that starts from Zeku departs around 07:00 on even numbered days, and one stops en route from Henan around 08:00 on odd numbered days.
*Tongren—Take a bus heading for Xining. Another option is to jump on a minibus that goes from Zeku to Tongren in the afternoon every day or so.

Local Transportation
There are no taxis, but there are occasional minibuses running around the town. Unfortunately, these have no destination indicated on them.

Accommodation & Restaurants
The *Xianzhengfu Zhaodaisuo* (County Government Guesthouse) is located behind the government building in the town. A bed in a 3-person room costs Y13.5, and one in a 4-person room will cost you Y8. When it gets cold, coal heaters are provided.

There are many Muslim restaurants in the town, or you can try reasonable Chinese meat and fish dishes at the *Jinxin Jiujia* (Restaurant), next to the Nongye Yinhang (Bank).

Places to See
Terton Choegar Gompa (Herisi)
This Nyingmapa order monastery is also known as

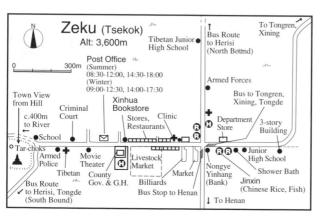

Hor Gompa, and it is 72km west, north-west of Zeku (Tsekok). You can get to the gompa by taking a bus heading for Tongde, and it is about a kilometer before you reach Hor (Heri). In the village there are a guesthouse, restaurant, and stores.

HENAN MONGOL AUTONOMOUS COUNTY (SOGWO)

Over the centuries many ethnic groups migrated to the Amdo region and assimilated with one another, thus shaping the Amdo-Tibetan people of today. However, some of the descendants of Mongolian settlers have clung more closely to their heritage.

In Henan County, 325km south of Xining, 90 percent of its 27,000 people are Mongolian. These nomadic horse riders are different from Tibetan nomads in culture and dress, and their Mongolian-style tents, or *Pao*, are to be seen all across the grassy plains in the area.

Access
From Xining
There is a bus to Henan that leaves Xining at 07:30 everyday. The 325km trip takes 11-12 hours.

From Henan
The buses all leave from the bus station in town.
*Xining (via Tongren and Zeku)—There is a daily bus that leaves at 06:00, and the trip takes 10-11 hours.
*Tongren (via Zeku)—There is a bus every 1-2 days that leaves at 06:00, taking 5 hours.
*Tongde (via Zeku)—It leaves at 06:30, but only on odd numbered days and takes 6-7 hours.

Lakha Gompa

*Xiahe (via Hezuo)—There is a bus every 1-2 days that leaves at 06:30, and the trip takes 8-9 hours.
*Linxia (via Hezuo)—It leaves at 06:00 every day, and the trip takes 9-10 hours.
*Ningmute—It leaves at 07:30 every day, and the trip is an hour.

Accommodation & Restaurants
The *Xianzhengfu Ganbu Zhaodaisuo* (County Government Guesthouse) has no showers, but the rooms are passable.

The *Zeyang Fandian* (Hotel) is located at the junction in the center of town, and this hotel has a distinctive Mongolian-style dome on its roof. A bed in a 2-person room costs Y17, one in a 3-person room costs Y13, and the cost of one in a 4-person room is Y8. The hotel staff are kind and helpful here.

There are many other guesthouses that are good if you are just planning to stay overnight in the town. Although there is a sign for it, the guesthouse at the bus station does not seem to be in business anymore.

AMDO

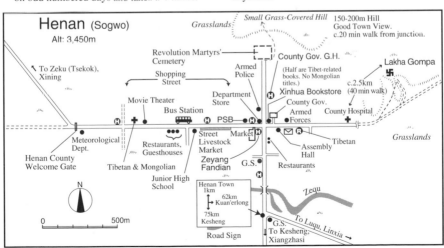

All the restaurants in Henan are Muslim, and you'll have trouble getting much in the way of variety in your diet while you are in the town, as there are no rice dishes on the menu.

Places to See
Lakha Gompa
About 3km east of the town is Lakha Gompa. The monastery is halfway up a small hill surrounded by grassland and is about 40 minutes on foot from the Zeyang Fandian (Hotel). The monastery is also known as Tsang-gar Gompa, and the incarnate lama here is still a young boy.

HAINAN TIBETAN AUTONOMOUS PREFECTURE

GONGHE (QIABUQIA) [CHABCHA]

Gonghe is the capital of Hainan Prefecture, but it once functioned as a trading town connecting Lhasa with Changan, the capital of Tang. It is like a watery oasis built in a depression and surrounded by the vast, bone-dry steppe. The Qiabuqia Shichang (Market) on the eastern side of the town and the Minzu Shichang (Market) to the west are always bustling with local people and traders. Although there are bus stations on both sides, the main one is the Gonghe Bus Station on the western side of town.

Access
From Xining
There are quite a number of buses and minibuses leaving from the bus station in Xining and from Changjiang Lu to the western side of Xining Binguan (Hotel), and the trip takes about 4 hours.

From Gonghe
There are buses to Guide, Gangcha (via Heimahe and Shinaihai), Xinghai, Guinan, Tongde, Dari (Jimai), Yushu (Jyekundo), etc.

Accommodation & Restaurants
The *Hainan Renmin Zhengfu Zhaodaisuo* (Prefecture Government Guesthouse) is the best place to stay in town, and it is in front of the Gonghe County Government Office. A dormitory bed here costs Y7-20, and double room rates are Y50-90.
The *Gonghe Xian Renmin Zhengfu Zhaodaisuo* (County Government Guesthouse) dormitory beds start from Y8, but there are no showers.
The *Gonghe Bus Station Guesthouse* is in the bus station, and beds cost from Y5-12. For the price, the rooms are quite clean, and for another Y2 you can have a hot shower. Out of the selection available, this one is recommended.
Many of the restaurants here are Muslim, and once again rice is difficult to find on the menus in town.

Places to See
In the north-west of the town there is a collection of religious sites made up of Kasar Gompa, Dungkar Gompa, the Gelukpa order's Chamru (Kyamru) Gompa, and a Bon temple.
A visit to 3 of these at once using a bike-taxi, takes about 5 hours and costs around Y90. The route runs through the airport on the way.

There are only 1 or 2 buses a day, and if you decide to take one, you'll have a lot of walking to do after you are dropped off.

Map labels:
c.5km to Kasar Gompa
Passage
Junior High School
Dongfeng Lu
To Xining
G.S.
Temple, c.2km
Teacher Training College
Provincial Gov.
Prefecture Committee
PSB (Provincial)
Museum & TV Station
PSB (County)
Buses to Xining
Movie Theater
Restaurants
Travel Agency
County Gov.
School of Sanitation
Square
Market
County Gov.G.H.
Prefecture Gov. G.H. (Best Hotel)
Lots of Taxis, Motor Cycles
Provincial
Busy Street
Food Market
Chabcha Market (+ Restaurants)
To Dungkar Gompa & Jamru Gompa
Muslim Stores
Xinhua Bookstore
Observation Platforms for Town View
Market
Prefecture Bus Station
Gonghe Bus Station
Slope
Revolution Cemetery
Restaurants
Toilet
Indoor Roller Skating Rink
Bus Stop for Shazhuyu (17:00), Niandi (10:00)
Street Market (Vegetable)
Playing Field
Busy Area
Junior High School
Gonghe Marble Co.
Chinese
Muslim Shower Bath
Teacher Training College
Dry River
Gonghe Market
Armed Police
To Yushu (Jyekundo), Maduo
Tibetan
0   500m

Gonghe (Chabcha)
Alt: 2,800m

AMDO

202

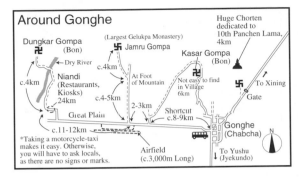

Around Gonghe

Dungkar Gompa (Bon)

(Largest Gelukpa Monastery) Jamru Gompa

Huge Chorten dedicated to 10th Panchen Lama, 4km

← Dry River

c.4km

Kasar Gompa (Bon)

Niandi (Restaurants, Kiosks) 24km

c.4km

c.4-5km

At Foot of Mountain

Not easy to find in Village 6km

To Xining

Gate

Great Plain

2-3km

Shortcut c.8-9km

Gonghe (Chabcha)

N

c.11-12km

*Taking a motorcycle-taxi makes it easy. Otherwise, you will have to ask locals, as there are no signs or marks.

Airfield (c.3,000m Long)

↓ To Yushu (Jyekundo)

XINGHAI (TSIGORTHANG)

Xinghai is a small town laid out in the middle of a great plain. If you go west, north-west of the town for about 30km, you will get to Serdzong (Treldzong) Gompa.

Access
From Xining
There are 3-4 buses from Xining every day, and the trip takes 7-8 hours.

From Xinghai
*Xining (via Heka)—There are 3 buses a day, and it is a 269km trip.
*Gonghe—There are minibuses on this route.
*Heka—There is a bus that leaves at 14:30, and this is a short 51km trip.
*Tangnaihai—There are 3 buses a day.
*Wenquan—The bus departs around 09:00.
*Tongde—Take a bus heading for Zhongtie that leaves at 10:00 or one for Queshian and then change at Queshian and take another on to Tongde. There are 1 or 2 buses a day for Queshian, and in many cases passengers on this route have to stay at Queshian overnight because the connections often don't match up. The trip is only 56km, but it takes about 3 hours, as the road conditions are pretty bad. From a cliff vantagepoint before you reach Queshian, you will get a view of the Yellow River (Huang He). Once you get to the town, there are a number of hotels and restaurants to choose from.

For the onward journey towards Tongde, there is a bus that leaves Queshian at 08:00. This stops at villages on the way, and the 50km trip takes just over 3.5 hours.

Accommodation
The *Xinghai Fandian* (Hotel) is a striking building in the center of the town, and a bed in a 4-person

room costs Y15.
There is a new guesthouse to the west of the Xinghai Fandian (Hotel). Beds in 4-person rooms cost Y21, and single rooms go for Y40. Heaters are available for guests.
The *Bus Station Guesthouse* has dormitory beds that cost Y5, and a double room bed here is Y10.

Places to See
Treldzong Gompa (Serdzong)
The monastery is about 30km to the west, north-west of Xinghai, and at 3,600m it is far from other human habitation. Behind the site there are rocky peaks, and the surrounding area is called *Drakar Treldzong*, or 'Monkey Fort made of White Rocks.' This is one of the most sacred places in the Amdo region, and there are many other famous sites connected with Guru Rinpoche (Padmasambhava) and Tsongkhapa in the area. The monastery itself belongs to the Gelukpa order, but the area is well-known as a place for trainee monks from the

To Gonghe, Xining

G.S.

G.S.

Kiosks

County G.H.

Armed Forces

Public Prosecutors Office

Tax Office

Army

To Serdzong (Treldzong)
← Gompa

Government

Renmin

PSB

To Tongde, Queshian

G.H.

Xinghai

Bus Station
(+ ⊕)

Sichuan

Xinhua Bookstore

Movie Theater

Shopping Street
(+Street Market & Guesthouses)

Tibetan Junior High School

G.H.

0

500m

Xinghai
(Tsigorthang)
Alt: 3,260m

AMDO

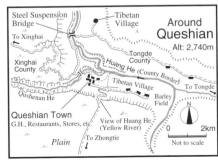

Steel Suspension Bridge

Tibetan Village

To Xinghai

Xinghai County

Tongde County

Huang He (County Border)

Tibetan Village

To Tongde

Qushenan He

Barley Field

Queshian Town
G.H., Restaurants, Stores, etc.

View of Huang He (Yellow River)

N

0

2km

Plain

To Zhongtie

Not to scale

Around Queshian
Alt: 2,740m

Nyingmapa order to practice asceticism.

At Xinghai there are some 4-wheel-drive cars available, and to charter one costs about Y200 for a round trip to the monastery. Sharing the cost of the car is advisable; otherwise, the cost is rather prohibitive, as it is only 2 hours to the gompa. The landscape on the way is somewhat reminiscent of the Grand Canyon.

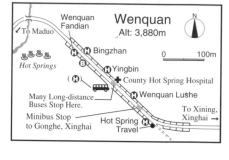

Wenquan (Hot Springs)

Located on the highway between Xining and Yushu (Jyekundo), this town just seems to function as a truck stop. To the north-west of the town center there are some hot springs, and about 30km to the west there is a monastery that also has hot springs.

GUIDE (TRIKA)

South, south-west of Xining, Guide is an oasis along the Yellow River (Huang He). The town stretches along the lush green valley and is surrounded by reddish-brown mountains. Guide consists of 3 parts, with Heyin at its center.

Roughly 3km to the west of the center there is Hexi, which is as a truck stop on the highway connecting Xining with Maqin (Dawu). The other section is Hedong, and this is some 3km to the east of the town center.

There are hot springs in the town, and both the Wenquan Binguan (Hotel) and Wenquan Yuchi (Public Bath) use this natural resource. At the village of Wenquan (Dratsang), around 13km south, south-west of Hexi, there is even a hot spring treatment center. Rungen Dratsang Gompa (Riansi) is across the river, opposite the center.

Access
From Xining to Guide
There are a lot of minibuses servicing this route.

From Guide
At Guide, the buses leave from the bus station.
*Xining—There are numerous minibuses daily, and the trip takes around 4 hours.
*Gonghe—There is a daily bus leaving at 09:00, and the trip takes 5 hours.
*Guinan—Departs at 08:30 on days with the numbers 2, 3, 5, 6, 8, and 9 in the date.

There are daily buses to Xinjie, Lihantang, and Donggou. Minibuses offer access to the towns and villages around Guide.

Accommodation
The *Wenquan Binguan* (Hotel) is a new 3-story building, 20 minutes from the bus station. As the name suggests, there are hot springs available here. Unfortunately there is an additional tariff for foreigners with dormitory beds costing Y14 and double room rates starting at Y120.

The *Jiaotong Lushe* (Traffic Hotel) is located in the bus station, and its rooms are not bad for the price. A dormitory bed costs Y6, and a single room is Y18. Although this is a good cheap option, foreigners are sometimes not allowed to stay here.

Places to See
Minyak Dratsang Gompa
This small monastery is around a kilometer to the north of the bus station. The monastery is also known as Minyak-dra Gompa and the *Minyak* in the name refers to the *Tangut* people, who are the original ancestors of the Amdo-Tibetan people.

Yuhuangge
In the north of the town, the tower here commands a good view of Guide. Right next door is the Minyak Gonkhang (Dafosi), but the site is currently in terrible condition.

Gongba Dratsang
If you go 6km to the south-west of Heyang, you will come to the monastery of Gongba Dratsang. You can get to here by a bus from Donggou or Changmu.

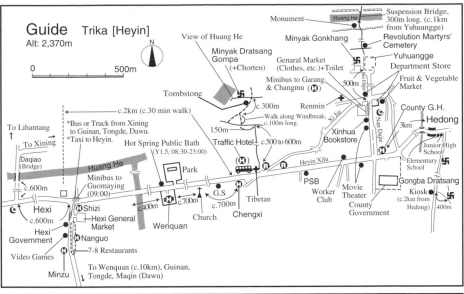

Guide Trika [Heyin]
Alt: 2,370m

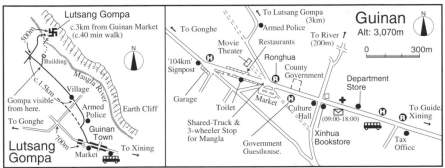

Thiwa Gompa
Another monastery in the area is at Tuanguocun, 6km south-east of Donggouxiang, where the bus will drop you off.

GUINAN (MANGRA) (CLOSED)

This is a small town about 250km south-west of Xining. The town itself is nothing special, but the setting is picturesque, with table-like cliffs and a desert framing it to the north across the river. Grassland and barley fields stretch out to the south, and 3km to the north of the town is Lutsang Gompa.

Access
From Xining
There are daily buses via Guide and also ones via Gonghe on even numbered days. The trip takes about 10 hours, and the road beyond Guide is graveled.

From Guinan
*Xining (via Gonghe)—The bus leaves at 08:00, but only on odd numbered days.
*Xining (via Guide)—There is a daily departure at 08:00.
*Gonghe—There are 2 buses a day, the first at 08:30 and the other at 15:30. The trip takes under 4 hours.
*Tongde—A bus from Gonghe stops at Guinan around 12:00 every 1-2 days.

Accommodation & Restaurants
The *Bus Station Guesthouse* has dormitory beds for Y4-6.

The *Xianroulianchang Zhaodaisuo* (Guesthouse)

AMDO

is opposite the bus station and has dormitory beds for Y10. There is only an outside toilet at the guesthouse.

The *Renminzhengfu Ganbu Zhaodaisuo* (Government Guesthouse) is another option for a short stay.

There are a number of restaurants serving Sichuanese and Islamic food in the town.

Places to See
Lutsang Gompa (Luzangsi)
Although the main temple at the monastery is still under construction, you will still meet a lot of pilgrims when you visit this gompa.

TONGDE (KAWASUMDO)

This town is on the northern side of the Baqu (Ba-chu), which meanders its haphazard path across the vast grasslands of this region. This long and narrow town spreads out from the east to the west, and in this area you will meet a lot of Tibetans on horseback. Tsang-gar Gompa (Shizangsi) and Serlak Gompa (Sailihaisi) are nearby, but they are quite a trek up into the mountains from here.

Access
From Xining
There is a bus that leaves Xining at 08:30 every day.

From Tongde
Buses leave from the bus station.
*Xining (via Guide (Hexi))—There is a daily departure at 07:00, and the trip takes 10-11 hours.

*Gonghe—There is a bus that departs at 07:00 on odd numbered days, and it takes 6-7 hours.
*Zeku—The bus leaves at 06:30, also only on odd numbered days. The trip takes 5 hours, and there is supposed to be a bus to Henan via Zeku every other day.
*Xinghai Area (Queshian)—There is a bus leaving at 08:00 every 1-2 days. The point of departure sometimes changes, with the bus leaving from close to the town center. This is an irregular thing, so it's advisable to check it out before you leave.
*Hebei—Take this bus to get to Shizangsi, but be careful, as they set off as soon as it has enough passengers, somewhere around 08:00 each day. There is also sometimes a bus on this route that departs from the town center.
*Maqin (Dawu)—There are a number of minibuses on this route every day.

Accommodation & Restaurants
The *Xianzhengfu Zhaodaisuo* (County Government Guesthouse) has double rooms for Y20.

The bus station has accommodation available for travelers that just need a place to sleep for the night, and a bed here costs around Y6.

Near the bus station you can get Sichuanese food, and there are also many Muslim restaurants in the town.

Places to See
Tsang-gar Gompa (Shizangsi)
Constructed in the 18th century, Tsang-gar Gompa is a Gelukpa monastery. It is said to house about 600 monks, and although it is very inconveniently located, it is definitely worth a visit. There is no

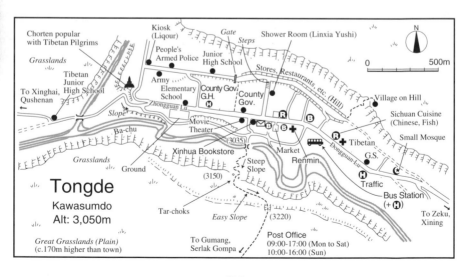

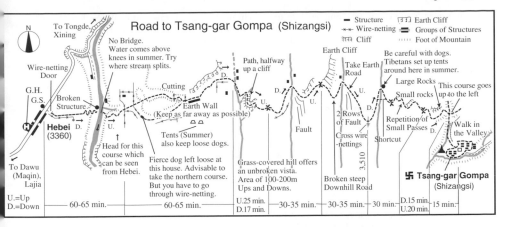

Road to Tsang-gar Gompa (Shizangsi)

Legend:
- ■— Structure
- ᠁᠁ Earth Cliff
- ⚡⚡ Wire-netting
- ᠌ Groups of Structures
- ᠌ Cliff
- ᠁᠁ Foot of Mountain

N

To Tongde, Xining

No Bridge. Water comes above knees in summer. Try where stream splits.

Path, halfway up a cliff

Earth Cliff

Take Earth Road

Be careful with dogs. Tibetans set up tents around here in summer.

Wire-netting Door

Large Rocks — This course goes

Cutting

Small rocks — up to the left

G.H.
G.S.

Broken Structure

Earth Wall (Keep as far away as possible)

2 Rows of Fault

Repetition of Small Passes

Walk in the Valley

Hebei D.   U.
(3360)

Tents (Summer) also keep loose dogs.

Fault

Cross wire -nettings

Shortcut

To Dawu (Maqin), Lajia

Head for this course which can be seen from Hebei.

Fierce dog left loose at this house. Advisable to take the northern course. But you have to go through wire-netting.

Grass-covered hill offers an unbroken vista. Area of 100-200m Ups and Downs.

Broken steep Downhill Road

3,510

卍 **Tsang-gar Gompa** (Shizangsi)

U.=Up
D.=Down

— 60-65 min.— — 60-65 min.— U.25 min. / D.17 min. — 30-35 min.— 30-35 min.— 30 min.— D.15 min. / U.20 min. — 15 min.—

---

accommodation available at the site, but there is a store.

Chartering a jeep to take you out to the monastery will cost you about Y400 one way. If there are no cars for hire, another option is to take a bus from Tongde bound for Hebei and then walk for around 5 hours to reach the site from the drop-off point. At Hebei there is a truck stop with accommodation and restaurants.

If you are going to tackle the walk, it would be a good idea to leave your main large backpack at one of the guesthouses, as it is quite a trek. If you follow this advice, be sure to take wet weather gear with you, as the weather in this region is extremely changeable. The pathway leading to the monastery is not very obvious, but you shouldn't worry about it too much, as the grassland here is very open and any local you meet won't hesitate to point you in the right direction. There is some wire fencing on the way to the gompa, but it is pretty easy to get over. In the summer, Tibetans pitch their tents in this area, and it is better not to approach these camps without making your presence known from a distance, as they often leave their dogs loose.

Serlak Gompa (Sailihaisi)
This important monastery belonging to the Gelukpa order monastery is 10km south-west of Gumangxiang, to the south-west of Tongde. There are no buses available on this route, so you will either have to tackle it on foot or charter a car.

GUOLUO (GOLOK) TIBETAN AUTONOMOUS PREFECTURE

For the deepest and wildest Tibetan experience in the region, Guoluo is the place to go. This prefecture is home to both the most sacred mountain in the Amdo region, Machen Kangri (Amnye Machen), and the source of the mighty Yellow River (Machu). This rugged area was also notorious for being home to bandits in ages gone by.

MADUO (MATO)

Five hundred kilometers to the south-west of Xining, the town of Maduo is located near the source of the Yellow River. Due to an altitude of around 4,270m it sometimes has snow even in the summer. Maduo itself is around 3km to the north of the main road, and from a hill to the south, the small and dreary town looks like a line of military barracks. Though there are few people around, the town has a massive white elephant of a movie theater, a size way beyond the needs of this small place. Maduo does get a trickle of tourists though, as it is a base for trips up to the source of Yellow River.

During the Qing (Manchu) Dynasty, it was an important place, as there was a main road starting from here that took traders and travelers on to Nakchu (Naqu) and Lhasa via both the Eling Hu and Zaling Hu Lakes.

Access
From Xining or Yushu (Jyekundo)
There are no buses actually terminating at Maduo.

AMDO

207

From Xining, you need to take one heading for Yushu (Jyekundo) that gets you to the town in around 14 hours. In the opposite direction you will need to catch the bus going from Yushu (Jyekundo) to Xining, and that trip will take you about 12 hours. At Maduo, the bus station is in the courtyard of the *Huang He Yan Bingzhan* (Military Depot).

Accommodation & Restaurants

The *Huang He Yan Bingzhan* (Military Guesthouse) is convenient for catching buses, and there is no problem for foreigners to stay here. Beds cost Y8-10, and there are coal heaters in the rooms. The guesthouse also has a restaurant.

The *Xianzhengfu Ganbu Zhaodaisuo* (Local Government Guesthouse) has an extra tariff for foreign guests, so you will have to pay Y30 for a bed here, and the guesthouse is far from the bus station. They also provide coal heaters, and there is a restaurant.

There are a lot of Muslim restaurants around the *Guoying Luguan* (Hotel) area. Chinese food is available, but it is extremely expensive, costing Y8-12 per dish.

Places to See

Huang He Daqiao (Yellow River Bridge) and Ayonggongma Tso (Lake)

Walk south-west from Maduo for an hour or so, and you will reach Huang He Daqiao (Yellow River Bridge), which spans the upper reaches of this mighty river. At this stage it is a narrow river with clear water, bearing little resemblance to the immense murky river that weaves its way across the plains of central China. The 84m-long bridge was completed in 1966.

Continue walking to a small lake and then go through a pass a little further on, and you will finally reach Ayonggongma Tso, a large lake with a small peninsula that runs out into its center. In summer the peninsular turns to pastureland.

Rather than taking the road there, walking along the lakeshore or climbing the small hill next to it will give you a much better view. The trip takes 2-3 hours in one direction, and it would be a good idea to take a little food along with you.

Eling Hu (Ngoring Tso)

Ngoring means 'Blue like the Color of the Dawn Sky.' The lake is about 30km across and is at an altitude of 4,271m. This massive lake, along with Zaling

Hu to the west, forms part of the Yellow River system. The river flows out of Eling Hu near a fishing spot at the northern end of the lake (52km from Maduo). Surrounded by grassy hills, the area also offers a distant view of the Kunlun Mountains.

At the small village of Caze, on the western side of the lake, is Tsowar Kartse Dokha Gompa (Cuowashenzeduosi), and there are a number of chortens of various sizes standing alongside one another in the monastery grounds. On top of the hill, on the western side of the monastery, there is a monument dedicated to the source of the Yellow River (Huang He Yuantou Jinianbei).

The roadway that comes up to the monastery continues on from this point. By car it is a 10km trip, but on foot this is shortened to 4-5km. You will also get a good view of Eling Hu, while Zaling Hu can be seen from another hill to the west.

Access

There seems to be only 1-2 trucks a day from Maduo to Caze and Ze. The trip to Caze takes about 4 hours, and the road conditions are pretty bad. There is no accommodation available along the way. If you just want to visit the monument marking the Yellow River source and then come back, you can charter a jeep from the *Governor's Office*

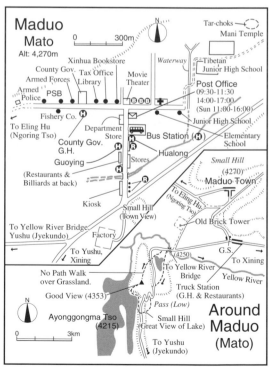

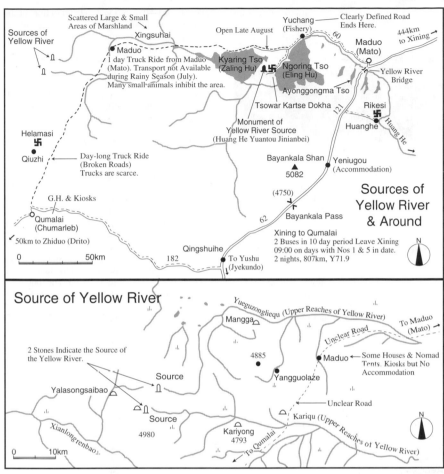

Sources of Yellow River & Around

Source of Yellow River

(Xianzhang Bangongshi) at the *County Government* building (Xian Renmin Zhengfu) in Maduo. These jeeps cost about Y600, and for example, a jeep leaving at 10:30 would get you back around 20:00. This makes for a fairly long day, and packing some food for the day is a good idea, as there is nothing in the way of food there.

Zaling Hu (Kyaring Tso) and Xingsuhai
About 20km further to the west from Eling Hu, you will come to another large lake, Zaling Hu (Kyaring Tso). *Kyaring* means 'Dawn,' and this lake is also part of the Yellow River system. The river flows into the lake at the western end and continues on its way from the southern end, finding its way next to Eling Hu. The path up to the lake is easy to follow and even allows you to access the area during the rainy season.

Continuing another 20-30km to the west from the western end of Zaling Hu, you will reach Xingsuhai, an area with numerous beautiful mountain pools scattered around it. This place is rather difficult to get to during the rainy season, which lasts from June to August. Although it is cold in the spring and fall, these are the seasons to visit, as the days are usually bright and clear.

Access
There are infrequent trucks heading for the small village of Maduo, beyond Xingsuhai. Chartering a car at the *County Government Offices* (Xian Renmin Zhengfu) in Maduo (Mato) costs Y600 per day.

The Source of the Yellow River
There are 2 monuments in this area that are

AMDO

209

Yellow River Source & Eling Hu

*Dari (Jimai)—The bus leaves from in front of the bus station at 07:00 each day. If there are too few passengers on any given day, the bus will be cancelled and you will have to take the one the following day. The trip takes 5-6 hours. There are also irregular buses organized by *Guoluo Minzu Luxingshe* (Travel).
*Banma (Padma), Jiuzhi (Jigdril)—There are no buses servicing these 2 towns, and the only way to get there is by hitching a ride.

Minibuses are also available for other neighboring towns and villages.

Accommodation & Restaurants

The *Xueshan Binguan* (Hotel) is the best in the town, but the building is really old. It is located about 150m before you get to the bus station. For foreigners, the rate starts at around Y16, and only the more expensive rooms are equipped with showers.

The *Chezhan Lushe* (Bus Stop Guesthouse) is, as the name suggests, located in the bus station itself, and a dormitory bed costs from Y5. The rooms are pretty good for the price, but there are no showers

dedicated to the source of the Yellow River. One traveler, after talking with the village headman, was able to hire a horse and spent 4 days visiting them both. Hiring a horse costs Y50-100 per day.

MAQIN (DAWU) [MACHEN (TAWO)]

This town is the capital of Guoluo Prefecture, and the buses that will get you there show their destination as Dawu. All of the major buildings in Maqin, such as guesthouses, the bus station, etc., are on the main street. Once you come off this street, there is only a gently sloping grassy area.

In the north of the town there is a *mani* temple, and behind that there is a hill decorated with fluttering *tar-choks*, where you can get a good view out over the town.

Access

From Xining and Tongde
*Xining—There is a daily bus, and also sleeping berth buses operating on this route.
*Tongde—A minibus leaves at 09:00 every morning.

From Maqin (Dawu)
*Xining—There is a bus every day leaving from the street in front of the bus station. There is also a night bus with sleeping berths operating on the same route.
*Gande (Gabde)—A minibus leaves from in front of the bus station at 07:00 every morning and takes 3 hours.

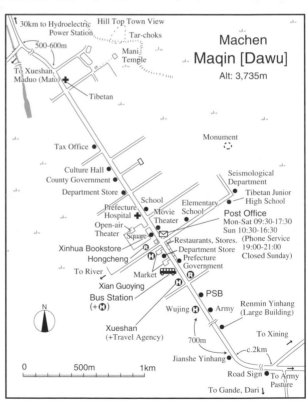

in the guesthouse.

The *Xian Guoying Lushe* (Hotel) seems to only be for a quick overnight stay, and beds cost Y6.

The *Hongcheng Fandian* (Restaurant) is in front of the Xian Guoying Lushe and serves good Chinese food. There are also a number of Muslim restaurants in the town.

Places to See
Machen Kangri (Amnye Machen)

With a peak rising to 6,282m, Machen Kangri is a sacred mountain that really symbolizes the Amdo region. As a place of pilgrimage, it is as important as Mt. Kailash in the far west of the country. The name of the town, *Machen*, is derived from the name of the peak and means 'The Greatest Source of the Yellow River.' *Kangri*, on the other hand, means 'Snowy Mountain,' and *Amnye* refers to the ancestors of the people of the region.

Rabgya Gompa (Lajiasi)

Sixty-six kilometers to the north-east of Maqin (Dawu) is the Gelukpa monastery of Rabgya. The gompa is built on the banks of the Yellow River and houses about 400 monks. There is a single bus daily from Maqin (Dawu), and the trip takes about 2 hours. From Hebei it is a 30km trip, and this takes about an hour and 20 minutes. The bus route passes right in front of the monastery, allowing easy access to the site. If you are asking for directions from local people, they pronounce the name of the monastery as *Rabjya*.

GANDE (GABDE) (CLOSED)

Gande is a small town surrounded by small hills. The town center is huddled around the movie theater, and you can buy general supplies here. There is little of special interest for foreign visitors in the town.

Access
To Gande

*Maqin (Dawu)—There is 1 bus each day.
*Dari (Jimai)—There is a minibus that stops near the movie theater in Gande every 1-2 days.

From Gande

*Maqin (Dawu)—There is a bus that leaves Gande between 11:00 and 12:00. A bus also arrives from Dari (Jimai) and continues on to Maqin (Dawu), stopping at Gande in the evening.
*Dari (Jimai)—A bus leaves the town every 1-2 days, and this arrives at 10:00-11:00. You should aim at catching it at the earlier time, as the driver doesn't hang around for long in the town.

Rabgya Gompa & Around
Alt: 3,050m
'Free Tibet' Written on Rock
Rabgya Gompa (Lajiasi)
Lajia Village
Kiosk
Lingkhor
To Xining, Hebei
Huang He
Truck Checkpoint
Jungong
Restaurant, Kiosk
c.25min walk to Rabgya Gompa.
Restaurants, Shared-truck Available.
To Dawu Kiosks Best to Hitchhike at Checkpoint.

Due to the lack of scheduled buses, many of the local Tibetans simply hitch lifts on passing trucks for both Maqin (Dawu) and Dari.

Accommodation & Restaurants

The *Liangyou Gongsi Zhaodaisuo* (Guesthouse) has beds for Y18, and although the rooms are good, the police are quick to turn up once a foreigner checks in.

The *Gandexian Lushe* (Hotel) is another possibility among a clutch of other places in town. This town functions much like a truck stop, catering to the drivers and passengers, and there are a lot of Muslim restaurants.

The *Jinhai Canting* (Restaurant) at the main junction is the place to check out for those in search of Chinese food.

Place to See
Donggyu Gompa (Donjiduokasi)

Twelve kilometers towards Dari (Jimai) from

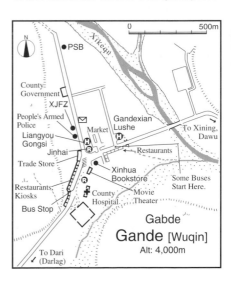

PSB
Xikequ
County Government
XJFZ
People's Armed Police
Liangyou Gongsi
Jinhai
Trade Store
Market
Gandexian Lushe
To Xining, Dawu
Restaurants
Xinhua Bookstore
Some Buses Start Here.
Restaurants, Kiosks
County Hospital
Movie Theater
Bus Stop
Gabde
Gande [Wuqin]
Alt: 4,000m
To Dari (Darlag)

AMDO

Gande is the Nyingmapa and Gelukpa monastery of Donggyu. There is easy access to the gompa, as the bus route passes only 200-300m from its entrance.

DARI (JIMAI) [DARLAG] (CLOSED)

Dari (Jimai), to the south of the Yellow River, is shown as Jimai on the buses that are heading here. The area is mainly populated by ethnic Tibetans, and in the western suburbs are the Chalang (Traling) Gompa (Chalangsi) and Nianmaosi (Temple).

Access
From Xining
There are buses leaving the bus station in Xining for Jimai on days with the numbers 2, 5, and 8 in the date. There is also a bus for Banma (Padma) that goes via Jimai leaving Xining on the 4th and the 10th of the month. The trip takes 2 days with an overnight stay at Heka.

From Maqin (Dawu)
There are 1-2 minibuses a day for this 5-6 hour trip, and they terminate at the Dari Bus Station.

From Dari (Jimai)
*Xining—Buses start from Dari on days with the numbers 4, 7, and 10 (e.g. on 4, 17, 27, 30, etc.) in the date. Those from Banma pass through around noon on the days when they are operated.
*Maqin (Dawu) —There is a bus every 1-2 days, departing at 13:00. There are also minibuses that service this route.
*Banma and Surrounding Area—There is a bus from Xining that stays at the Dari Bus Station overnight and leaves at 07:00 the following morning. It is operated on days with the numbers 1 (or 2) and 6 in the date, and the 169km trip takes 5 hours. Due to the infrequency of the bus service, many Tibetans decide to hitchhike to Banma.
*Jiuzhi (Jigdril)—There is no regular bus service on this route; therefore, you will have to hitch a lift. Once in a long while, there is a full-sized bus that is operated by *Guoluo Minzu Luxingshe* (Travel). When it does come through, it stays at the bus station overnight before departure.

Accommodation & Restaurants
The *Qinghai Dari Qichezhan Lushe* (Bus Station Guesthouse) has beds starting at Y8, and for a 2-

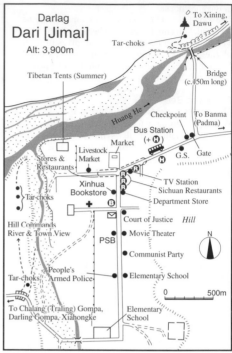

person room with a television, they charge Y13 per person. The building looks like an old-style terraced house, and its rooms are pretty dirty. The guesthouse is really just for people wanting an overnight stay.

There is not much of a choice when it comes to Chinese food in the town, though there are a couple of Chinese restaurants near the department store and dishes cost Y5-10. There are a lot of Muslim restaurants around the market area.

Places to See
Chalang (Traling) Gompa [Chalangsi]
This is a Nyingmapa monastery that is 16km to the west, south-west of Dari (Jimai). There are no buses on this route, but you may be able to hitch a lift part of the way.

Darling Gompa (Nyenmo Gompa)
This gompa is 10km further on over the mountain from Chalang (Traling) Gompa. You can get there directly by hitching a lift via Jianshe, and there seems to be a couple of trucks a day along this route.

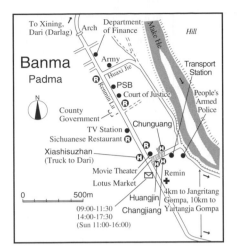

Map labels:
To Xining, Dari (Darlag) — Arch — Department of Finance — Hill — Mare He — Army — Huaxi Jie — Transport Station — **Banma** — Padma — PSB — Renmin Lu — Court of Justice — People's Armed Police — N — County Government — Chunguang — TV Station — Sichuanese Restaurant — Xiashisuzhan (Truck to Dari) — Movie Theater — Remin — Lotus Market — 0 — 500m — Huangjin — Changjiang — 4km to Jangritang Gompa, 10km to Yartangja Gompa — 09:00-11:30 14:00-17:30 (Sun 11:00-16:00)

BANMA (PADMA) [PARMA] (CLOSED)

Close to the border with Sichuan Province, Banma is at the south-east end of Qinghai Province, and the transportation system in this area is extremely poor. This is a small town, and its market area is deserted. Nonetheless, the Banma area is where the Golok (Guoluo) Tibetans trace their ancestry to.

There are many Tibetan monasteries with distinctive features in this region, and it is regrettable that Banma is still classified as a closed area for foreign visitors. It is 169km from Dari (Jimai), and the journey takes 4-5 hours by car.

Access
From Xining
There are only 2 buses during any given 10-day period, and these leave Xining on days with the numbers 4 and 10 in the date. They stay overnight at Heka and Dari (Jimai) and arrive at Banma in the afternoon on the third day.

From Banma
*Xining—There are buses on the days with the numbers 3 (or 2 if the month before had 31 days) and 7 in the date. These leave the Yunshuzhan (Bus Stop) at 06:00 in the morning, and the trip takes 2 days.
*Aba (Ngawa) and Rangtang (Zamthang) in Sichuan—Although the road leads to these towns, there are no buses on this stretch of the road, and trucks that go directly to them are very few and far between.
*Jiuzhi (Jigdril)—Most of the local people that are heading for the town get there by hitchhiking.

Accommodation & Restaurants
It is strange that there are 2 good-quality hotels that are well above the standard that one comes to expect from such a small town.
The *Huangjin Daxia* (Hotel) was built in the summer of 1995, and single rooms with a bathroom cost Y35, while doubles are Y30-35 per person. A bed in a 3-person room costs Y20, and one in a 4- to 5-person room is Y15.
The *Changjiang Daxia (Hotel)* is of similar quality but a little cheaper than the Huangjin Daxia.
The *Chunguang Lushe* (Hotel) is a hotel mainly for Tibetans, and the price of a dormitory bed is about Y5 here.
The *Xianshisuzhan* has dormitory beds costing Y5, and the rooms are dirty, but you can sometimes catch a lift in a truck from the courtyard of the hotel.

There are a number of Sichuanese restaurants where you can get Chinese food, and there are also many Muslim restaurants in the town.

Places to See
Jangritang Gompa (Jiangritangsi)
The Nyingmapa monastery of Jangritang is 4km to the east of Banma, and in the middle of the gompa there is a beautifully crafted wooden tower that you can actually see from Banma.

In the grounds of the monastery, there are about a hundred chortens of all different sizes. You will see many Tibetans making pilgrimage circuits around the site, and on the hillside there are many *tar-choks* fluttering in the breeze and also a small temple.

Yartangja (Akyong gya) Gompa (Ashijiang-jia-gongsi)
This Jonangpa monastery, an uncommon sight outside of the Amdo region, is set beside the road about 10km to the east of Banma. It has tower-like temples with eyes on them that are worth the trip, though the temple interiors are now in ruins.

The locals' pronunciation of the name sounds like *Akyonjya* or *Ajyanjya* Gompa.

Do Gongma Gompa (Duogongmasi)
This Nyingmapa monastery is right next to the bus route, 36km towards Dari (Jimai) from Banma. There are 4 square, pillar-like towers at the gompa that are reminiscent of the Milarepa Lhakhang at Hezuo (Tsoe in Gansu), only in miniature. There is also an interesting collection of rock chortens strung out in a line here.

Dodrubchen Gompa (Zhiqinsi)
Dodrubchen is an important Nyingmapa monastery, 57km to the south, south-west of Banma. The gompa's venerable incarnate lama, the 4th

AMDO

213

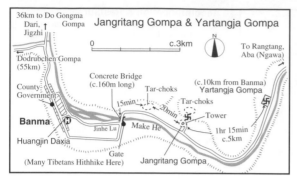

Jangritang Gompa & Yartangja Gompa

36km to Do Gongma
Dari, ↑ Gompa
Jigzhi
0   c.3km   To Rangtang,
Dodrubchen Gompa   Aba (Ngawa)
(55km)
County   Concrete Bridge   (c.10km from Banma)
Government   (c.160m long) Tar-choks Yartangja Gompa
                        15min   Tar-choks
Banma   20min   Tower
            Jinhe Lu   Make He
Huangjin Daxia   1hr 15min
                                        c.5km
              Gate   Jangritang Gompa
(Many Tibetans Hithhike Here)

Dodrubchen Rinpoche, no longer resides at the monastery and instead lives in exile in the Indian state of Sikkim. You can get to the site by hitching a lift on one of the trucks that are heading for Duokehelinchang, and there are usually 1 or 2 of these each day.

JIUZHI (JIGDRIL)

Although the town is administratively part of Qinghai Province, Jiuzhi is not connected with other towns in the province by bus. The only access to the town is from Aba (Ngawa) County, in neighboring Sichuan Province, and Jiuzhi has historically had strong ties with this county. Strangely, all the towns and villages surrounding Jiuzhi are closed to foreign visitors, and only the town of Jiuzhi is open and has been so for a long time.

Tarthang Gompa (Baiyusi) in this area is a Nyingmapa monastery and well worth visiting. There is also the sacred mountain, Nyenpo Yurtse (5,369m), which lies between the town and the gompa. There is 1 bus a day that takes you out here from Aba (Ngawa) County.

YUSHU TIBETAN AUTONOMOUS PREFECTURE (JYEKUNDO)

The Yushu (Jyekundo) Prefecture accounts for a quarter of the area of Qinghai Province, but it is geographically part of the Kham region. This is especially true of the southern part of the prefecture, including the areas of Yushu (Jyekundo), Nangqian (Nangchen), etc. These southern counties have a very strong connection with the Dege (Derge) region of Sichuan and Chamdo.

Among all the Tibetan areas that were annexed by China, the people of this region have managed

to maintain a very strong belief in their religion, and a large number of the monasteries that were devastated during the Cultural Revolution have been rapidly rebuilt. There are now about 200 monasteries active within the prefecture, and these are concentrated in Nangqian, Yushu, Chengduo (Trindu), and Zaduo (Dzato) Counties. Among the various religious orders with monasteries in the area, the Kagyupa order has particularly prospered.

On the second day of your trip from Xining, the bus goes through the desolate Guoluo area and then crosses the Bayankala Shankou Pass. The road conditions improve and at points it's even sealed. When you hit this sealed section, it marks the point where the main part of Yushu (Jyekundo) Prefecture starts.

YUSHU (JYEKUNDO)

Yushu is found along a tributary of the Tongtian He (Dri-chu), which helps form the upper reaches of the mighty Yangtze River (Chang Jiang). It is a town with a long tradition of trade and is famous as the site of the prestigious Jyegu (Kyigu) Gompa, an important Sakyapa monastery.

The famous Yushu horse-riding festival is held every year near the town during the last week of July and the first week of August.

Access
From Xining
There is a night bus with sleeping berths for Yushu (Jyekundo) that leaves Xining at 13:00 every day. There is also an ordinary bus that departs at 10:00 every morning. Without stopping for the night, the 819km journey takes about 25 hours.

From Yushu (Jyekundo)
*Xining—The daily bus leaves the Yushu (Jyekundo) Bus Station at 07:00.
*Xiewu (Zhiwu)—There are a lot of minibuses and jeeps available.
*Qumalai (Chumarleb), Zhiduo (Drito), Chengduo (Trindu), Zaduo (Dzato), Nangqian (Nangchen) —You can catch a lift in a shared-truck along with many of the local Tibetan people, as there is a very limited bus service for these towns and others in the surrounding areas. Many trucks leave at 07:00-08:00 from the junction in front of the Jiegu Shangchang (Department Store). To

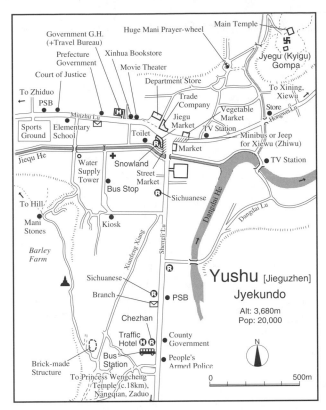

Map labels:
Government G.H. (+Travel Bureau)
Huge Mani Prayer-wheel
Main Temple
Prefecture Government
Xinhua Bookstore
Jyegu (Kyigu) Gompa
Court of Justice
Movie Theater
Department Store
To Zhiduo
PSB
Minzhu Lu
Trade Company
To Xining, Xiewu
Vegetable Market
Store
Hongwei Lu
Jiegu Market
Sports Ground
Elementary School
Toilet
TV Station
Jiequ He
Market
Minibus or Jeep for Xiewu (Zhiwu)
Water Supply Tower
Snowland
Street Market
TV Station
Bus Stop
Sichuanese
Dangdai He
Dangdai Lu
Mani Stones
Kiosk
Barley Farm
Xianfeng Xiang
Shengli Lu
Sichuanese
Branch
Chezhan
Traffic Hotel
County Government
Brick-made Structure
Bus Station
People's Armed Police
To Princess Wengcheng Temple (c.18km), Nangqian, Zaduo

Yushu [Jieguzhen]
Jyekundo
Alt: 3,680m
Pop: 20,000

N

0   500m

To Hill
To Zhiduo
PSB

---

arrange a lift, just ask one of the passengers or the driver, if they can be found, where they are going. After 8:00 there are a lot fewer trucks leaving the town. The cost of a lift is usually about Y10 for the 50-60km trip.

*Ganzi (Kandze), Sichuan Province—This service may be resumed in the future, and you should check out the situation locally.

*Shiqu (Sershul), Sichuan—Chartering a car from the parking area around Yushu Shangchang will cost you around Y300 during the summer and Y500 during the winter.

From Yushu to the Sichuan-Tibet Highway
There are a number of routes going south and connecting with the Sichuan-Tibet Highway that runs from Chengdu to Lhasa.

Yushu to Ganzi
Starting at Yushu, this route goes through Xiewu (Zhiwu) and Shiqu (Sershul) in Sichuan Province on to Manigango on the Sichuan-Tibet Highway and then heads for Ganzi (Kandze) to the east of Sichuan Province. There are a lot of trucks on this

section of the route. (For details, see the section on Ganzi in Sichuan Province.)

Yushu to Dege and onto Chamdo
After reaching Manigango (as detailed above), this route then heads west to Dege (Derge) in Sichuan Province. It continues in a westerly direction, crossing the Mekong River (Dza-chu) and finally reaching Chamdo (Changdu) in the TAR. This whole trip covers 767km. (See the Dege section for details.)

Yushu to Nangqian and onto Chamdo
Leaving Yushu, this route goes south-west, crosses the Mekong River (Zaqu or Dza-chu), and reaches Chamdo via Nangqian (Nangchen) and Riwoche (Leiwuqi) in the TAR. For reaching Chamdo, this route is shorter than the one via Dege, but the road conditions after Nangqian are pretty bad, and there are fewer trucks on this section. According to local truck drivers, the journey from Nangqian to Riwoche normally takes 2 days. The whole trip is about 450km (530km via Riwoche).

Accommodation
The *Zhengfu Zhaodaisuo* (Government Guesthouse) is the place that foreigners are advised to stay at, and foreign guests are charged Y25 for a bed in a 4-person room and Y100 for single rooms. Although the facilities are old, it is conveniently

Yushu (Jyekundo)

AMDO

215

located in the middle of the town, and there is a post office and telephone exchange nearby. The hotel has the Foreign Affairs Section of the PSB on the 1st floor, and the *Yushu Luyouju* (Travel Bureau) is in room 201.

The *Jiaotong Ludian* (Traffic Hotel) is a new 4-story hotel in the bus station, and this is convenient for those catching the early morning buses to Xining. The hotel is less convenient for guests that need to use the facilities in town, as it is a 15-minute walk to the town center.

There are heaters available, but the hot showers are in a different building than the rooms. Recently foreigners have not been allowed to stay here.

Restaurants
You will be struck by the large number of signs calling your attention to the many Muslim restaurants in the town, but if you are in the mood for Sichuanese cuisine, you can find restaurants serving this along the street between the Zhengfu

Jyegu (Kyigu) Gompa

Jyegu (Kyigu) Gompa

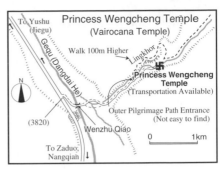

Zhaodaisuo (Guesthouse) and the bus station. Although Tibetan restaurants are not very common here, the *Snowland Restaurant*, behind Jiegu Shangchang (Department Store), is full of Tibetans, and understandably the menu is in Tibetan.

The *Chezhan Canting* (Restaurant) is next to the bus station, and this Chinese restaurant serves relatively good meals including rice dishes. The prices written on the menu are for large plates, and if you are alone, ask for a smaller dish, which is half the price, costing Y6-15.

Places to See
Jyegu (Kyigu) Gompa (Jiegusi)
Covering the hillside in the north of the town are clusters of lodging houses for the monks from this gompa, who are very friendly. Established in the 13th century, this huge Sakyapa monastery consists of a patchwork of the blue-gray lodging houses and dark-red temples. The combination of colors is just like that of Sakya Monastery in central Tibet.

There has been a lot of reconstruction here. However, up the hill there are the remains of a dzong (fortress) and a collection of old ruined dwellings that also used to house the monks from the monastery. The top of the hill commands a great view of Yushu.

Domkar Gompa (Dangkasi)
This impressive monastery belongs to the Karma Kagyupa order. It is perched on one of the northern hills around 15km outside of Yushu, on the route towards Xining. There is an easily-missed junction that branches off to the monastery, so you have to keep your eyes open. Take a minibus heading for Xiewu (Zhiwu) and get off en route, and from the drop-off point, it is roughly a 20-minute walk.

Princess Wengcheng Temple (Wencheng Gongzhu Miao) [Vairocana Temple]
In the 7th century, Princess Wengcheng, the daughter of the Tang Emperor, married into the Tibetan royal family. While she was on her way to Lhasa, she stayed at this temple for a month. Engraved on a cliff behind the monastery, there is a large image of Princess Wengcheng that is worshiped here. The Tibetan name of the site is Nampar Nangdze Lhakhang.

Catch a shared-truck that is heading towards Zaduo (Dzato) and Nangqian (Nangchen), and it will drop you off on the way. There are usually some around 08:00, and it takes about 20 minutes. Be careful, as it is easy to miss the stop even though the road goes straight past the front of the monastery. Make sure to tell the driver exactly where you want to get off when you are negotiating the price, which should be Y2-3. On the way you will see the Karma Kagyupa's Trangu Gompa (Changusi) on your left-hand side.

Lungshoe Gompa (Longxisi)
This is a huge Gelukpa monastery at Rabshi (Xialaxiu).

Princess Wengcheng Temple

CHENGDUO (TRINDU) (CLOSED)

This town is not so easy to get to, as it is well off the main road. The collection of monasteries that are tightly clustered around the town are interesting and will make your visit worthwhile.

Zhiwu Drogon (Duogansi)

The town of Xiewu (Zhiwu) is about 45km before you reach Yushu on the way from Xining. There are a number of minibuses every day, or you can take a shared-jeep between Yushu and Xiewu, and the trip costs Y7. For Shiqu, Sichuan Province, you can either take a shared-truck costing Y25 or a minibus for Y50.

The road from Xining branches off here, and the main route continues on straight to Yushu, while the road that veers off to the left leads to Shiqu (Sershul) in Sichuan Province. On a hill overlooking the junction is Zhiwu Drogon. You can get a good view from the road below. Like Jyegu (Kyigu) Gompa in Yushu, this monastery belongs to the Sakyapa order and has the same blue-gray and dark-red color combination of buildings. To the bottom left-hand side, you will also see Nyidzong Gompa (Nizongsi) halfway up the hill. If you want to stay in this area, there is accommodation here.

Jujye (Drubgyu) Gompa (Zhujiesi)

This monastery belongs to the Drigung Kagyupa order and is situated close to the bus route. In standard Tibetan the monastery is referred to as Drubgyuling Gompa (Zhenqinxiang in Chengduo County).

Karzang Gompa (Kazangsi)

The gompa is 5km to the east of the town of Chengduo and is administered by the Sakyapa order (Chenwenxiang in Chengduo County).

SUMANG (ZURMANG) REGION (CLOSED)

The area between Yushu and Nangqian is called Zurmang (Sumang), and there are quite a number of prominent monasteries of the Karma Kagyupa order concentrated here. Although it is a closed area, you can still arrange a visit by chartering a car at the *Luyouju* (Travel Bureau) in Yushu. There are so many monasteries in this area that regrettably there is only room here to introduce the main ones.

Zurmang Gompa (Sumangsi)

Zurmang Gompa is the general term used to refer to both Zurmang Dutsitil Gompa (Xiao Sumang-

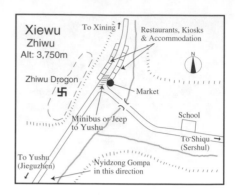

xiang in Yushu County) and Zurmang Namgyeltse Gompa (Maozhuangxiang in Nangqian County). These 2 huge monasteries are run by the Karma Kagyupa order, and the former is where the late Choegyam Trungpa Rinpoche (1939-1987), author of *'Born in Tibet,'* was from.

Karma Dargye Gompa

As the name infers, this is also a Karma Kagyupa monastery. The incarnate lama from here was one of the many that sought refuge abroad and founded branches in Western countries. Following the late 16th Karmapa (1923-1981), who escaped from the Chinese invasion, all the high lamas from this area fled to India and have since taken an active part in the propagation of the Karma Kagyupa-style of Tibetan Buddhism in the West. This has helped to make it the order with the largest international network and following abroad.

In addition to Karma Dargye Gompa, there are many other monasteries clustered around Nangqian (Nangchen).

TO THE SOURCE OF THE MEKONG RIVER (CLOSED)

The source of the Mekong River, called Zaqu (Dza-chu) in Tibet, can be found in Zaduo County. In Yushu you can catch a shared-truck to Zaduo (Capital of Zaduo County), 243km to the west, and the trip costs around Y25. If you decide to make your way out to the area, bear in mind that there is no public transportation for the other 230km on to Moyun, and the road conditions are terrible. For tourists, chartering a Land Cruiser in Yushu is really the only way to go.

In Moyun there is neither accommodation nor food available, and from Moyun to the source of the Mekong, you will have to hire a horse, as there is no access for cars.

ABA (NGAWA)

ABA (NGAWA) TIBETAN & QIANG AUTONOMOUS PREFECTURE, SICHUAN PROVINCE

Following the course of the Min Jiang River for only 100km to the north-west of Chengdu, the capital of Sichuan Province, you will reach the Aba (Ngawa) Prefecture, at the eastern end of the Tibetan Plateau that juts out into the Sichuan Basin.

A recent trend among travelers is to head north from Chengdu into the Tibetan Plateau and then to make for Gansu Province, through the vast grasslands of Hongyuan and Ruo'ergai (or in the

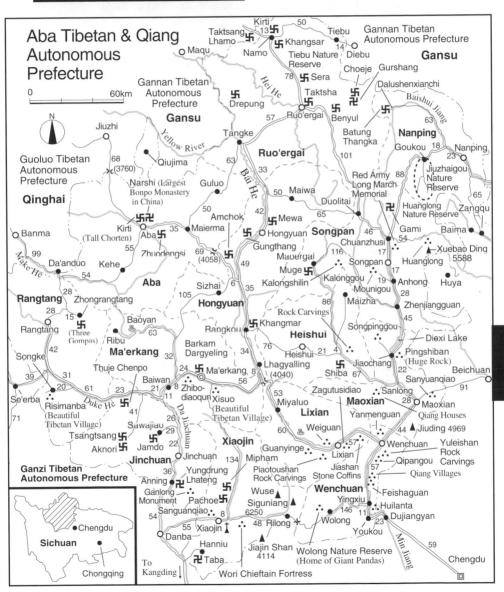

Aba Tibetan & Qiang Autonomous Prefecture

0 _____ 60km

N

Gannan Tibetan Autonomous Prefecture
Gansu

Guoluo Tibetan Autonomous Prefecture

Qinghai

Kirti 13
Taktsang
Lhamo
Maqu
Namo
Tiebu Nature Reserve
Sera 78
Drepung
Ruo'ergai 57
Tangke
Qiujima 63
Narshi (Largest Bonpo Monastery in China)
Kirti (Tall Chorten)
Aba
Zhuodengsi 55
Kehe
Da'anduo
Banma
Make He 99
54

Tiebu
Khangsar 14
Diebu
Choeje Gurshang
Dalushenxianchi
Baishui Jiang

Gansu
Benyul
Batung Thangka
Goukou 18
Jiuzhaigou Nature Reserve
Nanning
Nanping 23
63
65

Ruo'ergai
33
Maiwa 50
Duolitai
Amchok 42
Mewa
Hongyuan Songpan 46
Maierma 35
Gungthang
Maoergai 116
Muge
Kalongshilin
Kalonggou
Mounigou
Maizha 86
Songpan 17
Huanglong
Anhong
Zhenjiangguan

Red Army Long March Memorial 88
Huanglong Nature Reserve
Gami
Baima
Xuebao Ding 5588
Huanglong
Huya
Zangqu 65
54

Rangtang 28
Zhongrangtang
Rangtang 15 (Three Gompas)
Baoyan 63
Ribu
Songke
Se'erba
Risimanba (Beautiful Tibetan Village) 41
Sawajiao

Ma'erkang
Thuje Chenpo
Baiwan 21
Zhibodiaoqun 11
Xisuo (Beautiful Tibetan Village)

Hongyuan
Rangkou
Khangmar
Barkam Dargyeling 34
Heishui 21 4
Lhagyalling (4040)
Miyaluo
Lixian
Weiguan

Heishui 76
Jiaochang
Shiba 67
Zagutusidiao
Yanmenguan

Songpinggou 45
Diexi Lake
Pingshiban (Huge Rock)
Sanyuanqiao
Sanlong
Maoxian 28
Qiang Houses

Beichuan 91
Maoxian

Ganzi Tibetan Autonomous Prefecture

Tsangtsang
Aknori
Jamdo 22
Jinchuan
Anning
Ganlong Monument
Sanguanqiao 54
Danba

Jinchuan
Yungdrung Lhateng 36
Pachoe
Xiaojin 55
Hanniu
Taba
Wori Chieftain Fortress

Mipham 134
Piaotoushan Rock Carvings
Stone Coffins
Wuse
Siguniang 6250
Rilong 48
Jiajin Shan 4114

Guanyinge
Lixian 57
Jiashan 57
Feishaguan
Yingxiu
Wolong
Youkou

Wenchuan
Qipangou
Qiang Villages
Huilanta
Dujiangyan 23

Yuleishan Rock Carvings

Jiuding 4969
Wenchuan

146 11
Min Jiang
59
Chengdu

Wolong Nature Reserve (Home of Giant Pandas)

Sichuan
Chengdu
Chongqing

To Kangding

AMDO

other direction). At the foot of the Min Shan (Mountains) to the east are the well-known areas of natural beauty called Huanglong and Jiuzhaigou. These 2 draw large crowds of both Chinese and foreign visitors every year.

In Tibetan the name *Aba* is translated to *Ngapa* or *Ngawa*. During the 8th and 9th centuries, the region fell under the control of the Tibetan Kingdom, and since that time it has been strongly influenced by Tibet, especially within the religious sphere. In an area around the same size as Austria there is a population of only about 770,000, and around half of the people are Tibetans. The other half is made up of a mixture of Qiang, Hui, Han, and other smaller ethnic groups.

Broadly speaking, Aba (Ngawa) is part of the Amdo region. However, the southern mountainous area, where you will find Jinchuan, Xiaojin, Lixian, Danba, etc., is called *Gyarong*, meaning 'Valley of China.' As the name infers, this area is generally viewed in a different way.

In the area adjacent to the Sichuan Basin in the south of the prefecture, the ancient Bon religion and the Nyingmapa order have both maintained their deep-rooted influence over the spiritual and cultural lives of the people.

This southern area is covered in woodland. The climate here is temperate, and it tends to rain a lot. In contrast, the northern part of the prefecture is a world of nomads with big skies, wide horizons, and rich, rolling grasslands, which is the more common image of the Amdo region. This northern steppe spreads out towards Gansu and Qinghai Provinces.

Access

Although the prefectural capital is Ma'erkang (Barkam), Chengdu is the starting point for bus trips within the prefecture. For these buses you need to go to the Ximen Bus Station (Ximen Qichezhan) and not the Xinnanmen Bus Station (Xinnanmen Qichezhan), next to the Jiaotong Fandian (Traffic Hotel). (See the Chengdu section.) The prefecture is also connected with Gansu Province, Qinghai Province, Ganzi (Kandze) Prefecture in Sichuan Province, and other surrounding regions by bus.

Major Routes

*Huanglong and Jiuzhaigou
   Chengdu - Wenchuan - Songpan/Nanping
*The Great Grasslands
   Chengdu - Wenchuan - Hongyuan - Ruo'ergai
   (then to Gansu Province)

As there are buses between Ruo'ergai (Dzoge) and Songpan, you have the option to combine a trip to both of these popular tourist attractions. There are many group tours that visit Huanglong, Jiuzhaigou, and the Great Grasslands as a single package.

The following courses, though not very popular, will take you deep into the Tibetan world.

*Chengdu - Ma'erkang (Barkam) - Rangtang
   (Zamthang)
   (then to Banma in Qinghai Province)
*Chengdu - Xiaojin
   (then to Ganzi area in Sichuan Province)
*Chengdu - Aba (Ngawa) - Jiuzhi
   (in Qinghai Province)

WENCHUAN (LUNGU)

This is the gateway to the Aba (Ngawa) Prefecture if you are coming from the Sichuan Basin. Heading north from Chengdu along the Min Jiang River, the road splits here, and one branch goes out to Jiuzhaigou, while the other one continues on to Ruo'ergai.

There are a lot of buses to Wenchuan from the Ximen Bus Station in Chengdu, and the fare is Y16. There are also many buses that leave from Dujiangyan, a suburb of the city.

Wolong Nature Reserve

Wolong is a sanctuary for endangered Pandas, and there is also a Panda research center here. To get out to the nature reserve you will need to take a bus heading for Xiaojin from either Chengdu or Dujiangyan. This area is also home to a large number of Tibetan people.

MAOXIAN (MAOWEN QIANG AUTONOMOUS COUNTY)

Maoxian is a small town on the way from Chengdu to Songpan, and most residents here are from the Qiang ethnic group. You can get an insight into their traditional way of life by visiting the *Maoxian Qiang Museum* in the town.

The Qiang people are an ethnic group that settled in the area surrounding the upper reaches of the Min Jiang River. As early as the 4th century B.C., they entered the world stage as the Qiang. The Chinese character *Qiang* means 'The Sheep People,' and as this name suggests, they were probably a nomadic group.

They speak a Tibeto-Burmese language, but they are not Buddhists, preferring to follow their traditional animist and shamanist beliefs. The total number of Qiang people is around 130,000, and of this number, roughly 60 % live in Maoxian.

From Chengdu there are a number of buses each

Songpan

day that leave the Ximen Bus Station. At Maoxian, there are buses for Chengdu, Mianyang, Dujiangyan, Wenchuan, etc. There are a lot of guesthouses in the town, and one to check out is the *Maoxian Binguan* (Hotel).

Diexi Fengjingqu (Scenic Spot)
Heading 56km north of Maoxian towards Songpan, you will reach this well-known area. As your bus approaches, you will catch sight of the major attraction here, the famous Diexi Lake. The lake was created by a 7.5 magnitude earthquake in 1933. There is an observation platform that costs Y4.

A tragic element was added in August 1995 when a bus accident here led to the deaths of numerous foreign tourists.

HEISHUI (TROCHU) (CLOSED)

This town shares its name with the river that it is built beside, the Heishui He River. At Musuxiang, to the east of Heishui, there is the Karma Kagyupa order's Shiba Gompa (Xibasi).

A bus leaves Chengdu at 06:40, arriving at the town in the evening. There are also buses from Maoxian.

SONGPAN (ZUNGCHU)

Traveling along the Min Jiang River for 335km from Chengdu, you will come to this historical town, a popular starting point for trips to Huanglong and Jiuzhaigou. The town has an old castle, castle gates, etc., and is mainly populated by Han and Hui people. There are some Tibetan gift stores in the town.

Horse trekking to scenic spots in the surrounding areas, such as Mounigou (Tromje), Huanglong, etc., starts from here and agents come to the bus stop looking for business. You can also arrange these horse treks through travel agents or at hotels, and the guides are all experienced and look after you and the horses well.

Access
From Chengdu
Buses leave Ximen Bus Station at 07:00 every day, and the trip takes about 11 hours.

From Songpan
[Main Bus Station]
*Chengdu—Daily bus leaving at 05:30.
*Maoxian—Daily bus leaving at 06:00.
*Ruo'ergai—Daily bus leaving at 06:30.

[Eastern Bus Station]
There are buses for both Chengdu and Jiuzhaigou.
*In addition, buses from Chengdu heading for Nanping swing through Songpan around noon each day.
Many foreigners have been charged twice the local price for tickets here.

Accommodation and Restaurants
There are a lot of hotels in the town, as many group tours come here to take the trip to Jiuzhaigou. As might be expected, many of these hotels are

AMDO

expensive.

The *Beishun Luguan* (Hotel) is a cheap option with dormitory beds for Y6. The hotel is located near the main bus station and is run by a Hui family. They do not want to deal with Westerners, though travelers from other Asian countries don't usually have a problem. You can also arrange horse trekking here.

The *Xinxi Luguan* (Hotel) is another reasonably-priced place, with dormitory beds costing Y5.

The *Songpan Fandian* (Hotel) charges foreign guests Y78 for a room with a common shower and toilet.

The *Songpan Binguan* (Hotel) is a top-range hotel, and a foreign guest can expect to pay over Y100 per night.

Places to See
Mounigou (Tromje)
Mounigou is famous for the Zhaga Pubu (Waterfall) and Erdao Hai (Lake). At Anhong, 17km from Songpan on the way to Chengdu, there is a signpost marking the entrance to Mounigou. The distance between Anhong and Mounigou is 12km, and there are Tibetan villages on the way.

*Mounigou-Zhaga Pubu (Waterfall) (17km)

*Mounigou-Zhuzhuhai Wenquan (Hot Springs) (18km)

There are only 2 options for getting around, either on foot or on horseback, and there is no accommodation on the way. The horse trekking is probably the easier option, and a 1-2 night tour will allow you to visit all the places of interest. A 2-night tour costs about Y150, and admission for a foreign visitor is Y33 at both the Zhaga Pubu and Erdao Hai.

The Red Army Long March Memorial (Hongjun Changzheng Jinianbei)
Close to Chuanzhusi, 17km to the north of Songpan, is the 44.8m-high memorial tower dedicated to the thousands of Communist soldiers that participated in the Long March in 1934. At a shop in the memorial hall, Aba (Ngawa) Prefecture-related books and maps are available.

The town of Chuanzhusi has hotels that cater to Huanglong and Jiuzhaigou group tours, and they are expensive. Between Songpan and Chuanzhusi there are a lot of minibuses, and the fare is Y5. There is also a Bon monastery at Chuanzhusi (Tsotsang) called by the same name.

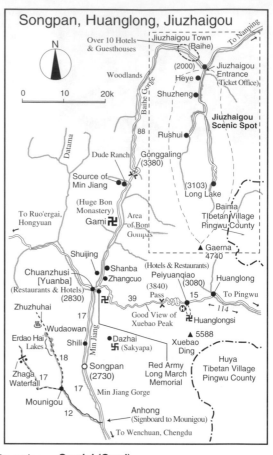

Songpan, Huanglong, Jiuzhaigou

Gamisi (Gami)
With the Tibetan name of Chadrul Gami, this great Bon monastery was founded in the 14th century. To get there, take the frequent minibuses from Songpan to Zhangcuo and then catch a lift on a tractor at Zhangcuo or walk there. At Zhangcuo there is another Bon monastery called Nogi. The Kyangthang Gompa is also nearby at Shanba on the way to Gami. This famous monastery is where the 33rd Menri Trizin, the highest priest of the Bon religion, stayed in his early days before fleeing Tibet and going into exile in India, where he still lives today.

HUANGLONG (SERTSO)

Sertso means 'Lake of Gold,' and there are around 3,400 emerald-green ponds laid out like terraced paddies on the side of Xuebao Ding (Mt. Shardungri, 5,588m), near its base. The area gets very crowded with tourists on group tours visiting Jiuzhaigou.

Access

If you decide to visit here independently, you will need to catch a tourist bus from Chuanzhusi, and there are a lot of these leaving around 09:00. Hitching is difficult on this route, as there are very few trucks making the trip. On the way to Huanglong, you get a good view of the top of Xuebao Ding. It may also be possible to take a group tour from Songpan to Huanglongsi. (For tours from Chengdu, see the Jiuzhaigou section.)

Huanglong Fengjingqu (Scenic Spot) & Huanglongsi

The admission charge at the entrance to the park (Peiyuanqiao) costs Y32 for Chinese citizens and Y96 for foreigners. From the entrance, you then walk up about 3.5km to Huanglongsi (3,430m), climbing around 360m on the way. Although Huanglongsi is a Taoist monastery, there are Tibetan-style *tar-choks* fluttering in the breeze.

A real highlight to your visit is getting to see the beautiful Wucaichi or 'Five-Color Pond' behind the monastery itself. Group tours usually spend about 4 hours in the grounds, and it is recommended that you take something to eat along with you, as there are no stores or restaurants here.

About 300m before you reach Peiyuanqiao, there is a Tibetan-style building, the *Sertso Binguan* (Hotel). During the summer there are a number of Tibetan-style tents erected here, where you can buy gifts, meals, etc.

JIUZHAIGOU

This area of natural beauty is in Nanping County. This 700-sq-km area is crammed with lakes, marshes, waterfalls, etc. There are 9 Tibetan villages nestling in the valleys, which gives the area its name. The people of Sichuan are rightly proud that Jiuzhaigou was beautiful enough for Zhao Ziyang (Chinese Premier 1980-1987 and general secretary of the Communist Party 1987-1989) to have ranked it higher than the world famous scenery of Guilin in southern China. In 1992 it was awarded world heritage site status. The region is well known throughout China, and it is a favorite destination

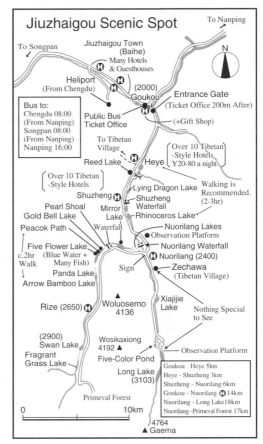

for Chinese honeymooners.

The altitude here ranges from 2,000 to 4,300m, and even in the summer you really need to bring warm clothing with you. The bus journey from Chengdu takes around a day and a half.

Access
Group Tour from Chengdu

On the western side of the square in front of Chengdu Station, there are a lot of travel agencies advertising group tours to these areas. A 6-day Jiuzhaigou and Huanglong tour costs Y200-225 by tourist bus and Y288-310 by minibus. These prices only cover the bus fare, and you will need to pay extras, such as admission fees, cost of accommodation, and any meals. If you factor in the entrance fees, a single room costing Y60-80 a night, plus meals for Y10-15 each, the total comes to Y800-1,000 for the 6 days.

Many of these group tours stay at expensive

hotels, but if you have a recognized student card, this may help to decrease the cost. Tours usually begin every day, except in the winter. In the summer the road conditions deteriorate due to the heavy rainfall at this time of year, and the tour schedules can be altered or cancelled altogether at short notice.

There are also agents selling tours in the *Jiaotong Fandian* (Traffic Hotel) and in the surrounding area. There is an additional charge of Y20 for insurance.

Sample Schedule- 6-day Jiuzhaigou & Huanglong Tour

Day 1: Chengdu - Huaxia Laxiangcheng - Songpan
Day 2: Songpan - Huanglong (4-5 hours free time) -Jiuzhaigou Entrance
Day 3: Jiuzhaigou Entrance - Changhai (Long Lake) - Wucaichi (Five-Color Pond) - Laoniuhai - Heye (2-3 hours on foot)
Day 4: Heye - Jianzhuhai (Arrow Bamboo Lake) - Nuorilang Pubu (Waterfall) - Chuanzhusi
Day 5: Chuanzhusi (Red Army Long March Memorial) - Diexi Lake - Wenchuan
Day 6: Wenchuan - Dujiangyan - Chengdu

Adding a trip to the Great Grasslands in the tour would make it a 7-day one, costing an additional Y30-50.

By Yourself

At the Ximen Bus Station in Chengdu or from Songpan, take a bus to Nanping and get off at the Jiuzhaigou entrance. From Chuanzhusi it costs Y10, and there are also a lot of minibuses from Nanping for the same price. If you are returning to Chengdu on an overnight sleeper bus, you might be better off to go to Nanping to secure a seat, which costs Y61.

Accommodation & Restaurants

In the town of Jiuzhaigouzhen (Bai He), before you enter the park, there are quite a number of hotels and guesthouses. In Jiuzhaigou there are 4 areas with accommodation, and a bed for the night costs Y20-40. At the hotels and guesthouses here, meals are served, but they are relatively expensive mainly because this is a tourist bottleneck. Many of the hotels have rooms with attached bathrooms. The Tibetan-style accommodation in Heye and Shuzheng is well recommended.

Sightseeing at Jiuzhaigou

You are required to buy a ticket on entry, and these can be purchased just after the gate leading into Jiuzhaigou. These tickets cost Y219 for foreigners and Y67 for Chinese people. You will need an identification card or your passport, and even if you

have a student card issued in China, you'll be unable to get a discount without a proper student visa.

The best approach for getting around is to hitchhike between the sights and then walk back down, as it is a fairly steep uphill climb from the gate to Changhai (Long Lake), at the southern end of the route, rising by 1,100m over this section. The Jiuzhaigou area is very broad, and it would take about 6 days to cover it all on foot.

*Entrance - Heye—There is nothing special to see on this leg.
*Heye - Nuorilang—There is a waterfall, and you can cross the river occasionally while following the roadway.
*Nuorilang Zhaodaisuo (Guesthouse) - Wucaichi (Five-Color Pond)—There is nothing of special interest to visit between these two. Wucaichi (Five-Color Pond) is a beautiful clear blue lake about 50m down from the road. If you walk a kilometer further up from here, you will reach Changhai (Long Lake), and there are rental boats at this lake.
*Zhenzhutan - Zhenzhutan Pubu (Pearl Shoal Waterfall)—There is a walkway along this course, circling around the area.
*Kongqiao Hedao (Peacock Path) - Xiongmaohai (Panda Lake)—There is also a walkway here, and you can walk on the other side of the road. Wuhuahai (Five Flower Lake) is one of the highlights on this section.
*At most of these locations you can rent authentic Tibetan clothes to give your photos a touch of the exotic.

NANPING (NAMPHEL)

From Chengdu & Songpan

At Ximen Bus Station in Chengdu there are buses to Nanping every day. A night bus with sleeping berths is also available on this route, and the trip takes 1 night. You can take a bus that leaves Songpan for Nanping around noon.

From Nanping

There is a bus for both Chengdu and Songpan each day, and it leaves around 08:00. Buses also leave for Wenxian and Pingwu. At Nanping there are a number of guesthouses, and a good option is the *Ximen Lushe* (West Gate Hotel).

LIXIAN (TASHILING)

Heading north from Chengdu towards Ruo'ergai,

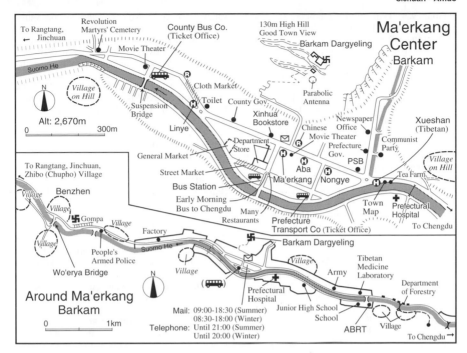

Around Ma'erkang
Barkam

0   1km

Mail: 09:00-18:30 (Summer)
08:30-18:00 (Winter)
Telephone: Until 21:00 (Summer)
Until 20:00 (Winter)

you will reach Lixian, the next town you come to after passing through Wenchuan. The town is in the valley of a tributary of the Min Jiang River. Miyaluo (Nyaklo), to the north, is famous as the largest area for viewing the colored fall leaves in China. There are also some hot springs nearby.

Access

From Chengdu Ximen Bus Station, there are buses leaving for Lixian at 07:20, 10:00, and 10:30 every day. The one departing for Miyaluo (Nyaklo) sets off at 07:20, and there are also buses from Dujiangyan and Wenchuan for Lixian and Miyaluo (Nyaklo). Another option is to catch one of the many minibuses between Lixian and Miyaluo (Nyaklo).

MA'ERKANG (BARKAM)

This large town is the capital of Aba (Ngawa) Prefecture, and as there are no famous tourist spots in the area, it is rarely visited by foreigners. However, the Tibetan-style houses constructed from rock in the suburbs are worth seeing. Those at Zhuokeji (Choktse), 10km before Ma'erkang on your way from Chengdu, are especially beautiful examples of this design.

Access
From Chengdu

There are a number of buses leaving Ximen Bus Station for Ma'erkang each morning. Though the buses are operated by different companies, they still depart at the same time. The buses stay overnight around Miyaluo (Nyaklo) and then arrive at Ma'erkang the following evening. The stretch between Lixian and Ma'erkang is covered in woodland, and you'll usually get a great view when crossing the 4,040m pass en route.

From Ma'erkang

In addition to the main bus station (Ma'erkang Qichezhan), there are 3 bus companies with ticket offices at Ma'erkang, and the pickup points for each company are different.

*Chengdu—Buses leave Ma'erkang Qichezhan, the *Prefectural No. 2 Transport Co. Stop*, and the *County No. 2 Bus Co.* office at 06:00. These buses arrive in Chengdu in around 13 hours. There is also a comfortable European-made bus that can be booked at the front desk of the Ma'erkang Fandian (Hotel). It leaves the hotel at 06:00 and arrives at Aba Binguan (Hotel), behind the Chengdu Ximen (West Gate), in about 11 hours.

*Dujiangyan—Daily bus departs at 06:00.
*Aba (Ngawa)—There is a bus leaving at 06:15 on even numbered days.
*Ruo'ergai (Dzoge)—This daily bus also leaves at 06:15.
*Wenchuan—Leaving at 06:30 every day.
*Xiaojin—There are 2 departures a day, one at 13:30 and the other at 15:30. The ticket office is opposite the Ma'erkang Fandian (Hotel), and it has a sign for minibuses costing Y30.
*Jinchuan—A bus leaves daily at 13:30 from the *County No. 2 Bus Co.* office. In addition, there is also a bus from Chengdu to Jinchuan, which stops here around noon.
*Rangtang (Zamthang)—A bus from Chengdu to Rangtang (Zamthang) arrives around noon.
*There are also buses to Sha'erzong (Sar Dzong) to the north and Guanyinqiao (Thuje Chenpo) to the west. There are sometimes departures for Dawei (Troye).

Accommodation & Restaurants

The *Ma'erkang Fandian* (Hotel) is a huge hotel only a couple of minutes from the main bus station. There is a tariff for foreigners, and a double room bed costs Y21, or one in a 3-person room is Y15. Although there are no showers, there is hot water available at night for washing. You can buy minibus tickets for Chengdu at the front desk, and there is a restaurant at the back of the hotel.

The *Aba Hotel* has beds starting at Y20, and there is a restaurant in the hotel.

The restaurant situation in the town is not too bad. There are a number of Sichuanese restaurants around the main bus station, and there are also many *Huoguo* (Hotpot) restaurants.

Places to See
Barkam Dargyeling (Ma'erkangsi)

Now belonging to the Gelukpa order, this small gompa was a Bon monastery up until the 19th century.

Zhibodiaoqun

At the village of Zhibo (Chupho), 10km to the west of Ma'erkang, there is a cluster of huge towers that were once used as lookout points for a fort. The tallest one is more than 40m high and is similar in design to the ones found in Maoxian, etc., an area settled by the Qiang minority people.

JINCHUAN (RABDEN) (CLOSED)

This is a small town located in the valley carved out by the Da Jinchuan River. The Dongnuguo Kingdom once flourished in this area, and this valley was once known as *Gyalmorong*, or 'Valley of the Queen.'

From the Ximen Bus Station in Chengdu there is a bus that leaves for Jinchuan at 07:40 every day. It stops at Ma'erkang and arrives at Jinchuan the following day, or alternatively, there is also a bus starting from Ma'erkang. At Jinchuan there is a minibus for Danba (Rongtrak) in Ganzi (Kandze) Prefecture every other day, which starts at 07:30 and takes 5 hours.

For accommodation, there are a number of hotels and guesthouses in the town. Beds at the guesthouse near the bus station cost Y9.

Yungdrung Lhateng
(Guangfasi, Jinchuan Zhongyongsi)

At the town of Anning you will find Yungdrung Lhateng, one of the most important Bon monasteries in Tibet. During the Qing (Manchu) Dynasty, when Bonpo was being purged, the monastery was superficially converted and handed over to the Gelukpa order. Subsequently it was devastated in the Cultural Revolution, and after the monastery was reconstructed, it reverted back to being a Bon monastery.

Thuje Chenpo (Guanyinqiao)

In the western part of Jinchuan, this sacred place is famous as a place of pilgrimage in the Gyarong area. The name *Thuje Chenpo* means 'Avalokiteshvara' (one of the Bodhisattvas of Compassion embodied in the Dalai Lamas). The Nyingmapa order's Thuje Chenpo Gompa here houses about 100 monks. You can get to this area by bus from Ma'erkang.

XIAOJIN (TSENLHA)

Xiaojin is located along the Xiao Jinchuan River, a tributary of the Da Jinchuan River in Jinchuan County. There are many Han Chinese in this town. At the eastern end of Xiaojin County, along the

Ma'erkang

boundary with Wenchuan County, you will find the highest mountain in Aba (Ngawa) Prefecture, Siguniang Shan (6,250m).

At the Chengdu Ximen Bus Station there is a bus to Xiaojin via Rilong every 1 or 2 days, which leaves at 07:00. Minibuses also connect Ma'erkang and Danba (Rongtrak) in Ganzi (Kandze) Prefecture with Xiaojin every day.

Kirti Gompa

RANGTANG (ZAMTHANG) (CLOSED)

The town faces toward Banma (Padma) in Qinghai Province and Seda (Serthar) in the Ganzi (Kandze) Prefecture of Sichuan Province. In a valley to the north of Rangtang is the Zhong Rangtang. (The name *Zamthang* is the same in Tibetan.) There are 3 Jonangpa monasteries at Zhong Rangtang, and their collective name is Zhong Rangtangsi. This is the center of the Jonangpa order in the Aba (Ngawa) area.

From Chengdu there is a bus every 2-3 days and the trip takes 2 days. There are 3 buses during each 10-day period that connect Aba (Ngawa) with the town. For Banma in Qinghai Province, there are no buses, and hitchhiking is the only option.

ABA (NGAWA) (CLOSED)

Although the name of the county is the same, this town is not the center of the Aba (Ngawa) Prefecture. The western side of Aba (Ngawa) County backs onto Qinghai Province, and there are many Gelukpa monasteries in this area. The county is also home to Narshi Gompa, which is said to be the largest Bon monastery in Tibet. Around the junction at the entrance to Kirti Gompa (Ge'erdengsi) is a meeting area that is usually crowded with many Tibetan people. There are many monasteries scattered around the town, and they are all worth visiting.

Access
From Chengdu
There is a bus that leaves Chengdu at 08:00 and another at 08:20 each day. They both arrive around noon the following day.

From Aba (Ngawa)
You can take a bus from the 3-road junction in front of the Luyuan Fandian (Restaurant). You can also buy a ticket at the same place, and these are available a day before departure.

*Chengdu—There is a daily bus leaving at 06:00

that arrives at Chengdu in the evening.
*Ma'erkang—The bus leaves on odd numbered days, and the trip takes 7 hours.
*Ruo'ergai—Hezuo in Gansu- Linxia
A daily bus sets off at 06:00 and makes its way to Ruo'ergai via Chali and Hongyuan. The trip takes about 12 hours. The ones for Hezuo and Linxia are operated every other day and stay overnight at Ruo'ergai.
*Jiuzhi (Qinghai Province)
This daily bus departs at 06:00.
*Guluo—The bus leaves at 07:00 every day.
*Rangtang (Zamthang)—A bus leaves at 07:30 on days with dates including the numbers: 2, 5, and 8 (i.e. 2, 12, 15, 28, etc.). There are 3 buses during each 10-day period.

Accommodation & Restaurants
The *Zhengfu Zhaodaisuo* (County Government Guesthouse) has single rooms for Y24, and doubles are Y24 per person. Beds in a 3-person room go for Y13, and one in a 4-person room is Y5. Both single and double rooms are equipped with hot showers, at least in theory, as the water heating system seems to be pretty temperamental. There are electric blankets available for guests.

Opposite the guesthouse there is a line of about 10 restaurants, and most of these serve Sichuanese food.

Places to See
Kirti Gompa (Ge'erdengsi)
This Gelukpa monastery acts as the center of the town, and it is one of the largest scale monasteries in Aba (Ngawa) County. It is a branch of Taktsang Lhamo Kirti Gompa (Nama Ge'erdesi) on the border with Gansu Province and is home to a famous 30m-high chorten. The gompa was founded in the 15th century. It now houses more than a thousand monks, and the monastery's incarnate lama lives in exile in India.

Ser Gompa (Saigesi)
This Jonangpa monastery is about a kilometer from the eastern end of Aba (Ngawa) Town and is also

227

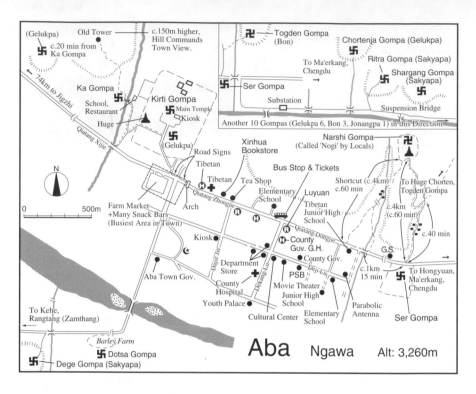

Map labels:

(Gelukpa) Old Tower — c.150m higher, Hill Commands Town View.
卐 c.20 min from Ka Gompa
74km to Jigzhi
Ka Gompa
卐 School, Restaurant
Huge
卐 Kirti Gompa
卐 Main Temple
Kiosk
(Gelukpa)
Qiatang Xijie
Road Signs
Tibetan
Tibetan
Xinhua Bookstore
Tea Shop
Elementary School
Luyuan
N
0   500m
Farm Market +Many Snack Bars (Busiest Area in Town)
Arch
Qiatang Zhongjie
Kiosk
☪
Department Store
Aba Town Gov.
County Hospital
Youth Palace
Dajie Jie
Dafang Lu
PSB
Movie Theater
Junior High
Cultural Center
Deji Lu
County Gov. G.H.
County Gov.
Qiatang Dongjie
Elementary School
Parabolic Antenna

卐 —— Togden Gompa (Bon)
Chortenja Gompa (Gelukpa)
To Ma'erkang, Chengdu →
Ritra Gompa (Sakyapa)
卐 Shargang Gompa (Sakyapa)
卐 Ser Gompa
Substation
Suspension Bridge
Another 10 Gompas (Gelukpa 6, Bon 3, Jonangpa 1) in this Direction
Narshi Gompa (Called 'Nogi' by Locals)
Bus Stop & Tickets
Shortcut (c.4km) c.60 min
To Huge Chorten, Togden Gompa
Tibetan Junior High School
c.4km (c.60 min)
c.40 min
G.S.
To Hongyuan, Ma'erkang, Chengdu
c.1km 15 min
Ser Gompa

To Kehe, Rangtang (Zamthang)
Barley Farm
卐 Dotsa Gompa
卐 Dege Gompa (Sakyapa)

Aba   Ngawa   Alt: 3,260m

known as Setenling. The monastery houses about 1,000 monks, and the incarnate lama is still in residence here.

Narshi Gompa (Langyisi)

Locally the gompa is called *Nogi*, and it is said to be the largest Bon monastery in Tibet. Narshi is a branch of Nogi (Duiansi) at Changla (Zhangcuo) in Songpan. To get to the site you walk for about an hour up the hill, opposite Ser Gompa. You can also take a shortcut up a path opposite the Xian Zangwen Zhongxue (Tibetan Junior High School). On a hill to the east of Nogi is also another Bon monastery, Togden (Topgyel) Gompa.

HONGYUAN (MEWA)

A grassy and marshland area, Hongyuan has been molded into shape by the Bai He (Kar-chu), which branches off from the Yellow River as its course makes one of its dramatic changes in direction. On the 1934 Long March, which saw the Chinese Communist Army crossing half of central China, this bottomless swamp area was the most trying

test for the participants. After their grueling ordeal in this quagmire, it was named *Hongyuan* or 'Red Plains.'

The town of Hongyuan, on the banks of the Bai He (Kar-chu), is set in grassland and surrounded by gentle mountains. As you wander around the streets of Hongyuan, you will see nomads on horseback coming into the town to pick up provisions, trade, and catch up with old friends and local news.

Access
From Chengdu

A bus leaves the Ximen Bus Station in Chengdu for Hongyuan at 08:00, and another follows it a little later at 8:20, arriving in Hongyuan the next day. You can also take one heading for Ruo'ergai at 08:20, and this stops off at Hongyuan on the way.

From Ruo'ergai

Take a bus at Ruo'ergai that is going out to Aba (Ngawa), Chengdu, or Ma'erkang, and these all stop over at Hongyuan en route.

From Hongyuan

There is a bus departing from Hongyuan for

Chengdu between 06:00 and 07:00 every morning. Another one from Ruo'ergai to Aba (Ngawa), Ma'erkang, and Chengdu leaves the bus station at Hongyuan between 10:00 and 11:00, every 1-2 days. Coming in the other direction, the buses from Aba (Ngawa) and Ma'erkang heading for Ruo'ergai leave here between 10:00 and 12:00. The one for Hezuo and Linxia, both in Gansu, sometimes stops at Hongyuan between 10:00 and 11:00.

Accommodation & Restaurants

The hotels that foreigners are permitted to stay in also have an additional tariff.

The *Hongyuan Binguan* (Hotel) has beds in 4-person rooms for Y35, and one in a 3-bed room costs Y30-120. The double room beds are Y80, and the single room rates are Y50-160. If you take a suite of rooms in the hotel, you will have to pay Y260-280. The rooms from the double upwards are equipped with hot showers, and there is a restaurant and a store in the hotel.

The *Hongmei Binguan* (Hotel) is a few minutes from the bus station, and a bed costs Y20-40 while a small single room costs Y40. The hot showers in the hotel are free.

Opposite the Hongmei Binguan (Hotel) there are a lot of Sichuan restaurants.

Places to See
Mewa Gompa

Also called Darchin Shenchen Choekhorling, this huge Nyingmapa monastery houses 1,500 monks. It was built in honor of Longchen Rabjampa, the 14th century scholar who laid the foundations of the Nyingmapa teachings.

You will find the gompa about 7km to the east of Amukeke He (Amokok-chu), which is around 25km north-east of Hongyuan. Some of the tours to Jiuzhaigou and the grasslands also visit here.

Gungthang Temple

A small Nyingmapa temple at Longrang, Gungthang Temple functions like a summer villa for the Gungthang Rinpoche, the great incarnate lama of the Labrang Monastery at Xiahe, Gansu Province. The temple is across the Bai He (Kar-chu) to the north of Hongyuan.

Amchok Gompa (Anqu Chalisi)

The monastery is located at Anqu, 30km to the south on the main route from Hongyuan to Ma'erkang. Although the town is administratively within Aba (Ngawa) County, Amchock Gompa is mentioned in this section due to the ease of access to the area from this direction.

This great Gelukpa monastery has around 1,000

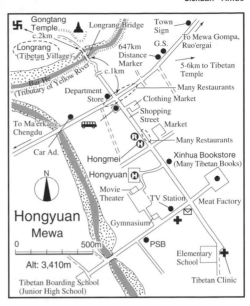

monks, and the incarnate lama, the 4th Amchok Rinpoche, often returns to the monastery from exile.

RUO'ERGAI (DZOGE)

Ruo'ergai is a town in the vast grassland area at the northern end of Aba (Ngawa) Prefecture. On the highway connecting Gansu Province with Sichuan Province, it is an important transportation hub for the region, but the town itself has a distinctly artificial feel about it. To the north-east of town is Taktsha Gompa (Dazhasi). Ruo'ergai is also well known for its eminent Tibetan medicine hospital.

Most of the grassland covering Ruo'ergai County is in fact marshland created by one of the many tributaries of the Yellow River. These waterlogged expanses are beautiful in the evenings when the surface reflects the colors of the setting sun.

Access
From Chengdu

At the Ximen Bus Station in Chengdu there is a bus every 1-2 days, and it is an overnight trip.

From Ruo'ergai

Most buses arrive at and depart from the bus station. Foreign passengers are subject to an additional tariff and are charged twice as much as local passengers.

AMDO

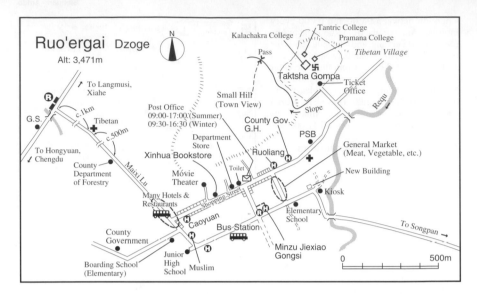

Ruo'ergai Dzoge

Alt: 3,471m

↗ To Langmusi, Xiahe

G.S.

c.1km

Tibetan

c.500m

To Hongyuan, Chengdu

County Department of Forestry

Maixi Lu

Post Office
09:00-17:00 (Summer)
09:30-16:30 (Winter)

Small Hill (Town View)

Department Store

Xinhua Bookstore

Movie Theater

Many Hotels & Restaurants

Shopping Street

Caoyuan

County Government

Boarding School (Elementary)

Junior High School

Muslim

Bus-Station

Kalachakra College

Pass

Tantric College

Pramana College

Tibetan Village

Taktsha Gompa

Ticket Office

Slope

County Gov.
G.H.

PSB

Ruoliang

Toilet

Minzu Jiexiao Gongsi

Elementary School

Kiosk

General Market (Meat, Vegetable, etc.)

New Building

Requ

To Songpan →

0   500m

*Chengdu—If there are a lot of passengers, this service is operated daily, departing at 06:00 or 07:00. Otherwise, the buses leave on odd numbered days. The bus arrives in Chengdu around noon the following day. There is another bus for Chengdu that also leaves from the area around the junction of Maixi Lu, near the Caoyuan Hotel.

*Ma'erkang—Leaving at 06:30 on odd numbered days, this bus arrives at Ma'erkang in the evening of the same day.

*Aba (Ngawa)— This bus leaves at 06:30 every day, and the trip takes 9-10 hours.

*Songpan—There is a daily bus leaving at 07:00, and the trip takes 5 hours.

To Gansu Province

*Hezuo—There is a daily departure at 06:30.

*Diebu—The bus sets off on this 5-hour trip at 06:30 every day.

*Linxia—A bus leaves at 06:40 on odd numbered days.

Buses from Linxia to Aba (Ngawa), Hezuo to Aba (Ngawa), and Hezuo to Songpan stay overnight at Ruo'ergai, and you may be able to arrange a seat on these depending on availability. For Hongyuan, you will need to take a bus heading for either Aba (Ngawa) or Chengdu. It takes about 4 hours to Hongyuan.

Accommodation

The *Zhengfu Zhaodaisuo* (County Government Guesthouse) takes less than 10 minutes on foot from the bus station, and a dormitory bed here costs Y10-25. There are electric heaters in the rooms.

The *Minzu Jiexiao Gongsi Zhaodaisuo* (Guesthouse) is about 100m to the east of the bus station, and you will see a sign in English for the guesthouse. A bed in the dormitory costs Y25, and you can get hot showers here.

The *Ruoliang Binguan* (Hotel) is the best hotel in town, and beds cost Y25-50. There are rooms in the hotel with hot showers.

Places to See
Taktsha Gompa (Dazhasi)

Taktsha is an 18th century Gelukpa monastery at the north-east end of the town. It is home to about 100 monks and also houses a school of Tibetan medicine.

Kirti Gompa (Dacannamo Ge'erdengsi)

This is a huge monastery on the border with Gansu Province. (See the Langmusi, Gansu Province section for details.)

AMDO

EASTERN KHAM
Ganzi Prefecture & Muli County
Sichuan Province

ཁམས།

At the eastern end of the Tibetan Plateau, roughly 150km to the west of Chengdu, the capital of Sichuan Province, you enter the prefecture right after tackling Erlang Shan (Yarla Namtse), a pass that used to mark the Chinese-Tibetan border. The region is a mountainous area twice as large as Ireland (Eire) or the same size as Michigan, with about 900,000 (1996 official figure) Tibetans living mainly in the valleys carved out by 3 north-to-south flowing rivers.

Compared to areas in central Tibet, the climate here is mild, and the land is fertile and covered in woodland. Kandze Prefecture, together with the area in and around Chamdo to the west across the Jinsha Jiang River (Dri-chu), is referred to as the Kham Region.

Generally, many people think of Tibetans as calm and peaceful people, but this image is challenged by the people of Kham, known as the *Khampa*. They are tall people whose bravery is legendary throughout the country, and you will see many of these people on the streets of Lhasa as well as in the region itself. The Khampa are given away by their red or black *Dashe*, a turban-like hair ornament, and their distinctive look is rounded off with the short sword strapped at their waist. If asked where they are from, they answer that they are from either Ganzi or Dege.

Although it is Tibetan, Kham has historically been rather separated from the areas ruled over directly by the government in Lhasa. The heads of the powerful families and the nobles in the area dominated the politics and religion of the region prior to the Chinese invasion. The Dalai Lama's Gelukpa order is the source of the Lhasa government's legitimacy, while in Kham the older schools of Buddhism, including the Karma Kagyupa, Nyingmapa, etc., have maintained their powerful footholds and continue to wield substantial influence throughout the region.

China started annexing parts of the Kham region as early as 1950, and since this process began, a large number of important monasteries have been systematically destroyed. Many of the high-ranking lamas from the area have fled into exile in neighboring India. Due to this treatment by the Chinese government and the strong will of the people, Khampa guerrillas offered stubborn resistance to the Communists, hampering their efforts to fully assimilate the area. Big cities, such as Dege, Chamdo, Litang, etc., ruled over by the heads of regionally powerful families, were the first to be attacked by the Communist military, and though the conventional war was quickly lost, the Khampas continued to fight on from their mountain bases.

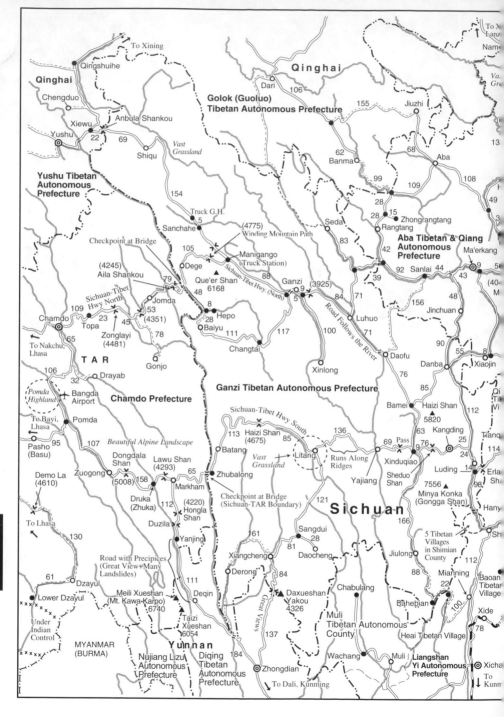

To Xining

Qinghai

Qingshuihe

Qinghai

Chengduo

Dari   106

Golok (Guoluo)
Tibetan Autonomous Prefecture

155

Jiuzhi

Xiewu   Anbula Shankou

Yushu

22   69

Shiqu

*Vast
Grassland*

62
Banma

68

Aba

108

13

49

3

**Yushu Tibetan
Autonomous
Prefecture**

154

99

109

Truck G.H.
5

Sanchahe

(4775)
Winding Mountain Path

28
28   15   Zhongrangtang
Rangtang

**Aba Tibetan & Qiang
Autonomous
Prefecture**

Ma'erkang

Checkpoint at Bridge

105

Manigango
(Truck Station)

Seda

83

42

92   Sanlai   44   43   9   5
40
M

(4245)
Aila Shankou

Dege

Sichuan-Tibet Hwy.   88

Que'er Shan
6168

Ganzi   (3925)

39

156

48

**Sichuan-Tibet
Hwy North**

79

48   8

9
5

84   71

Chamdo
109

Jomda
53
(4351)

Hepo

117

100

Luhuo

71

Jinchuan

23   45

Topa

28
Baiyu

111

Daofu

90

To Nakchu,
Lhasa

65

Zonglayi
(4481)

78

Changtai

76

Danba

55
Xiaojin

8

106

Gonjo

Xinlong

Ganzi Tibetan Autonomous Prefecture

85

Bamei   Haizi Shan

Qi
Ti
Vi

112

Drayab

32

*Pomda
Highland*

Bangda
Airport

Chamdo Prefecture

Sichuan-Tibet Hwy South

5820
Haizi Shan
(4675)

136

63   Kangding

Tiang

To Bayi,
Lhasa

Pomda

113

85

69   Pass   76   25

114

107

Beautiful Alpine Landscape

Batang

*Vast
Grassland*

Litang

Runs Along
Ridges

Xinduqiao   9   24

Pasho
(Basu)

95

Dongdala
Shan

Lawu Shan
(4293)

Yajiang

Sheduo
Shan

Luding   14

Erla
Sh

Demo La
(4610)

Zuogong
(5008)   158

65

Zhubalong

7556

98

Minya Konka
(Gongga Shan)

Hany

Markham

Druka
(Zhuka)

112

(4220)
Hongla
Shan

Checkpoint at Bridge
(Sichuan-TAR Boundary)

121

Sichuan

166

5 Tibetan
Villages
in Shimian
County

Sh

To Lhasa

130

Duzila

Yanjing

161

Sangdui
28

81

Daocheng

Jiulong

88   112

Baoan
Tibetan
Village

61

Dzayul

Xiangcheng

Derong

84

Chabulang

22

Mianning

*Road with Precipices
(Great View+Many
Landslides)*

111

Deqin

Daxueshan
Yakou
4326

Dahebian

100

Xide

Lower Dzayul

Meili Xueshan
(Mt. Kawa-Karpo)
6740

*Great
Views*

**Muli
Tibetan Autonomous
County**

Heai Tibetan Village

78

*Under
Indian
Control*

Taizi
Xueshan
6054

137

Wachang

Muli

**Liangshan
Yi Autonomous
Prefecture**

Xicha

**MYANMAR
(BURMA)**

Yunnan

Nujiang Lizu
Autonomous
Prefecture

Diqing
Tibetan
Autonomous
Prefecture

184

Zhongdian

To Dali, Kunming

To
Kunm

These same guerrillas protected the Dalai Lama during his 1959 flight into exile in India and continued to effectively harry the Chinese armed forces from their Mustang base, within present-day Nepal, until their American support finally dried up in the mid-1970s.

This strong spirit has survived among the Khampa, and the people are not intimidated by the Chinese, continuing to be rough-natured and short-tempered. Even though it may sound contradictory, the Khampa are also a high-spirited and religiously devout people.

Khampas can be found actively engaged in business throughout Tibet and China, and you will even encounter them as far away as Nepal and India. While they may sometimes be aggressive in their pursuit of money, they are often more than happy to turn around and donate the whole lot to their local monastery. This typifies what has come to be known as the 'Khampa spirit.'

Main Routes

*Sichuan-Tibet Highway North leading to Lhasa
Chengdu- Kangding - Ganzi - Dege - Chamdo - Lhasa
You will usually have to rely on hitching lifts on the route between Dege and Lhasa. Nonetheless, this remains a popular route for entering the TAR, and many travelers have completed the journey without serious incident.

*Sichuan-Tibet Highway South to Lhasa
Chengdu - Kangding - Litang - Markham - Pome - Bayi - Lhasa
Many travelers that have taken this route have subsequently been caught at either Markham or Bayi.

*North to Qinghai Province
Chengdu- Kangding - Ganzi - Manigango -Yushu (Jyekundo)
You will have to hitchhike between Manigango and points before Yushu.

*To Yunnan
Chengdu - Kangding - Litang - Xiangcheng - Zhongdian (Yunnan Province)
Taking this course in the opposite direction to get to Chengdu has become popular with travelers over recent years.

CHENGDU

Chengdu is the capital of Sichuan Province, and this large city seems to have more in common with Hong Kong or Shanghai with high-rise buildings

Sichuan-Tibet Highway North 2,421km
Chengdu-368-Kangding-388-Ganzi-204-Dege-340-Chamdo-795-Nakchu-326-Lhasa

Trucks run on this relatively stable road even during the rainy season.
From Ganzi to Chamdo - Tough mountain passes+ beautiful mountain views.
After Chamdo - Vast grassland areas.

Sichuan-Tibet Highway South 2,149km

Chengdu-368-Kangding-288-Litang-198-Batang Markham-335-Pasho-90-Rawok-120-Pome-240 Bayi-120-Kongpo Gyamda-285-Lhasa

After Kangding, this route rises and falls between 2,500-4,500m, which is hard going. During the rainy season, June - September, the section around Pome is closed due to landslides. Views are good - Grasslands around Litang and beautiful mountains from Markham to Nyangtri.

Nomads' Children

going up everywhere and fast-paced urban re-development.

In the neighboring highland areas, such as Ganzi Prefecture to the west and Aba (Ngawa) Prefecture to the north, Tibetan people still live quietly in their small villages and towns, a world away from the hectic lifestyle of modern China and its booming cities. Chengdu is one of the few places close to the Tibetan cultural sphere, where people are crowded together in such a limited area. There are only roughly 6 million Tibetans in total scattered across the globe, and yet here is a city in close proximity that on its own has a population of 10 million. Chengdu is not only a place to take direct flights to Lhasa, but is also a starting point for overland access to other areas within the Tibetan Autonomous Region and the Tibetan areas located in Sichuan and Gansu Provinces. This makes the city an important gateway to the Tibetan world.

Access
By Rail
*No. 7 Special Express
  Beijing West (Xi Zhan) 08:40-Chengdu 15:26
  (2 nights)
*No. 363 Express
  Beijing West (Xi Zhan) 19:45-Chengdu 07:24
  (2 nights)
*No. 382 & 383 Express
  Shanghai 07:35-Chengdu 06:09 (2 nights)
*No. 390 & 391 Express
  Shanghai 17:02-Chengdu 12:07 (2 nights)
*No. 92 & 93 Special Express
  Guangzhou 21:32-Chengdu 19:21(2 nights)
*No. 208 Special Express
  Kunming 13:28-Chengdu 10:50 (2 nights)

There are also daily trains from Xi'an, Lanzhou, Urumqi, Chongqing, and other major regional centers.

By Air
Flights are mainly on China Southwest Airlines (SZ), but there are flights provided by other carriers, including China Northwest Airlines (WH), Air China (CA), Sichuan Airlines (3U), and Shanghai Airlines (FM).

Daily flights from:
*Beijing—Minimum of 6 flights a day.
  (SZ, CA, 3U) Costs: Y1,550. (2 hrs)
*Shanghai—Minimum of 5 flights a day.
  (SZ, FM) Costs: Y1,610. (2 hrs)
*Guangzhou—Minimum of 6 flights a day.
  (SZ, 3U) Costs: Y1,310. (2 hrs)
*Shenzhen—1-2 flights a day.
  (SZ) Costs: Y1,350. (2 hrs)
*Hong Kong—1 flight (Monday-Saturday).
  (SZ & Dragon Air) Costs: Y2,510. (2 hrs 10 mins)
*Kunming—Minimum of 4 flights a day.
  (SZ, WH) Costs: Y720. (1 hr)

There are also flights from other major centers, such as Xi'an, Changsha, Lanzhou, Wuhan, etc. International flights come in from Bangkok and Singapore.

Airport to Town
The airport is at Shuangliu, around 15km to the south-west of the city. There are limousine buses from the arrival terminal that drop you off at the city office of China Southwest Airlines (SZ).

Local buses take you to Xinnanmen (New South Gate), and there are also minibuses and taxis available. The trip takes about an hour, though a taxi will take you straight to the Jiaotong Fandian (Traffic Hotel), for example, in less than 30 minutes.

Local Transportation
Chengdu is a huge, sprawling city with a radius of 20km, and there is a fairly good transportation system for getting around the place. Local buses and minibuses run along all the major routes within the city limits, and a really useful purchase on arrival at the station is one of the city maps showing the bus routes. You also have a lot of choice when it comes to hailing a cab in the street.

Accommodation
Guesthouses (Cheap Hotels)
The *Jiaotong Fandian* (Traffic Hotel) is a backpackers' hangout, and you will need to take a local bus (Wu Zhuan) from Chengdu Station (Bei Zhan) and get off at the last stop. Alternatively, you can take the #16 (Shiliulu) local bus until you reach the *Jinjiang Binguan* (Hotel). Jump off here, and it's about a 10-minute walk to the hotel. There are a bank and some travel agencies around the hotel as well as restaurants that cater to foreign visitors nearby. This conveniently-located hotel will look after your bags for a fee. A bed in a 3-person room costs Y50, and one in a room with a bath costs an

additional Y20. These prices include breakfast. You can make international calls, and there is also a fax service available. The hotel is a good place for exchanging travel information, and you'll get up-to-date, first-hand details of routes and the situation in the areas that you are planning to visit.

Top-Range Hotels

The *Jinjiang Binguan* (Hotel) is the most prestigious and longest running hotel in Chengdu. There is a post office here, convenient for sending parcels, and the building is also home to a popular Western-style bakery.

The *Minshan Fandian* (Hotel) is a 21-story hotel opposite the Jinjiang Binguan, and you can eat out in its Japanese restaurant.

Other Options

The *Chengdu Xizang Fandian* (Tibetan Hotel) has a branch of CITS Xigaze (Zhongguo Guoji Luxingshe) on the 9th floor.

The *Aba Binguan* (Hotel) is behind the Ximen Bus Station, which has buses for Aba Prefecture, and it is a good place to stay for those planning to take an early departure out to that area. There are also luxurious European-built minibuses that go out to Markham from this hotel. There is no dormitory here, and rooms cost Y120-200.

Restaurants

Above all else, Chengdu is the home of Sichuanese cuisine. If you want to try something else though, it is a large enough place to give you a pretty good choice of alternatives.

Public Security Bureau (PSB)

Visa extensions can be made at the Foreign Affairs Branch of the PSB at the end of Wenwu Lu. The

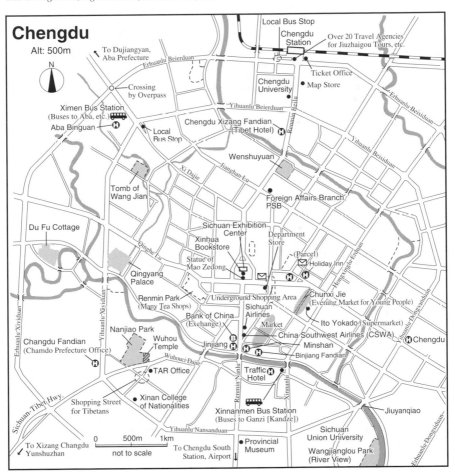

EASTERN KHAM

office can process 30-day visa extensions, though the cost of these can depend upon your nationality. The office is open from Monday to Friday.

CITS - China International Travel Service (Zhongguo Guoji Luxingshe)
The office is opposite the Jinjiang Binguan (Hotel). For train journeys, they can only help you if you want to reserve a ticket for the *Ruanwo* (Soft Sleeper) class.

China Southwest Airlines (SZ)
The office is north of the Minshan Fandian (Hotel), and this is also the place to catch limousine buses to take you out to the airport. You will find the ticket office on the 2nd floor, and though you can make international flight bookings here, foreigners are unfortunately unable to obtain tickets for Lhasa or Chamdo. If you want to book a ticket to fly with Sichuan Airlines, their office is about 100m to the north of here.

Tianfu Luyou
(Chengdu Tian-fu International Travel Service)
Tel: 0086-28-5562572 Fax: 0086-28-5543869
The agent can be found at the Jiaotong Fandian (Traffic Hotel), and it may be possible to arrange a ticket from Chengdu to Lhasa here.

Tibetan Places in Chengdu
About 200m to the south of Wuhou Temple, around the junction of Wuhouci Henjie and Ximianqiao Henjie, is a shopping area for Tibetans. This is a Khampa hangout, and there is a good selection of Tibetan stuff on sale, including everything from Buddhist altar paraphernalia to Tibetan clothes, photographs of high-ranking lamas, and music tapes.

Near to this area is the *Southwest Institute for Nationalities* (Xinan Minzu Xueyuan), which has many Tibetan students and also a government office of the TAR.

The area around the Aba Binguan (Hotel), behind the Ximen Bus Station, is also a hangout for Amdo-Tibetans from Aba Prefecture. This is another place that you can usually pick up Tibetan things.

From Chengdu to the Tibetan Areas
Flights from Chengdu to Lhasa
There are a 3-4 flights a day from Chengdu to Lhasa.
*Chengdu 06:30 - Lhasa 08:25 (Daily)
*Chengdu 07:00 - Lhasa 09:00
(Tuesday and Saturday)
*Chengdu 07:20 - Lhasa 09:20 (Daily)
*Chengdu 11:20 - Lhasa 13:10 (Daily)

The air fare for foreign passengers is Y1,580, decreasing to Y1,200 in the winter. A problem is that China Southwest Airlines (SZ) won't sell foreigners tickets to Lhasa and Chamdo, and the only way to get around this is to make an arrangement through a travel agency.

There are a number of travel agents that can arrange this for you, such as *Tianfu Luyou* at the Jiaotong Fandian (Traffic Hotel). You can usually get a ticket 2-3 days in advance. Depending on the season, these tickets cost Y1,600-2,000, which includes the minibus fare from the Jiaotong Fandian (Traffic Hotel) to the Chengdu airport and also the TAR entry permit fee. It also sometimes includes the hotel charge in Lhasa for your first night. The minibus leaves at 05:00 from the Jiaotong Ludian. The airport tax is Y50 for foreign passengers. Travel companies in Chengdu can also arrange either the air tickets or hire the car to take you onwards from Lhasa to Kathmandu.

Flights from Chengdu to Chamdo
In 1995 civil aircraft started flights to and from the previously military-only Pomda (Bangda) Airport, near Chamdo (Changdu) in the Tibetan Autonomous Region. There are only 2 services a week on this route, and these are on Tuesday and Friday. The plane leaves Chengdu at 07:28 and touches down in Chamdo at 08:40. The airfare is Y770, and unfortunately, tickets are not sold to foreigners at China Southwest Airlines (SZ) offices. Even travel agents can only arrange these for members of a group. The airport is around 120km from the town of Chamdo itself.

Chengdu to Kham (Ganzi, Chamdo) Overland
If you are heading for the Tibetan areas to the west of Chengdu along the Sichuan-Tibet Highway, you will have to go to Kangding (Dartsedo) first. The bus leaves from the Xinnanmen Bus Station, next to the Jiaotong Fandian (Traffic Hotel).
*Kangding—There are a number of buses each day. (See the Kangding section on the next page for details.)
*There are also direct buses for other towns in Ganzi (Kandze) Prefecture, including Daofu, Luhuo, Ganzi , Litang, and Batang.

Direct Buses to Chamdo & Lhasa
*Direct buses from Chengdu to Chamdo (Changdu) leave from the Xizang Changdu Yunshuzhan (Transport Station) near Xinan Jiaoqu Cuqiao. To get there, take a #14 (Shisi Lu) local bus from Wuhou Temple and stay on it until you reach a bridge on the left, about 5 minutes after the railroad. There are a couple of services a week, and the bus leaves at 06:00. The trip takes 4 nights and goes via Dege (Derge). At the time

of writing, foreigners were unfortunately unable to purchase tickets for this bus.

*There are direct buses from Chengdu to Lhasa along the Sichuan-Tibet Highway South, although these are irregular. The trip takes 9 nights and goes via Batang. The bus stand is at Baimasi Ersuo, Euhuan Lu Beiduan, which you can get to by taking a #16 (Shiliu Lu) local bus. Once again foreign passengers are not supposed to get on this bus either.

*There are also buses equipped with sleeping berths that go from Chengdu to Lhasa via Aba Prefecture, Xining, and Golmud. These take 4 nights, though the same restriction applies to foreigners, who are only allowed to use this option if they are traveling in the opposite direction.

Chengdu to Aba Overland
Buses from Chengdu to the Tibetan areas in Aba Prefecture leave from the Ximen Bus Station.

Chengdu to other Major Cities in China
[By Rail]
*No. 8 Special Express
  Chengdu 12:26 - Beijing West (Xi Zhan) 20:07 (2 nights)
*No. 364 Express
  Chengdu 18:07 - Beijing West (Xi Zhan) 06:02 (3 nights)
*No. 381 & 384 Express
  Chengdu 14:30 - Shanghai 12:59 (2 nights)
*No. 389 & 392 Express
  Chengdu 19:57 - Shanghai 12:44 (2 nights)
*No. 91 & 94 Special Express
  Chengdu 18:32 - Guangzhou 15:00 (2 nights)
*No. 207 Special Express
  Chengdu 11:08 - Kunming 08:21 (2 nights)

[By Air]
There are daily flights to many major Chinese cities. The ticket prices are as follows:

*Beijing (Y1,550)
*Shanghai (Y1,610)

Sleeping-berth Bus, Chengdu - Lhasa

*Guangzhou (Y1,310)
*Shenzhen (Y1,350)
*Hong Kong (Y2,510)
*Kunming (Y720)
*Lanzhou (Y910)
*Lhasa (Y1,580)

There are other services available including a flight from Chengdu to Xining (Y1,050), which operates on Monday and Friday.

GANZI (KANDZE) TIBETAN AUTONOMOUS PREFECTURE

KANGDING (DARTSEDO)

The town of Kangding, 368km to the west of Chengdu, is the capital of the Ganzi Tibetan Autonomous Prefecture. The town spreads out along a river in a narrow valley at an altitude of around 2,500m. There are a large number of 5- to 7-story buildings clustered together in the town, and Kangding is an important transportation center for those heading for other places in Ganzi Prefecture.

The Chinese characters that form the name *Kangding* mean 'Subjugation of Kham.' This was changed from the old Chinese name of *Dajianlu*, derived from the original Tibetan name *Dartsedo* or *Dardo*. For centuries the town prospered as a relay point for the trade between Tibet and China.

Besides the Tibetan monasteries in the town, there is also a Hui mosque. Along with Hui minority people, there are also many Yi people living here. Atop a hill on the southern side of the town is the Paoma Shan (Dentok Riwo) Park, which is home to a Tibetan monastery. There are also the Erdaoqiao Hot Springs to the north of the town.

Although Kangding is urbanized, you can still see the snow-capped mountains nearby, and the many old stores and houses give the place an atmosphere. The town is a Chinese-style one, but you can buy yak meat at the market and you will be served a cup of butter tea at any Tibetan home you visit.

Access
From Chengdu, buses leave the Xinnanmen Bus Station, next to the Jiaotong Fandian (Traffic Hotel). There are a number of buses leaving in the morning, and some buses with sleeping berths depart around 17:30. You can get tickets at the ticket office, but some tourists have reportedly been required to buy travel insurance prior to the issuing of the tickets. The cost of an ordinary bus ticket

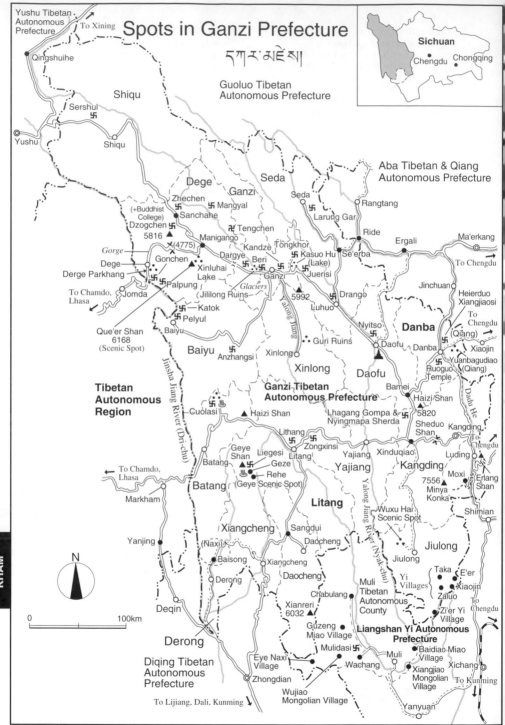

Spots in Ganzi Prefecture
དཀར་མཛེས།

Yushu Tibetan Autonomous Prefecture

To Xining

Qingshuihe

Shiqu

Sershul

Yushu

Shiqu

Guoluo Tibetan Autonomous Prefecture

Sichuan

Chengdu   Chongqing

Aba Tibetan & Qiang Autonomous Prefecture

Dege

Ganzi

Seda

Zhechen

Mangyal

Seda

Rangtang

(+Buddhist College)

Sanchahe

Larung Gar

Ride

Ergali

Ma'erkang

Dzogchen

5816 ▲

Tengchen

Se'erba

To Chengdu

Manigango

Kandze

Tongkhor

×(4775)

Dargye

Beri

Kasuo Hu (Lake)

Gorge

Dege

Gonchen

Xinluhai Lake

Ganzi

Juerisi

Jinchuan

Heierduo Xiangjiaosi

Derge Parkhang

Palpung

Glaciers

5992 ▲

Drango

Danba

To Chengdu (Qiang)

To Chamdo, Lhasa

Jomda

(Jililong Ruins

Luhuo

Xiaojin

Katok

Nyitso

Yuanbagudiao (Qiang)

Que'er Shan 6168 (Scenic Spot)

Pelyul

Baiyu

Guri Ruins

Daofu

Danba

Ruoguo Temple

Baiyu

Anzhangsi

Xinlong

Xinlong

Daofu

Bamei

Haizi Shan

Kangding

Tibetan Autonomous Region

Cuolasi

Haizi Shan

Ganzi Tibetan Autonomous Prefecture

Lhagang Gompa & Nyingmapa Sherda

5820 ▲

Sheduo Shan

Luding

To Chengdu

Lithang

Zongxinsi

Yajiang

Xinduqiao

Jinsha Jiang River (Dri-chu)

Geye Shan

Liegesi

Litang

Yajiang

Kangding

Moxi

Batang

Geze

Rehe

(Geye Scenic Spot)

7556 ▲

Minya Konka

Erlang Shan

Batang

Litang

Yalong Jiang River (Nyak-chu)

Wuxu Hai Scenic Spot

Shimian

Markham

Xiangcheng

Sangdui

Jiulong

Jiulong

Yanjing

(Naxi)

Baisong

Xiangcheng

Daocheng

Taka

E'er

Derong

Daocheng

Yi Villages

Xiaojin

Muli Tibetan Autonomous County

Zaluo

Deqin

Chabulang

Zi'er Yi Village

To Chengdu

0   100km

Xianreri 6032 ▲

Guzeng Miao Village

Liangshan Yi Autonomous Prefecture

Derong

Eye Naxi Village

Mulidasi

Muli

Baidiao Miao Village

Diqing Tibetan Autonomous Prefecture

Zhongdian

Wachang

Xiangjiao Mongolian Village

Xichang

To Kunming

Wujiao Mongolian Village

Yanyuan

To Lijiang, Dali, Kunming

Kangding

comes to Y62 without travel insurance.

After going through the Erlang Shan (Yarla Namtse) pass, you will get a good panoramic view of the majestic Dadu He (Ngul-chu) below. The trip to Kangding is supposed to take 15-16 hours, though this really depends on the driver and the time. This highway is good enough to have toll gates installed along the Chengdu to Ya'an stretch. But some western parts of the route past Ya'an are seemingly always undergoing construction work.

The mountainous section that brings you up to the Erlang Shan pass and then down again is also prone to landslides, and buses sometimes make a detour to avoid the pass altogether by going to the south from Ya'an and then heading north via Shimian. In this case, the trip from Chengdu to Kangding may take 1 or possibly 2 nights.

There are also direct buses available daily from Ya'an and Shimian. Xichang has a service 4 times a week, and there is a bus 3 times a week from Chongqing.

Accommodation

There is an additional tariff for foreign guests.

The *Kangding Binguan* (Hotel) is on the northern side of Jiangjunqiao (Bridge), 1.5km from the bus station. Opposite the hotel, there is a Tibetan monastery, Ngachu Gompa (Anjuesi). A single room here costs Y120, a bed in a double room is Y40, and one in a 3-person room is Y18. Both the single and double rooms are equipped with a hot shower,

toilet, and heater.

The *Gonggashan Lushe* (Hostel) is next to Ngachu Gompa (Anjuesi) and is run by a Tibetan. There is a communal toilet, and the showers don't have hot water. The store on the bottom floor is also the reception, and there is a restaurant next to it. The terrace of the hotel is a hangout for local Tibetans.

The *Jiaotong Lushe* (Traffic Hostel) is a convenient place to stay if you need to take an early morning bus, as it is in the bus station and buses from Chengdu terminate here. There are no showers available, and some foreigners have been turned away in the past.

If you are refused here, you can also try at the *Jiaotong Gongyu* (Traffic Apartment) building next door to the right. Beds at the Jiaotong Gongyu cost Y8.

The *Zhigong Zhaodaisuo* (Guesthouse) acts as an overflow place to sleep overnight for passengers when the Traffic Hostel is full, even though the guesthouse is dirty.

The *Paomashan Binguan* (Hotel) is next to the government building in town, and this middle range hotel is similar to the Kangding Binguan (Hotel).

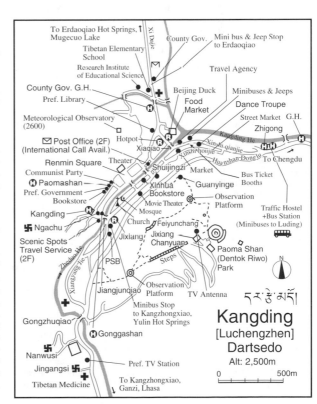

Kangding
[Luchengzhen]
Dartsedo
Alt: 2,500m

0   500m

र र ङे अर्दो

Restaurants

Kangding is the capital of the prefecture, and you can find good food here. The majority of what is available is Sichuanese, and there are also some Tibetan restaurants.

At the *Jixiang Fandian* (Lucky Restaurant) opposite the Jiangjunqiao (Bridge), the food isn't too bad.

Public Security Bureau (PSB)

Visa extensions are available here, and travel permits are no longer required, as all the places in Ganzi (Kandze) Tibetan Autonomous Prefecture are now open to foreign tourists.

Buses from Kangding

Long-distance buses for other towns in Ganzi, Chengdu, Chongqing, and Yunnan Province leave from Kangding Bus Station, and there is no problem with foreigners buying tickets. On the southern side of the Xiaqiao (Bridge), near the center of town, there are a handful of ticket offices. After they leave the bus station, the buses also stop and pick up passengers here. If you are staying at the Kangding Binguan (Hotel) or the Gonggashan Lushe (Hostel), it would be easier for you to catch the bus at this spot. When you buy one of the long-distance bus tickets, you are allocated a seat number.

For Tagong, Bamei, Guzan, Luding, Xinduqiao, and other surrounding towns and villages, there are minibuses and shared Land Cruisers waiting for passengers on the street opposite the ticket offices. At Guzan there is the Khampa University, but the PSB are sensitive about people going there.

For Tibetan Areas

[Daily Departures]
*Daofu—06:00 (8 hrs, 244km)
*Ganzi—06:00 (15 hrs)
*Litang—06:00 (13 hrs)
*Luhuo—06:00 (10-11 hrs)
*Danba—07:00 (6-7 hrs)
*Yajiang—07:00 (6-7 hrs)
*Luding—06:30-19:00 (1 hr 40 mins),
  10 buses a day.
*Moxi—13:30 (4-5 hrs)

[Other Departures]
*Baiyu - 06:00 Odd numbered days. (3 days there, 2 days back)
*Daocheng—06:00 Dates with the numbers 3, 7, and 0. (e.g. 3, 7, 13, 17, 20, etc.) (2 days)
*Dege—06:00 Dates with the numbers 1, 3, and 6. (2 days)
*Jiulong—06:00 Dates with the numbers 3, 6, and 9. (10 hours, 256km)
*Seda—06:00 Dates with numbers 2, 5, and 8. (2 days)
*Shiqu—06:00 Dates with the numbers 2, 5, and 8. (3 days there, 2 days back, 700km)
*Xiangcheng—06:00 Even numbered days.(2 days)
*Xinlong—06:00 Even numbered days. (2 days)
*Batang—07:00 Even numbered days. (2 days)

For Chinese Towns

*Chengdu—There are some buses that leave at 06:00-07:00 every morning. The 368km trip should take 15-16 hours, although this depends on the road conditions, and it actually can be anything up to 2 nights on the road.
*Chengdu (Sleeping Berth Buses)—There are some leaving around 17:00, and many will wait for the connecting bus arriving from Ganzi before departing. This is great for those wanting to head straight through from Ganzi to Chengdu without staying overnight in Kangding.
*There are also buses available for Chongqing, Xichang, and Shimian.

Places to See
Paoma Shan (Dentok Riwo)

To the south-west of the town, this mountain is the most famous place in Kangding. Kangding Guanyinge is the easiest place to find a path up the mountain, and on the peak itself there is a large chorten and Dentok Gompa (Jixiang Chanyuan). The mountain is also sacred to the Chinese, and there are also Confucian and Taoist temples here.

Ngachu Gompa (Anjuesi)

Opposite the Kangding Binguan (Hotel), Ngachu Gompa is a Gelukpa monastery that was built in the 17th century to function as a branch of the Drepung Losaling College, and it once housed around 100 monks. When the Dalai Lama traveled to Beijing in 1954, he stopped en route and stayed here. The head of the monastery now lives in exile in India.

Lhamo Tsering Gompa (Nanwusi)

Lhamo Tsering Gompa is another Gelukpa monastery to be found less than 10 minutes after you cross the Gongzhuqiao (Bridge) in the south of the town.

Dorje Drak Gompa (Jingangsi)

Make a right after the television station and continue on until you reach the monastery to the south of Lhamo Tsering Gompa. This gompa is a branch of the Dorje Drak Monastery, the head monastery of the Nyingmapa Northern Treasure tradition in central Tibet. The site was destroyed in 1959, but the main temple, Chanting Hall, and Jokhang have been fully reconstructed. In the main temple you can see a huge image of Guru Rinpoche (Padmasambhava).

Mani-stones with Buddhist mantras
painted on them. (HN)

Pilgrims making their circuit of the sacred Mt. Kailash. (HN)

Sacred Mt. Kailash (Kang Rinpoche). (SM)

The sacred Lake Manasarovar (Mapham Yutso),
revered by Hindus, Jains, Bonpos and Buddhists. (SM)

Sacred Mt. Kailash (Kang Rinpoche). (SM)

Preparing food along the pilgrimage route. (HN)

Dancers wearing turquoise headdresses perform at the popular Ladakh Festival. (HN)

A Dard woman from Dha Village, Ladakh. (HN)

Lamayuru Gompa in a desolate area sometimes referred to as 'Moon World.' (HN)

Erdaoqiao Hot Springs

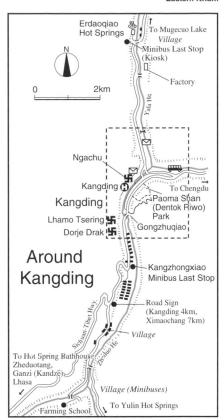

Around Kangding

Erdaoqiao Hot Springs

This natural spa is 4km to the north of Kangding, and you can get there by minibus from the Kangding Renmin Zhengfu Zhaodaisuo (Government Guesthouse). You will need to stay on the minibus until the last stop, and the fare is Y1. Admission to the hot springs is Y6, and there are private rooms where you can bathe without having to cover up. At the store here you can buy most of the things you will need, such as towels, soap, shampoo, etc. There are tables and chairs set out for visitors to relax and enjoy a cup of tea, and you can even get your hair done at the barbers here.

If you want to stay overnight, there are beds available for Y15. The hot springs are open at 11:00-18:00, and the minibus service seems to finish at 18:00.

MUGECUO LAKE (YEREN HAI) [SAVAGE'S LAKE]

This 4 sq km lake is at an altitude of 3,700m and located 37km from Kangding. The area surrounding Mugecuo is littered with over 30 lakes and marshes with names like Honghai (Red Sea), Heihai (Black Sea), and Baihai (White Sea). On the way to Mugecuo there is also another beautiful lake called Qisehai (Seven-Color Lake) from where you can get a distant view of the snow-covered mountains even in the summer. There are hot springs nearby.

Take a minibus from Kangding for Yumu, but you will need to be careful, as there are only 1 or 2 services a day. Alternatively, you could walk there, though this would take you 2 days each way. The best seasons to visit here are spring and fall, and it is better to avoid the period between June and August, as it rains a lot. You will find accommodation along the shore of Mugecuo Lake.

During the spring and fall there are group tours from Kangding, such as the popular 'One day trip

to Mugecuo Lake' arranged by *Kangding Luxingshe* (Travel) at the Jiaotong Lushe (Traffic Hostel). For advice on the latest tour offers, the staff at the *Fengjing Mingsheng Luyou Shiye* (Scenic Spots Travel Service) can give you up-to-date information.

EASTERN KHAM

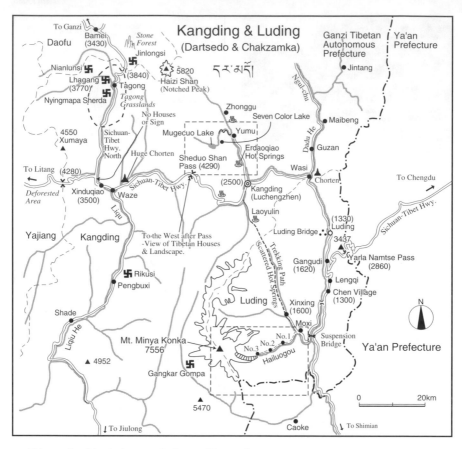

Kangding & Luding
(Dartsedo & Chakzamka)

To Ganzi
Daofu
Bamei (3430)
Stone Forest
Jinlongsi
Nianlunsi
Lhagang (3770)
Tagong (3840)
Haizi Shan (Notched Peak)
5820
Nyingmapa Sherda
Tagong Grasslands
Zhonggu
Seven Color Lake
No Houses or Sign
Mugecuo Lake
Yumu
4550 Xumaya
Sichuan-Tibet Hwy. North
Huge Chorten
Sheduo Shan Pass (4290)
Erdaoqiao Hot Springs
Guzan
To Litang (4280)
Wasi
To Chengdu
Deforested Area
Xinduqiao (3500)
Waze
(2500)
Kangding (Luchengzhen)
Chorten
Sichuan-Tibet Hwy.
Yajiang
Kangding
To the West after Pass -View of Tibetan Houses & Landscape.
Laoyulin
(1330) Luding
Luding Bridge
3437
Rikusi
Pengbuxi
Gangudi (1620)
Yarla Namtse Pass (2860)
Trekking Path Scattered Hot Springs
Lengqi
Chen Village (1300)
Shade
Luding
Xinxing (1600)
Moxi
Mt. Minya Konka 7556
No.1
No.3 No.2
Suspension Bridge
Ya'an Prefecture
4952
Hailuogou
Gangkar Gompa
5470
N
0 20km
To Jiulong
Caoke
To Shimian

Ganzi Tibetan Autonomous Prefecture
Ya'an Prefecture
Jintang
Maibeng
Ngul-chu
Dadu He

This area is said to be home to the human-like *Mugu* (in Tibetan), an elusive cousin of the Nepalese Yeti. The *Mugu*, unlike the mountain dwelling Yeti, is said to inhabit woodland areas.

AROUND KANGDING

LUDING (CHAKZAMKA)

The town stretches out from north to south, along the Dadu He (Ngul-chu) Valley, approximately 50km from Kangding, and most of the town's residents are Han Chinese. Luding is famous for the Ludingqiao (Bridge), a suspension bridge built in 1706. There is a charge for crossing the bridge, and from Guanyinge, on the other side, you can get a good view of the town.

Access
To Luding
*Chengdu—There are a lot of buses heading for Kangding that stop over at Luding leaving from the Xinnanmen Bus Station. There is also a bus that terminates at Luding.

*Kangding—There are many minibuses going to Luding, and these leave from the area opposite the bus station and the Xiaqiao (Bridge). The trip costs Y7 and takes about an hour and 40 minutes.

From Luding
There are 2 bus stations in Luding, and usually buses leave from the *Luding Keyun Zhongxin* (Passenger Transport Center), the northern one.

*Xingxin—There are daily departures at 07:30 and 14:00, and these go via Moxi. You need to take the one for Hailuogou.

242

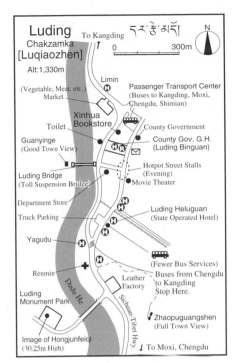

Luding [Luqiaozhen]
Chakzamka
To Kangding
ང་ར་རྩེ་མདོ།
N
0   300m
Alt:1,330m

(Vegetable, Meat, etc.)
Market
Limin
Passenger Transport Center
(Buses to Kangding, Moxi, Chengdu, Shimian)
Xinhua Bookstore
Toilet
County Government
Guanyinge
(Good Town View)
County Gov. G.H.
(Luding Binguan)
Hotpot Street Stalls
(Evening)
Luding Bridge
(Toll Suspension Bridge)
Movie Theater
Department Store
Truck Parking
Luding Heluguan
(State Operated Hotel)
Yagudu
Renmin
(Fewer Bus Services)
Buses from Chengdu
to Kangding Stop Here.
Leather Factory
Luding Monument Park
Dadu He
Sichuan-Tibet Hwy.
Zhaopuguangshen
(Full Town View)
Image of Hongjunfeiqi
(30.25m High)
To Moxi, Chengdu

*Chengdu—There are a number of buses every day.
*There are also many buses for Kangding, Wusihe (via Shimian), Yanshuixi, Guzan, and other regional centers.

Accommodation & Restaurants

The *Luding Zhengfu Zhaodaisuo* (Luding Binguan) (Government Guesthouse) has double rooms with bathrooms for Y42, and a bed in a dormitory is Y15-20. There is a restaurant here, and you can arrange tours to Hailuogou.
The *Yagudu Fandian* (Hotel) has single rooms costing Y50, and a bed in a double room costs the same.

Ludingqiao (Bridge)

*There are some other cheap guesthouses in the town. They range in price from Y3-18.
*Along with the restaurant at the Zhengfu Zhaodaisuo, there are many restaurants around the movie theater (Dianying). Food stalls spring up in the evenings selling *Huoguo* (Hotpot), and many of these also serve fish dishes.

MT. MINYA KONKA (GONGGA SHAN) [MINYAK GANGKAR]

At the eastern end of the Tibetan Plateau, this is the world's eleventh highest mountain and the highest in Sichuan Province at 7,556m. This is the only mountain over 5,500m in the area, making Mt. Minya Konka really stand out from the rest of the peaks.
Unfortunately, the mountain is often covered in clouds, and it's rare to get a full view of it, especially if you are in the area in summer during the rainy season. You have more of a chance during the spring or fall. At the western foot of the peak is the Gangkar Gompa (Gonggasi), belonging to the Karma Kagyupa order.
The area stretching from Sheduo Shan (Dardo La, 4,290m), to the west of Kangding, along to the Yalong Jiang River (Nyak-chu) is called the *Minyak* area, and the mountain itself has the other name, *Gangkar*, meaning 'White Snow' among the people of the area.

HAILUOGOU (HAILUOGOU GLACIER PARK)

This is a real draw for glacier fans. The glacier continues to flow below an altitude of 3,000m at Latitude 29°N, making it famous as the lowest glacier in the world. The area where the glaciers flow out from Mt. Minya Konka to the east, and the woodland surrounding it are real draws for tourists, and there are many group tours that flock to the area from Chengdu.
It is best to avoid the period between June and September, as this is the rainy season. For example, a trip to the area in early July found rain every day and a temperature around 7-8°C. The tourist season stretches from October to May, and in the winter the area is, of course, covered with snow. Nonetheless, you can still find accommodation, and you can get here by car even during the worst weather conditions.
Throughout the year it is necessary to take warm clothes with you, as the temperature can drop very low.

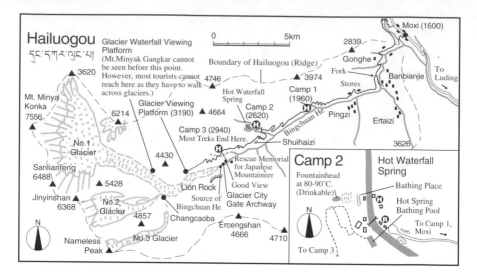

Hailuogou

རུང་དཀར་འུང་སེ།

Glacier Waterfall Viewing Platform
(Mt.Minyak Gangkar cannot be seen before this point. However, most tourists cannot reach here as they have to walk across glaciers.)

Boundary of Hailuogou (Ridge)

Mt. Minya Konka 7556

6214

Glacier Viewing Platform (3190)

▲ 3620

4746

▲ 4664

Hot Waterfall Spring

Camp 2 (2620)

Camp 3 (2940) Most Treks End Here.

Shuihaizi

No.1 Glacier

4430

Rescue Memorial for Japanese Mountaineer

Sanlianfeng 6488

▲ 5428

Lion Rock

Good View

Glacier City Gate Archway

Jinyinshan 6368

No.2 Glacier

4857

Source of Bingchuan He

Changcaoba

Ercengshan 4666

4710

Nameless Peak ▲

No.3 Glacier

Moxi (1600)

2839

Gonghe

▲ 3974

Fork

Stores

Camp 1 (1960)

Bingchuan He

Pingzi

Banbianjie

To Luding

Ertaizi

3626

0   5km

N

Camp 2
Fountainhead at 80-90°C. (Drinkable)

Hot Waterfall Spring

Bathing Place

Hot Spring Bathing Pool

To Camp 1, Moxi →

To Camp 3

N

Hailuogou Trip

Moxi is the starting point for a trip to Hailuogou, and a bus leaves Kangding at 13:30 every day, taking 4-5 hours. At Luding, take the daily bus for Xingxin that leaves at either 07:00 or 13:30 and stops off at Moxi. The ticket office in Luding charges foreigners twice the price that locals pay.

When you arrive at Moxi, you must pay an admission charge at the Moxi office of the *Luding Xian Luyou Gongsi* (Luding County Travel Co.). (See the map below.) The cost is Y70 for foreign passengers (Y30 for Chinese people). If you present your student ID to the clerks, they will give you the Chinese price. After you've made the payment, you will be issued your ticket, a pamphlet, and a

map. The ticket office also offers a baggage service, and they will look after your bag for Y2 per day.

Although there are no checkpoints for visitors in Hailuogou, you must produce a valid ticket whenever you check into a guesthouse. This is an added incentive not to forget to buy one at the office. You will only find accommodation at Camp 1, 2, and 3, and it is a good idea to have your name written on the ticket and to make sure it is officially stamped, especially at Camp 1, to avoid any confusion later.

You may be offered a horse ride by local people at the ticket office, and a round trip for 2 days costs Y100-200. There is a road covering the 22km from Moxi to Camp 1, but there is no public transportation available, and in the rainy season, landslides often disrupt the traffic on the road. By walking this section you can also take a shortcut between them.

Model Tour

You will need 2-4 days for the trip, but if you try to squeeze everything into a 2-day schedule, it will be very hard going. Visitors usually make it a 3-day trip, and this is the time frame taken for the following model tour.

*Day 1: Moxi-Camp 2 (Hot Springs) 6-7 hrs.
*Day 2: Camp 2-Camp 1 (Glacier Viewing Platform - Binghe Shijingtai - Round trip)
*Day 3: Camp 1-Moxi 7-8 hrs.

The cost of staying at Camp 1 is Y15, increasing to Y20 at Camps 2 and 3. The rooms are not very clean, and the toilet is outside. There are restaurants

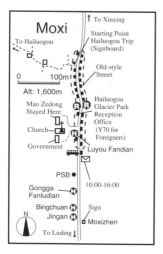

Moxi

To Xinxing

Starting Point Hailuogou Trip (Signboard)

To Hailuogou

Old-style Street

0   100m
Alt: 1,600m

Mao Zedong Stayed Here.

Hailuogou Glacier Park Reception Office (Y70 for Foreigners)

Church

Government

Luyou Fandian

PSB

10:00-16:00

Gongga Fanludian

Bingchuan

Sign

Jingan

Moxizhen

To Luding

N

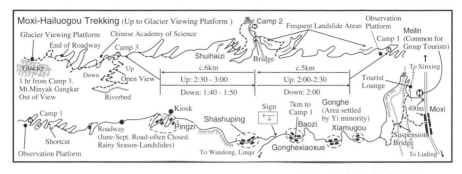

Moxi-Hailuogou Trekking (Up to Glacier Viewing Platform)

Glacier Viewing Platform — Chinese Academy of Science
End of Roadway — Camp 3
Glacier — Up — Open View
1 hr from Camp 3. — Down
Mt.Minyak Gangkar — Riverbed
Out of View
Shuihaizi
Camp 2
Frequent Landslide Areas
Observation Platform
Meilin
Camp 1 (Common for Group Tourists)
To Xinxing
Bridge

c.6km	c.5km
Up: 2:30 - 3:00	Up: 2:00-2:30
Down: 1:40 - 1:50	Down: 2:00

Tourist Lounge

Camp 1 — Kiosk — Shashuping — Sign — 7km to Camp 1 — Gonghe (Area settled by Yi minority) — Xiamugou
Roadway — Pingzi — Baozi
Shortcut (June-Sept. Road-often Closed. Rainy Season-Landslides)
Observation Platform
To Wandong, Linqu — Gonghexiaoxue — To Luding
Suspension Bridge
400m — Moxi
To Xinxing

at each of the camps, and a meal costs Y10-15. Beer, cola, and other beverages are also available, and you can also buy basic provisions at the small camp stores. The facilities all have electricity, but a flashlight is still a must.

From the Glacier Viewing Platform, you will get a great view of the glacier, but you will be unable to catch sight of Mt. Minya Konka. The mountain can be viewed from another observation platform, but most visitors are unable to reach it, as there is another glacier on the way. There are hot springs at Camp 2 with a waterfall. There is also a hot spring pool that costs Y5.

Access
From Moxi
There are 3 buses daily from Xingxin, and these stop in Moxi at 07:00, 08:00, and 11:00.
If you wait for one of these near the post office, you can usually get a seat.

Accommodation & Restaurants at Moxi
The *Meilin Binguan* (Hotel) is a new 3-story building that is popular with group tours, and the facilities are good. The hotel is not so convenient for an individual traveler though, as it is around 20 minutes to the north of the town.
There are also 4 or 5 places that are good just for overnight stays. A bed at the *Gongga Fanludian* (Guesthouse) costs Y8.
There are 10 or so restaurants in the town, and these serve quite a variety of food. The average cost of a dish is Y4-5.

By Group Tour
A group tour for Hailuogou is available from in front of the Chengdu Station and at travel agencies in the city. The cost of a 5-day trip is Y298-320, but this price only covers the cost of the minibus.

You will have to pay extra for accommodation, meals, hiring a horse, etc., and these additional expenses bring the cost up to Y400-600.

KANGDING TO GANZI, DEGE, ETC. (SICHUAN-TIBET HIGHWAY NORTH)

DANBA (RONGTRAK)

The town of Danba is 138km to the north of Kangding and is home to many Hui people. It is on the southern side of the area, where a number of tributaries, such as the Da Jinchuan River and the Xiao Jinchuan River, merge into the Dadu He (Ngul-chu). If you need everyday provisions, you will find most of the required things here.

The surrounding area, along with Jinchuan (Chuchen), Xiaojin (Tsenlha), and the neighboring Aba (Ngawa) Prefecture, is the region where the

Church, Moxi

EASTERN KHAM

245

Dongnuguo (Gyarong) Kingdom once flourished, and it is still called *Gyalmoron*, meaning 'Valley of the Queen.' *Gyarong*, on the other hand, means 'Valley of China.'

From Kangding, there is a single bus and a minibus each day. Depending on the road conditions at the time, one takes the route via Bamei, and the other one goes via Guzan. There is also a bus via Xiaojin that leaves Ximen Bus Station in Chengdu at 07:00 every couple of days, and the fare is Y46.9.

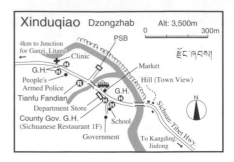

JIULONG (GYEZIL)

To the south of Kangding, this town is home to many Yi minority people. From Kangding there are roughly 3 buses during each 10-day period, and the 12-hour trip costs Y40. Wuxu Hai (Lake), 26km to the north-west of the town, is an interesting place to visit.

XINDUQIAO (DZONGZHAB)

You will stop at this small town on the way from Kangding to Ganzi, Litang, and surrounding areas. After Kangding and Sheduo Shan (Dardo La 4,290m), the scenery changes, and you get a real Tibetan feel, with grassland stretching out from the outskirts. Xinduqiao is home to many Tibetans. There are a handful of hotels in the town, and the cost of a bed averages Y8. For eating out you can try the good quality food available at the *Tianfu Fandian* (Restaurant).

Four kilometers beyond Xinduqiao is the junction with the road that heads north to Ganzi and west to Litang. There is nothing in the vicinity of the junction, not even houses.

TAGONG (LHAGANG) [HARGONG]

On the way from Xinduqiao to Ganzi, there is a cluster of chortens of various sizes, and this strange place is Lhagang Gompa (Tagongsi). On the hill above the road, a huge chorten welcomes pilgrims, and across the vast expanse of grassland stretching out to the east from the structure, there are *dar-shings* at intervals along the path to guide them.

To the east you can see Haizi Shan (Mt. Zhara Lhatse, 5,820m), a snow-covered peak, with a unique sharp, pointed shape. This mountain is also strongly connected with the stories of Guru Rinpoche (Padmasambhava). In summer there are

festivals held here, featuring horse racing on the plains surrounding the area.

To the west of the town there are 3 sacred mountains. These are from left to right: Jampeyang (Manjushri), Chenrezik (Avalokiteshvara), and Chakna Dorje (Vajrapani). The sides of the mountains are festooned with light-red and white *dar-shings*, the markings of a sacred mountain. One pilgrim said that these colored flags look like Bodhisattvas from a distance. The town is small, with only a few stores and restaurants scattered along the bus route.

Access
From Kangding
From the minibus stop at Xiaqiao (Bridge) there are minibuses and some shared-jeeps starting at around 10:00 and then again in the afternoon. Another option is to take a bus for Ganzi and get off on the way.

From Tagong
*Ganzi and the surrounding area—there are a number of buses coming from Kangding between 10:00 and noon.
*Kangding—there are minibuses and jeeps coming from and returning to Kangding around 07:00, 12:00, and again in the afternoon. Some of the buses from Ganzi and the surrounding area heading for Kangding stop here up until the evening.

Horse Racing, Tagong

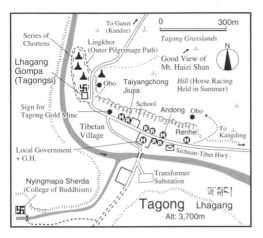

To Ganzi (Kandze)
0   300m
Series of Chortens
Lingkhor (Outer Pilgrimage Path)
Tagong Grasslands
Lhagang Gompa (Tagongsi)
N
Good View of Mt. Haizi Shan
Obo   Taiyangchong Jiujia
Hill (Horse Racing Held in Summer)
Sign for Tagong Gold Mine
School
Andong   Obo
Tibetan Village
To Renhe
To Kangding
Local Government + G.H.
Sichuan-Tibet Hwy.
Nyingmapa Sherda (College of Buddhism)
Transformer Substation
Tagong   Lhagang
Alt: 3,700m

Accommodation & Restaurants
The *Renhe Luguan* (Hotel) in the west of the town is truly Tibetan in style and has a warm atmosphere. Beds here cost Y4.

After the gate of the Tagong Township Government there is a building that has a guesthouse on the 2nd floor, and a bed in a double room costs Y9. There are neither showers nor heaters available though.

The *Taiyangchong Jiujia* (Restaurant) serves Chinese food, and you can get rice dishes here. The meals on the menu start from Y8. There are 7-8 other restaurants in the town mostly serving only noodles.

Places to See
Lhagang Gompa (Tagongsi)
This Sakyapa monastery is on the northern side of the town, and it is also known as *Tagongsi*. It is a very old monastery that is said to be the most easterly one of the 108 geomantic lhakhangs that radiate out from Lhasa in Tibet, which were built by the Tibetan king Songtsen Gampo in the 7th century. These temples were intended to subdue the great ogress that straddled the Tibetan lands, and they form 3 distinct groups, the *Runo* (Inner-sanctuary Temples), *Tandul* (Border-taming

Nyingmapa Sherda

Temples), and the *Yandul* (Further-taming Temples). Lhagang Gompa was constructed to act as one of the 4 further-taming *Yangdul*.

Although the main temple is interesting, the real highlight of a visit here is the Jokhang Chapel on the right of the complex. This houses an image of Shakyamuni, called *Lhagang Jowo*. The principle image of the Jokhang Temple in Lhasa is also an image of Shakyamuni that Princess Wengcheng, the daughter of the Tang Emperor, brought with her when she married into the Tibetan royal family. Legend has it that the most sacred image of Buddha in Tibet asked Princess Wengcheng to leave it in Hargong when she stayed here on her way to Lhasa — at least this is the story that locals believe. Indeed, when many pilgrims are present in the Jokhang Chapel, it seems to have an extraordinary atmosphere about it.

On the northern side of the monastery there are a large number of different size chortens all standing together. The number of these structures is said to be 124, but on counting them you'll find there are more than that.

Nyingmapa Sherda (Buddhism College)
This Nyingmapa monastery is brand new and still in very good condition, as reconstruction has been completed only quite recently. It houses more than a hundred monks, and the head lama lives on the hill next door. Looking from the town, the monastery is hidden behind the sacred Jampeyang (Manjushri) Mountain. Although it is only about a 30-minute walk from the town, you should be careful of dogs on the way, as you have to pass by a number of tents belonging to nomadic people.

At the foot of the hill on which the monastery is built, there is a huge *Mani Dophung*, a mound made up of a large number of beautiful *mani* prayer stones and definitely worth viewing.

BAMEI (GARTHAR) (CLOSED)

Bamei is at the junction of the road from Kangding to Ganzi and the one going up the Dadu He (Ngul-chu) via Danba (Rongtrak). As this is an important transit stop, the town has a lot of restaurants for its size, and there is also a guesthouse here. The vast majority of people in the town seem to be Han Chinese.

About 1km to the north-east of the junction, you will find Garthar Choede, a Gelukpa monastery built by the 7th Dalai Lama in the 18th century, and another claim to fame is that the 11th Dalai Lama was actually from Bamei (Garthar).

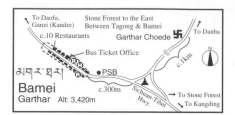

To Daofu, Ganzi (Kandze)
Stone Forest to the East Between Tagong & Bamei
To Danba
c.10 Restaurants
Garthar Choede
Bus Ticket Office
N
c.1km
སྨད་ར་ཐ་ར།
PSB
Bamei
Garthar
c.300m
Sichuan-Tibet Hwy.
Alt: 3,420m
To Stone Forest
To Kangding

the area between Daofu and Ganzi is called the Trehol region.

Access
From Kangding and Chengdu
There are a number of buses each day from Kangding, and the trip takes 8 hours. From Chengdu, there are a couple of direct services each week. In addition, those buses that are heading for Luhuo, Ganzi, Dege, Shiqu, Baiyu, Xinlong, and Seda also stop at Daofu.

From Daofu
To get to the Kangding area, there is a bus that leaves the bus station at 06:00, and the tickets are available here too. For the Luhuo area, there is a bus that stops here each night and then leaves the bus station at 06:00. Alternatively, you can catch a bus coming through Daofu between 14:30 and 15:00 on the street in front of the bus station.

Accommodation & Restaurants
The *Daofu Xian Zhaodaisuo* (County Guesthouse) is where foreigners are advised to stay. A single

DAOFU (TAWU)

About 8 hours from Kangding, Daofu is a town in a narrow basin along the Xianshui He River (Zhechu), a tributary of the Yalong Jiang River (Nyakchu). When you approach the town from Kangding, you will see a huge chorten to the left just before you reach the town. An immense 10m-sq pile of *mani* prayer stones is nearby, and the Nyitso Gompa (Lingqiaosi) is another place well worth visiting in the area. The bustling area between the bus station and the Daofu Nongmao Shichang (Agricultural Trade Market) is the busiest in the town.

There are Tibetan-style houses that seem to surround the newer sections of town. Daofu is renowned for its wood production, and there are a lot of newly-constructed, good-quality wooden houses here.

The mountains that can be seen from the town have all been stripped bare of trees, except for the 3 sacred ones, and the felling areas have now moved further beyond these.

On the other side of the Yalong Jiang River (Nyakchu) there is a village set among an area of pastureland, making it a pleasant place to take a stroll. The Daofu area is also famous for the apples that are grown nearby.

Tibetans in Daofu speak a unique dialect, differing substantially from any of the other languages spoken in the region, and

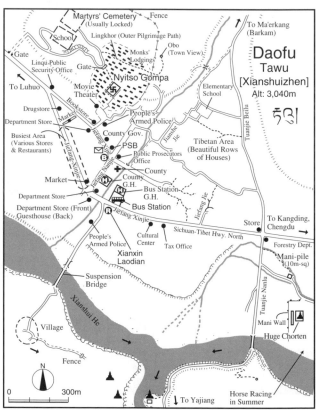

Martyrs' Cemetery
(Usually Locked)
Fence
Lingkhor (Outer Pilgrimage Path)
School
Gate
Obo (Town View)
To Ma'erkang (Barkam)
Monks' Lodgings
Linqu Public Security Office
Gate
Daofu
Tawu
[Xianshuizhen]
Alt: 3,040m
རྟའུ།
Nyitso Gompa
To Luhuo
Movie Theater
Elementary School
Drugstore
Bookstore
People's Armed Police
Department Store
Market
Busiest Area (Various Stores & Restaurants)
County Gov.
PSB
Public Prosecutors Office
Tibetan Area (Beautiful Rows of Houses)
Tuanjie Beilu
Jianshe Jie
Market
County G.H.
County
Department Store
Bus Station G.H.
Jiefang Jie
Department Store (Front)
Guesthouse (Back)
Bus Station
Jiefang Xinjie
Sichuan-Tibet Hwy. North
Store
To Kangding, Chengdu
People's Armed Police
Cultural Center
Tax Office
Forestry Dept.
Xianxin Laodian
Mani-pile (10m-sq)
Suspension Bridge
Tuanjie Nanlu
Mani Wall
Huge Chorten
Xianshui He
Village
Fence
N
0   300m
To Yajiang
Horse Racing in Summer

248

room costs Y40, and a bed in a 2-person room is Y15. Another Y2.5 gains you access to the hot showers that are located in another building. The staff is Tibetan, and they are kind and helpful. When foreigners stay here, there seems to be a level of surveillance by plain-clothes police officers.

The *Bus Station Hotel* is quite understandably found at the bus station, and it sometimes only allows bus passengers to stay. A single room costs Y11, and a dormitory bed is from Y4-9, though there are no showers here.

You can find Chinese food in the town, and the *Xianxin Laodian* (Restaurant) opposite the bus station is well recommended.

Places to See
Nyitso Gompa (Lingqiaosi)

This Gelukpa monastery plays a central role in Daofu. There used to be 400 monks living here, and the incarnate lama now lives in exile in India. At an observation point beyond the gompa you can see the 3 sacred mountains (Rigsum Gonpo), to the south over the river.

Great Chorten

This huge structure is as much as 30m-high, and in the summer there are festivals held here, with horse racing and other cultural events. The *Mani Dophung*, a massive pile of *mani* prayer stones nearby, is also worth a visit.

LUHUO (DRANGO)

Around 70km from Daofu along the river, the town of Luhuo is also called Luhuo Xinduzhen, and it is located where 2 rivers merge. It is a new town built on the ruins of the original one destroyed by an earthquake in the spring of 1973. Drango Gompa (Shoulingsi) is halfway up the mountain on the northern side of the river. The market area is the busiest part of the town.

Access

From Kangding, there are a number of buses each day, and the trip takes under 11 hours. You can also take one heading for the Ganzi area,

which stops over here. The bus for Kangding leaves at 06:00, and you can buy a ticket at the bus station. For the Ganzi area, if the bus arrives the day before and stays overnight here, it will then leave around 05:00. If you can't manage the early morning departure, you can catch one going to Ganzi on the street around 17:00 every afternoon.

Accommodation & Restaurants

The *Xincheng Luguan* (Hotel) is the one foreigners are advised to stay at. It is at the bottom of an alley opposite the bus station. It has dormitory beds costing Y8, and beds in double rooms are Y20. Its rooms are cleaner and more comfortable than those at the Qichezhan Luguan (Bus Station Hotel), and the staff here is also kind and helpful.

The *Luhuo Xianzhengfu Zhaodaisuo* (County Government Guesthouse) is 7-8 minutes to the west of the bus station. A bed in the dormitory costs from Y6-16, but there are no showers here.

The *Qichezhan Luguan* (Bus Station Hotel) is at the bus station and has beds that start at Y10. The rooms here are rather small.

There are a lot of restaurants around the bus station. If you want to eat cheaply, it would be good to check out the establishments along the Yanhe Dongjie (East Street) or Yanhe Xijie (West Street).

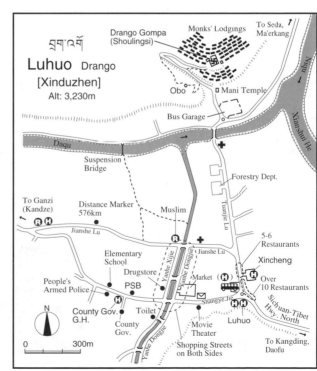

Luhuo Drango
[Xinduzhen]
Alt: 3,230m

EASTERN KHAM

You'll be able to find most of the usual selection of food on the menus in town, except for fish. You can get Tibetan meals and butter tea in this area too.

Places to See
Drango Gompa (Shoulingsi)
This is a 17th century Gelukpa monastery, and although it is kept locked, a monk will probably let you in if you ask nicely. If he likes the look of you, he may allow you to have a look at the rooms on the upper levels of the monastery buildings, and from that vantagepoint you can get a good view of the town. There are also some nuns at the gompa.

SEDA (SERTAL)

Along a tributary of the Dadu He (Ngul-chu), this town is 150km from Luhuo. The only thing of special interest here is the large chorten of the 10th Panchen Lama. Foreign visitors are requested to stay at the *Seda Xianzhengfu Zhaodaisuo* (County Government Guesthouse).

On the way from Luhuo to Seda there are a number of prominent Nyingmapa monasteries, such as Horshe Gompa, Nubzur Gompa, and Larung Gar Gompa. In the grasslands that stretch out from Seda towards Guoluo Prefecture in Qinghai Province to the north, there is also a scattering of large monasteries.

A bus from Kangding stays overnight at Luhuo and arrives at Seda the next day. From Chengdu, a bus leaving the Ximen Bus Station arrives here via Ma'erkang (Barkam) within 2 days. Both of these buses are operated 3 times during each 10-day period. Another convenient option is to take one of the shared-jeeps that sometimes leave from the Xincheng Luguan (Hotel) and some other places in Luhuo (Drango).

GANZI (KANDZE)

Although it is also the name of the prefecture, Ganzi is a small riverside town stretching out for 2-3km in a north-to-south direction and is about 1km wide. This is the largest town in the area, and there are many Tibetans here, with the men wearing red *Dashe* (Knitted Turbans) on their heads. Women also wear red cloths in a similar fashion to the men, and many of them also have black *Pandens* (Aprons). This is a trading town that attracts people and goods from the surrounding regions, such as Xinlong (Nyarong), Baiyu (Pelyul), Dege, and Amdo, among others.

Chorten of the 10th
Panchen Lama, Seda

On the northern side of the town is Kandze Gompa, with monks' lodgings spread out over the slope. The monastery commands a fine view of the snow-covered mountains to the south and over the town of Ganzi itself. The town center is in the area around the junction of Chuanzang Lu and Jiefang Jie. In the area near the Xinhua Bookstore on Jiefang Jie, is a Tibetan-style shopping street, where you can pick up various items, such as Tibetan clothes, swords, and ornaments.

Access
From Kangding there is a daily bus leaving at 06:30, which costs Y69 and takes around 15 hours. The bus arrives in Ganzi at 21:00-23:00. Foreigners are not supposed to stay at the Bus Stop Guesthouse, and you will have to stay at the Shunfeng Lushe (Hotel), the Xianzhengfu Zhaodaisuo (County Government Guesthouse), or possibly another one in town. There are also buses for Dege, Shiqu, and Baiyu that come to Ganzi and one for Baiyu that stays overnight.

From Ganzi, there is a bus for Kangding that leaves at 06:30, and tickets are available the day before the bus leaves. They also go on sale at 05:30 on the day of departure. There are also a number of minibuses each day for Xinlong and 1 or 2 a day heading out to Laima.

For Dege, Manigango, and the Baiyu area, there is only an intermittent service, and it would be better

Gompa, Seda Area

to hitch a lift on one of the passing trucks around the junction in front of Ganzi Minzu Shangchang (Market) early each morning. For Dege, a lift on a shared-truck costs Y25, and a mail truck is Y30.

Accommodation
The *Ganzi Xianzhengfu Zhaodaisuo* (County Government Guesthouse) is the best hotel in the town, set in a quiet area, 10 minutes on foot from the center of town. A single room costs Y30, a bed in a double room is Y20, and a bed in a 3- or 4-person room is Y14. There are no showers at the guesthouse, and although the beds are quite simple, they are clean, and there is a television provided in each room. There is a restaurant available for guests. Many of the staff at the hotel are Tibetan, and they are kind and helpful.

The *Shunfeng Lushe* (Hotel) is in the eastern end of town, and this Tibetan-run guesthouse is a good choice, as it is open until 24:00. A dormitory bed costs Y7, and it is a relatively clean place. The problem here is that there is neither a washing stand nor a washroom in the hotel, and you have to use the toilets at the Zhuode Fandian (Hotel), opposite.

Restaurants
Around the market on Chuanzang Lu there are about 10 restaurants, and there is also a cluster of others around the Shunfeng Lushe (Hotel) and the bus station.

The *Xueyu Fandian* (Restaurant), opposite the Guoying Luguan (Hotel), is popular with Tibetans, and the cost of a dish here is between Y3-5. Fish dishes are more expensive, costing about Y15.

Places to See
Kandze Gompa (Ganzisi)
Constructed in the 17th century, this massive Gelukpa monastery spreads out over the hill on the northern side of the town. Although many of the higher-ranking monks fled to India, the great incarnate lama has now returned to the monastery.

Places to See
Around Ganzi
Many of the places can be visited as a 1- or 2-day trip, and it is a good idea to take food with you, as there are no

restaurants in these areas. You may be able to pick up some supplies at the few stores that are around, though.

Kasuo Hu (Lake) and the Kasuo Ruins
At 3,455m, this lake is about 500m in each direction. You can get a good view of the lake from the bus route. The village of Chonggu is a base for your trip up to the area, and at Ganzi, you will need to take a bus for Kangding and then get off at Chonggu. The trip takes about an hour and 40

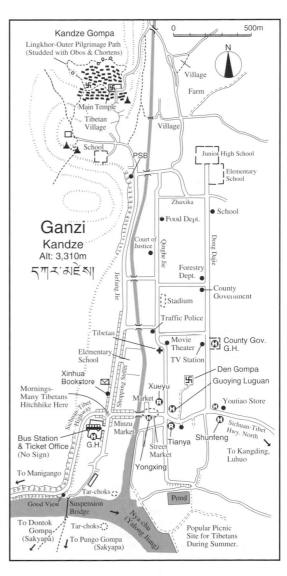

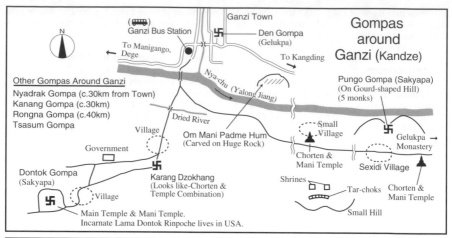

Gompas around Ganzi (Kandze)

Ganzi Town

(bus) Ganzi Bus Station

Den Gompa (Gelukpa)

To Manigango, Dege

To Kangding

Nya-chu (Yalong Jiang)

Pungo Gompa (Sakyapa) (On Gourd-shaped Hill) (5 monks)

Other Gompas Around Ganzi
Nyadrak Gompa (c.30km from Town)
Kanang Gompa (c.30km)
Rongna Gompa (c.40km)
Tsasum Gompa

Dried River

Village

Government

Om Mani Padme Hum (Carved on Huge Rock)

Small Village

Gelukpa Monastery

Chorten & Mani Temple

Sexidi Village

Dontok Gompa (Sakyapa)

Karang Dzokhang (Looks like-Chorten & Temple Combination)

Shrines

Tar-choks

Chorten & Mani Temple

Village

Main Temple & Mani Temple. Incarnate Lama Dontok Rinpoche lives in USA.

Small Hill

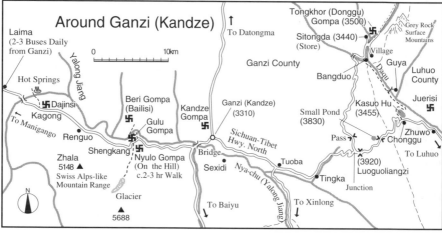

Around Ganzi (Kandze)

Laima (2-3 Buses Daily from Ganzi)

To Datongma

Tongkhor (Donggu) Gompa (3500)

Grey Rock Surface Mountains

Sitongda (3440) (Store)

Village

Guya

Luhuo County

0   10km

Hot Springs

Yalong Jiang

Dajinsi

Kagong

To Manigango

Renguo

Zhala 5148 ▲

Swiss Alps-like Mountain Range

Beri Gompa (Bailisi)

Gulu Gompa

Shengkang

Nyulo Gompa (On the Hill) c.2-3 hr Walk

Glacier

▲ 5688

Kandze Gompa

Ganzi (Kandze) (3310)

Bridge

Sexidi

Nya-chu (Yalong Jiang)

Ganzi County

Bangduo

Small Pond (3830)

Sichuan-Tibet Hwy. North

Tuoba

Kasuo Hu (3455)

Pass

(3920) Luoguoliangzi

Tingka

Junction

Juerisi

Zhuwo Chonggu

To Luhuo

To Baiyu

To Xinlong

minutes and costs Y7. If possible, it would be better to get off the bus at the point before Chonggu, when the lake comes into sight. It is said that there are some tombs at the Kasuo Ruins on the north-western side of the lake, but during previous visits, they weren't to be found. Local information is that they are now gone, though you can check this out for yourself. If you walk for about 4 -5 hours further on, you will get to Tongkhor Gompa (Donggusi).

Tongkhor Gompa (Donggusi)
With a never-ending stream of pilgrims visiting Tongkhor, this famous monastery in the area belongs to the Gelukpa monastery. The gompa is at Sitongda in Dongu, set deep in the mountains, and on the hillside there are a number of monks' lodgings that seem to surround it. Neighboring the

gompa to the east is a Tibetan village.

From Ganzi, there is a shared-truck heading out here every day, but the schedule is erratic. The trip takes a couple of hours and costs Y10. There are no official guesthouses or hotels here, but you may be able to arrange lodging at one of the stores or villagers' homes. There is a post office in the village.

Further to the east of the monastery is Kanshenshan, a sacred place consisting of 3 sharp-peaked mountains, from which sacred water flows.

Beri Gompa (Bailisi)
Until the 17th century, the gompa belonged to the Bon religion, but it is now controlled by the Gelukpa order. To get to the monastery you have to go to Shengkang on the northern side of the river,

15km to the west of Ganzi as you head for Manigango. From here, you can get a good view of a mountain with a number of glaciers on it. Gulu Gompa is also close by in a village higher up. It is a 2- or 3-hour walk from Shengkang toward the glacier to the south.

Dargye Gompa (Dajinsi)

Fifteen kilometers further to the west of Beri Gompa, you will reach this Gelukpa monastery on the northern side of the road. This gompa was built by Gushi Khan in the 17th century. You can take shared-jeeps from Ganzi to get here.

There are hot springs around 15 minutes on foot from the monastery, heading north over the river. The water is a bit tepid but clear, and both Tibetans and Han Chinese use the spa for bathing.

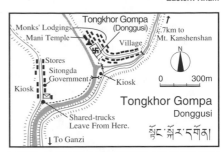

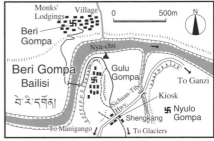

XINLONG (NYARONG)

Set deep in the valley of the Yalong Jiang River (Nyak-chu), the older religious orders, such as Bon and Nyingmapa, are still popular in this area. In the 19th century, the head of Xinlong (Nyarong), Nyarong Gonpo Namgyel, dominated all of eastern Tibet. The Guri Ruins are worth a visit. They are on a plateau on the eastern side of the Yalong Jiang River (Nyak-chu), 10km to the north of the town.

From Ganzi there are a few minibuses each day. From Kangding, there are 3 buses during each 10-day period. These buses stay overnight at either Luhuo or Ganzi and arrive at Xinlong the following day.

BAIYU (PELYUL)

On the eastern side of the Jinsha Jiang River (Dri-chu) that flows between Sichuan Province and the Tibetan Autonomous Region, this town is home to one of the largest power bases of the Nyingmapa order in the Kham region, Katok Gompa.

A bus from Kangding operates once every 2 days, and it stops overnight at Daofu (or Luhuo) and Ganzi and finally arrives at Baiyu on the third day. Although it is in a remote area, the town is larger than you might expect. The area was prosperous in the past and formed a part of the Derge (Dege) Kingdom.

To get to Baiyu, there is also a route that takes you down from Dege to the south, along the Jinsha Jiang River (Dri-chu). Although there are no buses on this route, you can catch a lift from trucks heading in this direction.

Katok Gompa

In the 8th century the first genuine monastery in Tibet, Samye Monastery, was constructed. During the ceremony that marked the start of construction, Guru Rinpoche (Padmasambhava), the founder of the Nyingmapa order, worked a miracle to produce a small temple in Kham. This miraculous temple is said to be the origin of the present-day Katok Gompa. Guru Rinpoche (Padmasambhava) foretold: 'A gompa called *Ka* will be built on a slope of a rocky *Senge* (Lion-shaped) mountain somewhere in Kham.' When the exact location of the slope was discovered at Baiyu (Pelyul) in the 12th century, as he predicted, there was even a rock on which the character *Ka* appeared. This became the site on which Katok Gompa was constructed, and the name *Katok* refers to this legend, meaning 'The Peak of *Ka*.'

The monastery housed more than a thousand

EASTERN KHAM

Manigango
Alt: 3,800m

To Yushu, Shiqu, Zhuqingsi
Islamic (Bed Y6, Noodle Y3)
Gas Station G.H.
Truck Guesthouses (Chinese Meals)
Hitchhike Point (Islamic Restaurants, Kiosks, etc.)
Wenjiao G.H. (+Chinese ℞)
To Ganzi
Shrine (+Kiosk)
20 min Walk to Laxiasi (Sakyapa)
Buses to Shiqu (Sershul) Stay Overnight Here
Nanchong (Kiosk, Chinese ℞)
Jixiang
To Dege, Chamdo
13km to Xinluhai (3hr Walk)
Yaorisi (Nyingmapa)
Wooden Bridge
Sichuan-Tibet Hwy.
N
0   300m

monks. Even after the Chinese invasion, the monastery has remained as a leading base for the order, and continual efforts have been made to rebuild the buildings. That's Khampa spirit!

Outside of Tibet, the monastery has more than a hundred branches in regions such as Mongolia, China, Sikkim, etc. There are a number of incarnated lamas at the gompa, such as Kato Kmoktsa and Katok Zhingkyong.

The gompa is about 30km to the north-east of Baiyu and this huge Nyingmapa monastery, which is also known as Katok Dorjeden Gompa.

Pelyul Gompa (Baiyusi)
This Nyingmapa monastery is located on a hill, on the northern side of the town, and it was built by the Derge King in the 17th century. Ranked along with Katok Gompa, this forms the solid base of the Nyingmapa order in the Kham region.

After fleeing to India in 1959, Penor Rinpoche re-established the monastery in Bylakuppe, southern India, and has kept the Nyingmapa traditions going there. After Dilgo Khyentse Rinpoche, the former head of Nyingmapa order, died in exile, Penor Rinpoche took over the position. Since 1982, he has often visited his home in Baiyu to oversee the reconstruction, and this has made the gompa a relatively lively place. In 1995, the new incarnation of Dilgo Khyentse Rinpoche was found.

Manigango is an important transportation hub, with the road from the Yushu area in Qinghai Province meeting the Sichuan-

Tibet Highway here. The town is home to the Nyingmapa Yazer Gompa (Yaorisi).

Buses from Kangding stay overnight at the *Bus Station Hotel*. (For a hitchhiking point, refer to the map.) The approximate cost of a lift to Dege is Y25 and to Ganzi is Y20.

XINLUHAI (YILHUN LHATSO)

It is a nearly 3-hour walk or a 15-minute drive from Manigango to the junction of Xinluhai. Walk for about 15 minutes after you cross the bridge, and you will see a muddy lake. Over the water is Que'er Shan (Mt. Chola, 6,168m) and its glaciers. The lake is regarded as a sacred place, and there are *tar-choks* fluttering on its banks.

DEGE (DERGE)

Famous for Derge Parkhang, a *sutra* printer, Dege (Derge Gonchen) is located near the Jinsha Jiang River (Dri-chu). It is a small town set in a valley, and it can be circled around on foot in less than half an hour.

In general, Ganzi men wear a red *Dashe* (Knitted Turban) on their heads, while the men of Dege wear a black one. The Kham region has always been relatively independent from the Lhasa government, and in Dege, the local rulers seized enormous power for themselves. In the 18th century, the Derge king, Tenpa Tsering, declared

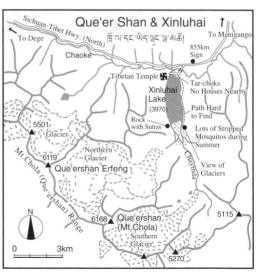

Que'er Shan & Xinluhai
Sichuan-Tibet Hwy. (North)
To Dege
To Manigango
855km Sign
Chaoke
Tibetan Temple
Tar-choks No Houses Nearby
Xinluhai Lake (3970)
Path Hard to Find
5501
Glacier
Rock with Sutras
Lots of Stripped Mosquitos during Summer
Northern Glacier
6119
Que'ershan Erfeng
View of Glaciers
Mt. Chola (Que'ershan) Range
N
6168
Que'ershan (Mt. Chola)
Southern Glacier
5115
Chayinda
5270
0   3km

EASTERN KHAM

Kham Man

that Derge Gonchen was the capital of both politics and religion in the region. Around the town, there are some trekking routes that have gained popularity recently.

Access
To Dege
There are 3 buses from Kangding during each 10-day period. These depart on days with the numbers 3, 6, and 9 in their dates, and the fare is Y114. The buses stay overnight at Luhuo and arrive at Dege the next evening.

From Dege
A bus for Kangding leaves at 07:00 on days with the numbers of 1, 5, and 8 in their dates. Tickets are available the day before it leaves. The trip to Manigango takes around 4 hours, and to get to Ganzi it takes 7-8 hours.

For the Chamdo area there are no buses available starting from the town. One from Chengdu heading for Chamdo passes through the town, but tickets are unavailable in Dege. Instead, you will have to take a shared-truck or hitchhike, and this costs Y50-80. To arrange a lift on a truck, it is a good idea to ask the guesthouse owner.

Accommodation & Restaurants
The *Dege Zhengfu Zhaodaisuo* (County Government Guesthouse) is opposite the offices of the Public Security Bureau. There are also a couple of privately-run guesthouses to the south of the bus ticket office. The cost of a bed in these is from Y6-8.

If you are on a really tight budget, the *Gucheng Luguan* (Hotel) has dirty dormitory beds for Y5.5. There are no toilets, but you will be given hot water here.

There are 5-6 Chinese restaurants around the ticket office on Hexi Jie, and these serve most of the usual fare.

Places to See
Derge Gonchen Monastery
Since it was founded in 1448, the monastery has kept strong ties with the Sakyapa order and its center at Ngor Gompa. The monastery and the private houses to the north are painted in the grayish-purple coloring of the Sakyapa. Its power and influence was built up under the protection of the Derge kings. During the Cultural Revolution, the monastery was totally leveled, but it has undergone fairly extensive reconstruction and now houses about 300 monks. The name *Gonchen* means 'Large Monastery,' but the name not only refers to the gompa but to the entire town as well.

Derge Parkhang (Dege Yinjingyuan)
Derge Parkhang is a printer of Tibetan Buddhist *sutras*, and although it used to belong to the Derge Gonchen Monastery, the institution is now a separate entity. The Tibetan Buddhist Canons that are printed here are delivered to monasteries all over Tibet, as the Parkhang now serves all the religious orders.

In the 18th century, the Derge king Tenpa

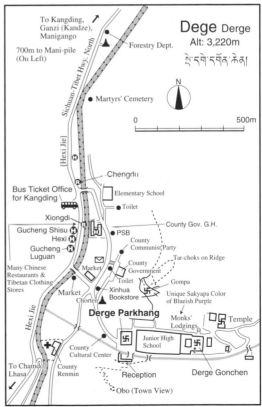

Dege Derge
Alt: 3,220m

ར་དགེ་དགོན་ཆེན།

To Kangding, Ganzi (Kandze), Manigango
700m to Mani-pile (On Left)
Forestry Dept.
Sichuan-Tibet Hwy. North
[Hexi Jie]
Martyrs' Cemetery
N
0   500m
Chengdu
Bus Ticket Office for Kangding
Elementary School
Toilet
Xiongdi
County Gov. G.H.
Gucheng Shisu
Hexi
PSB
County Communist Party
Gucheng Luguan
Many Chinese Restaurants & Tibetan Clothing Stores
Market
County Government
Tar-choks on Ridge
Toilet
Gompa
Market
Xinhua Bookstore
Unique Sakyapa Color of Blueish Purple
Chorten
Derge Parkhang
Monks' Lodgings
Temple
Hexi Jie
Junior High School
County Cultural Center
To Chamdo, Lhasa
County Renmin
Reception
Derge Gonchen
Obo (Town View)

Tsering sponsored a compilation of the Tibetan Buddhist Canons, which became known as the *Derge Version*.

Still now, craftsman chisel out woodblocks and print the *sutras* manually. The Parkhang is a 4-story building, including its attic. The 1st floor is where the printing blocks are made, and the 2nd and 3rd floors are used for storage and workshops. You can also buy paper-made *thangkas*, talismans, etc., on the 2nd floor.

To be allowed to visit the printing shop, it is necessary to obtain a permit at the Public Security Bureau, opposite the Parkhang, and these cost Y10. After leaving your bag at the entrance, you can then start your guided tour of the works in the capable hands of one of the guards.

Around the Parkhang you will always see many Tibetans making pilgrimage circuits, especially during the early morning and in the evening. It is a magnificent place, as the building is full to the rafters with the teachings of Buddha. At the stairs going up to the 2nd floor, black and red ink are given to visitors. Even the old ink and water mixtures are really appreciated, and some of the pilgrims take it home with them.

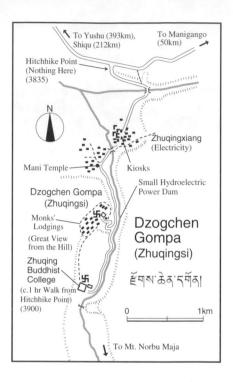

MONASTERIES AROUND DEGE

Tengchen Gompa (Dengqingsi, Dijinsi)
This is an old Bon monastery constructed between the 8th and 9th centuries.

Palpung Gompa (Babangsi)
One of the Karma Kagyupa's highest-ranking lamas, Tai Situ Rinpoche, established this monastery in 1727. The present rinpoche, who fled into exile in India, has been very active in spreading the teachings of the order both in India and Western countries. The only way to reach this area is by hitching a lift.

Dzogchen Gompa (Zhuqingsi)
Founded by Pema Rigdzin, the first Dzogchen Rinpoche, in the 17th century, Dzogchen Gompa is one of the most influential monasteries in eastern Tibet. It has not deviated from the *Dzogchen*, the most unique teachings from the Nyingmapa order.

The area is a pilgrimage place with many sacred sites that are connected with Mipam Rinpoche, Peltrul Rinpoche, and other leading religious figures. Still now, it is also a place for ascetics to learn the teachings of *Dzogchen*. Among the schools of Tibetan Buddhism, the teachings of *Dzogchen* are the most popular in the West.

You will reach the monastery after going about 2km to the south along the road connecting Manigango with Shiqu (Sershul). Be careful, as there are no signs along the bus route pointing to the path to Dzogchen Gompa and the village.

After giving a donation, you'll be able to stay at the Buddhist college, around 800m to the south of the monastery. Hot water is available, and there is a store here too. The monks here are kind to visitors, and some of them speak English.

Sometimes a shared-truck goes to Manigango from the village, and the monks can tell you the schedule. If, for some reason, there are no shared-trucks leaving on the day you want to leave, walk up to the main road and wait for a passing bus or another truck. There is a bus for Kangding from Shiqu that comes past at 11:00-12:00 on days with the numbers 1, 5, and 8 in the dates. Trucks are more likely to arrive here around 08:00, and a bus for Shiqu (Sershul) comes through around 08:20 on days with the numbers 4, 7, and 0 in the date.

Zhechen Gompa (Xieqingsi)
About 10km towards Shiqu (Sershul) from the junction of the path to Dzogchen Gompa, there is a road heading east along the Sancha He (Chusumdo) River. After taking this branch for a further 10km, Zhechen Gompa comes into view on the left-hand side.

This important Nyingmapa monastery was constructed in the 18th century and is where Dilgo Khyentse Rinpoche, the head of Nyingmapa, is from. It was destroyed during the Cultural Revolution, but recently there has been considerable reconstruction work at the site. The 7th Zhechen Rabjam Rinpoche, an incarnated lama in exile, founded a new Zhechen Gompa near Bodhnath in Nepal under the instruction of Dilgo Khyentse Rinpoche. This remains the largest Nyingmapa monastery outside of Tibet.

Shiqu

SHIQU (SERSHUL) [SERXU]

Only about 140km from Yushu (Jyekundo) in Qinghai Province, Shiqu is to be found at the upper end of the Yalong Jiang River (Nyak-chu), at the northern end of Ganzi Prefecture. The town is basically deserted, and there is nothing special to see or do there, though you might enjoy the expanse of grassland on the outskirts of the town. Tradition has it that Mongolian nomads from Amdo settled here about 500 years ago, and before the Peoples' Liberation Army took over the area, Shiqu was under the control of the Derge kings.

Access
To Shiqu
*Kangding—There are buses on days with the numbers 2, 5, and 8 in the date. The trip takes 3 days and costs Y114. Many buses stay overnight at Daofu and Manigango.
*Xiewu (Zhiwu), Qinghai Province—There is a daily shared-truck, which costs Y20.

From Shiqu
*Kangding—The buses operate on days with the numbers 1, 5, and 8 in the date. The bus stops at Ganzi around 18:00 the same day and arrives at Kangding within 2 days.
*Yushu (Jyekundo)—You will need to arrange passage on a shared-truck or a cargo truck, since there are no buses on this route. There is an occasional minibus service costing about Y50, but this shouldn't be relied upon. If you do decide to hang out for one of these, try to catch one around 07:00. Once you get to Xiewu, you should have no problems continuing on from there.

Accommodation & Restaurants
The *Shiqu Xianzhengfu Zhaodaisuo* (County Government Guesthouse) is on Dejidong Jie, and this is the best guesthouse in the town. However, the facilities leave something to be desired, and

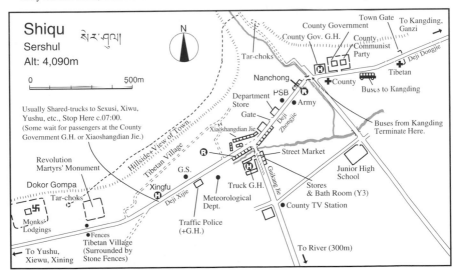

Shiqu
ཤི་ར་ཤུལ།
Sershul
Alt: 4,090m

0 _____ 500m

Usually Shared-trucks to Sexusi, Xiwu, Yushu, etc., Stop Here c.07:00.
(Some wait for passengers at the County Government G.H. or Xiaoshangdian Jie.)

N

Revolution Martyrs' Monument
Dokor Gompa
Tar-choks
Monks' Lodgings
Fences
Tibetan Village (Surrounded by Stone Fences)
To Yushu, Xiewu, Xining

Hillside View of Town
Tibetan Village
G.S.
Xingfu
Deji Xijie
Traffic Police (+G.H.)

Tar-choks
Nanchong
Department Store
PSB
Gate
Xiaoshangdian Jie
Deji Zhongjie
Meteorological Dept.
Truck G.H.
Street Market
Guihang Jie
Stores & Bath Room (Y3)
County TV Station
Junior High School

County Government
County Gov. G.H.
Army
County
County Communist Party
County
Tibetan
Buses to Kangding
Buses from Kangding Terminate Here.

Town Gate
To Kangding, Ganzi
Deji Dongjie

To River (300m)

EASTERN KHAM

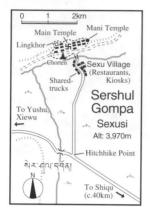

```
0    1    2km
```

Main Temple Mani Temple
Lingkhor
        Chorten Sexu Village
                 (Restaurants,
Shared-   Kiosks)
trucks

**Sershul
Gompa**
To Yushu,   Sexusi
Xiewu
←   Alt: 3,970m

                  Hitchhike Point

সེར་ཁུལ་དགོན།

N   To Shiqu
               (c.40km) ↘

there are no showers. A single room with an electric
stove and a television costs Y20, and the dormitory
beds go for Y7-14.

There is basic accommodation for truck drivers,
with beds costing Y10 for foreigners, but there are
no showers available here either.

The *Xingfu Ludian* (Hotel) is another cheap option
with beds costing Y10.

Although there are some Muslim restaurants
in the town, these are mainly dirty. Don't expect
too much from an eating experience here.

Places to See
Sershul Gompa (Sexusi)

In this area where the Nyingmapa and Karma
Kagyupa are the dominant religious orders, this
important monastery is proud to act as the base for
the Dalai Lama's Gelukpa order in the region, even
though it is a relatively new gompa, established
only about 180 years ago.

It is said to have housed more than 3,000 monks
prior to 1959, when the PLA destroyed it, and there
are now only about 900 monks living here.

At Shiqu, there is a shared-truck leaving for the
monastery around 07:00 every day, and the trip
takes an hour or so. The truck then returns to the
town at 09:00-10:00 the same morning. About an
hour on foot from the monastery is the junction
with the road to the Yushu (Jyekundo) area. The
morning is the best time to try to hitch a lift on this
route, as the traffic thins out substantially in the
afternoon.

Near the monastery there is a village consisting
of about 20 houses, and you should be able to buy
basic food here, such as noodles and vegetables.
There are also several other stores selling household
items. Unfortunately, there is no accommodation
here, but you may be able to stay at the monastery
itself if you ask politely.

YAJIANG (NYAKCHUKA)

This is a small town 150km to the west of
Kangding, which seems to hug the slope on the
western side of the Yalong Jiang River (Nyak-chu).
There are few Tibetan people in the town, and it is
mainly populated by Han Chinese. There is nothing
special to see in the town, and most travelers simply
pass through.

There is a bus from Kangding every day, and
the trip takes 6 hours. The bus goes through 2 high
mountain passes — one at 4,250m and the other at
4,280m. There are also buses for Litang, Batang,
Xiangcheng, and Xincheng that come through
Yajiang. The buses heading for Batang often stay
overnight here, and catering to those passengers,
there are beds at the bus station for Y6.

LITANG (LITHANG)

This small town can be found in a depression in
the grasslands, 137km further to the west of
Yajiang. Tibetan houses are spread out on the
northern side of the new town, and Lithang Gompa
is on a hill at the northern end. This area may be
the real Great Grasslands, and it is a good place to
relax for a while. To the south-west, you will see
Maoge Shan Mountain (5,064m) covered with
snow throughout the year.

Once Litang was said to be the world's second
highest town at 4,700m. However, this must have
been a mistake, as a benchmark on a hill to the
north-west indicates an elevation of only
3,993.27m.

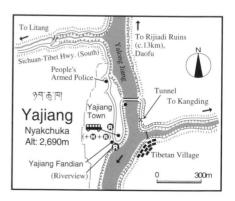

To Litang
                              To Rijiadi Ruins
                              (c.13km),
Sichuan-Tibet Hwy. (South)   Daofu   N

People's
Armed Police

ཉག་ཆུ་ཁ།   Tunnel
                              To Kangding
                   Yajiang
Yajiang   Town
Nyakchuka
Alt: 2,690m
                              Tibetan Village

Yajiang Fandian
(Riverview)   0   300m

In the town there are quite a number of Tibetans and only a few Han Chinese. The Litang summer horse racing festival is famous throughout the region, and it is held between July and August every year.

Among the Khampas with their reputation for bravery, those from Litang are definitely the vanguard. Gompo Tashi, the head of Chushi Gangdruk, the last guerilla group to stand up against the Chinese armed forces, was a member of the Andrugtsang family from Litang. The name *Chushi Gangdruk* means 'Four Rivers and Six Mountain Ranges,' another name for the Kham and Amdo regions.

Access
To Litang
From Kangding, there is a daily bus, and the trip takes 13-14 hours. When there are a lot of passengers, a couple of buses may leave for Litang at the same time. There are 3 high passes on the way, and the highest is the final one (4,405m) you go through after leaving Yajiang. After the pass, the scenery changes from woodland to grassland, and the bus continues along a ridge at around 4,000m until finally descending into the Litang basin. On arrival in the town, the bus passes the bus station and instead drops off passengers in front of the Xian Zhaodaisuo (County Guesthouse).

From Litang
*Kangding—The bus leaves from in front of the Xian Zhaodaisuo (County Guesthouse) at 06:00 and stops at the bus station to pick up other passengers. Tickets are available at both the bus station and the guesthouse.
*Batang Area—There is a bus available every other day. After staying overnight at Yajiang, the bus from Kangding runs along the road in front of the bus station at 12:00-13:00 and continues on to Batang.
*Daocheng and Xiang-cheng Areas—They often stay overnight at Litang. Check at the bus station at night if you're going to these areas.

Accommodation & Restaurants
The *Litang County Guesthouse* (Gaocheng Binguan) has beds in 3-person rooms costing Y60 for foreigners. It is in the center of the town, about 15 minutes on foot from the bus station. The bus for Kangding leaves from this hotel, and there are also tickets available here. The rooms are relatively clean, and electric heaters are available, but there are no showers.

The *Xiashan Fandian* (Hotel) has beds for Y7.

The *Litang Bus Station Hotel* is, as the name suggests, located at the bus station. The cost of beds range from Y7-12, and this is another hotel without showers.

There are a number of restaurants around the bus station and the market, including a few Tibetan ones.

Places to See
Lithang Gompa (Litangsi)
Also called *Ganden Thubchen Choekhorling*, though its formal name is even longer, this monastery belongs to the Gelukpa order. Following a request made by a powerful family from Lijiang in Yunnan Province, the 3rd Dalai Lama commissioned the building of the monastery in the 16th century. Later, during the rule of the 5th Dalai Lama, the site was expanded, and it became famous for the *Lithang Version* of the Tibetan Buddhist

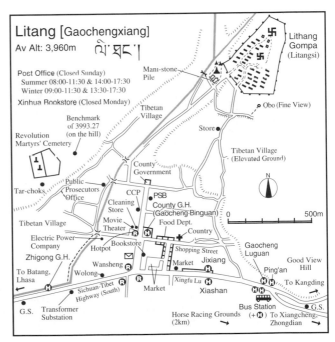

Litang [Gaochengxiang]
Av Alt: 3,960m

Lithang Gompa (Litangsi)

Post Office (Closed Sunday)
Summer 08:00-11:30 & 14:00-17:30
Winter 09:00-11:30 & 13:30-17:30

Xinhua Bookstore (Closed Monday)

Benchmark of 3993.27 (on the hill)

Revolution Martyrs' Cemetery

Mani-stone Pile

Tibetan Village

Obo (Fine View)

Store

Tibetan Village (Elevated Ground)

County Government

Tar-choks

Public Prosecutors' Office

CCP

PSB

Cleaning Store

County G.H. (Gaocheng Binguan)

Tibetan Village

Movie Theater

Food Dept.

Country

Electric Power Company

Bookstore

Hotpot

Gaocheng Luguan

Zhigong G.H.

Wansheng

Shopping Street

Jixiang

Good View Hill

To Batang, Lhasa

Wolong

Market

Ping'an

Sichuan-Tibet Highway (South)

Market

Xingfu Lu

Xiashan

To Kangding

G.S. Transformer Substation

Bus Station

Horse Racing Grounds (2km)

G.S.

(+⊕) To Xiangcheng, Zhongdian

500m

Canon. To add to this prestige, both the 7th and the 10th Dalai Lamas were from Litang. The monastery used to house more than 3,700 monks.

BATANG (BATHANG)

Two hundred kilometers to the west of Litang, this town is around 10km up a tributary of the Jinsha Jiang River (Dri-chu). Its western neighbor is Ma'erkang (Barkam) in the TAR, and Batang is home to many Hui people.

A bus from Kangding stops overnight at Yajiang and then arrives at Batang the following day. From here, there are also buses for Ma'erkang (Barkam) in the TAR across the Jinsha Jiang River (Dri-chu). There is accommodation available at the bus station, and in the area around it there are a few restaurants.

YUNNAN TO LITANG (LITHANG)

The route from Zhongdian (Gyalthang) in Yunnan Province up to Litang, via Xiangcheng (Chaktreng), has become popular in recent years. Between Zhongdian and Xiangcheng there is a bus every 1-2 days, and this arrives at Litang the same day. The bus route climbs into the mountains until it reaches a pass at over 4,000m, and the scenery is great. There seem to be no inspections along the way.

XIANGCHENG (CHAKTRENG)

Located on the route connecting Litang with Yunnan Province, this is a predominantly Tibetan town with a scattering of Han Chinese. There is a bus from Kangding every other day, and the trip takes 2 days, with the bus frequently stopping overnight at Litang. The fare is Y54 in either direction, and on the return journey the bus once again makes a stopover in Litang. A bus from Xiangcheng to Zhongdian is operated once every 1-2 days, and the trip takes 10-11 hours and costs Y48.5.

At the *Xiaxia Luguan* (Hotel) by the bus station, you can get a bed in a 4-person room for Y10.

DAOCHENG (DABPA)

The area around Daocheng is plateau country, with elevations varying between 4,000-5,000m, and most of the residents here are Tibetans.

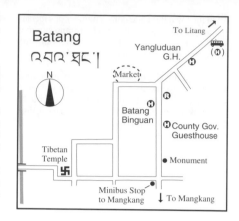

From Kangding, there are usually 3 direct buses during a 10-day period, and the trip takes a day and a half. These buses also frequently stay overnight at Litang. There is accommodation at the bus station.

DERONG

The smallest county in Ganzi Prefecture, Derong is to the south of Xiangcheng, and both face on to Dechen in Yunnan Province. From Zhongdian, there is a bus that leaves on even numbered days, and it takes 5-6 hours. There are no buses between Xiangcheng and Derong.

MULI TIBETAN AUTONOMOUS COUNTY, SICHUAN PROVINCE

Muli is a Tibetan autonomous county that makes up part of the Liangshan Yi Autonomous Prefecture in the south-west of Sichuan Province. The county is also home to numbers of Naxi, Miao, Mongolian, and other minority peoples.

It takes between 11-12 hours to reach the county capital, Qiaowa, from Xichang via the town of Yanyuan. The bus goes over 3 high passes at 2,560m, 3,130m, and 3,180m respectively, and in the last one there is a chorten, bringing home to you that you are in a Tibetan area. The hardest part of the journey comes after the pass when the bus continues on a hair-raising stretch of road gouged out of a cliff, 1,200m above a fast-flowing river below you. Three hours later, you will catch sight of the town of Muli spreading out over a slope in the mountains.

Tibetan House, Kham

It is likely to be more of a bustling town than you might have expected, and although there are many Tibetans, most of them do not wear their traditional clothing, and there is no Tibetan monastery here either. However, you may meet Yi and Miao people wearing their distinctive dress.

In the area surrounding the town there are few Tibetan villages. So to get a good look at some Tibetan villages and their monasteries, you will have to take a bus to Wachang and Chabulang. This service only operates once every 5 days. (Mulidasi is near Wachang.)

Access

At the bus station in Xichang there are buses leaving at 07:40, 08:00, and 08:30 daily for the 253km trip via Yanyuan. A seat on one of the larger buses costs Y35, and the journey takes 12-13 hours. Minibuses charge Y40 and take about 11 hours on the same route.

Buses from Muli

The larger buses leave from the bus station in Muli.
*Xichang (via Yanyuan)—There are 3 buses all leaving at 05:30.
*Wachang (Yiqu)—There is a bus every 5 days, and this leaves at 07:00. The 120km trip takes 6 hours and costs Y20.
*Chabulang (Sanqu, via Wachang)—This route also has only 1 bus every 5 days, and the 180km trip costs Y25. The bus stays overnight at Chabulang and returns the next day.

Accommodation & Restaurants

The *Xianzhengfu Zhaodaisuo* (County Government Guesthouse) has double rooms going for between Y25 and Y30. Guests have access to shared toilets and showers.
The *Muli Bus Station Hotel* is at the bus station, and a single room here costs Y13, while a dormitory bed is Y6. The staff at the hotel will wake you up if you need to catch an early bus.

There are some Chinese restaurants at the bus station and in the center of town. Food prices vary from Y4 -8 a dish, and a bottle of beer costs Y3.

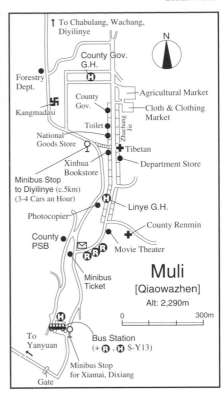

Wachang

Made up of 30-40 houses, this village is 120km to the north-west of Muli, and there is also a post office and a school here. For accommodation, you only have the *Gucheng Ludian* (Hotel), and its dormitory beds cost Y5. There are 2 restaurants that serve basic Chinese fare. Mulidasi is a Gelukpa monastery that is about 4km to the north-east of the village, and the walk should take you around an hour.

Mulidasi

Tibet Photos

Shintaro Matsui

Born in Tokyo, 1964. Since his first trip
to India during his school days, he has
repeatedly visited Nepal, Pakistan,
China and Tibet with his cameras.

Friday, September 12

I met a group of farmers who were taking a
rest on the roadside without removing the
bundles of barley strapped to their backs. With
the blue sky and the sunshine behind them,
the scene was too perfect for me to leave my
camera in its bag. After several shots they
asked me, 'Aren't you hungry? Why don't you
come to our village for some food?' I accepted
their kind offer.

With their help I pushed my bicycle along
the stony road to their village. On arriving, a
number of villagers came over, one after
another. Some women brought tsampa, butter
tea, and some other food and placed it in front
of me. Surrounded by them, I finished all the
food and found contentment in this village
near Dzogang, Chamdo Prefecture.

Extract from Travel Diary

DECHEN

Diqing Tibetan Autonomous Prefecture
Yunnan Province

བདེ་ཆེན།

From either Kunming or Dali in Yunnan Province you can get to the TAR by taking the Yunnan-Tibet Highway. This goes up along the valleys carved out by the Jinsha Jiang River (Dri-chu, the upper reaches of the Yangtze River) and the Lancang Jiang (Zaqu or Dza-chu, the upper reaches of the Mekong River). You then head for Lhasa after merging with the Sichuan-Tibet Highway South, which is one of the more appealing routes for entering the Tibetan region, even though there is no other option to hitching lifts on trucks in some sections.

The route is as follows:
Kunming - Dali - (Lijiang) - Zhongdian - Deqin - (TAR) - Yanjing - Markham (Mangkang)

There should be no problem with traveling in Yunnan Province, as the province is now completely open to foreigners. However, further on many travelers meet up with PSB officers at either Yanjing or Markham (Mangkang), just after entering the TAR.

Depending on how lucky you are with hitching lifts, and if everything goes well, it will take around 2 weeks to complete the trip from Kunming to Lhasa, as the road is in poor condition.

Yunnan Province is a melting pot of races, and Tibetans may not come to mind when thinking about the region. However, the northern part of the province, such as Diqing Tibetan Autonomous Prefecture (Dechen), has been under the influence of Tibet throughout its history. Tibetan Buddhism has also taken root among a number of ethnic groups other than Tibetans in the area.

Another connection between the 2 areas is the Yunnan-Tibet route, playing an important role in supplying Central Tibet with the tea that is a necessity for Tibetan life.

This chapter focuses on access information for Kunming, Dali, and Lijiang.

KUNMING

The provincial capital of Yunnan Province, Kunming is an international city connected with Hong Kong, Bangkok, Vientiane (Laos), and Yangon (Myanmar) by air. The city has undergone a lot of development recently and is now a large city of over a million people. Unlike other places in Yunnan, you will have to pay big city prices in

Kunming, but they are still fairly reasonable, compared to other large cities in China.

With an altitude of around 2,000m, Kunming avoids the heat of the lowland plains and is a city where tourists can stay in a pleasant climate with most of the creature comforts. One problem is that, due to the popularity of the city and the surrounding area, reasonable accommodation is difficult to secure. One way to avoid this is to arrive as early as possible and check in to a hotel prior to going off and exploring the city.

Access
By Air
There are daily domestic flights from Beijing, Shanghai, Guangzhou, Guilin, Xi'an, Chengdu, and other large centers. For international air routes, there are services from Hong Kong, Bangkok,

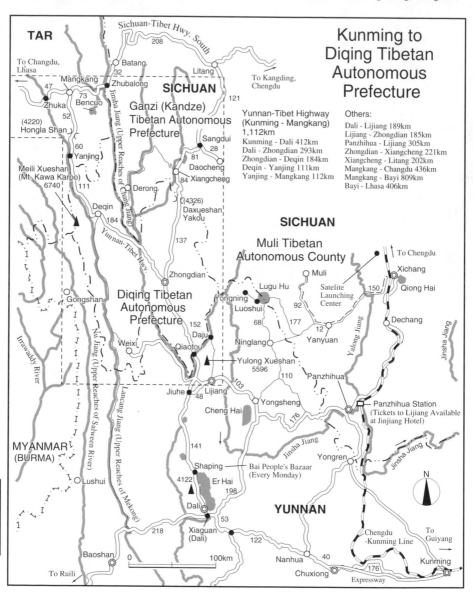

Kunming to Diqing Tibetan Autonomous Prefecture

Yunnan-Tibet Highway (Kunming - Mangkang) 1,112km
Kunming - Dali 412km
Dali - Zhongdian 293km
Zhongdian - Deqin 184km
Deqin - Yanjing 111km
Yanjing - Mangkang 112km

Others:
Dali - Lijiang 189km
Lijiang - Zhongdian 185km
Panzhihua - Lijiang 305km
Zhongdian - Xiangcheng 221km
Xiangcheng - Litang 202km
Mangkang - Changdu 436km
Mangkang - Bayi 809km
Bayi - Lhasa 406km

Chiang Mai, Vientiane, Yangon, and Singapore.

The airport is around 6km to the south of the city center, and from the airport you can take a limousine bus that connects the arrival terminal with the downtown area, dropping you off at the CAAC office. The bus fare is Y2, or for Y20 you can take a metered taxi into the center of the city.

From Kunming

You can make reservations at the CAAC office on Tuodong Lu, open 08:30-19:30. It is advisable to book your seats as early as possible, as flights are usually busy. At the junction in front of the Jinlong Fandian (Golden Dragon Hotel), there is a ticket office of China Southwest Airlines (SZ). Flight reservations can also be made with travel agents for a Y50 commission charge. Limousine buses for the airport leave from the CAAC office, and the airport tax is Y60 for a foreign passenger.

Major Domestic Flights (Daily.)

China Southwest Airlines (SZ), China Northwest Airlines (WH), China Northern Airlines (CJ), China Southern Airlines (CZ), Air China (CA), China Yunnan Airlines (3Q), China Eastern Airlines (MU), Xinjiang Airways (XO), Sichuan Airlines (3U), and Shanghai Airlines (FM).

*Beijing—3-5 flights a week
(CA, SZ, CY, CJ) Costs: Y1,970. (3 hrs)
*Shanghai—3-5 flights a week
(MU, FM, 3Q,) Costs: Y1,800. (3 hrs)
*Guangzhou—5 flights a week
(CS, 3Q) Costs: Y1,280. (2 hrs)
*Guilin—2-3 flights a week
(CS, 3Q, SZ) Costs: Y880. (1 hr 30 mins)
*Chengdu—5-6 flights a week
(WH, SZ, 3Q, MU, XO, 3U) Costs: Y720. (1 hr)
*Dali—2-3 flights a week
(3Q) Costs: Y340. (30 mins)
*Lijiang—1-2 flights a week
(3Q) Costs: Y420. (50 mins)

There are also flights to and from Xi'an, Nanning, Guiyang, Chongqing, Changsha, Shenzhen, and Wuhan.

International Flights

*Hong Kong—1-2 flights daily (CZ) (2 hrs)
*Bangkok—1-2 flights daily
(3Q, Thai Airways, Angel) (1 hr)
*Chiang Mai—Tue, Thu, and Sun
(Thai Airways) (35 mins)
*Vientiane—Thu (3Q) (1 hr 20 mins),
Sun (Lao Aviation) (1 hr)
*Yangon—Sat (Myanmar Airways) (1 hr)
*Singapore—Tue, Thu, Fri, and Sun
(Silk Air, 3Q) (3 hrs 30 mins)

By Rail

The ticket office at Kunming Station is open 08:30-12:00 and again at 14:00-17:00. Tickets are available 3 days prior to departure, and the ones sold on the day go on sale around 2 hours before the train leaves. You can also get tickets at travel agents.

From Kunming

No. 62 Special Express
Kunming 21:40-Beijing West 21:32 (2 nights)
No. 80 Special Express
Kunming 23:00-Shanghai 20:50 (2 nights)
No. 363 & 366 Express
Kunming 12:30-Guangzhou 08:40 (2 nights)
No. 208 Special Express
Kunming 13:28-Chengdu 10:50 (1 night)
No. 166 Special Express
Kunming 17:05-Xi'an 10:26 (2 nights)

To Kunming

No. 61 Special Express
Beijing West 10:53-Kunming 11:28 (2 nights)
No. 79 Special Express
Shanghai 10:10-Kunming 09:30 (2 nights)
No. 365 & 364 Express
Guangzhou 11:46-Kunming 08:33 (2 nights)
No. 207 Special Express
Chengdu 11:08-Kunming 08:21(1 night)
No. 165 Special Express
Xi'an 22:18-Kunming 13:18 (2 nights)

By Bus
Sleeping Berth Buses from Guangzhou

There are direct services from Guangzhou Provincial Bus Station to Kunming. The trip via Nanning takes 2 nights (about 44 hours) and finishes at the Sanye Fandian (Three Leaves Hotel) in Kunming. You can also stop over in Nanning and connect with a later bus for Kunming. This service is also available from Nanning to Kunming, and the buses are comfortable and not too crowded.

Major Buses from Kunming

In Kunming there are 6 bus stations, both large and small. Near the train station is the largest, the Kunming Bus Station, handling a large number of the arrivals and departures to and from the city. The buses with sleeping berths heading for Xiaguan, Jinghong, Ruili, etc. stop in front of the station or around the Sanye Fandian (Three Leaves Hotel). If there is an empty seat on one of these, you may get a very reasonable price by negotiating with the driver.
(For buses to Dali, see the Dali section.)

Accommodation

The *Kunhu Fandian* (Hotel) is popular with

backpackers and has beds in 4-person rooms costing Y25. A single room with a common toilet and shower is Y60, and a double room with attached bathroom starts from Y90. The receptionist speaks English, and there is a travel agency here. There is a handful of restaurants for tourists nearby. The hotel is at 44 Beijing Lu, about 15 minutes on foot to the north of Kunming Station.

The *Chahua Binguan* (Camellia Hotel) is a clean place with dormitory beds for Y30 and double rooms for Y140. Although it is not easily accessible, the hotel is still popular among backpackers. The building is also home to the consulates of Laos and Myanmar, convenient for those wanting visas to continue on to these countries.

Mid and Top-range hotels

The *Jinlong Fandian* (Golden Dragon Hotel) has a supermarket on the 1st floor.

The *Jinhua Dajiudian* (Hotel) is home to the Thai embassy, and visas are issued here.

The *Sanye Fandian* (Three Leaves Hotel) has double rooms for Y220, and there are travel agencies and airline ticket offices here. The hotel also works as a bus station for the sleeping buses for Guangzhou and Nanning. The department store next to the Holiday Inn has a wide variety of Western goods.

Restaurants

Around the Kunhu Fandian (Hotel) there are a number of restaurants for tourists.

The *Happy Restaurant* is popular among Westerners, as it has English menus. In the area there are a couple of the similar style restaurants, and at these places you can get both Chinese and Western dishes, with toast, omelets, and cake available.

The *Haha Canguan* (Wei's Place) is to the north of the Jinlong Fandian (Golden Dragon Hotel) and serves mainly Chinese and Western dishes.

Visa Extensions
These are available from the Foreign Affairs branch of the PSB at 93, Beijing Lu. You can get a single month extension as a rule, and this costs Y120.

Changing Money
Money changing is available at some *Bank of China* branches in town. Office hours are 09:00-11:45 and 14:30-17:00, but they are closed on Saturday and Sunday.

Post & Telecommunications
There is an international post office on Beijing Lu, opposite the Railway Hospital. Envelopes and packing boxes are available here.

DALI (DALI GUCHENG)

Famous for its marble production and the noted Santasi (Three Pagodas), Dali is very popular among backpackers for relaxing after a hard trip through the rest of China. There are a lot of Western-style restaurants, and many travelers stay for long periods here. There are quite a number of things to see in and around the town, including Nanchenglou, Santasi (Three Pagodas), Zhonghesi, and Erhai Lake.

Santasi

Access
To Dali
*Kunming—There are buses with sleeping berths operating on this route. Although several of these buses leave the Kunming Bus Station or from the square outside the train station at 19:00-20:00, most of them terminate at Xiaguan, the prefectural capital, 14km to the south of Dali. There are only a couple of buses going all the way to Dali. You may be able to negotiate a hefty discount for the bus to Xiaguan if you talk directly with the driver, as there is fierce competition on this route. There are some daytime buses leaving between 07:00-10:00, and

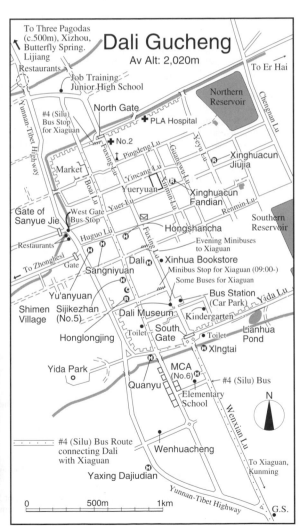

Dali Gucheng
Av Alt: 2,020m

To Three Pagodas (c.500m), Xizhou, Butterfly Spring. Lijiang
Restaurants
To Er Hai
Job Training Junior High School
Northern Reservoir
Chenghan Lu
#4 (Silu) Bus Stop for Xiaguan
North Gate
PLA Hospital
Yunnan-Tibet Highway
No.2
Pingdeng Lu
Guanying Lu
Yeyu Lu
Xinghuacun Jiujia
Market
Boai Lu
Fuxing Lu
Yincang Lu
Yueryuan
Yuer-Lu
Xinghuacun Fandian
Renmin Lu
Gate of Sanyue Jie
West Gate Bus-Stop
Huguo Lu
Hongshancha
Southern Reservoir
Restaurants
Evening Minibuses to Xiaguan
To Zhonghesi
Gate
Sangniyuan
Dali
Xinhua Bookstore
Minibus Stop for Xiaguan (09:00-)
Some Buses for Xiaguan
Yu'anyuan
Bus Station (Car Park)
Yida Lu
Shimen Village
Sijikezhan (No.5)
Dali Museum
Kindergarten
Honglongjing
South Gate
Toilet
Toilet
Lianhua Pond
Xingtai
Yida Park
MCA (No.6)
#4 (Silu) Bus
Quanyu
Elementary School
N
Wenxian Lu
#4 (Silu) Bus Route connecting Dali with Xiaguan
Wenhuacheng
To Xiaguan, Kunming
Yaxing Dajiudian
Yunnan-Tibet Highway
G.S.
0   500m   1km

267

a normal-sized bus costs Y30-40. Minibuses charge Y50, and a non-stop minibus to Dali is Y70 and takes 9-10 hours.

*Xiaguan—It takes around 40 minutes by a #4 (Silu) local bus. You can catch this bus every 5 minutes from 06:40-20:30, and the fare is Y1.2. Stop off at Nanmen (South Gate) for the popular MCA Guesthouse or at Huguolu-kou for the Hongshancha Binguan (Hotel). There are also minibuses leaving from near the Xiaguan Bus Station, and the cost of these is Y1.5.

*Lijiang, Zhongdian, etc.—For those coming from these towns, it would be better to stop off at Dali Ximen (West Gate).

There is also an airport about 15km to the east of Xiaguan and 30km from Dali. There are 1-2 flights a day that are operated from Kunming, and the fare is Y340. There is a newly constructed rail link to Xiaguan with Special Express trains No. 212 and No. 213 operating on this route.

From Dali
It is common for passengers to arrange their tickets for buses to Kunming, Lijiang, and other long-distance destinations at a travel agency. There are 6-7 companies around the Hongshancha Binguan.

*Lijiang—Minibuses leave Dali at 07:00, 07:20, 11:20, and 14:00, and the fare is about Y25. Also, a full-sized one starts from Xiaguan at 10:00 or 11:00, and the 6-hour trip costs Y20. You can make a reservation on the same day of departure.

*Zhongdian & Surrounding Area—Catch a bus coming from Xiaguan at the West gate of Dali around 07:30 each morning. You can make reservations at travel agencies in the town.

Accommodation
The *Hongshancha Binguan* (No. 2 Guesthouse) has dormitory beds starting at Y10 and up, singles are Y30, and double rooms start from Y30. If you stay here for more than a week, you can get a discount. Hot showers are available from 18:00-23:00. There is a rental bicycle service, and the guesthouse will look after your bags for Y1 a day.

The *Sangniyuan* (Sunny Garden Hotel) has a courtyard and a restaurant, but the rooms are rather dark. Dormitory beds are Y10, singles cost Y30, and a double room is Y40. The laundry is free of charge.

The *Yu'anyuan* (No. 4 Guesthouse) is very similar to the Sangniyuan with its courtyard, restaurant, and dark rooms, but this one is quite popular with Western travelers. Dormitory beds are Y15, singles cost Y30, and a double is Y50. Hot showers are available at any time of the day.

The *Sijikezhan* (No. 5 Guesthouse, Old Dali Inn)

is run by a Taiwanese guy, and although the guesthouse has a good atmosphere, you may get disturbed by your neighbors, as it is a wooden building with thin walls. Nonetheless, it remains popular among Western travelers. Dormitory beds are Y10, single rooms are Y30, and the double rooms are a little expensive at Y100. Hot showers are available from 08:00-13:00 and 15:00-23:00.

The *MCA Guesthouse* (No. 6 Guesthouse, Mekong Culture & Art) has dormitory beds starting at Y10 and single rooms for Y50. Double rooms also start from Y50. There is a swimming pool, museum, and restaurant at the guesthouse. You can catch up on what's been happening in the outside world, as they show BBC programs here. The guesthouse is quiet and relaxing, and it is understandably popular among travelers, even though it is a bit far from Huguo Lu, the center of the town.

The *Dali Binguan* (No. 1 Guesthouse) charges Y30 for a dormitory bed, Y100 for single rooms, and from Y110 for double rooms. The guesthouse is popular with tour groups.

The *Jinhua Dajiudian* (Hotel) has dormitory beds for Y20, and other rooms cost from Y210. This is another one that is popular with group tours.

Restaurants
Around Hongshancha Binguan there are over a dozen restaurants catering to foreign tourists.

The *Café de Jack* (Yinghuayuan) serves mainly Western food and shows Western videos too. The chocolate cake ice cream is good here, costing Y5.5, and the other goodies on the menu are pizzas and cookies.

The *Tibetan Café* is open 07:00-24:00 and has Western and Chinese food as well as Tibetan dishes. The prices are the most reasonable around, and the servings are substantial. Their soups, banana shakes, and cheesecakes are well recommended.

The restaurant at the *MCA Guesthouse* shows BBC programs while you dine in its fancy interior. They serve Western, Chinese, and Japanese food ranging from Y8-10.

The *Taibailou* also serves Western, Chinese, and Japanese food, and it will stay open as late as 01:00 if there are customers still eating.

The *Kikuya* charges from Y5-10 per plate for its Japanese food. There are also Western and Chinese dishes served here.

The *Happy Café* also has a good selection of different food.

LIJIANG (JANG SADAM)

At the center of Lijiang Naxi Autonomous County, this town is famous for the many Naxi who have their own unique written language, *Dongba*, a complex collection of over 2,000 of the pictographs that have recently been translated. At 2,400m, this region is cool even in summer, and the land continues to rise to the north of the town until it reaches Yulong Xueshan (Jade Dragon Snow Mountain) standing at 5,596m. The mountain can be seen clearly from the town, weather permitting.

In Tibet this place is known as Jang Sadam, and the ancient kingdom of Naxi (called *Jang* in Tibetan) that once dominated the area came under the control of Tibet in the 7th century. During the Yuan Dynasty in the 13th century the center was moved from Baisha to Lijiang, and it was during this period that the Karma Kagyupa and Nyingmapa schools of Tibetan Buddhism spread across the area.

Access

To Lijiang

*Kunming—There are sleeping berth buses leaving for Lijiang at 13:00 and 17:00 every day. The trip takes 18-19 hours.

*Dali—There are buses setting off on this 6-hour trip at around 07:00, 10:00, and 14:00. Booking the tickets through a travel agency costs Y22-25 for a minibus and Y20 for a normal-sized bus. These are usually available up to 20 minutes before departure.

*Panzhihua (Jinjiang, Sichuan Province)—A couple of buses leave daily for Lijiang, and the trip takes 9 hours.

Though Lijiang has a number of bus stations, you will probably arrive at the main Lijiang Passenger Transport Service Central Station in the southern end of town. Right outside is a stop for minibuses heading for the town center. Take a #1 (Yilu) local bus for the Lijiang Binguan (Hotel) or a #3 (Sanlu) local bus for the Guluwan Binguan (Hotel) and the Yuquan Binguan (Hotel). Both of these cost Y0.6.

From Lijiang

Buses at the Lijiang Passenger Transport Service Central Station

*Kunming—The night bus leaves at 14:00, and the bus with sleeping berths leaves at 17:15 for this 603km journey.

*Xiaguan (via Dali)—There are 8 buses a day from 06:45-14:10, and the trip is 203km.

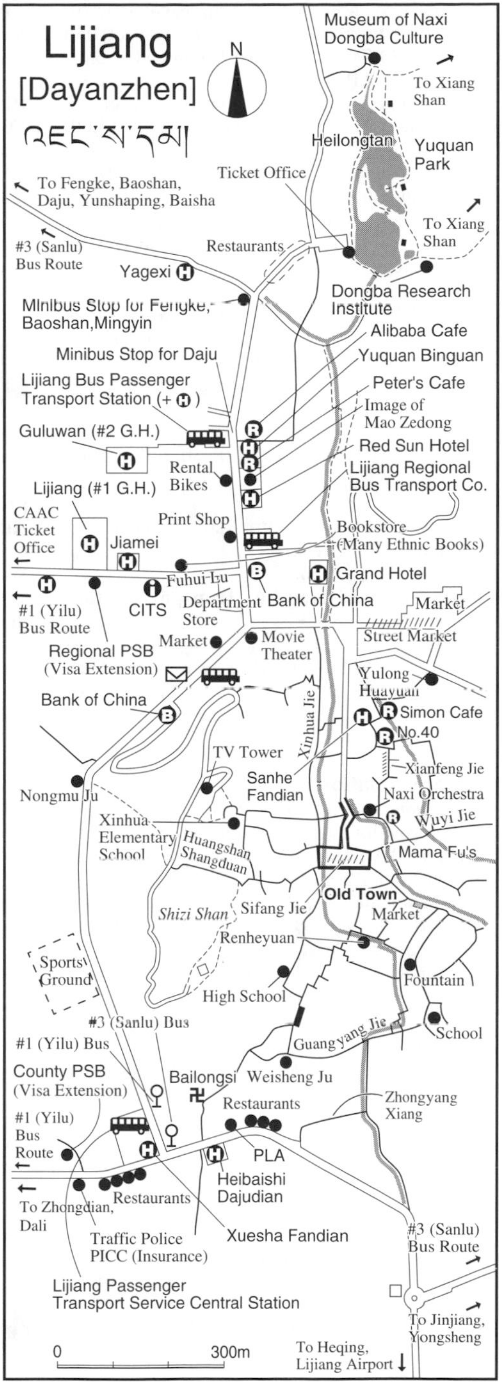

Lijiang
[Dayanzhen]
འཇང་ས་དམ།
N
Museum of Naxi Dongba Culture
To Xiang Shan
Heilongtan
Yuquan Park
Ticket Office
To Fengke, Baoshan, Daju, Yunshaping, Baisha
To Xiang Shan
#3 (Sanlu) Bus Route
Restaurants
Yagexi
Dongba Research Institute
Minibus Stop for Fengke, Baoshan, Mingyin
Alibaba Cafe
Minibus Stop for Daju
Yuquan Binguan
Lijiang Bus Passenger Transport Station (+ H)
Peter's Cafe
Image of Mao Zedong
Guluwan (#2 G.H.)
Red Sun Hotel
Rental Bikes
Lijiang Regional Bus Transport Co.
Lijiang (#1 G.H.)
CAAC Ticket Office
Print Shop
Bookstore (Many Ethnic Books)
Jiamei
Grand Hotel
Fuhui Lu
#1 (Yilu) Bus Route
CITS
Department Store
Bank of China
Market
Street Market
Market
Movie Theater
Regional PSB (Visa Extension)
Yulong Huayuan
Bank of China
Xinhua Jie
Simon Cafe
No.40
TV Tower
Sanhe Fandian
Xianfeng Jie
Nongmu Ju
Naxi Orchestra
Wuyi Jie
Xinhua Elementary School
Huangshan Shangduan
Mama Fu's
Old Town
Shizi Shan
Sifang Jie
Market
Renheyuan
Sports Ground
Fountain
High School
School
#3 (Sanlu) Bus
Guangyang Jie
#1 (Yilu) Bus
County PSB (Visa Extension)
Bailongsi
Weisheng Ju
Restaurants
Zhongyang Xiang
#1 (Yilu) Bus Route
PLA
Heibaishi Dajudian
To Zhongdian, Dali
Restaurants
Traffic Police PICC (Insurance)
Xuesha Fandian
#3 (Sanlu) Bus Route
Lijiang Passenger Transport Service Central Station
To Jinjiang, Yongsheng
0
300m
To Heqing, Lijiang Airport

*Zhongdian—A normal-sized bus leaves at 07:10, and then there are 2 minibuses leaving at 07:50 and 13:30. The 198km trip takes around 6 hours.

*Jinjiang—All 3 buses on this 305km route terminate at Panzhihua Station in Sichuan Province. They leave Lijiang at 06:45, 13:00, and 17:00.

*Weixi—There is 1 bus daily that departs at 07:30.

*In addition to these regular ones, there are also buses going out to Shigu, Judian, Qiaotou, Heqing, Jinding, and other towns and villages in the region.

Buses at the Lijiang Regional Bus Transport Co.

*Kunming—There is a bus with sleeping berths leaving at 17:00 every evening.

*Dali—There are 2 buses each day that leave at 07:00 and 12:30.

*Jinjiang—This route also has 2 buses servicing it. The first one sets off at 06:30, followed by one at 15:50.

There are also some buses for Xiaguan, Yongsheng, Zhongdian, Weixi, etc.

Buses at the Lijiang Bus Transport Station Ticket Office

Located at the gate of the Guluwan Binguan (Hotel), you can buy bus tickets for Kunming, Dali, and many of the other destinations here. Buses for the suburbs leave from around here and some other points in the town.

Accommodation

The *Lijiang Binguan* (Former No. 1 Guesthouse) is a hangout for backpackers, and a dormitory bed here costs Y12. Double rooms start from Y44, and a double room at the new building costs Y200.

The *Yuquan Binguan* (Hotel) has beds in a 4-person room for Y20, single rooms are Y40, and double rooms cost from Y70.

The *Sanhe Fandian* (Hotel) is a Naxi-style hotel in the old town. Sheets are changed every day, and the toilet here is clean. Dormitory beds are from Y30, and a double room costs Y60.

The *Hongtaiyang Jiudian* (Red Sun Hotel) has clean rooms and charges Y25 for a dormitory bed and Y180 for a double room.

Restaurants

The *Alibaba Café* near the statue of Mao Zedong has dishes for Y8-10.

Peter's Café is in the same area and serves pizza, steak, and other Western food.

The *Tower Café* is on Sifang Jie, and there is a good atmosphere here.

Mama Fu's, on Xianfeng Jie, is the place to get apple and fruit pies and delicious cheese pancakes. *Simon Café* nearby is a great place if you want good, wholesome sandwiches.

Places to See
Yufengsi

About 8km to the north of Lijiang there is a Naxi village called Baisha. If you carry on for half that distance again to the north-west of the village, you will come to the Karma Kagyupa's Yufengsi Monastery. There is a huge camellia tree here called *Wanduohuacha* that breaks out into over 20,000 beautiful blossoms each spring.

Diqing Tibetan Autonomous Prefecture, in the north-west of Yunnan Province, is where the province meets Sichuan and the Tibetan Autonomous Region. The prefecture consists of 3 counties, Zhongdian (Gyalthang), Deqin (Jol), and Weixi (Balung). Tibetans live in this autonomous prefecture alongside other ethnic groups, such as the Lizu, Naxi, Yi, and Bai.

Besides the Meili Xueshan Mountain (6,740m), there are a number of other peaks over 5,000m, and in fact, the region's lowest point is still at an altitude of 1,500m. The Jinsha Jiang River (Dri-chu, the upper reaches of the Yangtze River) and the Lancang Jiang (Zaqu or Dza-chu, the upper reaches of the Mekong River) have cut deep valleys between these towering peaks, and their waters feed the lush vegetation found here.

ZHONGDIAN (GYALTHANG)

Zhongdian is the capital of Diqing Prefecture, and it is also called Zhongxinzhen. The town is 709km from Kunming and is an important transportation center connecting Yunnan with Sichuan and the TAR, and half of the population of about 120,000

Zhongdian

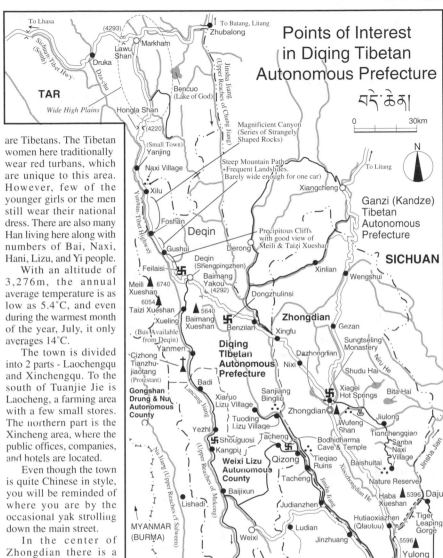

Points of Interest in Diqing Tibetan Autonomous Prefecture

བདེ་ཆེན།

0   30km

(Map labels:) To Lhasa; (4293); To Batang, Litang; Zhubalong; Markham; Lawu Shan; Druka; Sichuan-Tibet Hwy. (South); Dza-chu; TAR; Wide High Plains; Hongla Shan; Bencuo (Lake of God); (4220); Jinsha Jiang (Upper Reaches of Chang Jiang); Magnificent Canyon (Series of Strangely Shaped Rocks); N; (Small Town) Yanjing; Naxi Village; Steep Mountain Path + Frequent Landslides. (Barely wide enough for one car); Xiangcheng; To Litang; Xilu; Ganzi (Kandze) Tibetan Autonomous Prefecture; Foshan; Deqin; Precipitous Cliffs with good view of Meili & Taizi Xueshan; SICHUAN; Gushui; Derong; Deqin (Shengpingzhen); Xinlian; Wengshui; Feilaisi; Baimang Yakou; (4292); Dongzhulinsi; Meili 6740 Xueshan; 6054; Taizi Xueshan; 5640; Zhongdian; Gezan; Xueling; Baimang Xueshan; Benzilan; Xingfu; (Bus Available from Deqin); Yanmen; Sungtseling Monastery; Niru He; Diqing Tibetan Autonomous Prefecture; Cizhong; Tianzhu-jiaotang (Protestant); Dazhongdian; Nixi; Shudu Hai; Badi; Gongshan Drung & Nu Autonomous County; Lancang Jiang; Xiaruo Lizu Village; Sanjiang Bingliu; Xiagei Hot Springs; Bita Hai; Zhongdian; Yezhi; Tuoding Lizu Village; Wufeng Shan; Jiulong; Tianchengqiao; Shouguosi; Tacheng; Bodhidharma Cave & Temple; Sanba Naxi Village; Kangpu; Qizong; Tieqiao Ruins; Baishuitai; Weixi Lizu Autonomous County; Tacheng; Nature Reserve; Nu Jiang (Upper Reaches of Salween); Baijixun; Judianzhen; Haba 5396 Xueshan; Daju; Lishadi; Hutiaoxiazhen (Qiaotou); Tiger Leaping Gorge; MYANMAR (BURMA); Ludian; Jinzhuang; 5596; Weixi; Yulong Xueshan; Nujiang Lizu Autonomous Prefecture; Lijiang; Fugong; Zhongpai; To Dali; Jinsha Jiang; Xiaozhongdian He; Jinsha Jian

are Tibetans. The Tibetan women here traditionally wear red turbans, which are unique to this area. However, few of the younger girls or the men still wear their national dress. There are also many Han living here along with numbers of Bai, Naxi, Hani, Lizu, and Yi people.

With an altitude of 3,276m, the annual average temperature is as low as 5.4°C, and even during the warmest month of the year, July, it only averages 14°C.

The town is divided into 2 parts - Laochengqu and Xinchengqu. To the south of Tuanjie Jie is Laocheng, a farming area with a few small stores. The northern part is the Xincheng area, where the public offices, companies, and hotels are located.

Even though the town is quite Chinese in style, you will be reminded of where you are by the occasional yak strolling down the main street.

In the center of Zhongdian there is a market where you can pick up fruit and vegetables and most other everyday items. To the right of the market is the Zhongdian Passenger Transport Station (Long-distance Bus Station), and on the left-hand side are the post office and a telephone exchange where you can make international calls.

To the east of the town is Wufeng Shan (Mountain), and at its foot, the people of the region hold the biggest festival in Diqing Prefecture, at the time of *Duanwujie* (May 5th in the lunar calendar). On the south-east side of the mountain is Zangjing Tang (Scripture Library), constructed in 1724. An eclectic mixture of Tibetan and Han styles, this temple functions as the center of Tibetan religious and secular life in the area. Opposite the temple is the Daguishan Park from where you can get a good view of the town. In 1997 the prefecture opened a museum with local artifacts on display.

DECHEN YUNNAN

Access
To Zhongdian
*Xiaguan (via Dali)—The daily bus takes 9 hours. (293km)

*Qiaotou—There is a daily bus that takes 3 hours. (96km)

*Lijiang—This route has a number of buses each day, and it takes over 5 hours. You can buy a minibus ticket at the *Lijiang Bus Passenger Transport Station Ticket Office* in front of the Guluwan Binguan (Hotel), and you catch the bus in front of the hotel at 07:10 each morning.

*Kunming, Jinjiang (Sichuan Province)—There are sleeping berth buses available.

From Zhongdian
Buses leave from the Zhongdian Passenger Transport Station in the center of town, and the buses for Deqin and Xiangcheng are only operated seasonally.

*Kunming—There are 2 morning departures each day. The first one leaves at 06:30, and then a bus with sleeping berths leaves at 10:00. They usually take 18 or 20 hours. (709km)

*Lijiang—There are 3 buses operating on this route. They leave the bus station at 07:00, 12:00, and 13:30 daily. (185km)

*Xiaguan (via Dali)—A minibus leaves at 06:20, followed by a normal-sized bus at 07:10 every morning, and the trip takes 9 hours. (309km)

*Deqin (via Benzilan)—The journey takes 7 hours and has 1 bus a day that sets off at 06:50. At the Deqin County Bus Station there are also a number of buses. The services are suspended between January and April. (186km)

*Benzilan—The daily bus leaves at 15:00 and takes 3 hours. (82km)

*Sanba—Operating every other day, the bus leaves at 07:30 and takes 5 hours. (108km)

*Qizong (via Qiaotou, north side of the Jinsha Jiang River)—There is a daily one leaving at 07:20. (251km)

* Weixi (via Shigu, south of Jinsha Jiang River, Judian)—A bus leaves at 06:30 every other day. (338km)

*Jinjiang (Sichuan)—A daily bus with sleeping berths sets off at 10:00 and takes 16-20 hours. (485km)

*Xiangcheng (Sichuan)—This one takes 10 hours and leaves at 07:30 every morning. January-April the services are suspended due to snowfalls. (222km)

*Derong (Sichuan)—It leaves from the bus stop, 200m to the north of the main bus station at 08:00 on even numbered days, and the trip takes 6 hours.

For getting around the town there are local buses with Y1 fares. You can also catch minibuses to Xiaozhongdian.

Zhongdian-Xiangcheng (Sichuan)-Litang-Chengdu Route
This is a popular route among travelers, but both Xiangcheng and Litang are classed as closed towns. (See the Yunnan to Litang pages for details.)

Accommodation
The *Yongsheng Luguan* (Tibet Hotel) is a hangout for backpackers. There are dormitory beds here for Y16, and double rooms for Y42 with a communal bathroom. In the new building, a double room costs Y180, and a triple with a bathroom is Y240. Electric

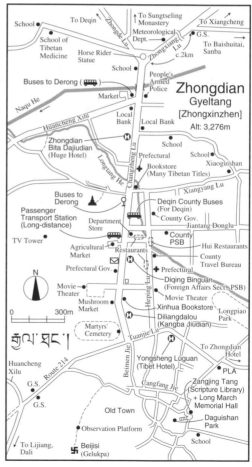

blankets are available for guests. To get there, walk 15 minutes along the Changzheng Lu to the south of the long-distance bus station and then make a left on Tuanjie Lu for another 5 minutes. You could also take a rickshaw, which will cost you Y3.

At the restaurant here you can choose to eat in rooms with a television, in an authentic Tibetan-style room, or out in the courtyard. The relatively pricey menu has both Chinese and Western food.

At the travel section in the hotel you can arrange a Tibet tour by Chinese jeep. For example, a 1-way 10-day trip from Zhongdian to Lhasa costs Y6,000 per car, and a 20-day round trip is Y8,000. These costs cover the car, fuel, and driver, but accommodation and meals are additional. Another expense to factor in is the cost of the travel permit, which is Y40 a day per person. Trips around Zhongdian and the surrounding area cost upwards of Y400 a day.

The *Diqing Binguan* (Government Guesthouse) is where you will find the Foreign Affairs Branch of the PSB.

The *Diliangdalou* (Kangba Jiudian) charges Y25 for a dormitory bed, Y128 for a single room, and Y140 for a double room.

The *Zhongdian Hotel* is a top-range, Tibetan-style hotel. Double rooms here cost more than Y300, including meals.

The *Zhongdian Bita Dajiudian* (Hotel) is another alternative that is relatively new.

Public Security

Although it is at the Government Guesthouse, the office is not easy to find. You should be able to get a second month-long extension here for Y120.

Places to See

Sungtseling Monastery (Songzanlinsi)

Housing around 600-700 monks, this Gelukpa monastery was built by the 5th Dalai Lama in 1679. The gompa is also known as Guihuasi, and admission to the main temple is Y2. On November 29 in the lunar calendar, there is a festival called *Gedongjie*, where you can see *Cham*, a dance

Sungtseling Monastery

performed by masked monks. The monastery is about 5km from the center of Zhongdian, and to get to the spot, walk about 20 minutes along the Changzheng Lu to the north from the long-distance bus station and make a left at the junction with a statue of a man on a horse. After about a hundred meters, turn right and continue along the paved road for another 40 minutes or so, and you will see the monastery.

Beijisi

On a small hill in the south of town stands this small Gelukpa monastery. From this spot you can get a good view of the town. It is about a 20-minute walk from the Tibet Hotel.

Saimahui

On May 5 in the lunar calendar, there is a horse festival held in this area of Zhongdian, lasting for a couple of days. There is an equestrian event, horse racing, Tibetan dances, and also a market. During this season, the grasslands on the outskirts of Zhongdian are covered with flowers.

Napahai

From winter through to spring there are dozens of small rivers that flow into this area and form Napahai (Lake). This marshy area changes in size between the rainy and dry seasons. In the dry season, it turns into a pasture with only small patches of marshland and pools dotted around.

This seasonal lake is around 8km to the north-west of Zhongdian. Walk about 2 hours along the road toward Deqin until you reach an open space on the left after a pass. From here climb the hill behind the village nearby, and you will get a view of the whole lake. The scenery on the way is also good, and it is well worth the trip.

Tianshengqiao and Xiagei Hot Springs

Crossing the Shudugang He River, 12km from Zhongdian, the Tianshengqiao is a naturally-occurring bridge of weathered limestone. This impressive structure stands 60m high, 10m wide, and around 200m in length. Around here there are a number of hot springs and the Xiagei Hot Spring, 5km east of the Tiansheng Bridge, is the largest among them. Admission to the bathing area is Y1, and if you want to stay here, you'll need to take a sleeping bag with you. At Zhongdian, take a bus for Sanba and then walk for 10 minutes after you are dropped off.

Bitahai Nature Reserve

Home to the *Bitachunyu* fish that has survived here since the last Ice Age, Bitahai is a beautiful lake about 32km to the east of Zhongdian. The lake stretches 3,000m from east to west and 700m from north to south and is surrounded by woodland.

Along the lakeshore there are groves of rhododendron bushes that burst into bloom in May. The flowers here are slightly poisonous, and it is said that the fish come to the surface during this season and act as if they are drunk due to the number of flowers that fall into the lake. The area has a wealth of flora and fauna, which has caused it to be declared an official nature reserve. There is a roadway up to the entrance of the nature reserve, but there are no buses operating on this route. It is a 7-km walk from the entrance to the lake area.

Baishui Terrace (Baishuitai)

The Naxi people's *Dongba* culture was born on this limestone plateau, and it still plays host to a Naxi festival on February 8, in the lunar calendar. The terrace is 104km to the south-east of Zhongdian, and admission is Y10.

At Zhongdian, jump on a bus heading for Sanba, leaving every other day and taking 5 hours. Baishuitai is to be found 4km before the last stop. There are bungalows that cost Y20 per bed, and meals are also available here. At Sanba, the last stop on the bus, there is the *Liangliang Zhaodaisuo* (Guesthouse), which charges Y15 for a bed. The town also has restaurants and a few stores. After an overnight stay here you can catch the bus leaving for Zhongdian at 08:15 the next morning.

Haba Snow Peak Nature Reserve

Another nature reserve in the area, this one serves to protect a number of rare and endangered species, such as the Jinsihou monkeys, snow leopards, and lesser pandas, among others.

The Haba Xueshan peak (5,396m) dominates the center of the reserve, and at the southern end is the famous Tiger Leaping Gorge. There are numerous glacial lakes and waterfalls in the reserve, and among these lakes, Heihai, Yuanhai, Huanghai, and Shuanghai are particularly beautiful. In the summer you will be treated to the spectacular sight of 2,000m-high waterfalls cascading off the mountain. If you visit the area from September to April, these are frozen.

A local legend has it that the Heilongtan in Lijiang will go dry if the natural spring in the area, called *Longwangbian* (Area of the Dragon King), runs out, as they are connected. The spring is an important place for the Naxi people, and they have an annual festival here on February 8 in the lunar calendar.

A road leads to the entrance of the nature reserve, but there is no bus service here either. It is 20km from the entrance to Heihai, where you will find accommodation, and this is also a good starting point from which to get out to the Longwangbian Spring on the southern side of the mountain, via

the 3 lakes of Yuanhai, Shuanghai, and the 2,000m-high waterfalls (Dadiaoshui).

Hutiaoxia
(Tiger Leaping Gorge)

This is the most popular trekking course along the gorge for travelers. There are mountains towering up to 5,000m above you as you go and the turbulent rapids of the Jinsha Jiang River (Dri-chu) are in the valley below. A detailed map and updated information is available at Mama Fu's in Lijiang and other travelers' hangouts in the town.

DEQIN (DECHEN) [JOL]

With a population of about 4,500, this small town is also known as Shengpingzhen. It connects Yunnan with the TAR, only about 100km away. The town is on a valley slope and is surrounded by snow-clad mountains. It is made up of a collection of various different Han-style buildings. However, the Tibetan villages in the area have managed to keep some of their authentic atmosphere, and in fact around 80% of the 56,000 people living in Deqin County are ethnic Tibetans.

Access

There is a daily bus from Zhongdian, though the service may be suspended up until April if it snows heavily early in the year. In that case, you can still get to the area by taking the route from Weixi. Deqin has 2 bus stations across the road from one other.

Deqin Bus Station

*Zhongdian—The only bus leaving from here goes at 07:00 and takes 7 hours.

Deqin County Buses

*Zhongdian—There is a daily bus leaving at 07:00.
*Yanmen—This bus leaves every other day at 08:00.

To the Tibetan Autonomous Region

For Yanjing, the first town in the TAR, there is a minibus going from the entrance of the mushroom market every day, and the trip takes 6-7 hours. To catch a lift on a truck, go to the gas station, about 500m to the south of the market. (See the map to the right.)

As you come into Yanjing, there is a checkpoint. (For information on traveling beyond Yanjing, see page 170.)

Accommodation

Foreigners are allowed to stay at the following hotels:

The *Meili Jiudian* (Hotel) has single rooms for Y90, doubles for Y110, and 5-bed rooms for Y200. The toilet is shared, and there are no showers. On the 2nd floor, there is the Foreign Affairs office of the PSB, where you pay your Y35 admission charge for the Meili Xueshan.

The *Xianzhengfu Zhaodaisuo* (County Government Guesthouse) charges Y14 for a bed in the dormitory and Y40 for a single room.

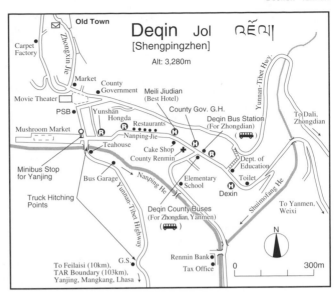

Places to See
Meili Xueshan
(Mt. Kawa Karpo)

There is an observation platform (3,480m) with *tar-choks* fluttering in the breeze about a kilometer beyond Feilaisi, which is 10km to the south-west of Deqin. This takes about 2-3 hours on foot, and from here you can get a good view of Meili Xueshan (6,740m), the highest mountain in Yunnan. There is a range of 13 snow-covered mountains over 6,000m that are collectively referred to as Taizishisanfeng. You may be able to hitch a lift on the return leg of the journey.

Dry season mornings, from November to March, are the best time to see the mountain, as in the afternoon the peak of Meili Xueshan is in shadows. The glacier on Meili Xueshan comes down to an altitude of about 3,000m.

Benzilan

By the Jinsha Jiang River (Dri-chu), this scenic Tibetan town is a good place to kick back and relax. You can get out to Benzilan from Zhongdian by bus, and the trip takes over 2 hours. Buses between

Meili Xueshan (Mt. Kawa Karpo)

Zhongdian and Deqin stop over here so that passengers can eat, and there are a number of restaurants and places to stay. Buses for Zhongdian leave at 08:30 from the street in front of the relatively new Duowen Luguan (Hotel).

Dongzhulin Temple (Dongdrubling)

This is one of the 13 Gelukpa monasteries that were constructed at the same time as Sungtseling Monastery in Zhongdian. You need to take the road towards Deqin from Benzilan, and it is around 23km. Unfortunately, there is no accommodation here.

Cizhong Tianzhujiaotang (Church)

This Protestant church is by the Lancang Jiang, the upper reaches of the mighty Mekong River, around 80km to the south of Deqin. It was originally constructed 15km to the south of Cizhong. However, it was rebuilt here in 1907 after the original one was destroyed by the anti-Christianity movement in 1905.

To get there you need to cross over the river using the suspension bridge, 10km to the south from Yanmen. Then walk up hill for about a kilometer, and you can't miss it.

WEIXI (BALUNG)

The capital of Weixi Lizu Autonomous County is heavily populated by Han Chinese, but there are

**DECHEN
YUNNAN**

Map labels:
To Deqin, Badi

To Lijiang, Dali, Xiaguan

Yongchun He

Bus Stop

Yongchun Store

Weixi
Balung
[Baohezhen]

N

Local Bank

Bei Jie (Shopping Street)

Food Co.

To Yongchun →

Shuncheng Beilu

Qinglong Lu

Junior High School

Xinhua Bookstore

Dept. of Finance

Culture Hall

Shizi Jie

Tax Office

Forestry Dept.

Agricultural Dept.

Theater

Xin Lu

Shuncheng Nanlu

Gov. G.H.

To Sanjia →

PSB

Sanitary Dept.

Renmin

Local Bank

County Government

To Schools

People's Armed Police

0   Not to Scale   300m

Bodhidharma Cave & Temple (Damozushidong)

Constructed in 1662, this Karma Kagyupa monastery seems to cling to the side of Damoshan (Mountain), about 100km from Weixi. There is a meditation cave here where Bodhidharma practiced asceticism. The monastery has 2 incarnated lamas in residence now.

Shuoguosi (Temple)

Established in 1728, this Karma Kagyupa monastery is located at Kangpuxiang, 73km from Weixi. There are many monks here from the Naxi people. You need to follow the course of the Lancang Jiang River, and Shuoguosi is about 500m up from the road.

LUGU HU (LAKE)

Where the provinces of Yunnan and Sichuan meet you will find this mysterious and beautiful lake. At an altitude of 2,688m and a depth of 93.6m, it has very clear water, unlike many other lakes in China. Although the area has become very popular for Chinese tourists, it has so far remained fairly unspoiled.

Around the lake live a minority people called the *Mosu*, who follow the teachings of Tibetan Buddhism. This group of people became famous for their traditional matrilineal society, in which they trace their family's descent through the female line. It is said that those living on Lige Island (Ligedao), at the north-west end of the lake, continue to practice this tradition even now.

There are 5 islands in the lake, and you can get out to Xiewae Island (Xiewaedao) and Liwubi Island (Liwubidao) by boat. The boats are rowed by traditionally-dressed Mosu men, who also sing to you along the way. The trip out to the islands costs Y15-20. On Liwubi Island (Liwubidao) there is a Gelukpa monastery.

still some Tibetans living here.

There is a daily bus from both Lijiang and Xiaguan, and there is also a fair amount of traffic from Deqin via Yanmen. Yanmen also has accommodation for travelers stopping overnight there.

From Weixi, a bus leaves for Lijiang at 07:00 every morning, and the trip takes 11 hours. There are also buses for Xiaguan departing around the same time. The one for Badi is a daily service, which is also available during the rainy season. Yanmen has a bus operating every other day, but these may be suspended at times during the rainy season.

There are a number of hotels in the town, such as the *Weixi Fandian* (Hotel), which charges from Y15 for a bed, and the hotel has its own generator providing the lighting and heating for the rooms.

Places to See
Dixia Migong (Underground Labyrinth)

This is an interesting cave close to Weixi. You can get there on foot, as it is only about 2km to the east of the town.

Mosu Women, Lugu Hu

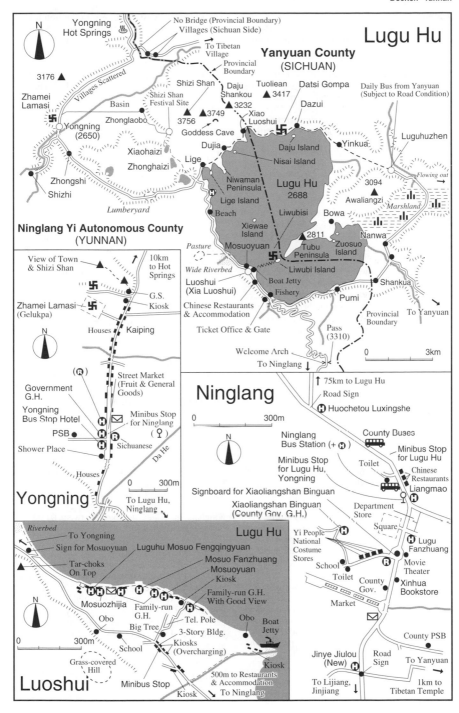

Lugu Hu

Yanyuan County
(SICHUAN)

Yongning
Hot Springs

No Bridge (Provincial Boundary)
Villages (Sichuan Side)

To Tibetan
Village

Provincial
Boundary

3176 ▲

Zhamei
Lamasi

Basin

Villages Scattered

Shizi Shan

Shizi Shan
Festival Site

Daju
Shankou

Tuoliean
▲ 3417

Datsi Gompa

Dazui

Daily Bus from Yanyuan
(Subject to Road Condition)

▲ 3232

▲3749

Xiao
Luoshui

Goddess Cave

Zhonglaobo

▲ 3756

Dujia

Daju Island

Nisai Island

Yinkua

Luguhuzhen

Yongning
(2650)

Xiaohaizi

Zhonghaizi

Lige

Niwaman
Peninsula

Lugu Hu
2688

Flowing out

Zhongshi

Shizhi

Lige Island

Beach

Lumberyard

Xiewae
Island

Liwubisi

Awaliangzi

3094

Marshland

Bowa

Nanwa

Ninglang Yi Autonomous County
(YUNNAN)

Pasture

Mosuoyuan

▲2811

Tubu
Peninsula

Zuosuo
Island

View of Town
& Shizi Shan

10km
to Hot
Springs

Wide Riverbed

Liwubi Island

Shankua

Zhamei Lamasi
(Gelukpa)

G.S.
Kiosk

Luoshui
(Xia Luoshui)

Boat Jetty

Fishery

Pumi

To Yanyuan

Houses

Kaiping

Chinese Restaurants
& Accommodation

Provincial
Boundary

Ticket Office & Gate

Pass
(3310)

0   3km

Welcome Arch

To Ninglang ↓

Street Market
(Fruit & General
Goods)

Ninglang

↑ 75km to Lugu Hu

Road Sign

Government
G.H.

Yongning
Bus Stop Hotel

Minibus Stop
for Ninglang

PSB ●

Sichuanese

0   300m

Huochetou Luxingshe

Shower Place

Houses

 Da He

0   300m

Ninglang
Bus Station (+)

County Buses

Minibus Stop
for Lugu Hu

Minibus Stop
for Lugu Hu,
Yongning

Toilet

Chinese
Restaurants

Yongning

To Lugu Hu,
Ninglang

Signboard for Xiaoliangshan Binguan

Xiaoliangshan Binguan
(County Gov. G.H.)

Liangmao

Department
Store

Square

Riverbed

To Yongning

Sign for Mosuoyuan

Lugu Hu

Luguhu Mosuo Fengqingyuan

Yi People
National
Costume
Stores

Lugu
Fanzhuang

Tar-choks
On Top

Mosuo Fanzhuang
Mosuoyuan
Kiosk

School

County
Gov.

Movie
Theater

Mosuozhijia

Family-run
G.H.

Family-run G.H.
With Good View

Toilet

Xinhua
Bookstore

Obo

Big Tree

Tel. Pole

Obo

Boat
Jetty

Market

3-Story Bldg.

Kiosks
(Overcharging)

County PSB

0   300m

School

Kiosk

Jinye Jiulou
(New)

Road
Sign

To Yanyuan

Luoshui

Grass-covered
Hill

Minibus Stop

Kiosk

500m to Restaurants
& Accommodation
To Ninglang

To Lijiang,
Jinjiang ↓

1km to
Tibetan Temple

**DECHEN
YUNNAN**

Access

The gateway for sightseeing in the area is Luoshui. First, you'll need to get to Ninglang, the county capital. From Kunming, there is a sleeping bus to Ninglang daily.

At Lijiang, Xiaguan, and Panzhihua (Jinjiang) buses are also available, and there are shared-taxis from Yanyuan. At Ninglang, take a minibus for Yongning and then get off at Luoshui. There are around 5 minibuses leaving from the street in front of the Ninglang Bus Station each day. Two of these leave between 07:00 and 08:00, and then 1 each at 10:00, 12:00, and 15:00. It is advisable to check out the latest schedule when you arrive. The trip to Luoshui takes 3 hours and costs from Y13-15.

Accommodation

There are many private houses providing beds and meals to visitors, and you can have fish meals for Y10-15. The following hotels are all popular with group tours, and when there is a group here, a *Mosu* dance is performed for them. It starts at 21:00 and lasts for about 90 minutes. During the latter half of the show, the audience is encouraged to participate in the singing and dancing. If you want some peace and quiet, these hotels are best to be avoided, and it might be better to stay at one of the private homes. The *Mosuoyuan* is very popular with tour operators, with single rooms costing Y18 and doubles starting from Y36.

The *Luguhu Mosuo Fengqingyuan* is owned by a village headman and has beds for Y13. This is another popular choice among group tours with clean rooms and good meals.

The *Mosuozhijia* has beds on the 1st floor for Y18, and the ones on the 2nd floor are Y15. There is a restaurant and a post office at the entrance.

The *Mosuo Fanzhuang* charges Y10-20 for a bed.

NINGLANG

The town is not as small as you may think, and there is a market where you will often catch sight of Yi women from the surrounding areas. There are half a dozen hotels available to foreigners.

The *Ninglang Bus Station Hotel* has clean rooms, and a bed costs Y10-20.

The *Liangmao Zhaodaisuo* (Guesthouse) costs Y8-15, and there is shared toilet.

The *Xianzhengfu Zhaodaisuo* (Xiaoliangshan Binguan) charges Y20-40 for a bed, and a double room at the new building costs Y140-200. The Foreign Affairs office of the PSB and the *Luguhu*

Zhaodaisuo (Guesthouse) are in the hotel. It is about 15 minutes on foot from the bus station.

Buses from Ninglang

[Ninglang Bus Station]

*Kunming—The sleeping berth bus leaves at 12:30 and goes via Panzhihua, costing Y110. There is also a night bus going via Yongsheng and Chuxiong, which leaves at 13:10 and costs Y73.

*Xiaguan—There is 1 bus leaving at 06:20 that costs Y40.

*Jinjiang—The daily bus at 06:40 costs Y40.

*Lijiang—There are 2 departures a day, one at 07:00 for Y21 and the other at 09:00 for Y29.

*Yongsheng—The 2 buses a day at 06:30 and 10:30 cost Y11.

[County Buses]

*Lijiang—A minibus costing Y25 leaves at 07:00.

*Yanyuan—When this bus is in operation, it leaves at 08:10 and costs Y25. Recently the service has been suspended.

*Yongning— Going via Luoshui, the bus leaves at 08:00 and costs Y15.

YONGNING

A kilometer to the north of the town is the Gelukpa monastery, Zhamei Lamasi (Tibetan Temple). Most of the monks here are from the Mosu minority. There is also a site of Kublai Khan's camp here. Yongning is 21km from Luoshui, about 1 hour by minibus costing Y5.

For accommodation, a room at the *Yongning Zhengfu Zhaodaisuo* (Government Guesthouse) costs Y30 with a common toilet. Many foreigners are advised to take a whole room for themselves even if they are alone. There is an additional charge for taking a shower, and it is really just a place for sleeping. A bed at the *Yongning Bus Stop Hotel* costs Y5, and there is a bus stop at the entrance. For Ninglang, there are 2 minibuses between 07:00 and 08:00, and one around 11:00 and again at 13:00.

Yongning Hot Springs

The water here is not so clean, but there is a restaurant and a guesthouse. You can see Sichuan Province from here, as it is just over the river. It is 11km to the north-east of Yongning, and there are a couple of shared-trucks each day. There are private rooms and a large bath in the hot springs building, and you must pay your Y1 admission fee at the store next door.

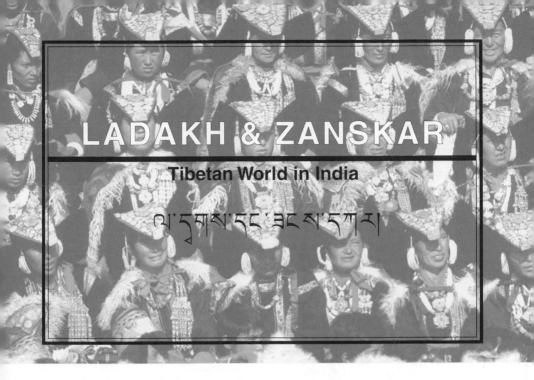

LADAKH & ZANSKAR

Tibetan World in India

ལ་དགས་དང་ཟངས་དཀར།

Located in the west of the Tibetan Plateau, Ladakh, Zanskar, and the Lahaul and Spiti Valleys are all Indian provinces, but they are distinctly Tibetan in their cultural makeup and have been influenced by Tibetan culture for a very long time. Fortunately, or simply by accident, they became Indian territories, not Chinese ones, thereby protecting these places from the cultural destruction that has taken place in much of central Tibet. This has also allowed them to retain many of their ancient Tibetan traditions, many of which still thrive throughout the region.

In the northern Indian states of Himachal Pradesh, Uttar Pradesh, etc., the descendants of the Tibetans, who migrated from eastern Tibet several generations ago, live closely together with the Indian people. Their number was swelled by over a hundred thousand refugees who refused to live under Chinese rule and who fled to India in the latter half of the 1950's.

DELHI

For many tourists, the capital city of Delhi is the gateway to northern India, especially those making for such areas as Ladakh, Manali and the Kullu Valley.

Access by Air

International flights arrive at the Indira Gandhi International Airport, 18km south-west of Connaught Place. To get from the airport to the center of town, you can take:

*Limousine bus by Delhi Transport Co —This leaves the international airport for the Inter-State Bus Terminal (ISBT) via Param Airport (for domestic flights) and continues on to Connaught Place in the center of New Delhi. The buses depart every hour-and a half throughout the day and cost 45Rs.

*Airport bus by ETS Ltd.—This also connects the airport with Connaught Place and takes around 40 minutes, stopping at the major hotels on the way. Buses leave every 30 minutes between 05:30 and 23:30 and cost 20Rs.

*Local bus—Number 790 will also take you into central Delhi and Connaught Place.

*Prepaid taxi—Go to the prepaid taxi counter in the airport. They cost about 150Rs and take around 30 minutes to get to the Main Bazaar. Be careful, as there are some unscrupulous taxi drivers about.

Access by Rail

The major railway terminals are New Delhi Station and Delhi Station (in Old Delhi). Some trains also depart from the Nizamuddin Station in the south-

INDIA

Formal Name of the Country
The Republic of India
Time Difference
5hrs 30mins ahead of GMT.
International Dialing Code
91
Currency
Rupees (Rs)=100 paise
Exchange Rates

Australian Dollar	25.30Rs
Bhutan Ngultrum	1.00Rs
British Pound	66.10Rs
Canadian Dollar	29.40Rs
Chinese Yuan	5.30Rs
Dutch Guilder	19.00Rs
French Franc	6.20Rs
German Mark	21.20Rs
Hong Kong Dollar	5.70Rs
Japanese Yen (100)	41.20Rs
Nepalese Rupee (100)	63.50Rs
New Zealand Dollar	21.00Rs
Pakistan Rupee (100)	86.00Rs
Singapore Dollar	25.50Rs
Swedish Krona	4.90Rs
Swiss Franc	28.40Rs
US Dollar	44.20Rs

Language
Besides Hindi, there are 14 other official languages, of which Urdu is widely spoken in the north. English is a semi-official language.
Inhabitants
In addition to the 2 major groups, the Dravida people in the south and Aryan people in the north, there are also minorities of Mongol and Turkish-Iranian descent. Over 80% of the population are Hindu and the next largest group is the Muslims, who account for over 10 % of the population. They are heavily concentrated in the north-western provinces. The remainder of the population consists of Sikhs, Christians, Jains & Buddhists.
Capital
New Delhi (Population of 10,000,000.)
Population
Over 1 billion people.
The population is growing rapidly and is estimated to be increasing by over 15 million per year.

Land Area
Approximately 3,298,000,000 sq km
Climate
It varies dramatically according to the region. Generally, the monsoon comes in from the Indian Ocean in the summer while the Himalayan weather system is dominant in the winter. The rainy season falls between June and September.
Electricity
AC230-240V, 50Hz
Office Hours
From Monday through Friday, public offices are open from 10:00 to 17:00. (closing at 16:00 during the winter). On Saturday, offices close around noon. Sunday is officially a day off.
National Holidays
January 26 (Republic Day)
August 15 (Independence Day)
October 2 (Gandhi's Birthday)
December 25 (Christmas Day)
Religious Festivals
There are hundreds of festivals throughout the year and the following list includes some of the major ones:
Ramadan --- Muslims must refrain from all manner of indulgences between sunrise and sunset for this month. This comes to an end with the Eid-ul-Fitr. The exact days are dependent upon time zones and moon-sightings but the provisional dates are:
November 27, 2000-December 27, 2000.
November 17, 2001- December 16, 2001.
Losar ------ Tibetan New Year held during February or March.
Iron Dragon Year (Year 2127) - February 6, 2000
Iron Snake Year (Year 2128) - February 24, 2001
*The Ladakhis celebrate the New Year 2 months before the rest of the Tibetan world.
Holi ----- A lively and colorful celebration held during the full moon in March.
Buddha Jayanti ------------ Celebrating the Buddha's birthday and enlightenment, held in May or June.
Dussehra ----------- A 10-day long festival held during September or October, celebrating the ascendancy of good over evil. Kullu in Himachal Pradesh is famous for its festival.
Diwali ---- This noisy festival is celebrated in October or November throughout India.

east and Sarai Rohilla Station in the north-west of the city. Reservations can be organized quickly and efficiently at the *International Tourist Bureau*, which is very used to catering to foreigners. The bureau's opening hours are from 07:30 to 13:30 and from 14:00 to 17:00, Monday to Saturday. The office is closed on Sundays. You will require a bank receipt and your passport to make a reservation.

Access by Bus
To travel on to the major cities in northern India, buses are convenient due to their frequency. For Dharamsala and Manali, you can catch a bus at the bus stop 5km to the north-east of the Main Bazaar. A 20-30Rs auto-rickshaw ride will take you out to the bus stop or you can take a local bus for just 2Rs.

Arranging Visas in Delhi

Chinese Embassy
50-D Shantipath, Chanakyapuri,
New Delhi, 110021
Tel: 11-687 1585/6/7 Fax: 11-688 5486
Hours are 09:00 to 12:00 Monday, Wednesday and Thursday. You can get a 1-month visa, valid for 3 months with single, double or multiple entry. The cost varies depending upon the nationality of the applicant. One photograph is required and it takes 4 days to issue. The visa section is at Gate No. 4, set back from Shantipath Road.

If you are planning to go on to China, it is advisable to get your visa in Delhi as the visa section in Kathmandu only issues visas to tourist groups.

Pakistani Embassy
2/50-G Shantipath, Chanakyapuri,
New Delhi, 110021
Tel: 11-467 6004/ 467 8467
Fax: 11-637 2339
Find a purple dome, which is 2 doors down from the Japanese Embassy. On the left-hand side is the visa section entrance. Applications are accepted between 09:00 and 11:00, and visas are issued from 11:00 to 13:00 either on the same day or by the following day.

You will be issued a 1-month tourist visa, valid for 3 months. The cost varies depending on the applicants' nationality and for some this is free. You are required to bring one photograph.

Nepalese Embassy
Barakhamba Rd, New Delhi 110001
Tel: 11-332 9969/ 7361/ 9218/ 8191
Fax: 11-332 6857

If you want to get a visa for Nepal in advance, go to the Nepalese Embassy in Delhi.

Visa applications are accepted from 10:00 to 13:00, and you can pick it up the following day from 10:00 to 11:00. A 2-month visa costs around 1,300Rs. You can get a visa at the border or at the airport, but you should have US dollars with you because other currencies are not accepted. For a 60-day visa, the charge is US$30. There is a 25% charge when you apply for one at the airport. One photograph is required.

Indian Visa Extensions
Foreign Registration Office - 1/f Hans Bhavan, Tilak Bridge.
In principle, those who entered the country on a 6-month visa cannot extend their visa dates.

Foreign Embassies in Delhi &
Indian High Commissions Abroad

See Appendix for the listings.

Tourist Information
Government of India Tourist Office - 88 Janpath
Tel. 11-332 0005/8
Open from 09:00-18:00 Monday to Friday and 09:00-14:00 on Saturday and bank holidays. The office is closed on Sunday. A 3-minute walk from Connaught Place, it is on the ground floor of a building on the left-hand side of Janpath St. as it stretches out towards the south. The area attracts a lot of less than trustworthy characters who claim their travel agency is an official government-run tourist office. The travel agencies in front of New Delhi Station are also notorious for this.

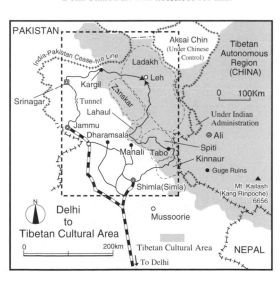

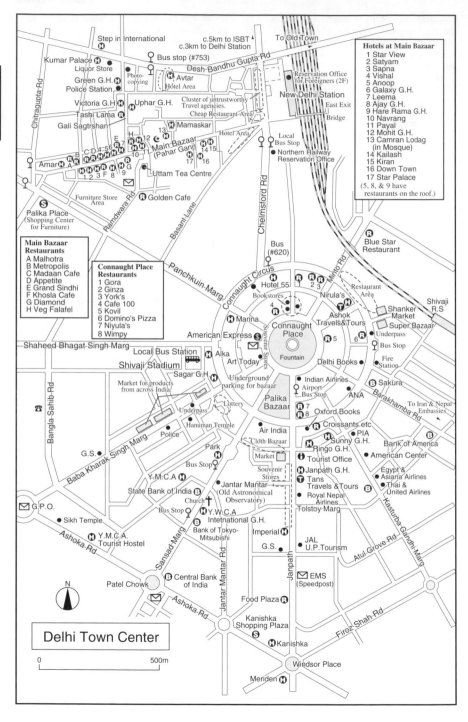

Step in International

c.5km to ISBT
c.3km to Delhi Station

To Old Town

Desh-Bandhu-Gupta-Rd

Bus stop (#753)

Kumar Palace H
Liquor Store
Green G.H. H
Police Station H

Photo-
copying

Avtar
Hotel Area

Reservation Office
for Foreigners (2F)

New Delhi Station

East Exit
Bridge

Victoria G.H. H
Tashi Lama R
Gali Sagtrshan

Uphar G.H. H

Cluster of untrustworthy
Travel agencies.
Cheap Restaurant Area

Mamaskar

Hotel Area

Local
Bus Stop

Northern Railway
Reservation Office

Main Bazaar
(Pahar Ganj)

Uttam Tea Centre

Amar

Golden Cafe

Furniture Store
Area

Palika Place
(Shopping Center
for Furniture)

Ramdwara-Rd

Basant-Lane

Chelmsford Rd

Blue Star
Restaurant

Main Bazaar
Restaurants
A Malhotra
B Metropolis
C Madaan Cafe
D Appetite
E Grand Sindhi
F Khosla Cafe
G Diamond
H Veg Falafel

Connaught Place
Restaurants
1 Gora
2 Ginza
3 York's
4 Cafe 100
5 Kovil
6 Domino's Pizza
7 Niyula's
8 Wimpy

Hotels at Main Bazaar
1 Star View
2 Satyam
3 Sapna
4 Vishal
5 Anoop
6 Galaxy G.H.
7 Leema
8 Ajay G.H.
9 Hare Rama G.H.
10 Navrang
11 Payal
12 Mohit G.H.
13 Camran Lodag
(in Mosque)
14 Kailash
15 Kiran
16 Down Town
17 Star Palace
(5, 8, & 9 have
restaurants on the roof.)

Panchkuin-Marg

Connaught Circus

Bus
(#620)

Minto Rd

Hotel 55
Bookstores

Nirula's

Restaurant
Area

Shivaji
R.S

Marina

Connaught
Place

Fountain

Ashok
Travels&Tours

Shanker
Market

Super Bazaar

Underpass

Bus Stop

Fire
Station

American Express
Art Today

Souvenir
Stores

Delhi Books

Sakura

Barakhamba-Rd

Shaheed-Bhagat-Singh-Marg
Local Bus Station
Shivaji Stadium

Alka

Sagar G.H.

Market for products
from across India

Underpass

Lottery

Underground
parking for bazaar

Palika
Bazaar

Indian Airlines
Airport
Bus Stop

ANA

Oxford Books

To Iran & Nepal
Embassies

Bangla-Sahib-Rd

Baba-Kharak-Singh-Marg

Hanuman Temple

Police

Park

Cloth Bazaar

Market

Croissants etc

Sunny G.H.
Ringo G.H.

PIA
Bank of America

American Center

G.S.

Y.M.C.A

State Bank of India

Bus Stop

Air India

Souvenir
Stores

Tourist Office

Janpath G.H.
Tans
Travels &Tours

Royal Nepal
Airlines

Egypt &
Asiana Airlines

Thai &
United Airlines

G.P.O.

Sikh Temple

Y.M.C.A.
Tourist Hostel

Ashoka-Rd

State Bank of India

Church

Bus Stop

Y.W.C.A

Intetnational G.H.

Bank of Tokyo-
Mitsubishi

Jantar Mantar
(Old Astronomical
Observatory)

Imperial H

Tolstoy-Marg

JAL
U.P.Tourism

Sansad Marg

Jantar Mantar Rd

Patel Chowk

Central Bank
of India

Ashoka-Rd

Janpath

Food Plaza

EMS
(Speedpost)

Atul-Grove-Rd

Kasturba Gandhi Marg

N

Delhi Town Center

0   500m

Kanishka
Shopping Plaza

Kanishka

Firoz-Shah-Rd

Windsor Place

Meriden

Changing Money

There are a lot of banks around Connaught Place but their exchange rates are all quite similar.

The *State Bank of India* is the most common but the service is terribly slow. *American Express* is much quicker and they don't charge a commission for cashing their own travelers checks. There is a 1% surcharge for others. *Bank of Tokyo-Mitsubishi* charges 100Rs on all travelers' checks. Most banks are open from 10:00 until 14:00 during the week and from 10:00 until 12:30 on Saturday mornings.

Post & Telecommunications

The GPO is in the roundabout at the bottom of Baba Kharak Singh Marg, about a 10-minute walk from Connaught Place. Business hours are 10:00 to 17:00 Monday to Saturday (the parcel service closes half-an-hour earlier), and it's closed on Sunday.

You can also send parcels from the post office in Connaught Place, which is more convenient. Prices vary according to size, weight, and destination and the postal workers here always seem to overcharge you for your parcels. For those too lazy or too busy to go to a post office, there are also packing service agents at the Main Bazaar that charge about 120Rs to send a parcel.

International calls are available at any store displaying an 'ISD' sign outside. The prices vary in these places and depend on the country you are calling. Be careful, as some places will overcharge you. An international call should cost between 65 and 85Rs per minute.

Accommodation

The cheap hotels and guesthouses for backpackers are mainly concentrated around the Main Bazaar (Paharganj) in front of the New Delhi Station.

The *Uphar Guesthouse* is cheap and a gathering place for Japanese travelers. It's a convenient place to collect travel information but extremely dirty. Dormitory beds are 35Rs, single rooms are 50Rs and doubles are between 70 and 90Rs. You must also pay 100Rs as a deposit.

Hotel Payal's rooms are small, but each is equipped with a shower and a toilet and the place is relatively clean. Dorm beds go for 70Rs, single rooms are 150Rs and doubles cost 200Rs. If you want an air-conditioned room, they cost between 250-300Rs.

The *Ringo Guesthouse* and *Sunny Guesthouse*, near the Government of India Tourist Office in Connaught Place, are also popular. There are also some mid-range hotels in this area.

Tibetan Places of Interest

Tibet House - This small building, out on the Lodi Road, holds lectures and exhibits photographs, *thangkas*, art objects, and goods for daily use. You can also buy books on Tibetan issues and other

Main Bazaar, Delhi

Tibetan products.

Majnukatila Tibetan Camp - Along the bank of the Yamuna River, a kilometer north of the ISBT, is this Tibetan refugee town with an interesting entertainment district. There are many restaurants and hotels where you can experience traditional food served with authentic Tibetan hospitality. Direct buses to Dharamsala leave from this camp.

FROM MANALI TO LEH

There are 2 land routes to Leh, Ladakh; one is from Srinagar in Kashmir and the other one is from Manali in Himachal Pradesh. Many tourists take the Manali route to reach Leh due to the worsening situation in Srinagar and Kashmir as a whole. To date, there have been a number of incidents involving tourists in the area. You must also be careful on the Manali route as many people suffer from altitude sickness on this section. Stopping overnight at Keylong can help to get used to the high altitude.

MANALI

Manali, in the Kullu Valley, is a famous Indian resort and many people take extended breaks in the town. Vashisht, with its hot springs, is very popular among foreign visitors.

Access

There are many public and private bus services from Delhi to Manali and the journey takes around 15-16 hours. The journey from Dharamsala to Manali takes around 9 hours, as does the trip from Chandigarh and Shimla. From Delhi, the buses depart from the western part of the Main Bazaar and you can pick up a ticket at a travel agency in the market.

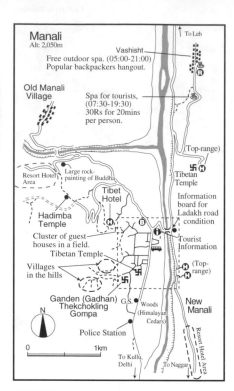

Manali
Alt: 2,050m

To Leh

Vashisht
Free outdoor spa. (05:00-21:00)
Popular backpackers hangout.

Old Manali
Village

Spa for tourists,
(07:30-19:30)
30Rs for 20mins
per person.

(Top-range)

卍
Tibetan
Temple

Resort Hotel
Area

Large rock-
painting of Buddha

Information
board for
Ladakh road
condition

Tibet
Hotel

Hadimba
Temple

Cluster of guest-
houses in a field.

Tourist
Information

Tibetan Temple

(Top-
range)

Villages
in the hills

卍

Ganden (Gadhan)
Thekchokling
Gompa

G.S.

Woods
(Himalayan
Cedars)

New
Manali

Police Station

N

0   1km

To Kullu,
Delhi

To Naggar

Resort Hotel Area

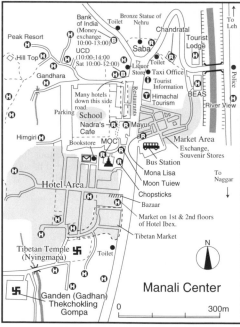

Bank
of India
(Money
exchange
10:00-13:00)

Bronze Statue of
Nehru

Toilet

Chandratal

To
Leh

Peak Resort

UCD
(10:00-14:00
Sat 10:00-12:00)

Saba

Tourist
Lodge

Hill Top

Toilet

Gandhara

Liquor
Store

Taxi Office

Tourist
Information

Police

Many hotels
down this side
road.

Himachal
Tourism

BEAS

River View

Parking

School
Nadra's
Cafe

Restaurants

Mayur

Himgiri

Bookstore   MOC

Market Area
Exchange,
Souvenir Stores

Bus Station

Mona Lisa

To
Naggar

Hotel Area

Moon Tuiew

Chopsticks

Bazaar

Market on 1st & 2nd floors
of Hotel Ibex.

Tibetan Temple
(Nyingmapa)

Toilet

Tibetan Market

N

Ganden (Gadhan)
Thekchokling
Gompa

Manali Center

0   300m

Accommodation

The number of hotels has been increasing in the
town because Manali is also a popular resort for
Indians. There are many guesthouses clustered
around Ganden (Gadhan) Thekchokling Gompa,
which is located in a farming area on a hill in the
town. The prices of these are quite reasonable at
50Rs to 150Rs a night. Many long-staying
backpackers prefer staying at Vashisht for its hot
springs.

Restaurants

The *MOC Restaurant* near the post office is run by
a Tibetan and serves *momos*, *tukpa*, and Western
food. There are also some Tibetan restaurants in
the market near the bus stand.

Places to See
Ganden (Gadhan) Thekchokling Gompa

Beyond the river is this new Tibetan monastery.
The gompa was constructed by the Tibetan refugees
who have settled in this area.

Vashisht

Built on the slope of a scenic hill, the Hindu temple
at the center of the village has an open-air bath.
There is no charge and it's open from 05:00 to
21:00. There is no mixed bathing allowed and you
are required to wear underwear while bathing.

There are more than 10 guesthouses in
Vashisht with prices ranging from 35Rs for a
single room to 50Rs for a double. There are
many visitors staying for extended periods and
therefore the usual selection of restaurants and
souvenir stores has sprung up in the village.

Travelling to Leh

Tourist buses are in operation between late June
and mid-September, depending on the weather.
Some local buses may even be available until
mid-October. The bus to Leh departs from the
Himachal Tourism office in Manali nearly
everyday. The trip is 2-3 days with overnight
stops under canvas. It costs about 800Rs

FROM SRINAGAR TO LEH

Srinagar has become a trouble spot due to the
ongoing dispute between the several separatist
groups operating in the Kashmir Valley and the
Indian government, which still refuses to
relinquish control of the only majority Muslim
state in the Union. The security situation has
been extremely bad and in 1995, tourists were
killed in a clash between armed militants and
the security forces.

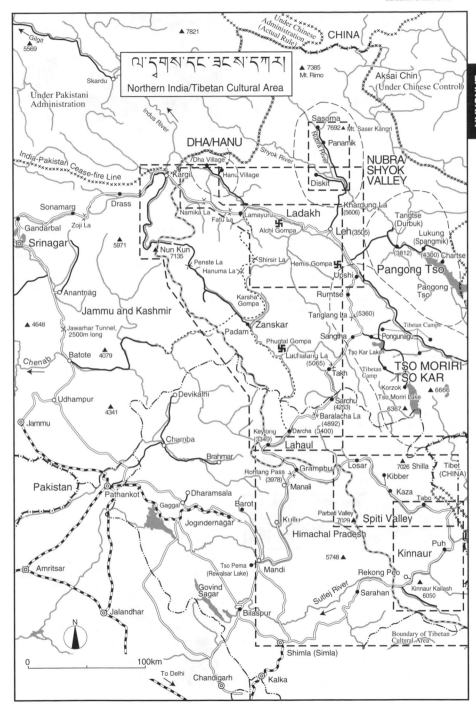

ལ་དྭགས་དང་ཟངས་དཀར།
Northern India/Tibetan Cultural Area

Gilgit
5569

Under Chinese
Administration
(Actual Rule)

CHINA

▲ 7821

Skardu

▲ 7385
Mt. Rimo

Aksai Chin
(Under Chinese Control)

Under Pakistani
Administration

Indus River

Sasoma
7692 ▲ Mt. Saser Kangri
Nubra River

DHA/HANU

Shyok River

Panamik

Dha Village

NUBRA
SHYOK
VALLEY

India-Pakistan Cease-fire Line

Hanu Village

Kargil

Diskit

Khardung La
(5606)

Tangtse
(Durbuk)

Sonamarg

Drass

Namika La

Lamayuru

Ladakh

Lukung
(Spangmik)

Gandarbal

Zoji La

Fatu La

Alchi Gompa

Leh (3505)

(3812)

(4300) Chartse

Srinagar

▲
5971

Nun Kun
▲ 7135

Shirsir La

Hemis Gompa

Pangong Tso

Penste La
Hanuma La

Upshi

Pangong
Tso

Anantnag

Karsha
Gompa

Rumtse

Jammu and Kashmir

Zanskar

Tanglang la (5360)

Tibetan Camps

▲ 4648

Jawarhar Tunnel,
2500m long

Padam

Phugtal Gompa

Sangtha

Pongunagu

TSO MORIRI
TSO KAR

Chenab

Batote 4079

Lachalang La
(5065)

Tso Kar Lake

Tibetan
Camp

Korzok

Udhampur

▲
4341

Devikalhi

Takh

Tso Moriri Lake

▲ 6666

6367 ▲

Jammu

Sarchu
(4253)

Baralacha La
(4892)

Chamba

Keylong
(3349)

Darcha (3400)

Brahmar

Lahaul

Pakistan

Rohtang Pass
(3978)

Gramphu

Losar

Manali

7026 Shilla

Kibber

Tibet
(CHINA)

Pathankot

Dharamsala

Kaza

Tabo

Gaggal

Barot

Kaza

Jogindernagar

Kullu

Parbati Valley
7029 ▲

Spiti Valley

Himachal Pradesh

Puh

Amritsar

5748 ▲

Kinnaur

Tso Pema
(Rewalsar Lake)

Mandi

Rekong Peo

Govind
Sagar

Sutlej River

Sarahan

Kinnaur Kailash
6050

Jalandhar

Bilaspur

Boundary of Tibetan
Cultural Area

N

Shimla (Simla)

0   100km

To Delhi

Chandigarh

Kalka

The nuclear tests carried out by both India and Pakistan in 1998 have heightened the tension and this may escalate the conflict over the coming years. Get as much information as possible in advance and be very careful when travelling in this area.

SRINAGAR

Access

Many buses bound for Srinagar depart from Delhi's ISBT. You can get a ticket at any of the travel agencies in the Main Bazaar and elsewhere. The journey takes about 30 hours from Delhi direct. There is another way to get to Srinagar that involves travelling to Jammu by rail and picking up a bus connection there to take you on to Srinagar. There are also 1-2 flights a day from Delhi to Srinagar.

Accommodation

Srinagar is famous for its houseboats on the Dal Lake. They are divided into 5 classes. Dormitory accommodation starts at around 15Rs, with singles going for anywhere between 30 to 300Rs. Double rooms range from 40 to 500Rs. If the houseboats don't grab you, there are guesthouses catering for backpackers around the Badshah Bridge.

Travelling to Leh

Make a seat reservation at the *Tourist Reception Centre*, from where the buses depart. You'll have to spend a night at Kargil on the way and then arrive at Leh in the evening of the following day as it's a 434km trip. The bus service operates between June and October, although it is dependent upon the weather conditions in the Zoji La Valley. When the weather is bad, buses still run on both sides of the valley, even though the direct service is unavailable.

LADAKH

Ladakh is known as 'Little Tibet' because it has maintained the Tibetan traditions that have been fast disappearing in central Tibet under Chinese rule. The Ladakh region was at times ruled over by Tibetan kings while on other occasions, Ladakhi kings governed the Guge area in Western Tibet. This allowed the region to maintain a relationship with the Tibetan monarchs and over time prosper as a Buddhist kingdom.

Ladakh's golden era, when the kingdom and its Buddhism flourished, was during the reign of

Polo Players, Ladakh

King Sengge Namgyal (1570-c.1642). The palace in Leh and Hemis Gompa were constructed around this time.

King Jamyang Namgyal (Sengge Namgyal's father), fell in love with Princess Gyal Katun of Balistan, which was a Muslim kingdom, and he welcomed her as his queen. This action protected the Ladakhi Kingdom. Ironically, while it was the Balistan ruler's intention to make the region Islamic, it was her son who became the most enthusiastic Buddhist king in Ladakhi history and the princess herself is praised as a manifestation of the Goddess Tara. In the 19th century, the Dogras from Jammu finally subdued the Ladakh nation and it was eventually merged into Kashmir.

More recently, the region has been in a difficult and complex political position, like so much of the rest of the Tibetan world. Tensions continue to be fueled by the 3 major powers in the region, India, Pakistan and China, as well as the separatist organizations that are active in Kashmir.

In Ladakh, the Drukpa Kagyupa school of Buddhism and the Dalai Lama's Gelukpa order are the most popular in the region. In the western areas, including Zanskar, Lahaul and Spiti, however, the teachings of the 11th century's great translator and monk, Rinchen Zangpo (958-1055), remain the dominant influence on the various religious orders here.

Rinchen Zangpo was sent to India by the ruler of the Guge Kingdom to revive Buddhism, which

Street Market, Leh

had been almost totally destroyed in central Tibet by the advocates of the ancient Bon faith. On his return, he became pivotal in the revival of Tibetan Buddhism, making him an enduring hero in the area. Along with Guru Rinpoche, who was invited from India in the 8th century, he remains the most popular figure among the people of this area.

LEH

Leh was once the capital of the Ladakh Kingdom, and the palace in the town center is a reminder of the town's past importance and prosperity. The current population stands at around 20,000 and though Islam has had a strong influence on the town, there is still a very Tibetan atmosphere about the place.

Access by Land
See the Delhi, Manali and Srinagar sections.

Access by Air
There are flights daily from Delhi to Leh, costing US$127. You can also fly in from Chandigarh (on Tuesday), Jammu (on Thursday and Sunday) and Srinagar (on Saturday). In summer, it is hard to get a confirmed ticket, although the aircraft are not necessarily full. Only about three-quarters of the seats can be occupied due to weight restrictions, even in late August just before the immensely popular *Ladakhi Festival* (which takes place during the first 2 weeks in September). Get your name on a waiting list or go to the airports early. With some patience and luck you'll get a seat.

When you arrive at Leh Airport, you are requested to fill out a simple form at the tourist information counter. This is a strange title, as you

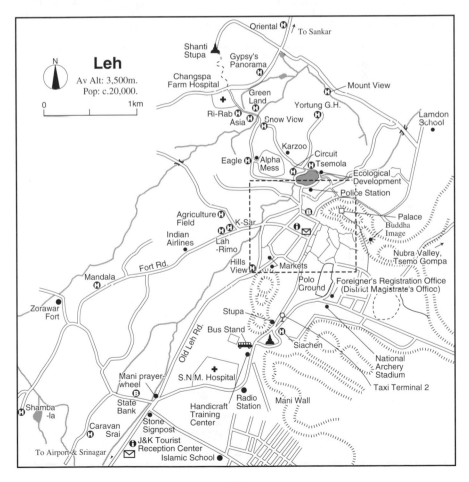

Shaman, Ladakh

can't get 'tourist information' here — they are the ones collecting the information. A taxi from the airport into the town center will cost you 70Rs.

Accommodation

You might have some difficulty in choosing a place to stay as there are more than 100 guesthouses and hotels dotted around the town. For a short stay, those near Fort Road or the Main Bazaar are the

most convenient. If you want to stay longer, the quiet Changspa area also would be good.

In winter, most guesthouses close, but you can still get some off-season discounts at the ones that stay open. Alternatively, local people are happy to make a little extra money, especially at this time of year, by having you stay at their homes in the town. The *Tak Guesthouse* offers double rooms for 150Rs and stays open during the winter, too. Off-season rates are around 50Rs for the same room.

The *Indus Guesthouse* single room charges start from 100Rs. After a long day looking around town you can enjoy unlimited hot showers in the evenings.

The *Ti-Sei Guesthouse*'s single rooms cost 120Rs and up, with doubles costing 150Rs and up. A friendly Ladakhi family runs this place and it has a traditional Ladakhi-style restaurant where you can enjoy a great dinner for around 25Rs, as long as you make a booking in advance. Rooms facing westward are particularly popular because of the great view. This guesthouse is also open year-round.

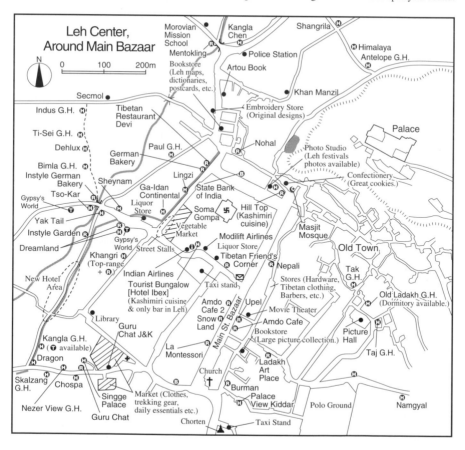

Leh Center, Around Main Bazaar

N

0   100   200m

The *Bimla Guesthouse*'s single rooms here start at 200Rs but the rooms are spacious and well-equipped.

The *Dreamland Hotel* used to be a popular hangout for Japanese backpackers.

The *Hotel Yak Tail*'s single room tariff is 1,000Rs, for which a meal is included. The restaurant is in the courtyard and has a good atmosphere.

Restaurants
There are a good variety of restaurants in the town with lots of Chinese, Tibetan and Western food available, though there are fewer Indian restaurants than you might expect. Drinks, such as beer, are sold at the more up-market establishments. Many of the restaurants unfortunately close during the low season.

The *Noral* is a very popular place for backpackers to meet up.

Dreamland Restaurant used to be a popular gathering place for backpackers.

Tibetan Friends Corner serves good food despite its appearance and the prices are reasonable. It's a little difficult to find as it has a very narrow entrance.

The *Guru Chat* serves good quality and reasonably priced curries and biriyani. It is famous for its owner, a well-known Japanese pop singer.

The *German Bakery* is popular among Westerners. You can get an apple pie here for 35Rs, and the large portions of pizza are a good take-away option if you're off on an outing for the day.

The *Instyle German Bakery* is full of tourists.

Changing Money
You have a couple of options for changing money in Leh. One is at the *FOREX Bureau* beside Hotel Ibex on Fort Road and the other is at the *State Bank of India*.

Mountain Sickness
This is a problem in Leh and quite a few tourists end up visiting the hospital. You should take it easy for the first couple of days after you arrive and drink

Leh Palace

plenty of water. It would also be better to lay off the alcohol and tobacco for a while. Even the more expensive hotels here do not have oxygen cylinders and masks.

Festivals
Among the many festivals held in the region, it is the *Tsechu* festivals that are especially popular with visitors. These are dedicated to Guru Rinpoche, who brought Tantric Buddhism from India in the 8th century.

Each gompa holds a celebration once a year, of which the one held at Hemis Gompa (June-July) is the most renowned. As you can imagine, this is easily the busiest time of the year in Leh [For a schedule of the major festivals, refer to the table in the Leh to the South section.]

In addition, the *State Tourist Office of Jammu & Kashmir* holds the annual *Ladakh Festival* from September 1-15. This is an attempt to extend the tourist season that ends in August and you can enjoy ethnic dances performed by villagers from throughout the region. Also on offer are Buddhist dances, concerts, polo matches, archery games, and a whole lot more.

Buses
Walk south from the Main Bazaar for about 20 minutes and you will reach the main bus stand. You can check the most recent timetables at the tourist information office in town. You don't have to get off the bus here since those buses arriving at Leh continue on to Taxi Terminal 2 near the Main Bazaar. Moreover, it is relatively easy to hitch a ride with a truck into Leh, so on returning to town after a trip, it would probably be better to hitch than wait for the infrequent buses.

Taxis
Taxis are also a convenient way to visit places such as Alchi and Lamayuru etc., where there are fewer bus connections. The taxi fares are not cheap but an association fixes them and neither booking one at the taxi office nor making a reservation through a travel agency makes any difference to the cost. There are various trips available or you can arrange one that fits with your own plans. Some of the more common routes and prices are as follows:

Likir-Alchi-Lamayuru 2,400Rs
Spituk-Phyang-Basgo-Likir-Alchi 1,550Rs
Chemre-Tak Tok-Hemis 1,115Rs
Stok-Matho 845Rs
*These prices are for 8 hours a day. For added hours, you should confirm the price in advance.

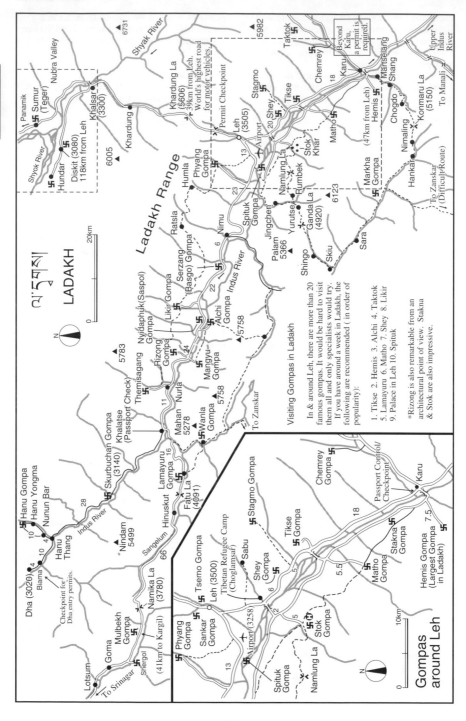

ལ་དྭགས།

LADAKH

Ladakh Range

6731
Shyak River
5982
Taktok
Upper Indus River
Beyond Karu, a permit is required.
Nubra Valley
Sumur (Teger)
Panamik
Khalsar (3300)
Khardung La (5606) 39km from Leh. World's highest road for motor vehicles.
Chemrey
Karu
18
Manselang Shang
To Manali
Khardung
Stagmo
Tikse
Konmaru La (5150)
Shyok River
Hundar
Diskit (3080) 118km from Leh
6005
Permit Checkpoint
Leh (3505)
Airport
13
20 Shey
Sakti
Matho
Chogdo
Hemis
(47km from Leh)
Nimaling
Humla
Phyang Gompa
Namlung La
Stok Khar
Markha Gompa
Hankar
To Zanskar (Difficult Route)
Ratsla
Nimu
Spituk Gompa
Jingchen
Yurutse
Ganda La (4920)
6123
Sara
5783
Serzang (Basgo) Gompa
6
22
5758
Palam 5366
Shingo
Skiu
Nyidaphuk (Saspol) Gompa
Likir Gompa
Alchi Gompa
Rizong Gompa
24
Mangyu Gompa
5758
Themisagang
11
Nurla
Skurbuchan Gompa (3140)
Khalatse (Passport Check)
Mahan 5278
Wanla Gompa
To Zanskar
Hanu Gompa
Hanu Yongma
Nunun Bar
Lamayuru Gompa
Hinuskut
Fatu La (4091)
28
Sangelum
Nindam 5499
Dha (3020)
Biama
Hanu Thang
10
4
10
4
Namika La (3780)
66
Checkpoint for Dha entry permits.
Mulbekh Gompa
Goma
Shergol
(41km to Kargil)
Lotsum
To Srinagar

20km
0

N

Visiting Gompas in Ladakh

In & around Leh, there are more than 20 famous gompas. It would be hard to visit them all and only specialists would try. If you have around a week in Ladakh, the following are recommended (in order of popularity):

1. Tikse 2. Hemis 3. Alchi 4. Taktok 5. Lamayuru 6. Matho 7. Shey 8. Likir 9. Palace in Leh 10. Spituk

*Rizong is also remarkable from an architectural point of view. Stakna & Stok are also impressive.

Gompas around Leh

Chemrey Gompa
Stagmo Gompa
Passport Control/ Checkpoint
Karu
Tikse Gompa
18
7.5
Tsemo Gompa
Sabu
Tibetan Refugee Camp (Choglamsar)
Shey Gompa
5.5
Stakna Gompa
Hemis Gompa (Largest Gompa in Ladakh)
Leh (3500)
6
5
Matho Gompa
Phyang Gompa
Sankar Gompa
Airport (3258)
2
5
Stok Gompa
Namlung La
13
Spituk Gompa

10km
0

N

290

Places to See
Leh Palace

The palace was considered fine enough to have been a model for the colossal Potala Palace in Lhasa. In the 16th and 17th centuries, when Leh was in its heyday, King Sengge Namgyal commissioned the construction of the building. It consists of 9 levels and looks down on the town from a rocky hill. The interior is almost in ruins and if you want to look around, the old monk who acts as a guard will unlock it for you. Admission is 10Rs.

Sankar Gompa

This Gelukpa monastery is about a 15-minute walk along the path beside the Himalaya Guesthouse and its quiet surroundings make it an ideal spot for a stroll.

Tsemo Gompa

On top of the same hill as the King's palace, this monastery was built in the 16th century and is home to a large sitting Buddha. This statue of Maitreya is the largest in Ladakh.

The Sonamling Tibetan Refugee Settlement at Choglamsar

About 5km south-east of Leh, you'll find this small village with its many stores, a Tibetan carpet factory, and other workshops which produce handicrafts. There is also a very large *Tibetan Childrens' Village*. It was established in 1975 and is home to around 2,000 children. The village has schools, a vocational training center and hostels for young and old people.
Tel: 01982-4124/ 4139/ 4140

LEH TO THE SOUTH
GOMPAS IN THE INDUS VALLEY

Spituk Gompa

This is the nearest gompa to Leh. There are minibuses to Spituk every 30 minutes from 07:00 to 19:00 and they cost 5Rs. Religious services are held around noon and there are sand *mandalas* on display here. Spituk Monastery holds a *Gustor* festival on the 28th & 29th of the 11th lunar month (December-January). There are no restaurants nearby and the admission charge is 15Rs.

Shey Gompa

This used to be the Ladakhi king's imperial summer villa but now it's almost in ruins. Inside, however, the wall paintings are splendid and it has a 12m-high statue of Buddha. Around the gompa, there are a large number of chortens standing together.

Tikse Gompa

Below the ruins, there is a marsh where horses and yaks are pastured. There is accommodation available and some restaurants around the monastery. To get to Shey, take a minibus going to Tikse Gompa.

Tikse Gompa

About 17km to the east of Leh lies Tikse Gompa. It stands on a hill and could even symbolize Ladakh itself. Some people will be satisfied with a stay in Ladakh if they simply see this one gompa. It is easy to get there from Leh as there are minibuses every 30 minutes from 08:30-19:00, costing around 8Rs. It would be a good idea to catch a religious service which start at 11:00 most days. Admission to the site is 15Rs. Each year on the 18th & 19th days of the 9th lunar month (October-November), a festival is held at the gompa. There are rooms and food available at the guesthouse near the foot of the monastery.

Hemis Gompa

This is the largest and most famous gompa in Ladakh. It was founded in the 17th century while the Ladakhi Kingdom flourished during the reign of King Sengge Namgyal (as were many other smaller monasteries throughout Ladakh). The *Tsechu* festival at Hemis Gompa, on the 10th & 11th days of the 5th lunar month (June-July) every year, is regarded as the most attractive event in the region. The monastery belongs to the Drukpa Kagyupa order and it costs 20Rs to enter. Minibuses leave Leh at 09:30 and 16:00 and it's a 2-hour trip.

Hemis Gompa

291

Stok Khar

Located on the opposite side of Choglamsar Bridge, this is where some of the kings of Ladakh used to live. Part of the palace is open to the public as a museum and the admission charge is 20Rs. There is also a *Tsechu* festival held at Gurphug Gompa in Stok every year on the 7th-9th days of the 2nd lunar month (March-April). Buses leave Leh at 08:00 and 17:00. Minibuses also go out to Stok Khar, leaving Leh at 14:00 and 16:30 and returning from Stok at 08:00 and 15:15.

Matho Gompa

This is a Sakyapa order gompa, which is uncommon in the Ladakh region. The *Nagrang* festival is held here on the 14th & 15th days of the 1st lunar month (February-March) each year. Buses taking you to Matho leave Leh at 07:30 and 16:30 and minibuses leave Leh at 14:00 and return from Matho at 08:00 and 16:00.

Stakna Gompa

This is a Drukpa Kagyupa gompa found between Tikse and Karu Village, which is located at the foot of Hemis Gompa's hill. The admission charge is 20Rs. You can get there by taking a bus to Hemis and many people combine a visit here with one to Matho Gompa.

Taktok Gompa

Taktok Gompa is the only Nyingmapa monastery in the area and holds its annual *Tsechu* festivities on the 9th & 10th days of the 1st lunar month (February-March). The *Angchok* festival is also held here on the 29th & 30th days of the 9th lunar month (October-November). Admission to the monastery is 20Rs.

Except on Sundays, a private bus leaves Leh at 08:00 for Taktok. You can also get there by taking a minibus to Sakti Village and then continuing on foot. From Leh, the minibuses leave at 09:30 and every half-hour between 14:00 and 16:00. Returning from Sakti, there are departures at 07:30, 10:30 and 16:00.

Ladakhi Festival

Chemrey Gompa

It is said that this gompa was built in 1645 to mourn the death of King Sengge Namgyal. The monastery also holds its *Angchok* celebrations on the 29th & 30th days of the 9th lunar month (October-November) each year. Admission costs 15Rs. You can get here by taking a minibus to Sakti.

Major Festivals in Ladakh and Zanskar		
Place (Festival)	Year 2004 / 2005 / 2006	

Place (Festival)	Year 2004 / 2005 / 2006
Spituk (Gustor)	Jan 19-20/Jan 8-9/Jan 27-28
Leh/Likir/Diskit (Dosmochey)	Feb 18-19/Feb 6-7/Feb 26-27
Stok Khar (Tsechu)	Feb 29-Mar 1/ Feb 17-18/Mar 8-9
Matho (Nagrang)	Mar 5-6/Feb 22-23/Mar 14-15
Hemis (Tsechu)	Jun 27-28/Jun 17-18/Jul 6-7
Karsha (Gustor)	Jul 14-15/Jul 3-4/Jul 22-23
Phyang (Tsedup)	Jul 19-20/Aug 7-8/Jul 27-28
Taktok (Tsechu)	Jul 27-28/Aug 15-16/Aug 4-5
Tikse (Gustor)	Oct 31-Nov 1/Nov 18-19/Nov 8-9
Chemrey/Taktok (Angchok)	Nov 10-11/Nov 29-30/Nov 18-19
All gompas (Ladakhi Losar-New Year)	Dec 12/Jan 1/Dec 21

LEH AND THE WEST
GOMPAS ON THE KARGIL ROUTE

Alchi Gompa

Sixty-four kilometers to the west of Leh, Alchi Gompa is famous for its precious Kashmiri-style Buddhist wall paintings. The exterior is in poor condition but inside, the artwork is a magnificent sight. It is said that Rinchen Zangpo founded the gompa in the 11th century and it has survived destruction at the hands of invading forces, unlike most of the area's monasteries that were decorated in this style. This was in part because Alchi Gompa is hard to reach. Admission is 15Rs and a flashlight is a must.

In Alchi, you'll find some guesthouses, restaurants, and souvenir stores. A minibus leaves Leh for Alchi at 16:00 and returns from Alchi to Leh at 07:00. If your schedule is tight, it would be better to take a taxi or to hitchhike. Another option is to take the bus leaving Leh for Kargil at 05:30 and get off at Saspul. From there you continue on foot for about an hour.

Likir Gompa

This gompa is nestled on a mountainside, set back about 5km from the main road. It was founded in the 14th century but the existing buildings are a lot more recent. This gompa is a Gelukpa monastery where about 150 monks are working hard on its reconstruction. Admission is not guaranteed. The monastery hosts a *Dosmochey* festival on the 28th & 29th days of the 12th lunar month (January-February) each year.

There is a guesthouse at the foot of the mountain and you can reach this gompa by taking a minibus that leaves Leh at 16:00 and returns at 07:00.

Serzang Gompa
Serzang Gompa is 42km to the west of Leh and lies in ruins on top of a cliff. The climb up to the monastery isn't easy and you have to be careful. There is a small village surrounding the site and beside it is a hut where an old monk lives. He acts as a guide and keeps the key for the room containing the great image of the Buddha. You can also see a very old but ill-defined statue of the Bodhisattva Maitreya. The gompa was built during the reign of King Sengge Namgyal and from this vantage you can get a great view of the surrounding area.

Rizong Gompa
This monastery and nunnery is 6km off the main road and up in the mountains. There are no hotels or guesthouses nearby but you can stay at the gompa itself. I was offered a single room with a solar-powered fluorescent lamp and a stove but be careful of the bedbugs. Meals are also served here and for breakfast, you'll be offered *tsampa* (*ngamphe* in Ladakhi) and leaf soup at 05:30. You get a heaped bowl of rice covered with *dal* for lunch at 09:00 and the same for supper at 21:00. Besides the 3 meals, butter tea and refreshments are served throughout the day.

To get to Rizong, you have to get off the bus at Uletokpo, about 9km from Saspul, though it would be advisable to tell the conductor in advance that you are going to Rizong Gompa. At the foot of the small bridge you will come to a sign reading 'Way to Rizong Gompa.' Walk 5-6km along the dreary mountain path and then suddenly this beautiful monastery will come into view.

Likir Gompa

Lamayuru Gompa

Lamayuru Gompa
This is an old but very typical Ladakhi gompa named *Yung Drung* meaning 'Swastika.' It lies in an area sometimes referred to as 'Moon World.' The monastery is along the Kargil to Leh bus route. There are a number of guesthouses in Lamayuru Village below the monastery. A popular route for trekkers is to head to the south-east from here and aim for Padam (Padum) in Zanskar via Wanla Gompa. Although there are no guesthouses in Wanla, on the way, you can still stay at people's houses in the village. There is also a bus service from Leh to Wanla that departs at 08:30 on Sunday.

TREKKING FROM LEH

Trekking Options
Unlike in Nepal, there are very few mountain huts or places to eat along the way. Camping and cooking your own food is the way things work in this area.

With a Guide & Pony
There seems to be no porter system; instead, a pony carries your bags and a pony-man acts as your guide and cook. Travel agencies and hotels in Leh can arrange these for you.

Trekking Alone
You carry all the equipment and food for the whole trek yourself. In large villages you may find places to stay and eat, or get some flour to make *chapattis* or buy some vegetables, but don't rely on it.

Season
From late May through to early June, you should be able to enjoy the calm villages and nature of Ladakh, however, snowfalls will prevent you from going to many areas. You can go anywhere in July and August, but the thawing of the mountain snows swells the rivers at this time of year and you may have to cross these icy obstacles using only a simple

piece of rope stretched across them. It can also rain heavily at this time of year (in June, you can cross these same rivers on foot.). Pony-men say that early June is better all-round for trekking.

Equipment
It is best to take a pair of trekking shoes because there are far fewer easy routes compared to similar areas in Nepal. A good sleeping bag is another recommended item, as a 3-seasons one didn't keep me warm enough, even in late May. Waterproofs are also a must.

Common Trekking Courses Starting at Leh
Namlung La Trekking (3 nights)
A short trekking course for crossing the Namlung La Pass (4,900m):

Day 1: Spituk-Jingchen
Day 2: Jingchen-Rumbek
Day 3: Rumbek-Namlung La-Stok Base Camp
Day 4: Stok-Leh

*This route can be closed until late May due to heavy snowfalls in Namlung La.

Markha Valley Trekking (7 nights)
A popular route for crossing Ganda La (4,920m) and Kongmaru La (5,150m) passes:

Day 1: Spituk-Jingchen
Day 2: Jingchen-Yurutse
Day 3: Yurutse-Ganda La-Skiu
Day 4: Skiu-Markha
Day 5: Markha-Hankar
Day 6: Hankar-Nimaling
Day 7: Nimaling-Kongmaru La-Shang
Day 8: Shang-Hemis

*If you have a couple of extra days, you can make the trip easier by staying at Shingo between Yurutse and Skiu, and at Chogdo between Nimaling and Shang.

Trekking Costs
Namlung La Trek (3 nights) for 1 person arranged by Bimla Guesthouse:

Tent rental 75Rs
Two ponies for 3 days 960Rs
(including the pony-man)
Food 900Rs
(including cooking fees)

Total 1,935Rs

Markha Valley Trek (7 nights) for 1 person arranged by Hotel Rafica:

Taxi from Leh to Spituk 115Rs
Food 2,200Rs
Two ponies for 8 days 3,200Rs
(including the pony-man)
Tent rental 185Rs
Commission 300Rs

Total 6,000Rs

*There is also a 15Rs fee required at the campsite in each village.

DHA/HANU VILLAGES

Right next to the India-Pakistan border (or cease-fire line) are the small villages of Dha and Hanu where an Aryan-related ethnic group, the Drokpa, lives. The Drokpa, also known as Dards, have a unique culture and they practice Tibetan Buddhism.

Dha Village
Dha is a small village of about 200 people located 160km to the west of Leh. Since 1994 it has been open to foreign tourists. One of the fascinating things about this village is the clothing worn by the women.

Although they are Buddhists, they wear neither Tibetan clothes nor *Peraks* (headdresses) like the women in other villages in Ladakh. Instead, they wear Punjabi dresses along with cardigans, both at home and in the fields. Another unusual custom peculiar to this area is the wearing of beautiful flowers and coins etc., in their plaited hair.

Permit
An ILP (Inner Line Permit) is required to enter the Dha/Hanu area. Individuals can get one of these from a travel agency in Leh and the prices can vary substantially. Sometimes it can cost 200Rs for a group and at other times it can cost 100Rs for just 1 person. It is said that a rule requires travel agencies to organize more than 4 tourists as a group for an application, thus affecting the prices per person. Apply for the permit in the morning and it will be issued in the evening of the same day. The permit allows you to stay in the area for up to a week.

Access by Bus
A bus heading for Dha/Hanu leaves Leh at 09:00 on Monday and Thursday. The rest of the week, the bus terminates at Biama, 4km away. You can't buy a ticket until around 08:00 on the day of departure. The bus arrives around 17:30 and returns to Leh the next day. Dha is on a hill so be careful

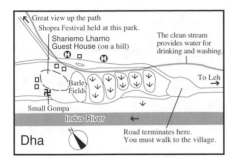

Dha

as it's not too easy to find the path up to the village, especially in the evening light when the bus usually arrives.

Chartering a Jeep
Hiring a jeep in Leh will make the trip a lot easier but also more expensive.

Accommodation & Restaurants
Shariemo Lhamo Guesthouse's beds are 40Rs.
Chunu Guesthouse's beds are 30Rs.
*There is food available at the guesthouses, with a dish of rice and vegetables costing 15Rs and tea 3Rs. Even so, it would be better to bring something to eat. If you get stuck, there is a small store near the bus stop at Biama.

Festivals
"When we visited Dha from July 11 to 14, we were lucky enough to catch a festival called *Shopra*, which is held to usher in a good harvest. It is celebrated over 4-5 days around the night of the full moon in July.

In the square, scores of men and women of all ages perform a deeply felt and moving dance called *Funla*. They dance in a circle accompanied by a sad melody played by between 3-7 musicians.

While we watched the dance, we were served *Chang* (a type of barley beer) and in a village without any electric light, the combination of moonlight and flickering torches made the festival feel very magical. There is another festival during harvest time around September."

Hanu Village
Fourteen kilometers towards Leh from Dha is the small village of Hanu. There is a small Indian army post here and a store that sells cigarettes, instant noodles, etc. A soldier even cooked a pot noodle for us while we

were there. There are fewer private houses here than at Dha. Hanu has a school but there is little else of interest in the village. The gompa is kept locked.

There is a trekking route from here to Masung Bali, Hanu Yongma, and Hanu Gompa and the path follows a cliff alongside a beautiful stream.

NUBRA VALLEY

The Nubra Valley is located 140km to the north of Leh and used to be a bustling trade route connecting Tibet with Turkestan. Now it's just a sleepy backwater. Khardung La pass, the highest point on the Beacon Highway from Leh to Nubra, is at 5,606m and this road is regarded as the highest road in the world open to motorized traffic. The tourist season is from early summer to early autumn but it has been extended recently due to snow clearing.

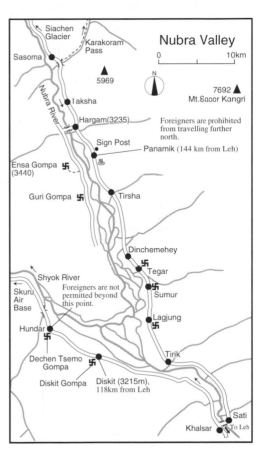

Permit

An Inner Line Permit is required for Nubra and there is a checkpoint on the way. You can get a 7 day permit from travel agencies in Leh and it will be issued within 1-2 days. The price is about 150Rs per person but once again, it will vary according to the agents and the number of applicants. No photograph is required. Although the permit is only valid for 7 days, verification of those leaving the Nubra area to return to Leh is not strict.

Panamik

There is a hot spring at the end of this village and if you want to take a dip, just ask any of the villagers as they all know it. You will find a place to take off your clothes and there are no problems with the water supply and temperature but a flashlight is necessary when it gets dark as there is no electricity. Ensa Gompa is on the other side of the river. The river looks shallow enough to cross on foot but don't be fooled as it is really too deep to ford. At Hargram, 5km upstream, you can cross a bridge, although this detour requires a couple of hours.

There are guesthouses in the village but you may enjoy staying at villagers' homes a bit more. A fair rate for this is about 65Rs per night. This includes meals. There are neither restaurants nor stores in Panamik.

Tegar & Sumur

There are 6 gompas in the villages of Tegar and Sumur on the way from Leh to Panamik. The most famous is Samtanling Gompa, a 10-minute walk to the east of Tegar Village. It is the second largest Gelukpa gompa in Nubra and is said to house about 70 monks.

Diskit

Diskit is the largest village in Nubra and even has a post office. Off to one side of the village there is Diskit Gompa which has a good view of the Nubra Valley. Diskit Gompa is the oldest and largest monastery in Nubra and there are countless

Chortens, Diskit

chortens around the site. The monastery holds its annual *Dosmochey* festival on the 28th & 29th days of the 12th lunar month (January-February). The monastery is about a 45-minute walk from the village.

The *Olthang Guesthouse* has only lukewarm showers but it is new, clean and prepares meals. A guy from the guesthouse comes to the bus stop to tout for customers and you'll find that it is a kilometer out of town, as opposed to other guesthouses nearer the center.

Khalsar

This village is located just before the turn-off for Panamik and Diskit and there are some guesthouses and restaurants here. This is a convenient place to hitch a lift from as most trucks, jeeps, and buses pull over for a rest stop here. If you're hungry, there is nothing more than *dal* and rice and omelets to be had.

Hundar

Hundar is the last place in this area that foreigners can visit. The village is home to Dechen Tsemo Gompa and a ruined fortress.

Access

Local bus services are available from the Government Bus Station in Leh and the road conditions are fairly good. Unless you get a ticket the day before, however, you may not get a seat and you'll miss all the stunning views along the way.

The tickets are sold from 15:00 the day before. To get to Diskit, there is a bus on Thursday (to Diskit) or Saturday (to Skuru Air Base) and the journey takes about 7 hours. To get to Panamik you'll have to take a bus on Tuesday (to Taksha) or Thursday (to Panamik). Alternatively, hitchhiking is relatively easy and will save you the hassle of hanging around for the limited bus services to these areas.

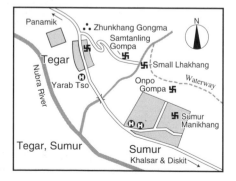

Tegar, Sumur

EAST LADAKH

At the eastern end of Ladakh, near the Tibetan border, there are 2 large lakes, Pangong Tso and Tso Moriri. The surrounding area is a wild nomadic land but it is relatively easy to get to the lakes by jeep if you arrange one through a travel agency in Leh. If you want to trek in this area, bear in mind that the going is tough in this remote region.

Tso Moriri

South from Leh on the Manali road after the Taglang La pass you'll come into the Tso Moriri area at an altitude of over 4,000m. Locals call this area *Changthang*, meaning 'Northern Plain.' There is no artificial sound here and only thin, extremely dry air and a huge deep blue sky.

In this area, where the temperature goes down to as low as -30°C in winter, sturdy nomads are the sole inhabitants along with their herds of sheep, goats, and yaks. They are continually moving around the region in search of the scarce grazing pasture and they warmly welcome the sudden arrival of any visitors.

There are very few villages on the way to Tso Moriri so be sure to bring a tent and plenty of food when you go trekking here. You should seriously think about packing a sleeping bag and warm clothes since the temperature drops sharply at night, even in summer. Having enough water is also a major concern and getting around isn't a simple matter, as you may not meet many people to ask for directions. In short, this is not an easy place for trekking, unlike around Zanskar.

If you take a local bus and get to Mahe Bridge along the Indus River, you can reach Tso Moriri in 3 days. If you don't join a group to travel to this area, you can't always get through the checkpoints on the way. You'll need a permit that can be issued in Leh, and a 1-week one will cost you 100Rs per person. You must have photocopies of the passports of 4 tourists before you can make an application.

A Tso Moriri jeep tour started in 1997 but many travel agencies are not too familiar with the area and the prices are still very high.

Tso Moriri Three-Day Jeep Tour

"We left Leh early in the morning and at the first checkpoint at Upshi we had no problem at all, unlike the situation if you take a local bus. Here, the real uphill section starts but our jeep quickly reached a valley with exposed brittle rock strata and we crossed Taglang La before noon. The pass, decorated with *tar-choks* fluttering in the mountain wind, is over 5,300m and it's still cold in mid-summer.

When our jeep got off the main road to Manali and we headed east, we came into the arid highlands at 4,500m and this area turned out to be the highlight of the tour. Although the car ran smoothly while churning up a cloud of dust behind us, the trip was still very tough. For the first night, we camped at Tso Kar Lake and as its name, which means 'White Lake', suggests, it's a salt lake with glittering white salt deposits on the shores and a surface that reflects the mountain vista in front of it.

On the second day, we encountered *Kyang* (Tibetan wild asses) galloping away from the noise of the jeep, yaks bolting from us despite their immense bulk and nomads chasing their scattering herds of sheep and goats. After another high pass, our jeep arrived at Sumdo, a Tibetan refugee camp with a school where nomadic children live and study together. Just before sunset, we finally reached Tso Moriri and after catching the last light over the lake, we prepared for our return trip the following morning.

Prices for the tours vary according to the travel agent. Our tour, including a tent, food and a driver/cook, cost US$ 80 per person per day."

Pangong Tso

Pangong Tso, three-quarters of which is in Tibet, is the highest salt lake in Ladakh and one of the highest in the world. Go from Leh to Karu on the eastern side of the Indus River and then take the road off to the north-east. The road stretching to the border used to be a trade route but now is mainly used by the army. To reach the lake you must cross the high Chang La Valley (5,599m).

A tour arranged by a travel agency in Leh takes you to Spangmik on the western side of the lake. It is said that there is also a local bus that can take you up to Tangtse just before Spangmik.

Tso Moriri Jeep Tour

ZANSKAR

Zanskar, in the south of Ladakh, tends to be isolated from the outside world for over 6 months each year due to heavy snowfalls in the highland valleys. This situation may be part of the reason why there was little effect here from the strong Islamic influence that swept across the rest of the region. Many of the old Buddhist temples built in the 10th century still remain intact.

Mosque, Padam (Padum)

There wasn't a road here open to motorized traffic until 1981 when the Padam (Padum)-Zanskar-Kargil route was finished. This road is only open to traffic between July and October, and even this depends on the weather conditions. The road is the main artery through to Zangla and the lack of other minor roads means that you'll have to trek to reach most places around the Zanskar area.

July to September is the best time to visit, though June might be better if you want to visit some of the quieter villages. Many tourists and trekkers crowd in after the road opens in early July. Besides, the villages are at their most beautiful in the early summer.

A tourist who entered Zanskar from Manali via Rohtang La and Shingo La in mid-June told me that there was still snow and frozen slopes which could be dangerous if you are trekking in the area. Also, there were dangerous roads on which ice beds had collapsed due to the heat of the early summer sun. To top it off, he also witnessed avalanches and a landslide while he was there. In the same area, there was a group of trekkers who had to abandon their baggage and donkey due to the bad weather. Visiting Zanskar doesn't require a permit.

PADAM (PADUM)

Padam (Padum) is in the center of Zanskar and has a population of about 1,000. For visitors, this is the starting point for trekking in the Zanskar area. The opening of the road has dramatically improved the supply of basic provisions and there is now even a trekking store in the town. Bottled water is still unavailable here.

Access
*From Leh, you will go through Kargil, in northern Ladakh, to reach Padam (Padum).
*Leh to Kargil—A bus to Kargil and onto Srinagar leaves the bus station in Leh at 06:00. There are also others available later in the day and the journey

takes around 12 hours. Kargil is the second largest town in Ladakh and has many stores and restaurants. There are hotels around the area of the bus stop. *Hotel International* has double rooms for 100Rs and is a 2-minute walk from the bus stop. It is located next to the *Crown Hotel*.
*Kargil to Padam (Padum)—A bus leaves Kargil at 03:00 every other day and you can buy a ticket at the Bus Booking Office, 1 minute from the bus station. To make sure you get a seat, you should buy a ticket when you first arrive in Kargil.

Accommodation & Restaurants
There are a number of hotels in Padam (Padum), such as the *Hotel Chorala* near the bazaar and others about 300m north of the bazaar. There are also some Chinese restaurants in the same area. Most of the hotels and restaurants are closed in the off-season but you can still stay at local peoples' houses.

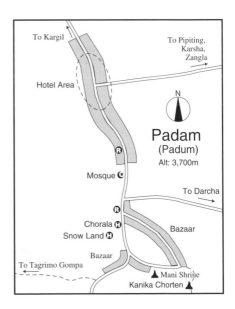

Trekking

Here are some common trekking routes starting from Padam (Padum).

Padam (Padum)-Phugtal- Darcha
.... (7 days or more)
Padam (Padum)-Zangla-Lamayuru
.... (10 days or more)
Padam (Padum)-Sani-Kargil
.... (7-9 days, access by car)

In the following section, the routes use Padam (Padum) as the starting point. You can also take routes that finish in Padam (Padum) or you can check for others on the map.

PADAM (PADUM)-PHUGTAL-DARCHA

You go south to the Tsarap River and then go upstream. A road extends about 2km beyond the village of Mune.
Sample trekking route for the area:

Day 1: Padam (Padum)-Mune Gompa
Day 2: Mune-Purne
Day 3: Purne-Phugtal Gompa-Purne-Testa (Teta)
Day 4: Testa (Teta)-Kargyak
Day 5: Kargyak-Lakong (Lakang)
Day 6: Lakong (Lakang)-Shingo La (5,080m)
        -Ramjak
Day 7: Ramjak-Darcha

*This route factors in around 6-8 hours trekking each day.

Bardan Gompa

Twelve kilometers to the south of Padam (Padum), this fort-like monastery stands on huge rocks in a riverbank. It belongs to the Drukpa Kagyupa order and has about 40 monks in residence. The main temple is a 3-story building and at the front is the Dukhang (assembly hall) with a Gonkhang (temple

Mask Dance, Bardan Gompa

that is home to the protector deities) to its left. The structures are surrounded by a walkway for pilgrims.

Mune Gompa

This is a small Gelukpa monastery, about 10km to the south of Bardan Gompa.

Phugtal Gompa

This is also a Gelukpa monastery that was established in the 15th century and is home to between 60 and 70 monks (some say that part of the gompa was actually built in the 11th century).

The white monks' residences stand in a lineup on the rock cliff, perched far above the river. There are also 3 temples in caves on the cliff; the Dukhang is to the right, and the Gonkhang and Kangyur are on the left.

At the eastern end, away from the caves, there is also the Tonpa Lhakhang honoring Shakyamuni (the Buddha of the history books, formerly known as Prince Siddhartha before he reached enlightenment).

There is a guesthouse and stores at Purne, where the Tsarap River changes course and merges with the Kargyak River. By going further up the Tsarap River, you will come to Tangtak Gompa, a branch of Phugtal Gompa. Alternatively, by going up the Kargyak River, you will find the path leading to Darcha on the Lch-Manali route.

PADAM (PADUM)-ZANGLA-LAMAYURU

Sample trekking route for the area:

Day 1: Padam (Padum)-Karsha
Day 2: Karsha-Pishu
Day 3: Pishu-Hanumil
Day 4: Hanumil-Snertse
Day 5: Snertse-Hanuma La (4,950m)-Lingshad
Day 6: Lingshad-Just before Singe La
Day 7: Singe La (5,060m)-Photosar
Day 8: Photosar- Shirsir La (4,800m)-Hanuputt La
Day 9: Hanuputt La (3,450m)-Wan La Gompa
Day 10: Wan La Gompa-Lamayuru

*This schedule is based on 4-6 hours of trekking per day, with an easy first day of 2-3 hours between Padam (Padum) and Karsha.

Karsha Gompa

This is the largest monastery in the Zanskar region and its buildings look as if they are hugging the rocky mountain slope on which they are built. It was reputedly founded during the 11th century. This monastery, north of Padam (Padum), belongs to the

Zanskar

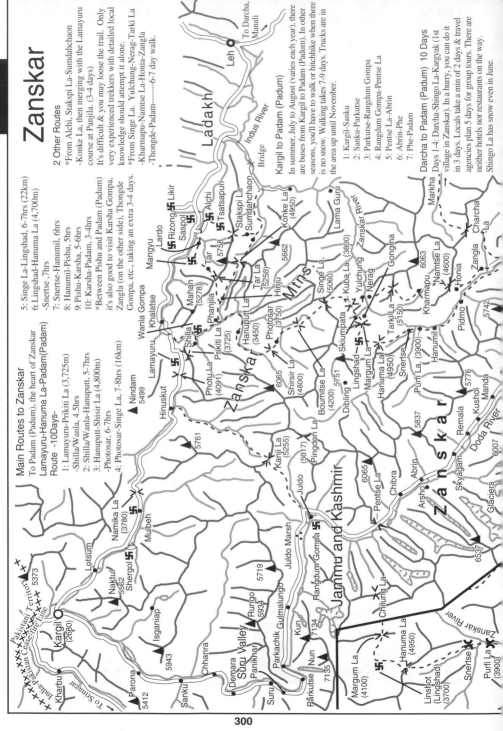

Main Routes to Zanskar

To Padam (Padum), the heart of Zanskar
Lamayuru-Hanuma La-Padam(Padam)
Route -10Days-

1: Lamayuru-Prikiti La (3,725m)
   -Shilla/Wanla. 4.5hrs
2: Shilla/Wanla-Hanuputt, 5-7hrs
3: Hanuputt-Shisir La (4,800m)
   -Photosar, 6-7hrs
4: Photosar-Singe La, 7-8hrs (16km)

5: Singe La-Lingshad, 6-7hrs (22km)
6: Lingshad-Hanuma La (4,700m)
   -Snertse .7hrs
7: Snertse-Hanumil, 6hrs
8: Hanumil-Pishu, 5hrs
9: Pishu-Karsha. 5-6hrs
10: Karsha-Padam, 3-4hrs
*Between Pishu and Padam (Padum)
it's also good to visit Karsha Gompa,
Zangla (on the other side), Thongde
Gompa, etc., taking an extra 3-4 days.

2 Other Routes

*From Alchi, Stakspi La-Sumdahchaon
-Konke La. then merging with the Lamayuru
course at Panjila. (3-4 days)
It's difficult & you may loose the trail. Only
very experienced trekkers with detailed local
knowledge should attempt it alone.
*From Singe La. Yulchung-Nerag-Tarki La
-Kharmapu-Namtse La-Honia-Zangla
-Thongde-Padam-------6-7 day walk.

Kargil to Padam (Padum)

In summer, July to August (varies each year), there
are buses from Kargil to Padam (Padum). In other
seasons, you'll have to walk or hitchhike when there
is no snow. Walking takes 7-9 days. Trucks are in
the area up until November.

1: Kargil-Sanku
2: Sanku-Parkutse
3: Parkutse-Rangdum Gompa
4: Rangdum Gompa-Pentse La
5: Pentse La-Abrin
6: Abrin-Phe
7: Phe-Padam

Darcha to Padam (Padum) 10 Days

Days 1-4: Darcha-Shingo La-Kargyak (1st
village in Zanskar). In a hurry, you can do it
in 3 days. Locals take a min of 2 days & travel
agencies plan 5 days for group tours. There are
neither hotels nor restaurants on the way.
Shingo La has snow even in June.

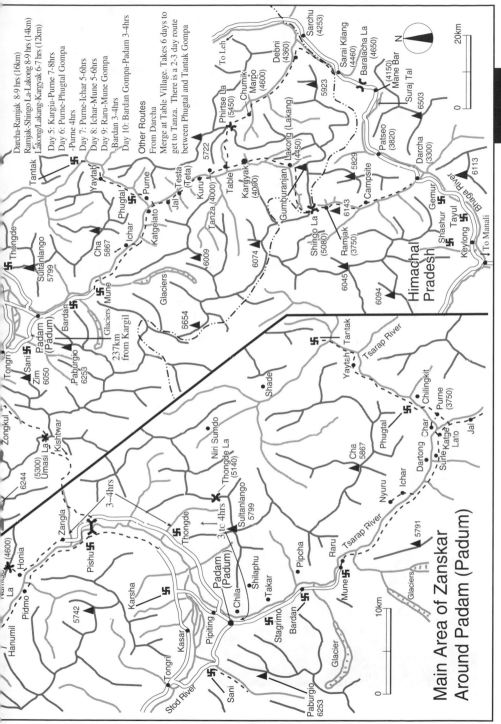

Main Area of Zanskar
Around Padam (Padum)

Gelukpa school and has about 200 monks now. The annual *Gustor* dances and festivities are held on the 29th & 30th days of the 5th lunar month (June-July). It is a 2-3 hours on foot from Padam (Padum) and also accessible by car. There are restaurants and stores here and you can stay at local peoples' houses overnight.

Thongde Gompa
After Karsha Gompa, Thongde is the second largest monastery in Zanskar. Established in the 11th century, this Gelukpa monastery houses about 30 monks. There are some temples surrounding a courtyard and when you look from the entrance, the new temple at the bottom right accommodates a 4-5m tall image of Tsongkhapa, the founder of the Gelukpa School. To reach the gompa, go up the hill at the back of Thongde Village. It's about 300m up a steep mountain path.

Zangla
The King of Zangla, who once ruled Zanskar along with the King of Padam (Padum), still lives in Zangla. The king's 3-story palace is in the center of the village and is the largest building here. On the south side of the village, there is an old palace, a fortress, and many chortens strung out in lines. There is no guesthouse but the local people are happy to put you up in their homes. The village is also without a restaurant or a store.

Pishu Gompa
On the other side of the river on the way to Zangla is this nunnery nestled behind the small village of Pishu. The village has only about 10 houses and little else of note.

Lingshad Gompa
This old monastery is located in a village just before Hanuma La and surrounded by 5,000m mountains.

It was founded about 500 years ago by Chensen Sherab Sangpo.

PADAM (PADUM)-SANI-KARGIL

Sani Gompa
Built in the 11th century, this is the oldest monastery in Zanskar and it has a peculiar style, with strong Indian Buddhist influences rather than the Tibetan Buddhist influences that were imported later. It stands beside the road on a flat piece of land unlike most other monasteries nearby, which were all built either on a hill or a slope. It is also famous for the Kanika Chorten, a 6m-tall Buddhist monument, built in the 2nd century by King Kanishka of the Kushan dynasty, which controlled the northern region of present-day Pakistan.

It is a 2-hour walk back from Padam (Padum) towards Kargil or you can get there on a bus that leaves for Kargil early in the morning every other day.

Zongkul Gompa
Walk up the Mulung Takpo River opposite Phey. It takes about 7 hours from Padam (Padum) and you will reach this Drukpa Kagyupa monastery which stands on a rock cliff beside the river. It is said that Naropa, the mentor to Kagyupa's founder Marpa (1012-1096), practiced asceticism in a cave in the craggy mountain here. If you pass the monastery and climb farther up the rock cliff, you will be able to visit the cave and view its wall paintings.

Another 7-hour walk up the river from Zongkul is Umasi La (5,300m). There is also a route to Kishtwar in Kashmir, though due to the activities of militants in the area, the section between Doda and Kishtwar is particularly hazardous at present.

Rangdum Gompa
Founded in the 18th century, this is the monastery of the 14th Dalai Lama's younger brother, Tenzin Chogyal Rinpoche, and of course it belongs to the Gelukpa order. If you are coming from the Kargil direction, this is the last monastery you will come to before entering the Zanskar region.

Karsha Gompa

LAHAUL

Across Rohtang La, which is 3,978m high, from Manali is the area called Lahaul/Spiti. The area consists of 2 major valleys, the Lahaul and the Spiti, and a trade route connects them with Ngari in Western Tibet. Along with Zanskar, this area used to be part of the ancient Guge Kingdom and half of the residences are Buddhist and the other half are Hindu. No permit is required to visit this region.

KEYLONG

This is the largest town in the Lahaul/Spiti districts and the road starts here and leads up to Leh via Zanskar. There are several buses a day from Manali to Keylong between June and October when the Rohtang La pass is accessible to cars. The 114km journey takes about 7 hours. There is a hotel area at the bazaar, which is about a 15-minute walk down from the bus stop.

Bus schedule from Keylong to:

04:00	Leh (from Manali via Keylong)
	* these run until early October
06:00	Raring (from Keylong)
	*a village beyond Darcha
	and an entrance to Zanskar
06:00	Kaza (from Keylong)
06:30	Delhi (from Keylong)
07:00	Gondhla (from Keylong)
07:30	Jahalman (from Kullu via Tandi)

07:30	Udaipur (from Kullu to Chandra-Bhaga River)
08:00	Mayar Nala (from Keylong via Udaipur)
	*2km before Udaipur
09:00	Darcha (from Kullu)
09:00	Udaipur (from Kullu via Tandi)
10:00	Lote (from Kullu via Keylong), Udaipur
10:30	Mayar Nala (from Keylong via Udaipur)
11:00	Delhi (from Udaipur via Keylong)
11:00	Dharamsala (from Triloknath via Keylong)
11:00	Triloknath (from Dharamsala via Keylong)
11:30	Rarig (from Manali via Keylong)
12:00	Shimla (Simla) (from Keylong)
12:00	Jahalmam (from Rarig via Koksar)
13:00	Manali (from Keylong)
14:30	Udaipur (from Kullu via Keylong)
15:30	Udaipur (from Manali via Tandi)
16:00	Udaipur (from Keylong)
17:15	Koksar (from Keylong)
17:15	Koksar (from Kullu via Keylong)
17:30	Jahalman (from Rarig via Wali)
17:30	Jahalman (from Kullu via Tandi)
17:30	Darcha (from Kullu)
17:30	Lote (from Kullu via Keylong)

* Udaipur here is in Himachal Pradesh (north-west of Keylong)
(Timetable from the Keylong booking office)

Places to See
Shashur Gompa
This 3-story Drukpa Kagyupa monastery stands on the slope of a mountain to the north of Keylong and was built in the 16th century. Unfortunately, there are no guesthouses, restaurants or shops around the monastery.

Khardong Gompa
This Drukpa Kagyupa monastery is halfway up a mountain across the Bhaga River to the south of Keylong. It has a 900-year history but little of the original structures remain, as the gompa was in ruins until its reconstruction in 1912. From this elevation you can get a good view of Keylong and the surrounding area. This gompa also has no guesthouse or restaurant.

Lama Gompa
This monastery is also called Lama Gozzangwa Gompa. At Khardong, there

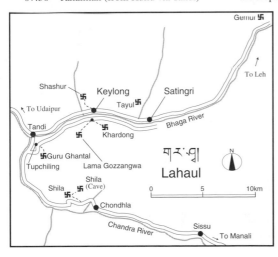

Lahaul

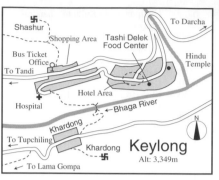

Shashur

Shopping Area

Tashi Delek
Food Center

Bus Ticket
Office

To Tandi

Hotel Area

Hospital

Khardong

To Tupchiling

Khardong

To Lama Gompa

To Darcha

Hindu
Temple

Bhaga River

N

Keylong
Alt: 3,349m

Shashur Gompa

is a sign stating 'Oldest Monastery 100m,' but it's actually a lot farther than that. It is said to be the oldest monastery in Lahaul, though at a glance, it is merely a private house, with another sign proclaiming 'Lama Gompa.' A new but small lhakhang is on the 1st floor of the building and supposedly there are 4 old nuns living here.

Tayul Gompa

Go 6km out of Keylong towards Darcha and you will arrive at Satingri at the foot of Tayul Gompa. If you want to take a bus to get there, there is one leaving Keylong for Darcha at the very convenient time of 09:00. This Drukpa Kagyupa monastery was established in the 17th century and has a huge image of Guru Rinpoche. A kilometer before

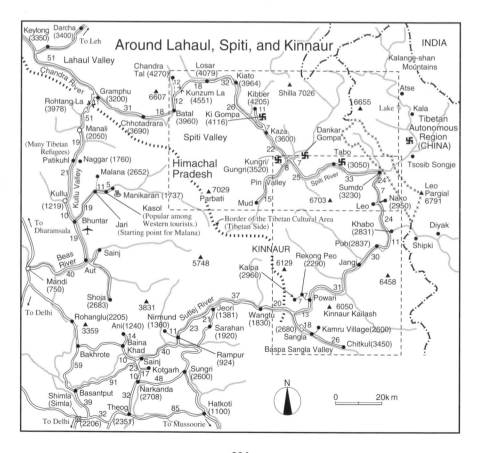

Satingri, there is a chorten on the mountainside above the road and this is where you need to start going up to reach Tayul Gompa. The walk to the monastery takes about an hour.

SPITI

Spiti, along with Lahaul and Zanskar, used to be part of the Guge Kingdom and most residences here are Buddhist and look very Tibetan. It is famous for Tabo Gompa, a noted monastery with a history stretching back over a thousand years. A permit is required to travel between Sumdo in Spiti and Jangi in Kinnaur. You can get a 7-day permit at Kaza, Keylong, Rekong Peo and other main centers in the area.

KAZA

Spiti Valley is across the Kunzum La, 4,551m, from Lahaul and the path is open between mid-May and mid-June. Kaza is the biggest town in Spiti and the usual starting point for monastery tours and trekking throughout the Spiti Valley. The town is clearly divided into 2 with New Kaza, the western section, home to public offices clustered together

resembling a Chinese town; and Old Kaza, the eastern section, much more like a Tibetan town with a lively bazaar. There is a Sakyapa monastery, Kaza Gompa, at the northern end of the town.

Bus services connect Kaza with Keylong, Manali, Kibber, Tabo (from Manali), Rekong Peo in Kinnaur, Chango and many other smaller towns and villages. It is better to book long-distance bus seats the day before you want to travel. If you want to charter a taxi, make a reservation at the taxi station in the bazaar. The rates are non-negotiable as a taxi association regulates the fares.

You can apparently get a permit to go to Kinnaur

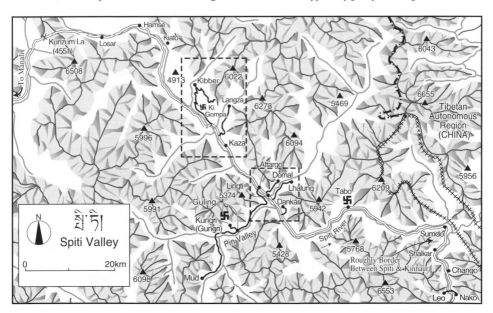

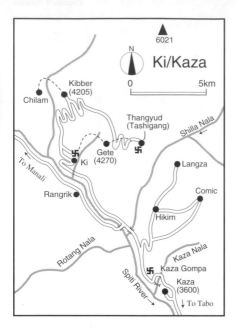

Ki Gompa

for Kibber at 09:00 everyday stops at Ki Gompa and takes about an hour. The last stop, Kibber (4,205m) is above Ki Gompa and it is claimed that this is the highest village in the world. As a matter of fact, the next village, Gete (4,270m), and Thangyud (Tashigang) Village are higher.

At Kibber, there are several hotels and restaurants and you can get to Thangyud from the village via Gete by going up a path behind Ki Gompa. At Thangyud Gompa, you can see old Kashmiri-style wall paintings on the ceiling inside the chorten on the roof of the monastery. A *Ngakpa*, or practitioner of the *mantras*, lives near the monastery and keeps a key.

Kungri (Gungri) Gompa

To the south of Kaza, there is the beautiful Pin Valley, which is great for trekking. Everyday the bus that leaves Kaza at 12:30 stops at Guling, and at Mud, where it changes direction and returns to Kaza.

To get to Kungri Gompa, get off the bus at Guling, about an hour from Kaza, and walk about 2 kilometers after a junction located not far after the bus stop. The gompa, reputedly founded by Guru Rinpoche, is a large and important Nyingmapa monastery. In the Pin Valley, there are 7 monasteries, all belonging to the Nyingmapa order and Kungri Gompa is chief among them. There seems to be no stores or restaurants in the small village of Guling or around Kungri itself.

at Kaza and it seems that a travel agency at the bazaar can arrange this, though this isn't confirmed. There are some cheap hotels in the Old Kaza area. The *Zambala Hotel*, nearest the bus station, has single rooms with private toilet for 100Rs.

Major bus destinations from Kaza:
04:00 Kullu via Manali
06:00 Manali (from Tabo)
07:00 Rekong Peo
07:30 Tabo (from Manali)
09:00 Kibber
12:30 Pin Valley
14:00 Chango

Ki Gompa

Twelve kilometers to the north-west of Kaza, Ki Gompa is the oldest and largest fort-like monastery in the Spiti Valley and it stands on a desolate mountain. At the top is the main temple, in which there are Dukhang, etc. The numerous buildings clustered on the hillside present an impressive sight. Although the buildings are not that old due to frequent reconstruction, the *thangkas* and other artwork in the Dukhang are supposed to hail from around the 11th century.

You can stay at the monastery where a dormitory bed costs 50Rs, and meals are also served, if required. At the next village, Ki, there is the *Samdup Tashi Khangsar Hotel & Restaurant* and there are also some stores. A bus leaving Kaza

Dankar Gompa

Dankar Gompa

Dankar used to be the center of Spiti up until Indian independence but now it's only a small village without a store. It's probable that Dankar Gompa also functioned as a fort since it stands on the hill commanding the high ground above the village. This powerful Gelukpa monastery was founded in the 12th century.

Chartering a car at Kaza gives easy access to Dankar, but if you take a bus, get off at Shichiling on the main road and you'll see Dankar to the north-west. It's about 7km by road or 4km via the path up the mountain. On the other side of the valley, there is a new building where the monks undertake their religious tasks. You can also go to Lhalung Gompa via Rama, which was established by Rinchen Zangpo (958-1055). The 30 monks and nuns here follow the teachings of the Gelukpa order.

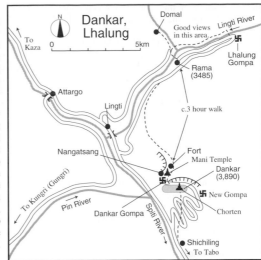

Tabo Gompa

In 996, Rinchen Zangpo established this monastery at Tabo. To commemorate its thousandth anniversary, it welcomed the Dalai Lama who held the *Great Kalachakra Initiation* there (one of the most important empowerment ceremonies, it can only be performed by the Dalai Lama himself). It is well known that Tabo Gompa houses the finest and most precious collection of Buddhist arts in all of the Tibetan cultural areas.

Several fine collections of photographs have been published using only the artwork housed in this monastery. It is regarded as the Himalayan 'Ajanta' (a collection of caves and monasteries decorated in Buddhist art in Maharashtra state and dating from between 200BC and 650AD) because its wall paintings were influenced by this earlier Ajanta-style.

Rinchen Zangpo, who was sent to India by the Guge Kingdom, brought back popular Kashmiri-style painters, as well as the Buddhist scriptures that he was sent to collect. At Tabo Gompa, the

works that these artists produced remain in good condition. There are only 2 monasteries that preserve this style of Kashmiri artwork: Alchi Gompa in Ladakh and Toling (Tsaparang) in Western Tibet, the rest having been destroyed by invading Muslim armies. Surrounded by walls, Tabo Gompa stands on a flatland area. There are 7 lhakhangs of various sizes, among which a number of chortens stand.

Sarma—Added to the monastery in the 17th century, this is the front temple leading to the main temple, the Tsuklakhang. It is covered with wall paintings from that period.

Tsuklakhang (Main Temple)—Here are 33 sculpted images of Buddha and various deities that surround the Dukhang, and which form a 3-dimensional *mandala*. The main statue is of Vairocana.

Ditsangkhang (Rear Shrine)—Behind the main statue, there is an Amitabha. The wall of the corridor is covered with impressive wall paintings.

Gonkhang (The Protector Deities' Shrine)—To enter the Gonkhang you have to go through the Sarma, and the deities are supposed to be honored here but the figures are hidden from sight.

Dromtonpa Lhakhang Chenmo (The Great Dromtonpa Temple)—This is to the south of the Tsuklakhang and was built in the 17th century. It is dedicated to Dromtonpa, a disciple of Atisha (982-1054), the Indian Buddhist scholar who helped revive the religion in Tibet.

Serkhang (The Golden Building)—It's to the south of the Dromtonpa Lhakhang Chenmo

Tabo Gompa

and was built when this monastery was founded. However, the intricate wall paintings were added between the 15th and the 16th centuries.

Kyilkhor Lhakhang (The Mandala Temple)— Built between the 15th and 17th centuries, it is behind the Dromtonpa Lhakhang Chenmo. Unfortunately, a leaking roof has led to a lot of damage inside.

Khardung Lhakhang—This is another small temple on the western side of the complex.

Dromtonpa Lhakhang (The Dromtonpa Temple) —It is said that Dromtonpa himself built this temple in the 11th century.

Jamchen Lhakhang (The Great Maitreya Temple) —In the front of the building, there is a 6m-high image of Champa seated on a chair (also known as Jampa, the Tibetan name for Maitreya). The statue is large enough for a person to get under the chair. The building has been here since the monastery was founded.

Accommodation
By the bus stop, the *Hotel Tabo Takchen Green Cave* has double rooms for 70Rs and there are also some places to stay in and around the monastery.

Access
A bus from Manali leaves Kaza at 07:30 everyday, or you can take one to Rekong Peo and others towards Kinnaur, and then get off along the way. To enter Kinnaur from here, a permit is required and there is a checkpoint at Sumdo.

KINNAUR

Travelling north-east of the Sutlej River from Shimla (Simla), which is the state capital of Himachal Pradesh, you will reach the Kinnaur region, where you will meet local people wearing distinctive green felt hats. Here, you will find the sacred mountain of Kinnaur Kailash at 6,050m. It is said that Shiva, who usually stays at Mt. Kailash in Tibet, comes to Kinnaur Kailash only in winter, just to smoke as much hashish as he wants. Not surprisingly, heavy smokers from around the world have flocked to the area. Hindus, however, come here on religious pilgrimages and they circle the holy mountain in a clockwise direction.

Although somewhat different from its northern neighbors, Lahaul and Spiti, the Kinnaur region used to be part of the Guge Kingdom and in the northern part of Kinnaur you will still see many small monasteries connected with Rotsawa

Rinpoche (the honorific title for Rinchen Zangpo) who was sent to India and contributed to the revival of Buddhism in Tibet in the 11th century.

From Kinnaur to Spiti, the following route is a rough guide:
Shimla (Simla)-Rampur (Jeori junction)-Sarahan (Sangla Valley)-Rekong Peo- Kalpa- Jangi- Puh-Nako- Chango- Sumdo (Spiti).
The tourist seasons are April to May and again from September to October.

Permit
Among the stops on the route mentioned above, the segment connecting Jangi to Sumdo requires an Inner Line Permit (ILP) and there is a checkpoint for foreign tourists on the way. You can get an ILP in Shimla (Simla), Keylong, Rekong Peo, Kaza and other larger towns. It's a 7-day permit but the period can be extended. To enter the area from Shimla (Simla), it's convenient to get your permit at Rekong Peo.

SHIMLA (SIMLA)

Shimla (Simla) is the state capital of Himachal Pradesh and most trips to Kinnaur start from here. In the mid-19th century this was the summer capital for the Raj (the British colonial administration of India). The city is home to a *Tibetan Refugee Self-Help Handicraft Society* in Kusumpti. Tel: 0177-78538.

There are many private and public buses from the ISBT in Delhi, which arrive at Shimla (Simla) day and night. The journey takes about 12 hours from Delhi. There are also buses from Dharamsala, Chandigarh, etc.

Buses to Kinnaur from Shimla (Simla) leave from the Rivoli Bus Stand in the north of the city and not from the main bus station. The buses for Sarahan leave at 10:00 and 14:00. There are many buses to Rampur and even some direct buses to Rekong Peo and Kaza in the Spiti Valley. There are a number of hotels located around the bus station but you need to be careful as they get expensive during the tourist season.

SARAHAN

When you reach Sarahan you're not quite in Kinnaur yet but the Hindu Bhimakali Temple is well worth the visit. There are 2 ways to get here and sometimes you will have to change buses at Rampur, even though it is supposed to go all the

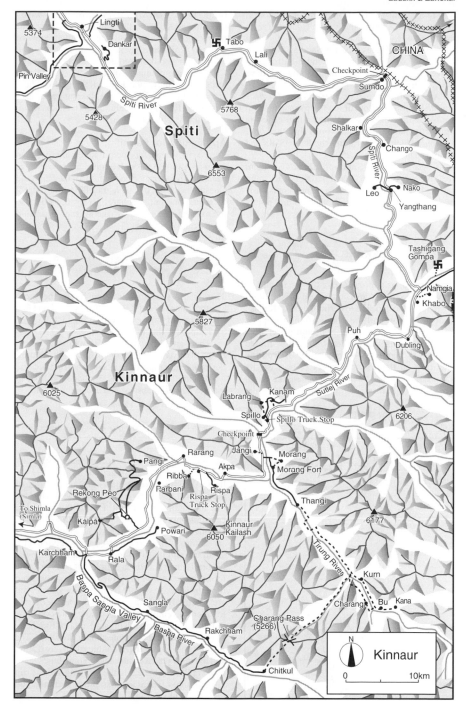

way to Sarahan. The bus from Rampur to Sarahan takes 2-3 hours. Alternatively, you can get to Jeori from Shimla (Simla) in about 7-8 hours, and then catch a bus that leaves Jeori for Sarahan every 1-2 hours and takes about an hour-and-a-half. If you arrive late in the afternoon though, you will have to take a taxi to Sarahan.

As for places to stay, there is the *Bushair Guesthouse* just in front of the temple's gate, with double rooms for 150Rs. Walk 2 minutes to the right from the bus stop and you'll find the *Hotel Sirkand*, which has dormitory beds for 55Rs and double rooms starting at 250Rs.

To get to Shimla (Simla) from Sarahan, there are 2 buses between 06:00 and 07:00. For Kinnaur, catch a bus to Jeori and wait there for a connection that will take you on to Rekong Peo and points beyond.

REKONG PEO

Rekong Peo, or simply *Peo* as the locals call it, plays a central role in Kinnaur and it is a larger town than expected. The towering Kinnaur Kailash appears nearby and the range of snow-capped mountains gives the town a very beautiful backdrop.

From the bus stop you can see a yellow-roofed gompa and a large golden statue of Buddha standing on the hillside. This is part of the monastery built for *Dukhor Wangchen*, the *Great Kalachakra Initiation* performed by the 14th Dalai Lama in 1992.

There are some guesthouses in the town; among

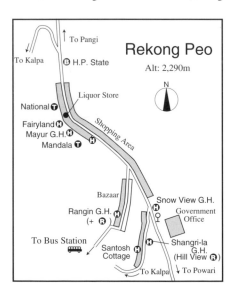

To Pangi

Rekong Peo

To Kalpa ⓑ H.P. State

Alt: 2,290m

N

Liquor Store

National ⓣ

Fairyland ⓗ
Mayur G.H.ⓗⓣ
Mandala ⓣ

Shopping Area

Bazaar

Snow View G.H.

Rangin G.H. ⓗ
(+ ⓡ)

Government
Office

To Bus Station

Santosh
Cottage

Shangri-la
G.H.
(Hill View ⓡ)

To Kalpa ↓ To Powari

them the *Fairyland Guesthouse* is well-recommended. From the windows of the south-facing rooms you can enjoy an excellent view of Kinnaur Kailash, especially in the morning and evening. It also has a quite reasonable restaurant.

If you are planning to move on to Spiti, you can get a permit for the area in Rekong Peo. There are many buses to Kalpa from Rekong Peo. Buses also go to Rampur, Shimla (Simla), Nako, Kaza, and elsewhere in the region.

Application for Permit
You can only apply for a permit for the area between Jangi and Sumdo through a travel agency, such as *National Travelers*, located in front of the Fairyland Guesthouse. Even if you are travelling alone, you'll be issued one but the charge varies according to the number of applicants (the average is around 200Rs each).

KALPA

This is the place where you'll get the most breathtaking views of Kinnaur Kailash. Rekong Peo is the center of Kinnaur nowadays but in times gone by, Kalpa was the main town.

There are plenty of buses from Rekong Peo to Kalpa everyday and the trip takes only 40 minutes. For your return trip, you can take a short cut because it's downhill all the way. The village has little in the way of reasonably priced accommodation.

SANGLA

Sangla is a beautiful and peaceful village, especially delightful in November when the apple trees bear fruit. Walking through the village at this time of year, you'll invariably meet people who will give you mountains of the fruit. During the *Dussehra* celebrations, between September and October, Sangla also has a colorful festival. Don't miss it!

Kamru Village seems to completely cover a small hill and it is a 10-minute walk from Sangla. Kamru Temple is a Hindu temple that is very similar looking to the one in Sarahan. Strangely, even though there are people living in the village that are Tibetan Buddhists, only Hindus are permitted to enter the temple. You can also get a good view of the southern face of Kinnaur Kailash from here.

In Sangla, there are 3 guesthouses available. The *Baspa Guesthouse* offers double rooms for 150Rs and the others have similar rates. Some buses leave Rekong Peo for Sangla in the morning and the trip takes 2 hours. There are also buses that take you up to Chitkul via Sangla.

Nako

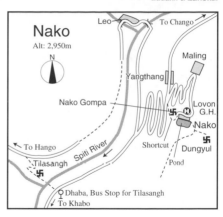

KANAM

Take a bus from Rekong Peo to Puh, Nako, or Kaza and you should get off at a truck stop called Spillo. There is a checkpoint for foreigners on the way, and there are some guesthouses and restaurants at Spillo. The starting point for going up to Kanam at 2,320m is at the foot of the bridge just before the Hindu temple. It is a short walk down the road towards Puh from the truck stop. From here, you walk up to the entrance of Kanam Village at 2,660m and there is a gompa another 100m farther on. At Kanam, there are several monasteries including the old Kanam Gompa that was founded by Rinchen Zangpo. It is a good idea to take some supplies with you as the village has only 1 small store.

Go west from Kanam and cross the valley made by a tributary of the Sutlej River and you will come to the distinctly Tibetan-looking village of Labrang. The large chorten and the gompa in the village are supposed to have been constructed by Rinchen Zangpo. Unfortunately, this village has no restaurant or store.

PUH

To reach the village of Puh you'll need to get on a bus from Rekong Peo heading for Nako, Kaza, Chango, and beyond. The village has a store and you can stay at the truck stop. The people in this area look really Tibetan. Near the entrance to their village is the Drukpa Kagyupa's Lotsabai Lhakhang, which is said to have been Rinchen Zangpo's monastery as it carries part of his full honorary name, *Lotsabai*.

The timetable for buses leaving Puh for places upstream on the Sutlej River is as follows:

Kaza	10:00	Chango	15:50
Nako	13:00	Yangthang	16:50

NAKO

A bus is available to take you as far as Yangthang, from where you can walk or take a jeep the rest of the way. The people, air, and atmosphere are very Tibetan here. There is a lake and Nako Gompa, a monastery supposedly built by Rinchen Zangpo in the 11th century. At the entrance to the village is *Lovon Guesthouse*.

CHANGO

Chango is a village built on an alluvial fan and the lush greenery here will definitely lift your spirits. There are a number of monasteries, including another founded by Rinchen Zangpo. There is a place to stay and a general store at the truck stop. At the entrance to the village there is a checkpoint.

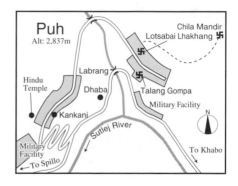

Chango
Alt: 2,658m

Labels in map: Spiti River, To Shalkar, N, Checkpoint, Kargo Gompa, Dhaba, Government Rest House, Tum Gompa, Mani Temple, Sheto Gompa, Loche Lhakhang, Chango Village, Village, Kyolon Gompa, To Yangthang

SHALKAR

Shalkar is about 5km from Chango and is also called Kyahar. This is the end of the Kinnaur region and it's divided into 2 parts. A hill on the southern side forms one part and the other is strung out along the highway to the north. The *Milan Hotel* on the northern side is the only place to stay and dormitory beds go for around 25Rs. The only restaurant in the village is in the hotel and there seems to be no store in the village.

You can see extensive remains of cellars and wall paintings on a cliff at the end of the village. The ruins are all that are left of a gompa that once stood on the site. A village on the hill to the south has a Gelukpa monastery called Sandup Choeling and this is home to a solitary Lama. Just after Shalkar, there is a checkpoint at Sumdo and this finally brings you into the Spiti region.

DHARAMSALA

When the British ruled India, Dharamsala was a summer resort for them. Now it's famous as the base for the Tibetan government-in-exile, led by Tenzin Gyatso, the 14th Dalai Lama who fled his homeland in 1959.

Even after 4 decades of Chinese rule, over 1,000 Tibetans each year brave a treacherous crossing of the Himalayas to head for Dharamsala. These illegal crossings are made by people who are unable to tolerate the Chinese occupation anymore, or by those who simply wish to be blessed by his holiness,

the Dalai Lama. In Dharamsala, there are about 8,000 resident Tibetans and over 2,000 refugee children lodging together and being educated at the *Tibetan Childrens' Village* (TCV).

After the Dalai Lama sought refuge here, many high-ranking Buddhist lamas followed him into exile, helping their religion to spread around the world and gain popularity in the West. Foreigners learning about Tibetan Buddhism or studying Tibetan arts go to Dharamsala and the town is popular with tourists because of its comfortable atmosphere and the chance to experience part of the Tibetan world in India.

Dharamsala is divided into 2 parts with Lower Dharamsala being a very Indian town and Upper Dharamsala (McLeod Ganj) comprising the Tibetan residential area. The upper section is the one that attracts most tourists.

Access
Most visitors make a reservation for the bus to Dharamsala at a travel agency in the Main Bazaar (Paharganj) near New Delhi Station. The place to catch the bus is at the western end of the bazaar and it departs every evening and costs around 230Rs. At the ISBT in Delhi, there are night and early morning buses. It takes 14-15 hours to reach Lower Dharamsala.

At Majnunkatila Tibetan Camp, about a kilometer to the north of the ISBT, there is a 'deluxe' night bus that goes to McLeod Ganj everyday. It leaves at 18:00 and arrives the next morning and costs 350Rs. You can get a ticket at *Potala Tours & Travels*, among others, in Majnunkatila.

This is the largest Tibetan town in Delhi and it has a Tibetan day school, workshops, etc. There are many Tibetan-run guesthouses and restaurants, and it is also famous for its entertainment district.

At Connaught Place in Delhi, there is also a night bus for McLeod Ganj. To make a reservation, go to the *Himachal Tourism* office or to a travel agency nearby. It leaves in the evening and arrives at McLeod Ganj the next morning.

If you want to go by rail, take a train from Delhi to Pathankot, which takes 12 hours. At Pathankot, catch a bus or taxi to Dharamsala and this takes another 3-4 hours.

Buses from Dharamsala
There is a deluxe bus to Delhi that leaves McLeod Ganj at 18:00 and arrives at Majnunkatila in Old Delhi the following morning. A ticket will cost you 350Rs and you can buy one at any travel agency in McLeod Ganj.

At the Lower Dharamsala Bus Station, there are also buses to Delhi, Kullu, Manali, Shimla (Simla), Pathankot, Chandigarh, etc.

Accommodation & Restaurants

The *OM Hotel* has single rooms for 50Rs and doubles for 60Rs. This is a backpacker's hangout and many Western travelers get together on its roof.
The *Kailash Guesthouse* has a restaurant and a good view of the sunset. Double rooms cost 70Rs.
The *Dream Land Guesthouse* also has a restaurant and its single rooms are 60Rs; doubles are 70Rs.
The *Ashoka Guesthouse* has good single rooms for 100Rs or doubles for 120Rs.
The *Green Hotel*'s single rooms cost 50Rs and the hotel also has a restaurant.
The *Kawachen House* is a bit far from the center of town but the rooms have great views. Double rooms here cost 450Rs.

Places to See
The Palace

The building looks very similar to the Potala Palace in Lhasa but it's a smaller version perched on a hill. The Dalai Lama gives his audiences here and the building acts as a 'temporary' palace until his return to Tibet, even though 40 years have already passed. Around the hill is a *Lingkhor* (A Path for Pilgrimage), which is lined with *mani*-stones and *tarchoks* just like those in Tibet. The area around the palace and the Tsuklakhang is called Thekchen Choeling.

Tsuklakhang
& Namgyal Monastery

Opposite the palace across the courtyard is the Tsuklakhang where the Dalai Lama makes his speeches and other ceremonies are held. Many festivals, such as the New Year's *Monlam* celebrations (The Great Prayer Festival), and festivities for the Dalai Lama's birthday are all held in the courtyard.

Namgyal Monastery, for which the Dalai Lama is directly responsible, was originally supposed to be in the Potala Palace but instead spreads over the hillside of Thekchen Choeling.

Institute of Tibetan Medicine and Astrology (Mentsikhang)

As you go down the northern slope from McLeod Ganj, the first building you will see is the Mentsikhang. This operates in the same way as the one in Lhasa, serving the refugees here as a hospital and an institution for calculating the Tibetan calendar.

Gangchen Kyishong

(Happy Valley in the Snowland)
Farther down the slope after the Mentsikhang, you will reach the Gangchen Kyishong area, where the government-in-exile offices are to be found.

Library of Tibetan Works and Archives (Pendzokhang)

Gangchen Kyishong is also the site for this gompa-like library in which you are free to read books and ask advice. They also offer courses to foreigners in the Tibetan language and the study of Tibetan Buddhism.

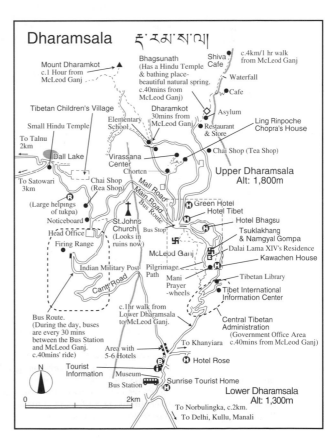

Dharamsala ད་རམ་ས་ལ།

Mount Dharamkot
c.1 Hour from
McLeod Ganj

Bhagsunath
(Has a Hindu Temple
& bathing place-
beautiful natural spring.
c.40mins from
McLeod Ganj)

Shiva
Cafe

c.4km/1 hr walk
from McLeod Ganj

Waterfall

Cafe

Tibetan Children's Village

Dharamkot
30mins from
McLeod Ganj

Asylum

Small Hindu Temple

Elementary
School

Restaurant
& Store

Ling Rinpoche
Chopra's House

To Talnu
2km

Dall Lake

Virassana
Center

Chai Shop (Tea Shop)

Upper Dharamsala
Alt: 1,800m

To Satowari
3km

Chorten

Chai Shop
(Rea Shop)

(Large helpings
of tukpa)

Green Hotel
Hotel Tibet

Noticeboard

Head Office

St.Johns
Church
(Looks in
ruins now)

Bus Stop

Hotel Bhagsu

Tsuklakhang
& Namgyal Gompa

Firing Range

McLeod Ganj

Dalai Lama XIV's Residence
Kawachen House

Indian Military Post

Pilgrimage
Path

Mani
Prayer
-wheels

Tibetan Library

Tibet International
Information Center

c.1hr walk from
Lower Dharamsala
to McLeod Ganj.

Bus Route.
(During the day, buses
are every 30 mins
between the Bus Station
and McLeod Ganj.
c.40mins' ride)

Area with
5-6 Hotels

To Khanyiara

Central Tibetan
Administration
(Government Office Area
c.40mins from McLeod Ganj)

Hotel Rose

Tourist
Information

Museum

Sunrise Tourist Home

Bus Station

Lower Dharamsala
Alt: 1,300m

N

0   2km

To Norbulingka, c.2km.

To Delhi, Kullu, Manali

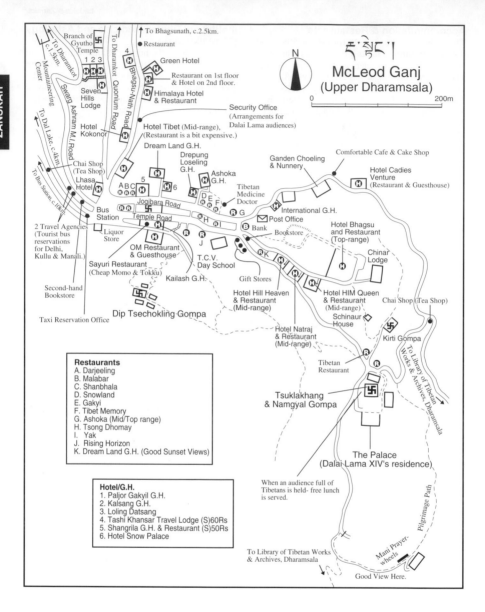

ད་སྲང་།

McLeod Ganj
(Upper Dharamsala)

0   200m

To Bhagsunath, c.2.5km.

Restaurant

Branch of
Gyutho Temple
c.1.5km.

Green Hotel

Restaurant on 1st floor
& Hotel on 2nd floor.

Himalaya Hotel
& Restaurant

Security Office
(Arrangements for
Dalai Lama audiences)

Mountaineering
Center

Seven
Hills
Lodge

Hotel Tibet (Mid-range),
(Restaurant is a bit expensive.)

Hotel
Kokonor

Dream Land G.H.

Drepung
Loseling
G.H.

Ganden Choeling
& Nunnery

Comfortable Cafe & Cake Shop

Chai Shop
(Tea Shop)

Ashoka
G.H.

Hotel Cadies
Venture
(Restaurant & Guesthouse)

Lhasa
Hotel

Tibetan
Medicine
Doctor

International G.H.

Post Office

Hotel Bhagsu
and Restaurant
(Top-range)

Bus
Station

Bank

Bookstore

2 Travel Agencies
(Tourist bus
reservations
for Delhi,
Kullu & Manali.)

Liquor
Store

China
Lodge

OM Restaurant
& Guesthouse

T.C.V.
Day School

Sayuri Restaurant
(Cheap Momo & Tokku)

Kailash G.H.

Gift Stores

Second-hand
Bookstore

Hotel Hill Heaven
& Restaurant
(Mid-range)

Hotel HIM Queen
& Restaurant
(Mid-range)

Chai Shop (Tea Shop)

Taxi Reservation Office

Dip Tsechokling Gompa

Schinaur
House

Hotel Natraj
& Restaurant
(Mid-range)

Kirti Gompa

Tibetan
Restaurant

To Library of Tibetan Works & Archives, Dharamsala

Tsuklakhang
& Namgyal Gompa

Restaurants
A. Darjeeling
B. Malabar
C. Shanbhala
D. Snowland
E. Gakyi
F. Tibet Memory
G. Ashoka (Mid/Top range)
H. Tsong Dhomay
I. Yak
J. Rising Horizon
K. Dream Land G.H. (Good Sunset Views)

The Palace
(Dalai Lama XIV's residence)

When an audience full of
Tibetans is held- free lunch
is served.

Hotel/G.H.
1. Paljor Gakyil G.H.
2. Kalsang G.H.
3. Loling Datsang
4. Tashi Khansar Travel Lodge (S)60Rs
5. Shangrila G.H. & Restaurant (S)50Rs
6. Hotel Snow Palace

Pilgrimage Path

To Library of Tibetan Works
& Archives, Dharamsala

Mani Prayer-
wheels

Good View Here.

Tibetan Institute of Performing Arts (TIPA)

Up a steep hill, on the left of the path to the Hotel Tibet, there is an institution called TIPA. Run by the government-in-exile, this cultural organization is dedicated to nurturing new and up-and-coming artistic talent. Performances are given in various places around the world, with traditional music, dance, and theater on offer. In the museum, you can also see the costumes worn for *Ache Lhamo* (Traditional Tibetan Opera).

Dip Tsechokling Gompa

This is a monastery on the southern hillside of McLeod Ganj. It is just below the OM restaurant and it was originally in the village of Dip, south of Lhasa.

Tibetan Childrens' Village (TCV)

The TCV is about an hour's walk from McLeod Ganj, and the buildings of the TCV are clustered near Dal Lake (actually more of a marsh than a lake). The village acts as a boarding school for refugee children. It was set-up by Tsering Dolma, the present Dalai Lama's elder sister, in 1960 and has grades from kindergarten to high school. The money to build this impressive center came from foreign aid grants.

Starved of anything but rudimentary education, such as Tibetan language, many children have made the dangerous journey from their homeland to study at this school. The children mostly have had to leave their families behind for this opportunity. The current number of students is around 2,000 and there are also branches in various other places in India.
Tel: 01892-21354/ 21204/ 21245
Fax: 01892-21670
E-mail: tcv@tcrclinux.tibdsala.org.in

There is also a *Handicraft and Vocational Training Center* for young adults attached to the school.
Tel: 01892-21592/ 21640 Fax: 01892-21670

Norbulingka Institute

Farther down from Lower Dharamsala, this is a large-scale Tibetan cultural center built in 1995. Taking a taxi from McLeod Ganj is much easier than walking all the way there. It is named, of course, after the famous Norbulingka in Lhasa and in its beautiful courtyard there are lhakhang and a museum where you can view Buddhist paintings, images of Buddha, etc. This collection shows the resilience of the exiled Tibetan community's spirit. Right next to the site is the Dolmaling Nunnery.

An Audience with the Dalai Lama

Even a passing foreign tourist can have an audience with the Dalai Lama among the throngs of Tibetans who have risked their lives to make it here. First, check at the security office between Hotel Tibet and the Green Hotel to find out whether the Dalai Lama is giving an audience in the near future. His frequent trips abroad and his religious activities make these audiences irregular events.

When an audience is scheduled, you can register at the security office; just take your passport and you can get a registration card. Confirm the exact date and time, then go to the palace with your passport and the registration card on that day. Leave your belongings, such as cameras and day packs, at the security check before the audience starts.

You can give the Dalai Lama neither a *katak* (a ritual scarf) nor any other gift directly. Just wait in line — you might have to wait for a long time

McLeod Ganj

because an audience can sometimes be given to hundreds of people at the same time. The ceremony is carried out like an assembly line. You shake hands with the Dalai Lama and then he gives you a red string as a blessing. A foreigner is given just a few seconds, shorter than Tibetans, and you might be able to say nothing more than *'Tashi Delek'* (Hello). If you have a conversation with him, you are really lucky and sometimes I even saw people floundering because they were given more time to talk to him than they had expected.

OTHER AREAS SETTLED BY TIBETAN REFUGEES IN INDIA

Tibetans live in other areas of India, not just in Ladakh, the Dharamsala region and eastern areas of Darjeeling, Kalimpong and Sikkim. Many of them have been relocated onto land that has been reclaimed from the jungle and there are settlements throughout Himachal and Uttar Pradesh, as well as in areas of southern and central India.

HIMACHAL PRADESH & UTTAR PRADESH [NORTH-WEST INDIA]

Bir/Suja

The 78km from Dharamsala to Bir takes about 4 hours by bus. Originally, Bir was a settlement solely for Khampas from eastern Tibet, but even people in Tibet know that this town has a Tibetan school for young people who have fled from Tibet or left temporarily for education.

The *Tibetan Childrens' Village* was completed in 1994 and is now home to over 350 children. The school in the village has been operating since 1986 and has around 500 students enrolled. All of these students attain at least a primary level education. There is also a vocational training center at the school where students learn the art of making *thangka*. If you would like further information, or would like to visit the school, you can call them. Tel: 01908-52620/21 / 42479

The *Bir Tibetan Society* can also be useful for information and assistance. Tel: 01908-8263. The town is also home to a couple of Tibetan technical institutes and there are a number of monasteries around the school.

Dalhousie

An old British hill station about 6 hours from Dharamsala to the north, this town has quite a large Tibetan population for its size. Dalhousie is often used as a base for exploring the beautiful Chamba Valley area. There is the *Phuntsokling Tibetan Handicraft Center* in town and this can be contacted through the *Tibetan Welfare Office* at 01898-22119.

Dalhousie is well serviced by buses and taxis from both Chandigarh and Delhi. The train station at Pathankot is around 80km from town.

Rewalsar

This sacred place is famous for its connection with Guru Rinpoche. The legend has it that the *Tsopadma* or *Tso-Pema*, meaning 'Lotus Lake,' was created by the great teacher to demonstrate his power and thus subdue the ruler of the region. The 7 islands in the center of the lake are revered as the home of 7 powerful Buddhist deities. In addition, Shugseb Jetsun Rongchen, a Nyingmapa female sage, was born in Rewalsar.

The lake area is also revered by the Hindus and Sikhs and their temples rub shoulders with the Tibetan Buddhist Tsopadma (Tso-Pema) Drikung monastery, which was founded in 1971 and which is now home to around 30 monks. This mixture of religions creates an unusual and unique spiritual atmosphere for the visitor.

To get to Rewalsar, take a bus to Mandi, which is an entrance to the Kullu Valley, from Shimla (Simla) or Dharamsala. There are frequent buses available from Mandi to Rewalsar.

Patlikuhl Village

This village is on the road halfway between Kullu and Manali. It is the site of one of the oldest Tibetan Refugee

schools outside of Dharamsala. The school was established in 1968 and holds classes for around 600 children. Tel: 01902-40175

Tashi Jong

Located in the Kangra district, it is famous for the Drukpa Kagyupa's Khampa Gar Gompa (Phuntso Chokhorling). There is also a *Tibetan Craft Community* in the area. Tel: 0198-3047. Nearby, there is a newly constructed *Tibetan Childrens' Village* at Gopalpur. Tel: 01894-52268/9

At Dharamsala, you'll need to take a bus to Mandi and get off after Palampur. The journey takes 2-3 hours.

Dolanji

Near Solan, south of Shimla (Simla), Dolanji is home to Tashi Menriling, the head of the Bon monasteries in exile. This village is also home to the *Tibetan Bonpo Foundation*. To reach Solan, there are buses from Chandigarh and Shimla (Simla). From there you can take a local bus to Kalghat and then walk the remaining 3-4km. There are also auto-rickshaws that will take you the whole way and these cost 100Rs for the 15km journey.

Dehra Dun

This historic town in the northern hills of Uttar Pradesh is home to a large number of Tibetan refugees. Built on reclaimed land to the south of Dehra Dun, is Clement Town, which is home to

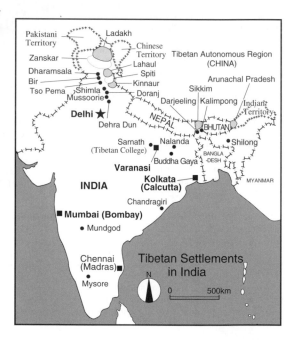

Tibetan Settlements in India

the *Dhondupling Tibetan Settlement*. The Mindroling Monastery, which is the head temple of the Nyingmapa school, has been rebuilt here and Minling Trichen Rinpoche is also based here.

The Tibetan settlement of *Doego Yougyaling* in Lakhanwala, and the *Dekyiling Handicraft Center* in Kulhan (Tel: 0135-72241), are also close to Dehra Dun.

In Rajpur, 12km north-east of the town, there is the Sakya Monastery, head temple of the Sakyapa school of Buddhism and where the Sakya Trizin Rinpoche lives. The *Sakya Center and Nunnery* are at 187 Rajpur Rd and the *Sakya College* can be found on the Mussoorie Road. You can also visit the *Tibetan Women's Handicraft Center* at 225 Rajpur Rd. Tel: 0135-842 201

For Dehra Dun, there are frequent buses from Delhi, Dharamsala, Mussoorie and most other main towns in the area. Also from Delhi, you can get there by train.

Mussoorie

Mussoorie was the first place the Dalai Lama settled after he fled Tibet. The town is close to Dehra Dun, and with an altitude of around 2,000 meters it was chosen by the British to function as a hill station in the mid-19th century. The buildings and layout of the town reflect this colonial influence. From the vantage of Gun Hill at 2,142m, and Lal Tibba at 2,438m, you can get good views of the surrounding area and of the Himalayas in the distance. The area, which is now called 'Happy Valley,' is the site of a large education center and a huge school for Tibetan refugees.

There are many buses from the Mussoorie Bus Station, next to Dehra Dun Station, and the trip takes around an hour-and-a-half.

KARNATAKA STATE [SOUTHERN INDIA]

Southern India has received a substantial number of Tibetan refugees and these relatively new settlements mentioned below actually house a large share of the total exile population.

A permit is required to visit these areas.

Mundgod

This town in North Kanara, is the site of the *Doeguling Tibetan Settlement*. Tel: 08301-84132. There are 2 large gompas in the area. The Ganden Monastery houses around 1,600 monks and the

Mindroling Monastery

Drepung Monastery has around 3,500 monks in residence.

Mysore

Bylakuppe is a suburb of Mysore and is where the *Lugsung Samdupling Tibetan Settlement* is located. Tel: 08276-74359. There is the large Sera Monastery, which is home to around 3,500 monks, and also the Namdroling Monastery, which was founded by Penor Rinpoche. With its 1,600 monks and nuns, this gompa is the largest Nyingmapa learning center in the world.

Bylakuppe is also home to a *Tibetan Childrens' Village*, founded in 1980 and which has over 1,500 children living there. The TCV also runs other facilities, including day care centers for the small children of farming families. Tel: 08276-74447.

The Mysore area has a number of other settlements including *Rabgyeling* in Hunsur Taluk, *Dbondenling* in Kollegal Taluk and *Dickyi Larso*.

CENTRAL INDIA

There are some sizable Tibetan refugee settlements in central India.

Maharashtra State

Norgyeling Tibetan Settlement in Pratapgarh, Bhandara district.

Madhra Pradesh State

Fendayling Tibetan Settlement, Karneswarpur, Mainpat, Sarguja district.

Orissa State

Phuntsokling Tibetan Settlement, Chandragiri, Ganjam district.

Tibet Photos — Hiroyuki Ishii

Born in Gunma, Japan, 1971. Hiroyuki is a photographer focusing on the people of the Himalayas.

The minority group of people living around Dha is called *Drokpa* or *Dards*. A complicated historical background, and precarious current political situation, has led these people to develop and defend their own unique culture. Once you step into the village, you will get a feeling that this is the very melting pot of races. This mixture has produced a group of people with no defining physical features. It seems to me that they confirm their racial identity through their traditions and customs, such as wearing coins, flowers and shell-works. They have been discriminated against because they are a minority but recently, they have started examining their own history and are trying to preserve their culture.

In Dha, they have a festival when they harvest their barley crop and I arrived and stayed there for some days before it was held. I went to see the practices, which were held at a vacant lot in the village. There, I saw young people proudly wearing their traditional costumes, which they reserve for festivals and other special occasions. At these practices the youngsters participating in the festival received instructions on how to perform the ritual dances and music from their village headman.

NEPAL

བལ་ཡུལ།

Nepal is the only kingdom in the world to be ruled over by a Hindu monarch. Sandwiched between 2 giant neighbors, the Chinese-controlled Tibetan Plateau to the north and the vast Indian plains to the south, Nepal has been strongly influenced by them both culturally and religiously. Buddhism and Hinduism continue to thrive side-by-side in the country and the different ethnic groups that make-up the country also co-exist peacefully.

The main areas settled by Tibetans and the descendants of Tibetan migrants are in the harsh mountain areas straddling the Tibetan border and around Mt. Annapurna and Mt. Everest. Their numbers have been substantially increased over the last 40 years by the tens of thousands of Tibetan refugees that have crossed into Nepal, fleeing from the Chinese invasion and occupation of their homeland.

The People of Nepal

Nepal is a country where both Indian and Tibetan cultures co-exist in their own unique way. Many Tibetans or direct Tibetan descendants live in the mountainous regions and elsewhere. These groups have clung onto their own identities and heritage and continue to live in much the same way as they have for centuries. Here is an overview of the distinctive groups of Tibetan descent:

Tamangs

Many Tamangs live in the Helambu and Langtang regions to the north of Kathmandu. These descendants of immigrants from Tibet mainly believe in Tibetan Buddhism and their language also reflects their northern roots.

Gurungs & Magars

The Gurung and Magar people have strong cultural and linguistic ties with each other and their Tibetan neighbors. The Gurung are commonly found in the highland regions in and around the Annapurna area.

The Magar are mainly found to the west of Annapurna in settlements in the Kali Gandaki Valley and surrounding area. The ranks of the Nepalese police and the military are full of Gurungs and Magars. This is also true of the Gurkha regiments in both the Indian and British Armies.

Sherpas

The Sherpa people migrated from Tibet to the Nepalese Himalayas over 500 years ago and are commonly found in the Solu Khumbu region, around the foot of Mt. Everest. They have also settled in many areas throughout eastern Nepal. Their Tibetan heritage is evident in the name *Sherpa*, which was derived from the Tibetan word *Shar-pa* meaning 'The Eastern People.'

NEPAL

Formal Name of the Country
Kingdom of Nepal
Time Difference
5hrs 45mins ahead of GMT.
International Dialing Code
977
Currency
Nepalese Rupee (NRs)= 100 paisa
Exchange Rates

Australian Dollar 39.7NRs
Bhutan Ngultrum (100) 157.00NRs
British Pound 102.50NRs
Canadian Dollar 46.50NRs
Chinese Yuan 8.40NRs
Dutch Guilder 29.90NRs
French Franc 9.70NRs
German Mark 32.70NRs
Hong Kong Dollar 8.90NRs
Indian Rupee (100) 157.00NRs
Japanese Yen (100) 64.80NRs
New Zealand Dollar 31.70NRs
Pakistan Rupee (100) ... 134.00NRs
Singapore Dollar 40.20NRs
Swedish Krona 7.60NRs
Swiss Franc 40.80NRs
US Dollar 69.60NRs

Language
The official national language is Nepali.
English is also understood in places that attract
a lot of tourists. In the mountainous areas of
the country each distinct ethnic group has its
own language.
Inhabitants
Over half of the population are Parvati Hindus
(53.2%), an Indo-Aryan people that have
settled in the Terai lowlands. The remainder is
made up of numerous ethnic groups including
the Bihari (18.4%), the Newars (3.5%) of the
Kathmandu Valley, and tribes in the mountains
such as the Tamangs (4.7%), Gurungs, Magar,
Thakalis, Sherpas, etc.
Capital
Kathmandu (Population approximately
800,000)
Population
Approximately 25,500,000 and growing at an
estimated rate of 2.5% per year.

Land Area
Approximately 145,000 sq km
Climate
Weather patterns in the sub-tropical south of
the country are dominated by the monsoon in
the summer while the mountainous north has
an alpine climate throughout the year. The
rainy season falls between June and September.
Electricity
AC220V, 50Hz
Office Hours
From Sunday through Thursday, public offices
are open from 10:00-17:00 (16:00 in winter).
On Friday, offices are open from 10:00-15:00.
Saturday is a bank holiday.
National Holidays
Most of the dates vary from year to year in
accordance with the Nepalese *Vikram* lunar
calendar. It is always advisable to check the
dates of these in advance as offices can be
closed for a number of days.

National Unity Day (January)
Martyr's Memorial Day (January)
National Democracy Day (February)
International Women's Day (March)
The Nepali New Year (mid-April)
Queen's Birthday (November 7)
The King's Birthday (December 29)

Religious Festivals
Nepal is famous for its many colorful festivals
throughout the year and the following list
includes some of the major ones:

Losar ------- The Tibetan New Year is held
during February or March. Iron Dragon Year
(Year 2127) - February 6, 2000. Iron Snake
Year (Year 2128) - February 24, 2001.
Holi (Fagu Purnima) ---------- A lively and
colorful celebration held during the full
moon in March.
Nawa Barsha ---------- Nepalese New Year
held in mid-April every year.
Buddha Jayanti --- The Buddha's birthday
and enlightenment, held in May or June.
Dasain (Dussehra) --------- A 10-day long
festival held between October and
November. This is the most popular festival
in Nepal.
Tihar (Diwali) ----------- Also held around
the same time as Dasain, this noisy festival
is celebrated for 5 days.

These people practice a form of Tibetan-style Buddhism and those who live deep in the mountains have managed to maintain much of their traditional way of life. If you are lucky enough to catch either of the *Mani Rimdu* festivals, you will definitely get an insight into the colorful traditions of these hardy mountain people.

Tibetans in Dolpo
Living in the Dolpo region, to the north of Mt. Dhaulagiri, they play an active part in the trade between Nepal and Tibet.

Lopas
Lopas are common in the Mustang (Lo Mantang) region. In Tibetan *Lo-pa* means 'The Southern People'. This group has mainly settled in the border areas between Tibet, Nepal and Bhutan. They are ethnically Tibetan and follow Tibetan-style Buddhism.

Thakalis
These people of Tibetan descent settled in the Kali Kandaki area and became wealthy through their control of the salt trade between Tibet and Nepal.

Tibetans
Kathmandu, Pokhara and many other large urban centers have been home to ethnic Tibetans for a considerable length of time and many of these early immigrants have established strong positions in the commerce and trade sectors.

Tibetan Refugees
The population of ethnic Tibetans living in Nepal has been significantly increased by the large influx of refugees who fled from Tibet after the Chinese took over the country in the 1950's. The Nepalese government has not proved to be as lenient with them as its Indian counterpart and in co-operation with Chinese authorities, the authorities exercise stricter control over the border crossings. This approach has enabled this small country to maintain relatively friendly relations with their huge northern neighbor.

Other Ethnic Groups
There are a large number of other ethnic groups throughout Nepal, some of which have been influenced by Tibetan culture and religion. The Newar people of central Nepal have been culturally and linguistically influenced by Tibetan traditions, though most of them are practicing Hindus. The Rai and Limbu people that live in the Solo Khumbu and Mt. Kangchenjunga regions have similarly been influenced by both cultures. The Jirels, populating the area to the east of Jiri, still have Tibetan-style Buddhist lama priests.

Sherpa Woman

Major Festivals in Nepal
The official religion of Nepal is Hinduism and around 90% of the people adhere to its teachings. Of the remainder, around 5% are practicing Buddhists and the other 5% are Muslims, Christians or Animists.

The dates for the religious festivals are formulated a year at a time and vary every year. The lunar calendar calculations are further complicated by the presence of inauspicious days, which can lead to festival dates being changed. Again, it is advisable to check on dates before arrival, especially if you are planning to arrive around October or November, as everything shuts down for the 10-day *Dasain* festival.

Prithvi Jayanti (January)
A celebration to commemorate the late King Prithvi Narayani Shah.

Magh Sakranti (January)
A Hindu festival held to thank the God Vishnu. People bathe and take gifts of flowers to Vishnu temples.

Basanta Panchami (January-February)
This festival celebrates the coming of *Basanta* (springtime). Official celebrations are held in Kathmandu's Durbar Square with the King of Nepal in attendance. There are also celebrations held at Swayambhunath.

Losar (February-March)
The Tibetan New Year is a time for Tibetans and Sherpas to celebrate with their families. Feasting and dancing are the main activities during this colorful festival. Swayambhunath and Bodhnath get very crowded with pilgrims at this time of year. Iron Snake Year (Year 2128) - February 24, 2001

Maha Shivaratri (February-March)
A Hindu festival dedicated to the God Shiva.

Holi or Fagu Purnima (February-March)
This Hindu festival lasts for the better part of a week and gets very messy with colored powder and water balloons thrown about.

Chaitra Dasain (March-April)
This festival is a smaller version of the hugely

NEPAL

popular 10-day *Dasain* festival held between October and November.

Nawa Barsha (mid-April)
These Nepalese New Year festivities last 3-4 days.

Bisket Jatra (mid-April)
The *Great Chariot Festival* in Bhaktapur that coincides with Nepalese New Year.

Ratu Maachendranath (April-May)
Another festival featuring a large chariot; this one is held at Patan. The temple of Maachendranath is considered sacred to both Hindus and Buddhists.

Buddha Jayanti (May-June)
While the Buddha's birthday is celebrated throughout Nepal, the Buddhist sites of Swayambhunath and Bodhnath are the real focal points. These sacred places are cleaned and decorated to welcome the pilgrims that start arriving from early in the morning.

Mani Rimdu [Thami Gompa] (May-June)
One of the 2 Sherpa festivals held high in the mountainous Solo Khumbu area. Dancing, eating and drinking are the main features of this 3-day festival.

Nag Panchami (July-August)
This ancient festival is dedicated to the Snake Gods of the Kathmandu Valley.

Teej (August-September)
Women are at the forefront of this festival, which celebrates the devotion of Shiva's wife, Parbati. These celebrations take place at the Hindu Pashupati Temple next to Bodhnath.

Gunla (August-September)
A Buddhist festival that is lavishly celebrated at Swayambhunath, among others. The month-long collection of festivities and ceremonies is held to express gratitude for the rains and for the rice crop.

Gai Jatra (August-September)
Funny costumes and generally amusing behavior feature heavily in this Hindu *Festival of the Cow*.

Krishna Jayanti (August-September)

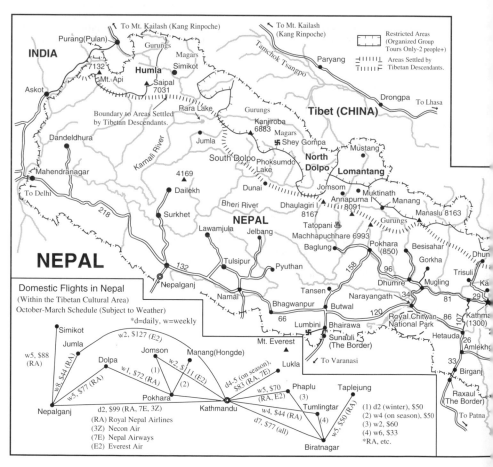

A celebration of Krishna's birthday.

Indra Jatra (September-October)

The festival lasts for a week or so and is dedicated to Indra, the God of Rain and King of the Heavens.

Dasain [Dussehra] (October-November)

The big brother of *Chaitra Dasain*, this 10-day festival is the most popular one of the year. All offices close and it is a time for families to gather together. Processions, animal sacrifices and visits to the temple are all performed during the celebrations.

Tihar [Diwali] (October-November)

Known as the *Festival of Lights*, this is the second most popular festival in Nepal and continues for 5 days.

Sita Vibhaha Panchami (November-December)

This festival features mock wedding ceremonies that mark the marriage of 2 Hindu deities.

Mani Rimdu [Tengpoche Gompa]
(November-December)

One of a pair of Sherpa festivals held high in the mountainous Solo Khumbu area. Dancing, eating and drinking are the main features of this 3-day festival.

Seto Maachendranath (December-January)

This is held in Patan and is connected to the Ratu Maachenranath festival though this ceremony is a cleansing one. The temple of Maachendranath is considered sacred to both Hindus and Buddhists.

ROAD TO NEPAL
Access by Air

For direct flights to Nepal, see the chart above. It

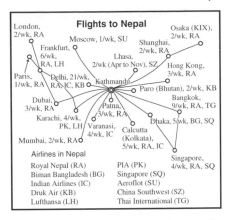

Flights to Nepal

Airlines in Nepal	
Royal Nepal (RA)	PIA (PK)
Biman Bangladesh (BG)	Singapore (SQ)
Indian Airlines (IC)	Aeroflot (SU)
Druk Air (KB)	China Southwest (SZ)
Lufthansa (LH)	Thai International (TG)

is about 7-8km from Kathmandu Airport to the downtown districts of Thamel and Jochne (Freak Street), where you'll find a large number of cheap hotels. Taxis charge between 150NRs and 200NRs during the day and 200NRs at night.

Arranging Visas

You can obtain a tourist visa at any Nepalese High Commission or Consulate in your home country. (See Appendix.) You can also get a visa while you are in India.

Nepalese Embassy - Barakhamba Rd,
New Delhi 110001.
Tel: 11-332 9969/ 7361/ 9218/ 8191
Fax: 11-332 6857.

Visa applications are accepted from 10:00 to 13:00 and you can pick them up the following day from 10:00 to 11:00. You can get a visa at the border or at Kathmandu Airport but you should have US dollars with you because other currencies are not accepted. There is also a 25% surcharge when you apply for visas at the airport.

Nepal introduced a simplified visa system in July 1999. A 60-day, single entry visa now costs US$30. If you want to re-enter the country, there is an extra charge. For each additional single re-entry you are charged US$25 (making a 60-day double entry visa cost US$55). If you require a triple entry visa, this costs US$70 (US$30+US$40 additional charge) and a multiple visa costs $90 (US$30+ US$60 additional charge).

A double entry visa for those intending to return to the country within 5 months of their first visit allows visitors a total of 30 days and costs US$50. One photograph is required.

If you only have a couple of days to look around Kathmandu and don't want to pay for the 60-day visa, there is also a transit visa option

that costs US$5 and allows a stay in the capital for 48 hours.

Visa Extensions
Visitors that want to extend their visas over the 60 days will now be able to extend it by 30 days. The cost of this extension is US$50 and is payable in Nepalese currency. To apply for the extension you will need to go to the *Department of Immigration*.

Geography, Climate & the Tourist Season
Nepal faces the Tibetan Autonomous Region (TAR) to the north across the great Himalayan mountain range. To the east are the Indian states of Sikkim and West Bengal, while Nepal's borders to the south and west are with the Indian states of Bihar and Uttar Pradesh. The south of the country is covered with a tropical rainforest that is home to tigers and elephants, which you can see on organized Safaris. The north of the country is dominated by the towering peaks of the Himalayas.

With altitudes ranging from lows of around 70m to over 8,800m on the summit of Mt. Everest (*Sagarmatha* to the Nepalese and *Jomolangma* to the Tibetans), the climate is extremely varied. The low-lying Tarai region has a sub-tropical climate that is affected by monsoon weather patterns, and with the amount of precipitation, flooding is a major problem in this area during the rainy season that stretches from June through to September. The mountain areas can have extremely harsh conditions throughout the year and the weather is very unpredictable.

Temperatures during the day in these areas are often comfortable but they plummet at night. The dry season is from October to May and there are usually many clear days between November to February, making this the best tourist season. For trekking, the 4-5 weeks between mid-October and mid-November are the best, as there are continuous bright and sunny days.

Access by Land
From India
Many disreputable travel agents in India will try to sell you tickets that take you all the way through to Kathmandu or Pokhara. Most of these ticket deals are frauds and in many cases tourists find that the ticket is worthless once they cross the Nepalese border. The only thing left to do in this situation is to kick yourself and purchase an onward ticket.

From Varanasi & Delhi
From these cities, your most accessible border crossing point will be at Sunauli and there are a number of buses travelling there each day. On reaching the border crossing, you walk to the Nepalese side through the immigration checkpoint.

Kathmandu

On the Nepalese side, there are a lot of day and night buses that take you directly to Kathmandu (10hrs) and Pokhara (8-9hrs) along 2 different routes.

From Patna & Kolkata (Calcutta)
Take a bus to Raxaul, which is the border town on the Indian side. It's then a 4km rickshaw ride from the bus station in Raxaul to the border. At Birganji, on the Nepalese side, there are regular buses that will take you directly to Kathmandu and the trip takes between 8 and 9 hours.

From Siliguri (West Bengal)
If you are coming from Sikkim, Bhutan or the northern hills of West Bengal, the transport hub of Siliguri is the best place to get a bus to take you to the Kakarbhitta crossing point. From there you can get to Kathmandu on direct buses, which take between 15 and 16 hours.

KATHMANDU

Kathmandu is like an 'oasis' in the Tibetan cultural area with a multitude of restaurants, places to stay and entertainment to choose from. Besides the Tibetan side of this sprawling city, there are also a large number of other attractions scattered throughout the various quarters. This chapter focuses on the more practical travel information concerning the city.

Access
Buses from Kathmandu
The long-distance bus terminal, referred to as the 'Kathmandu Bus Station,' is around 3km from Thamel (the northern end of town). Buses to Pokhara, the Indian border, etc, leave from there.

*Pokhara—Morning buses take 8 hours and cost 80NRs. There are also departures between 19:00

and 20:00 costing 90NRs.

*Sunauli—The buses depart every 30 minutes between 05:00 and 10:30, with the trip taking anywhere between 10 and 12 hours for 106NRs. For a slightly higher tariff of 132NRs, you can take one of the late afternoon buses that leave every hour between 16:00 and 20:00.

*Birganj—There are some departures in the morning, as well as between 19:00 and 21:00. The 10-12 hour trip costs around 100NRs.

*Kakarbhitta—Buses leave at 15:00 and 16:00. The journey takes 17 hours and costs 270NRs.

Central City Bus Station—This terminus has buses to Patan (20 mins for 3NRs), Bhaktapur (30 mins for 5NRs), Barabise (5 hrs for 41NRs) and Jiri (8-12 hrs for 110NRs). There are also services available to many other destinations throughout the country.

To connect between the Kathmandu Bus Station and the Central City Bus Station, you can take mini-buses that run through the north of the Thamel district and cost 3NRs.

Tourist Buses—There are tourist buses for many locations in Nepal, including Pokhara, and these depart from the front of the Fuji Restaurant on Kantipath in the center of town. There is a Pokhara bus that leaves at 07:00, costing around 200NRs.

GPO—There are some long-distance buses that depart from the GPO, which is also located on Kantipath.

By Air from Kathmandu to Tibet

China Southwest Airlines in Kathmandu won't sell Kathmandu-Lhasa tickets to independent travelers, even if they have a Chinese visa. Overland, many travelers with a Chinese visa are not allowed to enter the country, either, although there have been reports of individuals being successful. If you do decide to give it a go, don't have too high expectations.

An alternative that will get you into the country is to join an organized tour from Kathmandu and then leave it in Lhasa. By doing this you will need to change your visa status when you arrive to that of an independent traveler and this will cost a lot of money. Even if you are lucky, you will only be entitled to 7 days or so for your stay in China.

When the situation changes and independent travel once again becomes possible. you will need to take a morning bus going to Barabise and then change at the last stop for another to Kodari, where the immigration post is. After you pass through Nepali immigration and cross the Friendship Bridge, it is a 10km walk up to the Chinese immigration post at Dram (Zhangmu).

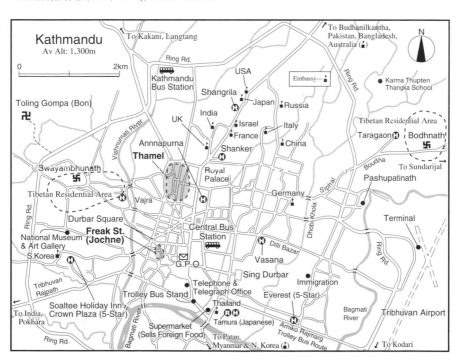

NEPAL

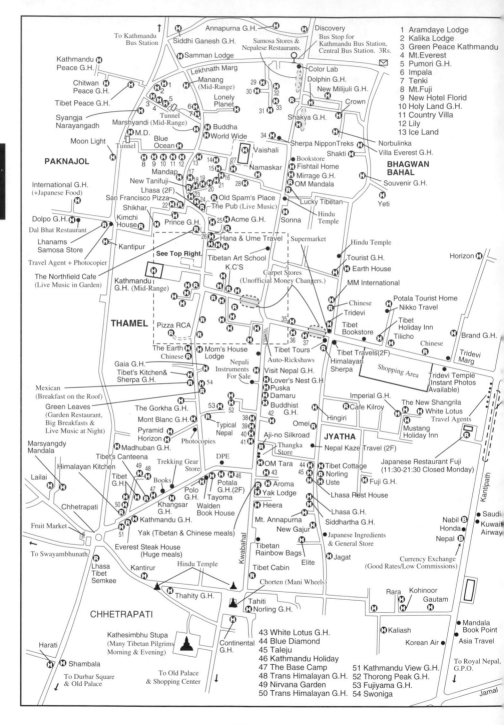

To Kathmandu
Bus Station

Annapurna G.H.
Siddhi Ganesh G.H.
Samman Lodge

Samosa Stores &
Nepalese Restaurants.

Discovery
Bus Stop for
Kathmandu Bus Station,
Central Bus Station. 3Rs.

Kathmandu
Peace G.H.

Lekhnath Marg

Color Lab
Dolphin G.H.

Chitwan
Peace G.H.

Manang
(Mid-Range)

New Milijuli G.H.

Tibet Peace G.H.

Lonely
Planet

Crown

Syangja
Narayangadh

Tunnel

Marshyandi (Mid-Range)

Shakya G.H.

Moon Light

M.D.

Tunnel

Blue
Ocean

Buddha
World Wide

Sherpa NipponTreks
Shakti

Norbulinka
Villa Everest G.H.

PAKNAJOL

Vaishali

Namaskar

Bookstore
Fishtail Home
Mirrage G.H.
OM Mandala

**BHAGWAN
BAHAL**

Souvenir G.H.

International G.H.
(+Japanese Food)

New Tanifuji
Lhasa (2F)

Yeti

San Francisco Pizza
Shikhar

Old Spam's Place
The Pub (Live Music)

Lucky Tibetan

Dolpo G.H.

Kimchi
House

Prince G.H.

Acme G.H.

Sonna

Hindu
Temple

Dal Bhat Restaurant

Lhanams
Samosa Store

Kantipur

Hana & Ume Travel

Supermarket

Hindu Temple

Travel Agent + Photocopier

See Top Right

Tibetan Art School
K.C'S

Tourist G.H.
Earth House

Horizon

The Northfield Cafe
(Live Music in Garden)

Kathmandu
G.H. (Mid-Range)

Carpet Stores
(Unofficial Money Changers.)

MM International

Potala Tourist Home
Nikko Travel

THAMEL

Pizza RCA

Chinese
Tridevi

Tibet
Holiday Inn
Tilicho

Brand G.H.

Tibet
Bookstore

Chinese

Tridevi
Marg

The Earth
Lodge

Mom's House

Chinese

Tibet Tours
Auto-Rickshaws

Tibet Travels(2F)
Himalayan
Sherpa

Gaia G.H.
Tibet's Kitchen&
Sherpa G.H.

Nepali
Instruments
For Sale

Visit Nepal G.H.
Lover's Nest G.H.
Puska
Damaru

Shopping Area

Tridevi Temple
(Instant Photos
Available)

Mexican
(Breakfast on the Roof)

The Gorkha G.H.

Imperial G.H.

Cafe Kilroy

The New Shangrila
White Lotus
Travel Agents

Green Leaves
(Garden Restaurant,
Big Breakfasts &
Live Music at Night)

Mont Blanc G.H.
Pyramid
Horizon

Typical
Nepal

Buddhist
G.H.

Hingiri

Omei

Mustang
Holiday Inn

Marsyangdy
Mandala

Madhuban G.H.

Photocopies

Aji-no Silkroad

JYATHA

Japanese Restaurant Fuji
(11:30-21:30 Closed Monday)

Lailai

Tibet's Canteena

Trekking Gear
Store

Thangka
Home

Nepal Kaze Travel (2F)

Himalayan Kitchen

Tibet
G.H.

Books

DPE

OM Tara

Tibet Cottage
Norling
Uste

Fuji G.H.

Chhetrapati

Polo
G.H.

Potala
G.H.(2F)
Tayoma

Aroma
Yak Lodge
Heera

Lhasa Rest House

Lhasa G.H.

Fruit Market

Khangsar
G.H.

Walden
Book House

Mt. Annapurna
New Gajur

Siddhartha G.H.

Japanese Ingredients
& General Store

Nabil
Honda
Nepal

Saudi
Kuwait
Airway

To Swayambhunath

Kathmandu G.H.

Yak (Tibetan & Chinese meals)

Everest Steak House
(Huge meals)

Tibetan
Rainbow Bags

Elite

Jagat

Currency Exchange
(Good Rates/Low Commissions)

Lhasa
Tibet
Semkee

Kantirur

Hindu Temple

Tibet Cabin

Chorten (Mani Wheels)

Rara

Kohinoor
Gautam

Thahity G.H.

Tahiti
Norling G.H.

Kaliash

Korean Air

Mandala
Book Point
Asia Travel

CHHETRAPATI

Harati

Shambala

Kathesimbhu Stupa
(Many Tibetan Pilgrims
Morning & Evening)

Continental
G.H.

43 White Lotus G.H.
44 Blue Diamond
45 Taleju
46 Kathmandu Holiday
47 The Base Camp
48 Trans Himalayan G.H.
49 Nirvana Garden
50 Trans Himalayan G.H.

51 Kathmandu View G.H.
52 Thorong Peak G.H.
53 Fujiyama G.H.
54 Swoniga

To Old Palace
& Shopping Center

To Durbar Square
& Old Palace

1 Aramdaye Lodge
2 Kalika Lodge
3 Green Peace Kathmandu
4 Mt.Everest
5 Pumori G.H.
6 Impala
7 Tenki
8 Mt.Fuji
9 New Hotel Florid
10 Holy Land G.H.
11 Country Villa
12 Lily
13 Ice Land

To Royal Nepal,
G.P.O.

Jamal

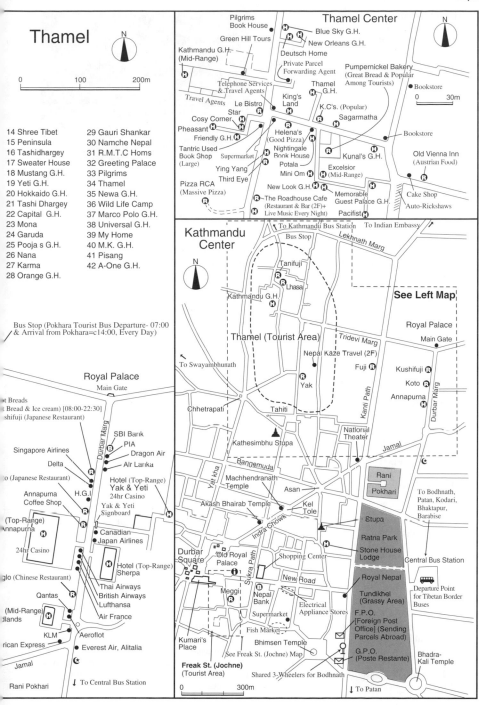

Tourist Information
Nepal Tourism Board, Tourist Service Center.
Bhrikuti Mandap, Kathmandu.
Tel: 01-256 909/ 229
Fax: 01-256 910 E-mail: info@ntb.wlink.com.np
The staff is very helpful and will reply to e-mail or
phone inquiries.

Ministry of Tourism
Ganga Path, Basantapur. Tel: 01-220 818
Sun-Thu 09:00-17:00 (16:00 in winter). Fri 09:00-
16:00. Closed Saturday and national holidays.
The office is near the old palace, to the west of
New Road. Free pamphlets, etc, are available.

Immigration Office
New Baneswar, Kathmandu.
Tel: 01-494 273 Fax: 01-474 267
Applications for visa extensions, trekking permits,
etc, are made at this office. A toilet is available for
applicants.
Sun-Thu 10:00-17:00 (16:00 in winter).
Fri 10:00-15:00.

Embassies & Visas
Indian Embassy
P.O. Box 292, Lainchaur, Kathmandu.
Tel: 01-411 940/699/466 Fax: 01-413 132
E-mail: inemb@mos.com.np
http://www.indiaexpress.com/embassy/
indemb.html

You can apply for a visa only after you have
requested a telex (09:30-17:15, Monday to Friday)
and the reply to it lists your name. The visa will be
delivered between 16:30 and 17:15 on the same
day of application. In total, you will have to visit
the office 3 times.
3-month visa (1,300NRs) + telex (300NRs)
=1,600NRs; 6-month visa costs 2,600NRs.
One photograph is required.

Chinese Embassy
P.O. Box 4234. Baluwatar, Kathmandu.
Tel: 01-411 740/958 Fax: 01-411 388
A visa can only be issued through a travel agent
for organized tour participants, not for independent
travelers.

[For other Foreign Embassies and Consulates in
Nepal, see Appendix.]

Post & Telecommunications
GPO (General Post Office)
On Kantipath, the operating hours are 10:00-17:00
from Sunday to Friday and 10:00-16:00 in the
winter. It is closed on Saturday and all national
holidays.

Kathmandu

There is a *Poste Restante* service provided and
you can pick up mail by producing your passport.
The counter is open from 10:30 to 15:00.

FPO (Foreign Post Office)
Open Sunday to Thursday at 10:00-13:00 and on
Fridays at 10:00-12:00. It is closed Saturday and
on national holidays.

If you are receiving a parcel from abroad, you
may be taxed on it and there are horror stories of
people paying up to 1,000NRs for a single package.
The office is about 100m north of the GPO building.

Changing Money
You can change cash and travelers' checks at most
banks and hotels. When you leave the country you
are permitted to change back into foreign currency
up to 15% of the amount shown on your bank
receipts. There is only a marginal difference if you
change money on the black market. The rate for
US$100 bills is only a coule of percent higher than
in the banks and travelers' check rates are even less.

Bookstores
Pilgrims Book House, Thamel.
Tel: 01-424 942/ 416 744
Fax: 01-424 943 E-mail: pilgrims@wlink.wa.com
This is the largest Western bookstore in the city
and it has a wide variety of books about Nepal and
Tibet. The bookstore also stocks many of the
Lonely Planet's titles, as well as other guidebooks.
It also has a fair selection of maps on offer.
Tantric Used Book Shop, Thamel. Tel: 01-416 633
This is the largest second-hand bookstore in town
and stocks many Nepal-related trekking maps,
books, and collections of photographs.

Travel Agents
Kathmandu has over 100 tour companies to choose
from and many of these agencies handle organized
trips to Tibet and trekking tours in the Himalayas.
This is a list of some of the more reputable travel
agents that have given good service over the years.

Tibet Travel & Tours
P.O.B. 7246 Tridevi Marg, Kathmandu.
Tel: 01-212 130/ 249 140/ 250 611
Fax: 01-228 986/ 249 986
E-mail: kalden@tibet.wlink.com.np
This is the place to arrange your trip into Tibet,
however, they don't arrange anything between
December to March.

Nepal Kaze Travel
(formerly 'Nepal Panorama Trek')
P.O.B. 4529, Jyatha Thamel, Kathmandu.
Tel: 01-240 393 Fax: 01-249 133
They are very experienced in organizing treks to
the Mustang and Dolpo regions.

Green Hill Tours (Pvt) Ltd.
P.O.B. 5072, Thamel, Kathmandu.
Tel: 01-414 803/ 416 596 Fax: 01-414 803
This agency is staffed by Bhutanese and as you
might expect, they specialize in arranging tours of
Bhutan.

Eco Trek & Expedition
P.O.B. 6438, Thamel, Kathmandu.
Tel: 01-231 184/ 224 067/ 417 420
Fax: 01-413 118
If it is discount air tickets that you are after, you
can usually get a good deal here.

Accommodation

Thamel and Jochne (Freak Street) are the 2 major
tourist areas in Kathmandu. Thamel is home to
more than 160 hotels and guesthouses ranging from
the very lowest standard up to mid-range quality.
The room rates at cheap guesthouses during the
tourist season (October to March) differ quite
considerably from those in the off-season (April to
September). Single rooms with a common toilet
and shower room cost from 60 to 150NRs during
the tourist season and double rooms of the same
standard start at around 100NRs.

Basantapur Square

Thamel

Alternatively, during the off-season you will
pay around 120NRs for a single room with a private
bath. By spending around 400-500NRs a night, you
will get a relatively neat room in a fairly good
quality hotel. For longer-term stays you will
normally be able to negotiate a discount on your
room rate.

Thamel

Kunal's Guesthouse & Tara Guesthouse- Single
rooms cost between 80 and 150NRs and doubles
are from 120 to 250NRs
The *Hotel Puska, Hotel Toyama & Hotel Mt. Fuji*-
Single rooms cost 100NRs and doubles are 200NRs.
The *Fuji Guesthouse, Hotel My Home, Hotel Shree
Tibet, Tibet's Kitchen & Sherpa Guesthouse*-
Singles cost 150NRs and doubles are 300NRs.

Swayambhunath

The *Northfield Cafe*, Thamel- You can sample their food while relaxing in the large garden where you also get treated to live music.

Everest Steak House, Thamel- The Everest has a good selection of steak dishes ranging from 180NRs to 250NRs. They also lay on Chinese, Indian and vegetarian meals.

Mexican Restaurant, Thamel- At the spicier end of the spectrum, you can enjoy their breakfast sets on the roof of the restaurant.

The *Roadhouse Cafe & Bar*, Thamel- You can enjoy their meals or prop up the bar along with live music every night.

Jochne (Freak Street)

For a reasonable price starting at around 100NRs for a double room, the *Himalaya Guesthouse* is a well-recommended choice.

Durbar Marg

Top-range hotels are found around Durbar Marg and the following are 5-star ones with casinos:

The *Hotel Del'Annapurna* has single rooms for US$110, doubles for US$120 and there is a 13% tax, which is not included in the price.

The *Hotel Yak & Yeti* has single rooms for US$140 and doubles for US$160. This hotel also has a 13% tax on top of the room price.

Restaurants

Kathmandu is second-to-none within the entire Tibetan cultural area when it comes to food. Even if you are totally into the Tibetan lifestyle and are comfortable living on *tsampa* and butter tea, this is the place to really go to town when it comes to eating out. The wide variety of restaurants means that almost any whim can be satisfied at a price that suits your budget.

Some of the restaurants also levy a 10% service charge, especially in the more expensive establishments. These are just a sample of what is on offer.

Tibetan Food

Lhasa Restaurant, Thamel- The servings are sizeable and the prices are reasonable. The prices for *momos*, *chop suey*, and *chang* (a type of barley beer) range from 35NRs to 45NRs. The restaurant also serves other Tibetan and Chinese meals.

Yak Restaurant, Thamel- Another restaurant that serves good-sized portions at reasonable prices.

Western Food

KC's Restaurant, Thamel- It has 2 floors on which to sample their well-recommended pizzas and steaks.

Pumpernickel Bakery, Thamel- This is a self-service restaurant serving great freshly baked bread.

Japanese Food

Aji-no Silkroad, Thamel- You can enjoy *katsudon* (pork cutlet on rice) and *tendon* (battered seafood on rice) for 130-140NRs and *maki-sushi* (raw fish with rice rolled in seaweed) for 190NRs. The restaurant's hours are 08:00-21:00.

New Tanifuji, Thamel- Opposite the Hotel Mandap, this restaurant has a fairly reasonably priced menu.

Fuji, Kantipath- Set meals are around 400NRs or you can choose individual dishes for 230-280NRs. The restaurant is closed Monday.

Kushifuji, Durbar Marg- This looks like a typical Japanese-style restaurant and the lunch box sets (*shokado-bento*) are highly recommended at 480NRs. A beer here costs 150NRs and the place is open until 22:30.

Koto, Durbar Marg- Real Japanese *tempura* (battered seafood and vegetables) is available.

Meggi Restaurant, Freak Street (Jochne)- This place serves good portions at very reasonable prices. You'll get a good feed for between 80 and 100NRs and a beer costs 80NRs.

Tibetan Language & Meditation Courses

Campus of International Languages, Tribhuvan University.
P.O.B. 8212. Tel: 977-1-330 433/ 331 592
Fax: 977-1-331 964

The school has both 1- and 2-year courses to offer to prospective students. This is not an easy option, as the courses are comprehensive and a strict record of attendance is kept. You are also required to sit for a series of examinations in order to complete the course.

The entrance fee is $525, the 1-year tuition $527, and a visa costs $40 a month. A bank statement verifying you are in possession of over $3,000 is required. There are also courses for Sanskrit and Nepalese.

Rangjung Yeshe Institute, the White Gompa (Chokyi Nyima Rinpoche's Gompa).
Tel: 997-1-470 993 http://www.shedra.com
There are irregular courses for Tibetan, meditation,

etc. Every Saturday there is a Buddhist teaching in English.

Himalayan Yoga Institute Tel: 977-1-413094
Meditation courses and yoga courses are on offer here. It is run by the Gelukpa order but also offers instruction for other schools of Tibetan Buddhism.

Meditation Buddhism Free Talking,
Nepalese Kitchen Restaurant, Thamel.
Classes are held 6 times a month.

Kopan Gompa
P.O.B. 817, Kathmandu.
Tel: 977-1-481 268/ 226 717 Fax: 977-1-481 267
http://www.kopan-monastery.com/
At certain times during the year, it has 1-week or 1-month long courses on offer. The cost of the 1-week course is 400NRs, including board and lodging. There are also courses for beginners.

Vaipassana Meditation Course
Burmese Buddhism. A 10-day course is held once a month. No conversation. This course is tough because it starts at 04:30 and finishes at 21:30. No fee. Donations only.

Thangka Courses
Karma Thupten Land of Snow Thangka School,
P.O.B. 2446 Tel: 01-483 979 Fax: 01-415 381
This is about 2km to the north-west from Bodhnath (a 30-min walk), near Kailash Boarding School. It costs 80NRs per hour and there is no extra charge over 3 hours.

Rok Chaitakar, Patan
Tel: 01-528 810/ 533 820
Newari-style.

Chitrokal Dipok, Swigha Stupa
Newari-style.

Others:
Karma Lama / Kalsang Lama at Durma Parlour Centre, near the Palace
Kegha Lama, Hotel Tashi Delek, Bodhnath

Places to See Around Kathmandu
Swayambhunath
When many people think of Nepal, it is this temple that comes to mind. This Buddhist chorten sits atop a hill to the west of Kathmandu and has large eyes painted on the top of it. The legions of monkeys that play in the grounds of the temple has led the site to also be known as the 'Monkey Temple.'

There are a number of Tibetan villages surrounding Swayambhunath with Buddhist gompas and also a Bon one. The temple is about 40 minutes on foot from the Thamel district and the hilltop location gives you a good view of Kathmandu below. Admission is 50NRs.

According to legend, the Kathmandu Valley was once a huge lake. One day a lotus flower floating on the lake's surface opened and gave out a streak of light. The bolt of light came from the deity Dorje Chang (Vajradhara) and symbolized the enlightened teachings of Mahayana Buddhism in Nepal. To gain access to this sacred place for his pilgrimage, the god Jampal (Manjushri) used his mighty sword to cleave the Chobar Gorge and create the Bagmati River Valley, which drained the water from the lake and shaped the Kathmandu Valley as is seen today. The temple's name comes from the word *Swayambhu*, meaning 'Self-birth,' and it was built on the exact spot where the lotus flower first opened.

Bodhnath
This huge religious structure, 7km to the east of Kathmandu, also has large eyes painted on it. At 38m high and stretching 100m on each side, there is little doubt that this is the largest chorten in Nepal. The site is sacred for both Tibetan and Nepalese Buddhists and there are many famous Tibetan Buddhist gompas surrounding it. All of the main religious orders are represented among these gompas.

You can get great views of the complex from the aptly named Stupa View Restaurant, and from the roof of the Himalayan Restaurant, both to the north of the chorten.

You can make a visit to Bodhnath into a simple 1-day excursion from Kathmandu, or if you really want to soak up the atmosphere, you can stay nearby in one of the many hotels in the area. Like Dharamsala, the seat of the Dalai Lamas' exiled Tibetan government, this sacred site also attracts a great number of foreigners who want to study Tibetan religion, language and culture.

From the GPO on Kantipath, you can catch a shared 3-wheel car that takes you to Bodhnath for

Bodhnath

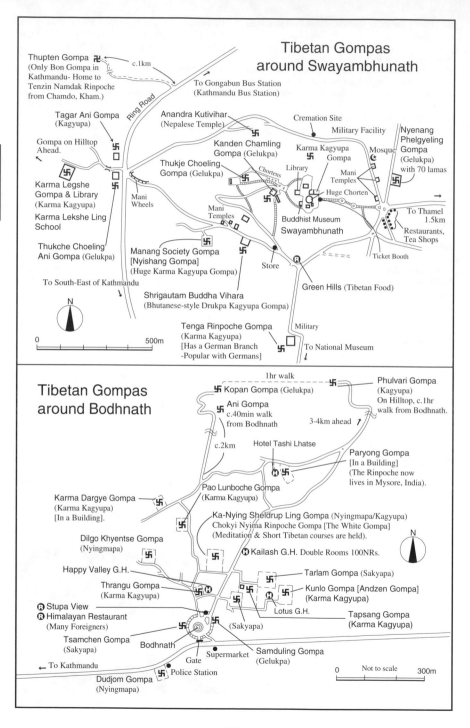

Tibetan Gompas around Swayambhunath

Thupten Gompa 卐
(Only Bon Gompa in
Kathmandu- Home to
Tenzin Namdak Rinpoche
from Chamdo, Kham.)

c.1km

To Gongabun Bus Station
(Kathmandu Bus Station)

Ring Road

Tagar Ani Gompa
(Kagyupa)

Gompa on Hilltop
Ahead.

Karma Legshe
Gompa & Library
(Karma Kagyupa)

Karma Lekshe Ling
School

Thukche Choeling
Ani Gompa (Gelukpa)

To South-East of Kathmandu

Anandra Kutivihar
(Nepalese Temple)

Kanden Chamling
Gompa (Gelukpa)

Thukje Choeling
Gompa (Gelukpa)

Chortens

Mani
Wheels

Mani
Temples

Manang Society Gompa
[Nyishang Gompa]
(Huge Karma Kagyupa Gompa)

Shrigautam Buddha Vihara
(Bhutanese-style Drukpa Kagyupa Gompa)

Cremation Site

Military Facility

Karma Kagyupa
Gompa

Library

Mani
Temples

Huge Chorten

Buddhist Museum
Swayambhunath

Store

Green Hills (Tibetan Food)

Mosque

Nyenang
Phelgyeling
Gompa
(Gelukpa)
with 70 lamas

To Thamel
1.5km

Restaurants,
Tea Shops

Ticket Booth

N

0   500m

Tenga Rinpoche Gompa
(Karma Kagyupa)
[Has a German Branch
-Popular with Germans]

Military

To National Museum

Tibetan Gompas around Bodhnath

1hr walk

Kopan Gompa (Gelukpa)

Phulvari Gompa
(Kagyupa)
On Hilltop, c.1hr
walk from Bodhnath.

Ani Gompa
c.40min walk
from Bodhnath

3-4km ahead

c.2km

Hotel Tashi Lhatse

Karma Dargye Gompa
(Karma Kagyupa)
[In a Building].

Pao Lunboche Gompa
(Karma Kagyupa)

Paryong Gompa
[In a Building]
(The Rinpoche now
lives in Mysore, India).

Ka-Nying Sheldrup Ling Gompa (Nyingmapa/Kagyupa)
Chokyi Nyima Rinpoche Gompa [The White Gompa]
(Meditation & Short Tibetan courses are held).

Dilgo Khyentse Gompa
(Nyingmapa)

Kailash G.H. Double Rooms 100NRs.

Happy Valley G.H.

Thrangu Gompa
(Karma Kagyupa)

Stupa View
Himalayan Restaurant
(Many Foreigners)

Tsamchen Gompa
(Sakyapa)

To Kathmandu

Bodhnath

Gate

Supermarket

Dudjom Gompa
(Nyingmapa)

Police Station

Tarlam Gompa (Sakyapa)

Kunlo Gompa [Andzen Gompa]
(Karma Kagyupa)

Lotus G.H.

(Sakyapa)

Tapsang Gompa
(Karma Kagyupa)

Samduling Gompa
(Gelukpa)

N

0   Not to scale   300m

6NRs. There are minibuses that leave from the Central City Bus Station to Bodhnath for 3NRs but they take over 30 minutes during the day. A metered taxi from Thamel to Bodhnath will cost you around 60NRs.

Pharping

The town of Pharping is around 20km to the south of Kathmandu along the Bagmati River. The area around this small quiet town is full of Hindu temples, Tibetan-style gompas and other Buddhist sacred sites. Many tourists flock to the Dakshinkali Temple, which is dedicated to the Hindu goddess Kali.

The Tibetan gompas are clustered close to the Gorakhnath cave where Guru Rinpoche, who brought Tantric Buddhism from India to the Tibetan lands in the 8th century, mastered the teachings of *Mahamudra*. One of the better-known gompas is the Nyingmapa monastery of Chadral Rinpoche.

You can get to the area by taking a bus to Dakshinkali from the Central City Bus Station in Kathmandu.

Namobuddha

Namobuddha is another stupa that is a destination for many Tibetan Buddhist pilgrims. The area is connected to the story of an incarnation of Buddha feeding a starving tiger with his own flesh.

The site is 4-5km south of Dhulikhel, to the east of Kathmandu. You'll need to take a bus to Dhulikhel from the Central City Bus Station in Kathmandu and get off at the last stop. From there it is an hour or so on foot.

TREKKING TO THE TIBETAN WORLD

To really experience the Tibetan world in Nepal you have to put on your trekking shoes and venture high into the snow-clad peaks of the Himalayas. The major routes are as follows:

From Kathmandu
- Solu Khumbu (the Everest Region)
  Jiri-Namche Bazaar-Everest
- Mt. Kangchenjunga
  Lukla-Hile-Mt. Kangchenjunga
- Langtang
  Dhunche-the Langtang Valley
- Manaslu
  Dhading-Manaslu

From Pokhara
- To the Annapurna Region
  The Annapurna Sanctuary/Jomsom-Muktinath-Manang

Dhaulagiri

- Lo Manthang (Mustang)
  Jomsom-Lo Manthang
- Dolpo
  The Tarap Valley-Phoksumdo Lake

Trekking Preparations
Seasons
The dry season stretches from October to March and the period from October to November is especially good for trekking. From December to February it gets cold at altitudes above 2,000m, but at this time of year the skies are clear and you can get stunning views of the peaks. Though many of the days are fine, most of the areas over 2,500m are covered with snow.

In the north-west of the country, in areas like Dolpo, Mustang and Humla, the weather is unaffected by the seasonal monsoons that drench much of the rest of Nepal. The best season to trek in these areas is from May to October, especially during the months of August and September. Winter in the region is best to be avoided as it gets bitterly cold.

Trekking Gear to Take
To minimize the weight of your baggage, pack only the essentials and leave the unnecessary stuff at your hotel. Most of them have secure storage space and are very used to people asking to do this — so much so that many hotels include this in their basic services and don't charge for it.

The basics that you will need are:
1) A good down sleeping bag.
2) A down jacket.
3) Sturdy trekking shoes and a couple of pairs of good hiking socks.
4) A reusable water bottle and water purification tablets.
5) Warm, tight-knit clothing.
6) A flashlight, small first-aid kit and other personal items.

If you are tackling areas like the Annapurna

NEPAL

Sanctuary or around Everest, you will need to kit yourself out for cold weather. Additional items should include: a woolen cap with ear flaps, mittens, thermal underclothes, sunglasses, suncream and waterproofs.

Trekking Permits

Up until July 1999, those wishing to trek in Nepal were required to purchase a trekking permit from the immigration offices in either Kathmandu or Pokhara. Many of these areas (Annapurna, Langtang, Everest, Rara areas, etc.) are now open to trekkers without the need for a permit as a result of the government's wishing to increase the number of tourists visiting the country.

Still, most areas that have a strong Tibetan feel to them are close to the sensitive Chinese border and these restricted areas require special permits (See the Permit Fees table below). For these areas you must also join an agency-organized tour with at least 2 group members. Applications for permits are accepted from 10:30 to 13:00, Sunday to Thursday, and from 10:30 to 12:00 on Friday. The permit will then be issued between 14:00 and 15:00 the following day.

To make an application for one of these permits, you must present the immigration official with your passport, 2 photographs, 2 application forms, and the money required to process the application. In the form you fill out, you must write in your personal details, along with the proposed date of departure, the intended length of your trip, the place of departure and the destination. You can apply for these permits a number of days before the date of departure.

Permit Fees (per person):

1. Mustang (Lo Manthang), North Dolpo
Group Tour Only- US$700 for 10 days. If you intend to extend your trip beyond that 10-day period, you will be charged US$70 per day.

2. Manaslu
Group Tour Only- The period from December to August is rated at US$75 per week. High season rates between September and November are US$90 per week.

3. Humla (Simikot-Yari) (See pages 147-149.)
Group Tour Only- US$90 for a week. If you intend to extend your trip beyond that 7-day period, you will be charged another US$15 per day.

4. Mt. Kangchenjunga, South Dolpo
You are charged US$10 for the first week and US$20 for each additional week.

5. Annapurna, Langtang, Everest, etc.
No Permit Required (previously the first 4 weeks cost you US$5 per week and it was then US$10 for each additional week).

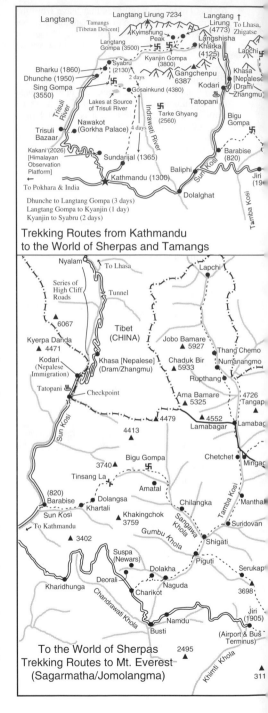

Dhunche to Langtang Gompa (3 days)
Langtang Gompa to Kyanjin (1 day)
Kyanjin to Syabru (2 days)

Trekking Routes from Kathmandu
to the World of Sherpas and Tamangs

To the World of Sherpas
Trekking Routes to Mt. Everest
(Sagarmatha/Jomolangma)

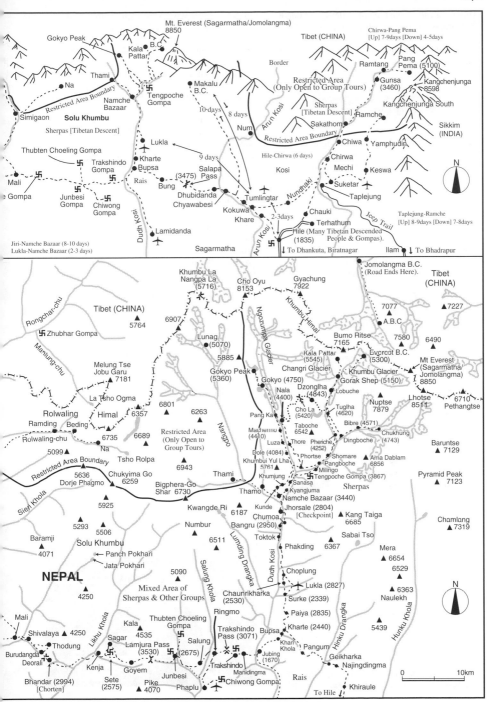

*There is an additional fee of 650NRs (1,000NRs for Annapurna) charged for admission into the National Parks. The most popular trekking areas in the regions mentioned above are in one of these many parks.

ROUTE TO BIGU GOMPA & SURROUNDING AREA

One of the starting points for trekking in the Solu Khumbu region is the small town of Jiri. You can reach Jiri by bus in about a half-day from Kathmandu. This route, however, is for those who dare to trek there from Barabise, which is just under halfway between Jiri and the capital. On the way, there is a Sherpa village with a large nunnery/monastery called Bigu Gompa.

Barabise to Jiri
Day 1: Barabise (820m)-Khartali
Day 2: Khartali-Thulo Tingsang
Day 3: Thulo Tingsang-Amatal
Day 4: Amatal-Saunepani
Day 5: Saunepani-Serukapti
Day 6: Serukapti-Mali-Jiri (1,905m)

EVEREST TREKKING

At the southern foot of the world's highest peak Mt. Everest (*Sagarmatha* to the Nepalese and *Jomolangma* to the Tibetans) is the Solu Khumbu region. This area is mainly populated by Sherpas who are said to have migrated from eastern Tibet centuries ago and settled this harsh land.

There are 2 popular trekking routes that start from the village of Namche Bazaar and take you deep into the Sagarmatha National Park. One of these will take you to Kala Pattar above Gorak Shep, and then onto the famous Everest Base Camp (5,300m). It will take you between 7 and 8 days to complete the round-trip.

The other less-traveled route goes out to Gokyo Peak (5,360m) to the west of Mt. Everest and it will take you around 7 days for the round trip.

Kathmandu-Namche Bazaar
Access by Air
During the high season, from late September to the end of November, the flights from Kathmandu into Lukla are always packed. You'll need to make a reservation on one of these as soon as you possibly can.

Factoring a couple of extra days into your schedule is advisable, as adverse weather conditions can play havoc with the flights and you may be grounded for a day or two.

Day 1: Kathmandu (1,300m)-Lukla (2,827m)
[By Air]
    *The flight takes about 40 minutes.
Day 2: Lukla-Chomoa (2,950m) 4-5 hrs.
Day 3: Chomoa-Namche Bazaar (3,440m) 4 hrs.

Access Overland
This trip is a combination of taking the bus from Kathmandu to Jiri and then trekking the rest of the way. Thubten Choeling Gompa is a large monastery and nunnery located a little north of Junbesi. Tulshi Rinpoche constructed the gompa after he came to the area as a Tibetan refugee, a few years after the Dalai Lama fled from Tibet. He was originally the abbot of the Rongbuk Monastery, which is situated on the Tibetan side of Mt. Everest. Close to the monastery is Pungmochhe, which is home to the *Traditional Sherpa Art Centre*. This organization promotes the skills of local *thangka* artists and their work is also on sale at the center.

Day 1: Kathmandu (1,300m)-Jiri (1,905m)
[By Bus]
    *The trip takes 10-12hrs and costs 110NRs.
Day 2: Jiri-Bhandar 7-9 hrs.
Day 3: Bhandar-Sagar/Sete (2,575m) 6-7 hrs.
Day 4: Sagar-Junbesi (2,675m) 7-8 hrs.
Day 5: Junbesi-Trakshindo (3,071m) 6-7 hrs.
Day 6: Trakshindo-Khari Khola 8-9 hrs.
Day 7: Khari Khola-Puiyan 5-6 hrs.
Day 8: Puiyan-Phakding 6 hrs.
Day 9: Phakding-Namche Bazaar (3,440m) 5 hrs.

Namche Bazaar to Kala Pattar & Everest Base Camp.
As the base for Everest trekking, Namche Bazaar is a large village with many hotels and lodges. There is a lively market held in the village every Saturday morning. About a 15-minute walk from the village is a museum, which concentrates on the beautiful nature of the Everest region and also has exhibits

Namche Bazaar

Everest
[Solu Khumbu Region]
Trekking Times.

For trekking in the Everest area, many tourists fly from Kathmandu to Lukla. They then walk a day and a half to Namche Bazaar, the base for treks to Kala Pattar, Chukhung & Gokyo Peak. Even with taking the Lukla flight, you will need at least 2 weeks for the tour. Access to the Everest region is not as easy as the Annapurna area. There is also a bus from Kathmandu to Jiri, but to continue onto Namche Bazaar will require a 7-8 day walk (One way).

A. By Air [Return]
With a round-trip flight between Kathmandu and Lukla, you could tackle either Kala Pattar or Gokyo Peak in about 2 weeks. To try for both you'll need an extra week. Make your return flight reservations as early as possible.

B. By Air [One Way]
Add 10 days to Schedule A.

*For planning, you should bear in mind that flights are sometimes suspended for a couple of days due to adverse weather conditions.

C. Walking [No Flying]
Add about 20 days to Schedule A. Trying both Kala Pattar and Gokyo Peak would take around 40 days in total. Cost-wise, there is little difference between flying and walking. To get to Namche Bazaar, you may spend as much as US$100 on hotels, meals, etc.

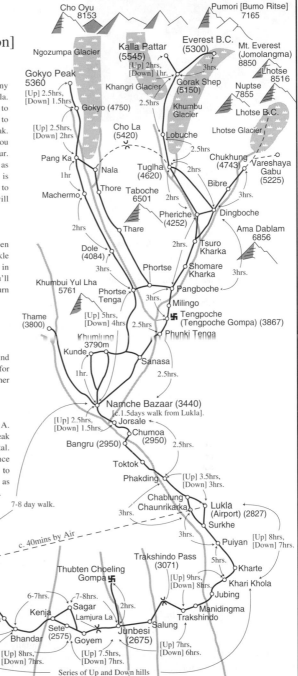

Cho Oyu 8153

Pumori [Bumo Ritse] 7165

Ngozumpa Glacier

Kalla Pattar (5545)
[Up] 2hrs, [Down] 1hr.

Everest B.C. (5300)

Mt. Everest (Jomolangma) 8850

Gokyo Peak 5360
[Up] 2.5hrs, [Down] 1.5hrs

Khangri Glacier

Gorak Shep (5150)

Lhotse 8516

Nuptse 7855

Gokyo (4750)

2.5hrs

Khumbu Glacier

Lhotse B.C.

[Up] 2.5hrs, [Down] 2hrs

Cho La (5420)

Lobuche

Lhotse Glacier

Pang Ka

Nala

Tuglha (4620)

2.5hrs

Chukhung (4743)

Vareshaya Gabu (5225)

1hr

2hrs

Bibre

Thore

Taboche 6501

3hrs.

Machermo

2hrs

Dingboche

Pheriche (4252)

Ama Dablam 6856

2hrs

Thare

2hrs.

Tsuro Kharka

Dole (4084)

Phortse

3hrs.

Shomare Kharka

3hrs.

Khumbui Yul Lha 5761

Phortse Tenga

3hrs.

Pangboche

Thame (3800)

[Up] 5hrs, [Down] 4hrs

2.5hrs

Milingo

Tengpoche (Tengpoche Gompa) (3867)

Khumjung 3790m

Phunki Tenga

Kunde

Sanasa

1hr.

2.5hrs.

Namche Bazaar (3440)
[c.1.5days walk from Lukla].

[Up] 2.5hrs, [Down] 1.5hrs.

Jorsale

Bangru (2950)

Chumoa (2950)

2.5hrs.

Toktok

Phakding

[Up] 3.5hrs, [Down] 3hrs.

Chablung
Chaunrikarka

Lukla (Airport) (2827)

3hrs.

7-8 day walk.

3hrs.

Surkhe

Barabise (820)

c. 40mins by Air

Puiyan

[Up] 8hrs, [Down] 7hrs.

Trakshindo Pass (3071)

Kharte

Kathmandu (1300)

Thubten Choeling Gompa

[Up] 9hrs, [Down] 8hrs.

Khari Khola

Mali

5hrs.

Jubing

Shivalaya

6-7hrs.

7-8hrs.

Sagar

2hrs.

Manidingma
Trakshindo

Jiri (1905)

Burudangda

Kenja

Lamjura La

Salung

c.10-12hrs by Bus. (2-3 Buses Every Morning)

[Up] 9hrs, [Down] 7hrs.

Sete (2575)

Junbesi (2675)

[Up] 7hrs, [Down] 6hrs.

Bhandar

Goyem

[Up] 8hrs, [Down] 7hrs.

[Up] 7.5hrs, [Down] 7hrs.

Series of Up and Down hills

NEPAL

Everest & Nuptse

showing the life of the Sherpa people.

The trek up from Namche Bazaar to Kala Pattar, the viewpoint for Mt. Everest, takes you past Tengpoche Gompa where the most important festival in the Sherpa's calendar, *Mani Rimdu*, is held during the full moon in either November or December. At this time, large numbers of local people gather at the monastery for 2 days of festivities, which feature dances by the monks from the gompa.

Day 1: Namche Bazaar (3,440m)-Tengpoche (3,867m) 5-6 hrs.
Day 2: Tengpoche-Pheriche (4,252m) 5-6 hrs.
Day 3: Pheriche-Lobuche 5-6 hrs.
Day 4: Lobuche-Kala Pattar (5,545m) 5 hrs./ Everest B.C. (5,300m) 6-7 hrs.

*The following route is a round trip to & from Chhukhung.

Day 2: Tengpoche (3,867m)-Dingboche 6 hrs.
Day 3: Dingboche-Chukhung (4,743m) 3 hrs.
Day 4: Chukhung-Lobuche 6-7 hrs.
For the descent, it will take you 2-3 days from Lobuche back to Namche Bazaar.

Namche Bazaar to Gokyo Peak
Gokyo Peak is a less-popular route and thus you'll meet fewer trekkers on the way, but it also commands an excellent view of Everest and Cho Oyu (8,153m).

Day 1: Namche Bazaar (3,440m)-Sanasa 2 hrs.
Day 2: Sanasa-Dole (4,084m) 5-6 hrs.
Day 3: Dole-Gokyo (4,750m) 6-7 hrs.
Day 4: Gokyo-Gokyo Peak (5,360m) 2.5 hrs.

LUKLA TO HILE

To reach the Mt. Kangchenjunga area on the border with Sikkim, you'll first need to make your way to Hile, the starting point for Mt. Kangchenjunga

trekking. The Lukla to Hile route doesn't attract many trekkers.

Day 1: Lukla (2,827m)-Puiyan
Day 2: Puiyan-Pangum
Day 3: Pangum-Najingdingma
Day 4: Najingdingma-Bung
Day 5: Bung-Sanam
Day 6: Sanam-Salapa Pass (3,475m)-Phedi
Day 7: Phedi-Dhubidanda
Day 8: Dhubidanda-Chyawabesi
Day 9: Chyawabesi-Khare
Day 10: Khare-Mangmaya Khola
Day 11: Mangyama Khola-Hile (1,835m)

THE MT. KANGCHENJUNGA AREA

This route starts at Hile (or Basantpur) and takes you up to the northern approaches of Mt. Kangchenjunga. It takes around 3 weeks to get to Pang Pema, the last stage on the route. At the foot of the mountain, there are many Limbu settlements and you can sample original *Thongba*, (a beer made from fermented barnyard grass). There is an airport at Suketar in an area settled by Sherpas.

Day 1: Hile (1,835m)-Basantpur (2,190m)
Day 2: Basantpur-Chauki (2,630m)
Day 3: Chauki-Gupa Pokhari (2,890m)
Day 4: Gupa Pokhari-Nesum (1,550m)
Day 5: Nesum-Thumma (1,010m)
Day 6: Thumma-Chirwa (1,140m)
Day 7: Chirwa-Sakathum (1,660m)
Day 8: Sakathum-Amjilassa (2,340m)
Day 9: Amjilassa-Kyapra (2,810m)
Day 10: Kyapra-Gunsa (3,460m)
Day 11: Gunsa
Day 12: Gunsa-Khambachen (3,980m)
Day 13: Khambachen
Day 14: Khambachen-Lhonak (4,720m)
Day 15: Lhonak-Pang Pema [End of this course] (5,100m)
Day 16: Pang Pema-Khambachen (3,980m)
Day 17: Khambachen-Gunsa (3,460m)
Day 18: Gunsa-Amjilassa (2,340m)
Day 19: Amjilassa-Chirwa (1,140m)
Day 20: Chirwa-Linkhim (1,510m)
Day 21: Linkhim-Suketar [Airport] (2,200m)

LANGTANG

The Langtang Valley is spread out to the north of Kathmandu, just below the Tibetan border. This area was settled by the Tamang people, who are

Tibetan Buddhists and who share their language and many of their customs with Tibetans.

In Helambu, to the south of Langtang, there are many Sherpas, though they differ from those inhabiting the Solu Khumbu region in both their clothes and customs. To trek up to the Langtang Valley, your starting point is Dhunche; then on the return you can branch off before getting back there and making your way to Sundarijal via Gosainkund.

In the Langtang area, the Kyanjin Gompa is a good staging point for exploring the area and also a place to rest up before the second leg of the trek. After swinging south at Syabru on the return leg towards Dhunche, you will come to Sing Gompa and the sacred Gosainkund Lake, which at 4,300m attracts both Hindu and Buddhist pilgrims.

Day 1: Dhunche (1,950m)-Syabru (2,130m) 6-7 hrs.
Day 2: Syabru-Lama Hotel 7-8 hrs.
Day 3: Lama Hotel-Langtang (3,500m) 7-8 hrs.
Day 4: Langtang-Kyanjin Gompa (3,800m) 4-5 hrs.
Day 5: Kyanjin Gompa- Moraine for a view of Langtang Lirung [Round-trip] 4-5 hrs.
Day 6: Kyanjin Gompa- Kyanjin Ri [Round-trip] (4,125m) 5-6 hrs.
Day 7: Kyanjin Gompa- Langshisha Kharka [Round-trip] 8-9 hrs.
Day 8: Kyanjin Gompa [Rest day]
Day 9: Kyanjin Gompa-Bamboo Lodge 6-7 hrs.
Day 10: Bamboo Lodge-Syabru (2,130m) 3 hrs.
Day 11: Syabru-Sing Gompa (3,550m) 4-5 hrs.
Day 12: Sing Gompa-Gosainkund (4,380m) 6 7 hrs.
Day 13: Gosainkund-Ghopte (3,495m) 6-7 hrs.
Day 14: Ghopte-Khutumsang 6-7 hrs.
Day 15: Khutumsang-Chisopani 7-8 hrs.
Day 16: Chisopani-Sundarijal (1,365m) 5-6 hrs.
*From Sundarijal it's an hour by bus to Kathmandu.

MANASLU NORTH

The northern side of Mt. Manaslu is also within the Tibetan cultural area. Tibetans and people of Tibetan descent, such as Gurungs, have settled throughout this area. Along the Manaslu trekking circuit, you will be able to visit Sama Gompa and at Ghap Village there is a beautiful *mani*-wall on which images of Milarepa have been engraved, as the great ascetic is said to have visited the valley. You need to get a permit to visit this area and these are only issued for organized group tours.

Kala Pattar Trekking

Manaslu Circuit

Day 1: Kathmandu (1,300m)-Dhading-Kafalpani
Day 2: Kafalpani-Arughat Bazaar (1,640m)
Day 3: Arughat Bazaar-Soti Khola
Day 4: Soti Khola-Labu Besi
Day 5: Labu Besi-Doban
Day 6: Doban-Jagat (1,341m)
Day 7: Jagat-Serson (2,300m)
Day 8: Serson-Deng
Day 9: Deng-Ghap (2,600m)

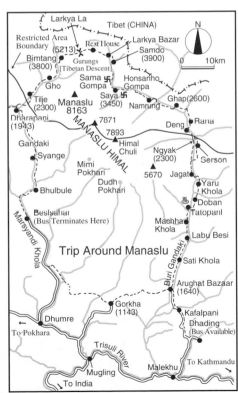

Trip Around Manaslu

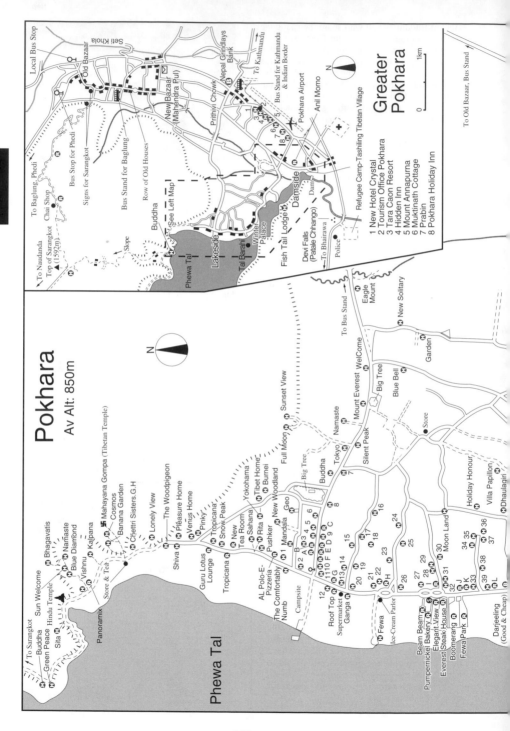

Pokhara
Av Alt: 850m

NEPAL

Greater Pokhara

1 New Hotel Crystal
2 Tourism Office Pokhara
3 Tara Caon Resort
4 Hidden Inn
5 Mount Annapurna
6 Muktinath Cottage
7 Prabin
8 Pokhara Holiday Inn

340

NEPAL

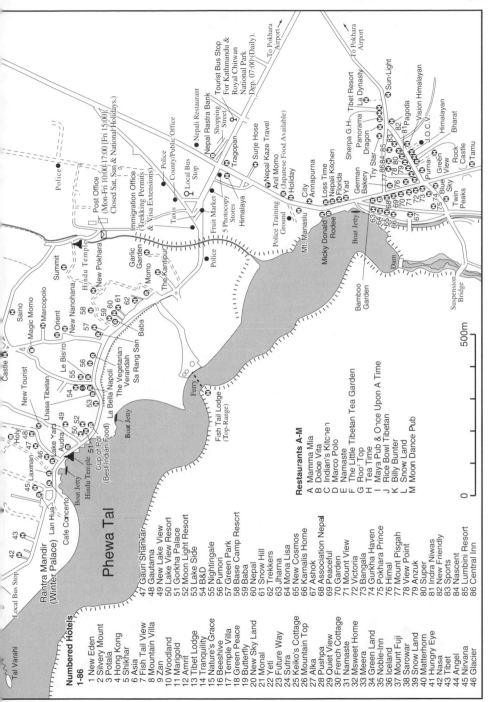

Phewa Tal

Rantra Mandir
(Winter Palace)

Lan Hua

Cafe Concerto

Boat Jetty

Hindu Temple
Cup of Pot
(Best Indian Food)

Boat Jetty

Tal Varahi

Local Bus Stop

Castle

Saino

Magic Momo

Marcopolo

Orient

New Tourist

Lhasa Tibetan

Lake Yard

Audra

Laxman

Holy

New Nanohana

Le Bistro

La Bella Napoli

The Vegetarian
Verandah

Sa Rang San

Baba

Fish Tail Lodge
(Top-Range)

Ferry

Boat Jetty

Summit

Hindu Temple

New Pokhara

Garlic
Garden

The Kantipur

Momo

Police

Police

Post Office
(Mon-Fri 10:00-17:00 [Fri 15:00].
Closed Sat, Sun & National Holidays.)

Immigration Office
(Trekking Permits
& Visa Extensions)

Police

Taxis

County/Public Office

Local Bus
Stop

Fruit Market

Photocopy
Stores

Himalaya

Police Training
Ground

Mt. Manaslu

Micky Donald

Rodee

Boat Jetty

Bamboo
Garden

Dam

Suspension
Bridge

Nepali Restaurant

Nepal Rastra Bank

Shopping
Street

Tragopan

Surje Hose

Nepal Kaze Travel

Anil Momo
(Japanese Food Available)

Holiday

City

Annapurna

Loss Time

Nepali Kitchen

Florida

Yad

German
Bakery

Try Star

Tourist Bus Stop
For Kathmandu &
Royal Chitwan
National Park
Dep. 07:00(Daily).

To Pokhara
Airport

To Pokhara
Airport

Sherpa G.H.

Panorama

Dragon

Tibet Resort

La Dynasty

Puma

Green

Himalayan

Sun-Light

Pagoda

Vision Himalayan

J.O.C.V.

Bharat

Rock
Castle

Tamu

Blue
Sky

Twin
Peaks

Suspension
Bridge

500m

0

Restaurants A-M

A Mamma Mia
B Dolce Vita
C Indian's Kitchen
D Marco Polo
E Namaste
F The Little Tibetan Tea Garden
G Roo² Top
H Tea Time
I Maya Pub & Once Upon A Time
J Rice Bowl Tibetan
K Billy Bunter
L Snow Land
M Moon Dance Pub

Numbered Hotels
1-86

1 New Eden
2 Silvery Mount
3 Potala
4 Hong Kong
5 Shikhar
6 Asia
7 Fish Tail View
8 Mountain Villa
9 Zan
10 Woodland
11 Marigold
12 Amrit
13 Tibet Lodge
14 Tranquility
15 Nature's Grace
16 Beeshive
17 Temple Villa
18 Green Peace
19 Butterfly
20 New Sky Land
21 Monal
22 Yeti
23 Future Way
24 Sutra
25 Keiko's Cottage
26 Mountain Top
27 Alka
28 Pushpa
29 Quiet View
30 French Cottage
31 Namaste
32 Msweet Home
33 Meera
34 Green Land
35 Noble-Inn
36 Iceland
37 Mount Fuji
38 Sarowar
39 Snow Land
40 Matterhorn
41 Hungry Eye
42 Nasa
43 Tibet
44 Angel
45 Nirvana
46 Glacier
47 New Lake View
48 Gautama
49 New Lake View
50 Lake View Resort
51 Gorkha Palace
52 Moon Light Resort
53 Lake Side
54 B&D
55 Nightingale
56 Pumori
57 Green Park
58 Base Camp Resort
59 Baba
60 Nepal
61 Snow Hill
62 Trekkers
63 Jharna
64 Mona Lisa
65 New Cosmos
66 Karnalis Home
67 Ashok
68 Association Nepal
69 Peaceful
70 Garden
71 Mount View
72 Victoria
73 Bangala
74 Gurkha Haven
75 Pokhara Prince
76 Himal
77 Mount Pisgah
78 View Point
79 Anzuk
80 Super
81 Indra Niwas
82 New Friendly
83 Sports
84 Nascent
85 Lumbini Resort
86 Central Inn

Day 10: Ghap-Namrung
Day 11: Namrung-Shyala (3,450m)
Day 12: Shyala-Sama Gompa
Day 13: Sama Gompa-Samdo (3,900m)
Day 14: Samdo-Larkya Bazaar-Larkya Rest House
Day 15: Larkya Rest House-Crossing Larkya-La
   (5,213m)-Bimtang (3,800m)
Day 16: Bimtang-Gho
Day 17: Gho-Tilje (2,300m)-Dharapani (1,943m)
   [Meets the route to Manang]
Day 18: Dharapani-Syange
Day 19: Syange-Bhulbule
Day 20: Bhulbule-Besisahar

POKHARA

Pokhara is around 200km to the west of Kathmandu and for those making for the Annapurna area for trekking, this will likely be your starting point. The town is famous for its lake known as 'Phewa Tal', as well as the stunning views of Machhapuchhare and the Annapurna range that form the backdrop to the town.

The tourist areas are basically divided into two, with the Lakeside area on the banks of the Phewa Tal, and the Damside area on the eastern bank of the Pardi Khola. The former is a much larger area and filled with Western tourists. There are over 200 guesthouses and hotels in this area alone and these are surrounded by numerous restaurants, souvenir stores, supermarkets, old bookstores and trekking gear stores.

Access
By Air
There are 8-10 flights a day from Kathmandu to Pokhara, although this number decreases during the rainy season. The flight time is around 40 minutes and the fare is US$61. If you can get a seat on the right-hand side of the plane coming into Pokhara, you will be treated to some great views of Mt. Manaslu and the Annapurna range.

Pokhara

By Bus
From Kathmandu, a minibus costs between 180NRs and 270NRs and it is around an 8-hour journey. The tourist buses take about the same amount of time and are slightly cheaper, costing 150-180NRs. Most tourists arrange these tourist bus tickets through a travel agency in Kathmandu.

The buses heading for Pokhara leave the bus stand in front of the Fuji Restaurant. The morning bus leaves at 07:00, arriving at Pokhara around 15:00, and there is a cheaper night bus that costs 95NRs and departs at 19:00. It gets you there between 03:00 and 04:00 the next morning.

Local Transportation in Pokhara
The local bus service in town connects the Lakeside and Damside tourist areas with the New Bazaar every 15 to 20 minutes and the fares range from 3-8NRs, according to distance. The fare system is rather complex and difficult to understand.

Rental Boats at Phewa Tal & Rental Bicycles
Rental boat fees depend on your negotiation skills and generally start around 100NRs per hour. You'll be offered cheaper rates at Damside. The rates for rental bicycles start at 5NRs per hour, or range from 30NRs to 50NRs a day.

Immigration Office
You can apply for special trekking permits and get your visas extended at the office just north of the Damside area. The office is open for applications from 10:30 to 13:00 Sunday through Thursday, and until 12:00 on Fridays. For collections, you need to return to the office the same day between 16:00 to 17:00 (14:00-15:00 on Friday). It is closed Saturdays and on national holidays.

The applications made in Pokhara follow the same routine as in Kathmandu and the rates are the same (the Annapurna entrance fee is still 1,000NRs). It is also possible to apply for these documents a few days prior to your trip.

Tourist Office
The office is next to Hotel New Crystal on a small hill near the airport and is open from 10:00 to 17:00 Monday to Thursday (10:00-16:00 from November 17 to February 12), and 10:00-15:00 on Fridays. This office is also closed on Saturdays and national holidays. The information available is not as useful as you might expect. A better option for trekking information is to check trekking gear stores or restaurants that are popular among tourists.

Accommodation
There are over 250 hotels or guesthouses to choose from in the town. Many Westerners prefer the Lakeside area while others, such as Japanese, tend

to stay in the Damside area, which has better views of the mountains. There are many lodges in this area with quiet courtyards.

There are 2 seasonal rates for the accommodation in the town. The peak season stretches from October to March and the off-season lasts from April to September. Many of the single or double rooms that charge less than 150NRs have no private bathroom. To get a bathroom you'll need to pay more, around 150-200NRs. If you are prepared to pay between 250NRs and 400NRs, you'll be able to get a fairly decent room.

The rates are generally open to negotiation and you should make sure that the price that you finally agree upon is inclusive of tax. For longer stays you can usually arrange a reduced tariff.

Lakeside

The *Hotel Access* has single rooms for between 150NRs and 250NRs while doubles go for between 200NRs and 300NRs. All the rooms in the hotel have private baths with hot showers.
Keiko's Hotel & Cottages has single rooms for 100-250NRs and doubles for 200-400NRs.

Damside

The *New Hotel Yad* has single rooms from 100NRs to 150NRs and doubles are 150NRs and up.
The Nascent's dormitory beds are 40NRs, singles are 60NRs and doubles start from 100NRs.

Restaurants
Lakeside

In the *Everest Steak House* a steak will cost you between 150NRs and 200NRs. If you are in the mood to try some Japanese food, the *Ajino Silkroad* has a selection of dishes ranging from 100NRs to 200NRs. The *Lan Hua* Chinese restaurant has meals that cost around 100NRs.

Some of the Lakeside restaurants also have live entertainment with Nepalese or Tibetan dancers. The performances usually start around 18:00.

Damside

The *Anil Momo* restaurant serves Japanese set meals for 80NRs. For a breakfast treat of freshly baked bread, the *German Bakery* is the place to check out.

Tashi Ling Tibetan Village

P.O.B. 24, Pokhara. Tel: 061-20447.
This is one of many Tibetan settlements in Nepal and is a couple of kilometers to the south-west of the Damside area on the opposite bank of the Pardi Khola. There are a lot of souvenir stores run by Tibetan women in the settlement, while many of the men are away in either India or Tibet laboring or trading goods.

There are a number of other Tibetan settlements scattered around Pokhara. *Tashi Palkhiel*, P.O. Box 7, Dhud Kharka (Tel: 061-21702), is near Hyangja, which is a couple of hours to the north of the town. The 2 other main Tibetan villages are the *Namgyaling* and *Jampaling Settlements*.

ANNAPURNA AREA TREKKING

Pokhara is the gateway for those interested in trekking in the Tibetan cultural areas around Annapurna. There are a number of routes available.

•The Annapurna Sanctuary
•Ghasa-Muktinath
•Dharapani-Manang-Muktinath

THE ANNAPURNA SANCTUARY

This course leads you towards the Annapurna Base Camp (A.B.C.). On the way, you will pass through Ghandrung, which is the second largest Gurung village in Nepal. You will also have a chance to have a soak in the hot natural springs at Jhinu. The view from the Annapurna Base Camp is spectacular, though it is advisable to wake up early and catch the clear morning sky as the visibility is often affected by the weather. From this vantage, weather permitting, you can also catch the glorious sight of Machhapuchhare aglow with the light of the setting sun.

Day 1: Pokhara (850m)-[By Bus]-Chandrakot (1,563m)-Ghandrung [Ghandruk] (1,920m) 5-6 hrs.
Day 2: Ghandrung (Ghandruk)-Chomrong 4-5 hrs.
Day 3: Chomrong-Hotel Himalaya (or Deorali) 7-8 hrs.
Day 4: Hotel Himalaya (or Deorali)-Machhapuchhare Base Camp 2.5-3 hrs.
Day 5: Machhapuchhare Base Camp-Annapurna Base Camp (4,130m) 1.5-2 hrs.
Day 6: Annapurna Base Camp-Bamboo Lodge 5-6 hrs.
Day 7: Bamboo Lodge-Jhinu Hot Springs 5-6 hrs.
Day 8: Jhinu-Tolka 3 hrs.
Day 9: Tolka-Dhampus-Pokhara (850m) 5-6 hrs.

*From Jhinu, it is possible to be back in Pokhara the same day. You'll need to go through Ghandrung and then get on a bus at Nayapur. The trip from Jhinu to Nayapur takes around 7hrs.

Trekking Routes to Mustang & Annapurna Region

Kore La (4400)

Takkiu-Chinese Checkpoint

Photu La(4200)

Mansail 6235

Nepalese Military Post

Namgyal Gompa

Garphu

LO MANTHANG (MUSTANG)
(Restricted to Travel Agency-Organized Group Tours +Special Permit.)

Ghar

Lo Manthang (Capital of Mustang Kingdom)

Tibetan Autonomous Region (CHINA)

NORTH DOLPO
(Restricted to Travel Agency-Organized Group Tours +Special Permit.)

Charang

Ghami

Lopas [Tibetan Descent]

Geling

Gaugiri 6111

Samar

Chele

Chhusang

Wide Dry Riverbed

Mustang Khola

Restricted Area Boundary

Kagbeni (2807)

Yakawa Kang 6482

Damodar Himal 6538

Hongde 6556

THAK KHOLA (Region)

Muktinath

Thorung La (5416)

Phugaon

Tukuche Peak ▲ 6920

Jomsom

Eklai Bhatti

Thorung Phedi (4500)

Marpha

Tukche

Jharkot

Chulu W. 6482

MANANG HIGHLANDS
(Restricted Area)

7126 ▲ Himlun Himal

Dhaulagiri I 8167

Thakalis [Tibetan Descent]

Mesokanto Pass (5099)

Chulu E. 6558

▲ Khobang

Kalopani

Nilgiri North 7061

Manang (3536)

Khangar Khola

Restricted Area Boundary

Kang Guru 6701

Thakali [Tibetan Descent] (Villages start around here to the North)

Lete

Annapurna I 8091 ▲

Ongre /Humde

Gurungs [Tibetan Descent]

Ghasa

Kali Gandaki River

Annapurna III ▲ 7555

Pisang (3333)

Tibetan Villages

Karche

Waterfalls

Dana

Annapurna South 7219 ▲

ABC (4130)

MBC

Annapurna II 7937 ▲

Chame

Koto

Tilje

Suspension Bridge

Tatopani (1189)

Magars

Dovan

Machhapuchhare ▲ 6997

Gurung Villages (Start around here to the North)

Thonje

Karte

Dharapani (1943)

Ratopani

Large Suspension Bridge

Tadapani

Bamboo

Gurungs [Nepalese Descent]

5181 ▲

Routes on both sides of the river.

To Dunai [South Dolpo]

Poon Hill 3194

Chomrong

Jhinu

GANDAKI

Tal

Rahughat Khola

Ghandrung (1920)

Main Route

Jagat (1341)

Ghorepani (2853)

Ulleri (2073)

Landrung/Landruk (1610)

Thanigaon

Beni

Pothana

▲ 2712

Long Suspension Bridge

Bahundanda (Village in a Valley)

Birethanti (1037)

Dhampus (1800)

Suspension Bridge

Baglung

Phedi

Bhulbhule

Naudanda

Sarangkot

Kusma

Chandrakot (1563)

Nayapul (1050)

Phewa Tal

Sarangkot

Pokhara (850)

Besisahar

To Tansen, Bhairawa

Begnas Tal

Rupa Tal

Chisankhu

0   10   20km

Large Bridge

Marsyandi Khola

From Pokhara to Thak Khola, Manang, & Mustang Regions.

*Pokhara-Ghorepani, Baglung-Tatopani-Jomsom (c.4-6 days)
*Pokhara-Besisahar-Thonje-Manang (c.6-7 days)
*Jomsom-Kagbeni-Lo Manthang (Mustang Palace) (5 days & Return-4 days)

Sankhar

Dhumre

To Kathmandu

NEPAL

Annapurna Trekking Times.

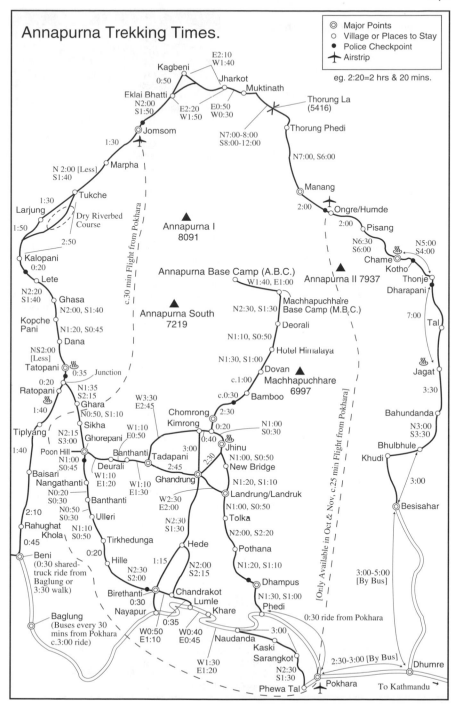

◎ Major Points
○ Village or Places to Stay
● Police Checkpoint
✈ Airstrip

eg. 2:20=2 hrs & 20 mins.

NEPAL

Kagbeni
E2:10
W1:40
0:50
Jharkot
Muktinath
Eklai Bhatti
N2:00
S1:50
E2:20
W1:50
E0:50
W0:30
Thorung La
(5416)
Thorung Phedi
N7:00-8:00
S8:00-12:00
Jomsom
1:30
N7:00, S6:00
Marpha
Manang
N 2:00 [Less]
S1:40
2:00
Ongre/Humde
Tukche
1:30
2:00
Pisang
Larjung
Dry Riverbed
Course
N6:30
S6:00
N5:00
S4:00
1:50
Annapurna I
8091
Chame
Kotho
2:50
Kalopani
0:20
Thonje
Dharapani
Lete
Annapurna Base Camp (A.B.C.)
W1:40, E1:00
Annapurna II 7937
N2:20
S1:40
Ghasa
Machhapuchhare
Base Camp (M.B.C.)
7:00
Tal
N2:00, S1:40
N2:30, S1:30
Kopche
Pani
Annapurna South
7219
Deorali
N1:20, S0:45
Dana
N1:10, S0:50
Hotel Himalaya
NS2:00
[Less]
N1:30, S1:00
Jagat
Tatopani
0:35
Junction
Dovan
Machhapuchhare
6997
0:20
N1:35
S2:15
c.1:00
3:30
Ratopani
Ghara
W3:30
E2:45
c.0:30
Bamboo
Bahundanda
1:40
N0:50, S1:10
Chomrong
Kimrong
2:30
N1:00
S0:30
N3:00
S3:30
Tiplyang
Sikha
N2:15
S3:00
W1:10
E0:50
0:20
Bhulbhule
Ghorepani
0:40
Jhinu
Khudi
1:40
Poon Hill
N1:00
S0:45
Banthanti
Tadapani
3:00
N1:00, S0:50
New Bridge
Baisari
Nangathanti
Deurali
W1:10
E1:20
2:45
N1:20, S1:10
3:00
N0:20
S0:30
W1:10
E1:30
Ghandrung
Landrung/Landruk
Besisahar
Banthanti
N0:50
S0:30
W2:30
E2:00
N1:00, S0:50
2:10
Ulleri
N1:10
S0:50
N2:30
S1:30
Tolka
Rahughat
Khola
Tirkhedunga
N2:00, S2:20
0:45
0:20
Hede
Pothana
Beni
(0:30 shared-
truck ride from
Baglung or
3:30 walk)
Hille
1:15
N2:00
S2:15
N1:20, S1:10
3:00-5:00
[By Bus]
N2:30
S2:00
Dhampus
Birethanti
Chandrakot
N1:30, S1:00
Baglung
(Buses every 30
mins from Pokhara
c.3:00 ride)
0:30
Lumle
Khare
Phedi
0:30 ride from Pokhara
Nayapur
0:35
W0:50
E1:10
W0:40
E0:45
Naudanda
3:00
Kaski
Sarangkot
2:30-3:00 [By Bus]
Dhumre
W1:30
E1:20
N2:30
S1:30
Pokhara
To Kathmandu
Phewa Tal

c.30 min Flight from Pokhara

[Only Available in Oct & Nov, c.25 min Flight from Pokhara]

345

JOMSOM & MUKTINATH AREA

The starting point for this trek is Tatopani, with its famous natural hot springs. You then walk up the road, which follows the course of the Kali Gandaki River. This road once flourished as an Indian-Tibetan trade route. While you are approaching the Thakali village of Tukche from Ghasa and Kalopani, you will pass through areas with a strong Tibetan atmosphere. Of these places, Marpha, Kagbeni, and Jharkot are well worth visiting.

Jomsom

Pokhara to Jomsom & Muktinath

Day 1: Pokhara (850m)-Nayapul [By Bus] 2 hrs
   -Ghandrung (1,920m) (4.5-5 hrs)
Day 2: Ghandrung-Tadapani 3 hrs.
Day 3: Tadapani-Ghorepani (2,853m) 3.5-4 hrs.
Day 4: Ghorepani-Poon Hill (3,194m) (R/T) 2 hrs.
   Ghorepani-Tatopani (1,189m) 6-7 hrs.
Day 5: Tatopani
Day 6: Tatopani-Ghasa 7-8 hrs.
Day 7: Ghasa-Tukche (2,586m) 7-8 hrs.
Day 8: Tukche-Marpha (2,670m) 2 hrs.
Day 9: Marpha-Jomsom (2,743m)-Kagbeni
   (2,807m) 5-6 hrs.
Day 10: Kagbeni-Jharkot (3,550m)-Muktinath
   (3,798m) 4-5 hrs.

Jomsom to Pokhara

Day 1: Jomsom (2,743m)-Marpha (2,670m)
   1.5 hrs.
Day 2: Marpha-Lete 6-7 hrs.
Day 3: Lete-Tatopani (1,189m) 8-9 hrs.

Day 4: Tatopani-Rahughat River 6-7 hrs.
Day 5: Rahughat River-Baglung (5-6 hrs.)-Pokhara
   (850m) [By Bus] 3 hrs.

TUKCHE

A 2-day walk from Tatopani, Tukche is a large Thakali village that has prospered the most from the Jomsom trading route. In the past here, the barley cultivated in the valleys of the area was exchanged for salt and wool brought from Tibet. A sign of the importance of the village is the presence of a number of gompas here.

At Tukche, one of the places to visit is the original *Sherchan's House*. This is where the Japanese monk and explorer, Ekai Kawaguchi, stayed over a hundred years ago. He stayed in the area to learn Tibetan so as to prepare himself for sneaking into Tibet, which was strictly prohibited to all outsiders at the time. The village is further connected to Japan as it has a sister village in the

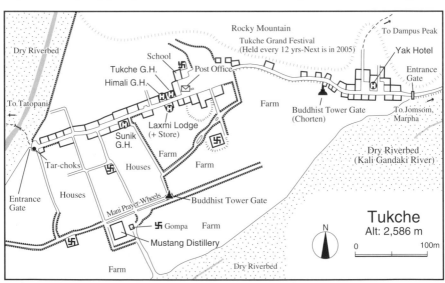

Japanese prefecture of Toyama and many of the residents of Tukche have been there. The village is also home to the Mustang Distillery, which produces brandy.

Accommodation

There are 5 hotels in Tukche and all of them are neat and clean. The standard price for a dormitory bed is 20NRs. A bowl of fried rice or *chow mein* will cost you around 40NRs.

The *Himali Guesthouse* has satellite television on offer. This is also the case with the *Yak Hotel*, which has a glassed-in terrace that commands a good view of Dhaulagiri I and serves good quality food.

The *Tukche Guesthouse* is also worth considering if you are staying in the village.

MARPHA

A 2-hour walk from Tukche, Marpha is an old Thakali village with a gompa. Its stone-paved street stretches along the highway, somewhat reminiscent of an old European village. It is perhaps because of the atmosphere that many visitors decide to stay here for a couple of days.

Try the good quality, locally produced apple wine, made from the apples harvested in the area. You can also get good dried fruit such as apples and apricots, as well as tasty apple jams, and almonds. A bag of dried apples goes for between 25NRs and 40NRs.

Accommodation

There are around 10 hotels in Marpha and rates are 45NRs for a bed in a dormitory and 20NRs for a hot shower. In addition, 65NRs will buy you a serving of *dal bhat* (lentil curry) while fried rice costs around 45NRs and an apple soda is 15NRs. The *Paradise Guesthouse* is a popular choice among foreign visitors and 2 other choices that are also comfortable are the *Neeru Guesthouse* and *Baba Lodge*. The *Hotel Trans Himalaya* is the only expensive hotel in the village.

JOMSOM

Jomsom is an hour-and-a-half walk from Marpha and is the center of the Thak Khola area. There is an airport here with daily flights to and from Pokhara and a few services a week connecting with Kathmandu. The town consists of 2 main areas and has a lot of good hotels near the air terminal.

At the eastern end of the new town is a police checkpoint and farther to the east you will see a military post. You can get to the old town by either going straight ahead or by crossing a suspension bridge near the barracks. Across the first bridge there is a post office on the right and the District Administration Office on the left.

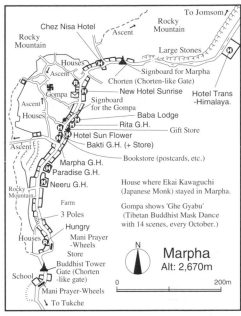

Farther to the east from the office, there is another bridge and this is the old town area. There is a bank here that can handle the changing of foreign currency and there are a couple of hotels, which are far cheaper than those near the airport. Keep going through the town and continue heading east and you will reach Kagbeni and Muktinath.

Accommodation
By the Airport

There are 13 hotels and guesthouses in this area. Good choices are *OM's Home*, *Trekker's Inn*, *Hotel Monalisa* and the *Hotel Himalaya Inn*. They all have clean restaurants and satellite TV. A single room with a hot shower costs 75NRs in these places and the prices for food and drink are pretty much standard, too: 65NRs for *dal baht*, 50NRs for *chow mien*, 90NRs for pizza and 110NRs for beer.

Old Town

There are 3 hotels in this area.

The *Dhaulagiri Lodge* has a restaurant and costs 10NRs a night.

The *Hotel Annapurna* is another option and it has rooms facing north that give you a good view.

KAGBENI

With an old fort and a Tibetan gompa, Kagbeni is a comfortable Tibetan-flavored village. It is a 3-hour walk from Jomsom and the village commands a great view of the north face of Nilgiri North and

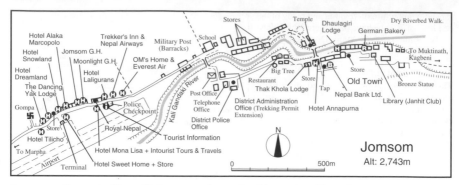

Jomsom
Alt: 2,743m

0   500m

Kagbeni
Alt: 2,807m

0   100m

the surrounding peaks. You will also get another excellent view at the police checkpoint on the way towards Mustang. The village attracts many tourists and the local people are very kind. The Tibetan gompa is only open to group tours.

Heading north from the police checkpoint you enter an area that requires a trekking permit. There are police in this area to check that visitors have these permits. The trip from Kagbeni to Mustang takes 4 days.

Accommodation
There are 9 hotels or guesthouses in the village and some of these are supplied with electricity.

The *Hotel Star* has a roof that commands a great view. The hotel has rooms that catch a lot of light and some that are quite dark. Dormitory beds here cost 20NRs a night.

The *Red House Lodge* has a glass-covered dining room on the roof, which has a good view and this hotel is popular with tourists.

The *Hotel Shangrila* has a restaurant that serves good *momos* and *tukpa*. The staff here is very nice and it is also a popular place for tourists to stay.

The prices for food are as follows: 65NRs for *dal bhat*, 40NRs for vegetable *chow mien*, 6NRs for milk tea and 35NRs for a potato omelet.

JHARKOT
This Tibetan village is located on a hill at 3,550m. There is an old fort and a precipitous cliff to the north. There is a great view of the village as you make your way to Muktinath.

Accommodation
There are 4 hotels and guesthouses in the village, all of which are supplied with electricity.

The *New Plaza Hotel* serves relatively good food and the prices are cheaper than those in Muktinath. You can see the village from the roof of the hotel. They have foot warmers on offer for the guests.

MUKTINATH
Muktinath is a pilgrimage center for both Buddhists and Hindus. Visitors to the sacred site usually stay at a nearby village called Ranipauwa, which is a 40-minute walk from Jharkot. Only a 10- to 15-minute walk from Ranipauwa, Muktinath is about halfway up a slope and the only place with trees on the mountain.

Surrounded by walls, this sacred place has 3 Buddhist temples and a 3-story Hindu pagoda (with a guard to collect donations from visitors wishing to enter the building) in the center. Right behind the temple, there are 108 taps from which holy water runs. On arriving at Muktinath, the pilgrims pay a visit to both the Buddhist and Hindu temples, regardless of their religion.

Don't miss the Jawala Mai Gompa, a Buddhist temple where you can see an eternal blue flame at the end of an altar. The flame is fueled by natural gas escaping from a hole along with a dribble of water. To see it, you will need to get the door

348

Mandala, Kagbeni

unlocked and the usual practice is for visitors to leave a donation.

Accommodation

There are 12 hotels and guesthouses in Ranipauwa Village. The room rates are reasonable starting around 20NRs for a bed, while food is unusually expensive, though the prices vary depending on the hotel.

The *Hotel Dhaulagiri* has a good view from its roof, though the meals at the hotel are expensive and not of very good quality. A dish of *dal baht* with an omelet costs 100NRs and a plate of fried rice is 85NRs.

The *Hotel North Pole* is popular among tourists with food that is a little cheaper and not too bad.

Rather than staying at Ranipauwa, using Jharkot as your base for visiting Muktinath will save you some money. If you are heading for Manang via Thorung La (5,416m), you should not leave a high-altitude village, such as Ranipauwa, for at least a couple of days before you get acclimatized. Taking a walking stick along with you will help you on the trail.

Muktinath-Changar-Dzong-Putra

At the Sakyapa gompa in Dzong, an artist from Ngawa in the Amdo region of Tibet has made a colorful wall painting and a statue of Buddha, etc. As with the Lo Manthang area, both Dzong and

Putra are closed. There have been reports that some tourists have managed to visit the area, though.

MANANG AREA

The Manang area, to the north of Annapurna, is home to many Tibetans and Gurungs. The Tibetans there are not refugees, having settled in the region hundreds of years ago. The stone-built chortens, gates and gompas with interiors made from a variety of wood, are more similar to those found in the villages of the Humla region (near Purang-Simikot) in western Nepal than those in the closer Mustang region.

Further to the north, after the Thorung La (5,416m), the combination of Gurungs and Tibetans gives way to the Thakali and Tibetan worlds.

BESISAHAR-MANANG-JOMSOM

This route starts to the east of Annapurna and heads for Jomsom.

Day 1: Besisahar-Bhulbhule 3 hrs.
Day 2: Bhulbhule-Jagat (1,341m) 7-8 hrs.
Day 3: Jagat-Dharapani (1,943m) 7-8 hrs.
Day 4: Dharapani-Chame (Hot springs) 4-5 hrs.
Day 5: Chame-Pisang (3,333m) 6-7 hrs.
Day 6: Pisang-Manang (3,536m) 4-5 hrs.

Jharkot

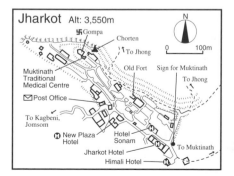

Jharkot Alt: 3,550m

Thakalis

Day 7: Manang
Day 8: Manang-Thorung Phedi (4,500m) 7-8 hrs.
Day 9: Thorung Phedi-Thorung La
    (5,416m)-Muktinath (3,798m) 7-8 hrs.
Day 10: Muktinath-Jomsom (2,743m) 4-5 hrs.
*It may be a good idea for you to stay at either
Jharkot or Kagbeni for a night.

At Pokhara, take a bus to Kathmandu and get off at
Dhumre (a 2-3 hour ride). The town has many
restaurants and stores, as it is a transport
hub, and there are also a number of hotels
available. From Kathmandu, take a bus
going to Pokhara and get off at Dhumre
(around a 5-hour ride). You will need to
change buses at Dhumre and this will take
you on to Besisahar. This second leg of
the trip takes 3-5 hours.
    There is a natural hot spring along the
river, a little to the north of Jagat. Walk
about 15 minutes from the highway
through some very tall grass and you will
see the water coming out of crevices in the
rocks close to the river. You cannot bathe
in the water as the pool is not big enough
for a person but you can have a refreshing
wash, as the water temperature is quite
high.
    At Chame, there is a prepared bathing
area beside the river but it doesn't have
enough water and is full of algae. Not to
worry, there is some fresh water among the
nearby rocks that will make for a small but
good bath that will fit 1 person at a time.
    The village of Pisang seems to cling to
the mountainside and there is a gompa
above it. The village commands a good
view of Annapurna II and IV. Until Pisang,
you often have a monotonous walk through
groves of trees that obstruct the view of
the mountains. The quality of both
accommodation and food in the areas
before Thorung La is nowhere near the

standard found on the western side of Annapurna.
    There is an airport at Ongre/Humde between
Pisang and Manang and in the high season, from
October to November, there are 3-4 flights a week
from Pokhara. The aircraft fly on a charter basis
the rest of the year. A 1-way ticket costs US$50
and it is advisable to check the most recent schedule
if you are planning to take this flight.
    On the route from Manang, via Thorung La to
Muktinath, there is a hotel at Thorung Phedi. After
your stay, you will have to walk 7-8 hours to reach
Muktinath (3,798m) via Thorung La (5,416m).
Make sure that you take food and water with you,
as there are no stores along this trail.
    In these passes decorated with *tar-choks* and
chortens, the wind always blows hard and cold. You
should get the most updated information on the
weather conditions as snowfalls may make the route
impassable. Some trekkers have reportedly taken
about 12 hours to cover this stage from Thorung
Phedi to Muktinath, while others have completed
it in only 8 hours.

*Be sure to acclimatize yourself before taking this
route so as to avoid altitude sickness. The best

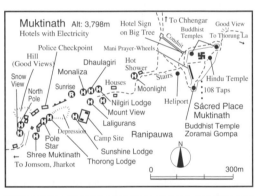

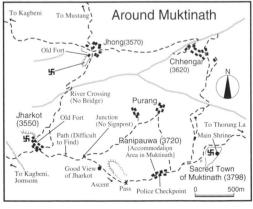

Lo Manthang (Mustang)

season for tackling Thorung La is from October to November. Snowfalls usually make it impassable in December, although some years don't see snow until as late as January.

There is another option off the main route at Chame (Day 5). You can try: Upper Pisang-Ghyaru-Ngawal-Mungji-Braga-Manang.

MANANG

At 3,536m, the large village of Manang has a great view of Annapurna III and Gangapurna. The village is also home to the Manang Gompa. The prices in Manang are relatively high compared to other places in the region. A bed in a dormitory will cost you 30NRs, and double rooms go for between 80NRs and 120NRs.

There are 10 hotels in the village and many of them, such as *Snati Guesthouse* and the *Yak Lodge* are clustered around the open space at the downstream end of the village. These hotels and guesthouses are all supplied with electricity.

LO MANTHANG (MUSTANG)

Lo Manthang, commonly called 'Mustang,' is located at the northern end of the Kali Gandaki River. This area used to be referred to as the 'Lo Kingdom.' To this day, locals call themselves the *Lopa*, meaning 'Southern people.' The capital of the Lo Kingdom was named *Manthang* and the combination of the two produced the name. On the other hand, the name *Mustang* was the result of a wrong pronunciation in a Nepalese dialect and the use of the name has persisted.

The Lo area, along with the Dolpo region to the west, was once a part of Ngari in the far west region of Tibet. Although there is no written record confirming it, Milarepa, the 11th century student of the great Buddhist teacher Marpa, is said to have visited Lo Manthang.

It was only after the Dalai Lama fled to India in 1959, following the Chinese occupation of his homeland, that the area suddenly appeared in modern history books. This area became the base from which thousands of Khampa guerrillas launched attacks against the Chinese forces in Tibet. These guerrillas received training and material support from the CIA during the 1960's, but were later abandoned by the Americans after President Nixon's landmark visit to China and the subsequent warming of relations between the 2 countries in the early 1970's.

Many of the Buddhist temples in Mustang belong to the Sakyapa order and the majority of these were established in the 11th century.

Trekking

To enter the Lo Manthang region you will require a permit, which costs US$700 per person for a 10-day trip. These permits are only issued to organized group tours with more than 2 participants. On top of this there is an additional charge of US$300 that pays for the porter, a guide, and the liaison officer that must accompany your group. Another hurdle to setting-up a trek in this area is the fact that the area accepts only 300 tourists a year.

A 12-day Lo Manthang trekking tour from Pokhara, using flights between Pokhara and Jomsom, costs around US$2,000 per person. You will also need to set aside a number of days in which

Lo Manthang (Mustang)

to make all the necessary arrangements and receive the permits before departure.

Jomson- Mustang R/T

Day 1: Kagbeni (2,807m)-Chele 6 hrs.
Day 2: Chele-Geling 6-7 hrs.
Day 3: Geling-Charang 6-7 hrs.
Day 4: Charang-Lo Manthang 5-6 hrs.
Day 5: Lo Manthang
Day 6: Lo Manthang
Day 7: Lo Manthang-Ghami 6 hrs.
Day 8: Ghami-Samar 7 hrs.
Day 9: Samar- Kagbeni 5 hrs.

*Between Kagbeni and Lo Manthang most of the areas you will pass through are easy for trekking. There are peddlers coming and going along this route everyday and there are numerous cheap lodging houses for them.

*This is a sensitive border region and at times the situation may mean that the area to the north of Lo Manthang will be closed. There are gompas scattered throughout this area, alongside a substantial Nepalese military presence. Although tourists must observe the official restrictions, the local people move quite freely across the border in both directions. There is also another route that brings you to Muktinath as an alternative for the return journey.

*If you go by yourself without a permit, you will definitely be discovered (unless you can successfully disguise yourself as a local and speak the language). There are police along the way and both the police and the military keep watch from the palace at Lo Manthang. Detection is only a matter of time and if you are caught, you will be taken to Kathmandu where you will have to pay the permit fee and a sizeable fine. One trekker caught and hauled back to Kathmandu had to pay the US$700 permit fee and a US$100 penalty, which was reduced from the original US$300 only by some serious negotiation.

LO MANTHANG TOWN

Lo Manthang is a fortress town surrounded by walls. There are 4 gompas within the walls, Champa Lhakhang, Tukchen Gompa, Chodi Gompa, and Nyimpa Gompa. Situated in the center of the town, the Lo Mantang Palace is a 4-story building where the present ruler, originally from Lhasa, and his royal family still reside.

To the south-west of Lo Manthang, there is the relatively large Garphu Gompa, which has a connection with the accomplished 8th century Indian spiritual master Guru Rinpoche (Padmasambhava). The gompa was reputedly

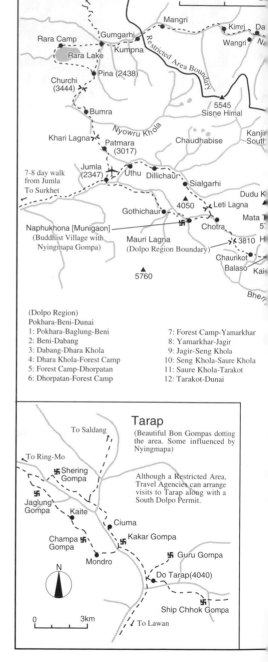

Dolpo

(Dolpo Region)
Pokhara-Beni-Dunai
1: Pokhara-Baglung-Beni
2: Beni-Dabang
3: Dabang-Dhara Khola
4: Dhara Khola-Forest Camp
5: Forest Camp-Dhorpatan
6: Dhorpatan-Forest Camp
7: Forest Camp-Yamarkhar
8: Yamarkhar-Jagir
9: Jagir-Seng Khola
10: Seng Khola-Saure Khola
11: Saure Khola-Tarakot
12: Tarakot-Dunai

Tarap

(Beautiful Bon Gompas dotting the area. Some influenced by Nyingmapa)

Although a Restricted Area, Travel Agencies can arrange visits to South Dolpo along with a South Dolpo Permit.

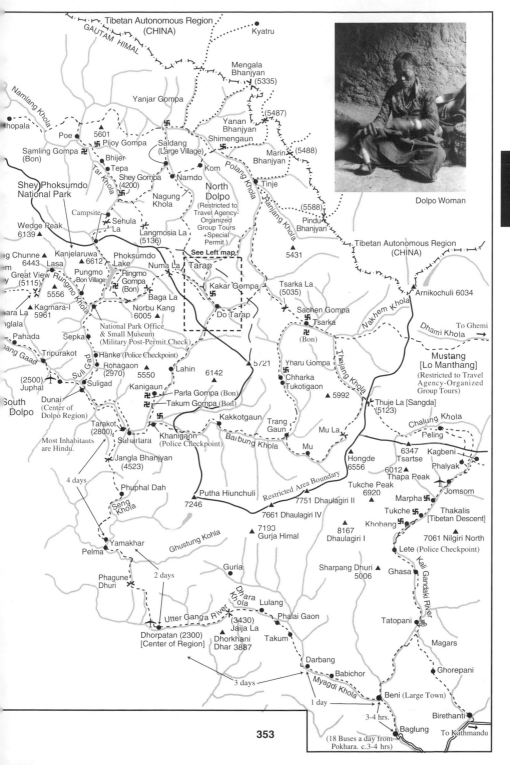

Tibetan Autonomous Region
(CHINA)

GAUTAM HIMAL

Kyatru

Namlang Khola

Mengala
Bhanjyan
(5335)

Yanjar Gompa

Yanan
Bhanjyan
Shimengaun

(5487)

Dhopala

Poe

5601

Pijoy Gompa

Saldang
(Large Village)

Marin
Bhanjyan

(5488)

Samling Gompa
(Bon)

Bhijer

Tepa

Shey Gompa
(4200)

Kom

Namdo

Polang Khola

Tinje

Shey Phoksumdo
National Park

Campsite

Nagung
Khola

North
Dolpo
(Restricted to
Travel Agency-
Organized
Group Tours
+Special
Permit.)

Pindu
Bhanjyan

(5588)

Tibetan Autonomous Region
(CHINA)

Wedge Peak
6139

Sehula
La

Langmosia La
(5136)

See Left map

Tarap

5431

Nanjang Khola

g Chunne

Kanjelaruwa

6443

Lasa

6612

Phoksumdo
Lake

Numa La

Kakar Gompa

Tsarka La
(5035)

Arnikochuli 6034

Great View
(5115)

Pungmo
(Bon Village)

Ringmo
Gompa
(Bon)

Baga La

Do Tarap

Nakhem Khola

Dhami Khola

To Ghemi

5556

Ruingmo Khola

Sachen Gompa

Kagmara-I
5961

Norbu Kang
6005

Tsarka
(Bon)

Mustang
[Lo Manthang]
(Restricted to Travel
Agency-Organized
Group Tours)

ara La

nglala

Pahada

National Park Office
& Small Museum
(Military Post-Permit Check)

5721

Yharu Gompa

Thaing Khola

Sepka

Tripurakot

Hanke (Police Checkpoint)

Lahin

6142

Chharka
Tukotigaon

5992

Thuje La [Sangda]
(5123)

Chalung Khola

Peling

ang Gaad

Suli Gad

Rohagaon
(2970)

5550

Kanigaun

Parla Gompa (Bon)

Takum Gompa (Bon)

Mu La

6347
Tsartse

Kagbeni

(2500)
Juphal

Suligad

Kakkotgaun

Trang
Gaun

Mu

Hongde
6556

6012
Thapa Peak

Phalyak

Dunai
(Center of
Dolpo Region)

Tarakot
(2800)

Khanigaon
(Police Checkpoint)

Barbung Khola

Tukche Peak
6920

Thapa Peak

Marpha

Jomsom

South
Dolpo

Most Inhabitants
are Hindu.

Sahartara

7751 Dhaulagiri II

Tukche

Thakalis
[Tibetan Descent]

Jangla Bhanjyan
(4523)

Putha Hiunchuli
7246

Restricted Area Boundary

7661 Dhaulagiri IV

Khobang

7061 Nilgiri North

4 days

Phuphal Dah

8167
Dhaulagiri I

Lete (Police Checkpoint)

Seng Khola

7193
Gurja Himal

Sharpang Dhuri
5006

Ghasa

Kali Gandaki River

Yamakhar

Ghustung Kohla

Guria

Pelma

Phagune
Dhuri

2 days

Dhara Khola

Lulang

Magars

Ghorepani

Utter Ganga River

(3430)
Jaija La

Phalai Gaon

Tatopani

Dhorpatan (2300)
[Center of Region]

Dhorkhani
Dhar 3887

Takum

3 days

Darbang

Babichor

Myagdi Khola

Beni (Large Town)

1 day

3-4 hrs.

Birethanti

Baglung

To Kathmandu

353

(18 Buses a day from
Pokhara. c.3-4 hrs)

Dolpo Woman

NEPAL

constructed to restrain a demon around the time that Samye Monastery, the first monastery in Tibet, was built.

DOLPO

With around 4,500 households, this area consists of the North Dolpo (Upper Dolpo) and South Dolpo (Lower Dolpo) regions. The southern part has been strongly influenced by Hindu culture, whereas the northern areas have a distinct Tibetan feel. Unfortunately, the North Dolpo region is a closed area.

Dolpo has been home to Tibetan people since the 10th century and was a part of Ngari in the far west region of Tibet until the 19th century. Even after becoming a Nepalese territory, it was still unable to communicate directly with the government in Kathmandu until 1963, due to its geographical separation from central Nepal. The rugged mountain environment has helped the people of the area to preserve old Tibetan customs.

The weather in the Dolpo region is similar to that found in many areas of Tibet and the precipitation in the region is minimal. The winter at this altitude is extremely cold and best to be avoided. The best months to visit Dolpo are May, September, and October.

Trekking Permits

The permit stipulations differ between North Dolpo and South Dolpo. You can go to the southern areas by yourself and simply pay US$10 per day for the first week and US$20 per day for the second and subsequent weeks.

For North Dolpo, the story is rather different. You must join an agency-organized tour with at least 2 participants and the permit costs US$700 per person for the first 10 days, and US$70 per day for each day thereafter. In the northern areas, you must be accompanied by a guide and a porter. Only 250 tourists a year are allowed to enter the region.

There are also other additional expenses to factor in as trekking in Dolpo requires a lot more heavy equipment, such as tents and food, than a similar trek in the Lo Manthang area. These extras push the total cost to US$4,000-5,000 for 30 days and this is one reason that the number of tourists on these treks is quite low. Most of the 250 tourist slots are taken up by scholars, photographers, etc.

Dolpo Flight Request *Hiroyuki Ishii*

Early in the morning we gathered at Juphal Airport with heavy bags and a fervent wish - 'Please, fly today!'

After trekking in Dolpo, I was really in need of some good news after spending 5 days eating nothing but *dal bhat* and instant noodles. I'd had enough and was dying for a cold beer.

A policeman with a stick started removing the local people who were relaxing on the weed-covered runway. This was it. Royal Nepal was on its way but I was feeling it was a little premature to get too excited. Two days before we had been in exactly the same situation only to be told that the flight had been cancelled. We watched the small aircraft approach with a desperate hope in our hearts.

Soon after its touch down, I finally said my good-byes to the depths of the Himalayas and imagined that all I had to do was just sit and wait for our arrival at Nepalganj Airport.

The 2 pilots were sitting in their evidently old-style cockpit and executed a smooth take-off. As the plane gained altitude, my hopes that everything was going to be fine rose, too. Unfortunately, my hopes did not reach the crew.

I watched incredulously as the co-pilot slowly spread a newspaper out over the window and then suddenly opened it. Wind howled into the small cabin and as I stared open-mouthed as I realized that he was trying fashion a sunshade out of the paper, even though the buffeting of the wind was making the job difficult. Was the sunlight this intolerable?

Once the storm was over and there was nothing but engine noise again, they acted as if nothing had happened at all. On behalf of the 20 passengers on board, I would like to make a simple request: 'Please do not open the window in flight. Thank you.'

Trekking Routes
There are 4 major routes in the Dolpo region.

South Dolpo
Route 1: Juphal (2,500m) [By Air]-Phoksumdo Lake-Tarap Valley (4,040m)-Tarakot (2,800m)-Juphal

Route 2: Jumla (2,347m) [By Air]-Kagmara La (5,115m)-Phoksumdo Lake-Tarap Valley (4,040m)-Tarakot (2,800m)-Juphal

Route 3: Baglung-Dunai-Phoksumdo Lake-Tarap Valley (4,040m)-Tarakot (2,800m)-Juphal (2,500m)

North Dolpo
Route 4: Jomsom (2,743m)-Chharka-Dolpo(Highlands)-Shey Gompa (4,200m)-Phoksumdo Lake-Tarap Valley (4,040m)-Tarakot (2,800m)-Juphal/ Jomsom (2,743m)

*For this course you must join an organized group tour and the route takes 30-50 days to complete.

Jumla to Dunai
Day 1: Jumla (2,347m)-Gothichaur
Day 2: Gothichaur-Naphukhona
Day 3: Naphukhona-Mauri Lagna (3,810m)-Balasa
Day 4: Balasa-Camp
Day 5: Camp-Tipurakot
Day 6: Tipurakot-Suphal (2,500m)-Dunai

Kaigaon, Kagmara La, Sumduwa to Ringmo (Recommended)
Day 1: Kaigaon-Toijem
Day 2: Toijem-Kagmara La (5,115m)
Day 3: Kagmara La-Lasa
Day 4: Lasa-Pungmo (Bon Village)
Day 5: Pungmo-Sumduwa-Ringmo

Dunai to Ringmo
Day 1: Dunai-Rohagaon (2,970m)
Day 2: Rohagaon-Ryajik
Day 3: Ryajik-Ringmo

Ringmo, Do Tarap to Dunai
Day 1: Ringmo- Baga La Phedi
Day 2: Baga La Phedi-Numa La Phedi
Day 3: Numa La Phedi-Tok Khyu
Day 4: Tok Khyu-Do Tarap (4,040m)
Day 5: Do Tarap-Campsite
Day 6: Campsite-Kanigaon
Day 7: Kanigaon-Namdo
Day 8: Namdo-Dunai

Pokhara, Beni to Dunai
(See the map on pages 352 & 353.)

Dolpo Woman

SOUTH DOLPO
Dunai
Dunai is a large town that also functions as the district center. There are some hotels in the town, such as *Phoksumdo Hotel, Blue Sheep Trekkers Inn*, etc.

Phoksumdo Lake
The lake covers an area of about 4.8km by 1.8km and it is located in the Shey-Phoksumdo National Park. At the entrance to the park there is a permit checkpoint and the admission fee is 650NRs. From the lake it is about a 3-hour walk to Ringmo Village where there is a Bon gompa.

The Tarap Valley
There are 4 villages in the valley and around 1,500 Dolpopas (People of Dolpo) live in them. The largest of the 4 is the village of Do. There are also a number of both Bon and Nyingmapa temples scattered around this area.

NORTH DOLPO
Day 1. Phoksumdo Lake-Phoksumdo Khola
Day 2. Phoksumdo Khola-Snowfields Camp
Day 3. Snowfields Camp-Shey Gompa

Shey Gompa
Since 1992, this gompa has been closed to foreigners due to the theft of a statue of Buddha from the monastery. The size of the building is not remarkable, but it is said to house an ancient scroll describing the origin of the gompa.

LUMBINI

Lumbini, south of Pokhara, is an important Buddhist pilgrimage destination, as Prince Siddhartha Gautama (Lord Buddha) is believed to have been born there about 2,500 years ago. In the center of the holy garden there is the Maya Devi Temple (named after his mother), which has a stone carving showing the birth of the prince. There is the Ashokan Pillar, erected over 2,000 years ago by the Indian emperor Ashoka, right next to the temple alongside the Sacred Pond, the Bodhi Tree, and various ruined stupas, etc.

There are a number of Nepalese and Tibetan temples that attract many pilgrims. And to the north of the garden, there are a growing number of new temples constructed by other Buddhist countries.

Access

*Bhairawa-Lumbini—At the junction to the north end of Bhairawa, there is a bus stop in front of a gas station. Buses depart from here for Lumbini every 30 minutes between 06:00 and 17:00. The buses take just under an hour to cover the 22km and the fare is 10NRs. The buses take a right at the Lumbini junction and then actually run through the Sacred Garden.

*Kathmandu/Pokhara-Bhairawa—To get to Bhairawa from either Kathmandu or Pokhara, take a bus heading for Sunauli and get off at the junction to the north end of Bhairawa.

*Sunauli-Bhairawa—There are a couple of buses to Butwal every hour and to catch them, you get off at Bhairawa. The ride takes around 15 minutes and costs 4NRs.

Accommodation & Restaurants

There is a pilgrim's lodge called *Dharamsala* in the sacred garden itself. Staying at the lodge is free, though making a donation of 50NRs or so is common practice. Meals are served there or you can try something at the food stalls near the main site's car park.

The *Lumbini Village Lodge* has single rooms for 150NRs and doubles for 250NRs.

The *Hotel Rainbow* is at the entrance of the town, around 3km from the main site. Single rooms are US$20 and the doubles are US$25.

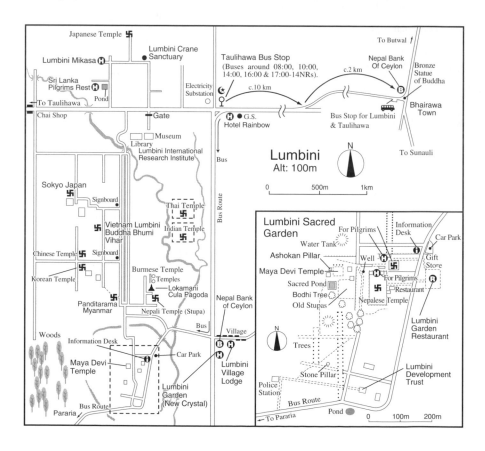

SIKKIM

འབྲས་ལྗོངས།

Sikkim and the area stretching down to Kalimpong and Darjeeling, along with Bhutan and Arunachal Pradesh, all have strong historical ties with Tibet and many Tibetans live in these areas. Surprisingly though, even with this strong cultural affinity, none of these areas have ever been part of Tibet itself.

Sikkim is bordered by Nepal to the west, Bhutan to the east, the Tibetan Plateau to the north and the Indian province of West Bengal to the south. Though the governments of Britain, India, and China have all had their designs on the Kingdom of Bhutan at various times, and thus actually allowed it to remain an independent kingdom (although under Indian military control), the fate of Sikkim and Arunachal Pradesh was to become Indian territories.

All the areas introduced in this section are border regions and thus visitors must abide by certain restrictions on traveling in these areas. Kolkata (Calcutta), Darjeeling and Kalimpong are exceptions and there are no restrictions on visiting these towns.

Indian Country Information
— See page 280.

KOLKATA (CALCUTTA)

Kolkata (Calcutta), the capital of West Bengal, is the usual starting point for people wishing to visit Sikkim and the surrounding areas. This sprawling city of over 10 million people contains a fusion of Indian and colonial British architecture, pointing to the fact that it was the seat of the British colonial government until 1912.

Access by Air
International flights come into Dum Dum Airport on the outskirts of the city. Kolkata (Calcutta) is famous as a place to purchase reasonably priced air tickets, especially for destinations throughout Asia. There are plenty of flights available for Bangkok, Dhaka and Kathmandu. There are many discount travel agents on Sudder Street, which is also home to many of the city's cheap hotels and backpackers' hostels. Be careful when buying tickets from some of these agents and check around with other travelers for the reliable ones. Two reputable ones are *Star Traveler's* and *Flics Travel*. Prices vary slightly depending on the agent and they may require that you present a bank receipt. For

international flights, the airport tax is 750Rs. Sample 1-way ticket prices for major destinations are as follows:

Bangkok .... $185 Royal Bhutan
Kathmandu .... $96* Indian Airlines
*25% off for those under 30
Istanbul .... $360 Aeroflot
Tokyo .... $346 Biman Bangladesh

Airline Offices

Aeroflot, 58 Chowringhee Rd. Tel: 033-242 3765
Air Canada, 230A AJC Bose Rd. Tel: 033-247 7783
Air France, 41 Chowringhee Rd. Tel: 033-242 6161
Air India, 50 Chowringhee Rd.
Tel: 033-242 2356/ 7358
Air Lanka, 230 AJC Bose Rd. Tel: 033-247 7783
American Airlines, 2/7 Sarat Bose Rd.
Tel: 033-475 1261
Biman Bangladesh Airlines, 1 Park St.
Tel: 033-292 844/293 709
British Airways, 41 Chowringhee Rd.
Tel: 033-293 454/ 453/ 430
Cathay Pacific, 1 Middleton St. Tel: 033-403 211
Continental, 3C Camac St. Tel: 033-292 092
Druk Air (Royal Bhutan Airlines), 1A Ballygunge
Circular Rd, 51 Tivoli Court. Tel: 033-247 1301
Indian Airlines, 29 Chittaranjan Ave.
Tel: 033- 262 417/ 909
JAL, 35A Chowringhee Rd. Tel: 033-298 370
KLM (Royal Dutch Airlines), 1 Middleton St.
Tel: 033-247 4593
Lufthansa, 30 A/B Chowringhee Rd.
Tel: 033-299 365
Malaysian Airlines, 3C Camac St. Tel: 033-292 092
Northwest, 1 Middleton St. Tel: 033-247 4593
Qantas, 235/1 AJC Bose Rd. Tel: 033-247 0718

Royal Nepal Airlines, 41 Chowringhee Rd.
Tel: 033-293 949
Singapore Airlines, 18D Park St. Tel: 033-299 297
Thai Airways, 18-G Park St. Tel: 033-299 846
United Airlines, 2/7 Sarat Bose Rd.
Tel: 033-747 622

The Airport to Downtown

Dum Dum International Airport is 13km from the city center and a pre-paid taxi carrying 4 passengers

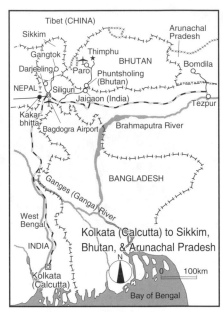

Kolkata (Calcutta) to Sikkim, Bhutan, & Arunachal Pradesh

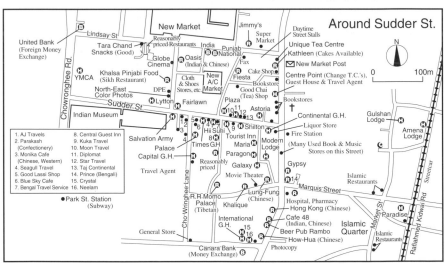

Around Sudder St.

1. AJ Travels
2. Parakash (Confectionery)
3. Monika Cafe (Chinese, Western)
4. Seagull Travel
5. Good Lassi Shop
6. Blue Sky Cafe
7. Bengal Travel Service
8. Central Guest Inn
9. Kuka Travel
10. Moon Travel
11. Diplomat
12. Star Travel
13. Taj Continental
14. Prince (Bengali)
15. Crystal
16. Neelam

costs around 100Rs from Sudder Street. Indian Airlines has an airport bus that travels to the downtown city airline office 7 times a day. The timetable of these buses is linked to the domestic flight schedule and subject to changes, accordingly. The bus fare is 20Rs and it takes around 50 minutes. A cheaper option is to take a local bus, either the #20B or #30B. It costs about 5Rs from the bus stop near the airport and takes you to the Esplanade downtown. Another alternative is to take a local bus to Dum Dum Station and then get on the subway.

Access by Rail

Howrah Station, on the west bank of the Hooghly River, is the main rail hub in Kolkatta (Calcutta). Most trains depart from, or terminate at, this station. For trains to Darjeeling and eastern India, though, you'll need to make your way to Sealdah Station on the eastern side of the city. In addition to arranging tickets at Howrah Station, you can also make reservations at the *Eastern Computerized Railway Reservation Centre*. It has an office that caters specially to foreign tourists where you won't have to join the long queues that the local people have to endure. Payments are made in rupees and you'll need to show a bank receipt and your passport.

Eastern Computerized Railway Reservation Centre 6 Fairlie Place B.B.D.Bagh. Tel: 033-700 001 Business hours: Monday to Saturday 08:00-20:00, Sunday 08:00-14:00

The Office for Foreign Tourists Business hours: Monday to Saturday 09:00-16:00, Sunday 09:00-14:00

Indian Visa Extensions

Foreign Registration Office - 237 Acharya Jagadish, Chandra Bose Rd. Tel: 033-124 3301 This is the office to apply for visa extensions. A 3-month visa is entitled to an extension of 3 more months. A 6-month visa cannot be extended.

Arranging Visas in Kolkatta (Calcutta)
Foreign Consulates in Kolkatta (Calcutta) & Indian High Commissions Abroad

(See Appendix for details.)

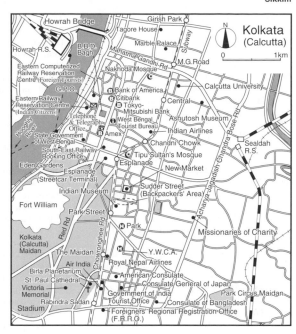

Tourist Information
Government of India Tourist Office
4 Shakespeare Sarani St.
Tel: 033-242 1402/ 5813/ 3521/ 1475
This office is located 2km south of Sudder Street. Maps and pamphlets covering Kolkata and other Indian cities are available here. The office staff is very kind and will help you with any problems.
Business hours: Monday to Friday 09:00-18:00, Saturday 09:00-13:00
West Bengal Tourist Bureau - 3/2 B.B.D.Bagh. Tel: 033-248 8271/ 5168/ 5917
Business hours: Monday to Friday 07:00-13:30/ 14:15-18:00, Saturday 07:00-12:30
Both offices also organize daylong or half-day long city bus tours. For those tours organized by the *National Tourist Office*, you can book a seat through *Ashoka Travel & Tour*. Tel: 033-242 0901

Changing Money
There are many places throughout the city to change money. These offices are reputable and offer good customer service.
American Express
The office is between B.B.D.Bagh and the Esplanade.
Tel: 033-248 5961/ 7947
Business hours: Monday to Saturday 09:30-18:30
Citibank
The bank has 2 offices in Kolkata. You can only

SIKKIM

change money at the branch near the Maidan Subway Station.
Tel: 033-299 220/ 293 456
Business hours: Monday to Friday 10:00-14:00, Saturday 10:00-12:00

Travelers Express Club
At the Centre Point Hotel, 20 Mirza Ghalib St. Tel: 033-244 8184. It offers better rates than the banks and prepares a bank receipt for you. The hotel is not far from Sudder Street.

R.R.Sen & Bros Veek
It has been reported that the best rates available are offered by R.R.Sen & Bros Veek at 18 Chowringhee Rd., located between the Oberoi Grand Hotel and the Y.W.C.A. There is a sign at the entrance to the building reading 'United Bank Foreign Exchange.'
Tel: 033-249 6077/ 7502. Business hours: Monday to Friday 10:00-17:00, Saturday 10:00-12:00

The State Bank of India
The branch at the airport is located behind the check-in counters in the new terminal building and gives an acceptable rate of exchange. This branch is also open 24 hours a day. Tel: 033-511 9030

Post & Telecommunications
The *GPO* is on the west side of B.B.D.Bagh.
Business hours: Monday to Saturday 07:00-20:30, Sunday 10:00-16:00
The post office near Sudder Street handles international parcels. The office also has rates for printed matter. 1kg packages cost 60Rs and 4kg parcels cost 140Rs (these rates are for most international destinations).
Business hours: Monday to Saturday 10:00-18:00 (Parcel Counter 10:00-15:30)
The *Telephone and Telegraph Office* is on the south side of B.B.D.Bagh. There isn't a big difference between the prices here and those offered by the private telephone services. The Kolkata area code is 033.

Accommodation
The most popular area in Kolkata for backpackers to stay is on famous Sudder Street. There is a wide selection of cheap hotels and backpacker hostels to choose from there.

The *Hotel Paragon* - 2 Stuart Lane.
Tel: 033-244 2445
Dormitory beds-60-65Rs, single rooms-120-130Rs, double rooms-150-180Rs.
The rates vary according to the floor. The hotel has a strongbox for guests' valuables.
The *Hotel Maria* - 5/1 Sudder St. Tel: 033-245 0860
Dormitory beds-50Rs, single rooms-150Rs, double rooms-250Rs.
The dormitory is spacious, airy, clean, and popular.

The *Salvation Army* (Red Shield Guest House) - 2 Sudder St. Tel: 033-442 895
Dormitory beds-50Rs, single rooms-100Rs, double rooms-280Rs.
Located in the middle of Sudder Street, it is well-equipped and administered for the price. Bags can be kept in a large locker room.
The *Hotel Palace* - 13 Chowringhee Lane.
Tel: 033-244 6214
Single rooms-175Rs, double rooms-300-600Rs.
The *Centrepoint Hotel* - 20 Mirza Ghalib St.
Tel: 033-244 8184
Dormitory beds-65Rs, double rooms-200Rs.
There is a moneychanger's office on the 1st floor. If you want a good view out across the city, check out the guesthouse roof.
The *Capital Guest House* - 11B Chowringhee Lane.
Tel: 033-245 0598
Single rooms-150Rs, double rooms-250Rs.
The *Astoria Hotel* - 6/2/3 Sudder St.
Tel: 033-226 1227
Single rooms-550Rs, double rooms-770Rs. Deluxe rooms are available for 1,100Rs. There is also a 11% tax that is added to your room charge. All rooms are equipped with a telephone and a TV.
The *YMCA* - 25 Chowringhee Jawaharlal Nehru Rd. Tel: 033-249 2192
Dormitory beds-260Rs, single rooms-365Rs. Air-conditioned single rooms are 605Rs.
Women are also allowed to stay here. All rooms are equipped with a shower. Breakfast and dinner are included in the room rates and there is a membership discount of 40Rs.
The *Lytton Hotel* - 14 Sudder St. Tel: 033-249 1872
Single rooms-1,290Rs-1,400Rs, double rooms-1,800Rs-2,500Rs. There is also a 20% tax added. If you miss tucking into a prime beefsteak, this may be the place for you. Although rare in India, this hotel has them on the menu.

WEST BENGAL

DARJEELING

Famous for its tea, Darjeeling used to be a British summer resort. At an altitude of 2,123m, India's colonial masters could escape the oppressive heat of the low-lying plains. Many other Tibetan areas, such as Dharamsala and Mussoorie, are also summer resorts that were developed when India was a British colony. Rows of houses in the hills of Darjeeling are reminiscent of Tibetan dwellings and the Darjeeling area was originally governed by the King of Sikkim.

Administratively, Darjeeling is part of West

SIKKIM

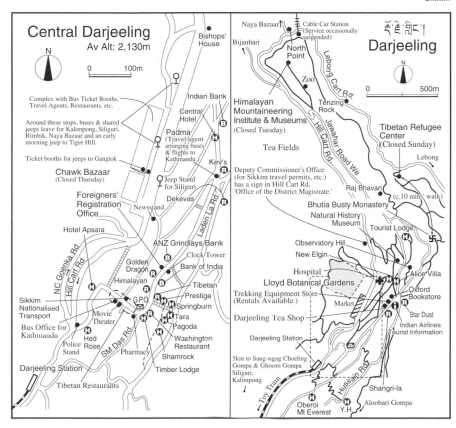

Central Darjeeling
Av Alt: 2,130m

N

0   100m

Complex with Bus Ticket Booths, Travel Agents, Restaurants, etc.

Around these stops, buses & shared jeeps leave for Kalimpong, Siliguri, Rimbik, Naya Bazaar and an early morning jeep to Tiger Hill.

Ticket booths for jeeps to Gangtok

Chawk Bazaar
(Closed Thursday)

Foreigners' Registration Office

Hotel Apsara

NC Goenka Rd
Hill Cart Rd

Sikkim Nationalised Transport

Bus Office for Kathmandu

Police Stand

Darjeeling Station

Tibetan Restaurants

Bishops' House

Indian Bank

Central Hotel

Padma
(Travel agent arranging buses & flights to Kathmandu)

Kev's

Jeep Stand for Siliguri

Dekevas

Newsstand

Laden La Rd

ANZ Grindlays Bank

Clock Tower

Golden Dragon

Bank of India

Himalayan

Tibetan

G.P.O.

Prestige

Springburn

Tara

Pagoda

Movie Theater

Hed Rose

SM Das Rd

Pharmacy

Washington Restaurant

Shamrock

Timber Lodge

Darjeeling

Naya Bazaar

Bijanbari

North Point

Cable Car Station
(Service occasionally suspended)

Zoo

Lebong Cart Rd

Himalayan Mountaineering Institute & Museums
(Closed Tuesday)

Tea Fields

Tenzing Rock

Hill Cart Rd

Jawahar Road We

Deputy Commissioner's Office
(for Sikkim travel permits, etc.)
has a sign in Hill Cart Rd,
'Office of the District Magistrate.'

Bhutia Busty Monastery

Natural History Museum

Observatory Hill

New Elgin

Hospital

Lloyd Botanical Gardens

Trekking Equipment Store
(Rentals Available.)

Darjeeling Tea Shop

Darjeeling Station

5km to Sang-ngag Choeling Gompa & Ghoom Gompa
Siliguri,
Kalimpong

Toy Train

Oberoi Mt Everest

Y.H.

Tibetan Refugee Center
(Closed Sunday)

Lebong

Raj Bhavan
(c.10 mins' walk)

Tourist Lodge

Alice Villa

Oxford Bookstore

Market

Star Dust

Indian Airlines Tourist Information

Hussain Rd

Shangri-la

Aloobari Gompa

N

0   500m

SIKKIM

Bengal and 80% of its population are Nepalese Hindus. The small numbers of Tibetans and Bhutanese (both populations of which are Buddhist), belie the strong cultural and economic influence the groups have had on the area.

Originally, the name *Darjeeling* came from the Tibetan word, *Dorje Ling* meaning 'The Place of Thunderbolts' and many Tibetan artisans and tradesmen had settled in the town before the Chinese invaded Tibet in 1950. After the invasion, and the flight of the Dalai Lama 9 years later, a large number of Tibetan refugees fled to Darjeeling, substantially swelling the number of Tibetans in the region.

The tourist season lasts from March to mid-June and occurs again from October to November. The latter period is when you'll get the beautiful views of Mt. Kangchenjunga, the third highest mountain in the world and India's tallest peak. The rainy season stretches from mid-June until September. Even in summer, the average temperature only gets as high as 15°C and the winters here are bitterly cold, although it only snows a couple of times a year.

Along the paved roads in town there are many flights of stairs criss-crossing the slopes. Local people will show you some shortcuts to the places where you want to go.

Access by Air
Bagdogra Airport near Siliguri is the closest airport to Darjeeling. It is about 90km from Darjeeling, or about a 4-hour direct bus ride. There are also regular flights from Delhi and Kolkata (Calcutta).

Access by Rail
Trains from Sealdah Station in Kolkata (Calcutta) will bring you into New Jalpaiguri, 8km south of the town of Siliguri. There are a number of direct trains from Kolkata:
  5657 *Kanchenjunga Express*. 06:25-18:10.
          2nd class 127Rs.
  3143 *Darjeeling Mail*. 19:15-08:15.
          2nd class sleeper 190Rs.

Bhutia Busty Monastery

The Toy Train

The famous narrow-gauge 'Toy Train' runs between New Jalpaiguri and Darjeeling. There are trains at 07:15-15:50 (Number 3D) and again at 09:00-17:30 (Number 1D) everyday from New Jalpaiguri. The 2 return trains from Darjeeling leave at 08:25 (Number 4D) and 10:00 (Number 2D).

These are the scheduled times for the summer but the trip can sometimes take as long as 12 hours, especially on the upward trip from New Jalpaiguri. In the winter, the service is usually restricted to the later 1D & 2D services.

Alternatively, you can take a bus that takes just over 3 hours. The bus station at Siliguri is not far from the station at New Jalpaiguri and the 5km journey costs around 15Rs by rickshaw.

Access by Bus

There are some buses that depart daily from the Esplanade Bus Station in Kolkata. The journey to Siliguri takes about 12 hours and the fare is 170Rs. From Siliguri to Darjeeling a bus runs every 30 minutes and gets you into Darjeeling in around 3 hours. Tickets cost 35Rs. A jeep taxi will get you there a little faster. They cost 45Rs and take 3 hours.

Changing Money

Banks usually only accept US Dollars and British Pounds. For travelers' checks, both Amex and Thomas Cook are acceptable and you can even exchange cash for local currency at some stores in town. Both Visa and MasterCard can be used in the banks and some teashops and the Oxford Bookstore will also accept them. If you want to send a package, the postal charges must be paid for in cash.

Accommodation

With so many slopes surrounding the bus station it is tough to walk around with your baggage once you arrive. Many travelers take the 15-minute walk to the Gandhi Road/Laden La Road area to the east of the GPO where there are a lot of cheap hotels.

The months of April, May, and October attract large numbers of domestic tourists and there is always a shortage of cheap rooms.

The *Shamrock Hotel* and *Pagoda Hotel* have reasonable room rates at around 200Rs for a double with a bathroom. There are also plenty of more expensive places catering to package tours, both in the same area and on the outskirts of the town.

The *Youth Hostel* on Zakir Hussain Road is the cheapest accommodation available although it is a little out of town. You'll get some great views for the money and there is also travel information posted by other backpackers. One drawback is that in winter it gets very cold because they don't seem to have any heaters. A dormitory bed costs 25Rs for members while non-members pay a small additional fee.

Restaurants

With the many Tibetans calling Darjeeling home, you'll find there is a good selection of Tibetan restaurants in town. They are centered around Laden La Road where the GPO is located. For a taste of good Tibetan food try the *Mili Restaurant* where the owner serves excellent *momos*. There are also a number of Chinese restaurants here.

Bookstores

The *Oxford Bookstore* has a good selection of books, maps, travel guides and postcards on Sikkim, Bhutan and Tibet. The staff is helpful and will recommend books covering the subjects you require.

Places to See
Bhutia Busty Monastery

A 30-minute walk down the CD Das Road from Chowrasta, this Karma Kagyupa monastery was founded in the 19th century and is regarded as a branch of the Phodang Monastery in Sikkim.

Tibetan Refugee Self-Help Centre

This was built in 1959 to provide self-supporting assistance for the Tibetan refugees who fled to Darjeeling after the Dalai Lama went into exile from Tibet. The former Dalai Lama is said to have stayed here when he visited India. This center manufactures and sells beautiful Tibetan carpets and handicrafts.

On a tour, you'll be taken to see wool spinning on the 1st floor of the center. Weaving is done on the 2nd floor and the dye works are behind the factory. The center offers classes in some traditional handicrafts and can help arrange Tibetan language courses, too.

The center is a 10-minute walk along the road behind the Bhutia Busty Monastery, located at 65 Gandhi Road. Tel: 091-354 2346. Also, about 15km

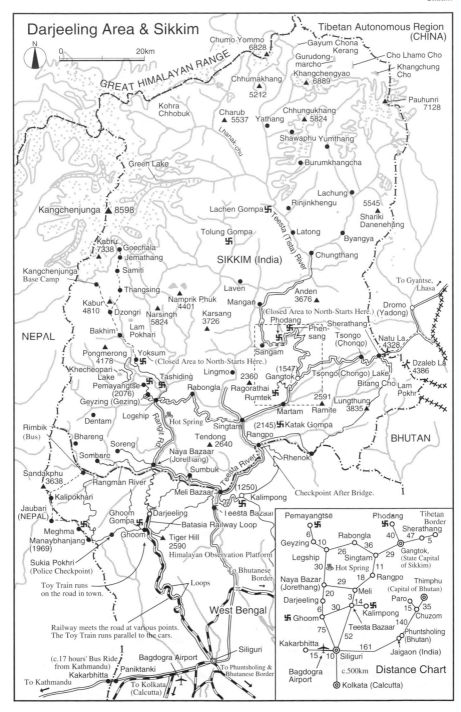

Darjeeling Area & Sikkim

N

0   20km

GREAT HIMALAYAN RANGE

Chumo Yommo
6828

Tibetan Autonomous Region
(CHINA)

Gayum Chona
Kerang

Gurudong-
marcho

Cho Lhamo Cho

Khangchung
Cho

Khangchengyao
6889

Chhumakhang
5212

Kohra
Chhobuk

Charub
5537

Yathang

Chhungukhang
5824

Pauhunri
7128

Lhanak-chu

Shawaphu Yumthang

Green Lake

Burumkhangcha

Lachung

Kangchenjunga ▲ 8598

Lachen Gompa

Rinjinkhengu

5545

Shariki
Danenehung

Tolung Gompa

Latong

Byangya

Kabru
7338

Goechala

Jemathang

Samiti

SIKKIM (India)

Chungthang

Kangchenjunga
Base Camp

Thangsing

Laven

Anden
3676 ▲

To Gyantse,
Lhasa

Kabur
4810

Namprik Phuk
4401

Mangan

Dromo
(Yadong)

Dzongri

Narsingh
5824

Karsang
3726

(Closed Area to North-Starts Here.)

Phodang

Sherathang

NEPAL

Bakhim

Lam
Pokhari

Phen-
sang

Tsongo
(Chonqo)

Natu La
4328

Pongmerong
4178

Yoksum

Sangam

(1547)

Dzaleb La
4386

Khecheopari
Lake

(Closed Area to North-Starts Here.)

Lingmo

2360

Gangtok

Tsongo(Chongo) Lake

Lam
Pokhri

Tashiding

Pemayangtse
(2076)

Rabongla

Ragorathai
Rumtek

Bitang Cho

Geyzing (Gezing)

Logship

Hot Spring

Singtam

2591

Martam

Lungthung
3835

Ramite

Rimbik
(Bus)

Dentam

Bhareng

Soreng

Tendong
▲ 2640

Rangpo

(2145)

Katak Gompa

Sombaro

Naya Bazaar
(Jorethang)

BHUTAN

Sandakphu
3638

Rangman River

Sumbuk

Rhenok

Kalipokhari

Meli Bazaar

(1250)

Kalimpong

Checkpoint After Bridge.

Jaubari
(NEPAL)

Ghoom
Gompa

Darjeeling

Teesta Bazaar

Batasia Railway Loop

Meghma

Manaybhanjang
(1969)

Ghoom

Tiger Hill
2590

Himalayan Observation Platform

Sukia Pokhri
(Police Checkpoint)

To Bhutanese
Border

Toy Train runs
on the road in town.

Loops

To Bhutan
Border

Railway meets the road at various points.
The Toy Train runs parallel to the cars.

West Bengal

(c.17 hours' Bus Ride
from Kathmandu)

Kakarbhitta

Paniktanki

Bagdogra Airport

Siliguri

To Kathmandu

To Kolkata
(Calcutta)

To Phuntsholing &
Bhutanese Border

Distance Chart

	Pemayangtse		Phodang		Tibetan Border
	6		40	Sherathang 47	5
Geyzing	10	Rabongla 36	29	Gangtok, (State Capital of Sikkim)	
Legship	26 Singtam	11			
	30 Hot Spring		Rangpo	Thimphu (Capital of Bhutan)	
Naya Bazar (Jorethang)	29	18		Paro	
	20	Meli	14	15	35
Darjeeling	6	3	Kalimpong	Chuzom	
Ghoom	30	75	Teesta Bazaar 52	140	Phuntsholing (Bhutan)
Kakarbhitta			161	Jaigaon (India)	
	15 10 Siliguri	c.500km			
Bagdogra Airport					
Kolkata (Calcutta)					

SIKKIM

out of town on the Pashok Road, there is the Tibetan settlement of Lama Hatta.

Ghoom Gompa
The gompa's claim to fame is that it is the largest Tibetan monastery in Darjeeling. It was built in 1875 by monks of the Dalai Lama's Gelukpa order and houses a 5-meter high statue of Maitreya. The monastery is about 5km south of the center of Darjeeling.

Thupten Sang-Ngag Choeling Gompa
This is the other main Tibetan monastery at Ghoom and it is the head monastery for the Drukpa Kagyupa order. It was originally located in Tsari in southern Tibet and the one there is now under reconstruction. The gompa here was founded by Drukchen Rinpoche after he sought refugee in this region.

Tiger Hill
This 2,590m high vantage point, 10km south of Darjeeling, is the highest peak in the area. The observation platform offers a full view of Mt. Kangchenjunga and you can also see Mt. Jomolangma (Everest), weather permitting. From Darjeeling, there is a shared-jeep service that leaves the town early in the morning and sometimes stops at Ghoom Gompa on the way back. There is also a hotel here mainly used by tours groups from Darjeeling.

Himalayan Mountaineering Institute & Museums
There are exhibits of equipment and photographs from many Himalayan mountaineering expeditions, including one from the first successful ascent of Everest. The Himalayan Zoological Park is next door.

KALIMPONG

This small town of around 40,000 inhabitants is at 1,250m and lies roughly 50km east of Darjeeling, close to the mighty Teesta (Tista) River. The moderate altitude, gentle climate and relaxed atmosphere have made Kalimpong a popular hill-station summer retreat.

Originally, Kalimpong was governed by the King of Sikkim but it was taken over by Bhutan in the 18th century. Later, after the war between Bhutan and the British in 1865, it became part of the Indian province of West Bengal. The town is home to many Tibetans, as well as to a large number of Bhutias and Lepchas, and the bazaar is a good place to pick up handicrafts such as locally handwoven cloth, Tibetan *thangkas* and silverware. The bazaar is held close by to where the buses arrive.

Access
From Darjeeling, there is a bus departing from the bus stand in the center of town. There is also a shared-jeep taxi that leaves from the taxi stand in town. It takes about 3-4 hours and the fare is 45Rs. From Siliguri, there are several buses a day and these will get you to Kalimpong in just over 2 hours. There are a couple of buses a day connecting Gangtok with Kalimpong and they take 3 hours.

Accommodation
There are some cheap guesthouses around the bus stand in Kalimpong. Among these, the *Deki Lodge* is recommended. It is run by a Tibetan and very homely. Dormitory beds start at 40Rs, singles go for 80Rs and up, and double rooms are 120Rs to 300Rs a night. There are also triple-bed rooms and deluxe rooms with hot showers available. The lodge also offers a 20% discount during the off-season (January-March and July-September). Walk 5-6 minutes along Rishi Rd to the east from the bus stand and then take a left turn. You will then see the signboard on the left. This lodge is popular among foreign travelers.

Places to See
Zong Dog Palri Fo-Brang Gompa
This is a Nyingmapa monastery on the hill called 'Durpin Dara,' located at the south-western end of town. The late Dudjom Rinpoche, the highest-ranking lama of the Nyingmapa order, fled from Tibet and founded the monastery in 1972. It was blessed by the current Dalai Lama in 1976.

There are other Tibetan-style lamaseries in Kalimpong, including Tharpa Choeling Gompa, which belongs to the Dalai Lama's Gelukpa order. This monastery was established just over 60 years ago. Tongsa Gompa is a much older Bhutanese monastery, having been founded in the 1690's.

Deolo Hill
From this vantage point above the town you can get good views of Mt. Kangchenjunga and Mt. Siniolchu, among other mountains. The viewpoint also looks out over Kalimpong and down the Teesta (Tista) River Valley. The walk to the hill takes around 2 hours and if you go for the clear early morning panorama, remember to dress warmly.

Dr. Graham's House
This school was established at the turn of the century by Rev Dr. John Anderson Graham to educate the tea plantation workers' children. The original school buildings and chapel are still in use

and the grounds are well-looked-after. If you are making for Deolo Hill, you will pass the school on the way from town.

Nature Interpretation Centre & Exotic Plant Nurseries
The interpretation center is an attempt by the Forestry Department to encourage local people in their efforts to live in harmony with the area's fragile ecology. Admission is free. Kalimpong is also famous for the growing of all kinds of exotic plants including gladioli, dahlias, orchids, and cacti in the numerous nurseries around the town.

Places to See around Kalimpong
If you are using the town as your base to explore the area, there are also some interesting sites a little further out, including the Teesta (Tista) River Valley about 15km outside the town. This is an area for relaxing, or for the more adventurous, river-rafting.

The village of Lava is 34km east of Kalimpong and a good gateway to the Neora National Park. At over 2,000m, this small village is home to a Bhutanese-style monastery and the entire area is covered in pine trees. About 50km further on from the village is the Samthar Plateau, which offers spectacular views of the surrounding area and is a great place for exploring the pristine nature and the small tribal villages that dot the landscape.

SIKKIM

Surrounded by Tibet (China), Bhutan, and Nepal, Sikkim is one of the few places where you can still get a taste of old Tibet. With Sikkim sharing a sensitive border with China, there are restrictions on foreigners' freedom of travel in the area.

In the 15th and 16th centuries, Tibetans (known as *Bhutia*) started migrating to Sikkim, which had been originally settled by the Lepcha people from Assam. While the Dalai Lama's Gelukpa government was established in Tibet, the Sikkim royal family, backed by high-ranking priests of the Nyingmapa order, came to power in Gangtok, the capital of Sikkim. Unlike their counterparts in neighboring Bhutan, the Sikkim royal family later established a friendly relationship with the government in Lhasa. These ties were strengthened through political marriages and other alliances.

The expanse of territory ruled over by the King of Sikkim once reached from the Chumbi Valley in Tibet through eastern Nepal and parts of Bhutan down to the area around Darjeeling. Throughout the 18th and early 19th centuries, the territory under the flag of Sikkim was diminished through conflicts with both Bhutan and then Gurkha invaders from

Nepal. By the end of the 19th century, the British had gained the lands around Darjeeling and Sikkim had become a British protectorate.

This relationship between British-ruled India and Sikkim continued with little change after Indian independence; indeed, the *Choegyal* (King) of Sikkim only lost his throne after the 1975 referendum when the people of Sikkim voted to become an integral part of India. Yet even after the British left, the border areas in this region have remained unstable. Chinese maps still show Sikkim as an independent country and the region's status has remained a thorny issue in the relations between India and China.

Although Sikkim exhibits a strong Tibetan influence, about 70% of its population is Hindu, due mainly to the migration of Nepalese into the area. The Tibetans call Sikkim *Drejong*, which means 'Rice Country.' The atmosphere surrounding Sikkim can be compared to that of Kham in eastern Tibet. The populated areas are at the lower altitudes and are blanketed in thick forest cover. This availability of timber enables the Sikkimese to build many of their houses and structures from wood. Conversely, the northern reaches of Sikkim are very mountainous and the area is home to the third largest mountain in the world, Mt. Kangchenjunga. The local people revere the mountain as a protective deity, as Mt. Kailash is amongst Tibetans and Hindus.

Rather than the 5-colored *tar-choks* that are common throughout Central Tibet, there are many white banner-like *dar-shing*, seen both in Sikkim and Bhutan. This is another similarity between these areas and the Tibetan province of Kham.

Arranging Travel Permits
Individual travelers are restricted from entering certain areas. To enter Sikkim, you are required to obtain a 'Restricted Area Permit.' The areas presently open to individuals are Gangtok, Rumtek, Phodang, Pemayangtse, Khecheopari and Tashigang. The permit allows a maximum stay of 15 days. For your permit application, a couple of passport photos and photocopies of your passport details and an Indian visa are required.

The permit can be requested when you apply for your Indian visa outside of the country or at the following offices in India itself:

Kolkata (Calcutta)
The *Sikkim Information Center* at 4 Poonam Bldg., 5/2 Russell St. Tel: 033-297 516/ 298 983
Delhi
The *Sikkim Information Center* at New Sikkim House, 14 Panchsheel Marg, Chanakyapuri. Tel: 011-611 5346
Darjeeling
Deputy Commissioner's Office, open Monday to

Friday 11:00-13:00, 14:30-16:00. The office is on the 2nd floor of the building with the signboard 'Office of the District Magistrate' that can be seen from Hill Cart Road.

Siliguri

Sikkim Information Center at the SNT Bus Station. Tel: 0353-432 646

Gangtok

Sikkim Information Center at the Department of Tourism. Mahatma Gandhi Marg.
Tel: 03592-23425/ 22064

It is also possible to arrange these permits at Foreigners' Registration offices and Immigration offices at major airports.

Areas Restricted to Group Tours

The following areas have checkpoints that only allow group tours organized by travel agents:

Trekking to Dzongri, West Sikkim.

Only group tours are allowed to apply for the 16-day permit for this area. Each group must then be escorted through the area by a military liaison officer.

Tsongo (Chongo) Lake, East of Gangtok.

Another restricted area that is only accessible for day trips organized as part of a group tour.

Mangan, Tong, Singhik, Chungthang, Lachung, Yumthang.

These are all to the north of Phodang in northern Sikkim. Those wishing to travel to these areas must join a 5-day group tour.

The main travel seasons in Sikkim are from mid-September until winter arrives in December. March through to May is also a peak time. Tours are available all year-round as the winters in the area are very mild. This is due to the altitude being below 2,000m. in many places, and the fact that it rarely snows in these areas.

The People of Sikkim

The Bhutia (Bhotia) People

Around 500 years ago these people migrated down from Tibet (Bhote) and settled mainly in the northern parts of present-day Sikkim and Bhutan. The Bhutias follow Tibetan Buddhism and make up around 5% of the population of Sikkim, although they form a majority in Bhutan.

Traditional Bhutia villages are characterized by their rectangular houses and the distinctive clothing of the inhabitants, with the men wearing long cloaks and the women gold jewelry. The Bhutia are mountain dwellers and practice terraced agriculture in the valleys where they make their homes.

The Lepcha People

Originally, the Lepcha were an animist tribe that retained a strong shamanist tradition until Buddhism was introduced by the Bhutia who migrated to the area. The *Lepcha* language and their rich written folklore reflect the Lepcha's close connection to the land and the nature around them. Lepcha villages are found mainly at high elevations in remote mountainous areas in central Sikkim and the people now constitute around 20% of Sikkim's population.

Their traditional way of life has survived and both the men and women continue to wear their distinctive cotton smocks and engage in their farming and cattle husbandry.

The Nepalese People

Nepalese migration occurred mainly during the last 150 years and their numbers have risen until they now make up over 70% of Sikkim's population. Most of these Nepalese immigrants are Hindu and have little interaction with the Buddhist Bhutia and Lepcha people. The Nepalese language is now spoken throughout the region and Nepalese continue to wear their traditional long double-breasted jackets while the men carry the famous heavy, curved *Khukri* knife.

Festivals in Sikkim

With over 190 large and small gompas scattered throughout the province, Tibetan Buddhism has had a major impact on the culture and everyday lives of the people of the region. The monks of the monasteries are renowned for their performances of the *Cham*, a ritual dance that depicts the victory of good over evil.

Bhum-Chu

Held at the Tashiding Gompa and Khecheopari Lake on the 15th day of the 1st lunar month in either February or March.

Saga Dawa (The Buddha Jayanti)

This festival celebrates 3 stages of the historical Buddha's life: his birth, his enlightenment and the reaching of Nirvana. It falls on the full moon of the 4th lunar month, around the end of May and the beginning of June. Gangtok is one of the best places to be on this day. There is a full procession of monks bearing sacred scriptures through the town. People from all over the region visit their local monastery to make offerings and light butter lamps.

The Rumtek Gompa 'Chams'
(Tse-Chu 'Chams')

These ritual dances are performed on the 10th day of the 5th lunar month, in June or July. The performers act out epic events from the life of Guru Rinpoche, who brought Buddhism to the area in the 8th century.

Drukpa Tseshi

Held on the 4th day of the 6th lunar month in late July or August.

Phang Lhabsol

This festival is unique to Sikkim as it is held to

thank the guardian deity of Sikkim, Mt. Kangchenjunga. This festival is held on the 15th day of the 7th lunar month, around the end of August and the beginning of September. The celebrations at Pemayangste stand out from the crowd.

Dasain
This is the Nepalese people's most important festival of the year and celebrations can become very hectic, especially in the southern areas of Sikkim where this ethnic group predominates. The festival is held at the end of October or in November.

Kagyat Dance
This is performed on the 28th and 29th days of the 10th lunar month between November and December and can be seen at the Palace in Gangtok and Rumtek, Pemayangste & Phodang Gompas.

The Enchey Gompa 'Chams'
These dances are held on the 18th and 19th days of the 11th lunar month between December and February.

Losong
This is the Sikkimese New Year and is celebrated all over Sikkim, usually at the end of December.

Winter 'Cham' (Guthor 'Cham')
These dances are held 2 days before the Losar celebrations at the end of the 12th lunar month in February or March.

Losar
This festival marks the Tibetan New Year and is held in February or March on the 1st day of the 1st lunar month. The Wood-Cock Year (year 2132) starts on February 9, 2005 and the Fire-Dog Year (Year 2133) begins on February 28, 2006.

Main Festivals in Sikkim

Year 2004 / 2005 / 2006

Enchey
Chams .... Jan 10-11/Dec 29-30, 2004/Jan 17-18
Winter Cham .... Feb 19/Feb 7/Feb 27
Losar .... Feb 21/Feb 9/Feb 28
Bhum-Chu .... Mar 6/Feb 23/Mar 14
Saka Dawa .... Jun 3/May 23/Jun 11
Rumtek Chams .... Jun 27/Jun 17/Jul 6
Drukpa Tseshi .... Jul 21/Jul 10/Jul 29
Phang Lhabsol .... Aug 30/Sep 18/Sep 7
Kagyat Dances ... Dec 10-11/Dec 29-30/Dec 18-19

These are provisional dates and can be subject to change (usually by only a day or two). If you are planning a trip to coincide with one of these festivals it is recommended that you check with a Tourist office to confirm dates. (See the Tourist Information section for contact numbers.)

Gangtok

CENTRAL & EASTERN SIKKIM

GANGTOK

Gangtok commands a good view of the sacred Mt. Kangchenjunga, the world's third highest peak. Many of the houses in the area are built to face north towards the holy mountain.

Gangtok, at 1,547m, is the state capital of Sikkim. This large town of 45,000 residents is similar in size to Darjeeling. There is electricity throughout the town, although the supply is intermittent at best. The town has many hotels and restaurants, as well as most other services you'll need. There is a selection of banks and money exchange services in the town. There are adequate medical facilities, and international calls are easy to arrange.

Gangtok has a relaxed atmosphere and seems far removed from other Indian towns down on the plains. The streets are peaceful and empty of obnoxious street vendors and persistent touts. The shopping experience is a refreshing one with few clerks asking unreasonable prices and you can expect the correct change without a fuss.

On the other hand, don't expect to be offered any discounts, either. Despite the sometimes traumatic experiences you'll have in the rest of India, the storekeepers in Gangtok are neither hard-nosed nor market-oriented. But they are not overly friendly with their customers, either.

Access by Bus & Taxi
From Siliguri
You won't have to wait long in Siliguri for the next bus to Gangtok. There are numerous departures throughout the day and the 60Rs journey will take you 4-5 hours.

From Darjeeling
There are 4 daily buses (or sometimes jeeps) that leave from the Bazaar Bus Stand in Darjeeling. Two buses leave between 07:00 and 08:00 and the other

2 leave between 13:00 and 14:00. The trip takes around 5 hours and costs 60Rs.

There is also a jeep service in the morning and one that leaves every half-hour between 07:00 and 12:30. The jeeps take just over 3 hours and cost 100Rs. Tickets are available from a couple of different companies that run booths in the complex next to Chawk Bazaar. In addition, there are some travel agents that lay on tour buses for Gangtok.

From Kalimpong
There are a limited number of buses for the daily 4-hour ride to Gangtok. There is a checkpoint at Rangpo on the state border. Passengers are required to report here on their way to Gangtok and on their return journey.

Leaving Gangtok
Shared-jeep taxis to Siliguri are available between 06:00 and 11:00. You'll pay around 80Rs for the 3-4 hour journey. There are also jeep services to Khakarbhitta on the Nepalese border. You can reserve a seat for this trip in advance at the booth in Chawk Bazaar.

Access by Air
The flight time from Delhi to Bagdogra Airport is about 2 hours and the fare is around US$140. Bagdogra has a good tourist information counter

Research Institute of Tibetology

for additional information about tours. Though there is a bus service from the airport to Gangtok, taking a taxi is recommended as you'll have to make a bus transfer on the way. A Suzuki multi-taxi can accommodate up to 5 passengers and the journey by paved road to Gangtok lasts around 5 hours. The cost per taxi is 1,500Rs and there is a checkpoint at Rangpo en route to the town.

Accommodation
The *Hotel Orchid* has a restaurant and is popular among backpackers. It is a convenient place to pick up travel information. The only drawback is that the blast of truck horns in the morning can be rather annoying since the hotel faces a main road. Single rooms are 50Rs and up. Doubles start at 80Rs.

The *Sunny Guesthouse* is located next to the bus stand. Single room rates start at 100Rs with doubles starting at 200Rs.

The *Green Hotel* is owned by an Indian and the Indian guests can be noisy. There are both e-mail and fax services available here. The former costs 60Rs while faxes (per page) are 150Rs. Single rooms cost 70Rs, 80Rs, or 120Rs. Double rooms cost 175Rs and 250Rs.

The *Hotel Tashi Delek*, Tel: 03592-22991/ 22038, is a relatively high-class hotel. What makes this hotel stand out are the 3 excellent meals a day that are included in the price. You'll be able to feast not only on Indian but also on Chinese and local cuisine. Single rooms at the hotel cost 1,150Rs and doubles cost 1,700Rs.

The *Nor-Khill Hotel*, Tel: 03592-23186/ 23187, is a common place for package tours and is a pricey 4-star government-approved hotel with all the modern conveniences.

Places to See
Gangtok Palace
This is the palace where the *Choegyals* of Sikkim resided from 1894 until 1975. The yellow-roofed Tskulakhang is located south of the palace and is the royal chapel and an important center of worship for the Sikkimese people. The building holds many

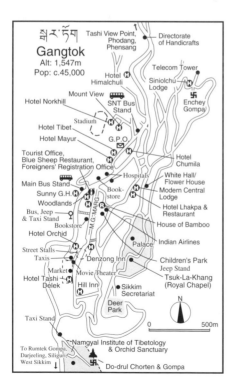

Buddhists scriptures, as well as a beautifully crafted interior. This is also the site of the famed New Year's festival (held during *Losar*, the Tibetan New Year celebration), featuring the sacred *Black Hat* dance. The dance portrays the battle between good and evil.

Research Institute of Tibetology

This is a museum dedicated to Tibetan Buddhism and is the repository for the *thangka* that was made for the present Dalai Lama's accession to the throne and later smuggled out of Tibet. There are also large numbers of books written in Sanskrit, Tibetan and local dialects covering Tibetan teachings on science, philosophy, medical matters, religion and astrology.

The institute is located on the road to the Rumtek Gompa and is closed in July, August and December. It is open from 10:00-16:00 throughout the week and the admission fee is 2Rs.

Orchid Sanctuary

Most of the 454 species of orchid that are native to the region can be viewed here in the sanctuary's landscaped gardens. The best seasons for viewing the plants when they are flowering are from April to May, July to August, and October to November. The sanctuary is accessible through the Research Institute of Tibetology.

Directorate of Handicrafts and Handloom

The center seeks to preserve the traditional arts and crafts of the region. You can see how the local people produce these handicrafts and much of the work is on sale. You can buy carpets, hand-woven shawls, bamboo crafts, *thangkas*, Lepcha fabrics and a wide variety of other authentic pieces.

You can visit the center from 09:30-12:30 & 13:00-15:00, except on Sundays. For other inquiries, call Tel: 03592-23126/ 22928

Do-Drul Chorten

The chorten and monastery were built by the Nyingmapa's high priest, Trulshi Rinpoche, in 1945. There are 108 *mani-khor* (prayer wheels) surrounding the chorten. This is also accessible through the Research Institute of Tibetology.

Enchey Gompa

This Nyingmapa monastery has a nearly 200-year history, with the site originally built by the great Lama Druptob Karpo (who, legend has it, could fly). The present buildings were constructed in 1909. The monastery, located at the eastern end of Gangtok, is the site of a *Cham* dancing festival performed by the 90 or so monks. It is held each year on 18th and 19th days of the 11th lunar month (December-January).

Enchey Gompa, Gangtok

The Flower House

This is the site for the annual *Orchid Festival*, held from mid-March to May. The admission fee is 5Rs and there is an additional 5Rs fee for cameras.

There are also some other flower festivals held here throughout the rest of the year. Check with the local tourist information in Gangtok for the dates as they vary. To reach the house, go up the Tibet Road and then take a shortcut up the stairs. From there you'll see it near the White Hall complex.

Places to See Around Gangtok
Rumtek Gompa

This is the biggest monastery in Sikkim and the seat of the Karmapa, the head of Karma Kagyupa order (founded in the 11th century), and the most influential sect in the area. Although the original buildings were constructed in 1740, the gompa was destroyed by an earthquake and later rebuilt.

In the 1960's, after he fled from Tibet along with Dalai Lama XIV, the late 16th Gyalwa Karmapa was based at this gompa and devoted himself to spreading the teachings of Buddhism throughout the world until his death in 1981. The next incarnation was designated by the Chinese government and ascended to his exalted position at the Tsurphu Gompa, near Lhasa. Nonetheless, Rumtek has still maintained a strong influence amongst the Kagyupa followers.

Rumtek Gompa

The site is also referred to as the *Rumtek Dharma Chakra Centre* (Tel: 03592-22663). With a bank and a research institute nearby, the monastery forms a village. On entry to the monastery you are required to register your name. The main temple is open to visitors and from the roof of the monks' residence there is a commanding view of Gangtok. There are *Cham* dances held annually on the grounds. These are held on the 10th day of the 5th lunar month.

There is a bus that leaves Gangtok at 14:00 and arrives at the gompa in 2-3 hours. A jeep costs 20Rs and covers the 24km in about 40 minutes. There are taxis available that will take you out for a fixed rate of 250Rs. In addition, there is a sightseeing bus that visits both the gompa and the botanical gardens. You can squeeze your visit into a day or you can break up the journey and stay at one of the guesthouses near the entrance to the gompa. The *Sangay Hotel* is right by the entrance to the monastery and single rooms start at 40Rs. There is also the similarly named *Sangay Guesthouse*, which has singles going for 90Rs and up.

Tsongo (Chongo) Lake

Forty kilometers east from Gangtok towards the Chinese border, this scenic kilometer long and 15m-deep egg-shaped lake is regarded as sacred among

Ngor Gompa

the local people. May through August is the best season to visit the area which, at 3,780m, abounds with flowering alpine plants at this time of year. If you're in the mood, there is yak riding available. A 15-minute ride down by the lake costs 20Rs.

There is a checkpoint on the way to the lake from Gangtok and there is also a substantial Indian military presence in the area due to its proximity to the sensitive border. Foreigners are required to carry a permit with their photograph displayed on it. To cut through the hassle, it is easier to join a 1-day tour organized by a travel agency in Gangtok. Permits are not supposed to be issued to groups with less than 4 members.

Many of the travel agencies in town are unwilling to deal with solitary visitors as they still have to find 3 others to fill up the quota. *Bayul Tours & Travel* accepts individuals and they will arrange a 1-day trip including lunch for US$12, which also takes care of the permit. The office is in the supermarket building, in front of the movie theater and the taxi stand.

Ngor Gompa

Luding Khen Rinpoche, the head priest of the Ngor Sakyapa order, founded this gompa in 1961. About 5km from the town, it is the only Sakyapa monastery in Sikkim. Many organized tours stop off at the gompa on their way back from Tsongo (Chongo) Lake.

NORTHERN SIKKIM

The area immediately north of Gangtok, up to the Phodang area, is open to visitors without joining a group tour or applying for the Inner Line Permit (ILP) that is required for destinations further to the north.

Tashi Viewpoint

Eight kilometers north of Gangtok, this is an observation platform for viewing the spectacular Kangchenjunga and Siniolchu peaks. If you can

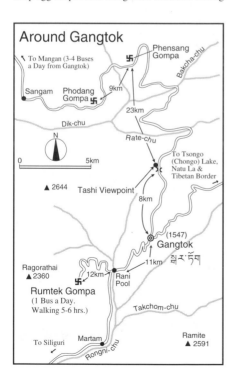

Around Gangtok

To Mangan (3-4 Buses a Day from Gangtok)

Phensang Gompa

Bakcha-chu

Sangam Phodang Gompa 9km

23km

Dik-chu

Rate-chu

N

0   5km

To Tsongo (Chongo) Lake, Natu La & Tibetan Border

▲ 2644 Tashi Viewpoint

8km

(1547)
Gangtok

ཤར་ཏོག

11km

Ragorathai
▲ 2360 12km Rani Pool

Rumtek Gompa
(1 Bus a Day.
Walking 5-6 hrs.)

Takchom-chu

To Siliguri Martam

Rongni-chu

Ramite
▲ 2591

drag yourself out of bed at 04:30, you will be rewarded by views of the mountains glittering in the morning sun. You'll need to make a taxi reservation at your hotel the night before and the rate varies from 75 to 150Rs, depending on your negotiating skills. The taxi is supposed to wait for you while you view the mountain and you'll definitely need your cold weather gear to fight off the early morning chill.

Phensang Gompa

This Karma Kagyupa monastery, on the road north of Gangtok, was established by Choegyal IV in 1721 but was extensively renovated in the 1940's after fire swept through the complex. The gompa is home to as many as 300 monks at any one time.

There are a couple of buses a day from Gangtok and the conveniently timed 09:40 departure from Gangtok will get you to Phensang Gompa at 11:00. The monastery is about a 5-minute walk up the hill from the bus stop.

Phodang Gompa

Another 9 km (or a 2-hour walk) from Phensang is Phodang Gompa. This renovated gompa is rated as one of the leading monasteries in Sikkim and it is a good place to see the *Kagyat* dancing festival (February-March). There are 3-4 buses a day from Gangtok that will take you there and the monastery is a little up from the bus stop.

If you walk up from Phensang and spend the afternoon at Phodang, there is a well-timed bus departing the monastery at 15:20 and which arrives in Gangtok at 16:50. If you want to stay at Phodang, there is a guesthouse in the monastery.

Chungthang, Lachung & the Yumthang Valley

Access to the northern parts of Sikkim has been tightly controlled in the past; however, there has been some relaxation in this policy and foreigners are able to apply for travel permits for areas north of Gangtok right up to Lachung and into the remote wilderness of the Yumthang Valley. The restrictions governing visits to these remote areas are subject to change and if you are planning to make the trip you must join a group tour organized by a travel agent. If you decide to make this trip while you're in Sikkim, you can easily organize these jeep tours in Gangtok.

To reach Chungthang you will pass through the administrative center of Mangan and then follow the Teesta (Tista) River up until you enter the picturesque Chungthang Valley where the Lachen-chu and Lachung-chu tributaries converge to form the Teesta (Tista). This valley, nearly 100km north of Gangtok, is connected to the legends surrounding the life of Guru Rinpoche and also figures

prominently in the folklore and history of the Lepcha people that live in this area.

Lachung is your next stop. It is a small village 35km further on from Chungthang and only about 20km from the Chinese border. From here it is a short hop up to the untouched Yumthang Valley. This valley, at over 3,500m, is covered by many of the 30 species of rhododendron found in Sikkim and the time to catch them in bloom is from late April until the end of May. There are also famous natural hot springs here that are worth a visit.

WESTERN SIKKIM

GEYZING

This is the main town in western Sikkim and though there are a couple of cheap hotels, there is little of interest in this tiny town. This is used as a jumping-off point for many of those wanting to explore the surrounding area.

Access by Bus & Taxi

There is at least 1 daily bus that connects Geyzing with Gangtok via Rabong La. The 140-km long trip takes 5-6 hours. There is also a jeep that leaves the jeep stand near the children's park in Gangtok at 12:30, daily. This trip takes around 4 hours and costs 90Rs.

From Geyzing to Siliguri, there are a couple of buses a day stopping en route at Naya Bazaar. If you just want to travel to Naya Bazaar, there are 4-5 buses a day and at the town you can get connections to Siliguri and Darjeeling. There also are buses directly to Darjeeling from Geyzing, or you can opt for one of the many shared-jeeps costing 50Rs per person and whose trip takes

around an hour.

Places to See Around Geyzing
Reshi Natural Hot Springs
On the road to and from Naya Bazaar there is a natural hot spring, about 5km south of the Legship checkpoint, near the river. The springs are actually down in the riverbed and it is an open-air spa. The baths are open to women during the day and to men at night. There are many stores and guesthouses in this area if you don't feel like spending the night in Geyzing.

Pemayangtse (Pelling)
There are shared-jeeps and a bus each day from Geyzing. If you feel like walking, it will take you just over an hour to cover the 5km to the town.

About a 20-minute walk east of town is Pemayangtse Gompa. The monastery you see now was built during the reign of Choegyal III of Sikkim in the late 17th century. The monastery is the head of the Nyingmapa order in Sikkim and is the best place to soak up the celebrations surrounding the *Phang Lhabsol* festival held throughout the region. The festival is held to thank Mt. Kangchenjunga, the guardian deity of Sikkim, on the 15th of the 7th lunar month (August-September). The monastery also hosts another special festival, the *Kagyat*, with magnificent dancing performed by the 100 or so costumed monks on the 28th and 29th days of the 10th lunar month (November-December). Pilgrims from all over Sikkim come to watch and worship at the gompa during these 2 days.

For those wanting to stay in the area, the *Hotel Garuda* with its fine view of Mt. Kangchenjunga is popular among backpackers. It has travel information in English and you can get meals there. The friendly staff will look after your bags while you are away trekking in the area.

Tashiding Gompa
Walk down from Pemayangtse to the river, and then follow it up the valley for 4-5 hours, and you will see a monastery perched on top of the mountain above. This Nyingmapa gompa, at 1,490m, has exceptionally large prayer wheel houses, *mani* stones, and houses made of rocks, all of which warrant inspection.

There is a winter festival held at Tashiding called *Bhum Chu*. It is celebrated on the 15th day of the 1st lunar month (February-March). You can get good views of the Himalayas that lay far in the distance and you can even spy the occasional pilgrim from your vantage point.

Khecheopari Lake
This sacred lake is on the road north from Pemayangtse towards Yoksum. The lake itself spreads out for about 500m on all sides and is decorated at intervals with *tar-choks*. There is also a gompa nearby. During the *Bhum Chu* festivities at the Tashiding Gompa, Khecheopari gets a little crowded with pilgrims making offerings to the lake's deities.

There is a guesthouse called the *Trekkers Hut* located about 10 minutes before the lake and the rate is 30Rs per night. You can also get meals there. At the entrance to the lake there is a store.

There are buses from Geyzing to Yoksum via Tashiding. The ride is about 3 hours. From Yoksum, there is 1 bus a day that leaves for Geyzing and another one that departs for Jorethang (Naya Bazaar). Both leave at 07:00. Near the bus stop there are a few hotels. The *Hotel Demazong* has double rooms for 50Rs. There is also the top-range *Hotel Tashi Gang*, which opened in 1997.

Dubdi Gompa
The gompa is about a 40-minute walk up a mountain path from the village. It was built in the early 18th century, making it one of the oldest Buddhist monasteries in Sikkim.

Trekking
Trekking is the major attraction to the Yoksum area and indeed, this village marks the end of the road system in western Sikkim. There is a trekking route that takes you up to Dzongri, Thangsing and onward right up to Mt. Kangchenjunga itself. If you are planning to take off into the mountains in this area, you'll require a trekking permit. Check the details of how to obtain these at the Sikkim Information centers in Gangtok, Siligiri, Darjeeling or other major cities (See Travel Permit section).

This province in the far north-east of India is wedged up against the borders of Tibet (China), Myanmar, and Bhutan. The actual line between India and China is still in dispute and this area saw heavy fighting during the brief 1962 Indo-China war. Although Arunachal Pradesh is currently under Indian administration, China still claims it as its territory.

Along with the Tsona area to the north, the north-western part of the state, including the great monastery of Tawang, was once part of the Monyul

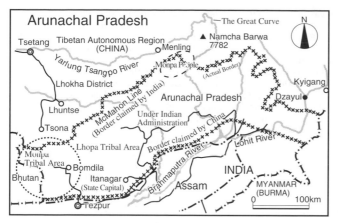

Arunachal Pradesh

Tel: 011-301 7909/ 3844
Calcutta- Roxi Cinema
Hall, Chowringhee Lane.
Tel: 033-286 500
Gawahati (Gauhati),
Assam, R.G.Baruah Rd.
Tel: 0361-62859

Access by Air
There are no commercial
airports in Arunachal
Pradesh but you can fly
into Gawahati (Gauhati),
Tezpur, Jorhat or
Dibrugarh in Assam.

Access by Rail & Bus
The nearest railway station
is in Tezpur. Once you

region. This area was within the Tibetan cultural sphere for hundreds of years but only politically controlled by Lhasa after the 17th Century. The border dispute between India and China has effectively cut-off this contact for the time being. However, the strong Tibetan influence is still evident, especially amongst the minority Monpa people that inhabit many of the border regions.

This remote province is sparsely populated and there are over 20 other distinct indigenous groups that have also made this region their home. The southern part of the province, near the lower reaches of Brahmaputra River (Yarlung Tsangpo in Tibet), is a sub-tropical jungle area. On the other extreme, the altitude of the rugged mountainous region in the north-west facing Tibet is over 3,000m and has the harsh climate that goes with it. The remoteness of the region has meant that the natural habitats of the many endangered species have remained intact, a fact that is now being discovered by more and more travelers every year.

Travel Permits
Up until recently foreigners weren't permitted to enter this highly sensitive area. You are now able to gain access if you have obtained a Restricted Area Permit from either the *Ministry of External Affairs* or the *Ministry of Home Affairs*. Travel agents can usually arrange the travel permits for this region. However, individuals can also apply for a permit at the *Foreigners' Regional Registration Offices (FRRO)* in Delhi, Calcutta, Mumbai, and Madras. Indian government offices abroad can also issue one along with your visa. You are allowed up to 10 days on your permit.

You can check the latest travel information at the *Tourist Office of the State Government of Arunachal Pradesh* at the following places:

Delhi- Kautala Marg, Chanakyapuri.

arrive in Tezpur there are regular buses to take you to Bomdila. You can also reach the area from the railheads at Rangapara, Dibrugarh and Tinsukia, and also in Assam.

Places to See
Tawang Monastery
For those in search of Tibetan culture, the big draw in this province is Tawang Gompa. Located near the Tibetan (Chinese) border, this huge Gelukpa monastery is 350 years old. The formal name of the monastery is *Ganden Namgyal Latse* and it can house up to 500 monks. It has strong ties with Drepung Monastery in Lhasa and was founded by the Mera Lama. Like many of the gompas in Tibet, it stands high on a mountain at over 3,000 meters. The monastery is well-fortified and from its commanding position it dominates the area.

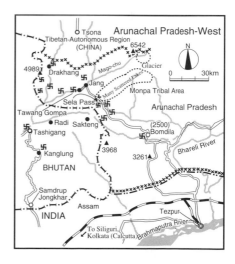

It is said that Buddhism was brought to the Monpa lands and then spread from Tawang after the great Buddhist master Guru Rinpoche visited there in the 8th century. The lamasery is the repository of many precious ancient Buddhist manuscripts and artwork, and is one of the leading centers of Buddhist learning in the world.

The 6th Dalai Lama, a writer of many love poems and son of a Nyingmapa ascetic, and fondly spoken of by Tibetans, was born near Tawang. In 1959, when the present Dalai Lama sought refuge from the Chinese, he made his way to Bomdila and Tezpur via the Tawang Monastery.

The distance between Bomdila and Tawang is about 180km and there are both public and private buses that service the route. There are also taxis available and during the journey you will get good views of the surrounding mountain range. There are some guesthouses in Tawang.

Namdapha National Park

For those in search of the great untouched wilderness of India, this is a must. The park to the north-east of the capital Itanagar, is home to snow leopards and tigers, as well as other endangered species, including the extremely rare 'Hoolock Gibbon.' Between the snow-capped mountains soaring to over 4,000m, and the inaccessible sub-tropical jungle, this park is also home to many of the 500 or so orchids that are found in Arunachal Pradesh. The best time to visit the park is between October and April.

The entrance to the park is located in the small town of Miao. Buses and taxis connect Miao with Dibrugarh and the trip takes around 3 hours. From Tezu it takes 4 hours to cover the 180km. For further information about the park you can contact the *Government of India Tourist Office* in Naharlagun, Tel: 0381-44328/ 44115.

BHUTAN

འབྲུག་ཡུལ།

The Buddhist kingdom of Bhutan, nestled at the eastern end of the Himalayas, is the most difficult part of the Tibetan cultural area in which to travel freely. You can enter the country on pre-arranged tours during which you are required to spend a minimum of US$200 a day. Entering the country as an independent tourist is another option at US$240 a day. Even by following these regulations there are still no guarantees that you'll get inside any of the monasteries in the country. Although many areas in mainland Tibet are officially closed to tourists, in practice there are many loopholes that allow you to move around fairly freely. This is simply not the case with a trip to Bhutan. Unless you have a special connection within the country, your travel plans will be mainly mapped out for you.

This does not mean that the Bhutanese government hates foreigners. Rather than a policy of 'development' and 'internationalization,' it follows one of 'appreciation' of the national culture and traditions. This policy is implemented through measures such as encouraging people to wear the national costumes, etc. For this mountainous kingdom, as small as Switzerland, and dwarfed by its neighbors India and China, it seems to be a wise strategy to protect Bhutan's national identity.

History

The 7th century Tibetan king, Songtsen Gampo, established the Kyerchu Lhakhang in Paro and the Jampa Lhakhang in Bumthang. It is believed that Bhutan became a Buddhist country when the Indian spiritual master Guru Rinpoche (Padmasambhava) visited the area in the 8th century. The various schools of Tibetan Buddhism continued to spread their influence throughout the region until the 17th century when Zhabdrung Ngawang Namgyal (1594-1651), the hierarch of the Drukupa Kagyupa order, fled to the south after losing a factional dispute in Central Tibet. He founded the unified state of 'West Bhutan' and created a theocratic regime that came to rule over the entire area that is present-day Bhutan.

From the date of its foundation until the late 18th century, Bhutan stood up against the Tibet that was ruled by the Dalai Lamas. In 1949, following the period of British 'influence' and 'guidance' that stretched from the 18th to the 20th century, Bhutan agreed to accept Indian advice in its external affairs. This situation changed somewhat in 1971 when the country obtained UN membership.

Bhutan's monarchy is still very young, having replaced religious rule of the country in 1907. The present king is Jigme Senge Wangchuck who

BHUTAN

Formal Name of the Country
Druk Yul
Time Difference
6 hrs ahead of GMT.
International Daialing Code
975
Currency
Ngultrum (Nu)= 100 chetrum. The Ngultrum is at 1:1 with the Indian rupee, which is also legal tender in the country.
Exchange Rates

Australian Dollar	28.50Nu
British Pound	69.10Nu
Canadian Dollar	29.30Nu
Chinese Yuan	5.10Nu
Dutch Guilder	18.80Nu
French Franc	7.00Nu
German Mark	23.40Nu
Hong Kong Dollar	5.50Nu
Indian Rupee	1.00Nu
Japanese Yen (100)	35.30Nu
Nepalese Rupee (100)	62.00Nu
New Zealand Dollar	24.00Nu
Pakistan Rupee (100)	93.00Nu
Singapore Dollar	25.00Nu
Swedish Krona	5.00Nu
Swiss Franc	28.40Nu
US Dollar	42.60Nu

Language
Official languages are Dzongkha (Tibetan origin), Sharchopkha, Kurtey and Nepali. English is also widely spoken throughout the country.
Inhabitants
Tibetan and Nepalese origin. The Bhutia (Bhotia), also known as the 'Drukpa' people, make up around 50 percent of the population. The ethnic Nepalese constitute about 35%, and the remaining 15% is made up of indigenous and migrant tribes. Three-quarters of the people in Bhutan follow Tibetan-style Buddhism while the others practice Indian or Nepalese-influenced Hinduism.
Capital
Thimphu (Population approximately 26,000).
Population
Estimates range from 600,000 up to 2 million.
Land area
Approximately 47,000 sq km.
Climate
Bhutan has 4 seasons and the monsoon brings heavy rain from June to the end of August. Summer temperatures in the lowlands can reach a very humid 30°C.
Even at this time of year it is still comfortable at night and the early mornings are mild. By September there is a perceptible chill in the air and you'll pat yourself on the back for packing that sweater. In the mountainous areas, the winter weather can be harsh and unpredictable, though the air is dry and the skies are usually clear.
Electricity
AC220V, 50Hz
Office Hours
Most offices follow a 09:00 to 17:00 regime, though stores tend to open a little earlier and close between 19:00 and 20:00.
Changing Money
Banks and major hotels will change money between 10:00 and 13:00 on weekdays.
National Holidays
Bhutanese New Year
  (Feb 6, 2000, Feb 24, 2001; varies each year)
June 2 (Coronation Day)
November 11-13
  (Present King's Birthday)
December 17 (National Day)
Religious Festivals
The most important festival in Bhutan is the *Tsechu* held on and around the 10th day of the lunar calendar months. These are celebrations of the events in the life of Guru Rinpoche (Padmasambhava) who brought Buddhism to the area. The regional dzong (fortress monasteries), located at various sites in Bhutan, celebrate this annual festival in different months. The festivals feature *Cham* dancing by the lamas from the dzong, with each dance being symbolic of various aspects of the Guru Rinpoche story.

ascended to the throne in 1972. He has continued many of the reforms that were instituted by his father, Jigme Dorje Wangchuck, who ruled from 1952 until his death. These reforms made the third king very popular amongst the people of Bhutan and the various anniversaries commemorating his life and death are celebrated throughout the land. The first 2 kings were Ugyen Wangchuck (1907-1926), who was elected by the people to the monarchy, and his son Jigme Wangchuck (1926-1952).

Religion still plays a large role in the affairs of state as well as in cultural and spiritual matters. The *Je Khenpo* is the elected head abbot of the Drukpa Kagyupa order and oversees the 6,000-7,000 monks that are officially supported by the state. The Bhutanese call their country *Druk Yul* which originally means 'Country of Drukpa Kagyupa.' The country is also called 'Land of the Thunder Dragon' in English since the original meaning of *Druk* is 'Dragon.'

Bhutanese Festival

The People of Bhutan

The people of Bhutan are proud of their traditions and devout in their religious beliefs. A symbol of this can be found in the fact that the wearing of the national dress is taken very seriously indeed.

The men wear a distinctive, long patterned robe called a *Kho* and the women wear long-patterned dresses called *Kera*. These garments are hitched up at the waist by a belt. When visiting religious sites, at festival time or on other formal occasions, the people break out their best quality clothes and wear traditional accessories such as scarves, sashes and elaborate footwear.

The Bhutia (Bhotia) People

The Bhutia (Bhotia) or Drukpa people are of Tibetan descent and make up around 50 % of the population. This ethnic group is divided into the Ngalop people who mainly inhabit the north and west, and the Sharchop people who are mainly settled in the east of the country. Although these 2 groups are ethnically distinct and speak different languages, the Sharchop have assimilated into much of the Ngalop-Tibetan culture and they share the same Buddhist faith. The Nagalop language *Dzongkha* is now the national language and is taught in the schools across Bhutan.

The Nepalese People

The Nepalese now make up over a third of the population and are mainly Hindus. They are concentrated in the southern areas of the country, their migration to the area having begun in the late 19th century. In recent years, the Bhutanese government has strictly controlled this mass movement of people.

Indigenous People & Minority Migrant Groups

These diverse groups make up around 15% of the population and are strongly connected to the groups that live in Sikkim, Assam and Arunachal Pradesh. These include the Lepcha, Drokpa and Monpa peoples. Most of these groups follow either Tibetan Buddhism, Hinduism or still practice their traditional shamanism.

The Tibetan People

Many Tibetan refugees, fleeing the Chinese invasion and subsequent occupation of Tibet, made their way into Bhutan. Although the government has accepted over 10,000 of them since 1959, they also later expelled to India a large number of refugees who refused to take up Bhutanese citizenship.

Major Festivals in Bhutan

The festival dates in Bhutan can change at short notice. Check with tour operators or tourist information bureaus for any last minute changes.

Spring

Punakha Dromche
   (Punakha, Western Bhutan)
   .... Feb 25-29, 2004 / Feb 13-17, 2005
Chorten Kora Tsechu
   (Tashi Yangtse, Eastern Bhutan)
   .. Mar 6 & 20, 2004 / Feb 23 & Mar 10, 2005
Gom Kora Tsechu
   (Tashi Yangtse, Eastern Bhutan)
   .... Mar 29-31, 2004 / Mar 18-20, 2005
Chukha Tsechu
   (Bumthang, Central Bhutan)
   .... Mar 29-31, 2004 / Mar 18-20, 2005

BHUTAN

377

Paro Tsechu -The biggest in Bhutan
(Paro, Western Bhutan)
.... Apr 1-5, 2004 / Mar 21-25, 2005
Ura Yak-Choey
(Bumthang, Central Bhutan)
.... Apr 30-May 4, 2004 / Apr 19-23, 2005

Summer
Nyimalung Tsechu
(Bumthang, Central Bhutan)
.... Jun 25-27, 2004 / Jun 15-17, 2005
Kurje Lhakhang Tsechu
(Bumthang, Central Bhutan)
.... Jun 27, 2004 / Jun 17, 2005
Thamshing Phala Choeba
(Bumthang, Central Bhutan)
.... Sep 22-24, 2004 / Sep 12-14, 2005

Fall
Thimphu Tsechu
(Thimphu, Central Bhutan)
.... Sep 23-25, 2004 / Sep 13-15, 2005
Wangdue Phodrang Tsechu
(Wangdue Phodrang, Western Bhutan)
.... Sep 21-23, 2004 / Sep 11-13, 2005
Tangbi Mani
(Bumthang, Central Bhutan)
.... Sep 27-29, 2004 / Sep 17-19, 2005
Jambey Lhakhang Drup
(Bumthang, Central Bhutan) ... Oct 28-31,
2004 / Oct 17-21 and/or Nov 15-19, 2005
Prakhar Tsechu
(Bumthang, Central Bhutan) ... Oct 29-31,
2004 / Oct 18-20 and/or Nov 16-18, 2005

Winter
Mongar Tsechu
(Mongar, Eastern Bhutan)
.... Nov 18-21, 2004 / Dec 7-10, 2005
Tashigang Tsechu
(Tashigang, Eastern Bhutan)
.... Nov 19-22, 2004 / Dec 8-11, 2005
Trongsa Tsechu
(Trongsa, Central Bhutan)
.... Dec 20-22, 2004 / Jan 8-10, 2006
Lhuntse Tsechu
(Lhuntse, Eastern Bhutan)
.... Dec 20-22, 2004 / Jan 8-10, 2006

*Early arrangements are recommended for the Paro
Tsechu and the Thimphu *Tsechu* since they are
extremely popular and the limited places on group
tours fill up quickly at these times of year.

Travel Conditions
Basically, the only area open to individual,
independent travelers without a guide is the Indian
border town of Phuntsholing. Those wishing to visit

the rest of the country should pre-arrange their
travels through a travel agent, either one abroad or
one in Bhutan. Generally the procedure is as
follows:
　　1) Draw up an itinerary and pay the national
tourist price (listed below).
　　2) Receive your 'visa clearance' issued by the
Ministry of Foreign Affairs through the travel
agency that is arranging your tour.
　　3) For air travel, you then present the visa
clearance in order to get an air ticket on the
national airline, Druk Air, at the airline agent's
office.
　　4) You must then present the visa clearance
at the Bhutanese border/airport and you will
receive a visa stamp in your passport. A 15-
day visa costs US$20.

These districts (dzongkhag), dzong (monastery
fortresses), lhakhang (Buddhist temples), along
with other places and events, are usually open to
foreign visitors and don't require special clearances.
Foreign Buddhist visitors can at times receive
special dispensations to visit otherwise restricted
areas.

Central Bhutan
Bumthang District - Ura Lhakhang (Ura), Mebar-
Tsho Gorge (Palrithang), Pelling Sermon Chorten
(Palrithang).
Chukha District - Zangdokpelri Lhakhang
(Phuntsholing), Kharbandi Lhakhang
(Phuntsholing), Kamji Lhakhang (Phuntsholing),
Chime Lhakhang (Phuntsholing), Chasilakha
Lhakhang (Phuntsholing), Chapcha Dzong
(Chapcha).
Thimphu District -Tashi Chodzong, November-
May (Thimphu), Changlimithang Lhakhang
(Thimphu), Memorial Chorten (Thimphu),
Jigmeling Lhakhang (Thimphu), Thimphu Tsechu
festival.
Trongsa District - Chendebeji Chorten (Nakarchu),
Trongsa Tsechu festival.

Western Bhutan
Paro District - Ta Dzong Museum (Paro), Taktsang
Monastery (Paro), Drukgyel Dzong (Paro), Bitekha
Dzong (en route to Ha), Paro Tsechu festival.
Punakha District - Punakha Dzong, June-October
(Punakha), Punakha Dromche festival.
Wangdue Phodrang District - Wangdue Choeling
Dzong (Wangdue Phodrang), Phobjikha and
Gangtey to see the Black-Necked Crane (Wangdue
Phodrang), Wangdue Phodrang Tsechu festival.

Eastern Bhutan
Mongar District - Mongar Dzong (Mongar).
Samdrup Jongkhar District - Zangdokpelri

Lhakhang (Samdrup Jongkhar).
Tashigang District - Zangdokpelri Lhakhang (Kanglung), Kanglung Lhakhang (Kanglung) Khaling Lhakhang (Khaling), Radi Lhakhang (Gamri-chu Valley), Tashigang Tsechu festival.
Tashi Yangtse District - Tashi Yangtse Dzong (Tashi Yangtse), Chorten Kora (Kulong-chu Valley).

The tour prices per person for an ordinary sightseeing 'cultural' tour are as follows:

4+ tourist group	US$200 per day
3 tourist group	US$220 per day
2 tourist group	US$230 per day
1 tourist	US$240 per day

All the prices quoted include accommodation, domestic transport, and meals (excluding drinks). Basically, there are only 2 gateways for travelers entering the country. Paro is the entry point if you're travelling by air and Phuntsholing is the entry point for those entering overland. On departure there is sometimes the alternative of going through Samdrup Jongkhar and into the Indian province of Assam.

On Tour Points
* You are permitted to make some changes to your pre-arranged itinerary after your arrival in the country.
* The guides that accompany your tour groups have a good command of English.
* Many of the stores, hotels, and even restaurants, accept American Express credit cards. You can also cash travelers' checks easily at banks and at the foreign currency exchange at the airport.
* If you need to buy negative film while in Bhutan, you can get color Konica film quite easily. If it is slide film you are after, you will need to go to one of the major hotels where they usually have a limited stock. Camera batteries are only available in the capital, Thimphu, so make sure you are carrying a spare when you travel elsewhere in the country.

Travel Agents in Bhutan
There is the option to book your trip through travel agents in Bhutan rather than one in your own country. One well-known example is the *Bhutan Yod Sel Tours & Treks*. PO Box 574, Thimphu, Bhutan. Tel: 975-2-323912, Fax: 975-2-323589. E-mail: dawa@travel.bt http://www.lightlink.com/cpost/. They offer tour quotes and answer e-mail inquiries.

Dealing directly with agents in Bhutan will mean savings on the commissions usually paid to the agents handling the arrangements from outside the country. One drawback is that you'll need to do more legwork and paperwork yourself. For payment, a remittance using *Citibank* is a convenient choice.

Bhutanese Embassies Abroad
These embassies don't handle visa applications directly but can give assistance if required.

Bangladesh
The Royal Bhutanese Embassy
58, Road No3A, Dhanmondi RA, Dhaka.
Tel: 880-2-545 018/ 605 840

India
The Royal Bhutanese Embassy
Chandragupta Marg, Chanakyapuri,
New Delhi, 110021.
Tel: 91-11-609 217/ 688 9230
Fax: 91-11-687 6710

The Royal Bhutanese Consulate
48 Tivoli Court, 1A Ballygunge Circular Rd,
Kolkata (Calcutta).

Switzerland
17-19 Chemin Du Champ D'Anier,
Ch-12209, Geneva.
Tel: 41-22-798 7971-73   Fax: 41-22-788 2593

United States
The Permanent Mission of the Kingdom of Bhutan to the UN
27F, 2 United Nations Plaza, 44th Street,
New York, NY 10017.
Tel: 1-212-826 1919/ 1990   Fax: 1-212-826 2998

Foreign Embassies & Delegations in Bhutan

India
Embassy of India
India House Estate, Thimphu.
Tel: 975-2-32162   Fax: 975-2-33195

Liaison Office of the Embassy of India in Bhutan
Phuntsholing. Tel: 975-5-32635

United Nations
The United Nations Development Programme
United Nations Building, Samden Lam,
PO Box 162, Thimphu.
Tel: 975-2-322 424   Fax: 975-2-322 657
E-mail: fo.btn@undp.org

Tourist Information
Tourist Authority of Bhutan
PO Box 126, Thimphu.
Tel: 975-2-323 251/2   Fax: 975-2-323 695

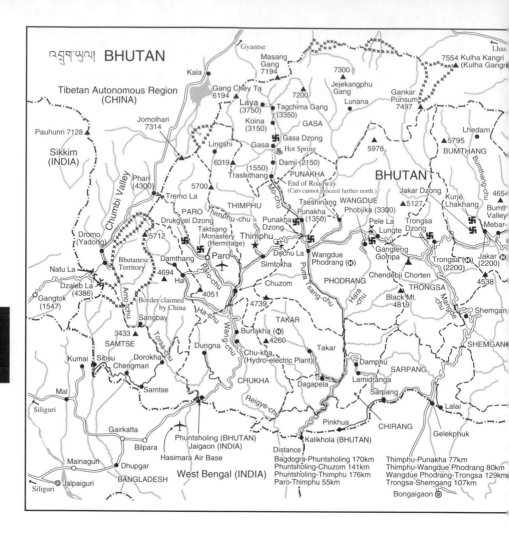

འབྲུག་ཡུལ། **BHUTAN**

Tibetan Autonomous Region
(CHINA)

Sikkim
(INDIA)

Pauhunri 7128 ▲

Kala

Gyantse

Masang
Gang
7194

Gang Chey Ta
6194

Laya
(3750)

Koina
(3150)

Jomolhari
7314

Lingshi

6319 ▲

Phari
(4300)

Tremo La

5700 ▲

PARO
Thimphu-chu

Drukgyel Dzong

Taktsang
Monastery
(Hermitage)

5712

Damthang
4694

Bhutanese
Territory

Ha

4051

4739

Bunakha (☉)

4260

Chu-kha
(Hydro-electric Plant)

Dungna

Dorokha

Chengmari

Samtse

Sangbay

3433 ▲

SAMTSE

Kumai

Sibsu

Chumbi Valley

Natu La

Dzaleb La
(4386)

Gangtok
(1547)

Dromo
(Yadong)

Border claimed
by China

Mal

Siliguri

Gairkatta

Bilpara

Mainaguri

Dhupgar

Jalpaiguri

Siliguri

BANGLADESH

Phuntsholing (BHUTAN)
Jaigaon (INDIA)

Hasimara Air Base

West Bengal (INDIA)

7300

Jejekangphu
Gang

7200

Tagchima Gang
(3350)

GASA

Gasa Dzong

Gasa

Hot Spring

Damji (2150)

(1550)

Trashithang

PUNAKHA
End of Roadway
(Cars cannot proceed further north.)

Tseshinang

Punakha
(1350)

Punakha
Dzong

Thimphu

THIMPHU

Dochu La

Simtokha

Chuzom

Wangdue
Phodrang (☉)

PHODRANG

Takar

TAKAR

Dagapela

Reigye-chu

Pinkhua

Kalikhola (BHUTAN)

Lunana

Gankar
Punsum
7497

5978

WANGDUE

Phobjika (3300)

Pele La

Lungte

Chendebji Chorten

Black Mt.
4819

Damphu

Lamidranga

CHUKHA

Distance
Bagdogra-Phuntsholing 170km
Phuntsholing-Chuzom 141km
Phuntsholing-Thimphu 176km
Paro-Thimphu 55km

Lhas

7554 Kulha Kangri
(Kulha Gangri

Lhedam

▲5795

BUMTHANG

465

Jakar Dzong

Kurje
Lhakhang

Bumth
Valley

Mebar-

▲5127

Trongsa
Dzong

Gangteng
Gompa

Trongsa (☉)
(2200)

TRONGSA

Jakar ☉
(2200)

4538

Shemgan

SHEMGAN

SARPANG

Sarpang

Lalai

CHIRANG

Gelekphuk

Thimphu-Punakha 77km
Thimphu-Wangdue Phodrang 80km
Wangdue Phodrang-Trongsa 129km
Trongsa-Shemgang 107km

Bongaigaon ☉

BHUTAN

Bhutan Tourism Corporation Ltd
PO Box 159, Thimphu.
Tel: 975-2-324 045/ 324 647   Fax: 975-2-323 392

Package Tours from Kathmandu
Travel agents in Kathmandu can arrange package tours to Bhutan all year round and even accept single tourists. A 4-night and 5-day tour by air costs around US$1,700.

Access by Air
The relatively new airport at Paro has flights coming in from Kolkata (Calcutta), Dhaka, Kathmandu, Delhi, Yangoon and Bangkok on the national airline, Druk Air.

	One Way	Return
Kolkata [Calcutta]		
(Eastern India)	US$165	US$330
Dhaka (Bangladesh)	US$175	N/A
Kathmandu (Nepal)	US$175	US$350
Delhi (Central India)	US$286	US$572
Yangoon (Myanmar)	US$286	N/A
Bangkok (Thailand)	US$340	US$680

There are flights a couple of days a week to each of these destinations and the scheduled times and flight availability vary according to the season. For the latest schedules you can contact the Druk Air offices at: *Druk Air Corporation Ltd.* PO Box 209, Thimphu. Tel: 975-2-322 215/ 322 825/ 323 420,

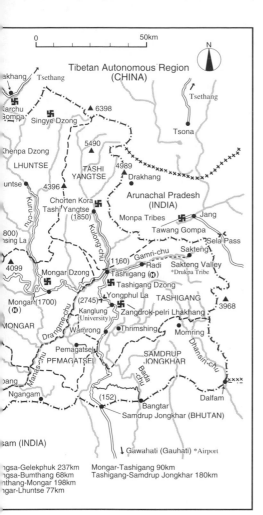

Pele La

agent but the actual document you will be issued is a 'visa clearance.' The visa itself will be affixed to your passport at the airport for an additional fee of US$20. Another additional charge is the airport tax collected on departure US$10 (or 420Nu). The guide and driver that pick you up at the airport will accompany you throughout your stay in Bhutan.

Access by Bus

For those entering Bhutan overland, the 'Free Zone' of Phuntsholing, 6-8 hours south of Thimphu, will be your entry point. The West Bengal town of Siliguri is the place to get bus connections for Bhutan. There are buses to Siliguri from Kolkata (Calcutta), Delhi and Kathmandu.

At Siliguri, you'll need to cross the bridge from the Tenzing Norgay Bus Station on the opposite side to the Sikkim Nationalized Transport building. Then at the junction near the Air View Hotel take the right-hand fork and you'll see the Bhutan bus stand. Buses to Phuntsholing take 3 hours and cost 41Rs. You will need to buy your ticket on the 2nd floor of the bus stand building.

On crossing into Phuntsholing, the Bhutanese border officials will board the bus to check that passengers have the correct documents and identification. Be sure to have your passport ready as passengers that are not carrying correct documents may be requested to get off the bus at this point.

What are Dzongs?

Dzongs are buildings that function as both monasteries and fortresses. Traditionally, they have been the centers of both politics and religion and are host to many of the *Tsechu* festivals. Visiting the dzongs across Bhutan is one of the highlights of any trip to the country. Unfortunately, foreign tourists are not allowed to go inside many of the buildings and have to satisfy themselves with just viewing their impressive exteriors.

Trekking

The trekking season in Bhutan is shorter than the one in Nepal. March through to May, and again

or check their homepage http://www.drukair.com/ The airline uses 2 British Aerospace e-146-100 aircraft, each of which can carry 62 economy passengers and 10 in executive class.

By taking the flights from Dhaka and Kolkata (Calcutta) to Paro, part of your in-flight entertainment will be catching the stunning views of 2 of the 3 highest peaks in the world. Mt. Kangchenjunga near the Sikkim-Nepal border and Mt. Everest (*Jomolangma* to the Tibetans and *Sagarmatha* to the Nepalese) straddles the Nepal-Tibet border and appears out of the left-hand side windows. On the return journey you'll be able to catch sight of Mt. Jomolhari on the right-hand side.

You'll need to arrange a visa through a travel

381

from October until November, are the best times to trek. There are various courses available ranging from short 1-day excursions to arduous expeditions lasting 20 days or more. Most of the travel agencies that arrange trips to Bhutan can arrange these treks. The rates include a guide, a cook, and a baggage horse or yak for your belongings. If you decide that you would like to do some trekking once you arrive in Bhutan, the routes mentioned below are easily accessible from either Thimphu or Paro.

Jomolhari Trekking
Paro-Lingshi (4,150m)-Thimphu (6 days/ 7 nights)
This trek starts in the Paro-chu Valley and ascends to over 4,000m as you approach Mt. Jomolhari (7,314m) on the Tibetan border. At this elevation you get stunning views of the mountain, as well as the rest of the peaks straddling the border. The trail then takes you towards Lingshi in the Mo-chu Valley and the start of the second leg of the journey onto Thimphu. From here, the start of the Thimphu-chu Valley is only one more high pass away. Once you reach the valley, the trail crosses the river at intervals as you descend and follows the river's snaking path down towards the capital.

The period from April through to May, and again in October, is the best time to tackle this one. Even at these times of year, the nighttime temperatures tend to be low and the weather can be unpredictable. Some of the passes that this course takes you through are well over 4,000 meters and you should be careful to acclimatize yourself so as to avoid mountain sickness. If you have only a limited amount of time in which to get used to the altitude beforehand, you should think of factoring in 1-2 days extra for the trek itself. This will allow you to take it easy on the first half of the route.

Phajoding Trekking
Thimphu-Phajoding Monastery-Paro
(3 days/4 nights)
You can tackle this one in either direction and it will give you some great views of both the Do-chu Valley and the town of Thimphu. This course is ideal for visitors with only a short time in the country and while it is not too arduous for an experienced trekker, there is a high pass (3,900m) along the route. The best time to try this route is between April and May.

Food
In general, the Bhutanese love to use a large amount of chilies and pepper in their cooking. One very common native dish is *Ema-datse*, which is a bowl of hot chilies covered in melted cheese. A less-explosive version of this is *Kewa-datse*, which replaces the chilies with potatoes.

Although the meat or *Sha* is not of the highest quality in Bhutan, it is still featured in many of the more popular dishes in the country. *Phak-sha* (pork) and *No-sha* (beef) are commonly stewed with vegetables and served with rice or occasionally noodles. Many Bhutanese meals contain rice and the region's specialty is a red rice that is unique to the country. Another eating habit that is unique to the Bhutanese is the taking of *Sippu* (dried rice) mixed with *Su-ja* (butter tea). If you can't stomach too much hot and spicy food, or simply need a break, there are other non-thermal alternatives. *Momo* (Tibetan-style dumplings), *Tukpa* (Tibetan-style noodle soup) and *Chowmein* (Chinese-style fried noodles) are widely available. You can also usually pick up various Nepalese and Indian dishes.

At an average restaurant, dishes cost between 25 and 40Nu and beer will cost you from 40 to 60Nu. The restaurants usually have a stock of 'Black Label,' which is one of the better Indian exported beers. If you want to sample something a little stronger, Bhutan produces a wide range of whiskies. The 'Special Courier' brand is good, though a little expensive at 160Nu. The prices quoted here tend to double or even triple when you drink in the hotels near the airport in Paro. If you are feeling adventurous, you can sample some of the locally produced *Chang*, which is brewed from barley. This stuff is strong and the quality varies from area to area, so be careful.

For the non-drinker, there are a number of soft drinks available, most of which have been imported from India. A bottle of mineral water will cost you around 15Nu. You can also treat yourself to a *Chai* (sweet milk tea) almost anywhere in the country for around 5Nu.

Dzongkha (National Language)
Dzongkha is basically old Tibetan and similar to the dialect spoken in eastern Tibet. The written language employs the Tibetan script.

Hello	kuso zangpo la
See you again	roku jege
Goodbye	legzembe joey
Yes	yoey
No	mey
Thank you	kadrinchey
What's your name?	choe ming gache mo?
My name is	nighi ming ....ying
How much?	gadechi mo?
What is this?	di gachi mo?
This is	di......ying

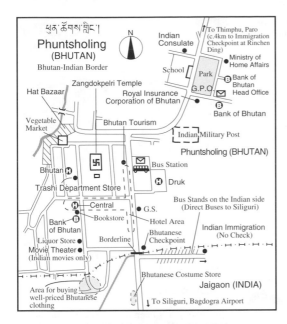

Phuntsholing
(BHUTAN)
Bhutan-Indian Border

immigration checkpoint is 4km from the town. It takes about an hour to get there and 40 minutes for the return journey. On the way you are treated to a good view of the town. At the immigration official's discretion, the *Ministry of Foreign Affairs* will issue you a 5-10 day visa for US$20. The formula applied to your application can vary, though. My visa was processed at the office using: US$200 x No. of Days + US$20. The advantage of going to the government office is that they will issue you the visa the same day. The *Bhutan Tourism Office* in the same town normally takes 5 days to complete the same procedure.

Buses Departing from Phuntsholing

*Thimphu (Local)—Daily departures: 07:30, 08:30, and 09:30 (8.5-hour ride) Cost: 53Nu.
*Thimphu (Mini Deluxe)—Daily departures: 10:00, 12:00, and 13:00 (6-hour ride) Cost: 80Nu.
*Paro (Mon, Wed, Sat)—Departure: 09:00 (10-hour ride).
*Siliguri—Daily departures: 07:00, 08:00 (3-hour ride), and 15:00 (3.5-hour ride).
*Kolkata (Calcutta)—Daily departure: 15:00 (17-hour ride); 200Rs (Indian bus), 250Rs (Bhutanese bus).

There are also buses to other destinations: Punakha (the old winter capital), Ha (to the west of Paro), Bunakha (between Phuntsholing and Thimphu) and the border towns of Sarpang, Gelekphuk and Samdrup Jongkhar (all to the east of Phuntsholing).

Accommodation

There is no shortage of cheap accommodation in Phuntsholing. These are concentrated right in the center of the town. The *Bhutan Hotel* near the Zangdokpelri Lhakhang has single rooms for 120Nu. The *Hotel Bongopa* has singles available for 60Nu. Just behind the bus station is the *Hotel*

PHUNTSHOLING (THE "FREE ZONE")

This is the only place in Bhutan that is open to independent travelers and it is easily accessible overland from India. The Bhutan-India border town of Phuntsholing is called a 'Free Zone' and tourists are allowed to enter the town without a visa. The actual border between Bhutan and India runs through the center of the town and the Indian part is called Jaigaon. Phuntsholing is the only option for those wishing to get a taste of a Bhutanese town without signing up for a costly package tour.

The atmosphere of Phuntsholing is one of a Bhutanese town heavily influenced by contact with India. However, unlike Indian towns, the streets are empty of stalls and hawkers selling their wares.

Although the town is full of Indian people and products, you are also reminded that you are in Bhutan when you see many of the men wearing *Kho* (the Bhutanese men's national dress). One thing that often catches people out is the time difference in the town. The whole of the free zone is on Bhutanese time, which is 30 minutes ahead of Indian time. Bear this in mind when you're making travel plans that depend on bus or train connections when you return to India.

Organizing a Visa

Those travelling into other areas of Bhutan will need to arrange a visa. The Rinchen Ding

Phuntsholing

Druk, Tel: 975-5-426/8, where a single room costs 850Nu and the hotel has a store selling postcards (12Nu) and small gifts.

Places to See
Zangdokpelri Lhakhang
The lhakhang is a new 3-story building in town, a few minutes from the bus station. The Buddhist master Guru Rinpoche (Padmasambhava) is featured on the 1st floor. The compassionate Avalokiteshvaraon, of whom the Dalai Lama is the incarnation, is on the 2nd floor, and the Amitabha Buddha is on the third. Unlike other temples in Bhutan, this one is relatively easy to visit and will give you a taste of the country.

There are other lhakhang and dzong outside of Phuntsholing on the road to Chuzom, including Kharbandi and Kamji Lhakhangs and Chapcha Dzong, though to visit these you must enter the country fully.

Paro Dzong

allows you to savor the fine morning views as you eat your breakfast.

The *Sonam Thopel Food & Lodge* is run by a very friendly landlady who has a good command of English. The rooms at the lodge are both bright and clean, though the restrooms leave some room for improvement.

Places to See
Paro Dzong
This dzong has been the fortress of Zhabdrung Ngawang Namgyal (1594-1651) and his descendants since the 17th century. A fire in 1905 gutted the dzong but Guru Rinpoche's *Tongdrol Thangka*, an intricately painted scroll depicting religious events in his life, thankfully survived the blaze.

The dzong hosts the largest *Tsechu* festival in the country, which is held in either March or April each year. On the last day of the festivities, the famous *thangka* is unveiled to the public. This dzong has another more unorthodox claim to fame. The buildings were used as the backdrop for Bernardo Bertolucci's 1994 film, 'The Little Buddha.'

Dungtse Lhakhang
This temple is found on the way to the National Museum from Paro. The lhakhang was constructed by Thangtong Gyalpo in 1421. Thangtong Gyalpo (1385-1464) was the founder of traditional Tibetan opera, *Ache Lhamo*, and the builder of 108 bridges throughout the Tibetan world.

Ta Dzong (National Museum)
Above the dzong is the old watchtower called 'Ta Dzong.' This 4-story building now exhibits *thangkas* and other works of religious art. There are also general everyday objects on show here, along with farming implements, stamps, jewelry, etc.

Photography is not permitted inside the building and the museum is closed on Mondays.

WESTERN BHUTAN

PARO

Paro is the gateway for those entering Bhutan by air on most package tours. The actual village of Paro, down in the valley, is quite small with perhaps a score of stores, a bank and some hotels, all surrounded by fields. There are a number of hotels for foreign tourists scattered on the outskirts of the village.

Access By Bus
From Paro to Thimphu, there are 3-4 buses a day that take you out to the capital and the trip takes about 2 hours.
From Paro to the Phuntsholing 'Free Zone,' there are 3 buses a week.

Accommodation
Hotel Olathang is built on a hilltop about 3km out of town. This hotel is commonly used by many of the package tour operators and is definitely a top-range establishment.
The *Gantey Palace* is a cheaper hotel built by the hillside at the western end of the village. The rooms each have a bath and a hot shower but the small electric heaters provided are insufficient for the chilly nights.
The *Hotel Druk* is a fairly new hotel that is designed to look like a dzong. It is located on the slope above the village and commands a good view of the valley below. The facilities are good and the restaurant

Kyerchu Lhakhang

A 20-minute ride from Paro, this temple, along with Jampa Lhakhang in Bumthang, is one of the 108 geomantic lhakhang that radiate out from Lhasa in Tibet and which were built by the Tibetan king Songtsen Gampo in the 7th century. These temples were intended to subdue the great ogress that straddled the Tibetan lands and they form 3 distinct groups: the *Runon* (Inner-sanctuary Temples); the *Tandul* (Border-taming Temples); and the *Yangdul* (Further-taming Temples).

Kyerchu was constructed to act as one of the 4 further-taming *Yangdul*. This lhakang is meant to pin down the left foot of the evil monster and so help maintain the peace and harmony in the land.

The temple now belongs to the Drukpa Kagyupa order. In 1968, a new building housing deities from the Nyingmapa order was donated by the Queen Mother of Bhutan.

Taktsang Monastery

Farther above the Paro Valley, this monastery stands on the face of a cliff. The spectacle of it clinging to the rocks makes it one of the most striking temples or dzongs in the country. *Taktsang* means 'Tiger's Lair' and legend has it that in the 8th century, Dorje Drolod, the incarnation of Guru Rinpoche, flew there on a tiger's back and wiped out the demons that were fighting against Buddhism. Later, many other notable Buddhist figures from Tibet, such as Milarepa, Phadampa Sangye, Machik Labdron, and Thangtong Gyalpo, came to Taktsang to lead an ascetic life. Taktsang Monastery is one of the greatest power centers in the Tibetan world. In April 1998, parts of the monastery were razed by fire but luckily the sacred cave where Guru Rinpoche meditated was unscathed.

To reach the monastery, it's a 30-minute ride

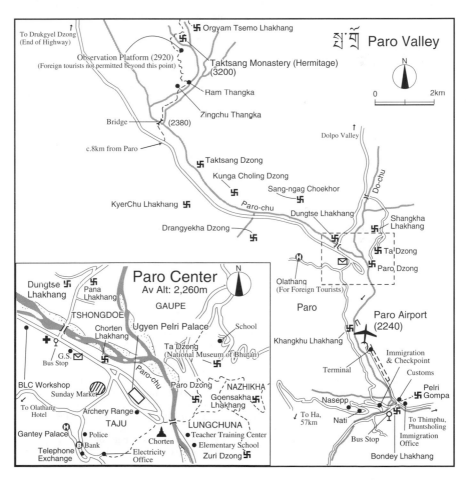

from Paro until you reach the end of the sealed road. Then it will take you between an hour-and-a-half and 2 hours to reach the teahouse near the top of the mountain. From the teahouse, it's another 30 minutes up to the observation platform. After you've taken in the view it will take you another half-hour up the path to finally get to the temple.

The basic rule is that foreigners are not allowed to enter the buildings. However, those with a profound understanding of Buddhism may gain admittance.

Drukgyel Dzong

This dzong is 18km north-west of Paro. The dzong was built by Zhabdrung Ngawang Namgyal in 1644. After fleeing from Tibet and founding the Bhutanese Kingdom, Namgyal and his army routed both the Tibetan and the Mongolian armies and in commemoration, a dzong was constructed and given the name of *Drukgyel* (The Victorious Drukpas). In 1951, the buildings were scorched by fire and then in 1985, a shingled roof was put up to protect the remains of the original buildings from further damage. You can enjoy a great view of Mt. Jomolhari from here.

THIMPHU

The small town of Thimphu, with a population of around 26,000, is the capital of Bhutan. Although a town of this size would probably not be classed as a small regional center in most developed countries, the white office buildings scattered throughout Thimphu give it the look of a city, especially after you have visited either Paro or Punakha (the old winter capital). There is no old town center to speak of, but there are many bars, discos, etc. scattered throughout the town.

Most of the goods on sale in Bhutan are imports from India and the price of these commodities tend to be higher than you'll find across the border, except that is, for liquor. The main street in Thimphu is Nordzin Lam, which stretches the length of town.

Accommodation

The *Hotel Druk* is a high-class hotel that has been around for years. Rooms start at around 1,500Nu a night. Although some of the rooms still have old-style facilities, the rooms are all well-heated. The hotel is well-located, facing the square in the center of town.

The *Hotel Jomolhari* is next to the Hotel Druk and is also one that was established many years ago. The interior has been renovated recently and a single room will cost you around 1,000Nu a night.

Movie Theater, Thimphu

The *Moti-thang Hotel* is located in a less convenient spot, far from the city center. The hotel is run by the Bhutan Tourist Corporation Ltd. and the room rates here are also in the 1,000Nu range.

The *Norling Hotel* is in the heart of town and the hotel has a restaurant that serves good Indian food. They have single rooms for 100Nu a night while the doubles are 150Nu.

Restaurants

Lanam's Restaurant - The friendly staff at this restaurant will serve you excellent *momos* (Tibetan-style dumplings) and *tukpa* (Tibetan-style noodle soup). Pork *momos* cost 15Nu, *tukpa* costs 20Nu and you can also buy Bumthang apple juice for 16Nu.

Hasty Tasty - Very few restaurants in Bhutan can touch the well-decorated interior of this place. The well-dressed staff and the music all add up to a great atmosphere. The restaurant closes at 20:00 and if you want to indulge yourself with an espresso be sure to get in early as the supply is limited. A good dish of *tukpa* costs from 15Nu-25Nu.

Centrepoint Restaurant - This eatery, which opened in January 1997, is on the 2nd floor of the Centrepoint shopping mall. The restaurant is in the white building to the left of the movie theater. Be careful when you're looking for the entrance to the mall as it isn't too obvious. From the window, the restaurant has a fine view of Zangdokpelri Lhakhang and the River View Hotel across the river. The restaurant is a good place to sample local food and the atmosphere and staff are friendly. A serving of *phak-sha* (pork) costs 25Nu, *jya-sha* (chicken) is 35Nu and pork *tukpa* is 17Nu. The portions of *ema-datse* (chillies with melted cheese) and *kewa-datse* (potatoes with melted cheese) are both 25Nu. You can get Japanese cuisine here including breaded pork cutlets for 40Nu, bowls of rice with fried pork cutlets on top that are 45Nu, and Japanese-style croquettes which cost 40Nu. There is also a good selection of Chinese dishes on the menu. For a great dessert you can try the Centrepoint special donuts for 25Nu.

Swiss Bakery - Serves great bread. A sandwich will

cost you about 25Nu which is not cheap, but it's well worth it. Fresh bread is served each day around 9 in the morning and there is a microwave if you want to warm your purchase at other times of day. *Hotel Gahsel* - On the opposite side to the parking lot on Nordzin Lam, this vegetarian restaurant with a friendly Tibetan hostess attracts both Indian and Nepali customers and the restaurant also has a bar. The entrance to the building is behind the shopping complex.

Dekeling Restaurant - This restaurant has a good atmosphere but the price of the food is a little high. The spicy *phak-sha* has good meat and plenty of vegetables for 39Nu a plate. A nice touch is the English-language Indian newspapers at the counter that you can read for free while you eat your food. The entrance to this place is also a bit difficult to find. Other dishes here include *ema-datse* and *kewa-datse* for 35Nu, chicken *tukpa* for 28Nu, pork *tukpa* for 22Nu and 2 types of rice. The white rice costs 10Nu and the red rice is 15Nu.

The Dekeling is open from 10:00 until 22:00 and it is closed on Sundays.

Plum Café - This cafe is the place to hang out if you're into desserts. It is on the 2nd floor of the building opposite the Taktsang Hotel. The Black Forest gateau is 15Nu, a slice of chocolate cake is 10Nu and eclairs are 10Nu each.

Bookstores

Pekhang- Next to the movie theater, this bookstore is an old-timer with a stationery section.

DBS Book Store- This bookstore has the largest collection of books in Thimphu. It also has public telephones, rental videos, and a stationery section. At the back of the store, on the right-hand side, there is a whole section of books about Bhutan. There are plenty of English and Hindi dictionaries on sale, as well as English-language newspapers from India, which are delivered a couple of days after their publication dates. The newspaper

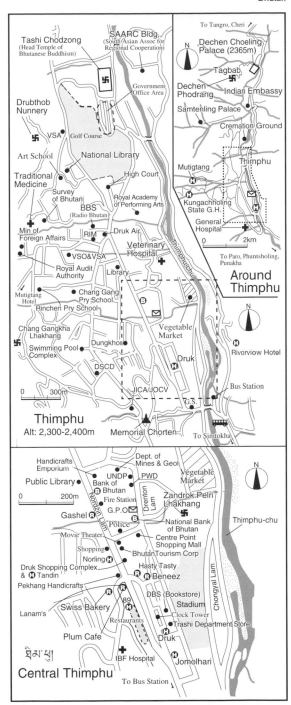

Around Thimphu

Thimphu
Alt: 2,300-2,400m

Central Thimphu

BHUTAN

Shopping in Thimphu

Mito Masayoshi

In Thimphu, the number of folk handicraft stores has increased substantially in recent years. This trend is a convenient one for tourists lacking the time to travel around the country. One drawback is that you have to pay for the convenience as the prices are certainly higher in the capital than they are in the provinces.

There are 2 major souvenir-shopping areas in Thimphu: one is around the movie theater and the other is around the clock tower. Many of these stores are closed on Tuesdays.

Handicrafts Emporium

This is the largest store for buying handicrafts in Thimphu and is run by the government. The store has a good selection of wares but it is worth shopping around. You'll find the store about a 5-minute walk from the town center, traveling north on the Nordzin Lam. It's not far after you pass the Bank of Bhutan on your right.

Druk Trin Rural Handicraft Centre

Second only to the Handicrafts Emporium, this is the largest privately owned souvenir store in Thimphu. It is a bit difficult to find, though. You'll need to take the road to the clock tower at the junction where the Plum Café is. You will see the signboard for the store at the next junction but this is not it. From there you have to take the road to the taxi stand and find the Sakten Health Club on the left, just before the Changlingmithang National Stadium. The store is on the 3rd floor of the club.

The prices tend to be high but the quality of the products is good, especially the brocade from Lhuntse, the *Kira* (traditional women's dress) from Kaling, and the *Yatra* cloth from Bumthang.

There is also a mini-museum exhibiting the owner's private collection. You can watch demonstrations of dyeing, (you'll need to reserve a place) and weaving at the center. All the major travelers' checks are acceptable but unfortunately only AMEX credit cards can be used here. Shipping services with DHL are available.

There is also a branch of the center at the Hotel Druk, but the selection and quality is far better at the original center.

Kelzang Kurtoe Handicrafts

On Nordzing Lam, the store is next to the Druk shopping complex.

Anonymous

There is a souvenir store without a nameplate, 2 doors down from Kelzang Kurtoe Handicrafts.

Norling Handicraft

This store is on the 1st floor of the Norling shopping mall, opposite the Druk shopping complex. A large part of the selection here is made up of accessories.

Anonymous

Another store without a nameplate is located next to a drug store on the same side of the road as the Norling Hotel. This souvenir store seems to specialize in antiques.

Druk Handicraft

This store is at Booth A8 in the Druk shopping complex, next to the movie theater. When you enter the complex through the entrance facing Nordzin Lam, take a right and you'll soon find it. Besides fabrics such as *Kira*, the store also stocks a wide selection of handicrafts. If you are in the market for national costumes, there is a store just after the entrance that has a good variety.

Gyalzang Handicraft

Right next to Etho Metho Handicrafts, this store is in Booth D19 on the 1st floor of the Druk shopping complex. It is a relatively new store, having opened in late 1997. You can pick up bookmarks for 35Nu, wallets for 150-280Nu, soft pencil boxes for 95Nu and hard pencil boxes for 35Nu.

Etho Metho Handicrafts

Located between the Druk shopping complex and the movie theater, this store doesn't have a great variety of goods but it does have books about Bhutan.

CIU Handicrafts Bhutan

This store is near the taxi stand on Chang Lam. The interior of the store is spacious and there is a room where you can watch both *Yatra* and *Kira* being woven on weekdays.

The Art Shop Gallery

This small handicraft store is next to a restaurant at the end of the clock tower plaza.

Bhutan Arts & Crafts Center

This store is next to the Swiss Bakery.

BHUTAN

prices start at 2Nu and those on the right-hand side at the entrance are for subscribers only.

National Library Bookstore- This has a basic collection of *sutras* and other Buddhist writings.

Places to See
Tashi Chodzong
This palace is the center of the Bhutanese government. The government is headed by King Jigme Senge Wangchuck, who ascended to the throne in 1972. The palace also acts as the summer residence of the top religious authority in the country, Je Khenpo.

While Je Khenpo and his monks are away at Dechen Phodrang Dzong in Punakha from November to May, tourists are allowed to enter the courtyard after 17:00 each day, though they are not usually permitted to enter the buildings. Tashi Chodzong is also the place for watching the Thimphu *Tsechu* celebrations in the fall.

Drubthob Nunnery
Drubthob is the popular name for Thangtong Gyalpo, the famous bridge-builder of Tibetan history. A later incarnation of Thangtong Gyalpo built the nunnery in the 15th century and hence the title. There is also a nunnery in Lhasa that shares the same name.

Changangkha Lhakhang
Built on the side of a hill, this building may remind you of the Potala Palace in Lhasa. It is said to have been built in the 15th century and to be one of the oldest temples in Thimphu.

Dechen Choeling
Four kilometers north of Tashi Chodzong, this royal palace is the home of the King's mother.

Dechen Phodrang
This phodrang (or palace) is in the suburbs of Thimphu, north of Drubthob Nunnery. This was Thimphu's dzong until 1772. It now functions as a monastery and religious training center for young monks.

Pangri Zampa
This temple is to the north of Dechen Choeling. After his defeat in the factional fighting that ravaged Central Tibet, Zhabdrung Ngawang Namgyal (1594-1651) fled Tibet in 1616 and went on to become the founding father of Bhutan. On first arriving in the country he took up residence at Pangri Zampa.

Memorial Chorten
This eye-catching 3-story chorten or stupa was built by the present king's mother in 1974 to

Changangkha Lhakhang

commemorate her husband, King Jigme Dorje Wangchuk III, who died 2 years earlier. The monument contains religious *mandalas* and statues that can be viewed by visitors.

Tangro & Cheri
Both of these temples are on the top of a mountain some 20km north of Dechen Choeling. Tangro was constructed in the 13th century and Cheri in the 17th century. *Tangro* means 'Horse's Head' and the temple hugs the side of the rock face, looking just like the head of a horse.

Vegetable Market (Sabji Market)
The market is open on the weekends and the produce on sale is mainly vegetables. You can also buy cheese, *tang* tea (tea leaves for butter tea), animal skins, prayer wheels and other assorted souvenirs.

National Library
This library, at the northern end of Nordzin Lam, is primarily used for housing a collection of valuable Buddhist *sutras* and other religious writings.

National School for Buddhist Arts
Near the library you can visit this art school where students learn how to make *thangka* and traditional masks, as well as how to play traditional Bhutanese instruments. The school allows enrollment of students from elementary school age onwards and sells the *mandalas* made by them at very reasonable prices. These start at around US$20 each.

Hospital of Traditional Medicine
The Himalayan range of mountains is a real treasure trove of medicinal herbs and the traditional methods of treatment have continued to flourish in Bhutan. In addition to treating patients, the hospital also exhibits a wide variety of herbs and basic drugs.

Post Office
One of Bhutan's sources of earning foreign exchange comes from selling beautiful and bizarre

BHUTAN

postage stamps. You can buy selections of these at the post office and they make good souvenirs. Stamps designed by the Japanese designer, Kohei Sugiura, are also available here.

Mutigtang Zoo
This zoo is on the slope of a mountain to the west of town. This is one of the places that you'll be able to see the curious *Takin* (Budorcas taxicolor), the national animal of Bhutan. These animals appear to be a mixture of cow, horse, and sheep and their normal habitat is in the highlands above 4,000m. They are only found in Bhutan and parts of the Tibetan Plateau now in the Sichuan Province of China. These strange looking animals are not easily domesticated and will often attack people.

Simtokha Dzong
Six kilometers south of Thimphu, this is the oldest dzong in Bhutan and was built in 1629 by Zhabdrung Ngawang Namgyal. The dzong has become a training school for Bhutanese (*Dzongkha*) language teachers. If the dzong seems familiar to you, this is because it appears on the back of the 1Nu bank notes. The road from here to Punakha and Wangdue Phodrang takes you up through the breathtaking Do-chu La pass (3,000m).

PUNAKHA

The present capital of Bhutan is Thimphu but up until about 40 years ago, Thimphu was only the summer capital while the winter capital was in Punakha, 70km east of Thimphu. This all changed when the King Jigme Dorje Wangchuk III made the decision to settle in Thimphu in 1955.

The actual village of Punakha is so small that it's quite easy to count the number of houses that make up the village. After crossing the Do-chu La pass, it is about a 2-hour journey to the village. Punakha is a small village, but it gets very crowded during the *Tsechu* festival in the spring (February-

Cham (Mask Dance)

March). Accommodation at this time of year is understandably scarce.

Accommodation
The *Hotel Zangdok Pelri* is up in the mountains, quite far from the actual village, and there is little of interest surrounding the hotel. Even though the cottage-style hotel is high above the village, the Punakha area's low altitude still allows you to take a late-night shower without getting frozen.

Places to See
Punakha Dzong (Dechen Phodrang Dzong).
It stands at the confluence of the Pho-chu (Man's River) and the Mo-chu (Woman's River) and is a beautiful sight. This is another monastery-fortress constructed by Zhabdrung Ngawang Namgyal, the unifier of Bhutan, and was established in 1637. Within the complex is the temple where his mummified body is held in state.

Punakha Dzong was where the government sat during the winter months until Thimphu became the sole capital. Now only the monks move from Punakha to Thimphu in the summer months. Tourists are not allowed to visit the dzong from October to April because the monks, including Je Khenpo, the Head Monastic Leader of Bhutan, are in residence.

Wangdue Phodrang Dzong
After a 30-minute ride from Punakha along the river, you'll reach Wangdue Phodrang Dzong. This fortress is atop a rocky cliff and was also built by Zhabdrung Ngawang Namgyal in the 17th century. This one was constructed in response to a divine revelation of the protector deity Mahakala (Gonpo). It used to function as the guard post on the border between western and central Bhutan.

The extended village of Wangdue Phodrang has a few stores and is a good place to buy the carved stone and bamboo work that the area is well-known for. The village celebrates its *Tsechu* festival between September and October every year.

Punakha Dzong

CENTRAL BHUTAN

TRONGSA

Trongsa (2,200m) is in the center of Bhutan and is home to the present king's family. The town is dominated by the Trongsa Dzong, which controlled the former main route through the Pele La pass connecting eastern and western Bhutan. This impressive dzong is visible for a long time as you approach the town along the looping road from the pass. It is no exaggeration to say that Trongsa was the virtual capital of Bhutan during the 19th century because the dzong exerted a huge influence over central and eastern Bhutan due to its strategic importance. The Trongsa *Tsechu* festival is celebrated between November and December. The dzong is 209km east of Thimphu and the trip takes 7-8 hours by bus.

Accommodation
The *Yangkyil Hotel* rooms have a view of the dzong and the food served is good. Beds start at 35Nu with shared amenities for the guests.

Places to See
Trongsa Dzong
Once the site of a temple dating from the 16th century, Trongsa Dzong is the largest and arguably the most impressive dzong in Bhutan and was also established by Zhabdrung Ngawang Namgyal in the 17th century. Gradually expanded over the years, it now has a total of 23 temples. Although tourists are unable to enter the actual fortress, you can get an excellent view of it from the watchtower (known as a *Ta Dzong*) behind it. During the summer, the monks of the dzong move to Kurje Lhakhang in the Bumthang Valley.

Chendebji Chorten
This religious site, at 2,830m, lies halfway along

Trongsa Dzong

Chendebji Chorten

the winding mountain road between Trongsa and the Pele La pass, which cuts through the Black Mountains. Not far from the road are 2 stupas: a Nepalese-style chorten built in the 18th century and a Bhutanese one added in 1982. They stand near a long *mani* wall; the older one was built to commemorate the defeat of a demon on this spot.

Gangteng Gompa
In the Phobjika Valley, to the west of Pele La, this gompa is the only Nyingmapa monastery to the west of the Black Mountains. Pema Trinley, a grandson of the great *sutra*-finder, Pema Lingpa (1450-1521), founded it in 1613. The valley is where the northern Black-Necked Cranes migrate to escape the harsh winters there. This area is open to tourists during the migration season.

THE BUMTHANG VALLEYS

Travelling nearly 70km east from Trongsa, you will reach the Bumthang Valleys. The 2 hour 30 minute bus ride takes you out of the mountains into an area of relatively flat, spacious, and gently sculpted panoramas, unlike anywhere else in Bhutan. Bumthang is the name given to the area consisting of 4 fertile valleys: the Chokhor (Jakar), Tang, Ura, and Chu-Me. The altitude in the district ranges from 2,600m to 4,000m. The Chokhor and the Chu-Me Valleys are both used for growing crops, while the people of the Tang and Ura Valleys mainly tend to livestock on their land.

In the 8th century, Buddhism was introduced to the Bumthang region by Guru Rinpoche and from the 14th to the 15th centuries 3 Nyingmapa lamas, Longchen Rabjampa, Dorje Lingpa, and Pema Lingpa, played active and important roles throughout the region. The dominance of the Nyingmapa order in this area is another factor that sets this area apart from the rest of Bhutan, where the teachings of the Drukpa Kagyupa order are the most influential.

BHUTAN

The Bumthang area is famous for its archery, which is the national sport of Bhutan. Contests are held regularly and often coincide with the many festivals held in the region. The Ura *Yak-Choey* festival is held between April and May and this is followed by the Nyimaling festival in June or July. There are also a number of other festivals that are open to tourists in the region. (See the Major Festivals in Bhutan section for details.)

Jampa Lhakhang

This is the oldest temple in Bumthang and is located about 5km north-west of the Jakar Dzong in Chokhor, the center of the Bumthang area. Like Kyerchu Lhakhang in Paro, it was built by the Tibetan king Songtsen Gampo in the 7th century as one of the 108 geomantic lhakhang that radiate out from Lhasa in Tibet. These temples were intended to subdue the great ogress that straddled the Tibetan lands and they form 3 distinct groups, the *Runon* (Inner-sanctuary Temples), *Tandul* (Border-taming Temples) and the *Yangdul* (Further-taming Temples). Jampa, one of the *Yangdul* lhakang, was constructed to pin down the left knee of the ogress and so help to maintain the peace and harmony in the land.

The temple is dedicated to Jampa (the Tibetan name for Maitreya [in Sanscrit]), the future Buddha. There is an annual festival held at Jampa Lhakhang between October and November.

Kurje Lhakhang

Located to the north of Jampa Lhakhang, the temple's name *Kurje* means 'an imprint,' for Guru Rinpoche is said to have left the imprint of his body in the rock here. Among the 3 temples at the site, the oldest one was built in the 17th century and is said to hold the *Kurje*. There is a huge 10-m high image of Guru Rinpoche in the middle temple. The lhakhang hosts a summer festival every year between June and July.

Mebar-Tsho

This sacred pool is located about 10km east of Jakar Dzong, in the Tang Valley. *Mebar-Tsho* or 'Blazing Fire Lake' is said to be the place where the great *sutra*-finder Pema Lingpa (1450-1521) found a *sutra* at the bottom of the lake. Then in full view of the onlookers, he went into the water with a lamp in his hand and it was still burning when he came out with his prize.

This area is about 200km east of the Bumthang region. You must cross 2 high mountain passes to reach Mongar and the bus takes around 8 hours from the Bumthang area. The roads to 3 dzongs, Lhuntse to the north, Bumthang to the west and Tashigang to the east, meet at Mongar Dzong. The dzong was constructed in the 19th century but unlike other old dzongs, this one allows tourists to enter and look around. You can also watch the *Tsechu* festival that is usually held in the town between November and December.

LHUNTSE

About 80km along the Kuru-chu, upstream from Mongar, is the 17th century Lhuntse Dzong. This is also the site of a festival that is usually held sometime in December. If you continue along the Kuru-chu, you will eventually reach Lhodrak in Tibet.

TASHIGANG

The town is 90km, or a 3-4 hour bus ride east of Mongar. The town is the center of the Tashigang Dzongkhak and is the most populated administrative region in Bhutan. The town is spread out, with its roads built on the slopes along the Gamri-chu. The town's festival is also held during the winter.

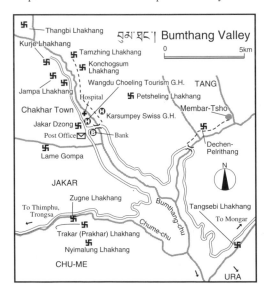

There are bazaars on both sides of the river where you can pick up beautifully hand-woven local cloth. Tashigang and the village of Radi to the east are renowned for the quality of the fabric produced there. The bazaars are also a draw for the hill tribes from the Sakteng Valley and can be a very colorful shopping experience.

To the east is the Indian state of Arunachal Pradesh and many of the people that live in the area are related to the ethnic groups across the border. Tashigang also shares the sub-tropical climate of its eastern neighbor.

SAMDRUP JONGKHAR

A 7-hour bus ride south of Tashigang takes you to the cross-border trading town of Samdrup Jongkhar. There is a border crossing into the Indian state of Assam here. The altitude in the area is as low as 200m and the town has an almost Indian feel about it.

About 20km down the road towards Samdrup Jongkhar is Bhutan's only school of higher education, Kanglung University. In the same area there is a Zangdok-pelri Lhakhang and 20km further to the south is Khaling where Bhutan's only school for the blind is located.

TASHI YANGTSE

About 50km north of Tashigang lies Tashi Yangste. This is a popular day trip for tourists, as Tashi Yangtse is well-known for its Chorten Kora, one of the largest chortens in Bhutan. This Nepalese-style stupa was built in 1782 in accordance with one of Guru Rinpoche's prophecies that a temple and chorten would be built on the site. Chorten Kora, and Gom Kora just to the south, are the sites of festivals held between February and March. The festival at Chorten Kora is the larger of the two.

Historically, the Tashi Yangtse Dzong was connected with the Tsona area in Tibet and there was once a thriving trade route between them. The monks at the dzong are only in residence after the winter snows have melted in March or April.

BHUTAN

Born in 1965, Mie, Japan.
Hiroyuki Nagaoka is a photographer
who goes deep into remote areas.
'Portrait of Tibet' (Manyosha, 2000) is
the latest collection of his work, much
of which has appeared in a number of
magazines.

Over 10 years have passed since I started
working with the people and nature of the
Tibetan Cultural Region. I've trekked into
the Himalayas to meet the people and
camped alongside nomads for days at a time.

For this kind of traveling, a portable
stove is an essential item. Without it, you
can neither drink tea nor cook your meals.
In Tibet, a kerosene-stove is useful, as the
fuel is relatively easy to obtain in the region;
however, the unpurified kerosene you can
buy often causes the jets to become clogged
up. So, 'Manaslu,' a relatively heavy and
bulky kerosene-stove, has recently joined me
as my travel companion. Though it is
cumbersome, it produces a good flame even
with Tibetan fuel.

But what about Tibetans? Without
anything like a stove they can easily make a
fire from animal dung, even if all they have
is a single match. This is nothing special for
them and their lifestyle really shows you
how hardy they are to survive in such a harsh
environment.

My wish is that my portrayals will do
justice to these people and their way of life.

Survival Tibetan

Useful Expressions		
All the best.	tashi delek	བཀྲ་ཤིས་བདེ་ལེགས།
Thank you.	thuk jay chey	ཐུགས་རྗེ་ཆེ།
Goodbye (said when leaving).	ghaley shu	ག་ལེ་བཞུགས།
Goodbye (said to the person who is leaving).	ghaley phey	ག་ལེ་ཕེབས།
See you.	ja yong	མཇལ་ཡོང་།
That's it.	rey	རེད།
No, it's not.	ma rey	མ་རེད།
Need.	gin	དགོས།
Don't need.	magoo	མི་དགོས།
Please (drink it or eat it).	nen ro nang	གནང་རོགས་གནང་།
Did you understand?	ha kho song ai?	ཧ་གོ་སོང་ངས།
Understood.	ha kho song	ཧ་གོ་སོང་།
Didn't understand.	ha kho ma song	ཧ་གོ་མ་སོང་།
How much (Yuan or Rupees)?	gormo khatseur rey?	སྒོར་མོ་ག་ཚོད་རེད།
It's expensive.	khong chenbo du	གོང་ཆེན་པོ་འདུག
Give me a discount.	khong doktsam jakthang	གོང་ཏོག་ཙམ་བཏང་དང་།
What is this?	di kha rey rey?	འདི་ག་རེ་རེད།
Is it there?/Do you have?	duk gey?	འདུག་གས།
Yes, it's there/we have.	du	འདུག
No, it's not there / we don't have.	min du	མི་འདུག
My name is	ngey ming la .... yin.	ངའི་མིང་ལ་......རེད།
What's your name?	kheyrang khi ming la kha rey rey?	ཁྱེད་རང་གི་མིང་ལ་ག་རེ་རེད།
Where are you from?	phayul kha nai yin?	ཕ་ཡུལ་ག་ནས་ཡིན།
I'm from	...... nai yin	...... ནས་ཡིན།
Sorry.	gonda	དགོངས་དག

Pronouns			Address Form			Interrogative		
I	nga	ང་	Sister	acha la	ཨ་ཅག་ལགས།	When?	kadu	ག་དུས།
You	kheyrang	ཁྱེད་རང་	Teacher	gen la	རྒན་ལགས།	Where?	kaba	ག་པར།
He/She	khong	ཁོང་	Elder brother	jhola	ཇོ་ལགས།	Who?	su	སུ།
Mother	ama la	ཨ་མ་ལགས་	Mr/Mrs	kusho la	སྐུ་ཞབས་ལགས།	What?	kha ray	ག་རེ།
Father	pala	པ་ལགས་	Aunt	ani la	ཨ་ནི་ལགས།	Which one?	kha gi	ག་གི།
Uncle	akha	ཨ་ཁུ།				How?	khan dres	ག་འདྲས།

Accommodation

English	Tibetan (roman)	Tibetan	English	Tibetan (roman)	Tibetan
Hotel	drongkhang	མགྲོན་ཁང་	Key	dey mi	ལྡེའུ་མིག
Room	khangpa	ཁང་པ	Lost the key	day mi la song	ལྡེའུ་མིག་བརླག་སོང་
Toilet	sengchue	གསང་སྤྱོད	Electricity	lo	གློག
Shower	chu khang	ཆུ་ཁང་	Candle	yang la	ཡང་ལའ
Bed	nyitri	ཉལ་ཁྲི	Material things, belongings	ja la	ཅ་ལག

Food & Drink

English	Tibetan (roman)	Tibetan	English	Tibetan (roman)	Tibetan
Dining room	za khang	ཟ་ཁང་	Sugar	chey ma ka ra	ཅེ་མ་ཀ་ར
Tea room	ja khang	ཇ་ཁང་	Salt	tsa	ཚ
Food	khala	ཁ་ལག	Chili	seben	སི་པན
Drink	tungyag	འཐུང་ཡག	It's delicious.	shimbo du	ཞིམ་པོ་འདུག
Milk	omma	འོ་མ	It's sweet.	ngar mo du	མངར་མོ་འདུག
Milk tea	cha ngamo	ཇ་མངར་མོ	It's hot (spicy).	khatsapo du	ཁ་ཚ་པོ་འདུག
Tibetan tea	pur cha	ཇ་ བོད་ཇ་	It's hot (in temperature).	tsapo du	ཚ་པོ་འདུག
Meat	sha	ཤ	It's cold.	trangmo du	གྲང་མོ་འདུག
Yak meat	yak sha	གཡག་ཤ	There's a lot of it.	mangpo du	མང་པོ་འདུག
Vegetables	tsel	ཚེལ	That's enough/ that's alright.	dik song	འགྲིག་སོང་།
Fish	nya	ཉ	Highland barley wine	chang	ཆང་
Fruit	shingto	ཤིང་ཏོག	Tibetan dish	pur ba khala	བོད་པའི་ཁ་ལག
Yoghurt	sho	ཞོ	Chinese dish	gyemi khala	རྒྱ་མིའི་ཁ་ལག

Moving Around

English	Tibetan (roman)	Tibetan	English	Tibetan (roman)	Tibetan
Road	lamka	ལམ་ཁ	Snow	khang	གངས
Mountain	ri	རི	Rain	charwa	ཆར་པ
Mountain pass	la	ལ	Hot spring	chutsan	ཆུ་ཚན
River	chu/tsangpo	ཆུ་ གཙང་པོ	Bus	basey	སྤ་སེ
Lake	tso	མཚོ	Car, motor vehicle	motra	མོ་ཊ
Valley	lung shong	ལུང་གཤོང་	Ticket	pasey	པ་སེ
Nomad	drogpa	འབྲོག་པ	Tractor	tho la	ཐོ་ལ་ཅེ
East	shar	ཤར	Yak	yak	གཡག
West	nub	ནུབ	Horse	ta	ཏ
South	lho	ལྷོ	Yes, I'm going to Lhasa.	nga...Lhasa... la drogi yin	ལ་འགྲོ་གི་ཡིན
North	chang	བྱང་	Where is it?	kaba yorey?	ག་པར་ཡོད་རེད
Right	yey	གཡས	Where are you going?	kaba phe kha?	ག་པར་ཕེབས་ཀ
Left	yin	གཡོན	It's quite far.	tha ringpo du	ཐག་རིང་པོ་འདུག
Tent	gur	གུར	It's close by.	nyepo du	ཉེ་པོ་འདུག
Village	trongsep	གྲོང་གསེབ	Please go to....	la pheb rog nang	ལ་ཕེབས་རོགས་གནང་།
Town	gyangtra	གྲོང་ཁྱེར	Please stop here.	kag rog nang	བཀག་རོགས་གནང་།

Time

What's the time?	chutso khatsoe rey?	ཆུ་ཚོད་ག་ཚོད་རེད།	This year	thalo	ད་ལོ་
At present/ now	thanda	ད་ལྟ་	Next year	thusang	དུས་སང་
Afterwards/in the future	jeyla	རྗེས་ལ་	Tomorrow	san yi	སང་ཉིན་
Quickly	gyog po	མགྱོགས་པོ་	The day after tomorrow	nan nyin	གནངས་ཉིན་
Slowly	khaley khaley	ག་ལེ་ག་ལེ་	Morning	shokhai	ཞོགས་ཁད་
Today	te ring	དེ་རིང་	Afternoon	nyin gung	ཉིན་དགུང་
Yesterday	kay san(g)	ཁ་ས་	Night (evening)	gongmo	དགོང་དག

Monastery

Monastery	gompa	དགོན་པ་	Buddhism	nangchoe	ནང་ཆོས་
Chapel/Temple	lhakhang	ལྷ་ཁང་	Buddhist	nangpa	ནང་པ་
Lama/Monk	lama/trawa	བླ་མ་ / གྲྭ་པ་	New	sarpa	གསར་པ་
Reincarnation/Incarnation	trulku	སྤྲུལ་སྐུ	Old (thing, material)	nyingpa	རྙིང་པ་
Rinpoche	rinpoche	རིན་པོ་ཆེ་	Statue of Buddha	kundrag	སྐུ་འདྲ
May I take a photo?	par gyab dig gi ray peh?	པར་རྒྱབ་ན་འགྲིག་གི་རེད་པས།	Scripture	paycha	དཔེ་ཆ་
			His Holiness the Dalai Lama	gyalwa rinpoche	རྒྱལ་བ་རིན་པོ་ཆེ་

Hospital

Hospital (clinic)	menkhang	སྨན་ཁང་	Stomach ache	trokho nagi du	གྲོ་ཁོག་ན་གི་འདུག
Medicine	men	སྨན་	I'm suffering from diarrhoea.	trokho shey khey du	གྲུ་ཁོག་བཤལ་ཁྱི་འདུག
Doctor	amchi	ཨམ་ཆི་	I've caught a cold.	champa chapsong	ཆམ་པ་བརྒྱབ་སོང་།
Oxygen	yanglong	ཡང་ལུང་	I was bitten by a dog.	khi sochobsong	ཁྱིས་སོ་རྒྱབ་སོང་།
I have a headache.	go nagi du	མགོ་ན་གི་འདུག	I feel dizzy.	goyou khorgi du	མགོ་ཡུར་འཁོར་གི་འདུག

People & Places

Tibet	pür	བོད་	Friend (male)	trokpo	གྲོགས་པོ་
Tibetan	püba	བོད་པ་	Friend (female)	trokmo	གྲོགས་མོ་
China	gya na	རྒྱ་ནག	That's good.	yapo du	ཡག་པོ་འདུག
Chinese	gya mi	རྒྱ་མི་	That isn't good.	yapo mindu	ཡག་པོ་མི་འདུག
India	gyag gar	རྒྱ་གར་	I like it (I'm happy).	la gapo du	ལ་དགའ་པོ་འདུག
Nepal	pha yul	བལ་ཡུལ་	I don't like it (I'm not happy).	la gapo mindu	ལ་དགའ་པོ་མི་འདུག
Other Countries	Pronunciation from English. [America, England, Swiss, France...]		I feel happy/ I'm glad.	kyipu du	སྐྱིད་པོ་འདུག

Numbers

0	leka	০	6	drug	৬	12	ju nyi	১২	60	drug chu	৬০
1	chig	১	7	dun	৭	13	ju sum	১৩	70	dun chu	৭০
2	nyi	༣	8	gyey	৪	20	nyi shu	২০	80	gyey chu	৪০
3	sum	༣	9	goo	৯	30	sum shu	৩০	90	goop chu	৯০
4	shi	৪	10	ju	১০	40	ship chu	৪০	100	gya tanba	১০০
5	nga	৫	11	ju chick	১১	50	ngap chu	৫০	1000	chick dong	১০০০

Survival Chinese

Useful Expressions

Hello.	nǐ hǎo	你好
What's your (family) name?	nín gùixìng?	您贵姓？
My (family) name is ...	wǒ xìng ...	我姓 ...
Yes.	shì	是
No.	búshì	不是
Goodbye.	zàijiàn	再见
Thank you.	xìexie	谢谢
You're welcome.	búkèqi	不客气
Do you want (need) ...?	yào ... ma?	要 ... 吗？
I want (need) it.	yào	要
I don't want (need) it.	búyào	不要
I am sorry.	duìbuqǐ	对不起
How much is it?	duōshǎoqián?	多少钱？
Where is the...?	... zài nǎlǐ?	...在哪里？
What is this?	zhè shì shénme?	这是什么？
I want this.	wǒ yào zhège	我要这个
It's expensive.	tàiguì	太贵
I	wǒ	我
You	nǐ	你
Name	xìng /míngzì	姓、名字

Public Offices

Bank of China	zhōngguó yínháng	中国银行	Police	jǐngchá	警察
Post Office	yóujú	邮局	Public Security Bureau	gōng'ānjú	公安局
Telephone Office	diànhuàjú	电话局	Foreign Affairs Branch	wàishì kē	外事科

Moving Around

Airport	fēijīchǎng	飞机场	Ferry	dùchuán	渡船
CAAC	zhōngguó mínháng	中国民航	Bicycle	zìxíngchē	自行车
Bus	gōnggòngqìchē	公共汽车	Ticket	piào	票
Bus Station	qìchēzhàn	汽车站	Luggage	xíngli	行李
Train	huǒchē	火车	Left-luggage room	jìcún chù	寄存处
Railway Station	huǒchēzhàn	火车站	Near	jìn	近
Taxi	chūzūqìchē	出租汽车	Far	yuǎn	远

398

Accommodation

Hotel	fàndiàn/bīnguǎn	饭店/宾馆	Twin room	shuāngrénfáng	双人房
Guesthouse	zhāodàisuǒ	招待所	Key	yàoshi	钥匙
Daoban	dàobān	道班	Shower	língyù	淋浴
Toilet	cèsuǒ	厕所	Boiling water	kāishuǐ	开水
Room	fángjiān	房间	Do you have it?	yǒu ma?	有吗?
Dormitory	duōrénfáng	多人房	I have it.	yǒu	有
Single room	dānrénfáng	单人房	I don't have it.	méi yǒu	没有

Food & Drink

Meat	ròu	肉	Mineral water	kuàngquán shuǐ	矿泉水
Fish	yú	鱼	Beer	píjiǔ	啤酒
Steamed white rice	mǐfàn	米饭	Coffee	kāfēi	咖啡
Rice gruel	xīfàn	稀饭	Coca-Cola	kěkǒu kělè	可口可乐
Tea	chá	茶	Hot, peppery	là	辣
Water	shuǐ	水	Nice, delicious	hǎo chī	好吃

Hospital

Hospital	yīyuàn	医院	Fever	fāshāo	发烧
Doctor	yīshēng	医生	Headache	tóuténg	头疼
Cold, flu	gǎnmào	感冒	Medicine	yào	药

People & Places

Tibet	xīzàng	西藏	Germany	déguó	德国
Tibetans	zàng zú	藏族	Israel	yǐsèliè	以色列
China	zhōngguó	中国	Japan	rìběn	日本
Hans	hàn zú	汉族	New Zealand	xīnxīlán	新西兰
Australia	àodàlìyà	澳大利亚	Switzerland	ruìshì	瑞士
Canada	jiānádà	加拿大	UK	yīngguó	英国
France	fǎguó	法国	USA	měiguó	美国

Numbers

0	líng	零	7	qī	七	21	èrshíyī	二十一	90	jiǔshí	九十
1	yī	一	8	bā	八	30	sānshí	三十	100	yìbǎi	一百
2	èr/liǎng	二/两	9	jiǔ	九	40	sìshí	四十	1,000	yìqiān	一千
3	sān	三	10	shí	十	50	wǔshí	五十	2,000	liǎngqiān	两千
4	sì	四	11	shíyī	十一	60	liùshí	六十	30,000	sānwàn	三万
5	wǔ	五	12	shí'èr	十二	70	qīshí	七十	100,000	shíwàn	十万
6	liù	六	20	èrshí	二十	80	bāshí	八十	200,000	èrshíwàn	二十万

Chinese Place Names

Provinces

Gansu, *G*	甘肃	
Guangdong, *Gd*	广东	
Guangxi, Gx	广西	
Qinghai, *Q*	青海	
Shaanxi, *Sx*	陕西	
Shandong, *Sd*	山东	
Sichuan, *S*	四川	
Tibet (TAR), *T*	西藏	
Xinjiang, *X*	新疆	
Yunnan, *Y*	云南	

Aba (Linggongli), *X* 零公里

Aba (Ngawa), *S* 阿坝

Ali (Shiquanhe), *T* 阿里(狮泉河镇)

Amdo (Anduo), *T* 安多

Baiyu (Pelyul), *S* 白玉

Bamei (Garthar), *S* 八美

Banma (Padma), *Q* 班玛

Basong Tso 巴松错
  (Draksum Lhatso), *T*

Batang (Bathang), *S* 巴塘

Bayi, *T* 八一

Beijing, - 北京

Boyu (Boeyul), *G* 博峪

Chamdo (Changdu), *T* 昌都

Chang Jiang 长江
  (Yangtze River), -

Chengdu, *S* 成都

Chengduo (Trindu), *Q* 称多

Chongqing, *S* 重庆

Chongye (Qiongjie), *T* 琼结

Chusum (Qusong), *T* 曲松

Dahongliutan, *X* 大红柳滩

Dali, *Y* 大里

Damzhung (Dangxiong), *T* 当雄

Danba (Rongtrak), *S* 丹巴

Daocheng (Dabpa), *S* 稻城

Daofu (Tawu), *S* 道孚

Dari (Jimai), *Q* 达日 (吉迈)

Dawu (Tawo), *Q* 大武
  [Maqin (Machen), *Q*] [玛沁]

Dege (Derge), *S* 德格

Deqin (Dechen), *Y* 德钦

Derong, *S* 得荣

Diebu (Thewo), *G* 迭部

Diexi, *S* 叠溪

Diqing (Dechen), *Y* 迪庆

Domar (Duoma), *T* 多玛

Dram (Zhangmu), *T* 樟木

Dranang (Zhanang), *T* 扎囊

Dromo (Yadong), *T* 亚东

Drongpa (Zhongba), *T* 仲巴

Drotoe (Shangyadong), *T* 上亚东

Druka (Zhuka), *T* 竹卡

Dunhuang, *G* 敦煌

Dzayul (Chayu), *T* 察隅

Dzogang (Zuogong), *T* 左贡

Gande (Gabde), *Q* 甘德

Gannan, *G* 甘南

Ganzi (Kandze), *S* 甘孜

Ganjia, *G* 甘加

Gertse (Gaize), *T*	改则	Kangding (Dartsedo), *S*	康定
Golmud (Ge'ermu), *Q*	格尔木	Kangxiwar (Kangxiwa), *X*	康西瓦
Gonghe (Chabcha), *Q*	共和	Kashgar, *X*	喀什
Gongkar (Gongga), *T*	贡嘎	Khangmar (Kangma), *T*	康马
Guangzhou, *Gd*	广州	Kongpo Gyamda, *T*	工布江达
Guide (Trika), *Q*	贵德	Kuda (Kudi), *X*	库地
Guilin, *Gx*	桂林	Kunming, *Y*	昆明
Guinan (Mangra), *Q*	贵南	Kyirong (Jilong), *T*	吉隆
Guoluo (Golok), *Q*	果洛		
Gyantse (Jiangzi), *T*	江孜	Lanzhou, *G*	兰州
Gyatsa (Jiacha), *T*	加查	Ledu (Drotsang), *Q*	乐都
		Lhakhang (Lakang), *T*	拉康
Hailuogou, *S*	海螺沟	Lharigo (Jiali), *T*	嘉黎
Hainan, *Q*	海南	Lhasa, *T*	拉萨
Heiqia Daoban, *X*	黑恰道班	Lhatse (Lazi), *T*	拉孜
Heishui (Trochu), *S*	黑水	Lhodrak (Luozha), *T*	洛扎
Henan (Sogwo), *Q*	河南	Lhorong (Luolong), *T*	洛隆
Hezuo (Tsoe), *G*	合作	Lhuntse (Longzi), *T*	隆子
Hong Kong, -	香港	Lijiang (Jang Sadam), *Y*	丽江
Hongyuan (Mewa), *S*	红原	Lintan, *G*	临谭
Hotan (Hetian), *X*	和田	Linxia, *G*	临夏
Hualong (Bayan Khar), *Q*	化隆	Litang (Lithang), *S*	理塘
Huang He	黄河	Lixian (Tashiling), *S*	理县
(Yellow River), -		Luding (Chakzamka), *S*	泸定
Huanglong (Sertso), *S*	黄龙	Lugu Hu (Lake), *Y*	泸沽湖
Huangnan, *Q*	黄南	Luhuo (Drango), *S*	炉霍
Huangzhong (Tsongkha)	湟中	Lunang (Lulang), *T*	鲁郎
[Lushaer], *Q*	[鲁沙尔]	Luoshui, *Y*	落水
Hutiaoxia	虎跳峡	Luqu (Luchu), *G*	碌曲
(Tiger Leaping Gorge), *Y*			
Huzhu (Gonlung), *Q*	互助	Ma'erkang (Barkam), *S*	马尔康
		Maduo (Mato), *Q*	玛多
Jinchuan (Rabden), *S*	金川	Manigango, *S*	马尼干戈
Jiulong (Gyezil), *S*	九龙	Maoxian, *S*	茂县
Jiuzhaigou, *S*	九寨沟	Maqu (Machu), *G*	玛曲
Jiuzhi (Jigdril), *Q*	久治	Markham (Mangkang), *T*	芒康

Mazar, *X*	麻扎	Rangtang (Zamthang), *S*	壤塘
Meldro Gungkar, *T*	墨竹工卡	Rawok (Ranwu), *T*	然乌
Menling (Milin), *T*	米林	Riwoche (Leiwuqi), *T*	类乌齐
Montser (Menshi), *T*	门士	Ruo'ergai (Dzoge), *S*	若尔盖
Mounigou (Tromje), *S*	牟尼沟	Rutok (Ritu), *T*	日土
Moxi, *S*	磨西		
Mugecuo Lake, *S*	木格错	Saga, *T*	萨嘎
Muli, *S*	木里	Sakya (Sajia), *T*	萨迦
		Samye (Sangye), *T*	桑耶
Nakchu (Naqu), *T*	那曲	Seda (Sertal), *S*	色达
Namling (Nanmulin), *T*	南木林	Shanghai, -	上海
Nang Dzong (Lang) [Langxian], *T*	朗县	Sharsingma (Xiasima), *T*	下司马
Nangartse (Langkazi), *T*	浪卡子	Shelkar (New Tingri) [Xindingri], *T*	新定日
Nanping (Namphel), *S*	南坪	Shenzhen, -	深圳
Nedong (Naidong), *T*	乃东	Shigatse (Rikaze), *T*	日喀则
Ngamring (Angren), *T*	昂仁	Shiqu (Sershul) [Serxu], *S*	石渠
Ninglang, *Y*	宁蒗	Sok Dzong (Suoxian), *T*	索县
Nyalam (Nielamu), *T*	聂拉木	Songpan (Zungchu), *S*	松潘
Nyangtri (Nyingtri) [Linzhi], *T*	林芝	Sumang (Zurmang), *Q*	苏莽
		Sumzhi (Songxi), *T*	松西
		Sunan, *G*	肃南
Paryang (Payang), *T*	帕羊		
Pasho (Basu), *T*	八宿	Tagong (Lhagang) [Hargong], *S*	塔公
Pelbar (Bianba), *T*	边坝	Taktsang Lhamo (Langmusi), *G*	郎木寺
Pemako (Metok) [Motuo], *T*	墨脱	Tang-me [Tongmai], *T*	通麦
Phenpo Lhundrub (Linzhou), *T*	林周	Tashi Dargyeling (Tiantangsi), *G*	天堂寺
Ping'an (Tsongkha Khar), *Q*	平安	Tengchen (Dingqing), *T*	丁青
Pomda (Bangda), *T*	帮达	Tianshuihai, *X*	甜水海
Pome (Powo) [Bomi], *T*	波密	Tianzhu (Pari), *G*	天祝
Purang (Pulan), *T*	普兰	Tingri (Dingri), *T*	定日
Qingdao, *Sd*	青岛	Toelung (Duilongdeqingxian), *T*	堆龙德庆县
Qinghai Hu (Lake Kokonor), *Q*	青海湖		

402

Tongde (Kawasumdo), *Q*	同德	Xining, *Q*	西宁
Tongren (Repkong), *Q*	同仁	Xinlong (Nyarong), *S*	新龙
Trakdruka (Dazhuka), *T*	大竹卡	Xinluhai (Yilhun Lhatso), *S*	新路海
Tsamda (Zhada), *T*	扎达	Xunhua [Dowi], *Q*	循化
Tsethang (Zedang), *T*	泽当		
Tsochen (Cuoqin), *T*	措勤	Yajiang (Nyakchuka), *S*	雅江
Tsona (Cuona), *T*	错那	Yamdrok Yumtso Lake, *T*	羊卓雍错
		Yanjing, *T*	盐井
Urumqi, *X*	乌鲁木齐	Yangpachen, *T*	羊八井
		Yarkant (Shache), *X*	莎车
Wachang, *S*	瓦厂	Yecheng, *X*	叶城
Weixi (Balung), *Y*	维西	Yongning, *Y*	永宁
Wenchuan (Lungu), *S*	汶川	Yushu (Jyekundo), *Q*	玉树
Wolong, *S*	卧龙		
		Zangzang (Sangsang), *T*	桑桑
Xi'an, *Sx*	西安	Zeku (Tsekok), *Q*	泽库
Xiahe (Sang-chu), *G*	夏河	Zhangye, *G*	张掖
Xiangcheng (Chaktreng), *S*	乡城	Zhethongmon	谢通门
Xiaojin (Tsenlha), *S*	小金	(Xietongmen), *T*	
Xiewu (Zhiwu), *Q*	歇武	Zhongdian (Gyalthang), *Y*	中甸
Xinduqiao (Dzongzhab), *S*	新都桥	Zhouqu (Drukchu), *G*	舟曲
Xinghai (Tsigorthang), *Q*	兴海	Zhuoni (Cho-ne), *G*	卓尼

Foreign Embassies in Beijing, China (Area code 010)

Australia-21 Dongzhimenwai Da Jie, Sanlitun Tel: 6532 2331/7
Canada-19 Dongzhimenwai Da Jie, Chaoyangqu Tel: 6532 3536/ 4311
Denmark-1 Dongwu Jie, Sanlitun Tel: 6532 2431-9
France-3 Dongsan Jie, Sanlitun Tel: 6532 1331/ 4841
Germany-5 Dongzhimenwai Da Jie, Sanlitun
Tel: 6532 2161/5 Fax: 6532 5336
India-1 Ri Tan Dong Lu, Jianguomenwai
Tel: 6532 1908/ 1856
Fax: 6532 4684
Ireland-3 Ritandong Lu, Jianguomenwai
Tel: 6532 2691/ 2914
Japan-7 Ritan Lu, Jianguomenwai Tel: 6532 2361/ 4625
Nepal-1 Xi Liu Jie, Sanlitun Tel: 6532 1795/ 3251
Netherlands-4 Liangmahe Nan Lu Tel: 6532 1131-4
New Zealand-1 Donger Jie, Ritan Lu, Chaoyangqu Tel: 6532 2731-3
Pakistan-1 Dongzhimenwaida Jie, Sanlitun Tel: 6532 2715/ 6660
Singapore-1 Xiushuibei Jie, Jianguomenwai
Tel: 6532 3143/ 3926
Sweden-3 Dongzhimenwai Da Jie Tel: 6532 3331/ 3803
Switzerland-3 Dongwu Jie, Sanlitun Tel: 6532 2736-8
United Kingdom-11 Guanghua Lu, Jianguomenwai
Tel: 6532 1937/ 7967
United States of America-3 Xiushuibei Jie, Jianguomenwai Tel: 6532 3831/ 3431

Chinese Embassies Abroad

Australia-15 Coronation Dr, Yarralumla, A.C.T. 2600
Tel: 0262-273 4780/ 3 Fax: 273 4878
Canada-515 St. Patrick St, Ottawa, Ont.K1N 5H3
Tel: 613-789 3434 Fax: 789 1911
Denmark-Oregards Alle 25, 2900 Hellerup, Copenhagen
Tel: 045-3961 9889/ 3946 0889
Fax: 3962 5484
France-11 Ave George V, 75008 Paris
Tel: 01-4723 3677 Fax: 4720 2422
Germany-Märkischer Ufer 54, 10179 Berlin
Tel: 030-275 88-0 Fax: 2758 8221
India-50-D, Shantipath, Chanakyapuri, New Delhi 110021
Tel: 011-687 1585-7 Fax: 688 5486

Ireland-40 Ailesbury Rd, Dublin 4. Tel: 01-269 1707 Fax: 283 9938
Japan-4-33, Moto-Azabu 3-chome, Minato-ku, Tokyo 106-0046
Tel: 03-3403 3389 Fax: 3403 3345
Nepal-P.O.B. 4234 Baluwatar, Kathmandu
Tel: 01-411 740/ 958 Fax: 414 045
Netherlands-Adriaan Goekooplaan 7, The Hague.
Tel: 070-306 5061 Fax: 355 1651
New Zealand-2-6 Glenmore St, Wellington
Tel: 04-721 383 Fax: 990 419
Pakistan-Diplomatic Enclave, Ramna 4, Islamabad
Tel: 051-822 540/ 824 786
Fax: 821 116
Singapore-70-76 Dalvey Rd, Singapore 259470 Tel: 0065-734 3200/ 7880 Fax: 734 4737
Sweden-Lidovagen 8, 115 25 Stockholm
Tel: 08-5793 6437 Fax: 5793 6454
Switzerland-Kalcheggweg 10, 3006 Berne
Tel: 031-352 7333 Fax: 351 4573
United Kingdom-49-51 Portland Place, London W1N 4JL
Tel: 0171-636 2580 Fax: 636 2981
United States of America-2300 Connecticut Ave N.W. Washington, D.C. 20008
Tel: 202-328 2500/ 2517
Fax: 588 0032

Foreign Embassies in Delhi (Area code 011)

Australia-1/50-G Shantipath, Chanakyapuri
Tel: 688 8223/ 5556 Fax: 688 5199
Bangladesh-56 Ring Rd
Tel: 683 4668/ 9209 Fax: 683 9237
Bhutan-Chandragupta Marg, Chanakyapuri
Tel: 609 217 Fax: 687 6710
Canada-7/8 Shantipath, Chanakyapuri
Tel: 687 6500 Fax: 687 0031
China-50-D Shantipath, Chanakyapuri
Tel: 687 1585-7 Fax: 688 5486
Denmark-11 Aurangzeb Rd
Tel: 301 0900 Fax: 301 0961
France- 2/50-E Shantipath, Chanakyapuri
Tel: 611 8790 Fax: 687 2305
Germany-6/50-G Shantipath, Chanakyapuri
Tel: 687 3117 Fax: 687 3117
Ireland-230 Jor Bagh Rd
Tel: 462 6733/ 41 Fax: 469 7053
Japan-50-G Shantipath, Chanakyapuri
Tel: 687 6581-2 Fax: 688 5587

Nepal-Barakhamba Rd
Tel: 332 9969/ 7361 Fax: 332 6857
Netherlands-6/50 F Shantipath, Chanakyapuri
Tel: 688 4951-4 Fax: 688 4956
New Zealand-50-N Nyaya Marg, Chanakyapuri
Tel: 688 3170 Fax: 687 2317
Pakistan-2/50-G Shantipath, Chanakyapuri
Tel: 600 601-3 Fax: 687 239
Singapore-E -6 Chandragupta Marg, Chanakyapuri
Tel: 688 5659/ 6506 Fax: 688 6798
Sri Lanka-27 Kautilya Marg, Chanakyapuri
Tel: 301 0201-3 Fax: 301 5295
Sweden-Nyaya Marg, Chanakyapuri
Tel: 687 5760/ 608 135
Fax: 688 5401
Switzerland-Nyaya Marg, Chanakyapuri
Tel: 604 225 Fax: 687 3093
United Kingdom-Shantipath, Chanakyapuri
Tel: 687 2161 Fax: 687 2882
United States-Shantipath, Chanakyapuri
Tel: 600 651 Fax: 672 476

Foreign Consulates in Kolkata (Calcutta) (Area code 033)

Australia-96/1 Sarat Bose Rd
Tel: 475 2795
Bangladesh-9 Circus Ave
Tel: 247 5208 Fax: 247 2263
Bhutan-48 Tivoli Court, 1A Ballygunge, Circular Rd
Tel: 446 952 Fax: 434 527
Denmark-3 Netaji Subhas Rd, McLeod House Tel: 248 7476-8
France-26 Park Mansions
Tel: 290 978-9 Fax: 292 793
Germany-1 Hastings Park Rd, Alipore
Tel: 479 2150/ 1141-2 Fax: 479 3028
Japan-12 Pretoria St
Tel: 242 2241/ 5 Fax: 242 0954
Nepal-1 National Library Ave, Alipore
Tel: 479 1224/ 1154 Fax: 479 1410
Netherlands-31 Netaji Subhas Rd, RPG Enterprises
Tel: 220 8948/ 9281 Fax: 248 1614
Singapore-8 A.J.C Bose Rd
Tel: 247 4990/ 0400
Sri Lanka-2 Hare St
Tel: 248 5102 Fax: 220 9443
Sweden-5/2 Russell St
Tel: 470 1594 Fax: 293 643
Switzerland-113 Park St
Tel: 295 542-3/ 549/ 557
Fax: 296 248
Thailand-18B Mandeville Gardens
Tel: 440 7836 Fax: 440 6251

United Kingdom- 1 Ho Chi Minh Sarani Tel: 242 5171/ 5175 Fax: 242 3435 **United States of America-** 5/1 Ho Chi Minh Sarani Tel: 242 3611/ 3615 Fax: 242 2335

Indian Embassies Abroad

Australia- 3-5 Moonah Place, Canberra, ACT 2600. Tel: 06-273 3999/ 3774 Fax: 273 1308 h t t p://www.ozemail.com.au/ indoaust/indi.htm
Bangladesh- 120 Rd 2, Dhamondi, Dhaka Tel: 02-865 373/ 966 Fax: 863 662
Bhutan- India House Estate, Thimphu Tel: 0975-22 162 Fax: 23 195
Canada- 10 Springfield Road, Ottawa, Ont.K1M 1C9 Tel: 0613-744 3751-3 Fax: 744 0913 http://www.docuweb.ca/India
China- 1 Ri Tan Dong Lo, Beijing 100600 Tel: 01-532 1908/ 3127 Fax: 532 4684 http://www.gcinfo.com/indembch
Denmark- Vangehusvaj 15, 2100 Copenhagen Tel: 045-3118 2888 Fax: 3927 0218
France- 5 Rue Alfred Dehodenoq, 75016, Paris Tel: 01-4050 7070 Fax: 4050 0996
Germany- Adenauerallee 262-264, 53113 Bonn Tel: 0228-54 050 Fax: 540 5153 http://www.bn.shuttle.de/essente-eoi
Hong Kong- 16-D United Centre, 95 Queensway Tel: 2528 4028/ 9 Fax: 2529 0421 http://www.hk.super.net/comind1
Ireland- 6, Leeson Park, Dublin-6 Tel: 01-497 0483/ 0959 Fax: 497 8074
Japan- 2-2-11 Kudan Minami, Chiyoda-ku, Tokyo 102 Tel: 03-3262 2391 Fax: 3234 4866 http://www2.gol.com/indembjp
Nepal- P.O.B. 292, Lazimpat, Kathmandu Tel: 01-411 699/ 410 900 Fax: 413 132 http://www.indiaexpress.com/ embassy/indemb.html
Netherlands- Buitenrustweg-2, 2517 KD, The Hague Tel: 070-346 9771 Fax: 361 7072
New Zealand- 180 Molesworth St., P.O.B. 4045, Wellington Tel: 04-473 6390/ 1 Fax: 499 0665
Pakistan- G-5 Diplomatic Enclave, Islamabad Tel: 051-814 371-5 Fax: 820 742

Singapore- India House, 31 Grange Rd, P.O.B.9123, Singapore 0923 Tel: 65-737 6777/ 6809 Fax: 732 6909 http://www.allindia.com/hcisin
Sri Lanka- 36-38 Galla Rd, P.O.B. 882, Colombo 3 Tel: 01-421 605/ 422 788 Fax: 446 403
Sweden- Adolf Fredricks Kyrkogata 12, Box 1340, 11183 Stockholm Tel: 08-107 008 Fax: 248 505 http://www.indianembassy.se
Switzerland- Effingerstrasse 45, CH-3008 Berne Tel: 031-382 3111 Fax: 382 2687
Thailand- 46 Soi, 23 Sukhumvit Rd, Bangkok 10110 Tel: 02-258 0300-6 Fax: 258 4627 http://www.indianemb.or.th/
United Kingdom- India House, Aldwych, London WC2B 4NA Tel: 0171-836 8484 Fax: 836 4331
United States- 2107 Massachusetts Ave NW, Washington DC 20008 Tel: 202-939 7000 Fax: 265 4351 http://www.indianembassy.org

Foreign Embassies in Kathmandu, Nepal (Area Code 01)

Australia- P.O.B 879, Bansbari Tel: 411 578/ 413 076 Fax: 417 533
Canada- Lazimpat Tel: 01-415 193/ 391 Fax: 410 422
China- P.O.B. 4234, Baluwatar Tel: 411 740/ 958 Fax: 414 045
Denmark- Lalita Niwas Rd, P.O.B. 5598, Baluwatar Tel: 413 010/ 020 Fax: 411 409
France- P.O.B. 452, Lazimpat Tel: 412 332/ 414 734 Fax: 419 968-9
Germany- P.O.B. 226, Gyaneswor Tel: 416 527/ 832 Fax: 416 899
India- P.O.B. 292, Lainchaur Tel: 411 466/ 699/ 940 Fax: 413 132 http://www.south-asia.com/Embassy-India
Japan- P.O.B. 264, Maharajgunj Tel: 225 813/ 226 061 Fax: 228 638
Netherlands- P.O.B. 1966, Lagankel Tel: 522 915
New Zealand- P.O.B. 224, Dilli Bazaar Tel: 412 436
Pakistan- P.O.B. 202, Panipokhari Tel: 411 421-2 Fax: 419 113
Sweden- Khichapokhari Tel: 220 939
Switzerland- P.O.B. 4486, Jawalakel Tel: 523 468
United Kingdom- P.O.B. 106 Lainchaur Tel: 410 583/ 414 588 Fax: 411 789
United States- P.O.B. 295,

Panipokhari Tel: 411 179/ 604/ 613 Fax: 419 963 http://www.south-asia.com/USA/

Nepalese Embassies Abroad

Australia- 3F, 441 Kent St., Sydney. NSW Tel: 02-264 5909 Fax: 261 1974
Bangladesh- U.N. Rd #2, Baridhara, Dhaka Tel: 02-601 790/ 890 Fax: 886 401
Canada- 310 Duport St., Toronto, Ontario, M5R IV9 Tel: 416-968 7252
China- 1, Xi Liu Jie, Sanlitun, Beijing Tel: 01-532 1795 Fax: 532 3251
Denmark- 2 , Teglgaardstraede, 1452 Copenhagen Tel: 045-3312 4166 Fax: 3315 1045
France- 45 Bis rue des Acacias, 75017 Paris Tel: 01-4622 4867 Fax: 4227 0865
Germany- Im Hag 15, 53179 Bonn Tel: 0228-343 097-9 Fax: 856 747
India- Barakhamba Road, New Delhi 110001 Tel: 011-332 7361/ 9218/ 9969 Fax: 332 6857
Japan- 14-9-7 Todoroki, Setagaya-ku, Tokyo 158 Tel: 03-3705 5558/ 9 Fax: 3705 8264
Netherlands- Kaisergracht 463, 1017 DK Amsterdam Tel: 020-624 1530/ 1580 Fax: 266 795
New Zealand- 278A Remuera Rd., Auckland 5 Tel: 09-520 3169 Fax: 520 7847
Pakistan- #506, St. 84, Attaturk Ave., Ramna g-6/ 4, Islamabad Tel: 051-210 642 Fax: 217 875
Sri Lanka- 153 Rd., Colombo 8 Tel: 01-689 656 Fax: 689 555
Sweden- Eriksbergsgatan 1A, S-11430 Stockholm Tel: 08-679 8039 Fax: 611 0901
Switzerland- P.O.B. Asfylstrasse 81, 8030 Zurich Tel: 01-475 993 Fax: 251 9152
Thailand- 159 Sukhumvit 71 Rd, Bangkok 10110 Tel: 02-391 7240 Fax: 381 2406
Tibet (China)- Norbulingka Rd. 13, Lhasa, T.A.R., P.R.C. Tel: 0891-36 890/ 22 881 Fax: 633 6890
United Kingdom- 12A, Kensington Palace Gardens, London, W8 4QU Tel: 0171-229 1594 Fax: 792 9861
United States- 2131 Leroy Place, N.W., Washington, D.C. 20008 Tel: 202-667 4550/ 1551 Fax: 667 5534

Tibet & China

A
Aba 158
Aba (Ngawa) Prefecture 177, 219-29
Ache Lhamo 60
Aksobhya 46, 48
Akyong Gya 213
Ali Prefecture 140
Amchok Gompa 229
Amdo 175-229
Amdo 108
Amitabha 46, 48, 114
Amoghasiddhi 46, 48
Amrita 48, 50
Amnye Machen 211
Anduo 108
Ani 44
Ani Longchen 96
Ani Tshamkhung Nunnery 77
Anjuesi 240
Anqu Chalisi 229
Atisha 95, 99, 149
Avalokiteshvara 46-7, 74, 80, 166, 226, 246
Ayonggongma Tso 208

B
Babangsi 256
Baisha 270
Baishui Terrace 274
Baiyu 253
Balung 275
Bam Tso 131
Bamei 247
Banma 213
Bangda 169
Barabise 128
Bardo Thoedrol 45
Barkham 225
Barkhor 75
Basong Tso 163
Basu 169
Batang / Bathang 260
Bayan Khar 195
Bayi 162
Bayi Pelri, Mt. 163
Beijisi 273
Beishansi 193
Benzilan 275
Beri Gompa 252
Bhaisajyaguru 46, 47
Bianba 174
Bitahai Nature Reserve 273
Bodhicitta 36
Bodhidharma 276
Bodhisattvas 46
Boeyul 187
Bomi 168
Bon 37-8
Bonri, Mt. 166

Boyu 187
Buddhism 36-54
Bumpa 50

C
Cha 51
Chabcha 202
Chadrul Gami 222
Chadur 57
Chalang Gompa 212
Chaka Salt Lake 197
Chakna Dorje 46, 153, 246
Chakpori Hill 81
Chaktreng 260
Chakzamka 242
Chamdo 169-74
Chamru Gompa 202
Chang 56
Changdu 169-74
Changkhang 56
Changkya Lama 194
Changthang Plateau 106
Changzhusi 94
Chayu 169
Chedezhol 97
Chemar 58
Chengdu 220, 233-37
Chengduo 218
Chenrezik 46-7, 77
Chikhor 145
Chimphu Hermitage 92
Chingwa Taktse Dzong 95
Chiu Gompa 145
Cho Oyu, Mt. 126
Chod 96
Choeding Khang 84
Choekyong 42, 47
Choeme 43
Choepa 43
Chogu Gompa 143
Chogyel Drupuk 80
Chokhorgyal Gompa 104
Cho-ne 186
Chongye 95
Chuanzhusi 222
Chuba 55
Chuku Gompa & Rinpoche 143
Chumbi Valley 131
Chung Riwoche 129
Chunga Choepa 59
Chusin 51
Chusum 103
Chuwori, Mt. 96
Cintamani 47, 51
Cizhong 275
Cuona 106

D
Dabpa 260
Dacanglangmu Saichisi 186
Dacangnama Ge'erdisi 186, 230

Daduka 167
Dago Kani 81
Dahongliutan 158
Dakini 47, 48, 143
Dakpa Shelri, Mt. 105
Dalai Lama 35, 78-82, 104, 106, 194-5, 273
Dali 267-8
Damaru 50
Damzhung 106
Danba 245
Dangkasi 217
Dangxiong 106
Daoban 22 129
Daocheng 260
Daofu 248
Darchen 141
Darchin Shenchen Choekhorling 229
Dardo 237
Dargye Gompa 253
Dari / Darlag 212
Darling Gompa 212
Darpoche 143
Dar-shing 41
Dartsedo 237
Dashe 56
Dawa Lhakhang 91
Dawu 210
Dazhasi 229, 230
Dechen 263
Dechen Chokhor 95
Dege / Derge 254
Demchok 153
Demo Chemnak 167
Dengqingsi 256
Dentok Gompa 240
Dentok Riwo 240
Deqin 170, 270, 274
Derge Parkhang 255
Derong 260
Desi Sangye Gyatso 35, 78
Deyang Tratsang 83
Dharma 36
Dhunche 130
Diebu County 187
Diexi Fengjingqu 221
Dingpoche Gompa 145
Dingqing 173
Dingri 126
Diqing Tibetan Autonomous Prefecture 270-8
Dixia Migong 276
Do 37
Dodrubchen Gompa 213
Do Gongma Gompa 213
Dolma 46, 48, 81, 83
Dolma La 143
Dolma Marpo 48
Domar 156, 158
Domkar Gompa 217
Dongba 269, 274
Dongdrubling 275
Dongguan Qingzhen

Dasi 193
Donggyu Gompa 211
Dongzhulin Temple 275
Donyo Drupa 48
Dorje 49, 97
Dorje Chang 46, 118
Dorje Drak Gompa 97, 240
Dorje Jigje 47, 153
Dorje Jigje Lhakhang 153
Dorje Phagmo 52, 102
Dorje Sempa 46
Drachi Valley 92
Drak Lhalupuk 81
Drak Yangdzong 97
Drak Yerpa 99
Drakar Treldzong 203
Drakda 98
Draksum Tso 163
Drakyul Caves 97
Dram 66, 127
Dramnyen 49
Dranang 92
Drango 249-50
Dratsang 204
Drayab 174
Drepung Monastery 82-3
Dresi 58
Dri 55
Drib Tsechokling 78
Driguk 50
Drigung Kagyupa 39, 98, 105
Drigung Kyabgon Rinpoche 98
Drigung Til Gompa 98
Drilbu 49
Drirapuk Gompa 143
Drotoe 131
Drotsang Gompa 195
Drubtob Lhakhang 81
Druk 51
Druka 171
Drukchen Rinpoche 106
Drukchu 187
Drukpa Kagyupa 39, 105-6
Drukpa Tsezhi 60
Drul 51
Dudjom Rinpoche 164
Duk 50
Dukhang 42
Dukhor Lhakhang 80
Dukhor Wangchen 53
Dung 50
Dungdor 166
Dungkar 153
Duogansi 218
Duogongmasi 213
Duoma 156, 158
Duringma Lhakhang 153
Dzaleb La 131
Dzarongpu Gompa 126
Dzayul 169
Dzitho 174

Dzo 55
Dzogang 171
Dzogchen 39
Dzogchen Gompa 256
Dzoge 229
Dzomo 55
Dzong Kumbum 98
Dzonggyab Lukhang
    Temple 81
Dzongka 130
Dzongzhab 246

E
Erdao Hai 222
Erdaoqiao Hot Springs
    237, 241
Erlang Shan 231, 239
Everest 109, 123

F
Four Regency Temples 77
Friendship Bridge 127

G
Gala 131
Gamisi / Gami 222
Gande / Gabde 211
Ganden Choekhorling 93,
    119
Ganden Monastery 85-8
Ganden Ngawang Ziktrul
    Rinpoche 174
Ganden Podrang 82-3
Ganden Tripa 40, 85, 186
Ganga-chu 146
Gangkar Gompa 243
Gangri Toekar, Mt. 96
Ganjia / Ganja 183
Gannan Prefecture 181-7
Gansu Province 177-89
Ganzi Tibetan Autonomous
    Prefecture 237-60
Ganzi 250
Garthar 247
Garuda 51
Garuda Valley 156
Gashari 198
Gau 43
Gautama Siddhartha 46, 48
Ge'ermu 197-8
Gelukpa 39-40, 80, 83,
    85, 99
Gendun Drupa 35
Gendun Gyatso 35
Gesar Lhakhang 81
Geshe 44
Godemchen 97
Golmud 197-8
Gomar Gompa 199-200
Gompa 41
Gonchen Shedrubling 186
Gongba Dratsang 204
Gongga Shan 243
Gonggasi 243

Gonghe 202
Gongkar 65, 95
Gongpori, Mt. 92-3
Gonkhang 42
Gonlung Jampaling 194
Gonpo 47
Guangfasi 226
Guanyinqiao 226
Guge 149, 156
Guide 204
Guihuasi 273
Guinan 205
Gun 130
Gungthang Temple/
    Rinpoche 229
Guoluo Tibetan
    Autonomous Prefecture
    207-14
Guomarisi 199
Gurla Mandhata 146
Guru Rinpoche 38, 80,
    91-2, 97-8, 102, 156,
    163, 203, 240, 253
Gurubum Lhakhang 75
Gya Khache Lhakhang 78
Gyala Pelri, Mt. 167
Gyalthang 270-4
Gyaltsen 50
Gyalwa Ngapa 35
Gyamda 173
Gyangdrak Gompa 145
Gyantse 114-18
Gyathuk 56
Gyatsa 104
Gyezil 246
Gyu 37
Gyume Tratsang 77
Gyuto Tratsang 77, 99
Gyuzhi 78

H
Haba Snow Peak Nature
    Reserve 274
Haidong Diqu (District)
    193
Hailuogou 243-5
Hainan Tibetan
    Autonomous Prefecture
    202
Hamdong Khangtsang 84
Hargong 246
Hayagriva 47, 84, 143,
    153
Hebu 88
Heishui 221
Henan Mongol
    Autonomous County
    201
Hepori 91
Herisi 200
Hexi 204
Heye 224
Heyin 204
Hezuo 183-4

Hongyuan 228
Huanglong 222
Huanglong Hui
    Autonomous County
    195
Huangnan Tibetan
    Autonomous Prefecture
    198-202
Huangzhong 193
Humla Region 147
Hutiaoxia 274
Huzhu Tu Autonomous
    County 194

I
Incarnated Lama 44
Institute of Tibetan
    Medicine and Astrology
    78

J
Ja 56
Ja Ngarmo 56
Ja Thang 56
Jakhyung Gompa 195
Jamchen Choeje Sakya
    Yeshe 83
Jamkhang Chenmo 114
Jampa 47-8, 74, 77, 83-4
Jampa Thongdrol
    Lhakhang 83
Jampal Gyatso 35
Jampaling Monastery
    172-3
Jampeyang 46-7
Jamyang 48
Jamyang Choeje 82-3
Jamyang Lhakhang 83
Jamyang Zhepa 183
Jang 269
Jang Sadam 268
Jangchup Sempa 36, 46
Jangritang Gompa 213
Jangsem Sherab Zangpo
    172
Je Rinpoche
    See Tsongkhapa
Je Rinpoche Lhakhang 74
Jetsunma Rinpoche 96
Jetsunpei Gyencho Zhengsa
    194
Jiacha 104
Jiali 174
Jiangzi 114-8
Jigdril 214
Jilong County 130
Jimai 212
Jinchuan County 226
Jingangsi 240
Jiulong 246
Jiuzhaigou 223, 224
Jiuzhi 214
Jokhang Temple 71-5
Jol 274

Jomda 174
Jomolangma, Mt.
    See Everest
Jomonang Gompa 120
Jonang Kagyupa 39, 120
Jonang Kumbum 120
Jorkhe Ritro 174
Jowo Rinpoche 74-6
Jowo Shakyamuni
    Lhakhang 75
Jujye Gompa 218
Jyegu Gompa 217
Jyekundo 214

K
Kadampa 95, 99, 119
Kaga 129
Kagyupa 39
Kailash, Mt. 137-40, 141-
    45
Kalachakra Mandala 53
Kamthok 174
Kandro Sanglam Pass 143
Kandroma 47, 48
Kandze 250
Kangding 237
Kang Rinpoche
    See Kailash, Mt.
Kangyur 44, 187
Kapala 50
Kapse 58
Karghalik 156-7
Karma Dargye Gompa 218
Karma Gompa 173
Karma Kagyu Zhamarpa
    100
Karma Kagyupa 39, 100
Karma Kawdi. 53
Karmapa 100
Karmashar Monastery 77
Karzang Gompa 218
Kasar 198
Kasar Gompa 202
Kashgar 157
Kashyapa 48
Kasuo 251
Katak 43, 75
Kathmandu 128
Katok Gompa 253
Kawa Karpo, Mt. 275
Kawasumdo 206
Kelzang Gyatso 35
Kelzang Lhakhang 114
Kermi 148
Khache Lhakhang 78
Kham 231-78
Khamsum Sangkhang Ling
    91
Khangmar 131
Kharchu Gompa 103
Khasa 127
Khedrub Gyatso 35
Khenpo 44
Khon Family 39, 121

Khora 41
Khorlo 49-50
Khothing Lhakhang 103
Khyung 51
Khyunglung 156
Khyungpo District 173
Kings' Tombs 95
Kirti Gompa 185, 186, 227, 230
Kodari Border Crossing, 128
Kokonor, Lake 196
Konchok Gyalpo 39, 121
Kongpo 159-69
Kowa 78
Kulha Kangri, Mt. 100, 102-3
Kumbum 118, 193
Kunchok Sum 36
Kundeling Gompa 78, 81
Kundung Lhakhang 114
Kunkhyen Tashi Namgyal 99
Kunlun Mountain Range 156
Kunming 263-7
Kusinagara 84
Kyamra Chenmo 74
Kyamru Gompa 202
Kyangcha 42
Kyangthang Gompa 222
Kyaring Tso 209
Kyilkhor 43, 52-3, 105
Kyilkhor Lhakhang 153
Kyirong 130

L
Labrang Gyaltsen Tonpo 114
Labrang Monastery 182
Lakha Gompa 202
Lama 43, 46
Lama Dondrub Rinchen 195
Lamrim 80, 99
Langa Tso 145
Langchen Tsangpo 146-7
Langdarma, King 99, 103, 156
Langmusi 185
Lang / Langxian 105
Langyisi 228
Lanzhou 177-9
Lapchi Gang 126
Lazi 122
Ledu 195
Leiwuqi 173
Lhabab Duechen 60
Lhagang 246
Lhakhang / Lakang 103
Lhakhang Chenmo 122
Lhakhang Karpo & Marpo 150, 153
Lhakhangs 42

Lhalung Gompa 103
Lhalung Peldor 99, 103
Lhamko 56
Lhamo Latso Lake 104
Lhamo Tsering Gompa 240
Lharampa Geshe 59
Lharigo 174
Lhasa 63-84
Lhatse 122
Lhodrak 100, 103
Lhokha Prefecture 88-95
Lhorong / Luolong County 174
Lhuntse 106
Lianhuashan 186
Lijiang 268
Ling Gesar, King 81, 163
Ling Shi 77
Lingka 57
Lintan 186
Linxia Hui Autonomous Prefecture 179
Linzhi 165
Linzhou 99
Litang / Lithang 258-60
Lixian 224-5
Lizu 270
Lobzang Gyatso 35
Lodro Rinchen 84
Long March Memorial 222
Longchen Ranbjampa 39, 92, 96, 106, 229
Longwangbian 274
Longwusi 198-9
Longzi 106
Losar 58
Loseling Tratsang 83
Lower Tantric College 77
Lu 51
Luding 242
Lugu Hu 276
Luhuo 249
Lunang / Lulang 167
Lungshoe Gompa 217
Lungta 40
Lungtok Gyatso 35
Lungu 220
Luqu 184
Luozha 103
Luri Langkar 156
Lushaer 193
Lutsang Gompa 205, 206
Luzangsi 206

M
Machen Kangri 211
Machik Labdron 48, 96
Maduo 207
Ma'erkang 220, 225-6
Mahakala 47, 58
Mahatma Gandhi 145
Maitreya See Jampa
Makala 51
Manasarovar, Lake 145

Mandala 43, 46-54, 80, 88, 103
Mangkang 170
Mangra 205
Manigango 254
Mani Prayer-wheel 42
Manikhor 42
Mani-stones 41
Manjughosa 46, 47
Manjushri 48, 246-7
Manjushri Meditation Cave 83
Mantra 47-8
Maowen Qiang Autonomous County 220-1
Maoxian 220
Mapcha Tsangpo 146-8
Mapham Yutso See Manasarovar, Lake
Maqin 210
Maqu / Machu 187
Markham 170
Marpa 39, 100, 103, 184
Marpori, Mt. 81
Martsang Kagyupa 174
Mato 207
Matisi Monastery 189
Mazar 158
McMahon Line 167
Meili Xueshan 270, 275
Melong 50
Memo Nani 146
Mengda Tianchi Lake 195
Menla Sangye 83
Menlha Desheg Gye Lhakhang 74
Menling 162, 166
Menri Trizin 119
Mentsikhang 70, 78
Meru Nyingba Temple 77
Meru Sarpa Tratsang 77
Metho Dusang 187
Metok 167
Mewa 229
Mikyopa Dorje Sempa 48
Milarepa 39, 100-101, 103, 127, 143-4, 184
Milarepa Lhakhang 184
Milarepa Monastery 127
Milin 166
Mindroling Monastery 92, 126
Minhe 195
Minling Trichen 92
Minling Trichen Rinpoche 92
Minya Konka, Mt. 243
Minyak Dratsang Gompa 204
Minzu Shichang 202
Miyalang 225
Momo 56
Monastery 41

Mongolia 54
Monk 43
Monlam 59, 75, 183
Mosu 276
Mounigou 222
Moxi 244
Muchu 147
Mugecuo Lake 241
Mugu 242
Muli Tibetan Autonomous County 260-1
Myrobalan 47

N
Naga 51
Naidong County 92
Nakchu 108
Nalanda Gompa 99
Nama Ge'erdesi 227
Namcha Barwa, Mt. 162, 167
Namde Osung 149, 156
Namling 119
Nampar Nangze 48
Namphel 224
Namri Songsten 30
Namru 153
Namse Zampa 163
Namtso Lake 106-8
Nang Dzong 105
Nangartse 102
Nangkhor 145
Nanping 224
Nanwusi 240
Napahai 273
Naqu 108
Naro Bonchung 143-4
Narshi Gompa 227, 228
Narthang Monastery 119
Naxi 268-276
Nechung 47
Nechung Monastery 83
Nedong 92
Neten Lhakhang 81
New Rutok 158
Newar 118, 152
Ngachu Gompa 240
Ngadrak 98
Ngakpa 44
Ngakpa Tratsang 83, 84
Ngamring 129
Ngari 133-58
Ngawa 177, 219-29
Ngor Monastery 118
Ngor Sakyapa 118
Nguldung Lhakhang 122
Niaodao 196
Nielamu 126
Ninglang 278
Nogi 222, 228
Nojin Gangzang, Mt. 102
Norbulingka 81-2
Nyalam 126-7
Nyakchuka 258

Nyame Sherab Gyaltsen 119
Nyangtri 165
Nyarong 253
Nyatri Tsenpo 94, 166
Nyenchen Tanglha 106
Nyentok 198
Nyetang Dolma Lhakhang 95
Nyima Lhakhang 91
Nyinggong 88
Nyingmapa 38, 91-2, 96, 253-4
Nyingmapa Sherda 247
Nyingthig of Dzogchen 96
Nyiseb Gompa 174
Nyitso Gompa 249
Nyiwo Shar Ganden Nangsel 79

O
Old Rutok 156
Old Thongmon 120
Om Mani Padme Hum 41, 47
Opame 48
Orgyen Lingpa 92
Othang Gyatso Lhakhang 74
Othang Lake 74, 81

P
Padma / Parma 213
Padmasambhava
    See Guru Rinpoche
Pakchen 58
Palden Lhamo 47, 60, 75
Palpung Gompa 256
Panchen Lama 40, 91, 104, 109, 113-4, 132, 193, 195
Panden 56
Panggong Tso 158
Paoma Shan 237, 240
Pari 188
Parikrama 143
Parmari 78, 81
Pasho 169
Pata 49
Pawangka Gompa 84
Pe 167
Pecha 44
Pelbar 174
Pelbeu 50
Pelkhor Choede 115
Pelkhu Tso 131
Pelyul 253
Pema 51
Pemako 167
Pemaling Tso 103
Peruche 123
Phak 51
Phakmodrupa Dorje Gyalpo 105

Phakmodrupa Kagyupa 105
Phakpa 39, 122
Phakpa Lhakhang 80
Phakpa Wati Lhakhang 130
Phakpalha Gelek Namgyel 173
Phari 131
Phelung 167
Phenpo Lhundrub 99
Phuma Yumtso Lake 101-2
Phuntsoling 120
Phurbu 50
Ping'an County 194
Piyang 153
Podrang Karpo 79
Podrang Marpo 80
Poe 43
Pomda 169
Pome / Powo 168
Potala Palace 78-81
Potowa of Kadampa 99
Powo 168
Princess Wengcheng 30, 74, 77, 194, 196, 217
Princess Wengcheng Temple 217
Pulan 148
Purang 147-8, 156

Q
Qiabuqia 202
Qijiachuan 194
Qinghai Hu 196
Qinghai Province 190-218
Qisehai 241
Quanshuigou 158
Qushui 88
Qusong 103
Qutansi 195

R
Rabden 226
Rabgya Gompa 211
Raga 129
Rakshas Tal 145
Ramoche Temple 76
Rangjung 41, 80
Rangtang 227
Ratnasambhava 46, 48
Rawok / Ranwu 169
Rechungpa 94, 127, 130
Rechung Puk Gompa 94
Red Hat Sect
    See Nyingmapa
Red Palace 80
Relpachen, King 77
Repkong 198
Reting Gompa 99
Reting Rinpoche 77, 99, 104
Rigdzin Lhakhang 80
Rikaze 109-14

Rimotang 156
Rinchen Jungne 48
Rinchen Zangpo 149-50
Rinchentse Gompa 120
Rinding Temple 115
Rinpoche 44
Rinpung 119
Risum 156, 158
Riting 196
Riwo Dechen Monastery 95
Riwoche 99, 173
Riyueting 196
Rong Jamchen Gompa 119
Rongbo Gompa 198, 199
Rongbo Kyabgon 199
Rongbuk Monastery 126
Rongton Sheja Kunrig 99
Rongtrak 245
Rungen Dratsang Gompa 204
Ruo'ergai 229
Rutok 156

S
Sachen Kunga Nyingpo 121-2
Saga 129
Saga Kawa Gompa 88
Saigesi 227
Saimahui 273
Sakya 120-2
Sakya Pandita 31, 39
Sakya Trizin Rinpoche 122
Sakya Yeshe 84
Sakyapa 39, 120
Samding Dorje Phagmo 102
Samding Gompa 102
Samtenling Gompa 108
Samye 88-92
Sang 41
Sangak Choeling 106
Sang-chu 182-3
Sangha 36
Sangke Grasslands 183
Sangsang 129
Sangye 88
Sangye Lingpa 163-4
Sangye Marmedze 48
Sangye Menla 46-7
Sangyesi 91
Santisi 267
Sapan 39
Sarasvati 47
Seda 250
Sekhar Gutok 103
Selung Gompa 145
Senge 51
Senge Magotsang 199
Senge Tsangpo 146-7
Senge Yagotsang 199
Sengeshong 198-200

Ser Gompa 227
Sera Monastery 83-4
Serdung Dzamling Gyenchik 80
Serdzong 203
Serkhyim La 167
Serlak Gompa 207
Sernya 51
Sershul / Serxu 257-8
Sertri Gompa 185-6
Sertso 222
Sertal 250
Setenling 228
Shakya Thubpa 46
Shakyamuni 46, 48, 74-5, 95, 118, 141, 143
Shamar Rinpoche 100
Shang Valley 119
Shannan 88, 92
Shantaraksita 38, 91
Shaobei Hu 197
Shardungri, Mt. 223
Sharsingma 131
Sheldrak Drubpuk 94
Shelkar 123
Shenrab Mibo 166
Shenrab Miwoche 37, 141, 145
Shiba Gompa 221
Shide Tratsang 77
Shigatse 109-14
Shiqu 257
Shiquanhe 140
Shishapangma, Mt. 126
Shitsang Monastery 184-5
Shizangsi 206
Sho 58, 62
Shoga 163
Shugseb Ani Gompa 81, 96
Shugseb Jetsun Rinpoche 96
Shuoguosi 276
Sibsib 148
Sichuan Province 177, 219-230
Simbiling Gompa 148
Simikot 147
Simpo Ri Gompa 96
Six Realms 37
Sky Burial 57
Sogwo 201
Sok Dzong 173
Sok Tsanden Gompa 173
Sonam Gyatso 35
Songpan 221
Songtsen Gampo, King 30, 65, 71, 74, 77, 80, 84, 94-5, 99, 103-4
Songzanlinsi 273
Sumang Region 218
Sumeru, Mt. 91
Sunan Yugurzu Autonomous County 189

Sungtseling Monastery 273
Suoxian 173
Sust 157
Sutras 37
Syabunbesi 130

T
Ta'er Monastery 193
Tagong 246
Taje Gompa 189
Taklakot 148
Taklung Kagyupa 39, 99, 173
Taklung Tangpa Tashipel 99
Takten Podrang Palace 82
Taktsang Lhamo 185
Taktser 194
Taktsha Gompa 229-30
Tamdrin 47, 153
Tamdrin Dronkhang 143
Tamdrin Lhakhang 84
Tanakpu Valley 120
Tanggu La Shankou 195
Tang-me 167, 168
Tangpoche Gompa 94
Tangyur 187
Tantra 37, 118
Tantric College 83
Tara 46, 81, 166
Tar-choks 40, 143
Tarting Gompa 120
Tashi Dargyeling 188
Tashi Gomang Tratsang 83
Tashi Menri Gompa 119-20
Tashi Tagye 50
Tashidor Gompa 106-8
Tashilhunpo Monastery 113
Tashiling 224-5
Tathagata 46
Tatopani 129
Tawo 210
Tawu 248
Tekmen 36
Tekpa Chenpo 36
Tengchen 173
Tengchen Gompa 256
Tengyeling 78
Tengyur 44
Tenthuk 56
Tenzin Gyatso 35
Terdak Lingpa 92
Terdrom 98
Terma 44, 92, 99
Terton 44
Terton Choegar Gompa 200
Thai Gompa 102
Thangka 43, 49-51, 88, 94
Thangtong Gyalpo 81, 96, 129
Thewo 187

Thiwa Gompa 205
Thuje Chenpo 226
Thuje Chenpo Lhakhang 74
Tianshengqiao 273
Tiantangsi 188
Tianzhu 187
Tianzhu Tibetan Autonomous County 187
Tibetan Book of the Dead 45
Tibetan College of Medicine 81
Tibetan Medical & Astrological Institute 70
Tidrom Gompa *See Terdrom*
Tiger Leaping Gorge 274
Tingri 123, 126
Tirthapuri 153
Tobgyal 119
Toelung 100
Togden Gompa 228
Toling 150
Tongde 206, 207
Tongkhor Gompa 252
Tongmai 167
Tongren 195, 198
Tongwa Donden Lhakhang 114
Tonmi Sambhota 77
Topgyel Gompa 228
Torea 148
Torma 43, 50
Tradruk Temple 94
Trakdruka 119
Trapa 43
Tratsang 42
Treldzong Gompa 203-4
Trena 166
Trengwa 50
Trika 204
Tri Relpachen, King 31, 77
Trindu 218
Trinle Gyatso 35
Trisong Detsen, King 30, 91, 98
Trochu 221
Trongmo 56
Trugo Gompa 145
Trulnang Temple 74
Trulzhik Rinpoche 126
Tsaka Salt Lake 197
Tsalung 130
Tsamda 149-52
Tsampa 56
Tsang 109-31
Tsang-gar Gompa 202, 206
Tsangyang Gyatso 35
Tsaparang 152-3
Tsari 105

Tsatsa 41
Tsawarong 174
Tsekok 200
Tsenlha 226
Tsethang 88, 92-5
Tsezang Duezang 57
Tshamkhung 77
Tsigorthang 203
Tso Ngonbo 196
Tsoe Gompa 183-4
Tsogyal Latso 98
Tsokar Lake 106
Tsokchen 42, 83, 84
Tsokchen Nub Sizhi Phuntsok 80
Tsokchen Shar 80
Tsomonling 78
Tsona County 106
Tsongkha 193
Tsongkha Taktser 194
Tsongkhapa 39, 74, 82-5, 99, 153, 175, 193, 195, 203-4
Tsongkhapa Lhakhang 74
Tsongpa 55
Tsosum Gompa 163
Tsuglagkhang 71-5
Tsultrim Gyatso 35
Tsurphu Gompa 100
Tubten Gyatso 35
T'u-Fan 30
Tukpa 56
Tulku 44

U
U 109
Udumbara 48
Umdze 44
Unjuk 62
Upper Tantric College 77, 99
Utse 91

V
Vairocana 46, 48
Vaishravana 47
Vajra 49
Vajrabhairava 47, 153
Vajrapani 46, 153
Vajrasattva 46
Varadhara 46

W
Wachang 261
Wanzi 56
Weixi Lizu Autonomous County 275
Wendo Gompa / Wendusi 195
Wencheng Gongzhu Miao 217
Wenchuan 220
Wenquan 204
Wheel of Dharma 48-9

White Palace 79
White Tara 48
Wolong Nature Reserve 220
Wopame Lhakhang 74-5
Wucaichi 223, 224
Wutun Shangzhuang / Xiazhuang 199

X
Xiagei Hot Springs 273
Xiahe 182-3
Xiangcheng 260
Xiaojin 226
Xiaqiongsi 195
Xiasima 131
Xicangsi 185
Xietongmen 120
Xieqingsi 256
Xiewu 218
Xindingri 123
Xinduqiao 246
Xinghai 203
Xingsuhai 209
Xining 190-5
Xinlong 253
Xinluhai 254
Xuebao Ding 223
Xunhua Salar Autonomous County 195

Y
Yabyum 47, 118
Yadong 131
Yajiang 258
Yalbang 147
Yamalung Gompa 92
Yamdrok Yumtso Lake 100-1
Yangar 148
Yangchenma 47
Yangpachen 100
Yanjing 170, 274
Yarlung Tsangpo 88, 133, 146-7
Yarlung Valley 88
Yatangja Gompa 213
Yecheng 156-8
Yellow Hat Sect *See Gelukpa*
Yeren Hai 241
Yeshe Tsogyal 92, 98-9, 156
Yeshe-o 149
Yeshung Valley, 120
Yeti 167, 242
Yidam 47
Yilhun Lhatso 254
Yongning 278
Yongpado Gompa 102
Yonten Gyatso 35
Youningsi 194
Yueting 196
Yufengsi 270

Yuhuangge 204
Yumbu Lagang 94
Yungdrung 38
Yungdrung Lhateng 226
Yungdrungling Monastery
  119-20
Yunnan Province 263-78
Yushu Tibetan Autonomous
  Prefecture 214-18

Z
Zaling Hu 209
Zamthang 227
Zangjing Tang 271
Zangzang 129
Zeku 200
Zhaba 195
Zhabten Gompa 108
Zhada 149-52
Zhalu Monastery 118
Zhalupa 115
Zhamar Rinpoche/
  Zharmapa 100
Zhamei Lamasi 278
Zhanang 92
Zhangcuo 222
Zhangmu 127
Zhangye 189
Zhangzhung 133, 156
Zhechen Gompa 256
Zhedang 92
Zher 147
Zhethongmon 120
Zhibo 226
Zhibodiaoqun 226
Zhingpa 55
Zhiqinsi 213
Zhiwu Drogon 218
Zhol 79
Zhong Rangtang 227
Zhongdian / Zhongxinzhen
  270-4
Zhouqu 187
Zhujiesi 218
Zhuka 171
Zhuoni 186-7
Zommug 123
Zungchu 221-2
Zuogong 171
Zurmang Region 218
Zutrulpuk Gompa 143

India, Nepal & Bhutan

A
Alchi Gompa 292
Amjilassa 338
Annapurna 343, 350-1
Arughat Bazaar 339
Arunachal Pradesh 372-74
Atisha 307, 310, 313

B
Baga La Phedi 355
Baglung 346, 355
Balasa 355
Barabise 336
Bardan Gompa 299
Basantpur 338
Besisahar 342, 349
Bhairawa 356
Bhandar 336
Bhandara 317
Bhimakali Temple 308
Bhulbhule 349
Bhutia 364, 366, 377
Bhutia Busty Monastery
  362
Bigu Gompa 336
Bodhnath 321, 331
Bomdila 374
Braga 351
Bumthang Valleys 391
Bung 338
Butwal 356

C
Calcutta See Kolkata
Chamba Valley 316
Chame 349, 350
Champa 308
Champa Lhakhang 352
Chandrakot 343
Changangkha Lhakhang
  389
Changar 349
Chango 311
Changspa 288
Changthang 297
Chapcha Dzong 384
Charang 352
Chauki 338
Chele 352
Chemrey Gompa 292
Chendebji Chorten 391
Chensen Sherab Sangpo
  302
Cheri 389
Chharka 355
Chirwa 338
Chisopani 339
Chitkul 311
Cho Oyu 338
Chobar Gorge 331
Chodi Gompa 352

Choegyal 365, 368, 371
Chomoa 336
Chomrong 343
Chongo Lake 360, 370
Chorten Kora 393
Chukhung 338
Chumbi Valley 365
Chungthang 366, 371
Chyawabesi 338
Clement Town 317

D
Dakshinkali Temple 333
Dalai Lama 315, 369, 374
Dalhousie 316
Dankar Gompa 307
Darcha 303
Dards 294-5, 318
Darjeeling 360-64
Dechen Phodrang 389
Dechen Tsemo Gompa 296
Dehra Dun 317
Delhi 279-83
Deng 342
Dha 294
Dhading 339
Dhaka 357
Dhampus 343
Dharamsala 312-15
Dharapani 342, 349
Dhubidanda 338
Dhulikhel 333
Dhunche 339
Dickyi Larso 317
Dingboche 338
Dip Tsechokling Gompa
  314
Diskit 296
Do Tarap 355
Doban 339
Doda 302
Do-Drul Chorten 369
Dole 338
Dolmaling Nunnery 315
Dolpo 354-5
Dorje Chang 331
Dorje Drolod 385
Dorje Ling 361
Dorje Lingpa 391
Dram 325
Drejong 365
Drepung Monastery 317
Drokpa See Dards
Dromtonpa Lhakhang
  307-8
Drubthob Nunnery 389
Drubtop Karpo 369
Druk Yul 377
Drukgyel Gompa 386
Drukpa Kagyupa 286, 364
Drukpa Tseshi 366
Dubdi Gompa 372
Dudjom Rinpoche 364
Dunai 355

Dungtse Lhakhang 384
Durbar Marg 330
Durpin Dara 364
Dzongkha 377, 382
Dzongri 366

E
Enchey Gompa 369
Ensa Gompa 296
Everest 336-8, 364

G
Gadhan Thekchokling
  Gompa 284
Gai Jatra 322
Ganden Monastery 317
Ganden Namgyal Latse 373
Ganden Thekchokling
  Gompa 284
Gangapurna 351
Gangchen Kyishong 313
Gangteng Gompa 391
Gangtok 367-70
Garphu Gompa 352
Geling 352
Gete 306
Geyzing 371-72
Ghami 352
Ghandruk 343
Ghandrung 343
Ghap 339
Gho 342
Ghoom Gompa 364
Ghopte 339
Ghyaru 351
Gokyo Peak 336, 338
Gom Kora 393
Gondhla 303
Gonpo 390
Gopalpur 316
Gorak Shep 336
Gothichaur 355
Guling 306
Gungri Gompa 306
Gunla 322
Gunsa 338
Gupa Pokhari 338
Gurphug Gompa 292
Guru Rinpoche 287, 304,
  316, 333, 366, 371, 374,
  384-5, 391, 392
Gyalwa Karmapa 369

H
Hanu 295
Hargram 296
Helambu 339
Hemis Gompa 291
Hile 338
Himachal Pradesh 283,
  308, 315-7
Humde 350
Hundar 296
Hunsur Taluk 317

I

Institute of Tibetan
Medicine and Astrology
313

J

Jagat 339, 349
Jahalman 303
Jamchen Lhakhang 308
Jampa 308
Jampa Lhakhang 375, 392
Jampal 331
Jamyang Namgyal 286
Jawala Mai Gompa 348
Je Khenpo 377, 389, 390
Jharkot 348
Jhinu 343
Jiri 336
Jochne 329-30
Jomolangma, Mt.
See Everest
Jomolhari, Mt. 382
Jomsom 346, 347
Jorethang 372
Jumla 355
Junbesi 336
Juphal 355

K

Kafalpani 339
Kagbeni 346, 347, 352
Kagyat 372
Kaigaon 355
Kala Pattar 336
Kalghat 317
Kali 333
Kalimpong 364-5
Kalpa 310
Kamji Lhakhang 384
Kamru 310
Kanam 311
Kangchenjunga, Mt. 338,
361, 365-7, 370-2
Kanigaon 355
Kanika Chorten 302
Kargil 292, 298
Karma Kagyupa 369
Karmapa 369
Karnataka 317
Karneswarpur 317
Karsha Gompa 299
Karu 292, 297
Kashmir Valley 284
Kathmandu 324-33
Kaza 303, 305-8
Keylong 303-5
Khaling 393
Khalsar 296
Khambachen 338
Khampa 316, 351
Khampa Gar Gompa 316
Kharbandi 384
Khardong Gompa 303
Khardung La 295

Khardung Lhakhang 308
Khare 338
Khari Khola 336
Khartali 336
Khecheopari Lake 372
Khutumsang 339
Ki Gompa 306
Kibber 306
Kinnaur 308-12
Kinnaur Kailash, Mt. 308,
310
Kodari 325
Koksar 303
Kolkata 357-60
Kollegal Taluk 317
Kopan Gompa 331
Kullu Valley 283
Kungri Gompa 306
Kurje Lhakhang 392
Kyahar 312
Kyanjin Gompa 339
Kyapra 338
Kyerchu Lhakhang 375,
385
Kyilkhor Lhakhang 308

L

Labrang 311
Labu Besi 339
Lachung 366, 371
Ladakh 286-97
Lahaul 303-05
Lakhanwala 317
Lama Gompa 303
Lamayuru Gompa 293
Langshisha Kharka 339
Langtang Valley 338-9
Larkya Bazaar 342
Lasa 355
Leh 287-91
Lepcha 364-6, 377
Lete 346
Lhonak 338
Lhuntse 392
Library of Tibetan Works
and Archives 314
Likir Gompa 292
Limbu 321, 338
Lingshad Gompa 302
Lingshi 382
Lo Manthang 351-54
Lobuche 338
Longchen Rabjampa 391
Lopas 321, 351
Losong 367
Lote 303
Lower Dolpo 354
Luding Khen Rinpoche 370
Lukla 336, 338
Lumbini 355-6

M

Machhapuchhare Base
Camp 343

Machik Labdron 385
Maitreya 308, 364, 392
Majnukatila Tibetan Camp
283, 312
Mali 336
Manali 283-4
Manang 349-51
Manaslu 339
Mangan 366
Mangmaya Khola 338
Manjushri 331
Markha Valley 294
Marpa 302, 351
Marpha 346
Masung Bali 295
Matho Gompa 292
Mauri Lagna 355
Maya Devi Temple 356
Mayar Nala 303
McLeod Ganj 312
Mebar-Tsho 392
Memorial Chorten 389
Mentsikhang 313
Milarepa 339, 385
Mindroling Monastery 317
Minling Trichen Rinpoche
317
Mongar 392
Muktinath 346, 348-9
Mulung Takpo River 302
Mune Gompa 299
Mussoorie 317
Mustang See Lo Manthang

N

Najingdingma 338
Nako 311
Namche Bazaar 336
Namdapha National Park
374
Namdo 355
Namdroling Monastery 317
Namgyal Monastery 313
Namlung La 294
Namobuddha 333
Namrung 342
Naphukhona 355
Naropa 302
Naya Bazaar 372
Nayapul 346
Nepal 319-56
Nesum 338
New Jalpaiguri 362
New Kaza 305
Nga Lhakhang 378
Ngawal 351
Ngor Gompa 370
Ngor Sakyapa 370
Nilgiri North 348
Norbulingka Institute 315
North Dolpo 354-5
Nubra Valley 295
Numa La Phedi 355
Nyimpa Gompa 352

P

Padam / Padum 298
Padmasambhava
See Guru Rinpoche
Paharganj 312
Panamik 296
Pang Pema 338
Pangong Tso 297
Pangri Zampa 389
Pangum 338
Parbati 322
Paro 380-1
Patan 322, 323
Patlikuhl 316
Pelling 372
Pema Lingpa 391, 392
Pema Trinley 391
Pemayangtse 372
Pendzokhang 314
Penor Rinpoche 317
Peo 310
Phadampa Sangye, 385
Phajoding Monastery 382
Phakding 336
Pharping 333
Phedi 338
Phensang Gompa 371
Pheriche 338
Phewa Tal 342
Phobjika Valley 391
Phodang Gompa 371
Phoksumdo Lake 355
Phugtal Gompa 299
Phuntsholing 381, 383
Pin Valley 306
Pisang 350
Pishu Gompa 302
Pokhara 342-3
Prithvi Narayani Shah 321
Puh 311
Puiyan 336, 338
Punakha 390
Pungmo 355
Putra 349

R

Radi 393
Rangdum Gompa 302
Ranipauwa 348
Rarig 303
Raring 303
Rekong Peo 310
Research Institute of
Tibetology 369
Reshi Hot Springs 372
Rewalsar 316
Rinchen Zangpo 286, 292,
307-8, 311
Ringmo 355
Rizong Gompa 293
Rohagaon 355
Rok Chaitakar 331
Rongbuk Monastery 336
Rotsawa Rinpoche 308

Rumtek Gompa 369
Ryajik 355

S
Sagar 336
Sagarmatha *See Everest*
Sakathum 338
Sakteng Valley 393
Sakti 292
Sakya Monastery 317
Sama Gompa 339, 342
Samar 352
Samdrup Jongkhar 393
Samtanling Gompa 296
Samthar Plateau 365
Sanam 338
Sanasa 338
Sandup Choeling 312
Sangla 310
Sani Gompa 302
Sankar Gompa 291
Sarahan 308-10
Sarma 307
Saspul 293
Satingri 304
Saunepani 336
Sengge Namgyal, King
    286, 291-3
Sera Monastery 317
Serkhang 307
Serson 339
Serukapti 336
Serzang Gompa 293
Sete 336
Shakyamuni 299
Shalkar 312
Shashur Gompa 303
Shey Gompa 291, 355
Shey-Phoksumdo National
    Park 355
Shimla 308
Shugseb Jetsun Rongchen
    316
Shyala 342
Sikkim 365-74
Simtokha Dzong 390

Sing Gompa 339
Singhik 366
Siniolchu, Mt 364, 370
Solu Khumbu 336
Sonamling Tibetan Refugee
    Settlement 291
Songtsen Gampo 375
Soti Khola 339
South Dolpo 354-5
Spangmik 297
Spillo 311
Spiti 305-08
Spituk Gompa 291
Srinagar 286
Stakna Gompa 292
Stok Khar 292
Suja 316
Suketar 338
Sumduwa 355
Sumur 296
Sunauli 356
Suphal 355
Swayambhunath 321-2
Swigha Stupa 331
Syabru 339
Syange 342

T
Ta Dzong 384, 391
Tabo Gompa 307
Taglang La 297
Taktok Gompa 292
Tangro 389
Tangtak Gompa 299
Tangtse 297
Tarakot 355
Tashi Chodzong 389
Tashi Jong 316
Tashi Ling Tibetan Village
    343
Tashi Menriling 317
Tashi Viewpoint 370
Tashi Yangste 393
Tashiding Gompa 372
Tashigang 306, 392-3

Tatopani 346
Tawang Monastery 373
Tayul Gompa 304
Tegar 296
Tengpoche Gompa 323,
    338
Tenzin Chogyal Rinpoche
    302
Tezpur 374
Thak Khola 347
Thamel 329
Thami Gompa 322
Thangtong Gyalpo 384,
    385, 389
Thangyud 306
Tharpa Choeling Gompa
    364
Thekchen Choeling 313
Thimphu 386-90
Thongde 302
Thubten Choeling Gompa
    336
Thulo Tingsang 336
Thumma 338
Thupten Sang-Ngag
    Choeling Gompa 364
Tibetan Childrens' Village
    291, 312, 315-7
Tibetan Institute of
    Performing Arts 314
Tihar 323
Tikse Gompa 291
Tilje 342
Tipurakot 355
Toijem 355
Tok Khyu 355
Tolka 343
Tong 366
Tongsa Gompa 364
Tonpa Lhakhang 299
Toy Train 362
Trakshindo 336
Triloknath 303
Trongsa 391
Trulshi Rinpoche 369
Tsemo Gompa 291

Tsering Dolma 315
Tso Moriri 297
Tsongkhapa 302
Tsongo Lake 366, 370
Tsuklakhang & Namgyal
    Monastery 313
Tsurphu Gompa 369
Tukche 346
Tukchen Gompa 352
Tulshi Rinpoche 336

U
Ugyen Wangchuck 377
Uletokpo 293
Upper Dharamsala 312
Upper Dolpo 354

V
Vaipassana 331
Vairocana 307
Vajradhara 331
Vashisht 284

W
Wangdue Phodrang 390
Wanla 293
West Bengal 360-65

Y
Yarlung Tsangpo 373
Yoksum 372
Yumthang 366, 371
Yung Drung 293

Z
Zangdokpelri Lhakhang
    384, 393
Zangla 302
Zanskar 298-302
Zhabdrung Ngawang
    Namgyal 375, 384, 386,
    389-91
Zhangmu 325
Zong Dog Palri Fo-Brang
    Gompa 364
Zongkul Gompa 302

Map Index

A
Aba 158
Aba (Ngawa) 228
**Aba Tibetan & Qiang
Autonomous
Prefecture   219**
Aba Tibetan & Qiang
Autonomous Prefecture
- Location 219
Ali (Shiquanhe) 140
Amdo 176-7
**Amdo - Central -
Gannan Tibetan
Autonomous
Prefecture (Gansu),
Qinghai 180-1**
Amdo - Location 177
Amdo Tibetan
Autonomous
Prefectures -
Location 181
Annapurna Trekking
Times 345
Arunachal Pradesh 373
Arunachal Pradesh-West
373

B
Bamei (Garthar) 248
Banma (Padma) 213
Batang 260
Bayi 162
Beri Gompa (Bailisi) 253
Bhutan 380-1
Bodhnath - Tibetan
Gompas 332
Bumthang Valley 392
**Bus Service Routes in
Tibetan Cultural Area
16-7**

C
Chamdo (Changdu) 172
Chango 312
Chengdu 235
Chumbi Valley 131
Chusum (Qusong) 104

D
Dali Gucheng 267
Dankar, Lhalung 307
Daofu (Tawu)
[Xianshuizhen] 248
Darchen 141
Dargye Gompa (Dajinsi)
253
Dari (Jimai) [Darlag] 212
Darjeeling 361
Darjeeling - Central 361
**Darjeeling Area & Sikkim
363**

Darjeeling Area & Sikkim
- Distance Chart 363
Dege (Derge) 255
**Delhi to Tibetan Cultural
Area 281**
Delhi Town Center 282
Deqin (Jol)
[Shengpingzhen] 275
Dha 295
Dharamsala 313
**Diqing Tibetan
Autonomous
Prefecture 271**
Dolpo 352-3
Dorje Drak 97
Drak Yerpa 99
Dram (Zhangmu)
[Khasa-Nepalese] 128
Drepung Monastery 83
Drigung Til Gompa &
Tidrom Hot Springs 98
Drongpa (Zhongba) 138
Druka (Zhuka) 171
Dzogang (Zuogong) 171
Dzogchen Gompa
(Zhuqingsi) 256

E
**Everest [Jomolangma]
Trekking & Shelkar
(New Tingri) - Dram
Route 124-5**
Everest [Jomolangma]
Trekking Distance
Chart 124
Everest [Solu Khumbu
Region] Trekking
Times 337
**Everest Trekking Routes
-To the World of
Sherpas 334-5**

F
Freak St. (Jochne) 329

G
Gande (Gabde) 211
Ganden Monastery 85
**Ganden—Samye Trekking
89**
Gangtok 368
Gangtok Area 370
Ganzi (Kandze) 251
Ganzi (Kandze) Area 252
Ganzi (Kandze) Area -
Gompas 252
Ganzi Prefecture 238
Ganzi Prefecture - Location
238
Golmud (Ge'ermu) 197
Gonghe (Chabcha) 202
Gonghe (Chabcha) Area
203
Gongkar Choede 96

Greater Pokhara 340
Guge Ruins (Tsaparang)
152
Guge Ruins - Access 152
Guide (Trika) [Heyin] 205
Guinan 205
Gyantse (Jiangzi) 115
Gyantse Kumbum
(Pelkhor Chorten) 118
Gyatsa (Jiacha) 105

H
Hailuogou 244
Hailuogou - Camp 2 244
Henan (Sogwo) 201
Hezuo (Tsoe) 184
Hongyuan (Mewa) 229
Huangzhong [Lushaer]
194

J
Jangritang Gompa &
Yartangja Gompa 214
Jharkot 349
Jiuzhaigou Scenic Spot
223
Jokhang (Tsuglagkhang)
74
Jokhang Temple Area 72-3
Jomsom 348

K
Kagbeni 348
Kailash, Mt - Distances
138
**Kailash, Mt. & Guge
Ruins 136**
Kailash, Mt.
(Kang Rinpoche) 144
**Kailash, Mt.
(Kang Rinpoche) -
Access 138-9**
Kailash, Mt.
(Kang Rinpoche)
[Western Tibet] -
Location 134
**Kailash, Mt.
(Kang Rinpoche)
[Western Tibet] -
Routes 134-5**
**Kailash, Mt.
(Kang Rinpoche) Area
142**
**Kangding & Luding
(Dartsedo &
Chakzamka) 242**
Kangding [Luchengzhen]
(Dartsedo) 239
Kangding Area 241
**Karakorum Highway &
Kashgar to Western
Tibet 154-5**
Karakorum Highway &
Kashgar to Western

Tibet-Distance Chart
155
Kashgar 154
Kathmandu 325
Kathmandu Center 327
**Kathmandu to the World
of Sherpas and
Tamangs - Trekking
Routes 334-5**
Kaza 305
Keylong 304
Kham 232-3
Ki/Kaza 306
Kings' Tombs 95
Kinnaur 309
Kolkata (Calcutta) 359
**Kolkata (Calcutta) to
Sikkim, Bhutan, &
Arunachal Pradesh
358**
**Kongpo - Around
Nyangtri (Linzhi)
164-5**
**Kongpo & Chamdo
(Eastern TAR) 160-1**
Kongpo & Chamdo
(Eastern TAR)-
Location 161
Kongpo Gyamda 163
Kunming 266
**Kunming to Diqing
Tibetan Autonomous
Prefecture 264**
Kyirong (Jilong) 130

L
Ladakh 290
Lahaul 303
**Lahaul, Spiti, and
Kinnaur Area 304**
Lanzhou 178
Leh 287
Leh Area - Gompas 290
Leh Center, Around Main
Bazaar 288
Lhamo Latso Lake 104
Lhasa 68-9
Lhasa Area 86-7
Lhasa Mid-distance Bus
Station Route Bus 86
Lhasa Minibus Route Map
68
**Lhasa to Kathmandu
110-1**
Lhasa-Kathmandu
Location 110
Lhatse (Lazi) [Quxiazhen]
122
Lhatse Area 116
Lhopas 166
Lijiang (Dayanzhen) 269
Linxia 179
Litang [Gaochengxiang]
259

414

Luding (Chakzamka)
[Luqiaozhen] 243
Lugu Hu 277
Luhuo (Drango)
[Xinduzhen] 249
Lumbini 356
Lunang (Lulang) 166
Luoshui 277
Luqu (Mawen or Qiaotou)
185
Lutsang Gompa 205

M
Maduo (Mato) 208
Maduo (Mato) Area 208
Ma'erkang (Barkham) Area
225
Ma'erkang (Barkham)
Center 225
Manali 284
Manali Center 284
Manasarovar 146
Manaslu - Trekking Route
339
Manigango 254
Maqin (Dawu) [Machen]
210
Markham (Mangkang) 170
Marpha 347
McLeod Ganj
(Upper Dharamsala)
314
Menling (Milin) 166
Moxi 244
Moxi-Hailuogou Trekking
245
Mugecuo Lake
(Savage's Lake) 241
Muktinath 350
Muktinath Area 350
Muli [Qiaowazhen] 261
**Mustang & Annapurna
Region - Trekking
Routes 344**

N
Nakchu (Naqu) 108
Nako 311
Namling (Nanmulin) 120
Namtso Lake 107
Nang Dzong (Langxian)
105
Nangartse (Langkazi) 102
Nepal 322-3
Nepal - Domestic Flights
322
Nepal - Flights 323

Ninglang 277
Norbulingka 82
**Northern India/Tibetan
Cultural Area 285**
Nubra Valley 295
Nyalam (Nielamu) 127
Nyangtri (Nyingtri or
Linzhi) 164

P
Padam (Padum) 298
Panggong Tso 157
Paro Center 385
Paro Valley 385
Paryang (Payang) 138
Pasho (Basu) 169
Phuntsholing 383
Pokhara 340-1
Pomda (Bangda) 170
Pome (Bomi) 168
Potala Palace -
Main Parts 80
Potala Palace
(Podrang Potala) 79
Potala Palace Area 68
Princess Wengcheng
Temple 217
Puh 311
**Purang - Simikot Border
Crossing 148-9**
Purang (Pulan) [Taklakot]
150

Q
Qinghai Hu
(Lake Kokonor) 196
Que'er Shan & Xinluhai
254
Queshian Area 203

R
Rabgya Gompa & Around
211
Rawok (Ranwu) 168
Rekong Peo 310
**Road Condition and
Distance Charts
(China) 18-9**
Ruo'ergai (Dzoge) 230

S
Saga 129
Sakya (Sajia) 121
Sakya South Monastery
122
Samye (Sangye) 90
Samye Monastery

(Sangyesi) 91
Sera Monastery 84
Serdzong (Treldzong)
Gompa 204
Sershul Gompa (Sexusi)
258
Shigatse (Rikaze) 112
Shigatse Area 116-7
Shiqu (Sershul) 257
Shugseb Ani Gompa 97
Sikkim - West (Around
Pemayangtse) 371
Sok Dzong (Suoxian) 173
Songpan (Zungchu) 221
Songpan, Huanglong,
Jiuzhaigou 222
Spiti Valley 305
Sudder St. Area 358
Swayambhunath - Tibetan
Gompas 332

T
Tagong (Lhagang) 247
Taktsang Lhamo
(Langmusi) 186
Tang-me 168
Tarap 352
Tashilhunpo Monastery
113
Tegar, Sumur 296
Thamel 326-7
Thamel Center 327
Thimphu 387
Thimphu - Central 387
Thimphu Area 387
Tiantangsi (Tashi
Dargyeling) Area 188
Tianzhu (Huacangsi) 188
Tibet (Chinese Admin
Division) 9
Tibet (Lhasa) - Access 8
Tibet-Latter half of 19th
Century 32
Tibet-Latter half of 8th
Century 31
Tibetan Cultural Area -
Model Tour 1 24
Tibetan Cultural Area -
Model Tour 2 25
Tibetan Cultural Area -
Model Tour 3 27
Tibetan Placenames 9
**Tibetan Settlements in
India 316**
Tingri (Dingri) 126
Tirthapuri 156
Tirthapuri Gompa & Hot

Springs 156
Toling Area 151
Tongde (Kawasumdo) 206
Tongkhor Gompa
(Donggusi) 253
Tongren (Repkong)
[Longwusi Zhen] 199
Tongren Area - Gompas
200
Tsamda (Zhada) 151
Tsamda (Zhada) Area 151
Tsang-gar Gompa
(Shizangsi) - Access
207
Tsethang (Zedang) 93
Tsethang Area 94
Tukche 346

W
Weixi (Balung)
[Baohezhen] 276
Wenquan 204

X
Xiahe (Sangchu) 182
Xiahe Area & Sangke
Grasslands 183
Xiewu (Zhiwu) 218
Xinduqiao (Dzongzhab)
246
Xinghai (Tsigorthang)
203
Xining 191

Y
Yajiang (Nyakchuka) 258
**Yamdrok Yumtso Lake to
Lhodrak Region 101**
Yanjing 170
Yellow River Source 209
Yellow River Source Area
209
Yongning 277
Yungdrungling Monastery
119
Yushu (Jyekundo)
[Jieguzhen] 215
**Yushu (Jyekundo)
Prefecture 216**

Z
Zanskar 300-1
**Zanskar - Around
Padam (Padum) 300-1**
Zeku (Tsekok) 200
Zhongdian (Gyeltang)
[Zhongxinzhen] 272